Song Lin   Xiong Huang (Ed

Advanced Research on Computer Education, Simulation and Modeling

International Conference, CESM 2011
Wuhan, China, June 18-19, 2011
Proceedings, Part II

 Springer

Volume Editors

Song Lin
International Science & Education Researcher Association
Wuhan Branch, No.1, Jiangxia Road
Wuhan, China
E-mail: 30978376@qq.com

Xiong Huang
International Science & Education Researcher Association
Wuhan Branch, No.1, Jiangxia Road
Wuhan, China
E-mail: 499780828@qq.com

ISSN 1865-0929   e-ISSN 1865-0937
ISBN 978-3-642-21801-9   e-ISBN 978-3-642-21802-6
DOI 10.1007/978-3-642-21802-6
Springer Heidelberg Dordrecht London New York

Library of Congress Control Number: 2011929161

CR Subject Classification (1998): J.1, I.6, H.2, I.4, I.2, F.1-2, H.3-4

Typesetting: Camera-ready by author, data conversion by Scientific Publishing Services, Chennai, India

Printed on acid-free paper

Springer is part of Springer Science+Business Media (www.springer.com)

Preface

The International Science & Education Researcher Association(ISER) puts its focus on the study and exchange of academic achievements of international researchers, and it also promotes educational reform in the world. In addition, it serves as an academic discussion and communication platform, which is beneficial for education and for scientific research, thus aiming to stimulate researchers in their work.

The CESM conference is an integrated event concentrating on computer education, simulation, and modeling. The goal of the conference is to provide researchers working in the field of computer education, simulation, and modeling based on modern information technology with a forum to share new ideas, innovations, and solutions. CESM 2011 was held during June 18-19, in Wuhan, China, and was co-sponsored by the International Science & Education Researcher Association, Beijing, Gireida Education Co. Ltd, and Wuhan University of Science and Technology, China. Renowned keynote speakers were invited to deliver talks, giving participants the chance to discuss their work with the speakers face to face.

In these proceeding, you can learn more about the field of computer education, simulation, and modeling from the contributions of several international researchers. The main role of the proceedings is to be used as a means of exchange of information for those working in this area. The Organizing Committee made great efforts to meet the high standards of Springer's *Communications in Computer and Information Science (CCIS)* series Firstly, poor-quality papers were rejected after being reviewed by anonymous referees. Secondly, meetings were held periodically for reviewers to exchange opinions and suggestions. Finally, the organizing team held several preliminary sessions before the conference. Through the efforts of numerous individuals and departments, the conference was successful and fruitful.

During the organization, we received help from different people, departments, and institutions. Here, we would like to extend our sincere thanks to the publishers of CCIS, Springer, for their kind and enthusiastic assistance and support of our conference. Secondly, the authors should also be thanked for their submissions. Thirdly, the hard work of the Program Committee, the Program Chairs, and the reviewers is greatly appreciated.

In conclusion, it was the team effort of all these people that made our conference such a success. We welcome any suggestions that may help improve the conference in the future and we look forward to seeing all of you at CESM 2012.

April 2011   Song Lin

Committee

Honorary Chairs

Chen Bin	Beijing Normal University, China
Hu Chen	Peking University, China
Chunhua Tan	Beijing Normal University, China
Helen Zhang	University of Munich, Germany

Program Committee Chairs

Xiong Huang	International Science & Education Researcher Association, China
Li Ding	International Science & Education Researcher Association, China
Zhihua Xu	International Science & Education Researcher Association, China

Organizing Chair

ZongMing Tu	Beijing Gireida Education Co. Ltd., China
Jijun Wang	Beijing Spon Technology Research Institution, China
Quan Xiang	Beijing Prophet Science and Education Research Center, China

Publication Chairs

Song Lin	International Science & Education Researcher Association, China
Xiong Huang	International Science & Education Researcher Association, China

Program Committee

Sally Wang	Beijing Normal University, China
Li Li	Dongguan University of Technology, China
Bing Xiao	Anhui University, China
Z.L. Wang	Wuhan University, China
Moon Seho	Hoseo University, Korea
Kongel Arearak	Suranaree University of Technology, Thailand
Zhihua Xu	International Science & Education Researcher Association, China

Co-sponsored by:

International Science & Education Researcher Association, China
VIP Information Conference Center, China

Reviewers of CESM 2011

Chunlin Xie	Wuhan University of Science and Technology, China
Lin Qi	Hubei University of Technology, China
Xiong Huang	International Science & Education Researcher Association, China
Gang Shen	International Science & Education Researcher Association, China
Xiangrong Jiang	Wuhan University of Technology, China
Li Hu	Linguistic and Linguistic Education Association, China
Moon Hyan	Sungkyunkwan University, Korea
Guang Wen	South China University of Technology, China
Jack H. Li	George Mason University, USA
Marry Y. Feng	University of Technology Sydney, Australia
Feng Quan	Zhongnan University of Finance and Economics, China
Peng Ding	Hubei University, China
Song Lin	International Science & Education Researcher Association, China
XiaoLie Nan	International Science & Education Researcher Association, China
Zhi Yu	International Science & Education Researcher Association, China
Xue Jin	International Science & Education Researcher Association, China
Zhihua Xu	International Science & Education Researcher Association, China
Wu Yang	International Science & Education Researcher Association, China
Qin Xiao	International Science & Education Researcher Association, China
Weifeng Guo	International Science & Education Researcher Association, China
Li Hu	Wuhan University of Science and Technology, China
Zhong Yan	Wuhan University of Science and Technology, China
Haiquan Huang	Hubei University of Technology, China
Xiao Bing	Wuhan University, China
Brown Wu	Sun Yat-Sen University, China

Table of Contents – Part II

Table of Contents – Part I

The Reform and Practice of Open Teaching for Micro-Computer Principle and Interface Technology

Zheng Nong

College of Education Science, Guangxi University for Nationalities, 530006 Nanning, China

Abstract. Taking into account the requirements of individual differences and individuality development of students, this paper makes a hierarchically teaching goal and an open teaching content, realizes the open teaching of Micro-Computer Principle and Interface Technology through the multiplicative teaching forms of the class teaching, the second class activity and the network autonomous learning, which will fully satisfy the need of the individuality development of the students and will be good for individual training.

Keywords: Micro-Computer Principle and Interface Technology, Open Teaching, Personalized Training.

1 Introduction

"Microcomputer Principle and Interface Technology" is an important basic course for electronic and electric information major students, the purpose of the course is to enable students to initially have a grasp of the basic principles of computer and interface technology, a calculated thinking and scientific thinking and an ability to develop and apply the software and hardware, build the foundation for the following related curriculum. Proceeding from the individual discrepancy of the students, according to the students characteristic study and development needs, making difference teaching goals and teaching contents, carrying out the hierarchically teaching aim, providing a prolific, optional content of course, will help to meet the requirements of the independent development, give full play to students' initiative, enthusiasm and creativity, embody "students-centered".

2 The Basis of Making Open Teaching

2.1 To Understand the Students' Individual Characters

To guide of the students' formulating individual learning plans, development goals and cultivating their independent development and innovation capability must be premised on the understanding of students' characters, hobbies, personalities, learning needs and academic motivation. It was just like someone said, "There are no two leaves are the same in the world, nor do sands". Students' individual differences are not inherent, so it should need to teach students in accordance of their aptitude. In terms of analysis of the view of learning, American professors Sharon E. Smaldino,

S. Lin and X. Huang (Eds.): CESM 2011, Part II, CCIS 176, pp. 1–6, 2011.
© Springer-Verlag Berlin Heidelberg 2011

James D.Russell, etc, point out that the characteristics of learners can be divided into General Characteristics, Entry Competencies and Learning Styles in their classical ASSURE Teaching Mode[1]. The analysis and understanding of the characteristics of learners will be the foundation of formulating teaching goals, designing teaching contents, selecting teaching media and approaches.

(1) General Characteristics: Generally, college students, who have certain learning and practical experience, strong self-discipline, the abilities of independence and clear goals, are one group that pay more attention to teaching efficiency and desire to participate in teaching decision. Individually, there are differences among gender, grades (age), places (students come from), domestic background, social relationships and ethnic customs. These fundamental characteristics will have an effect on the students' learning goals, learning motivation and personalized development.

(2) Entry Competencies: This course is generally opened in the second year of college; the students have already learnt some foundation courses such as the fundamentals of electronic technology, the digital logic and the fundamentals of computer application, so they have possessed entry competencies to handle this course. For individual, students' entry competencies are relevant to some factors, such as individual talent, the basis knowledge of discipline, the ability of practice, the grasp of studying tools, the abilities of application, the interest of academic majors, hobbies and learning motivation. Students' entry competencies will affect teachers who formulate and modify teaching goals, choose and ensure teaching contents, implement and adjust teaching schedule.

(3) Learning Styles: Learning styles mainly represent learners' psychological characteristics of perception preferences and strength, information processing habits, learning motivation factors and physiological factors, etc, which will affect a person's consciousness in learning environment and a person's response and interaction of environment. Thus, it should require the teachers to select proper teaching aids, teaching media and teaching approaches, in order to meet the learning needs of students who have different learning styles and different characteristics.

2.2 To Formulate the Teaching Objectives with Varied Levels

So-called teaching objectives, when viewed as a whole, is that the teaching practice is to achieve the expected results, the expected result by conceptual forms exist in the thoughts of teachers and students; From every body content to say, summarizing, it include the normally" knowledge" and" skill" and the" attitude" projects [2].Whether teachers or students, to comprehend and grasp the teaching goal is essential, teachers only understand the teaching goal can be very good to schedule or design the teaching work of each link, students only understand the teaching goal, can centralized independent of time and energy to improve autonomous learning continuously, then obtain the greatest possible development.

The teaching goals of gradation mean that the teaching aims to satisfy all students' learning requirements as the foundation, on this basis, realizing the individuation development goals. Namely, the teaching goals duty to have basic targets (up to the basic requirements of academic knowledge, to master and apply subject knowledge to solve practical problems) and expansion of the target (to meet the development needs of individual learners ,to achieve independent development) requirements, the basic goal is for all students to learn the most basic tasks and requirements, development of the goal is the development of the different requirements of individual students, gives optional learning objectives and tasks.

Therefore, the level of teaching goal is to be flexible, optional, is according to the teaching syllabus and teaching content requirement, that the differences of both students and teaching feedback information to be adjusted, is a dynamic generative process. It will give the individuation development opportunities, make everyone to get maximum development and realize the developments of all.

3 The Design of Open Teaching Contents

The Open Teaching contents mean that the open teaching contents are rich, having basic content, expanding the sexual contents and individualized learning contents, such as target of points, exhibition times being dynamic, teaching contents to be chosen.

"Microcomputer Principle and Interface Technology" includes the teaching of theory courses and practice courses, into two parts are divided into the basic of contents and the development of content. The basic contents are the basic requirements for the students, all the students are required to fully understand and master basic knowledge and skills, microcomputer is requests each student must master, compulsory content; the develop contents are the choice of contents to study for the students, according to different professions, different students' level, the requirements for teaching different content in the teaching has taken care to meet the students' interest, hobbies and personality development as the main purpose. The Open Teaching contents of the course are shown in table 1 [3].

Table 1. Open teaching contents of the course

Teaching contents	Basic contents	Develop contents
Theory teaching	.CPU principle and structure; .Instructions and programming; .Interface Chips and application.	.Technology for Bus, Cache, Assembly, Parallel and USB. .CPU of dual-core and multi-core. .Computer systems of dual CPU and multiple CPU.
Experiment teaching	.The basic of principles and interface experiment, including: .Basic of principle, programming and interface experiment.	Comprehensive design experiments, For example: .WDM Driver programming; .Data collection and distance transmission system; . Step motor distance control.

With the continuous advancement of computer technology, micro-computer has been from the original 16-bit, 32-bit fully access to 64-bit. From the CPU perspective of the development, it has developed from single-core, dual-core to multi-core; from the aspect of computer components and structure, but also by a single CPU, dual CPU to multiple CPU. Computer theory has undergone tremendous changes. Many problems have been related to the composition and structure of computer knowledge. However, traditional teaching materials and teaching contents is mainly 16 or 32 bits primarily, therefore, in the teaching process, reflecting the introduction of new ideas and the development of computer content is necessary. For example, introduced 64-bit Pentium processor, Pentium IV, 20-stage pipeline, Harvard computer parallel structure and so on, to enable students to understand the current situation and development of computer technology, so the trend line with the computer, but also to satisfy the desire to learn, open the horizons of students, to stimulate students interest in learning. Theory of teaching generally implemented in the classroom, individual development of knowledge, as an optional learning content, courses on the Internet for students reference.

"The microcomputer principle and Interface Technology "is a strong practical course, combining theory with practice, the theoretical teaching and experimental teaching synchronization. Whether theory teaching, or experiment content, must have a hierarchy and be optional, make the teaching contents appear richness with depth and the breadth to meet different levels students wants to achieve the knowledge system structure, professional knowledge structure and the course content, in the teaching goal of the hierarchy, the dynamic elastic to request, can choose the teaching content, which can better satisfy all student everyone development, individuality development needs. Let the students in the open teaching environment learning from each other, exchanging and discussion, give full play to students' autonomy, and cultivate students' interest and practical innovation spirit.

4 Open Teaching Mode

What we called open teaching mode which means it includes classroom teaching, extracurricular experiment, extracurricular activities, web online teaching and so many types of learning activities not just limited to teach in the classroom.

4.1 Innovative Approach to Teaching

Currently, the main educational method of the universities is teaching in the class, learning during the class is the most important way that students gain knowledge. The quality of class teaching all depends on the teachers' educational method.

When teaching in the classroom, teachers can using heuristic, exploratory, discussion and participatory teaching methods and so on., these methods all fully reflect the thinking of teaching science concepts and the modern learning theory of self-exploration and the core idea of cooperative learning, which is in line with education laws and laws of human growth, is the gateway to teach students how to learn and help students know effective ways of learning. Teaching should be an important part of the reform and practice. Efforts in teaching should do the following points:

First, focus on interaction, inquiry learning. Such as "Why use a port?", "Why there is contradiction between the computer core and peripheral equipments when transfer the data?" and so on, this thinking's lead students to question the learning content, and then the teachers aim at each questions to analyze, students and teachers discuss together, there's a question, there's an answer.

Second, teachers should guide students to discuss, self-explore and gain new knowledge. Teachers give students some time that they can discuss and learn with each other and get new knowledge through self-exploration. This arrangement not only let the teachers know how much the students have grasped, but also can mobilize the enthusiasm of the students, reflecting the dominant position of students.

Third, play multimedia teaching strengths, to achieve human-computer interaction. Such as: build the situation like" How does DMA replace CPU to finish the assignment of transferring data?", Simulate the image of the vivid images of DMA data transfer, so that students can feel a lively animated demonstration, the students would be quickly attracted the attention of the class. Continuously infecting students, make the dry, abstract knowledge into lively, animated images, so that students can observe, think, express and so on. Mobilize a variety of senses of students to participate in learning, inspire the students' interest, activate the students thinking and then help students solve the main and difficult problems.

Fourth, pay attention to feedback and scientific evaluation. Teachers' design of teaching content of the lesson should based on students' existing knowledge and experience, during the process of decomposing knowledge, it's right to fully use the multi-media presentation so that we can observe and record the performance of students in the learning process.

4.2 Make Enrich Activities for the Second Class

The second class activities are an important and effective teaching method to develop the creativity and independent learning ability of students. The technical activities month, professional competition activities and students' innovative plan has become the important classroom to cultivate the operation ability and the practice ability of students, the major carrier to enhance comprehensive quality and innovative ability of students, the effective platform to train the research ability of students.

Students must complete the comprehensive design task in the open lab, which will be used as study result, outstanding works will directly be the entries of technical activities month. The design titles can be chose independently by students, if they meet with the teacher approval, the design works may be used as innovative projects and professional competitions, and as the comprehensive design achievement. The second class activities embody the synthesis of knowledge, the investigation of question and the independent innovation and personal development of students.

4.3 Autonomous Learning by Network Courses

The network course can provide students with a broader study space, a variety of teaching resources would be dropped onto the network. The students can know the learning content and requirements through the network information and select learning content development goals according to their own preferences.

"Thick basis, wide bore, high quality, strong adaptability" must be learn the knowledge and skills training for the college students, Require of students with broad knowledge structure and solid foundation of knowledge, including innovative business knowledge, professional characteristics technical knowledge, theoretical and technical knowledge, moral, economic and legal knowledge of humanities and social sciences, and so on [4]. Students also have to learn foreign historical, cultural, political, economic and international norms and international practice knowledge and accomplishment. Networked autonomous learning is not only the important way to learn the course knowledge and cultivate professional skills, but also the way to cultivate students' innovation ability and creation ability, the key to develop the habit of lifelong learning of students, the chief signs that students know how to learn.

5 Closing

The reform of the open teaching can not only provide students with a broader study space, realize personalized training, enhance students' capacity for independent innovation and creativity, but also build up the ranks of teachers and raise their professional ethics and competence, promote the open laboratory building and improve management of the laboratory, its theoretical and practical significance are well worth studying.

Acknowledgement

Supported by New Century Higher Education Teaching Reform Project of Guangxi China (No.2010JGB029).

References

1. Smaldino, S.E., Russell, J.D.: Instructional Technology And Media For Learning, 8th edn., p. 48. Higher Education Press, Beijing (2005)
2. Shi, Z.-Y.: Education Philosophy, p. 166. Beijing Normal University Press, Beijing (2007)
3. Le, J.-C.: New 16/32Bit Micro-Computer Principle and Application. Tsinghua University Press, Beijing (2007)
4. He, X., Jiang, H.: Educational Reform and Innovation for Undergraduate in Computer Specialty. Computer Education (1), 34–37 (2011)

Numerical Simulations on Fire and Analysis of the Spread Characteristics of Smoke in Supermarket

Daijian Ling and Kaihui Kan

College of Civil Engineering, Yangzhou University
196 West Huayang Road, Yangzhou, Jiangsu Province, P.R. China, 225127

Abstract. In order to get the special characteristics of fire spread and smoke movement inside supermarket, a typical fire scenario in supermarket model is established in this paper. Fire spreading and smoke movement inside the building is simulated by FDS (Fire Dynamic Simulator) software, and the simulation results are displayed in Smokeview. By studying the process of fire spread and smoke motion in different cases of smoke evacuation, the laws of smoke spread and temperature, speed, concentration of various components distribution is analyzed. It provides some results for performance-based fire protection design in supermarket buildings.

Keywords: Supermarket, Fire, FDS, Smoke Spread.

1 Introduction

Based on the specific function, the building structure of large supermarket has some characteristics. Because of the higher story, hot smoke will go down before rising to the ceiling during fire, and it leads to the air filling with smoke. The horizontal distance is longer which makes the diffuse speed reduces during the process of smoke spread, and it results the deposition of poisonous gas in the local field. The temperature near the ceiling is higher which prevents smoke from going up to the top of the room, which is often called the heat barrier phenomenon. Because of the above characteristics, the thermal convection will speed up inside fire area. In addition, fire spreads quickly under the influence of wind action and chimney effect caused by staircase, lift shaft and conduit shaft. It will make difficulty for fire protection and deliverance[1-3].

The given fire scenario in a large supermarket is simulated by FDS in this paper. The results incarnate aspects characters of fire, such as the law of fire spread and smoke motion, temperature, velocity and concentration of various components changed with time[4-5]. The simulation results will be helpful for fire performance-based designs, including fire compartment, exit passageway and lift, ventilation system, fire alarm, spray system and so on.

2 Software Brief Introduction

FDS[6] is the abbreviation for Fire Dynamics Simulator. It is a computational fluid dynamics model of fire-driven fluid flow, and is developed by NIST (National Institute

S. Lin and X. Huang (Eds.): CESM 2011, Part II, CCIS 176, pp. 7–13, 2011.

of Standards and Technology) of American. FDS solves numerically a form of the Navier-Stokes equations appropriate for low-speed, thermally-driven flow with an emphasis on smoke and heat transport from fires. The theory is based on the conservation of mass, momentum and energy, and the law of chemical reaction. A differential equation is summarized from the above theories. The temperature and concentration field at different times and locations can be calculated according to the border conditions[7]. Smokeview is a separate visualization program that is used to display the results of an FDS simulation. The first version of FDS was publicly released in 2000, and the latest version is FDS5.5.3.

In an FDS simulation, an FDS input text file should be established, including building parameters, such as the size, composition, window and door and furniture, parameters of heat, heat boundary conditions. Meanwhile, the other parameters, such as mesh density, location, type and heat release of fuel. This paper finishes calculation through inputting model from PyroSim software to FDS directly.

By studying the process of fire spread and smoke motion in the supermarket, the law of temperature distribution and smoke spread will be analyzed quantitatively. It expects to provide a basis for fire safety-evaluation and achieves some useful results for performance-based fire protection design in buildings.

3 Modeling

3.1 Architectural Status

The full-sized scale model is considered in this paper, and the size of building is 90000mm × 50000mm × 9000mm (length, width, height). The material of constructional elements of floor and wall is concrete. The characteristic parameters for all kinds of furniture can be set from different materials.

According to the nation code[8], the biggest area of fire compartment above ground is no more than $4000m^2$, therefore, the building is divided into two fire compartments; combining with the former, smoke prevention compartment is designed by vertical wall. Because smoke will not spread along horizontal direction until up to the ceiling, it sets a vertical wall with 50 centimeter-high at least. It is divided into eight smoke prevention compartments, and ten exhaust ports are installed. The thermal detectors in the model are used to monitor temperature, velocity and density changing with time.

3.2 Modeling

Considering the limitation of computer configuration and operation time, it is feasible to choose the model mesh as 180 × 100 × 185 and modeling time is 360s after some tests. 3D image is shown in Fig.1.

3.3 Fire Design

Suppose the fire source position is in a desk of supermarket. The fuel is coal gas, and heat release rate $2000kW/m^2$, the mass fraction of smoke released 0.042. It is

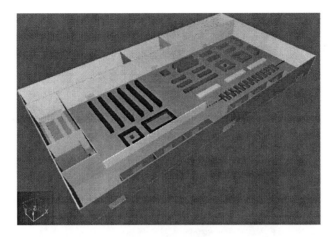

Fig. 1. Supermarket 3D Mode

supposed that all of the doors in the building are open. The simulation is made in the following two cases: exhaust ports are closed all the time and open at 60s.

4   Simulation and the Result Analysis

4.1   Fire Smoke Spread and Concentration Distribution

Through FDS simulation, four diagrams of smoke spread in the building at different time can be obtained from Smokeview. Based on the above two cases, the simulation is shown in Figure2 (a) and (b). Once the burn occurs, smoke moves straight up from fire source. When smoke reaches a certain thickness under the ceiling, it will diffuse along horizontal direction. With the increase of motion distance and entrainment of flesh air, smoke will become rare gradually.

It is found that smoke flow will collide with the vertical wall when it rises to the middle of ceiling. And then it moves down quickly, which slows down the speed of smoke spread. The vertical wall designed for smoke prevent play an important role to prevent the hot smoke from spreading rapidly.

When smoke flow moves to the end of ceiling, it will collide with the wall of building. Momentum is increased with the limit of ceiling. It makes smoke go down along the wall and store to be thicker. This can be used to explain why people may be poisoned away from fire source and in the room on the edge.

From the comparison between the above two cases, the significant difference is observed in distribution of smoke density. Considering main materials of decoration be plastics and chemical fiber, it is easy to burn and give off a large of poisonous gas. As a result, the exhaust ports should be designed according to the correlative code strictly.

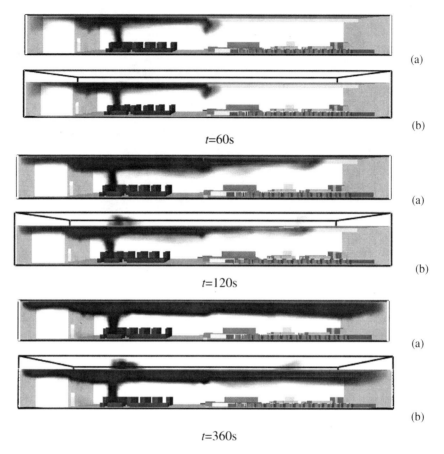

(a)

(b)

t=60s

(a)

(b)

t=120s

(a)

(b)

t=360s

Fig. 2. Smoke spread at different time, (a) Exhaust ports are closed, (b) Exhaust ports open at 60s

4.2 Temperature Distribution in X Direction

The diagrams of temperature distribution at 120s and 360s in X direction are shown in Figure 3.

In the position of $X = -25m$ near the fire source, high temperature area is in vertical distribution over the hot flame, the peak is about 210^0C. Contrast with temperature distribution between $X = -25m$ and $X=25m$ at 120s and 360s, it is found that the hotter smoke is discontinuous at 120s, whereas the hotter is continuous at 360s. This is mainly due to the temperature of smoke flow is lower and rarer in the early period of fire, and the function of cooling and entrainment from cold air is strong. With the development of fire, hot smoke is added continuously and gas cloud is stable, so temperature distribution is continuous.

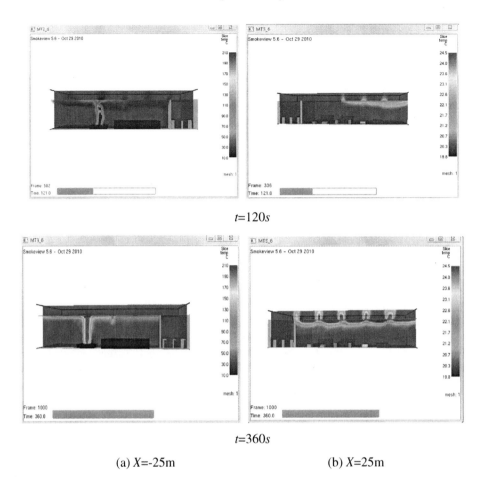

$t=120s$

$t=360s$

(a) X=-25m   (b) X=25m

Fig. 3. Temperature distribution in X direction at different time

4.3 Smoke Velocity

The variation of smoke velocity with time and variation of heat release velocity with time have a similar trend. The flow direction of smoke is the paths of fire spread. The velocity of smoke is about five times more than the speed of fire spread. Fig.4 shows the change curve of temperature at different height. The temperature jumps to a certain value after burning, and goes up to the peak with time gradually. The velocity keeps a bigger increase because of the entrainment of hot smoke at $Z = 8m$. The curves in the figure is fluctuating because of the heat transfer and temperature and momentum attenuation under heat convection on one hand, and resistance and friction force from ceiling to hot smoke on the other hand. Comparatively speaking, the velocity of smoke grows gently at $Z = 2m$.

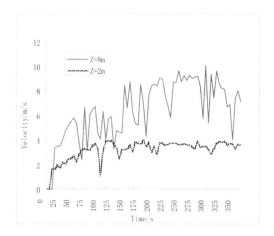

Fig. 4. Variations of smoke velocity with time $(X = -25m)$

4.4 O_2 and CO Density Variation

Figure 5 and 6 are the change curves of O_2 and CO density with time under the two cases of exhaust ports close or open. In the figures, A means the exhaust ports are open, and B means they are closed. In the initial stage of fire, the density of O_2 decreases with time owing to consumption for burning. It returns later. When exhaust ports open, ventilation improves the density of O_2. It goes up at 60s. Density in the case of exhaust port open is higher comparing with exhaust port close.

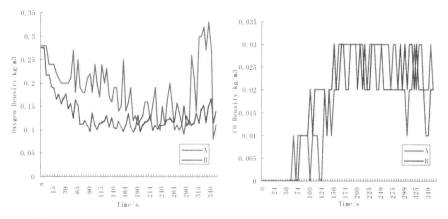

Fig. 5. Variation of O_2 density with time   **Fig. 6.** Variation of CO density with time

With the sustainable burning and the consumption of O_2, the poisonous gas of CO is produced from the incomplete combustion of fuel. This is one factor of casualties. The change rule of CO density is alike substantially. Exhaust port open makes flesh air entrainment, which postpones the time of CO production effectively. In addition, it can exhaust poisonous gas and achieve time for fire suppression and personnel evacuation.

5 Conclusions and Recommendations

Fire spread and smoke movement inside the supermarket is simulated by FDS and the law of smoke flow is analyzed in the paper. The hot smoke released by fire burning goes up vertically under the function of buoyancy force. When smoke rises to the ceiling, it forms ceiling jet in horizontal direction. After accumulating to a certain thickness, it will move down along the wall. It also leads to phenomena of backward flow in horizontal direction. With the supplement and entrainment of cold air continuously, temperature and peak velocity of hot smoke intend to decrease. Exhaust port open or not directly influence thickness of smoke and density of O_2 and CO.

When designing fire protection for large supermarket, the vertical wall in smoke bar should be added to delay the hot smoke spread. It is important for engineers to design smoke extraction system according to both the code and the simulation results, which can be useful for speed up the spread of smoke and the performance-based fire safety design.

References

1. Huo, R., et al.: Building Fire Safety Engineering Introduction. Chinese University of Science and Technology Press, Hefei (1999) (in Chinese)
2. Zhong, M.-H.: Dynamics Analysis of Fire Process. Science Press, Beijing (2007) (in Chinese)
3. Feng, R., et al.: Simulation studies on Smoke Spread and Occupant Evacuation for Shopping Mall Fire. Journal of Safety and Environment 1, 22–25 (2006)
4. Tewarson, A.: Nonthermal Fire Damage. Fire Science 10, 188–241 (1992)
5. Hietaniemi, J., Kallonen, R., Mikkola, E.: Burning Characteristics of Selected Substances Production of Heat, Smoke and Chemical Species. Fire and Materials 3(4), 71–185 (1999)
6. Wu, W.-Y., et al.: Physically-based Model for Fire Scenario in FDS. Journal of System Simulation 17(8), 1800–1802 (2005)
7. Grattan, K.B.M.C., Baum, H.R., Rehm, R.G., et al.: Fire Dynamics Simulator Reference Guide. Building and Fire Research Laboratory (2002)
8. Ministry of Public Security of the People's Republic of China. Code of Design on Building Fire Protection and Prevention GB 50016—2006 (2006) (in Chinese)

Numerical Simulation of Nonlinear Filtering Problem

Zhen Liu[1], Fangfang Dong[2], and Luwei Ding[3,*]

[1] Department of Mathematics
Zhejiang University of Technology, Hangzhou 310023, China
[2] School of Statistics and Mathematics
Zhejiang Gongshang University, Hangzhou 310018, China
[3] School of Science
Huazhong Agricultural University, Wuhan 430070, China
deer@mail.hzau.edu.cn

Abstract. In the paper, we give the numerical simulation of nonlinear filtering problem. We introduce the basic filtering problem and review the reduction from robust Duncan-Mortensen-Zakai equation to Kolmogorov equation firstly. Then the difference scheme of the Kolmogorov equation is given to calculate the nonlinear filtering equation. We derive the result that the solution of the difference scheme convergences pointwise to the solution of the initial-value problem of the Kolmogorov equation. Numerical experiments show that the numerical method can give the exact result.

Keywords: Nonlinear filtering equation, DMZ equation, Kolmogorov equation.

1 Introduction

In 1961, Kalman and Bucy [1] published a historically important mathematics paper on filtering that are highly influential to the modern industry. Since then, the Kalman-Bucy filtering has proved useful in many areas such as navigational and guidance systems, radar tracking, solar mapping, and satellite orbit determination. Ever since the technique of the Kalman-Bucy filtering was popularized, there has been an intense interest in developing nonlinear filtering theory. In the 1960s and early 1970s, the basic approach to nonlinear filtering theory was via "innovation methods" originally proposed by Kailath [2] and Frost and Kailath[3] and subsequently rigorous developed by Fujisaki, Kallianpur, and Kunita[4] in 1972. But the difficulty with this approach is that innovation process is not, in general, explicitly computable. In the late 1970s, Brockett and Clark [5], Brockett [6] and Mitter [7] proposed the idea of using estimation algebras to construct a finite dimensional nonlinear filtering. Yau and his coworkers have finally classified all finite dimensional estimation algebras of Maximal rank ([8],[9],[10]).

Although it is an interesting and challenging problem to classify all finite dimensional filtering, it appears that from Yau's previous works, finite dimensional filtering simply does not exist for many practical situations. In [11], Yau and Yau

---

* Corresponding author.

S. Lin and X. Huang (Eds.): CESM 2011, Part II, CCIS 176, pp. 14–19, 2011.
© Springer-Verlag Berlin Heidelberg 2011

proved the existence and decay estimates of the solution to the DMZ(Duncan-Mortensen-Zakai) equation under the assumption that the drift terms of the signal dynamic and observation dynamic respectively have linear growths. Later they [12] showed that the real-time solution of DMZ equation can be reduced to off-time solution of Kolmogorov equation if the drift terms have linear growths. Recently Yau and Yau [13] finally proved that the real-time solution of DMZ equation can be reduced to off-time solution of Kolmororov equation if the growth of the drift term of observation dynamic at infinity is faster than the growth of the drift term of signal dynamic at infinity.

In section 2, we recall the basic filtering problem and review the reduction from robust DMZ equation to Kolmogorov equation of Yau-Yau method. In section 3, we shall use finite difference method to derive the solution of Kolmororov equation. The numerical simulation of Yau-Yau method is shown in section 4.

2 Introduction of Yau-Yau Methods for Nonlinear Filtering Problem

The filtering problem considered here is based on the signal observation model

$$dx(t) = f(x(t)) + g(x(t))dv(t), \qquad x(0) = x_0. \tag{1}$$

$$dy(t) = h(x(t)) + dw(t), \qquad y(0) = 0. \tag{2}$$

in which x, v, y and w are R^n, R^p, R^m and R^m valued processes and v, w have components that are independent, standard Brownian processes.

Let $\rho(x,t)$ denote the conditional probability density of the state given the observation $\{y(s) : 0 \le s \le t\}$. Then $\rho(x,t)$ is given by normalizing a function $\sigma(t,x)$ that satisfies the following Duncan-Mortensen-Zakai equation

$$d\sigma(t,x) = L_0\sigma(t,x)dt + \sum_{i=1}^{m}L_i\sigma(t,x)dy_i(t), \ \sigma(0,x) = \sigma_0(x). \tag{3}$$

Where

$$L_0 = \frac{1}{2}\sum_{i=1}^{n}\frac{\partial^2}{\partial x_i^2} - \sum_{i=1}^{n}f_i\frac{\partial}{\partial x_i} - \sum_{i=1}^{n}\frac{\partial f_i}{\partial x_i} - \frac{1}{2}\sum_{i=1}^{m}h_i^2. \tag{4}$$

and L_i is the zero degree differential operator of multiplication by h_i $i = 1, 2, \cdots, m$. From the robust algorithms proposed by Davis [14], it define a new unnormalized density

$$u(t,x) = \exp(-\sum_{i=1}^{m}h_i(x)y_i(t))\sigma(t,x). \tag{5}$$

Then we can reduce the equation (3) to the following equation, which is called robust DMZ equation,

$$u_t = \frac{1}{2}\Delta u + F(t,x)\cdot\nabla u + V(t,x)u, u(0,x) = \sigma_0(x). \tag{6}$$

where drift function $F(t,x) = -f(x) + \nabla k(t,x)$, source function

$$V(t,x) = -divf(x) - \frac{1}{2}|h(x)|^2 + \frac{1}{2}\Delta k(t,x) - f(x) \cdot \nabla k(t,x) + \frac{1}{2}|\nabla k(t,x)|^2 .$$

The fundamental problem of nonlinear filtering theory is how to solving the robust DMZ equation (6) in real time and in memoryless manner. Suppose $u(t,x)$ is the solution of robust DMZ equation. Let $T_k = \{0 = \tau_0 < \tau_1 < \cdots < \tau_k = \tau\}$ be a partition of $[0,\tau]$ and $u_i(t,x)$ be a solution of the following equation for $\tau_{i-1} \leq t \leq \tau_i$

$$\frac{\partial u_i}{\partial t}(t,x) = \frac{1}{2}\Delta u(t,x) + F(\tau_i,x) \cdot \nabla u + V(\tau_i,x)u \tag{7}$$

$$u_i(\tau_{i-1},x) = u_{i-1}(\tau_{i-1},x) . \tag{8}$$

Theorem 1. [Yau-Yau] Let $u(t,x)$ and $u_k(t,x)$ be the solutions of (6) and (7) respectively. For any given $\varepsilon > 0$ and sufficiently large n,

$$|u(t,x) - u_k(t,x)| \leq \varepsilon T e^{CT} . \tag{9}$$

and

$$u(\tau,x) = \lim_{|\tau_k| \to 0} u_k(\tau_k,x) \quad \text{uniformly in } x . \tag{10}$$

Where C is the constant and $|T_k| = \sup_{1 \leq i \leq n} \{|\tau_i - \tau_{i-1}|\}$.

So the solution of (7) approximate the solution of robust DMZ equation very well in the point wise sense. Therefore it remains to describe an algorithm to compute $u_k(\tau_k,x)$, which is based on the following property.

Proposition 1. [Yau-Yau] $\tilde{u}(t,x)$ satisfies the following Kolmogorov equation

$$\frac{\partial \tilde{u}}{\partial t}(t,x) = \frac{1}{2}\Delta \tilde{u}(t,x) - \sum_{i=1}^{n} f_i(x)\frac{\partial \tilde{u}}{\partial x_i}(t,x) - (\sum_{i=1}^{n}\frac{\partial f_i}{\partial x_i}(x) + \frac{1}{2}\sum_{i=1}^{m} h_i^2(x))\tilde{u}(t,x) . \tag{11}$$

for $\tau_{i-1} \leq t \leq \tau_i$ if and only if $u(t,x) = \exp(-\sum_{i=1}^{m} h_i(x)y_i(\tau_i))\tilde{u}(t,x)$ satisfies the robust DMZ equation with observation being fixed at $y(\tau_i)$

$$\frac{\partial u}{\partial t}(t,x) = \frac{1}{2}\Delta u(t,x) + F(\tau_i,x) \cdot \nabla u + V(\tau_i,x)u . \tag{12}$$

3   Numerical Method for the Kolmogorov Equation

Consider the Kolmogorov equation (11), we use finite difference method to approximate the solution of the equation. We take the Kolmogorov equation

$$\frac{\partial u}{\partial t}(t,x) = \frac{1}{2}\frac{\partial^2 u}{\partial x^2}(t,x) + p(x)\frac{\partial u}{\partial x}(t,x) + q(x)u(t,x) . \tag{13}$$

as example to explain the method, where $p(x) = -f(x), q(x) = -(\frac{\partial f}{\partial x}(x) + \frac{1}{2}\sum_{i=1}^{m} h_i^2(x))$.

To approximate the equation (13) by finite difference, we discretize the spatial and time domain by placing a grid over the domain. For convenience, we use a uniform grid, with grid spacing Δx and Δt. The space-time domain of our problem then is approximated by the lattice of points. We will attempt to approximate the solution to our problem at the points on the lattice. We define v_k^n to be a function at the point $(k\Delta x, n\Delta t)$. To arrive at the finite difference equation used to approximation the Kolmogorov equation, we use the approximation

$$u_t(n\Delta t, k\Delta x) \approx \frac{v_k^{n+1} - v_k^n}{\Delta t} \tag{14}$$

$$u_{xx}(n\Delta t, k\Delta x) \approx \frac{v_{k+1}^n - 2v_k^n + v_{k-1}^n}{\Delta x^2} \tag{15}$$

$$u_x(n\Delta t, k\Delta x) \approx \frac{v_k^n - v_{k-1}^n}{\Delta x} \tag{16}$$

We see that

$$u_t - \frac{1}{2}u_{xx} - p(x)u_x - q(x)u =$$

$$\frac{u_k^{n+1} - u_k^n}{\Delta t} - \frac{1}{2}\frac{u_{k+1}^n - 2u_k^n + u_{k-1}^n}{\Delta x^2} - p(x_k)\frac{u_k^n - u_{k-1}^n}{\Delta x} - q(x_k)u_k^n. \tag{17}$$

where the above expression assumes that the higher order derivatives of u at $(k\Delta x, n\Delta t)$ are bounded.

Then we have the following theorem,

Theorem 2. Suppose $q(x_k) < 0$, and

$$1 - \frac{1}{2}\frac{2\Delta t}{\Delta x^2} + \frac{\Delta t}{\Delta x}p(x_k) + \Delta t q(x_k) \geq 0, \frac{1}{2}\frac{\Delta t}{\Delta x^2} - \frac{\Delta t}{\Delta x}p(x_k) \geq 0. \tag{18}$$

then the solution of the difference scheme

$$v_k^{n+1} = v_k^n + \frac{1}{2}\frac{\Delta t}{\Delta x^2}(v_{k+1}^n - 2v_k^n + v_{k-1}^n) + \frac{\Delta t}{\Delta x}p(x_k)(v_k^n - v_{k-1}^n) + \Delta t q(x_k)v_k^n \tag{19}$$

convergences pointwise to the solution of the initial-value problem

$$\frac{\partial u}{\partial t}(t,x) = \frac{1}{2}\frac{\partial^2 u}{\partial x^2}(t,x) + p(x)\frac{\partial u}{\partial x}(t,x) + q(x)u(t,x) \tag{20}$$

4 Numerical Simulation for the Nonlinear Filtering

Let $f(x) = \cos(x), h(x) = \sin(x)$, and $f(x) = x^2, h(x) = \sin(x)$ respectively, we can have figure 1 and 2, where $\sigma_0 = \exp(-10 * x^2)$. The dashed line denotes the mean of the conditional probability density ρ and the solid line is generated from discrete extended Kalman filtering equations. Figure 3 and 4 show the numerical behavior of the conditional probability density ρ in different time.

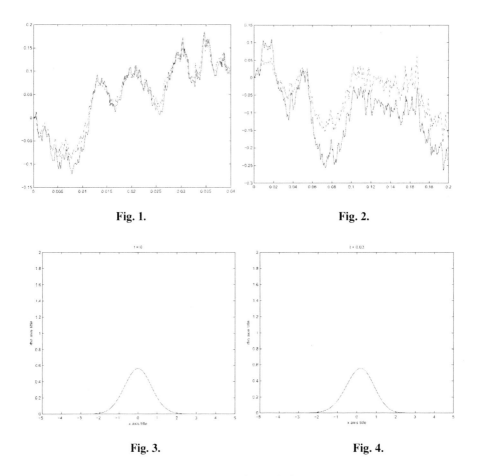

Fig. 1.   Fig. 2.

Fig. 3.   Fig. 4.

Acknowledgement. This work is supported by Zhejiang Provincial Natural Science Foundation of China (Grant No. Y6100526) and by National Natural Science Foundation of China (Grant No.10801045).

References

1. Kalman, R.E., Bucy, R.S.: New results in linear filtering and prediction theory. Trans. ASME Series D, J. Basic Engineering 83(196), 95–108
2. Kailath, T.: An innovations approach to least-squares estimation, Part I: Linear filtering in additive white noise. IEEE Transactions on Automatic Control 13, 646–655 (1986)
3. Frost, P.A., Kailath, T.: An innovations approach to least-squares estimation II. IEEE Transactions on Automatic Control 16, 217–226 (1971)
4. Fujisaki, M., Kallianpur, G., Kunita, H.: Stochastic differential equations for the nonlinear filtering problem. Osaka Journal of Mathematics 2, 19–40 (1972)
5. Brockett, R.W., Clark, J.M.C.: The geometry of the conditional density functions. In: Jacobs, O.L.R., et al. (eds.) Analysis and Optimization of Stochastic Systems, pp. 299–309. Academic Press, New York (1980)

6. Brockett, R.W.: Nonlinear systems and nonlinear estimation theory. In: Hazewinkel, M., Williams, J.C. (eds.) The Mathematics of Filtering and Identification and Application, pp. 479–504. Reidel, Dordrecht (1981)
7. Mittar, S.K.: On the analogy between mathematical problems of nonlinear filtering and quantum physics. Ricerche Automat. 10, 163–216 (1979)
8. Yau, S.S.-T., Hu, G.-Q.: Classification of finite dimensional estimation algebras of maximal rank with arbitrary state-space dimension and Mitter Conjecture. International Journal of Control 78(10), 689–705 (2005)
9. Chen, J., Yau, S.S.-T.: Finite dimensional filters with nonlinear drift VI: Linear structure of Ω. Mathematics of Control, Signals and Systems 9, 370–385 (1996)
10. Yau, S.S.-T., Wu, X., Wong, W.S.: Hessian matrix non-decomposition theorem. Mathematical Research Letter 6, 1–11 (1999)
11. Yau, S.-T., Yau, S.S.-T.: Existence and uniqueness and decay estimates for the time dependent parabolic equation with application to Duncan-Mortensen-Zakai equation. Asian Journal of Mathematics 2, 1079–1149 (1998)
12. Yau, S.-T., Yau, S.S.-T.: Real time solution of nonlinear filtering problem without memory I. Mathematical Research Letter 7, 671–693 (2000)
13. Yau, S.-T., Yau, S.S.-T.: Real time solution of nonlinear filtering problem without memory II (preprint)
14. Davis, M.H.A.: On a multiplicative functional transformation arising in nonlinear filtering theory. Z. Wahrsch Verw. Gebiete 54, 125–139 (1980)

An Wavelet Multi-scale Edge Detection Algorithm Based on Adaptive Dual Threshold

Ni Zhao and HuaPeng Zhang

Luoyang Institute of Science and Technology, Luoyang, China
chewchew@yeah.net,
lygzzhp@163.com

Abstract. This paper, firstly researches the wavelet module maximum edge detecting algorithm, then puts forward the adaptive dual threshold method aiming at advantages and disadvantages of threshold, and make threshold partial self-adaption come true. For the pixels of module between two thresholds, this method can improve the detection accuracy by using the difference between edge and noise for further selecting candidate edge. The paper integrates multi-scale structural elements of filtering and denoising image with morphological sharpening algorithm, and makes the self-adaptive integration for edge information with different directions through the calculation of edge variance. The result shows that the method can efficiently filter noise interference, sharpen image edge, remain image edge information and improve the result of edge detection.

Keywords: Edge Detecting, Adaptive Dual Threshold Method, Multi-scale, Wavelet.

1 Introduction

Image edge contains most part of information, and it is where serious comparison of image gray scale takes place and is also the important basis of image segmentation, image compression and recognition. It is very difficult for image edge diction because of noise similar to edge dot frequency, so the difficulty and hot spot of research is to improve the edge detection accuracy and simultaneously suppress image noise[1].

Wavelet transform is a mathematical tool used widely in recent years. It has the characteristics of multi-scale and good localization properties in time domain and frequency domain. Also, it applies refined sample steps to high frequency components so that any subject detail can be focused[2]. Therefore, wavelet transform is a powerful tool for detecting singularity signals. Singularity in the area of wavelet transform correspond to maxima or zero-crossing of wavelet transform modulus, edge detection based on wavelet transform is to apply wavelet transform on original image and divide it into different frequency bands, the selected modulus of high frequency is the edge.

S. Lin and X. Huang (Eds.): CESM 2011, Part II, CCIS 176, pp. 20–25, 2011.

2   Edge Detection Algorithms Based on Wavelet Transform

2.1   Method of Wavelet Transform Modulus Maxima

Wavelet is localized in time and frequency domains, so modulus maxima correspond to singularities which can be found through detecting modulus maxima. Image multi-scale edge detection can be carried out by detecting signal singularities of wavelet transform.

Given two-dimensional differentiable smooth function is $\theta(x, y)$, two requirements should be met.

$$\iint_R \theta(x, y)dxdy = 1 \tag{1}$$

$$\lim_{x,y\to\infty} \theta(x, y) = 0 \tag{2}$$

First-order partial derivatives of smooth function $\theta(x, y)$ in the directions of x and y should be the basic wavelet function[3].

$$\begin{cases} \psi^1(x, y) = \dfrac{\partial\theta(x, y)}{\partial x} \\ \psi^2(x, y) = \dfrac{\partial\theta(x, y)}{\partial y} \end{cases} \tag{3}$$

It can be resulted according to equation (1), equation(2)and equation(3):

$$\begin{cases} \iint_R \psi^1(x, y)dxdy = \int_R [\theta(+\infty, y) - \theta(-\infty, y)]dy = 0 \\ \iint_R \psi^2(x, y)dxdy = \int_R [\theta(x,+\infty) - \theta(x,-\infty)]dx = 0 \end{cases} \tag{4}$$

So $\psi^1(x, y)$, $\psi^2(x, y)$ is two-dimensional wavelet

Wavelet basis function can be created by basis wavelet shrinkage[3][4].

$$\begin{cases} \Psi_a^1(x, y) = \dfrac{1}{\alpha^2}\Psi^1(\dfrac{x}{\alpha}, \dfrac{y}{\alpha}) = \dfrac{\partial\theta_\alpha(x, y)}{\partial x} \\ \Psi_a^2(x, y) = \dfrac{1}{\alpha^2}\Psi^2(\dfrac{x}{\alpha}, \dfrac{y}{\alpha}) = \dfrac{\partial\theta_\alpha(x, y)}{\partial y} \end{cases} \tag{5}$$

Where in: $\theta_\alpha(x, y) = \dfrac{1}{\alpha^2}\theta(\dfrac{x}{\alpha}, \dfrac{y}{\alpha})$ 。

In discrete algorithm, only scale $\alpha = 2^j$, $j \in Z$ should be considered, here, wavelet is translated into dyadic wavelet. Image $f(x, y)$ dyadic wavelet is transformed:

$$\begin{bmatrix} W_{2^j}^1 f(x, y) \\ W_{2^j}^2 f(x, y) \end{bmatrix} = \begin{bmatrix} f(x, y) * \Psi_{2^j}^1(x, y) \\ f(x, y) * \Psi_{2^j}^2(x, y) \end{bmatrix} = 2^j \begin{bmatrix} \dfrac{\partial}{\partial x}[f(x, y) * \theta_{2^j}(x, y)] \\ \dfrac{\partial}{\partial y}[f(x, y) * \theta_{2^j}(x, y)] \end{bmatrix} \tag{6}$$

$$= grad|f(x, y) * \theta_{2^j}(x, y)|$$

In the formula, $W_{2^j}^1 f(x, y)$ represents horizontal detail components with scale 2^j, $W_{2^j}^2 f(x, y)$ represents vertical detail components with scale 2^j. This formula shows the wavelet transform of image in the directions of row and line is the grads after smoothing when image passes smooth function, so edge points are the modulus maxima of result function. Modulus of gradient vector can be derived through formula (6):

$$M_j f(x, y) = \sqrt{[W_{2^j}^1 f(x, y)]^2 + [W_{2^j}^2 f(x, y)]^2} \qquad (7)$$

The angle between gradient vector and horizontal direction:

$$A_j f(x, y) = \arctan\left[\frac{W_{2^j}^2 f(x, y)}{W_{2^j}^1 f(x, y)}\right] \qquad (8)$$

Local modulus maxima creation: in the direction of gradient vector, process the detection in some area, keep the maxima and delete non-maxima. Therefore, for the image pixel (x, y), modulus $M_j f(x, y)$ in the angle direction $A_j f(x, y)$ is compared with the one of two adjacent pixels so as to judge if $A_j f(x, y)$ is the local maximum and determine candidate edge point and then modulus maximum image.

2.2 Scale Product Function

Noise and edge of signal belong to singular points, and represent local modulus maxima of signal wavelet transform coefficients, to distinguish detected singular points, the difference between edge and noise should be found. But under the effect of wavelet transform and because of the signal regularity, signal edge and noise will show different characteristics with the increasing scale. When edge is detected under small-scale wavelet transform, the edge localization is correct, but will cause strong response for noise and signal edge, and overmuch fake edge; while detecting edge under big-scale wavelet transform, the noise could be filtered efficiently, but excess smooth will be caused, and edge information will be lost, then edge localization will not be correct[5]. Therefore, according to different scale characteristics between noise and edge signal, differences between edge and noise should be strengthened by multiplying adjacent scale wavelet modulus. In this way, edge response would be stronger and noise response be weaker, then multi-scale edge detection is realized. Scale function is therefor defined:

$$\begin{cases} Pf_j^1(x, y) = W_j^1 f(x, y) \cdot W_{j+1}^1 f(x, y) \\ Pf_j^2(x, y) = W_j^2 f(x, y) \cdot W_{j+1}^2 f(x, y) \end{cases} \qquad (9)$$

In the formula, $Pf_j^1(x, y)$ and $Pf_j^2(x, y)$ separately represent corrected horizontal detail component and vertical detail component.

Now, modulus and angle at the point of (x, y) will be:

$$M_j f(x, y) = \sqrt{[Pf_j^1(x, y)]^2 + [Pf_j^2(x, y)]^2} \qquad (10)$$

$$A_j f(x, y) = \arctan\left[\frac{Pf_j^2(x, y)}{Pf_j^1(x, y)}\right]$$ (11)

According to new wavelet coefficients constructed by scale product, modulus and angle can be derived, modulus maximum image can be derived by selecting candidate edge points by means of local maximum as shown in 1.1.

2.3 Selecting Adaptive Dual Threshold

In the maximum image, there is edge signal as well as unexpected noise. Though the frequency of signal and noise could be overlapped, but their power is not the same. Wavelet transform makes the power of edge signal centralize in few wavelet transform coefficients, those coefficients values are much greater than the ones of noise whose power is scattered on many wavelet coefficients, wavelet coefficients are under the process of threshold value, and noise with low amplitude and unexpected signal can be reduced within the domain of wavelet transform. The selection of threshold value is vital, if the value is too small, the noise will be filtered incompletely and edge or fake edge will be introduced; if the value is too big, expected local edge signal will deleted, so the edge information will be lost so that detection effect will be influenced. In addition, if the same threshold value is applied to the whole image, weak edge will be removed together with noise, which will influence image edge detection. Ege is the image local characteristic with continuity, while noise is commonly isolated, therefore, based on such difference, this paper puts forward a new adaptive dual threshold according to Canny's dual threshold thought.

- Definition of adaptive high threshold: 3x3 window, scan modulus maximum image point by point, threshold of pixels lie in the central window can be derived by using wavelet coefficients in the window, and can be defined as below:

$$Th(x, y) = T_0 + \sum_{i,j} M_{i,j} / (3 \times 3)$$ (12)

In the formula, Th is the high threshold at the point (x, y), T_0 is initial threshold, $M_{i,j}$ is the corresponding wavelet coefficient. Because the best threshold lies in between half average value of image pixel and half maximum value of pixel, this paper selects half average value of image pixel as initial

- Determining adaptive low threshold

$$Tl(x, y) = 0.1 \times Th(x, y)$$ (13)

- Determination of edge points. If $M(x, y) > Th(x, y)$, (x, y) is the edge point. If $M(x, y) > Th(x, y)$, then (x, y) is the noise point. For the pixels between high and low threshold, that is $Tl(x, y) \leq M(x, y) \leq Th(x, y)$, we should judge if there will be edge points around adjacent domain, if edge points exist, they will be edge point, if not, they should be noise point, and image edge point will be derived.

3   Concrete Steps for Improving Algorithm

The concrete steps for edge detection algorithm are shown as below:

- Proper wavelet basis and wavelet decomposing scale are selected for wavelet transform, and then a series of high-frequency and low-frequency images can be obtained.
- Modulus maximum image can be obtained by using corrected wavelet coefficients of scale product function and choosing corrected modulus maximum of wavelet coefficients extracted in formulas (10) and (11) as the candidate edge points.
- Edge points can be obtained by selecting candidate edge points in the way of improved adaptive dual threshold and filter noise points.
- Image edge curve is formed. Connecting edge points. The principle is adjacent points. The points with similar grey are connected, and the direction is vertical with the direction of angle.

4   Simulation Experiment

This paper add 30-level Gaussian white noise into 256×256 Lena testing image and uses quadric B-spline wavelet to process 3-decomposition, and uses 2-scale and 3-scale wavelet coefficients to construct scale product function to correct wavelet coefficients. In order to test the effect of edge detection algorithm, this paper makes the comparison among wavelet edge detection algorithm based on adaptive single threshold, traditional Sobel algorithm and Canny algorithm, the results are shown as Fig.1:

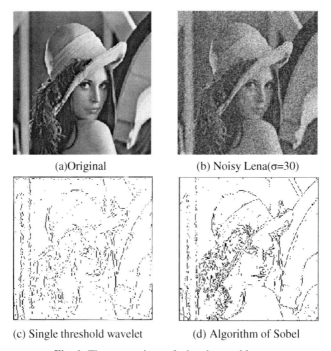

(a)Original   (b) Noisy Lena(σ=30)

(c) Single threshold wavelet   (d) Algorithm of Sobel

Fig. 1. The comparison of edge detected Lena

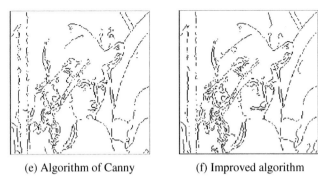

(e) Algorithm of Canny   (f) Improved algorithm

Fig. 1. (*continued*)

Fig.1. shows that the result of wavelet edge detection algorithm based on adaptive single threshold is the worst, there are lots of noise around the edge. The edge of crowns is detected by using Sobel method, which is not detected by using other methods, and the edge is complete, but there is still little noise as shown in Fig. 1.(d). Canny algorithm has strong denoising effect as shown in Fig.1.(e). But algorithm this paper uses can extract completely the edge of right side of background image, and has a better continuity than single threshold method and Soble method. In summary, the denoising effect and continuity of algorithm used in this paper with less edge loss are all better than other methods.

5 Conclusion

This paper introduces the basic information of wavelet analysis, and establishes a theoretical foundation for edge detection by using wavelet transform. According to different characteristics caused by edge signal and noise signal with scale change, scale product function is introduced to enhance edge and suppress noise. Based on dual threshold algorithm of Canny operator, a new adaptive dual threshold algorithm is put forward, which has the advantage of adaptive single threshold and also considers the difference between noise and edge signal, improves the accuracy of determining threshold modulus maximum pixel and detection accuracy. This method can realize automatically determining threshold, eliminates the man-made factors. The result of simulation experiment shows this method is effective.

References

1. Shyu, M.-S., Leou, J.-J.: A genetic algorithm approach to color image enhancement. Pattern Recongnition 31(7), 871–880 (1998)
2. Hankyu, M., Rama, C., Azriel, R.: Optimal Edge_ based Shape Detection. IEEE Trans. on Image Processing 11(I1), 1209–1227 (2002)
3. Gonzalez, R.C., E·Woods, R.: Digital image Processing, 2nd edn. Publishing House of Electronics Industry, Beijing (2003)
4. Hou, Z., Koh, T.: Robust edge detection. Pattern Recognition 36(9), 2083–2091 (2003)
5. Ruzon, M., Tomasi, C.: Alpha estimation in natural images. In: Proceedings of the IEEE Conference on Computer Vision and Pattern Recognition, vol. 1.1, pp. 18–25 (2000)

Credibility Evaluation of Information Service Platform Based on SOA-Extended

JingJing Yan[1,*], TingJie Lv[1], LongFei Guo[1], and ZiMu Zhang[2]

[1] Key Laboratory of Information Management and Economy,
Beijing University of Post and Telecommunication, Beijing 100876, China
[2] State Key Laboratory of Intelligent Technology and Systems,
Tsinghua, Beijing 100084, China

Abstract. The current information service platforms often consider service providers and users to be credible, causing that the service quality of platform is not high, but in the actual web, the parties involved in the service may be false and malicious. Thus low degree reputation seriously affects the quality of services and other issues of information service platform. In this paper, based on KMRW, firstly we evaluate the credibility of the information source, and then, using the double-Rating credit evaluation model, we effectively describe the service and feedback trust evolutionary relationship between information service platform and users.

Keywords: SOA, Information Service Platform, reputation model, KMRW, trust of service, trust of feedback.

1 Introduction

Service-oriented architecture (SOA) provides a standard programming model, making the software components on the network to be published, discovered and invoked. This model generally involves three roles: Service Provider (SP), Service Registry (SR) and Service Consumer (SC). Among them, the service consumer needs to use the service application or other services, through the service registry to search for the demanded services and bind with the service provider to invoke the service.[1] Service providers establish services to publish the service interfaces to the service registry, and provide the consumer corresponding service. Service registry take a predominant part to store service information, for the service consumers' searching for the demanded services and service providers' registering the services offered.

In this open architecture, users can freely register, find and bind services. But with the increasing applications, information services available on the network also show a growth trend, so it becomes the current key issue to identify the fraud uncertain services. In the traditional SOA structure, the credibility issue of service has not been focused on. Therefore, this paper introduces the credibility service module to the SOA architecture, presenting a SOA-extended architecture on the information service platform.

---

* Corresponding author.

S. Lin and X. Huang (Eds.): CESM 2011, Part II, CCIS 176, pp. 26–32, 2011.

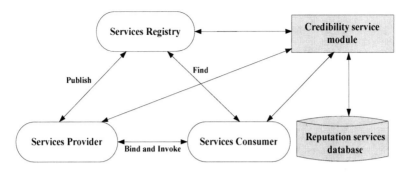

Fig. 1. Extended SOA model [2]

2   Credibility Model of the Credibility Service Module

In the information service platform, its reputation services include two aspects: (1) For the open information services platform based on SOA-extended, it is very needed to develop some constraint mechanisms to protect the credibility of information sources, so the perspective of the credibility of information source based on KMRW reputation model can be used to research the credibility of the information service platform; (2) After the platform provides service to user, the user should give an evaluation of this service feedback to the platform. But there commonly exists the situation that some malice consumer gives false evaluation, so it is very necessary to build a double credit evaluation of services trust and feedback trust based on dual-ratings credit evaluation model between service platform and users. The credit rating relationship of information service platform based on SOA-extended shown in Figure 2:

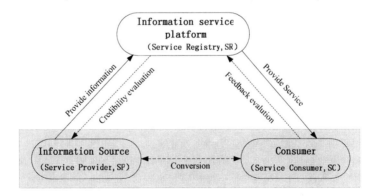

Fig. 2. Credit rating diagram of information service platform based on SOA-extended

Based on the true reliability of information provided by users and fairness of score after interaction, the users can be divided into the following 4 types:

(1) Sincere user, which provides authentic services to other users in the system, and provides a fair rating for each other in the end of the interaction. [3]

(2) Traitorous user, which sometimes provides truthful services and fair score to other users in order to accumulate the credibility value of their own, but sometimes provides unreal or non-credible service to seek illegal interests, and denigrate the value of service through give the unfair credit score to the other.

(3) Malicious user, which always provides unreal or non-credible service and gives unfair credit score to other user.

(4) Collusive user, which is a group formed by the part of illegal users, usually bids up the credit score of each other, while slander the reputation value of legitimate users, in order to deceive other users to trust him and refuse interact with the legitimate users.

3   The Reputation Evaluation of Information Sources

KMRW reputation model is a classical model in the reputation theory, established by David M. Kreps, Paul Milgrom, John Roberts and Robert Wilson. This model made a good explanation for the effect of reputation (ie, co-phenomenon) in limited repeated games. [4] The reputation model shows that incomplete information of payoff function or strategic space from the participants to other participants has an important influence on the equilibrium outcome, cooperative behavior will appeared in finitely repeated games if the game repeated long enough. Therefore, we use this model to analyze the quality of information sources. [5]

Assume that there are two sides on the market: information sources and service platform. Information source are two types, i.e. honest and cheating users. Assume only the information source knows the type of itself, the service platform do not know. Consider a two-period model (t =1,2), information source chooses in the low-quality $s=0$ and high-quality s =1. The cost of information source to provide high-quality is c_1, while low-quality is c_0, ($c_1 > c_0 \geq 0$). The average utility of each period is $(\theta s_t - p_t)$, if the information sources used are the same, otherwise will be 0. The probability of honest information sources sets x_1, and the probability of dishonest sets $1 - x_1$.

Information source can save the cost of $(c_1 - c_0)$ by providing low quality information or services in the first phase, on this situation the platform inferred that the information sources may be dishonest and will provide low quality information in the second period, so in the second phase, the profit of information sources is 0.

On the contrary, if the information source provide high quality information or service in the first period, he can gets profit up to $\delta(\theta - c_0)$ (θ is the discount rate) in the second period, because in the best case, consumers believe that he is honest and willing to pay the highest price of θ, therefore, information sources could earn a reputation of $(\theta - c_0)$ in the second period.

Then, in the $c_1 - c_0 < \delta(\theta - c_0)$, due to the cost saving from low-quality being less than reputation value, information sources will provide the high quality to disguise himself as an honest type in the first period. Since both types of information sources are provided for the same quality, the probability of the service platform to encounter an honest information source is still x_1 in the second period, and it may willing to pay the price of $E(\theta s_2) = \theta x_1$. That is, information sources are willing to provide the high quality if $c_1 - c_0 < \delta(\theta - c_0)$. Even with the information sources of opportunistic tendencies will provide high quality information to build reputation.

In many of the cases, the equilibrium will tend to generalize. Assume the game repeated T times, the probability for the service platform see the information sources as the high-quality is y_t, balanced as $y_t = x_t$. According to the Bayes Rule, if the information sources provide a high quality in the t period, then the posterior probability of the platform see the information source as the honest in the $t+1$ period is:

$$P_{t+1}\left\{s_{t+1} = 1 \middle| s_t = 1\right\} = \frac{p_t \times 1}{p_t \times 1 + (1 - p_t)y_t} \geq p_t \qquad (1)$$

If the information source provides the low quality in the t period, then the posterior probability of service platform in the t +1 period is:

$$P_{t+1}\left\{s_{t+1} = 1 \middle| s_t = 0\right\} = \frac{p_t \times 0}{p_t \times 0 + (1 - p_t)y_t} = 0 \qquad (2)$$

It can be seen that, service platform will adjust upwards the probability to see the information source as an honest type if it provides the high quality. But once the platform observed low-quality information, this information source will be identified as a dishonest type that will always provide the low quality.

Consider the game in the last two stages. In the T stage, the information source to keep its reputation has no meaning, so it will provide low quality and get a gain of $(c_1 - c_0)$. In the stage of $T+1$, the low-quality information sources can save the cost of $(c_1 - c_0)$ in the current period, but the loss of $\delta(\theta y_t - c_0)$, while if the information source maintain the reputation of high quality, $(\theta y_t - c_0)$ will be available in the T stage). Because of $c_1 - c_0 < \delta(\theta y_t - c_0)$, so the equilibrium results at this time is that the information sources will provide high quality to maintain reputation and maximize his inter-period profits. Under the Backward Induction Rule, information sources in each period will provide high quality services, to maintain the reputation of high quality until the last period to reduce the quality and access the reputation. In the mixed strategy case, the conclusion is the same, as long as T is sufficiently large, the information source must provide high-quality information or services at least until the t period.

So in the market economy, the information sources of economic rationality will actively improve product quality, create and maintain the reputation in order to obtain the maximum inter-period profits. Therefore, reputation mechanism will have a positive effect to improve the quality of information.

4 The Credibility Evaluation of Service and Feedback between the Platform and Consumer

After served by the platform, the consumers need to feedback an evaluation or a rate for this service, honest consumers will give a true evaluation to the platform, but also malicious consumers may give false evaluation that does not meet the actuality, so it is needed to take some measures of credibility evaluation to make sure the feedback rating are authentic. In this case, the platform and consumers formed a dual credit evaluation based on the two sides of service and feedback. In a certain extent, information source also can be a user of platform, and the credibility evaluation between information source and platform can be abstracted as the users with the platform.

Service confidence expressed the reliability of the rating provided by platform; Feedback confidence is about the authenticity and honesty of the rating from consumers. Papaioannou has proposed a feedback treatment mechanism based on double-ratings in 2005, and it reflects the reliability of ratings from the node (including the server and consumer) by ncr factor. If the two ratings are consistent, the service trust of server will increase, and if not, server and consumer should be punished that they can neither request a service, nor provide services. [6]

Parasuraman, Zeithaml and Berry (1985, 1988) (referred as the PZB) has divided service quality into 10 factors: reliability, responsiveness, competence, Access, courtesy, communication, Credibility, security, understand and crallgibles. [7][8]According to these factors, the model set the quantitative parameters of service information, including: reliability (indicated by A), response speed (indicated by B), availability (indicated by C), stability (indicated by D), security (expressed by E), courtesy (indicated by F), interactive (indicated by G) and so on. For the different aspects of the service, this model makes a comprehensive evaluation using the method of assigning different weights. Let the weights assigned by K_A, K_B, K_C, K_D, K_E..., satisfy $-1 < K_A$, K_B, K_C, K_D, K_E...< 1. The attribute service of each types are m_A, m_B, m_C, m_D, m_E..., the range of $-1 < m_A$, m_B, m_C, m_D, m_E...< 1. The reported service evaluation (rating) from the information service platform (SR) and consumer (SC) can be expressed as:

$$L = m_A K_A + m_B K_B + m_C K_C + m_D K_D + m_E K_E + \cdots \tag{3}$$

Set L_R and L_C are the service evaluation (ratings) of information service platform (SR) and consumer (SC), respectively. Set k presents the consistency of the service evaluation between L_R and L_C, so $0 < k \leq 1$ is that L_R and L_C are give the same service evaluation, exactly the same when $k = 1$; $-1 \leq k < 0$ is that L_R and L_C are inconsistent of their service evaluation, exactly the opposite when $k = -1$; $k = 0$ is that one of L_R and L_C did not respond a service evaluation, that is $L_R ==$ null or $L_C ==$ null.

Meanwhile, set U_R as the service trust of information service platform (SR), T_C is the feedback trust of consumer (SC). T_θ is the critical value to determine T_C is true evaluation or false, i.e., the feedback trust is false when $T_C < T_\theta$, while the feedback trust is true when $T_C \geq T_\theta$. [9]

To prevent the ups and downs of service trust and feedback trust, through the introduction of penalty constraints N_{punish}, reward factors of α and punish factors of β to reflect the reward and punishment to corresponding node ($0 < \alpha \leq \beta < 1$). When both of evaluations are received, the reputation system will update the service trust of information service platform as follows:

$$U_R^{new} = \begin{cases} U_R^{old} + \alpha N_{punish}, & \text{if } T_C \geq T_\theta \&\& k \neq 0, \\ U_R^{old}, & \text{if } T_C < T_\theta \&\& L_R \neq \text{null}, \\ U_R^{old} - \beta N_{punish}, & \text{if } T_C < T_\theta \&\& 0 < k \leq 1, \\ U_R^{old} - N_{punish}, & \text{if } L_R == \text{null}. \end{cases} \quad (4)$$

Where U_R^{new} refers to service trust updated by information service platform (SR), U_R^{old} is the service trust before updated. [9] When the assessment of SR consistent with the SC, if $T_C \geq T_\theta$, it means that the feedback of SC is true, so the service provided by SR is true and the service confidence of SR will be increased; but if $T_C < T_\theta$ that the credibility of SC is very low, it is possible that the rating is untrue, so the service trust of SR will not arise which can resist collusion.

When the evaluation of SR is inconsistent with SC, if $T_C \geq T_\theta$ that the feedback of SC is true, then the service trust of malicious SR will drop; [9]However, if $T_C < T_\theta$ that SC may be a liar, which intent to harm the service trust of SR, therefore set U_R^{new} to remain U_R^{old} can reduce the unfair to SR.

When it is only one evaluation reply from SR and SC, if $L_R == \text{null}$ that means the SR is attempt to do some malicious behavior through not to submit the feedback, so we reduce the service trust of malicious SR to curb such attempts. However, if $L_C == \text{null}$ that means the traitorous SC do not want to improve the service trust of SR, so we reduce the feedback trust of SC to severely punish it.

5 Summary

Based on web service, the service reputation model is described in detail in the paper, and a credit evaluation model of information service platform was built on the SOA-extended architecture. For the low quality of information sources, we proposes an evaluation system of information source based on the classic KMRW reputation model, and the equilibrium result shows that the information source will maintain a high-quality situation high reputation to maximum cross of income, so the reputation mechanism will have a positive effect on the quality of the provided information.

For the transaction relationship between information service platform and users, and even the possibility of the false evaluation, the evaluation mechanism of service and feedback trust was established based on dual-ratings credit evaluation model, which can deal effectively with the problem of false feedback and collusion attacks, and furthermore verify the validity and reliability of the reputation model based on SOA-extended architecture.

The information service platform should provide the hard environment (technical conditions, system characteristics, etc.) and soft environment (system security, reputation security, etc.) for protecting the users, according to which, the trust issue of information service system should be researched from the consumer respect. Our future study will focus on the information collection, evaluation and prediction of historical behavior in the system, and establish the evaluation index and evaluation system, to protect the reputation and credibility of consumers.

References

1. Gou, X., Qu, F., Yan, J.: SOA-based interactive graduate design system constructive programs study. In: 2009 International Conference on New Trends in Information and Service Science, NISS 2009, pp. 439–443 (2009)
2. Jing, Z., Wenjing, T.: On Extended SOA Based Credibility Evaluation Model. Journal of Shenyang Normal University (Natural Science Edition) (01), 64–67 (2010)
3. Zhang, H., Duan, H., Liu, W.: An incentive reputation model. Science in China (Series E: Information Sciences) (10), 1747–1759 (2008)
4. Kreps, D., Milgrom, P., Roberts, J., Wilson, R.: Rational Cooperation in the Finitely Repeated Prisoners Dilemma. Journal of Economic Theory (27), 245–252 (1982)
5. Zhang, W.: Game theory and information economics, pp. 214–223. Shanghai People's Publishing House (2004)
6. Papaioannou, T.G., Stamoulis, G.D.: An incentive mechanism promoting truthful feedback in peer-to-peer systems. In: Proc. of the 2005 IEEE Int'l Sympon Cluster Computing and the Grid, pp. 275–283. IEEE Computer Society Press, Los Alamitos (2005)
7. Parasuraman, A., Zeithaml, V.A., Berry, L.L.: A conceptual model of service quality and its implications for future research. Journal of Marketing 49(4), 41–50 (1985)
8. Parasuraman, A., Zeithaml, V.A., Berry, L.L.: SERVQUAL: A Multiple-Item Scale for Measuring Consumer Perceptions of Service Quality. Journal of Retailing 64(1), 12–40 (1988)
9. Wang, X., Ding, X., Liang, P.: Reputation model of dual ratings. Computer Engineering and Design (10), 2234–2236 (2010)

Saving Energy Control of Auxiliary Fan

Xian-wei Xu[1], Jin-bao Xu[1], Yang Liu[1], Nan Hu[1], and JIan-xin Gao[2]

[1] College of Safety Science and Engineering Liaoning Technical University Fuxin, China
[2] HongMiaoCoal mine PingZhuang energy company limited corporation
1984xuxianwei@163.com

Abstract. Auxiliary Fan is one of the major electric equipments. Reasonable intelligent control Auxiliary Fan plays key role in mine energy efficient and safe operation. In this paper, according to the scene of the realities, analysis the matter between the quantity of auxiliary fan and gas concentration change of driving, use the PID control function of Siemens S7-200PLC to control Frequency Converter, not only realize the auxiliary fan frequency conversion adjusting speed, but also have the function of automatic fault diagnosis, discover fault, fault alarming. We guaranteed the mine safety production with energy saving, low cost, automatic control.

Keywords: Auxiliary Fan, PLC, PID control, Frequency Converter.

1 Introduction

The driving of mine workface is a place where gas and coal dust accidents occur frequently, Auxiliary Fan is the major electric ventilation equipments in the driving process, that use of the flexibility and performance a direct impact on the gas safety discharge. Traditional Auxiliary Fan is in contact with manual controls, Auxiliary Fan speed is not change as gas concentration and the light of actual conditions. This paper designs Adjustable Speed System that works as the change of gas concentration with PLC controller, PID close-looped controller and Frequency Converter. The PID close-looped control of PLC was carefully introduced, and united with hardware design and software design of the system, the purpose of automatically regulating was achieved by laboratory simulate. The design is to improve automation of mine and decrease operation mistakes, which provides guarantee for coal mine safety efficient production.

2 Design of Overall System

According to the changes of gas concentration that gas sensors detecting, the Auxiliary Fan is controlled automatically in order to the gas emission control and without congressional excesses gas emissions. The gas sensors should arrange in air intake, workface and return current as shown in Fig. 1.

The T2 gas sensor detect the intake air gas concentration, that less than 0.5% the Auxiliary Fan will start, more than 0.5% will be alarm, more than 0.6% will be power failure and restart less than 0.5%. The T1 gas sensor detect driving workface ($\leqq 5m$),

S. Lin and X. Huang (Eds.): CESM 2011, Part II, CCIS 176, pp. 33–39, 2011.
© Springer-Verlag Berlin Heidelberg 2011

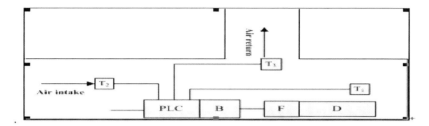

Fig. 1. Distribution of gas sensors. B-Frequency Converter, F-Auxiliary Fan, D-Air Tube, T-Gas Sensors

the alarm gas concentration is 1.0%, the power failure gas concentration is 1.5%, restart gas concentration is 1.0%. The T3 gas sensor installs near the entrance of driving workface that detects the gas concentration in return current, the alarm gas concentration is 1.0%, the power failure gas concentration is 1.1%, restart gas concentration is 1.0%. Plc have been collected data from T1, T3 sensors and compared to the setting data of PID, When the density is less than the concentration is not work, as the concentration of the larger the concentration that control Frequency Converter, a change in output, at last realize the implementation of the most efficient gas emissions.

In addition, The TD 200C Connects with the plc can modify the PID level and displays the realized gas concentration, motor speed and air-quantity. Fig. 2 shows the overall structure of the system.

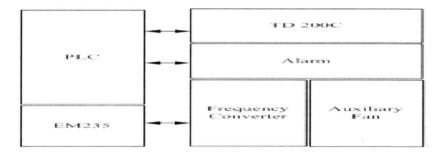

Fig. 2. System architecture

3   The PId Control of PLC

In industrial production, the analog temperature, pressure and flow are often controlled by closed-loop, both models use a measure of the controller a control system and computer digital control systems (including PLC), the PID control have been widely used. PID controller is short for Proportional Integral Derivative. Its advantage is not need precise control system of mathematical model, have great flexibility and adaptability, and pid controller of the typical, programming is a simple, easy to implement projects and for readjustment. In the closed system, the PID close-looped control system as in Fig. 3.

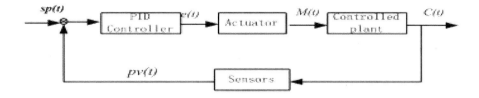

Fig. 3. Continuous closed control system

$sp(t)$ is given value, $pv(t)$ is feedback quantity, c (t) is the output of the system, The PID controller I/O relationship as(1).

$$M(t) = Kc\left[e(t) + \frac{1}{T_I}\int_0^t e(t)\,dt + \frac{1}{T_D}\frac{de(t)}{dt}\right] + M_0 \qquad (1)$$

$M(t)$ -Output of controller, M_0 -initial value of output, $e(t) = sp(t) - pv(t)$ is error signal, Kc -factor of proportionality, T_I -integral time constant, T_D -derivative time constant. The right of the equal the first three items are integral parts of proportion, and differentiation are and error, the integration and differential proportional.

The siemens S7-200 PLC PID close-looped control as in Fig. 4.

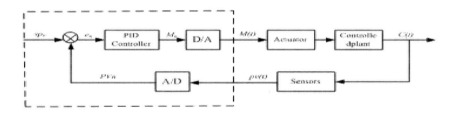

Fig. 4. Continuous closed control system of PLC

In the analog closed control system, $C(t)$ are continuously changing of analogue, some executing agency asks for the output signal of the plc was analogue $M(t)$ and the plc only deal with digital. First, $C(t)$ first is the measuring elements (sensors) and change to the converted into standard range of a direct current or voltage signal $PV(t)$, Plc analog input module uses A/D to translate that into digital PVn. Plc collects feedback according to regular intervals and PID calculation. The time interval was known as the sampling period (sampling time).

The dashed part in the PLC, sp_n, pv_n, e_n, M_n are all the n sampling digital, $PV(t)$, $M(t)$, $e(t)$ are continuous change of analogue. In many control system, the PID control needs only one or two. For example, may only ask for the control or scale of proportion with the control, the set a parameter to return the control type of selection.

4 Hardware

The hardware of the system includes: S7-200 PLC, EM231 Analog expansion module, MM420 Frequency Converter, Test display TD 200C and so on.

4.1 S7-200PLC

Programmable logic controller (Abbreviation PLC) is a operating digital electronic computers system, designs for the industrial environment. It uses programmable memory to realize internal storage implementation of logical, sequential control, timing, counting and arithmetic operations, such as operating instructions, and through digital input and output module to control various types of machinery or production process.

The system uses siemens S7-200 cpu222 that integrated 24V load power supply can directly connected to the sensor, CPU222 has a 180mA output, an integrated 8 inputs/6 outputs, a total of 14 digital I/O points. That can connect to two expansion modules. Have 6K bytes of program and data storage space. 4 independent high-speed counters of 30 KHz, 2-way separate 20 KHz high-speed pulse output. A communication and programming port RS485, with PPI protocol, MPI communications protocols and free communication ability.

4.2 EM231 Analog Input Module

EM231 is the most commonly used analog expansion module, which implements the 4 analog inputs Fig. 5 shows the wiring diagram of the sensor and EM231.

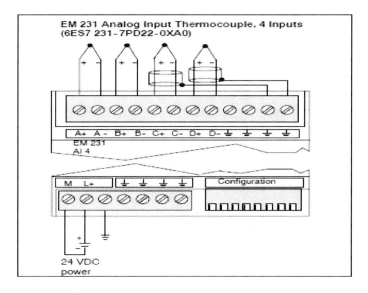

Fig. 5. Wiring diagram of sensor with the EM231

Gas sensors signal output is 4 ~ 20mA, so the DIP switch settings as shown in Table 1.

Table 1. DIP Switch Settings of EM231

Unipolar						Full-scale input	Resolution
SW1	*SW2*	*SW3*	*SW4*	*SW5*	*SW6*		
ON	OFF	OFF	OFF	OFF	ON	0~20mA	5μA

4.3 MM420 Frequency Converter

MM420 is a frequency converter of series productions of Siemens, for the control of three-phase ac motor speed. Here Inverter is controlled by microprocessor, and modern advanced Insulated Gate Bipolar Transistor (IGBT) is used as power output devices. Therefore, they have high operation reliability and function diversity. In addition, its switching frequency of pulse width modulation is optional, reducing the noise of motor running. As a result, the transducer and motor were provided with comprehensive and perfect protection.

4.4 Text Displays TD 200C

Text displays (abbreviation TD) are used to display Numbers, characters and Chinese characters, also used to modify the Parameter setting of PLC. TD 200C is the special text display of S7-200, used to check, monitor and modify process variables of S7-200 user program. TD 200C displays 2 text lines with a maximum of 10 Chinese characters and it has a maximum of eight special function keys. With the Text display guide in software MicroWIN STEP7 V4.0 of S7-200 programming, TD 200C can be easily configured, for simple operating which can be conveniently facilitated to small control system.

5 Software

This system program is designed with modular and function structured. Mainly composed by control main program, analogue collection calculation program, PID control procedures, alarm, subroutines process and so on, It is easy to be debugged and extended. While Siemens PLC programming software MicroWIN STEP7 V4.0 is used on programming. PID function instructions consisted in the software and an analog input/output module EM231 used together, PID process control function could be realized.

TD 200C is connected to S7-200 CPU through cables TD/CPU, and default address of TD equipment is 1, while default address of CPU is 2. S7-200 programming software MicroWIN STEP7 provides text display guide for TD equipment to configure. and only after a few simple settings, configuration information screen and alarm messages of parameters block can be automatically generated for TD equipment storage, and Parameters are blocked in CPU V storage area. TD equipment reads parameters block, a part of a data block, from the CPU of S7-200. Data generated by text display guide should be downloaded to S S7-200 pieces.

6 Laboratory Simulation

We download the program designed to PLC through programmable software STEP7 MicroWIN V4.0 and Connects the electricity line as Fig. 6.

Gas sensors output signals are current from 4 to20mA, which are converted by EM231 to acceptable signals of PLC. Calculated by PID controller, output turns to Voltage of 0~10V to control the Frequency Converter, and control Auxiliary Fan.

We use G110 to instead of MM420 Frequency Converter, because of G110 Frequency Converter drive 200V~240V, 0.2kW~3kW motor, MM420 drive large power motor. The settings of G110 Frequency Converter as shown in Table 2.

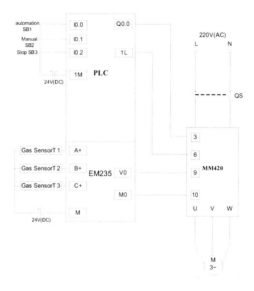

Fig. 6. Water storehouse online table control menu

Table 2. The G110 Frequency Converter Settings

Number of Parameter	Name of Parameter	Setting	Instruction
P0304	Rated voltage	220V	
P0305	Rated electricity	0.5	Uint, A
P0306	Rated power	0.75	Uint, kW
P0310	Rated frequency	50	Uint, Hz
P0311	Rated revolution	1460	Uint, r/min
P0700	Source of command	2	Input from board
P1000	Setting of bands	2	Analog Setting
P1080	Frequency min	5	Uint, Hz

7 Conclusion

Laboratory simulation proves that local-ventilator energy-saving control system composed of PLC, PID controller, frequency converter runs well and has good reliability.

The application of PLC and inverter not only realizes the automatic regulation of fan speed according to the gas concentration, but also fulfills motor soft start. What's more, impact on grid and load can be eliminated, avoiding to injuring motor for operating over-voltage, prolonging the service life of fan. While in PID control, density value can be arbitrarily set through TD 200C, and the operation is more flexible.

References

[1] Siemens, A.G.: Study siemens S7-200 PLC step by step. People Post (2004) (in press)
[2] Siemens, A.G.: WinCC V6 getting started. Siemens, Germany (2007)
[3] Dong, N.P., Zhou, S.W.: Application of S7-300 and WinCC in Dense Phase System. In: Proceedings of the 2009 Third International Symposium on Information Technology Application Workshops, pp. 352–355 (2009)
[4] Ogawa, M., Henmi, Y.: Recent Developments on PC+PLCbased ControlSystems for Beer Brewery Process Automation Applications. In: International Joint Conference, SICE-ICASE, pp. 1053–1056 (2006)
[5] Honda, A.: Application of PLC to dynamic control system for liquid He cryogenic pumping facility on JT-60U NBI system. Fusion Engineering and Design (2008)
[6] Cao, Y.-P., Xie, J.-Y.: Design of Remote Supervisory System Based on FieldBus. Process Automation Instrumentation J. 25, 23–25 (2004)

The Denotational Semantics Definition of PLC Programs Based on Extended λ-Calculus

Litian Xiao[1,2,*], Ming Gu[1], and Jiaguang Sun[1]

[1] National Laboratory for Information Science and Technology,
Key Laboratory for Information System Security, Ministry of Education,
Department of Computer Science and Technology,
School of Software, Tsinghua University, Beijing 100084, China
[2] Beijing Special Engineering Design and Research Institute, Beijing 100028, China
{xlt05,guming,sunjg}@mails.tsinghua.edu.cn

Abstract. PLC is widely used in the field of automatic control. The correctness verification methods of PLC programs include software model checking and theorem proving, etc. To use formal methods verifying the correctness of PLC programs, denotational semantics needs to define and then PLC programs can be modeled, model checking and verified. Based on the extended λ-calculus definition, the paper has researched and defined the architecture and denotational semantics of PLC programs. The work is the basis of model checking and theorem proving for correctness verification on PLC programs.

Keywords: PLC Program, Extended λ-Calculus, Architecture, Program Modeling, Denotational Semantics.

1 Introduction

With the increasing requirements for embedded applications, the complexity and the scale of PLC programs is also increasing and becoming larger. As the applications of embedded system in a wide range of security field, relevant to its correctness guarantee becomes more urgent. In terms of PLC, the hardware logic of its foundation has high reliability, but its software correctness is much difficultly guaranteed due to the function complexity of PLC program.

In order to eliminate bugs as possible and verify the correctness of a program, the main methods are test [1]-[3] and formal verification. Although the testing technology is an effective method to find out bugs, it has incompleteness. Finite test cases are difficultly utilized to cover all the accessible codes of a program. Thus, the researchers try to use the formal methods to verify the correctness of program.

One type of formal verification method is model checking which to be verified by state space search based on specified features (such as safety and activeness etc.) upon the abstract model. This method is reliable and complete. However, it faces the biggest problem of "state space explosion" [4]-[6]. The other is the formal verification

---

*Corresponding author: Litian Xiao, P.O. Box 4702, Beijing 100028, China.

S. Lin and X. Huang (Eds.): CESM 2011, Part II, CCIS 176, pp. 40–46, 2011.

method of theorem proving. It firstly describes the characteristics of system behaviors with a series of logical formulae. Then it proves the specified objectives correct or falsification by the means of deductive methods with inference rules provided by the logical system (or proof tools).

The theorem proving is well suitable for the verification of infinite state system. The most of the proof tools (such as PVS [7], Coq [8] and Nqthm [9], etc) provides the basic logic that is high-order logic possessed of the function of describing the infinite data structure, i.e., insensitive to the scale of state space. But this type of method has relatively higher requirements to the verification personnel.

For PLC program, its formal verification has its own characteristics:

a. PLC program is used in the most embedded hardware environment, so its logic structure is relative simple, the sentence categories is few in program, its program is relative short.

b. PLC program is written in hardware machine instruction (or ladder diagram). It is convenient for the abstracted process of model, even in some times it can be used directly as models for verification (similar to assembly language, Verilog, VHDL, etc.).

c. Although PLC program is simple, but it still has the most mechanism of high-level programming language.

d. PLC program completes in sequence within a scan period, and then out images are refreshed and next scan period is started. From the interior of the scan period, it has characteristics of sequence program. From the whole scan period, what showed by PLC is the output response to the various input signals. Its response is not fixed — because the accumulation of many kinds of timers and counters is span-scan period, a PLC program is not simply regarded as the fixed transformation logic of input-output. Compared with the verification of general assembly or high-level language program, PLC programs' has the advantages that are relative small scale, relative simple structure, relative clear control logic and close to mathematical representation.

In order to verify the correctness of PLC program and the temporal sequence feature of it within span-scan period, we address the research for verification approach based on Coq which is a theorem proving tool. To using the Coq, PLC program need to be modeled at first. The paper defines the denotational semantics of the typical PLC program based on extended λ-calculus definition, i.e. it defines the mapping function from the input configuration to the output. It deals with the transformation policy from denotational semantics to symbolic transition system. Theses work has established the foundation of Coq verifying PLC program.

2   The Architecture Definition of PLC Program

The cyclic scanning mode is adopted in PLC. When in operation, each scan period is divided into five stages such as internal processing, program communication, input scanning, program performing and output processing. Among the stages internal processing, program communication are auxiliary. The primary units composed in PLC system hardware are input relay unit (X), output relay unit (Y), auxiliary relay unit (M), status register (S), timer (T), counter (C), data register (D), PLC pointer (P) and so on. The various series of PLC typical instructions are basically similar, including the normal opened/closed contacts connecting to the control bus (I/O: *LD/LDI*), series connection to the normal opened/closed contacts (*AND/ANDI*), parallel connection to the normal opened/closed contacts (*OR/ORI*), block operation (*ANDB/ORB*), negating (*INV*), special element set 1/0 and remaining (*SET/RST*), non-operation (*NOP*), main program end (*END*), stepping (*STL* or *RET*), push stack / read stack / pop stack (*MPS/MRD/MPP*), condition jump (*CJ*), loop (*For...NEXT*), subprogram call and return (*CALL/SRET*), arithmetic operation (*ADD, SUB, MUL, DIV, INC, DEC*), digitwise logical operation (*WAND, WOR, WXOR, NEG*), comparison (*CMP*), data transfer (*MOV*), etc. The detailed instructions can be referred to the related manuals and reference [10].

The exact mathematical description of PLC program architecture can be defined as following:

a. To introduce an argument $V_z \in \{0, 1\}$ to every I/O relay unit, aux relay unit and status register Z, e.g. the input unit X0 corresponding to V_{x0}.

b. To introduce a corresponding argument $V_z \in \mathbb{N}$ (the domain of natural numbers) to every data register unit and counter unit Z.

c. To regarding the pointer value (such as subprogram jump entry address, conditional jump statement address) as constant value.

d. Not considering the mathematical description of the timer due to the verification technology in this paper not related to the real-time problem.

e. The above arguments are divided into two types: global argument and local argument. Among them, the unit operated by *SET/RST* command and the counter unit are global arguments, and the rest are local arguments. *GV* and *LV* are separately denoted as the sets of global and local arguments.

f. In addition, for the counter units, because a scheduled counting value is required and this value will be set for many times. A temporary argument E_C will be set for each counter C, which E_C value is effected by *OUT* command. For example, *OUT C0 K200*, when E_C is assigned as 200.

g. Due to stack operation exiting, a structure $S_M \in \{0, 1\}^*$ used to record the current changes of bus stack. To consider the following codes,

```
LD      X0
MPS
AND     X1
OUT     Y1
MRD
AND     X2
MPS
AND     X3
MPP
```

Supposed $V_{X0}=1$, $V_{X1}=1$, $V_{X2}=0$, $V_{X3}=1$, then after implementing the codes stack values are respectively ε, 1, 1, 1, 1, 1, 1·0, 1·0, 1. where empty string ε is expressed that stack is empty.

h. There are a large number of commands similar to *AND/OR/ANDB/ORB/ANDI /ORI*, which results of the implementation rely on the current bus connecting status. Meanwhile, the implementation of these commands can change the current bus status, as well as the block series and parallel commands rely on bus connection status prior to some steps. Therefore, it is necessary to set a stack for the current bus connecting status.

Generally V is expressed as an argument and C is constant, which may be with subscript. A quad $<\omega_M, \omega_T, \sigma_G, \sigma_L>$ is expressed as the current Configuration. Where, ω_M is bus stack and ω_T is current connecting stack, σ_G is assignment functions of global variables and σ_L is local, i.e. the current value of every global variable V is assigned as $\sigma_G(V)$ and the value of every local variable V is $\sigma_L(V)$.

Because there is the configuration in a stack structure, the following defines some operations and the related function. Given the alphabet Σ, a stack on it is a finite word $\omega \in \Sigma^*$ in the alphabet. The empty letter ε is expressed as empty stack. ω^0 is expressed as the first letter of ω, called the top of ω. If $\omega = a_1 \cdot a_2 \cdot \ldots \cdot a_n$, the stack $a_2 \cdot \ldots \cdot a_n$ is expressed as ω', i.e. ω' is the stack which removes an element from the top of the stack ω. Analogically, $a_0 \cdot \omega$ is expressed as a new stack after a_0 being pushed into ω. Besides, the following abbreviation will be quoted: $\omega^1 = (\omega')^0$, $\omega^2 = (\omega')^1 = (\omega'')^0$, ... etc.

In order to give the denotational semantics of PLC program, BNF paradigm is introduced as following:

$$e ::= V$$
$$| \ C$$
$$| \ e+e \ | \ e-e \ | \ e\times e \ | \ e\div e$$
$$| \ e^\wedge \ e \ | \ e \quad e \ | \ e\oplus e \ | \ \neg e$$
$$| \ e\&e \ | \ e|e \ | \ e^\wedge e \ | \ \bar{e}.$$

Where $+$, $-$, $\times$ and $\div$ are corresponding arithmetic operation symbols of "plus, minus, multiplication, division". Symbol $\wedge$, , $\oplus$ and $\neg$ are logic operation of "and, or, XOR, not". Symbol $\&$, $|$, $^\wedge$ and $^-$ are bit operation of "bit and, bit or, bit XOR, bit not".

Given configuration $CF = <\omega_M, \omega_T, \sigma_G, \sigma_L>$, the semantics value under an expression e is denoted by $[\![e]\!]_{CF}$. The inductive definition is as follows.

- $[\![C]\!]_{CF} = C$.

- $[\![V]\!]_{CF} = \begin{cases} \sigma_G(V), V \in GV \\ \sigma_L(V), V \in LV \end{cases}$.

- $[\![e_1 * e_2]\!]_{CF} = [\![e_1]\!]_{CF} * [\![e_2]\!]_{CF}$, where $* \in \{+, -, \times, \div, \wedge, \quad , \oplus, \&, |, ^\wedge\}$, its operation definition is same to normal.

- $[\![\ !e]\!]_{CF} = ! \ [\![e]\!]_{CF}$, where $! \in \{\neg, ^-\}$, its operation definition is same to normal.

3   The Denotational Semantics Definition of PLC Program

Data domain is limited on natural number domain $\mathbb{N}$ expressed constant quantity of natural number (with symbols) by C, C_i $(i=1,2,\ldots)$ and argument or variable of which value is a natural number by V, V_j $(j=1,2,\ldots)$. $\vec{C}$ and $\vec{C}_i$ $(i=1,2,\ldots)$ express constant vectors (ordered pair). $\vec{V}$ and $\vec{V}_j$ $(j=1,2,\ldots)$ express variable vectors (ordered pair).

A constant $\perp$ is introduced for expressing "undefined value". In addition, a "flat partial order" is defined as $<$ and is stipulated by that for any natural number C, $\perp < C$ works. But this partial order between two natural numbers is not comparable as shown in Fig. 1, where the relation of $<$ is reflexive.

Fig. 1. Flat Partial Order on Natural Number

This partial order relation may be raised to ordered pair (tuple), string and function naturally. For example, for ordered pair, there are $(\perp,5)<(3, 5)$, $(3,\perp)<(3, 5)$, $(\perp,\perp)<(\perp,5)$, $(\perp,\perp)<(3,\perp)$, etc. For string, there are $0\cdot\perp\cdot3<0\cdot1\cdot3$ etc. For function, if and only if $F_1<F_2$, $\forall X. F_1(X)<F_2(X)$ works.

$N_\perp$ is expressed as the set of $N\cup\{\perp\}$, and then, $<$ can be further raised on the ordered pair composed of tables or (multiple variables) function on $N_\perp$. $\vec{X}$ and each $\vec{X}_i$ $(i=1,2,...)$ are expressed such a ordered pair in general. Obviously, every configuration is such one.

A complete PLC program is divided in structure according to statement block (always assuming that sub-program call statement has already been expanded equivalently and step instruction has been converted into equivalent bus operating instructions) and be classified into four types:

a. Basic statement block: it only includes the statement block of a PLC instruction.

b. Synthetic sequence statement block: it is constituted by some statement blocks in sequence.

c. Branch statement block: instruction block is introduced by *JC* statement, i.e. it is with the following forms. Where, *Cod1* and *Cod2* are instruction blocks.

```
            JC        L
            Cod1
    L:        Cod2
```

d. Loop statement block: instruction block is introduced by *FOR* statement, i.e. it is with the following forms. Where, *Cod* is an instruction block.

```
            FOR        Z (or K)
            Cod
            NEXT
```

For each (well-formed) statement block *Cod*, its denotational semantics *M(Cod)* is mapping function which maps one configuration to another, i.e. if the configuration is *CF* before statement block *Cod* executing, then the configuration is *M(Cod)(CF)* when *Cod* has executed (if normal end). In order to give the formal definition of *M(Cod)*, the grammar definition is based on the extended λ-calculus as following.

$$F ::= \vec{X} \mid \Phi$$
$$\mid [\lambda \vec{X}.F]$$
$$\mid F \circ F$$
$$\mid F(F)$$

$$/ \overrightarrow{x} \ ?F{:}F$$
$$/ \ \mu\Phi.F \ .$$

Where, Φ is a function argument, $[\lambda \overrightarrow{x} .F]$ is λ-abstract, $F_1 \circ F_2$ is the synthesis of functions assumed that output type of F_2 match with the input of F_1. $F_1(F_2)$ is the application of functions, where only allowed the type of F_2 to be same as the input type of F_1. $\overrightarrow{x} \ ?F_1{:}F_2$ is selection function with the conditions, where only allowed to $\overrightarrow{x} \in \mathbb{N}_\omega$—If $\overrightarrow{x} \in \mathbb{N} \ | \{0\}$, then function is equivalence to F_1, otherwise, the function is equivalence to F_2. $\mu\Phi.F$ is the least fixpoint where Φ is generally required to appear in F.

Kleen iteration is adopted in calculation process like $\mu\Phi.F$, i.e. the least fixpoint (relative to partial order $\prec$) of formula $\Phi \equiv F(\Phi)$ calculated process is as followings:

a. Let $F_0 = F \perp$, i.e. function values is the function of $\perp$.

b. Let $F_{i+1} = F[\Phi/F_i]$, i.e. Φ in F is substituted by F_i.

c. If $F_k = F_{k+1}$, then the iteration is stopped and let $\mu\Phi.F = F_k$.

Because every chains is finite for the flat partial order, above iteration can be proved that it certainly finishes in finite steps.

Additionally, semantic function is transformation mapping from configurations, thus the input of function is a configuration $<\omega_M, \ \omega_T, \ \sigma_G, \ \sigma_L >$. The following simple form can be adopted in λ- expression.

$$\lambda <\omega_M, \ \omega_T, \ \sigma_G, \ \sigma_L >.F \triangleq \lambda x.let \ x{:=} \ <\omega_M, \ \omega_T, \ \sigma_G, \ \sigma_T >.in \ F$$

$M(Cod)$ is defined as following. At first, synthetic sequence, condition branch and loop statement are discussed.

a. Synthetic sequence: If $Cod = Cod_1 Cod_2$, then $M(Cod) = M(Cod_2) \circ M(Cod_1)$.

b. Branch statement: If $Cod = $ JC L; Cod_1; L: Cod_2, then

$$M(Cod) = \omega_T^0 ? M(Cod_2) {:} M(Cod_1 \ Cod_2).$$

c. Loop statement: If $Cod = $ FOR D; Cod_1; NEXT and D is data register name, then

$$M(Cod) = \mu\Phi.(\ \lambda <\omega_M, \ \omega_T, \ \sigma_G, \ \sigma_L >. \ [\![V_D]\!] \ _{<\omega_M \ . \ \omega_T \ . \ \sigma_G \ . \ \sigma_L >} ?$$

$$\Phi \circ M(DEC \ D) \ \circ M(Cod_1)(\ <\omega_M, \ \omega_T, \ \sigma_G, \ \sigma_L >){:}<\omega_M, \ \omega_T, \ \sigma_G, \ \sigma_L >).$$

If D is constant, then $M(Cod) = (M(Cod_1))^D$, i.e. $M(Cod_1)$ synthesizes its own for D times.

4 Conclusion and Further Work

With the example of typical PLC, the paper abstractly describes the architecture and working modes of PLC program and has given the denotational semantics of PLC program based on the extended λ-deduction. It is the foundation of verification and theorem proving for PLC program. Given the denotational semantics of PLC program, we have further studied that the semantics is transformed into other mathematical model, i.e. the transition system (model) need to use in model checking technology. Specifically, the research further develops PLC program modeling based on Gallina language of Coq platform and defines the Coq description for each PLC syntax elements. It is utilized to prove some program natures and verify practical feasibility of the definitions dicussed above. The part of the work will be introduced in another paper because of paper length limit.

Acknowledgement

This research is sponsored by NSFC Program (No.90718039) and 973 Program (No.2010CB328003) of China.

References

1. Zipori, H., et al.: Approaches and execution of software test and development system for embedded computer systems. Embedded System Design 35(6), 30–39 (2005)
2. Lee, E.A.: Computing for embedded systems. In: Proceeding of IEEE Instrumentation and Measurement Technology Conference, Hungary, Budapest, pp. 100–105 (2001)
3. Kang, B., et al.: A Design and Test Technique for Embedded Software. In: Proceedings of the 2005 Third ACIS Int'l Conference on Software Engineering Research, Management and Applications, pp. 160–165. IEEE Press, New York (2005)
4. Clarke, E.M., Emerson, E.A.: Design and Synthesis of Synchronization Skeletons Using Branching Time Temporal Logic. In: Kozen, D. (ed.) Logic of Programs 1981. LNCS, vol. 131, pp. 52–71. Springer, Heidelberg (1982)
5. Queille, J.P., Sifakis, J.: Specification and Verification of Concurrent Systems. In: Dezani-Ciancaglini, M., Montanari, U. (eds.) Programming 1982. LNCS, vol. 137, pp. 216–230. Springer, Heidelberg (1982)
6. Lamport, L.: Proving the Correctness of Multiprocess Programs. IEEE Trans. on Software Engineering (1977)
7. Owre, S., Rajan, S.P., Rushby, J.M., Shankar, N., Srivas, M.K.: PVS: combining specifications, proof checking and model checking. In: Alur, R., Henzinger, T.A. (eds.) CAV 1996. LNCS, vol. 1102, pp. 411–414. Springer, Heidelberg (1996)
8. The Coq toolkit, http://coq.inria.fr/
9. Boyer, R.S., Moore, J.S.: Proving theorems about lisp functions. Journal of the ACM 22(1), 129–144 (1975)
10. John, K.-H., Tiegelkamp, M.: IEC 61131-3: Programming Industrial Automation Systems. Springer, Heidelberg (2001)

ADRC with Synthesis Tuning Algorithm
for Main Steam Pressure of CFBB

Qiang Ma, Qi Xv, and Weishu Wang

Institute of Electric power, North China University of Water resources and electric power,
450011, China
mqiang1977@hotmail.com

Abstract. Auto-Disturbance-Rejection-Controller (ADRC) with synthesis tuning
algorithm is designed for main steam pressure of Circulation fluidized bed boiler
(CFBB). There are 8 parameters in ADRC, so auto-tuning algorithm is necessary.
The synthesis tuning algorithm in this paper includes NSGA_II algorithm for
Extended State Observer (ESO) and Levenberg-Marqudart algorithm for Non-
linear Feedback (NLF). Tuning of TD is according to set transient time.
Mathematic simulation with disturbance shows satisfactory disturbance-rejection
character, and simulation with different load shows satisfactory robustness of
ADRC.

Keywords: ADRC, CFB, main steam pressure, synthesis tuning algorithm.

1 Introduction

The Circulating Fluidized Bed (CFB) Boiler with the advantages of widely fuel
adaptation and less air pollution emission had been widely applied in power industry.
Main steam pressure is critical parameter of CFB and it reflects process safety and
economical operation. However, main steam pressure is always coupled with bed
temperature. That is change of flue input will influence main steam pressure and bed
temperature. So many decoupling researches had been applied and some decoupling
control system has been designed. In these systems, flue input is applied to main
steam pressure regulation to meet thermal load and first air input is applied to bed
temperature regulation. However, characterized by large time delay and inertia,
traditional control strategy of main steam pressure cannot work well.

Auto-disturbance-rejection-controller is developed from traditional PID controller
[1], and can work well for the control problem with large delay which can not be
controlled by the PID controller. However, there are many parameters in this
controller. So parameter tuning is the key mater blocking its aboard appliance. In this
paper, Extensive State Observer (ESO) of ADRC will be tuned with NSGA-II and
NLF will be tuned with non-linear least square algorithm. [7]

The rest part of this paper is organized as following: in section 2, the main steam
pressure system of CFB is introduced; in section 3, ADRC controller and synthesis
tuning algorithm is introduced; section 4 shows mathematic simulation result; section
5 concludes this paper.

S. Lin and X. Huang (Eds.): CESM 2011, Part II, CCIS 176, pp. 47–52, 2011.
© Springer-Verlag Berlin Heidelberg 2011

2 Main Steam Pressure System of CFB

The main steam pressure is influenced by flue input of boiler and regulation valve of turbine. So there are two regulation measures according to unit work measure: regulated with flue input with boiler follow and regulated with regulation valve of turbine with turbine follow. In these two measures, the last will arose larger fluctuate of main steam pressure. So regulation with flue input is better.

Identification with experiment shows that the model of main steam pressure with flue input disturbance is

$$W(s) = \frac{K(1-as)}{(Ts+1)^2} e^{-\tau s} \qquad (1)$$

Here K is $6 \sim 4$, T is $300 \sim 100s$, a is 20, τ is $100 \sim 60s$ and the boiler load from 25% to 100%. [8]

Four typical work conditions with 25%, 50%, 75% and 100% load are derived with linear approximation algorithm and the parameters are as following:

$$
\begin{aligned}
25\% &: K = 6, T = 300, \tau = 100 \\
50\% &: K = 5.33, T = 250, \tau = 86.7 \\
75\% &: K = 4.67, T = 200, \tau = 73.3 \\
100\% &: K = 4, T = 100, \tau = 60
\end{aligned}
\qquad (2)
$$

3 ADRC and Synthesis Tuning Algorithm

3.1 ADRC

ADRC comprises three main components: Tracking Differentiator (TD), Extended State Observer (ESO) and Nonlinear Feedback (NLF) [1]-[4]. TD is able to output a transient signal with a step input. ESO is able to estimate the value of state parameters with the input and output of the plant system. Additionally the uncertain part of transfer function and disturbance of plant system can estimate as the extensive state parameter by ESO. And this ensures the performance of the controller. NLF is the realization of control theory with output of ESO, in which control signal is generated with nonlinear feedback structure. So performance of ADRC should be small exceeding value, fast response and strong robustness with well tuned parameters.

Where, is the control objective, is its track signal of and is its differential signal; are the estimation of output and its differential signal, is the estimation of the uncertain part of transfer function and disturbance; are the error and its differential; is the output of NLF.

The structure of 2-level ADRC is shown as Fig1.

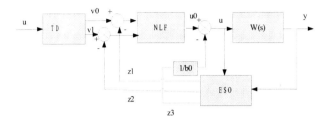

Fig. 1. Structure of 2-level ADRC

Here, $W(s)$ is the control objective $\{z_1, z_2, z_3\}$ is estimation of state value and extensive state value; $\{v_0, v_1\}$ is the transient signal and its differential signal.

The discrete algorithm realizations of the 2-level ADRC are as following:
TD:

$$\begin{cases} v_1(k+1) = v_1(k) + hv_2(k) \\ v_2(k+1) = v_2(k) + hfst(v_1(k) - v_0, v_2(k), r, h) \end{cases} \tag{3}$$

ESO:

$$\begin{cases} e = z_1(k) - y(k) \\ z_1(k+1) = z_1(k) + h(z_2(k) - \beta_{01}e) \\ z_2(k+1) = z_2(k) + h(z_3(k) - \beta_{02}fal(e, 0.5, d)) + bu(k) \\ z_3(k+1) = z_3(k) - h\beta_{03}fal(e, 0.25, d) \end{cases} \tag{4}$$

NLC:

$$\begin{cases} e_1 = v_1(k) - z_1(k) \\ e_2 = v_2(k) - z_2(k) \\ u_0 = \beta_1 fal(e_1, \alpha_1, d) + \beta_2 fal(e_2, \alpha_2, d) \\ u = u_0 - \dfrac{z_3}{b} \end{cases} \tag{5}$$

3.2 Synthesis Tuning Algorithm of ADRC

3.2.1 NSGA_II for ESO
According to equation (4), we can get that the performance of ESO reflect on the error between states value and their estimation. So tuning of ESO is a multi-objective optimization problem. NSGA_II shows satisfactory performance on multi-objective optimization [5][6]. In this algorithm, all the individuals of the solution population is sorted according to dominance. Then crowding distance is assigned to the individuals. From the second iteration, the population to genetic computation is selected from the parent population and now population according to the dominance class and crowding distance. As the optimization result, a Pareto optimal set is produced, which is a set of optimal solution and can not compare each other. In this paper, the result with first dominance class and best crowding distance is selected as tuned parameters.

3.2.2 Non-linear Least Square Algorithm for NLF

With tuned ESO the performance of NLF shows on the dynamic performance of control system output. So the Non-linear least square method - Levenberg-Marqudart algorithm, which shows good performance on tuning of PID controller, should work well.

4 Mathematic Simulation Result

As a typical work condition, parameters with 75% load are chosen as the parameters of plant system, and the transfer function is

$$W(s) = \frac{4.67(1-20s)}{(200s+1)^2} e^{-73.3s} \tag{6}$$

The parameter of TD is set as $r = 2$ to ensure transient time to 1.4 seconds.

With NSGA-II algorithm, 20 optimization parameters of ESO are generated after 100 generations, and one of them is chosen as tuned parameters of ESO.

$$\beta_{01} = 10.025, \beta_{02} = 77, \beta_{03} = 0.103$$

After 50 generations, parameters of NLF are tuned with the orient value $\beta_1 = 1, \beta_2 = 0$. The tuned parameters are $\beta_1 = 0.8, \beta_2 = 0.4$.

4.1 Response with Step Disturbance

Fig. 2 shows the close output response of ADRC and PID controller with step disturbance. From this figure, ADRC is better than PID controller on response rapidity and exceeding value.

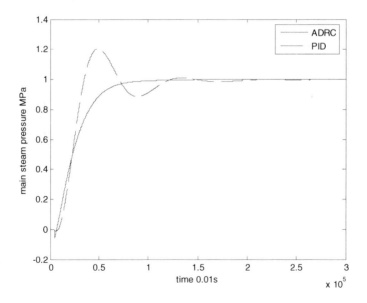

Fig. 2. Response with step input

4.2 Robustness and Disturbance Rejection

To determine the robustness of ADRC on main steam pressure, parameters of four work condition with various loads are set to transfer function. Fig. 3 shows the simulation result. From this figure, the robustness of ADRC is satisfactory.

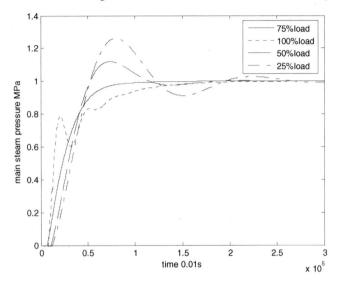

Fig. 3. Response with step input of various load

To determine the disturbance rejection ability of the controller, a step disturbance is set at 2000s with value of 0.2. Fig 4 shows the simulation result. From this figure, ADRC has good performance on disturbance rejection.

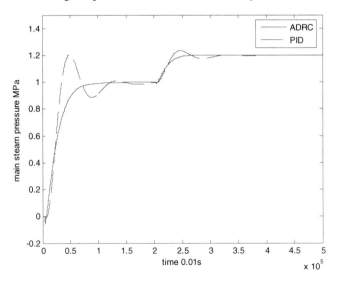

Fig. 4. Response with step disturbance

5 Conclusion

ADRC controller tuned with synthesis algorithm is applied on the main steam pressure system of CFBB. Mathematic simulations demonstrate that response rapidity, exceeding value, robustness and disturbance rejection of ADCR are satisfactory. It should be good solution for the main steam pressure system of CFB with large time delay and inertia. The synthesis tuning algorithm in this paper ensures the performance of this controller.

References

[1] Huang, Y., Zhang, W.: Development of active Disturbance rejection controller. Control Theory and Applications 19(4), 485–491 (2002)
[2] Han, J.: From PID Technique to Active Disturbances Rejection Control Technique. Control Engineering of China 9(3), 13–18 (2002)
[3] Liu, Z., Li, S.: Two-order Active Disturbance Rejection Control Algorithm for Permanent Magnetic Synchronous Motor. In: Proceeding of 26 Chinese Control Conference
[4] Lin, Y., Guan, Z., Wang, B.: Study of the bed temperature system for a circulating fluidized bed boiler based on a selfdisturbance-resistant control. Journal of Engineering for Thermal Energy and Power 25(5), 514–516, 575 (2010)
[5] Deb, K.: A Fast and Elitist Multiobjective Genetic Algorithm NSGA-II. IEEE Transaction on Evolutionary Computation 6(2), 182–197 (2002)
[6] Sehadri, A.: Multi-objective optimization using Evolutionary algorithms (MOEA). IEEE Transactions on Evolutionary Computation 6, 526–526 (2002)
[7] Ma, Q., Xu, D., Shi, Y.: Research of synthesis tuning algorithm of Active-Disturbance-Rejection Controller. In: Proceedings of the 7th World Congress on Intelligent Control and Automation, WCICA 2008, pp. 2788–2793 (2008)
[8] Niu, P.: An intelligence combustion process control system application and research for circulating fluidized bed boiler of giant domestic manufacture. In: Proceedings of CSEE, vol. 20(12), pp. 62–66, 71 (2000)

Comparing and Analyzing on Value-Passing between Pages in ASP.NET

Jin Wang

Guilin University of Electronic Technology, Teaching Practice Department, China
access_wj@163.com

Abstract. This paper reviews various methods of value-passing between the pages in ASP.NET, describes the concepts, roles and characteristics of the objects that are necessary for realizing. Through sample code, we illustrate the basic applications of these methods. Finally, the paper analyzes and compares the advantages and disadvantages all of them unified. Conclusion: no matter which kind of method about value-passing between web pages in ASP.NET all has its own application scope.

Keywords: ASP.NET, Value-Passing, Page, Method, Object.

1 Introduction

When carrying on a dynamic web application, how to deal with the issues about data transfer between web pages is the problem that we usually need to face. The efficiency of its implementation has a direct-acting impact on procedure performance. Traditional solution is by means of Get or Post method. However, now, we use programming model based on event-driven in ASP.NET, and the page adopts PostBack techniques, some traditional methods are already inapplicability. ASP.NET with its excellent structure provides more methods on passing value. Different implementation methods based on different principles, and possess their own characteristics. In terms of function realizing, resource utilization, time efficiency and security, they all have different effects. In-depth understanding of these methods would help us solve practical problems and improve the quality and efficiency of procedures.

2 ASP. NET's Three-Tier Architecture

Before we introduce value-passing methods between web pages, it is necessary to understand the development method of ASP.NET Three-Tier architecture. In this architecture, front-end includes html, asp, aspx etc, mainly responsible for dealing with the input of users and the outputting to the users. The middle layer is the link of two layers, used to establish database connection, generate SQL sentences for realizing retrieve or updating database according to the user's requests, and in the end, return the results to client, it usually exists in form of dynamic link library .Dll. Rear is a database

S. Lin and X. Huang (Eds.): CESM 2011, Part II, CCIS 176, pp. 53–58, 2011.

server, responsible for actual data storage and retrieval. In the three-tier architecture, database through middle layer to link and operate, front-end transmit parameters to the middle, and receive parameters from the middle. Here mainly concern with the data communication between the middle layer and the front-end.

3 Methods of Value-Passing between Pages

For convenience of description, make the following convention: all the examples are based on c #; The source page and the target page have already imported the necessary namespace; The date existing in the TextBox control of source page (SrcForm.aspx) is transferred to the target page (DstForm. aspx), and through the Label control of the target page to display, the transport dot of value are established at Click event of Button control named Btn, the reception dot of value are located in Page_Load event of this page.

3.1 The Usage of QueryString

QueryString is a very simple transfer mode, it puts transmitted data value in a query string, and displays in browser's address bar, it's easy to achieve. But, there are some disadvantages: it can not deliver complicated objects, only appropriate for less value and less safety requirements. Specific implementation code segments are as follows:

SrcForm.aspx

```
Private void Btn_Click(object sender, System.EventArgs e)
{strUrl ="DstForm.aspx? id="+ TextBox.Text;
 Response. Redirect (strUrl);}
```

DstForm.aspx:

```
Private void Page_Load (object sender, System.EventArgs e)
{Label.Text = Request.QueryString ["id"];}
```

3.2 The Usage of Session

Session object is used to store variables of the across web procedure, and provides information for the current user session. Through its attributes can easily set and retrieve ASP.NET session state variables.

During the process of using Session variable, its value remains unchanged, and can be visited by all pages of the same session. It will disappear only when user close the browser or exceed the valid time. If Session variable store too much data would consume large amounts of server resources. So, particular attention should be paid to control its number when using. We shall make use of clean-up action to free up some unnecessary session to reduce consumption. Session variable is relatively localized, and its effective range is the page that defines them. Examples are as follows:

SrcForm.aspx:

```
Private void Btn_Click (object sender, System.EventArgs e)
{Session ["id"] =TextBox.Text;
 Response. Redirect ("DstForm.aspx");}
```

DstForm.aspx:

```
Private void Page_Load (object sender, System.EventArgs e)
{Label. Text=Session ["id"].ToString ();
 Session. Remove ("id");}
```

QueryString and Session possess their own advantages, and also possess defects that can not to be overcome respectively. QueryString is quite simple, Session is relatively complicated; QueryString's security is poor, but Session is high; QueryString would achieve various web pages simple data transfer, and commonly, it's only string type. However, session could realize complex data transfer, etc.

3.3 The Usage of Application

Application object generates state variable on server side to store information that needed, it is overall, and can realize value transfer between web pages. Comparing with Session objects, both are similar on data storage and access. The difference lies in: each web application only generates one Application case, and is applied to all users and sessions, its validity is the life cycle of the whole web. The method is suitable for storing commonly data such as little quantity, and remains unchanged with user. Meanwhile, for it is overall, means that it can only store some information that will be announced, so involving personal security information can not use it.

Application object variable has two commonly usage: Lock and Unlock, mainly responsible for problem that multiple user writing on the date stored in the application simultaneously. Lock method locks all Application variables, and prevent other users from modifying. Then, Unlock method relieves the lockup. Examples are as follows:

SrcForm.aspx:

```
Application ["id"] =Textbox. Text;
Server.Transfer (DstForm.aspx);
```

DstForm.aspx:

```
Application. Lock ();
Label. Text=Application ["id"].ToString0;
Application. Unlock ();
Application. Remove ("id");
```

3.4 The Usage of Cookie

The variables of Application objects and Session objects are all generated on the server side. Different from them, cookie is stored on the client, contains less information, and could permanently exist or to be end at the set time. It cooperates with ASP.NET built-in object Response and Request to complete value-passing. In addition, Cookie is associated with web site rather than a particular page. No matter which page that the user requires in the website, browsers and servers will exchange the Cookie information. For reading and writing at the client, users should pay more careful attention on cookie's safety and access privilege. Examples are as follows.

SrcForm.aspx:

```
Private void Btn_Click (object sender, System.EventArgs e)
{Response. Cookies ["id"].Value=TextBox.Text;
 Response. Redirect ("DstForm.aspx");}
```

DstForm.aspx:

```
Private void Page_Load(object sender, System.EventArgs e)
 {Label.Text=Request. Cookies["id"].Value;}
```

3.5 The Usage of Transfer Method

Transfer is a server-side data transmission method. On the server, by calling server object's Transfer method, redirect to the target page programmatically. The advantages are that they can deliver large amounts of data, and can access data and public attribute values that exist in the controls of the source page. This method is fully object-oriented, concise and effective. Defects: the operation is more complex, and the life cycle is only limited to the current request. Examples are as follows:

SrcForm.aspx:

```
Public string id {get {return TextBox.Text;}}
private void Btn_Click(object sender,System. EventArgs e)
  { Server. Transfer ("DstForm.aspx");}
```

DstForm.aspx:

```
<%@ Reference VirtualPath ="~/SrcForm.aspx" %>
Private void Page_Load (object sender, System.EventArgs e)
{ScrForm srPage;
 srPage = (ScrForm) Context.Handler;
 Label.Text=srPage.id;}
```

3.6   The Usage of Class Static Properties

In ASP.NET, each page corresponds to a class. This method makes use of class static properties to achieve value-passing between two pages. Such static variable will be allocated fixed storage space during the application running time, it exists by class not class instance, and could be accessed by class name while using.

Advantages: putting good use could effectively improve the efficiency of data transfer; Defects: if abuse, it would lead disturbance to the users or data, and could cause tremendous hidden trouble. Example of this method is as follows:

SrcForm.aspx:

```
// first define a class contain static properties and the
source page should be introduced namespace;
Private void Btn_Click(object sender, System.EventArgs e)
   {Srct.id=TextBox.Text; //Srct is static class
     Response.Redirect("DesForm.aspx");}
```

DesForm.aspx

```
Private void Page_Load (object sender, System.EventArgs e)
   {Label.Text=Srct.id;}
```

3.7   The Usage of Cache

Caching mechanism in application can be used for values-passing. Different from others, it needs to set cache item priority and cache time. Because when lack of system memory, caching mechanism will automatically remove items which seldom use or lower priority, and then would cause value-passing failure.

The advantage is that the size and the number of transfer data are unlimited and quickly. Defects: caching mechanism operation is relatively complicated. In ASP.NET, caching mechanism is realized through Cache class. Example is as follows:

SrcForm.aspx:

```
Private void Btn_Click (object sender, System.EventArgs e)
   {Cache ["id"] =TextBox.Text;
     Response.Redirect ("DstForm.aspx");}
```

DstForm.aspx:

```
Private void Page_Load (object sender, System.EventArgs e)
   {If (Cache ["id"]! =NULL)
    Label. Text=Cache ["id"].ToString ();
    Cache. Remove ("id") ;}
```

4 Compare and Analysis

Ground on all discussions, we can find out: QueryString is most convenient when transferred data is simple and without confidentiality; It's only Transfer method when pass on data by control directly; Session is most appropriate when deliver specific data which only relate to the users; It is rather convenient by using Application when share data among all users; Static variable could keep data for long time, and Cache could automatically remove the data; If want to preserve data for long term, can only choose from Cookie database or documents; generally, all these methods would not form performance bottleneck if properly designed. Overall, each of them has its own characteristics and advantages. In practical application, select which method should be based on particular case particular analysis, can not generalize.

5 Conclusions

In the web program development, we often need to consider the following factors: the accessibility of program function, the efficiency of server operation and the safety of procedures, etc. Therefore, the choice of method for value-passing between web pages is the issue that requires developers carefully consideration. In fact, no matter which method all has its scope of application, and also has its weaknesses. In actual development, our choice must according to the demand that faced. Generally, such as data confidentiality, data type, data size, use scope and retention time length, etc, are the factors we should take to consider. In addition, the method would be simple, and its application performance optimization is also important. In practice, only keep on trying, continually analyzing and summarizing, can we fully understand and flexible to use them.

References

1. Wang, C.-Z., Min, P.: The Research on Passing the Values Method between ASP. NET Page. Journal of Hubei University of Technology 21, 49–51 (2006)
2. Millett, S.: Professional ASP.NET Design Patterns. Wrox (2010)
3. Evjen, B., Hanselman, S., Rader, D.: Professional ASP.NET 3.5 SP1 Edition. In C# and VB. Wrox (2009)
4. Several methods on value-passing between ASP.NET web pages,
   http://tieba.baidu.com/f?kz=89180898

A Retrieval System of Internet Audio Public Opinion Based on Dynamic Keyword Spotting

Bo Xie, Dongliang Dai, and Xiaojun Li

College of Computer Science & Information Engineering,
Zhejiang Gongshang University, Hangzhou, China
boxie@mail.zjgsu.edu.cn, a2792275@163.com,
lixj@mail.zjgsu.edu.cn

Abstract. Audio retrieval of internet public opinion is an important component of public opinion monitoring and management. It can improve the utilization and retrieval rate. This paper proposes a retrieval system of internet audio public opinion based on keyword spotting which consists of audio public opinion collection, the dynamic reference template definition and online search. The keyword spotting model uses the dynamic technology of keywords increment to generate dynamic vocabulary to achieve the keywords of public opinion online decision-making and flexible definition of reference templates. Last, the mixed confidence algorithm is designed to confirm the results. Experimental results show that this keyword spotting based on dynamic reference template can automatically complete the training and optimization of system via the accumulation of retrieval times. On the other hand, the mechanism also improves the system detection rate.

Keywords: Audio Retrieval, Public Opinion, Keyword Spotting, Viterbi Algorithm, Mixed Confidence Algorithm.

1 Introduction

Internet public opinion is the opinions and views on some hot real life through the internet, which have a strong influence and bias [1]. The formats of internet public opinion have both structured text and non structured audio and video documents. Previous public opinion research focused on the text. With the rising of video sites, video is becoming the important way to get and publish information for internet users. In addition, the audio files include the most information of the public opinion in video. Audio has become another important form of public opinion after the text. It is necessary to study audio public opinion with the substantial increase.

Audio data stream has rich semantic information. However, audio retrieval is a hard problem, and at the time there are fewer schemes known to us that can satisfy audio retrieval. We eventually develop our own techniques that meet all the operational constraints. A retrieval system based on keyword spotting (RDBKS) is proposed to retrieve audio public opinion in this paper. The user experience is as follows: First, user submits the search keywords to the system. Then, an identification of the dynamic

S. Lin and X. Huang (Eds.): CESM 2011, Part II, CCIS 176, pp. 59–66, 2011.

reference template (DRT) is performed, and the system uses the new DRT to search audio that have been collected. Finally, the system outputs the audio that contains the retrieved keywords.

Keyword spotting is a very forward-looking and promising branch of speech recognition [2]. It needs some fixed vocabulary and is applied to search the input audio data [3], whereas the RSBKS has to perform the recognition quickly over a database of the audio with nearly 2.1G audio files. Therefore, a new model of keyword spotting based on dynamic reference template (DMKS) is put forward to search audio public opinion in this paper. DMKS generates a new DRT for each entry keyword via the dynamic technology of keywords increment. The technique ensures that the process of allocating words is flexible and dynamical within the template. All the database audio files are subjected to the same analysis via the new syntax diagrams and vocabulary library which are generated from new template. The system is suitable for audio retrieval. The candidate audio are subsequently evaluated for correctness of match via mixed algorithm confidence.

2   System Framework

RSBKS detects the audio from the database via research keyword. It addresses the problem of audio retrieving via human voice. Figure 1 illustrates that RSBKS system consists of three fundamental modules. The audio public opinion collection module is offline operation, and the DRT definition module and online search module which belong to DMKS model are synchronous online operation.

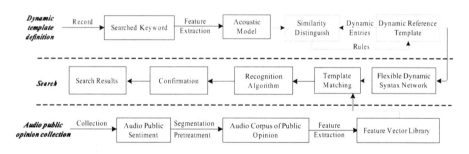

Fig. 1. The Framework of RSBKS

2.1   Audio Public Opinion Collection

The video documents are collected from the news websites which focus on public opinion information, such as the People's Daily, Xinhua, Sina, and they are stored with flv format. Audio files are extracted on 16KHZ sampling rate and 8bit quantitative by professional conversion software. The audio files are stored in wav format. They will generate the corpus that has cleared semantic after segmentation and preprocessing. Speech is determined by its start and end via zero crossing rate and energy entropy. The method of double threshold is used to detect the start of voice automatically [4]. The end of the voice is very easy to detect according to previous studies.

The system has to perform the recognition over the corpus of public opinion events with nearly 2.1G audio files. Every event contains 2 to 5 keywords which can convey this public opinion event. The number of files corresponding to each keyword is different. For instance, there are three keywords in so-called "XiongMao ShaoXiang" event, they are "XiongMao ShaoXiang", "WuHan NanHai" and "LiJun". In our test, we use the set of search keywords recorded by different people to search the public opinion database included 10 categories of public opinion., they are called "XiongMao ShaoXiang BingDu", "ShanXi HeiZhuanYao", "WenChuan DiZhen", "SanLu NaiFen", "HuaNanHu JiaZhao", "DuoMaoMao", "ChongQing DingZiHu", "GuiZhou WenAn 6.28 ShiJian", "Zhu LiuGan" and "XiangJiang DaZha ShiJian".

2.2   The Reference Template of DMKS

A variety of keyword spotting models has been sprung up recently. DMKS takes advantage of the garbage network model. The reference template definition is static in traditional KS, but DMKS makes the reference template definition to be dynamic by the dynamic technology of keywords increment. DMKS uses this technique to distinguish similarity of keywords, and allocates the entries. This makes sense that the acoustic models of dynamic entries have been recycled.

The speech signal is sampled with a frequency of 16 kHz, and 400 samples at a time are combined to frames with a frame period of 10ms. A total number of 30 mel-filtered cepstral coefficients and their time derivatives of first and second order are calculated, giving a feature vector with 64 components. This vector is optimized by use of a linear discriminate analysis.

The template may contain the entries which are similar to the current search keywords because of continuous searching by different user. View of this, as shows in figure 2, the DRT is defined as the dynamic keyword template, dynamic filler template and fixed-fill template. The entries of dynamic keyword templates and dynamic filler template are called as "dynamic entries". To perform discrimination between the similarities of keywords, this step is performed via dynamic keywords incremental algorithm. Then the map of dynamic vocabulary and flexible syntax diagram are used to search at syntax level, shows in figure 2.

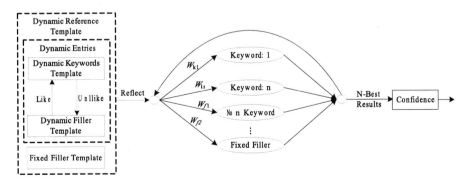

Fig. 2. The dynamic reference template (DRT) and the syntax diagram

The dynamic algorithm of keywords increment contains keywords similarity discrimination and dynamic reference template storage. Keywords similarity discrimination is based on the acoustic model. This paper defines the probability distance measure $d(k, \lambda_\tau)$ to describe the similarity of current keyword and dynamic entry, moreover system takes as discrimination threshold, last generates the DRT according to storage rules.

2.2.1 Keywords Similarity Discrimination

The recorded keywords are labeled as k. The total number of dynamic entries are denoted as t, choosing the acoustic model of dynamic entries and make them as λ_τ, $\tau \in t$, and the system generates keywords set (KW) and non-keywords set (NKW) after traversing each dynamic entry model via the keywords similarity discrimination algorithm. KW set and NKW set are stored in the dynamic keyword template and dynamic filler template.

if $\forall \tau \in t$, $\exists \lambda_\tau$, and $d(k, \lambda_\tau) < \theta$, then k and λ_τ are similar. So we define the set of keywords as formula (1).

$$KW = \{\tau \mid d(k, \lambda_\tau) < \theta, \tau \in t\}. \tag{1}$$

if $\forall \tau \in t$, $\exists \lambda_\tau$, and $d(k, \lambda_\tau) \geq \theta$, then k and λ_τ are not similar. So we define the set of non-keywords as formula (2).

$$NKW = \{\tau \mid d(k, \lambda_\tau) \geq \theta, \tau \in t\}. \tag{2}$$

2.2.2 Storage Rules of Dynamic Reference Template

The KW set and NKW set can be gotten via formula (1) and (2) in keywords similarity discrimination. The entries of KW set and NKW set take as the new retrieve entries in current DRT, and the new entries are allocated dynamically according to the stored rules in the template. The rules suggest that the recorded keyword model and the words' models of KW set are all stored in dynamic keyword template; The non-keywords of NKW set are stored in dynamic filler template.

The probability distance measure $d(k, \lambda_\tau)$ [5] is used to describe the acoustic models similarity between the current keywords and the dynamic entries.

The probability distance measure of two HMM is $d(\lambda_1, \lambda_2)$:

$$d(\lambda_1, \lambda_2) = \lim_{k \to \infty} \frac{1}{K} \sum_{k=1}^{K} \{\log P_{Y_1^{(k)}}[\lambda_1] - \log P_{Y_1^{(k)}}[\lambda_2]\} \cdot \tag{3}$$

Their model parameters of HMM are $\lambda_1 = \{a_1, A_1, B_1\}$ and $\lambda_2 = \{a_2, A_2, B_2\}$, $Y_1^{(k)}$ is a feature vector sequence produced by λ_1.

$d(\lambda_1,\lambda_2)$ can not determine the similarity directly because it is a asymmetric mea sure that $d(\lambda_1,\lambda_2) \neq d(\lambda_2,\lambda_1)$. The symmetry distance measure $d_s(\lambda_1,\lambda_2)$ is use d to define the similar in this paper.

$$d_s(\lambda_1,\lambda_2) = \frac{1}{2}\{d(\lambda_1,\lambda_2) + d(\lambda_2,\lambda_1)\} \cdot \tag{4}$$

2.3 Search Online

First, the user submits the recorded keywords to the system, and then search keywords are stored in the module of public opinion keywords after feature extraction and HMM construction, the system distinguishes the similar between the recorded search keywords and dynamic entries at last. The updated DRT is utilized to match the audio. The dynamic syntax diagram is used to search at syntax layer when decode with the Viterbi algorithm [6]. The system will output the results finally through analyzing the candidate sequence with mixed confidence algorithm.

At present, the main confidence algorithms are confidence analysis based on acoustic model [7] and cell-based method confidence (cell can be a word, phoneme, etc.) [8]. We propose a new confidence algorithm that merge word-based confidence and confidence based on acoustic model in this paper. It adopts complementary advantages of two confidence algorithm.

We sign the confidence based on acoustic and MAP word-based confidence as M_{CM1}, M_{CM2}. Due to their different score range, calculating directly the sum of them does not work. This paper incorporates a weighting factor to balance the two confidence score. The mixed confidence M_{CM} is defined:

$$M_{CM} = \beta M_{CM1} + (1-\beta)M_{CM2} \cdot \tag{5}$$

We use the acoustic confidence based on the normalized state length in this paper. Its acoustic confidence score marked by the normalized observation distribution probability M_{CM1} shows in formula 6.

$$M_{CM1} = \frac{1}{N}\sum_{i=1}^{N}[\frac{1}{e[i]-b[i]+1}\sum_{t=b[i]}^{e[i]}\log b_i(o_t)]. \tag{6}$$

There are N states in HMM altogether. Where O is a particular input vector sequence for observing. Where b[i] and e[i] are the starting and ending frame number corresponded to state i. $b_i(o_t)$ is the probability at state i.

The main thing that finds a link objective functions between the entries for MAP word-based confidence [9]. Its locality is more outstanding compared with acoustic confidence. W^{n-1} is the path of trace back. If $\{\omega_n;\tau,t\}$ is the next link word, τ, t are the starting and ending moment of this word. Then the objective function $f(W^n)$ linked $\{\omega_n;\tau,t\}$ to W^{n-1} can get by formula (7), (8).

$$f(W^{n-1},[\omega_n;\tau,t]) = g(W^{n-1},t) + h(W^n,t) . \tag{7}$$

$$f(W^n) = \max f(W^{n-1},[\omega_n;\tau,t]) . \tag{8}$$

Where $g(W^{n-1},t)$ is the cumulative likelihood sore of trace back process from the path tail to the first. $h(W^n,t)$ is called the sub-inspired likelihood generated through frame synchronization Veterbi decoding in the previous process. In this way, we can calculate the confidence of keyword ω_n with results obtained above in the decoding process.

$$M_{CM2} = e^{f(W^{n-1})} / \sum_{W_c} e^{f(W^{n-1},[\omega_n;\tau,t])} . \tag{9}$$

3 Experiment and Result Analysis

To perform an experiment, this step is performed on the collected corpus that introduced in chapter 2.1. In order to address the problem of testing correctness, we set 50 persons to retrieve the audio library of public opinion; there are 30 males and 20 females. Each one pronounces a keyword to retrieve the corresponding audio documents. The total number of the keywords in the corpus is 33. This process is repeated until this person finish recording a collection of keywords corpus, that the person completed the search task. Searching order of 50 persons is random. The record and retrieval processing all completed in a laboratory environment.

To avoid too many spurious entries to occur, we assume that experiment will determine the similarity threshold θ as the optimal threshold., with the justification that the optimal threshold ensures the entries' similarity is optimal in the KW set, namely, there are all right keywords of public opinion in KW collection, and NKW collection contains all non-keywords without confusion term when θ is the optimal threshold. Experiment records the average detection rate of the system per person in retrieval process. Finally depicts graph of the relationship between people cumulative and performance of system, shown in Figure 3.

The Average Detection Rate: $ADR = \dfrac{1}{nKeys} \sum\limits_{i=1}^{nKeys} DR_i$, the DR_i is the detection rate of i_{th} keyword to somebody, the $nKeys$. is the total number of the keywords.

$$DR_i = \frac{\text{The number of output documents contained keyword i}}{\text{The total number of files contained search keyword i}} . \tag{10}$$

Figure 3 curve is divided into three sections. In the first 11 people to retrieve, the average detection rate float of 61.2% ~ 64.5%, the curve does not show regular changes. The average detection rate of the latter are higher than the previous 0.8% to 1.5% after the first 12 people, an average growth rate reaches 1.2%. This growth rate maintains to 41.The average detection rates are stable after the first 41, the highest average detection rate reaches to 85.6%.

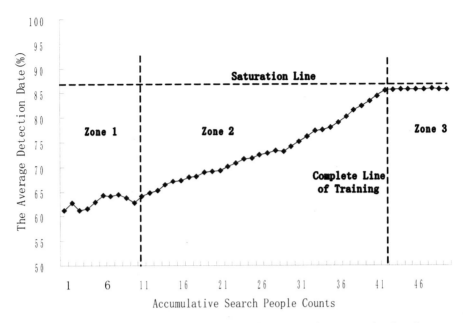

Fig. 3. The relationship of accumulative search people counts and system retrieval performance

The instability in zone 1 demonstrates that system triggers the dynamic reference template to allocate the initial term at 10 people accumulation of searching. But the low reference of initial template causes the template definition and distribution quality are not obvious. So we can call the region 1 as debug period. The changes of region 2 demonstrate that the dynamic template is at the optimization stage which is from the beginning to the completion of training. Since the increase in the number of search and experimental conditions in the optimal similar threshold, entries' models of KW and NKW sets are enriched. The system expands the retrieved range as well as increases the detection rate. The solid growth in zone 2 also shows that system has the higher robustness. We call zone 2 as training period. The accumulative search people count 41 is the training critical point, templates have been trained at 41st people searching, and the detection rate of public opinion corpus is also stable. Training critical point will change relative to the experimental keywords set of corpus. Zone 3 is called saturated period. This makes clear that the DRT can optimize automatically for a particular corpus via the accumulated search times, and the system detection rate is maintained a stable and relatively high state.

4   Conclusion

This paper proposes a retrieval system of internet audio public opinion based on dynamic keyword spotting. The system makes use of the DMKS based on dynamic reference template. Experiment shows that the dynamic reference template has a good performance. Its searching and optimization are synchronous. The system achieved good recognition results when used in searching internet audio public opinion. How to improve the accuracy and speed of keywords similarity discrimination in dynamic incremental technique and how to improve the performance of the MAP word-based confidence algorithm effectively and reduce the complexity of the algorithm are the main content of the late.

References

1. Din, G.L., Qing, Z.J., Wang, G.S.: A flexible mining model oriented view of internet public opinion crisis. J. Information 28(10) (2009)
2. Han, J., Liu, X.X., Pan, J.L.: A keyword spotting system for network and information security. In: China Network and Information Security Technology Conference, Beijing (2004)
3. Huang, E.F., Wang, H.C.: A Fast Algorithm for Large Vocabulary Keyword Spotting Application. IEEE Transactions on Speech and Audio Processing, 449–452 (1994)
4. Rabiner, L.R., Juang, B.H.: Fundamentals of Speech and Speaker Recognition. Murry Hill, New Jersey (1993)
5. Knill, K.M., Young, S.J.: Fast implementation methods for Viterbi-based word-spotting. In: Proceedings of IEEE International Conference on Acoustics, Speech and Signal Processing, Atlanta, USA, pp. 522–525 (1996)
6. Juang, B.H., Rabiner, L.R.: A Probabilistic Distance Measure for Hidden Markov Models. AT&T Technical Journal 64(2), 391–408 (1985)
7. Kamppari, S.O., Hazen, T.J.: Word and phone level acoustic confidence scoring. In: Proceedings of IEEE International Conference on Acoustics, Speech and Signal Processing, Istanbul, Turkey, pp. 1799–1802 (2000)
8. Evermann, G.: Minimum Word Error Rate Decoding. Cambridge University, Cambridge (1999)
9. Lu, S.Q., Sun, C.L.: Study of keyword recognition system for speech based on streaming media. Journal of Beijing Institute of Machinery (2006)

An Image De-noising Algorithm Based on Improved Wavelet Threshold Scheme

Li Zhang and Bing Tang

School of Computer Science and Engineering,
Hunan University of Science and Technology,
Xiangtan 411201, China
zlhncdsy@163.com

Abstract. Based on the analysis of image de-noising by soft and hard threshold functions, this paper presents a new threshold function and an adaptive threshold scheme with β coefficient. Simulation experiments prove that the new de-noising method gives better performance than the previous schemes based on soft or hard threshold functions. Furthermore, the paper also discusses how does the constant m in the proposed method influence the de-noising effect, and the result shows that there exists different m that could produce the best de-noising effect for different noise intensity.

Keywords: Wavelet Transform, Image De-noising, Threshold Functions.

1 Introduction

Image is usually corrupted by noise more or less during the transfer period, which may cause the Signal Noise Ratio (SNR) to be decreased. Once the SNR decreases to some extent, image quality would be affected and noises would become visible coarse grains. Generally, image de-nosing is the first step for image processing operation. From the perspective of noise stochastic analysis, noise is randomly added to image, and it can be considered as image details which are independent of host image. Traditional de-noising methods adopt linear techniques such as Wiener filter. Though termed as the typical method, the Wiener filter appear demerit in large of the image de-noising applications because of its linearity and the fact that image data are rather sparsely distributed. Nowadays, non-linear techniques are widely used. In 1995, Donoho proposed a wavelet-based threshold method, which obtained an excellent de-nosing effect. Since that, wavelet-based threshold method has been attracted many attentions. The Donoho method is just trying to optimize the hard or soft threshold function [1][2]. However, both of these functions have some shortcomings. For example, both the hard threshold function and the derivative of the soft threshold function are discontinuous, and the estimated wavelet coefficients have invariable error with original wavelet coefficients. Hence these shortcomings restrict the further application of hard and soft threshold method.

In this research, a new energy-adaptive threshold function is presented, which overcomes the disadvantages of classic hard and soft threshold method. Simulating

S. Lin and X. Huang (Eds.): CESM 2011, Part II, CCIS 176, pp. 67–72, 2011.

results demonstrate the effectiveness and advantages of the proposed function. The rest of the paper is organized as follows. Section 2 reviews the classic Donoho threshold de-nosing method. The proposed de-nosing algorithm is introduced in Section 3, and Section 4 presents the simulation results and analysis of new de-noising algorithm. Finally, Section 5 concludes the whole paper.

2 Donoho Threshold De-noising

2.1 Signal Model

It is supposed that $X(k)$ denotes original signal, and $V(k)$ stands for random noise, while noised signal is represented by $Y(k)$, therefore one dimensional signal can be modeled as follow,

$$Y(k)=X(k)+V(k), k=0,1,2,\ldots,n\text{-}1 \tag{1}$$

Usually, the useful signal is represented by low frequency parts, while noise is represented by high frequency parts. Therefore the main task for de-noising is that decomposing signal according to their characteristics and then removing the high frequency noise while preserving most of useful signal so as to achieving the objective of de-noising with inconspicuous distortion.

2.2 Wavelet-Based Threshold De-noising

The idea of wavelet-based threshold de-noising algorithm proposed by Donoho is that, when wavelet coefficient $w_{j,k}$ is smaller than a specified threshold, the wavelet coefficient is considered to be noise and it should be dispelled. Otherwise, when $w_{j,k}$ is larger than the threshold, it is considered to be signal, and it must be preserved directly (namely Hard Threshold Method) or it can be shrank to zero according to a fix value (named as Soft Threshold Method). Subsequently, denoised signal is constructed by new wavelet coefficients. The Donoho's de-noising procedure can be realized by three steps as follows.

Step 1: Apply discrete wavelet transform (DWT) to noised signal $y(k)$, and obtain a group of wavelet coefficients $w_{j,k}$;

Step 2: Perform a threshold process on $w_{j,k}$, and obtain estimated coefficient $\hat{w}_{j,k}$ which makes the value of $\|\hat{w}_{j,k} - w_{j,k}\|$ as small as possible. Equation (2) and (3) present hard threshold function and soft threshold function respectively [1][2],

$$\hat{w}_{j,k} = \begin{cases} w_{j,k} & |w_{j,k}| \geq \lambda \\ 0 & |w_{j,k}| < \lambda \end{cases} \tag{2}$$

$$\hat{w}_{j,k} = \begin{cases} \mathrm{sgn}(w_{j,k})(|w_{j,k}| - \lambda) & |w_{j,k}| \geq \lambda \\ 0 & |w_{j,k}| < \lambda \end{cases} \tag{3}$$

where λ is the specified threshold which can be calculated as $\lambda = \sigma\sqrt{2\lg(N)}$, and sgn(*) represents the symbol function, while σ is the noise standard deviation, and N is the length of signal.

Step 3: Reconstruct signal using $\hat{w}_{j,k}$ by inverse discrete wavelet transform(IDWT), and obtain estimated signal $\tilde{y}(k)$ which indicates the de-noised signal.

3 Proposed De-noising Algorithm

3.1 Improved Threshold Function

Hard and soft threshold schemes have been used widely in practice. Generally, soft threshold method out performs hard threshold method in terms of visual quality of reconstructed image. In hard threshold function, $\hat{w}_{j,k}$ is un-continuous at the position of $\pm \lambda$, which leads to a result that some coefficients near threshold value are preserved while some may be set to zero. In contrast with hard one, soft threshold function overcomes this disadvantage in a certain extent, with continuous wavelet coefficients range, however there always exists an invariable error λ between $\hat{w}_{j,k}$ and $w_{j,k}$, which would affect the reconstruction precision [3]. Nevertheless, reducing the error λ to zero maybe also not a good solution, because $w_{j,k}$ is composed of low frequency part $u_{j,k}$ and high frequency part $v_{j,k}$, and it is possibly affected by $v_{j,k}$, which leads to $|w_{j,k}| > |u_{j,k}|$. Thereby, the goal of threshold function is making $\|\hat{w}_{j,k} - w_{j,k}\|$ as small as possible, and making the value of $\hat{w}_{j,k}$ ranged from $|w_{j,k}| - \lambda$ to $|w_{j,k}|$. In this way, the estimated wavelet coefficient $\hat{w}_{j,k}$ may be more closer to $u_{j,k}$. Based on the above analysis, this paper proposes a new semi-soft-semi-hard threshold function as you see in Equation (4) which is similar to hard and soft methods but improves their shortcomings.

$$\hat{w}_{j,k} = \begin{cases} \text{sgn}(w_{j,k}) \left[|w_{j,k}| - m\lambda + \dfrac{(m-1)\lambda}{\exp(w_{j,k}^2 - \lambda^2)} \right] & |w_{j,k}| \geq \lambda \quad (0 < m < 1) \\ 0 & |w_{j,k}| < \lambda \end{cases} \tag{4}$$

(1) When $w_{j,k} \rightarrow \pm \lambda$, Equation (5) comes into existence.

$$\frac{(m-1)\lambda}{\exp(w_{j,k}^2 - \lambda^2)} = (m-1)\lambda \tag{5}$$

Combining Equation (5) with Equation (4), we are aware that $\hat{w}_{j,k}=0$, and the proposed threshold function is considered to be continuous at the position of $\pm \lambda$.

(2) When $w_{j,k} \rightarrow \pm \infty$, it can be concluded that $\hat{w}_{j,k} \rightarrow w_{j,k} \pm m\lambda$, as well as $|\hat{w}_{j,k} - w_{j,k}| \rightarrow m\lambda$. This means that with the increase of $w_{j,k}$, the deviation between $\hat{w}_{j,k}$ and $w_{j,k}$ will be reduced to $m\lambda$, which is smaller than the error produced by soft threshold function. Thereby, the demonstrated new function can promote image reconstruction precision and improve denoising effect. Comparing with hard and soft function, the proposed function is superior and more flexible, better denoising effect can be obtained as long as adjusting the value of m between 0 and 1.

(3) Because the square of wavelet coefficient is directly proportional to signal energy, the proposed threshold function $\exp(w_{j,k}^2 - \lambda^2)$ contains energy information [4]. During coefficient processing, the new function can consider about the energy distribution character and adjust energy distribution adaptively.

3.2 Threshold Value Selection

Current threshold value selection strategies for most de-noising algorithms are divided into four types [5]: 1) based on the maximum and minimum principle; 2) based on the Stein's unbiased risk estimator; 3) based on fixed threshold $\sigma\sqrt{2\lg(N)}$; 4) based on heuristic threshold.

When we make wavelet decomposition for pure noise, it will also produce high frequency coefficients, thus high frequency coefficients of noised signal include both signal and noise information. If only a few high frequency coefficients are produced by noise, threshold value selection strategy 1) and 2) only set part of coefficients to zero, which can preserve most of actual signal and extract slim signal, while strategy 3) and 4) can make de-noising more effective, but useful high frequency coefficients maybe filtered as a part of noise. In this paper, a threshold value with coefficient β is adopted.

$$\beta = \sqrt{\lg\frac{L_K}{2^{J-1}}}$$ (6)

$$\lambda = \frac{\beta\sigma^2}{\sigma_X}$$ (7)

$$\sigma_X = \sqrt{\max(\sigma_Y^2 - \sigma^2, 0)}$$ (8)

$$\sigma_Y^2 = \frac{1}{n^2}\sum_{i,j=1}^{n} w_{i,j}^2$$ (9)

In Equation (6)-(9), L_K denotes the length of the Kth level decomposition subband image, and J stands for the total decomposition levels, and σ^2 denotes the noise variance, where that $\sigma = median(|w_{j,k}|)/0.6745$. σ_X is denoted as the signal standard deviation. We also define that, $w_{i,j} \in subband$ HH$_1$, and $n \times n$ is the size of current subband. λ is just the threshold value. All the foregoing parameters are acquired according to each subband data. Utilizing spatial relativity of wavelet coefficients, threshold value can distinguish signal from noise more accurately so as to get better de-noising effect.

4 Simulation Results and Analysis

A The standard grayscale image "baboon", "lena", "boat" and "goldhill" are used in experiment as you see in Fig. 1(a)-(d). The size of all images is 512×512. Noised images have different noise intensity, respectively $\sigma = 10, 20, 30, 40$. Wavelet "db3" is used to for three level wavelet decomposition.

Fig. 2(a)-(d) show the noised images with $\sigma = 30$, and the corresponding de-noising effect using proposed algorithm is presented by Fig. 3. The proposed function and threshold value with β coefficient is compared with hard and soft threshold methods in terms of *PSNR* (Peak Signal-to-Noise Ratio) value, and the comparison result is shown in Table 1. The simulation results demonstrate that the proposed method out performs soft and hard threshold method.

| (a) baboon | (b) lena | (c) boats | (d) goldhill |

Fig. 1. Original image

| (a) baboon | (b) lena | (c) boats | (d) goldhill |

Fig. 2. Noised image ($\sigma = 30$)

| (a) baboon | (b) lena | (c) boats | (d) goldhill |

Fig. 3. De-noised image by proposed method ($\sigma = 30$)

Table 1. The comparison of three methods for PSNR

	σ	Noised image	Proposed method	Soft method	Hard method
baboon	$\sigma = 10$	19.5142	21.8631	20.8302	21.1898
	$\sigma = 20$	16.8988	20.7377	20.3616	20.4404
	$\sigma = 30$	15.3686	20.2227	20.0353	19.9682
	$\sigma = 40$	14.3444	19.8634	19.7821	19.6689
lena	$\sigma = 10$	19.5927	26.8787	26.3844	26.4856
	$\sigma = 20$	17.0101	25.3870	25.2206	25.1023
	$\sigma = 30$	15.5040	24.4133	24.3550	24.0512
	$\sigma = 40$	14.4532	23.6628	23.6657	23.3708
boats	$\sigma = 10$	19.7862	26.4439	25.6159	25.8508
	$\sigma = 20$	17.1229	24.7343	24.3969	24.2858
	$\sigma = 30$	15.5635	23.7034	23.5791	23.2151
	$\sigma = 40$	14.4893	22.9826	22.9324	22.4892
goldhill	$\sigma = 10$	19.6896	26.3761	25.9900	25.9895
	$\sigma = 20$	17.1167	24.9834	24.9412	24.7725
	$\sigma = 30$	15.6702	24.1753	24.1916	23.8932
	$\sigma = 40$	14.6358	23.4735	23.5005	23.1253

Furthermore, in proposed threshold function, we are aware of that different m would lead to different *PSNR*. Different σ means there certainly existing an optimum m which makes the *PSNR* value reach the maximum value. Taking "goldhill" image as an example, we perform the image de-noising using proposed threshold. Fig. 4 shows *PSNR* curve graphs varying with m when σ equals 10 and 40, respectively.

(1) when $\sigma = 10$, $m = 0.35$ make *PSNR* reach the maximum value 26.3761;

(2) when $\sigma = 40$, $m = 0.25$ make *PSNR* reach the maximum value 23.4735.

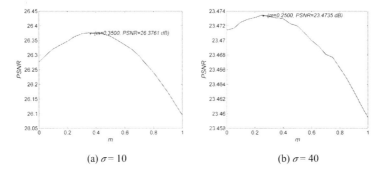

(a) $\sigma = 10$ (b) $\sigma = 40$

Fig. 4. PSNR varying with m and optimum PSNR

5 Conclusion

On the basis of analyzing hard and soft threshold methods presented by Donoho, this paper proposes a novel threshold function and an improved threshold value with β coefficient which overcomes the shortcoming of hard and soft threshold methods. Simulation results show that the proposed de-noising scheme has better de-noising effect than traditional Donoho threshold schemes.

Acknowledgments. This paper is supported by Start-up Research Fund for Doctoral Employee in Hunan University of Science and Technology under grant no. E51097.

References

1. Donoho, D.L.: De-Noising by Soft-Thresholding. IEEE Transactions on Information Theory 41, 613–627 (1995)
2. Donoho, D.L., Johnstone, I.M.: Adapting to Unknown Smoothness via Wavelet Shrinkage. Journal of the American Statistical Association 12, 1200–1224 (1995)
3. Cui, H., Song, G.X.: A Kind of Modified Project Based on the Wavelet Threshold Denoising Method. Modern Electronics Technique, 8–10 (2005)
4. Zhou, Y.M., Lai, X.Z., Lai, S.L.: An Energy Self-adaptive Threshold Function on Denoise. Control and Automation 24, 288–290 (2008)
5. Xie, J.C., Zhang, D.L., Xu, W.L.: Overview on Wavelet Image Denoising. Journal of Image and Graphics 7, 209–217 (2002)

Experiences on Teaching "Computer Program Design" in Military Academy by Applying Constructivism

MeiJuan Wang, YaQing Shi, ZhengHong Qiao, and XiaoYu Lei

Dept. of Fundamental Electronics, PLA University of Science and Technology,
NanJing, 211101
Wangmeijuan1984@hotmail.com

Abstract. "Computer Program Design" is the core course of computer-related majors, and is the foundation of many advanced courses .Under the union informationization condition application demands and the compliance requirements of the teaching objectives the authors put forward the Constructivism theory into the course of "Computer Program Design", with amount of hand-on practices, and achieved good teaching effect and experiences.

Keywords: Computer Program Design, Constructivism, Individualized.

1 Introduction

One important feature of the information society is information flow and accumulation. Enabling students to have good information awareness and information ability is the basic requirements of education. The so-called information literacy education is for the purpose to improve the Human's information quality, training the learners with the ability of using information technology to acquire effectively, analyze and use information, making learners in information consciousness, information ability and information morality, etc to adapt to the information society and level. Information technology quality is not a purely technical education, but a new educational model reconstruction.

The "Computer Program Design" is one of the important basic courses of the science and engineering major. It is the basis for many advanced courses, and occupies an important position in the entire study. Different from the software engineering program design, we focus more on teaching the theory of knowledge consistently. Consquently, the teaching of this course is mainly about introducing the programming algorithms and programming languages, raises the students' procedure thinking, which has the bright teaching characteristics. Depending on the real experience in teaching students to master the program design with C language in the information age, this paper discuss the concrete question, and then into the constructivist approach to solve the problem to meet the teaching requirements better, and train more outstanding talented students.

2 Pros and Cons of the Existing Teaching Modes

2.1 Traditional Teaching Methods

Traditional teaching method is the most widely used education as a means of teaching, which can be summed up into four steps: "put forward the concept--explain

S. Lin and X. Huang (Eds.): CESM 2011, Part II, CCIS 176, pp. 73–78, 2011.

the concept – examples -- summarizing". This textbook-based teaching mode has many advantages, such as clear, rhythmic steady. But it can't conducive to divergent thinking, and therefore, is obviously not applicable to "Computer Program Design", which is characterized with strong practicality and rich changes in the content.

The course of program design requires students not only to understand the basic C language syntax, but also to develop programming ideas. By traditional teaching method, all students in the classroom are targeted to the thinking of only one method, which will lead that codes are copied rigidly, using the same lines, the same algorithm, or even the same variable definition in the follow-up experiment. In addition, we teach a wide range of students, whose basis are different, the difficulty degree of example and homework is difficult to grasp in the classroom, which is also the reason that both individualized and traditional methods is difficult due to defects.

2.2 Project Teaching Method

Project teaching method is popular because of combination of theory and practice. It was first proposed as an instance by Professor Fred Heinrich, who is the education expert, in "Quality education report performance of Germany and the European and American countries". First, the method selects a related project in the real world by students or teachers. Second, grouping students to discuss the needs analysis about the project and write their own plans and complete implementation. Third, explaining through their demonstration of the mechanism by groups, and finally assessing by teachers. Students would learn more from each other by discuss. Through joint implementation of a complete work of teaching activity, this method becomes a teacher-student projects, in which the theory is converted to the actual demand to allow students to use, and in large part to explore the creative potential of students to enable them to understand and grasp the knowledge and skills course requirements better. Currently, promoting program design courses within part local universities has achieved very good effectiveness.

However, for the "computer program design" course in military academy, to promote the project teaching method is difficult, especially for the class as a wide range of students with big difference and weak foundation. Our teaching objects are lack of engineering exercise because of their military background. Without the conception and knowledge of programming, achieving a complete project in a short time is difficult. They have litter chance to come into contact with project information because of limited off-school time.

3 Several Ponders about the Course

3.1 Emancipate the Minds and Clarify the Goals

The teaching objectives of military college are different from the general higher colleges or vocational colleges. We respect the choice of the learner, focusing on general knowledge education. Students focus on the spirit of innovation and cooperation in culture and so on. Therefore, the key point of teaching the course of "computer program design" can not just stay in the model of teachers' teaching and students' learning. We need to further update the concept and free from the traditional teaching model, in order to establish the new ideas for the needs suited to social development and the future high-tech warfare. The talent in the information age will be "Only those, who have sense of innovation and ability of innovation to achieve the value of innovation, are most needed in our military in the future information age."

3.2 Focus on Methods and Individualized

Individualized teaching philosophy of education has been proposed for more than one thousand years. When facing different students, different teaching methods and enough communication were necessary. Confucius proposed that the method of researching human beings needs the acknowledgement of existent differences between them for the premise. As a teacher, he knows the characteristics of each student, and consequently could require students studying and thinking, learning and behaving in different ways, which also reflected the spirit of modern teaching and educating.

Teachers should respect the characterisics of students and help them to develop skills. The practical ability of divergent thinking can be practiced through teaching and guiding by individualized. With the improvement of teaching conditions, the traditional teaching model has developed from "speaking without practice" to "talking and doing". Confirmatory test after theoretical classroom, which requires Individualized must be used in teaching. "Experiment practice and theory combining, stresses the practice experiment teaching to promote discipline theory knowledge learning. "Based on the different level of students, teachers should stimulate their own motivation to learn.

3.3 Education Innovation of Student-Oriented

Marxist philosophy is human-oriented philosophy, and believes the real world is based on human being, whom is distinguished based on its own practice and emotional event .No practice, no human being. Person is the subject of practice, which is the foundation of all the world including people, and knowledge is the product of practice.

In society today, quality-oriented education, innovative education and elite education have become dominant. The so-called innovative education, as the result of people-oriented philosophy combining with other various methods, is for the real to cultivate people's innovation sense and thinking, creativity and creative ability, and innovative personality. The innovative education is proposed for the needs within the incoming knowledge economy age and future competition, which can give full play to that education is to train the national innovation system, and promoting quality-oriented education.

4   Experience of Practicing Constructivist

As talked above, individualized and innovative education is an important means of teaching. How to achieve is a major topic in the implementation process. Through the course "Computer Program Design" of different classes with different levels of students, the authors used the constructivist mode to discuss the comparative analysis of improvement, achieving good effect and promotion of teaching experiences.

4.1 Constructivist in Teaching

Constructivist learning theory, accompanied by the criticism and development of cognitive psychology in the end of 20th century, is an important branch of psychology. It is learner-centered, and emphasizes the learner's active exploration of knowledge and the active construction of the significance of knowledge they learned.

In the teaching-and-learning process guided by Constructivists, learners must learn new knowledge by their own initiative and interactive way. Corresponding changes are thus to teachers, who are no longer a "provider" of knowledge but a "facilitator" They have to provide the opportunity for the students to discover the differences between the new and old knowledge (which is vertical), and the gap with superior in the environment around (which is lateral). The ultimate purpose is to encourage and motivate students to study actively.

4.2 Construction Analysis of "Computer Program Design"

"Computer Program Design" is a practical course. It is not only necessary to grasp the concept, but also hands-on programming, debugging and running on the machine. Practice is an effective way to acquire knowledge in any activity, which is deeply accepted by the authors, including the younger who teach for the first time and the elder who have many years of teaching experiences. Despite the different classes and distinguish levels of students, the teaching effectiveness points out that, thinking and doing are important. No matter the original foundation, those who grasp knowledge solid ultimately must be good at summing algorithm, being a seriously debugger, and continue to explore the practice.

Teachers usually come to be not only the "guider" of teaching in the traditional philosophy of education, but the also the "facilitator" in the constructivist model. With programming of C language for example, what teachers need to do from work assignments to checking just includes: selecting the appropriate operation for examples of student's ability, requiring students to find out the guiding principles and requirements before the experiment. However, students have to type in the program on computer and check the grammar by VC6.0 editing environment, then compile and check the running results. At the same time, they have to record the encountered problems and solutions in the program debugging process, and finally submit the laboratory test report after the inspection.

The focus of this method is to understand the process of debugging, accumulate and consolidate up the experience in the debugger gradually. From explaining the algorithm to guiding student to test, and then helping them to complete the process design, teachers should play the role of assistant of practice in order to fully inspire the enthusiasm of the students. Finally, teachers may require the better students to further optimize of their algorithms and procedures, thus to help them improve the practical ability.

4.3 Implementation of Construction Practice

Learning by Constructivist is that learners don't passively receive external information, but actively build the meaning of current things by the cognitive structure of previous construction and selective perception of external information. Therefore, before teaching the scientific knowledge of "Computer Program Design", teachers have to seriously consider the learner's knowledge and experience, in order to ensure the scientific knowledge be fell within the scope of the learner's construction area. Combining with learner's experience closely is the only way to assist their meaningful learning.

During the teaching process of practicing Constructivist, the authors have experiences as following:

● Our "Computer Program Design" course have 40 the oretical lessons and 20 practical lessons. As a result student would not have enough time on programming practice. Consequently teachers should remind and let student to prepare for the practical lessons. Better to form a thought of flow chart or get the algorithm like C-language ready on the lab report. Knocking and testing directly is rather than waiting until class. Typing the code but without thinking has no effect to learner. This advice can improve not only teaching efficiency but also the learner's thinking ability.

● For the compilation errors and warnings in the process of debugging, teachers should teach effective methods, such as step debugging, equivalence class partition, boundary value of the debug, placement of test statements, etc. this means teachers should facilitate students to understand error and correct mistakes, rather than help them to modify the program directly.

● After the experiment, students have to turn in the lab report with complete specification, including algorithmic ideas, source code, debugging data and results, ultimately the self experience. In particular, how to find the error in debugging and how to modify are very important. As a result, even though student can't accomplish the final success of a program due to the insufficient class-time, they still can learn practical knowledge.

● To some students of better foundation and stronger practical ability, teachers should recommend more difficult comprehensive experiments of relatively complex algorithm for their selective study ,in order to extend thinking power

5 Concluding

As a bridging course, the "Computer Program Design" is rather important. The teaching methods directly impact the final result. With the clear objective, teachers must take into account of searching for the individualized education methods. Proved by experience of teaching, the method of Constructivist could help student build their own knowledge structure by themselves, which can fully mobilize the initiative of students and the practical ability. More important, Students learned not only knowledge, but also methods to learn knowledge. In the future, we will continue to promote and draw more experiences on the teaching philosopher.

References

1. Yin, S.: Discussion about C Language Learning. Computer Knowledge and Technology (September 2008)
2. Chen, Z.: Discussing on Teaching Method of C. Computer Knowledge and Technology (November 2008)
3. Liu, J.: The Research of Teaching Methods in "C Programming Language". Computer Knowledge and Technology (November 2008)
4. Yang, L.: Applying of Study Method with Constructivist in Education Design. Education Exploration (August 2004)

IT Infrastructure, E-commerce Capabilities and Firm Performance: A Empirical Test Based on China Firm Data

Kuang Zhijun

School of Economic and Management, East China Jiaotong University, Nanchang, Jiangxi China
kuang1130@tom.com

Abstract. In recent rapidly changing competitive environment, E-commerce plays an important role on value chain. Many firms invest IT to ensure their success on e-commerce. However, how affect the firm performance when using information systems in supporting organizational e-commerce activities is still a question. The purpose of the research is to explore how the IT infrastructure and e-commerce capability affect firm performance. The paper proposes and test a research framework to analyze the relationship among IT infrastructure, e-commerce capability and firm performance based resource-based view. At last, the paper points out some research suggestions for the future study related to the e-commerce capability and business value research.

Keywords: firm performance, IT infrastructure, e-commerce capability, resource-based view.

1 Introduction

Considering the rapidly changing competitive environment today, developing direct access to customers via IT infrastructure is the dominant e-commerce strategy among firms. The strategic value of IT infrastructure has generally been associated with its ability to allow a firm to adapt successfully to changes in the external environment (Broadbent et al., 1999; Byrdand Turner, 2001b; Weill et al., 2002), but the mechanisms by which IT infrastructure impact firm performance when using IT in supporting organizational e-commerce activities are still not well understood. A potential framework for analyzing the relationship between IT infrastructure, e-commerce capability and firm performance is the resource based view. In this paper we present a research model to analyze the relations among IT infrastructure capabilities and e-commerce capability in the aim for better firm performance. The paper is structured as follow: The background literature is briefly examined to build the rationale for our research model. The research method including data collection and data analysis approaches is discussed in the following section. This is followed by the study results and discussion in the subsequent section. These are followed by a brief set of conclusions and directions for future research.

S. Lin and X. Huang (Eds.): CESM 2011, Part II, CCIS 176, pp. 79–85, 2011.

2 Literature Review

2.1 IT Infrastructure Capability

IT infrastructure is viewed as a platform technology consisting of the processing hardware and operating system, networking and communication technologies, data, and core data processing applications (Dunkan, 1995; Weil and Broadbent, 1998). IT infrastructure is used in all e-business initiatives to connect different parts of the firm and to link to suppliers, customers, and allies (Weill et al., 2002).

IT infrastructure capability is a integrated set of reliable IT infrastructure services available to support both existing applications and new initiatives (Weill et al., 2002). IT infrastructure capability is reflected in the range and number of IT infrastructure services (Broadbent and Weill, 1997; Broadbent et al., 1999). Reach refers to the locations that can be connected via the IT infrastructure from local workstations and computers to customers and suppliers. Range determines the level of functionality that can be shared automatically and seamlessly across each level of "reach", and answers the question of "what services can be offered." (Keen, 1991). Another dimension is data management capability. The capability to manage the data is an important measure of IT infrastructure capability.

2.2 E-commerce Capability

E-commerce is defined as business activities conducted over the Internet, continues to penetrate the enterprise value (Zhu 2004). The purpose of the adoption of e-commerce is predominantly to broaden their customer base by exploring new marketing channels, or to create competition for the traditional channels (Amit and Zott 2001, Chircu and Kauffman 2000). E-commerce capabilities reflect a company's strategic initiatives to use the Internet to share information, facilitate transactions, improve customer services, and strengthen supplier integration. E-commerce functionalities may range from static information to online order tracking and from digital product catalogues to integration with suppliers' databases.

Upon resource-based view, it is how firms leverage their IT infrastructure to create unique e-commerce capabilities that determines a firm's overall performance. Regardless of how commodity-like the technology components may be, the architecture that removes the barriers of system incompatibilities and makes it possible to build a corporate platform for launching e-business applications is clearly not a commodity. Moreover, e-commerce capabilities are often tightly connected to the the firm's resource base and embedded in the business processes of the firm. Therefore, e-commerce conveys to the firm a resource that cannot be substituted for or easily imitated (such as customer proprietary data and shared information). The exploitation of these resources will lead to performance advantages for net-enhanced organizations (Lederer et al. 2001).

3 Concept Framework and Hypotheses

The theoretical discussions above lead us to believe that e-commerce capabilities which combine with IT infrastructure can explain performance variance across

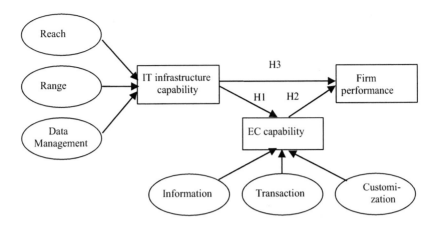

Fig. 1. Concept Model

firms.The concept framework used for this study is showed in Fig.1. Following we will discuss the Hypotheses about the relationship among IT infrastructure capability, E-commerce capability and firm performance.

3.1 IT Infrastructure Capability and Firm Performance

IT infrastructure capability of firms tends to be highly firm specific and evolves over long periods of time, during which gradual enhancements are made to reflect changing business needs (Scott-Morton 1991). The possibility that IT will enhance business performance and bring sustainable competitive advantage is through the development of efficacious IT infrastructure capabilities which cannot be readily assembled through markets, instead, they must be built over time (Weill et al., 2002). These arguments suggest:

Hypothesis 1 (H1): Greater IT infrastructure capability is associated with higher level of firm performance.

3.2 E-commerce Capability and Firm Performance

E-commerce capability is the capabilities of a firm to provide information, facilitate transactions, offer customized services, and integrate the back end and fulfillment (zhou, 2004). E-commerce capability can be viewed as a firm's ability to deploy and leverage e-commerce resources to support e-commerce activities. Therefore, e-commerce capability cannot be substituted for or easily imitated (such as customer proprietary data and shared information). The exploitation of these capabilities will lead to performance advantages for net-enhanced organizations (Lederer et al. 2001). These arguments suggest:

Hypothesis 2 (H2): Greater e-commerce capability is associated with higher level of firm performance.

3.3 IT Infrastructure Capability and E-commerce Capability

IT infrastructure is used in all e-business initiatives to connect different parts of the firm and to link to suppliers, customers, and allies. The reach, range and data manangent capabity of IT infrastructure is considered to be key for initiating e-commerce activity (Weill et al., 2002). Zhu (2004) also shows that IT infrastructure capability exhibit positive relationships to e-commerce capability measures. These arguments suggest:

Hypothesis 3 (H3): Higher levels of IT infrastructure capability is associated with greater e-commerce capability.

4 Methods

4.1 Data Collection

A survey design was used for this study and questionnaires were sent to 300 top or senior IT executives (CIO, vice president of IT, director of IT) in a variety of industries randomly when a IT application meeting is held in shanghai in 2009. A total of 210 usable responses were received, resulting a response rate of about 70 percent. There were totally 138 valid questionnaires after the deduction of incomplete ones. We conducted a Chi-square test to determine whether responses varied by the industry and their revenues. No significant differences in Chi-square at the .05 level were noted, which suggests that perceptual measures are unbiased by variations in the industry and their revenues.

4.2 Operationalization of Measures

According to the literature review in the section 2, IT infrastructure capability is a second-order construct based on several levels of reach, range and data management capability. E-commerce capability is defined as a high-level, multidimensional construct generated from a set of specific variables measuring e-commerce functionalities. Firm performance is a first-order construct which measure financial indicators of the firm.

All of the questions were asked from a scale ranging from 1 to 7, where 1 refers to the lowest score in the measure and 7 represents the highest score on the measure. The scales for various constructs were adopted from a review of the literature. If existing measures were not available, a list of items covering the domain of the variables under investigation was developed.

4.3 Reliability Analysis

Cronbach's alpha, composite reliability, and the average variance extracted were computed to assess the internal consistency of each dimension (Hair et al. 1998). The results in Table 1 show that all Cronbach's alpha and composite reliabilities exceeded Nunnally's (1978) criterion of 0.7 while the average variances extracted for these constructs were above the recommended 0.5(Hair et al. 1998).

Table 1. Assessment of consistency reliability indices of each construct

Construct/dimension	Cronbach' α	Composite Reliability	Average Variance Extracted
IT infrastructure	0.8573	0.896	0.610
Reach（3）	0.7638	0.763	
Range（3）	0.8290	0.724	
Data Management（3）	0.7895	0.735	
E-commerce capability	0.8665	0.866	0.723
Information（3）	0.7813	0.902	
Transaction（3）	0.8211	0.815	
Customization（4）	0.8404	0.772	
Firm performance（6）	0.8525	0.813	0.683

4.4 Convergent Validity

Convergent validity ensures that all items measure a single underlying construct. To test the convergent validity, we performed confirmatory factor analyses of the eight multiple- items constructs using LISREL 8.7. As shown in Table 2, a high value of composite reliability, ranging from .724 to .902, suggests the convergent validity of the constructs. The model fit indices (Table 3) also provide adequate evidence of the unidimensionality of the items. All indices were quite close to their criterion level.

Table 2. Assessment of Convergent Validity for the Measurement Model

Goodness of Fit Indices	Desired Levels	IT infrastructure	E-commerce capability	Firm performance
χ^2/df	<2	1.871	2.118	2.478
GFI	<0.9	0.913	0.921	0.929
AGFI	<0.9	0.927	0.932	0.932
NFI	<0.9	0.909	0.919	0.919
RMSEA	<0.05	0.056	0.054	0.051

4.5 Testing the Structural Models

Having demonstrated that our measures possessed adequate validity and reliability, we then proceeded to test hypotheses in a structural equation model. Fig.2 shows the standardized loadings of the items on each construct, as well as the path loadings between constructs. The overall model fit (RMSEA =0.049, CFI=0.962, AGF=0.912 and χ^2/d.f.=2.872) shows that our structural model has good model validity. Therefore, the model is acceptable. The hypotheses have been proved for the results show that all the hypotheses are supported at the P<0.001level.

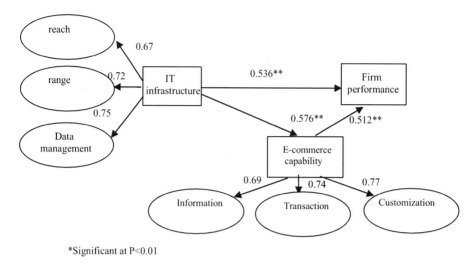

*Significant at P<0.01

Fig. 2. SEM Analysis Result

5 Discussion and Conclusions

During the past years, the rise of the Internet era prompted most corporations to reexamine their strategic logic and the role of information technologies in shaping their business strategies. Many firms begin to share a common understanding that IT play a fundamental role in their ability to enhance their business performance through e-commerce capabilities in products, services, channels, and customer segments. Therefore, the goal of this paper has been to develop a theoretical perspective for understanding the connections among IT infrastructure, e-commerce capability and firm performance. We construct a theory framework that describes IT infrastructure can enhance the e-commerce capability which can improve firm performance. But more importantly, e-commerce is a dynamic capability that requires firms to build and then dynamically reconfigure in order to align with changing technology and business environments.

Although this study provided a profound theoretical foundation for investigating the value of IT and a thoroughly empirical data analysis, there is still more work to do in the future. First, we could adopt qualitative methods such as case study to strengthen the potential for greater generalizability of the research findings. Second, since we examined the path element of IT infrastructure and e-commerce capability with cross-sectional data, we do not examine the long-term role of IT infrastructure. Longitudinal research is needed to trace the dynamics of business activities over time. In conclusion, this study provides not only a profound theoretical foundation for investigating the value of IT but also examines these empirical findings in a way which might help companies make wise decisions about IT adoption and use.

Acknowledgments. The research was supported by the National Natural Science Foundation of China under Grant 70761003.

References

1. Zhu, K.: The complementarity of Information Technology Infrastructure and E-Commerce Capability: A Resource-Based Assessment of Their Business Value. Journal of Management Information Systems 21(1), 167–202 (2004)
2. Pires, G.D., Aisbett, J.: The Relationship between Technology Adoptionand Strategy in Business-to-Business Markets: The Case of E-Commerce. Industrial Marketing Management 32(4), 291–300 (2003)
3. Melville, N., Kraemer, K., Gurbaxani, V.: Review: Information technology and organizational performance: An integrative model of IT business value. MIS Quarterly 28(2), 283–322 (2004)
4. Grant, R.M.: The resource-based theory of competitive advantage: Implications for strategy formulation. California Management Review 33(3), 114–135 (1991)
5. Bharadwaj, A.S.: A Resource-Based Perspective on Information Technology Capability and Firm Performance: An Empirical Investigation. MIS Quarterly 24(1), 169–196 (2000)
6. Sambamurthy, V., Zmud, R.W.: Arrangements for information technology governance: A theory of multiple contingencies. MIS Quarterly 23(2), 261–288 (1999)
7. Broadbent, M., Weill, P., Clair, D.: The Implications of Information Technology Infrastructure for Business Process Redesign. MIS Quarterly 23(2), 159–182 (1999)
8. Bhatt, G.D., Grover, V.: Types of Information Technology Capabilities and Their Role in Competitive Advantage: An Empirical Study. Journal of Management Information Systems 22(2), 253–278 (2005)
9. Daniel, E.M., Wilson, H.N.: The role of dynamic capability in e- business transformation. European Journal of Information Systems (12), 282–298 (2003)
10. Devaraj, S., Kohli, R.: Measuring information technology payoff: a meta-analysis of structural variables in firm-level empirical research. Information Systems Research 14(2), 127–145 (2003)
11. Zhu, K., Weyant, J.: Strategic Decisions of New Technology Adoption under Asymmetric Information. Decision Sciences 34(4), 643–675 (2003)
12. Eisenhardt, K., Martin, J.: Dynamic Capability: What are they? Strategic Management Journal (21), 1105–1121 (2000)
13. Teece, D.J., Pisano, G., Shuen, A.: Dynamic Capability and Strategic Management. Strategic Management Journal (18), 509–533 (1997)

Remote Sensing Image Segmentation Using Mean Shift Method

Fang Wan[1,2,*] and Fei Deng[3]

[1] Computer school of Hubei university of Technology
wanfangwan@gmail.com
[2] Computer school of Wuhan university
[3] School of geodesy and Geomatics of Wuhan university

Abstract. Mean shift is a Feature space analysis algorithm widely used in natural scene images and medical image segmentation. It is also used in the high-resolution remote sensing image segmentation process. But one bottleneck of the mean shift procedure is the cost per iteration, especially in the huge data processing. We present an improved mean shift based image segmentation algorithm for the remote sensing images. Given initial parameter of windows, in each iteration step, the algorithm can adaptively adjust window size, which makes the iteration times reduce and speed up the segmentation process. Experiments proved the method can bring good result and satisfying performance.

Keywords: Mean shift, segmentation, remote sensing, adaptive adjustment.

1 Introduction

According to statistics data, people used only quite few of all remote sensing information they have accessed, not to mention depth information to be developed, which greatly limits the practical applications of remote sensing technology. Traditional remote sensing image information extraction methods used pixel as the basic unit of recognition data and depend on spectral data composition difference in the statistics. It is suitable for multi-spectral and high spectral resolution remote sensing images. For the analysis of low-resolution remote sensing image which always change in a large area it may get better results, However, it is lack of processing capacity for high resolution mass data.

High-resolution remote sensing image can record rich details of surface features. Spectrum characteristics based pixel-level low-resolution image interpretation methods often have a variety of errors and mistakes when used in the high-resolution images. Because the spatial feature of texture of ground objects and topological relations are essentially the regional level characteristics, feature extraction in the homogeneity region of the obtained image is obviously more reasonable than feature extraction in any given square window in the region. Therefore, image segmentation

---

* Corresponding author.

S. Lin and X. Huang (Eds.): CESM 2011, Part II, CCIS 176, pp. 86–90, 2011.

has become the first processing steps in the high-resolution remote sensing image interpretation, also has become important content in surface features extraction of high-resolution images.[1,2]

The mean shift algorithm is a nonparametric clustering technique which does not require prior knowledge of the number of clusters, and does not constrain the shape of the clusters. In recent years, the mean shift algorithm in image segmentation receive much concern[3,4,5]. MS-based segmentation algorithm is of good capacity of noise immunity and suitable for parallel processing. But as an iterative algorithm, MS algorithm has high computational complexity, which became a bottleneck when used in remote sensing images with massive data feature.

Our algorithm is an optimization of MS, utilizing the inherent heuristic characteristics. In the iteration, we adopted adaptive bandwidth adjustment to improve the efficiency. At the beginning of iteration, bandwidth is set to be small, which can gradually increase in the process of iterations. In this way, the iteration number can be reduced. We use EDISON[7] framework and optimize the algorithm. We have applied the algorithm on multiple remote sensing images and got good results in efficiency and segmentation effect.

2 Mean Shift Method

Given n data points x_i, i = 1,2..., n on a d-dimensional space R^d, the multivariate kernel density estimate obtained with kernel $K(x)$ and window radius h is[6]

$$f(x) = \frac{1}{nh^d} \sum_{i=1}^{n} K\left(\frac{x - x_i}{h}\right).$$ (1)

For radial symmetric kernels, it suffices to define the profile of the kernel $k(x)$ satisfying

$$K(x) = c_{k,d} k(\|x\|^2)$$ (2)

where $c_{k,d}$ is a normalization constant which assures $K(x)$ integrates to 1. The modes of the density function are located at the zeros of the gradient function $f(x) = 0$.

The gradient of the density estimator (1) is

$$\nabla f(x) = \frac{2c_{k,d}}{nh^{d+2}} \sum_{i=1}^{n} (x_i - x)g\left(\left\|\frac{x - x_i}{h}\right\|^2\right)$$

$$= \frac{2c_{k,d}}{nh^{d+2}} \left[\sum_{i=1}^{n} g\left(\left\|\frac{x - x_i}{h}\right\|^2\right)\right] \left[\frac{\sum_{i=1}^{n} x_i g\left(\left\|\frac{x - x_i}{h}\right\|^2\right)}{\sum_{i=1}^{n} g\left(\left\|\frac{x - x_i}{h}\right\|^2\right)} - x\right].$$ (3)

Where $g(s) = -k'(s)$. The first term is proportional to the density estimate at x computed with kernel $G(x) = c_{g,d}g(\|x\|^2)$ and the second term is the mean shift.

$$m_h(x) = \frac{\sum_{i=1}^{n} x_i g\left(\left\|\frac{x - x_i}{h}\right\|^2\right)}{\sum_{i=1}^{n} g\left(\left\|\frac{x - x_i}{h}\right\|^2\right)} - x$$ (4)

The mean shift clustering algorithm is a practical application of the mode finding procedure.

3 Segmentation Algorithm Analysis

3.1 Selection of Kernel Function

If the image dimension is p, when the position vector and the color vector integrate into the "space-color" field, the dimension is p+2, then, each pixel corresponds to a p+2 dimensional vector. $x=(x_s, x_r)$ as the radial symmetry kernel and Euclidean multi-core kernel is expressed as:

$$K_{h_s, h_r}(x) = \frac{C}{h_s^2 h_r^p} k\left(\left\|\frac{x^s}{h_s}\right\|^2\right) k\left(\left\|\frac{x^r}{h_r}\right\|^2\right)$$

3.2 Mean Shift Based Image Segmentation Algorithm

First, the mean shift segmentation algorithm need to convert image from RGB color space to LUV feature space in order to achieve better separation of the feature space [8,10]. This is because non-linear RGB space does not have good correspondence between space statistical capacity and scale, while the LUV could be better applied in image segmentation process to differ pixel spectral and statistical information [1, 2].

Selection of Nuclear function and the corresponding parameters (h_s and h_r) of LUV images is feasible. Then mean shift filtering can be applied on the image, which is a clustering process. For grayscale images, the brightness data can directly be used instead of LUV data.

Mean shift based image segmentation process is as follows: Let xi for the d-dimensional input image, z_i (i = 1,2 ..., n) for filtering images, L_i is the image pixel, the segmentation process is as followed:

(1) Mean filter, filtering data are stored in d-dimensional $z_i = y_{i, c}$;

(2) Iterate the mean shift procedure until convergence. Clustering the data where in the space field the value is less than h_s and value in domain field is less than hr. {Cp}, p= 1, ..., m;)

(3) For each i = 1,2, ..., n, calculate $L_i = \{ p \mid z_i \in Cp \}$;

(4) Merge the scale region. Region in continuous space filed where the scale less than M will be merged.

When using mean shift algorithm in image smoothing, usually a square of side length 2^r window will be used to traverse each pixel in the image. So the sampling points in operation are different if spatial bandwidth is different. Commonly, big spatial bandwidth brings more sampling points and the derivation of filtered image with original image pixel will be great. To big derivation will result in the image seriously distorted. In the other way, if the sampling points are too few, smoothing objective cannot be achieved. So, in the paper, we take a method as showed in Fig.1. At the beginning, we set a initial value to space field bandwidth a R0. Then in each iteration step, the bandwidth increase to fit the image data. The bandwidth will be R1,R2,R3,R4..., when a iteration end, r value will be recalculated.

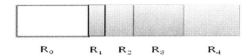

Fig. 1. Adaptive bandwidth adjusted according to the specific image data

In this way, bandwidth can be adaptive to greatly improved efficiency of image processing and enhance the result effect.

4 Experiments

Algorithm is developed on the framework of EDISON. The experiment is carried out on a PC machine, with Intel 2G CPU, 2G memory and Gefore9600 graphics card. In order to test the mean shift algorithm in the application of remote sensing image segmentation, we selected some city's image from Google Earth as the experimental data. The figure is the result using mean shift algorithm for image segmentation.

Fig. 2. Image segmentation result using SIFT algorithm

Fig.3 is segmentation results using improved SIFT algorithm. It can be seen that although the new algorithm using the adaptive bandwidth adjustment, it did not affect the segmentation effect, and the segmentation result is very similar to the result using original algorithm.

Fig. 3. Image segmentation result using improved SIFT algorithm

Table.1 is the comparison of execution time of the two algorithms. For the bandwidth can be adaptive, the new algorithm will reduce the number of iterations, so the speed of the algorithm has been improved.

Table 1. Comparison of SIFT and improve SIFT algorithm in segmentation block and speed

Resolution	Parameter	SIFT		new SIFT	
		block number	time	block number	time
512*512	hs=5,hr=4.5	2455	0.97	3521	0.58
800*600	hs=5,hr=4.5	3837	1.48	4093	1.03
1024*768	hs=6,hr=5	5793	2.54	6022	1.97
1024*1024	hs=6,hr=5	6946	3.22	7352	2.35

5 Conclusion and Future Work

Mean shift segmentation algorithm has good adaptability and robustness. The algorithm can be easily fit multi-scale segmentation requirements in different applications and be widely used in high-resolution remote sensing image information extraction. But the initial parameters need to be set according to different demand, and the iterative process is often implemented in the region which usually has many repeated calculations. In this paper, we analyzed the principle of the mean shift algorithm and presented adaptive window mean shift segmentation algorithm. We take case testing to verify the segmentation accuracy and performance. From the result we find the speed improved significantly and the segmentation effect is similar as the SIFT algorithm.

Acknowledgments. This work is supported by the National Science Foundation of China (Grant No. 41001305).

References

[1] Dell'Acqua, F., et al.: Exploiting spectral and spatial information in hyperspectral urban data with high resolution. Geo-science and Remote Sensing Letters 1(4), 322–326 (2004)

[2] LeiGuang, W., Wenbo, W., QinLing, D., Qianqing, Q.: Remote sensing image texture classification based on Gabor wavelet and support vector machine. SPIE, San Jose (2006)

[3] Comaniciu, D., Meer, P.: Mean Shift Analysis and Applications. In: Proceedings of the 7th IEEE International Conference on Computer Vision, vol. 2, pp. 1197–1203 (1999)

[4] Cheng, Y.: Mean shift, mode seeking, and clustering. IEEE Trans. Pattern Analysis and Machine Intelligence 17(8), 790–799 (1995)

[5] Georgescu, B., Shimshoni, I., Meer, P.: Mean shift based clustering in high dimensions: A texture classification example. In: Proc. ICCV, pp. 456–463 (October 2003)

[6] Comaniciu, D., Meer, P.: Mean shift: A robust approach toward feature space analysis. IEEE Trans. Pattern Anal. and Machine Intelligence 24, 603–619 (2002)

[7] Christoudias, C.M., Georgescu, B., Meer, P.: Synergism in low level vision. In: 16th International Conference on Pattern Recognition, Quebec City, Canada, vol. IV, pp. 150–155 (2002)

An Image Registration Method Based on Feature Matching

Fang Wan[1,2,*] and Fei Deng[3]

[1] Computer school of Hubei university of Technology
wanfangwan@gmail.com
[2] Computer school of Wuhan university
[3] School of geodesy and Geomatics of Wuhan university

Abstract. In this paper we present an effective algorithm for automatic image registration by matching features in images made from different viewpoint. For the SIFT detector can assure local variant of image features such as translation, scaling and rotation, we use SIFT to implement the image registration. But the SIFT usually bring too many matching points and outliers removing process is needed. We present an SIFT based algorithm which get rid of redundant matching points by an estimated threshold from multiple experiments. From the experiments, we found our algorithm produce much less match points and the correctness rate increased significantly.

Keywords: SIFT, bandwidth, registration, Feature extraction.

1 Introduction

Harris corner detection method is very sensitive to the changes in image scale. For the transformation such as translation, rotation of small-scale image, Harris feature point based method can get accurate registration results, but when facing large scale images transformation, this approach does not guarantee the correct registration and stitching. Researchers have proposed scale invariant feature point detection method [1], affine invariant feature point detection method [2], local invariant feature detection method [3] which are detection technology based on invariant feature.

David.Lowe [4,5] proposed a scale space based local features which can keep invariant on image translation, rotation, scaling, or affine transformation, and introduce the descriptor. He named the method as Scale Invariant Feature Transform, as SIFT.

SIFT algorithm first detect feature in the scale space, determine the location of feature point, and use the main gradient direction of the neighborhood feature points as the feature point's main direction, as to promise the independence of operator with scale and direction. Features extracted from the image using SIFT can be used to for a reliable match between images for its invariance to scaling, rotation, illumination changes, noise and affine transformation. In addition, the local characteristics of the image are special, so it can provide a very high probability of correct match. Since SIFT algorithm need multiple convolution computation, multi-scale space calculation is slow, and the feature points detected is sometime not stable.

---

* Corresponding author.

S. Lin and X. Huang (Eds.): CESM 2011, Part II, CCIS 176, pp. 91–95, 2011.
© Springer-Verlag Berlin Heidelberg 2011

In this paper, we present an improved SIFT algorithm for image registration. The speed and accuracy are better than SIFT algorithm. Paper structure is as described: First, introduce SIFT feature extraction principles and methods. Then, introduce our algorithm. At last, we use experiment to validate the algorithm and give some improvement plan in future.

2   Sift Feature Representation

2.1   Feature Extraction

In order to make the features scale invariant, feature point detection is done in a multi-scale space. Scale space theory first appeared in the field of computer vision. Its purpose is to simulate multi-scale features of the image data. Koendetink[6] proved that the Gaussian convolution is the only change kernel to achieve the scale transformation, and Lindeberg[7,8] prove the Gaussian kernel is the only linear kernel. So scale space of a two-dimensional image is defined as:

$$L(x, y, \sigma) = G(x, y, \sigma) * I(x, y)$$

Where G (x, y, σ) is the scale variable Gaussian function

$$G(x, y, \sigma) = \frac{1}{2\pi\sigma^2} e^{-(x^2 + y^2)/2\sigma^2}$$

Symbol * denotes convolution, (x, y) is the pixel position, σ is the scale space factor, the smaller the value, less the image is smoothed, and smaller is the corresponding scale. Large-scale corresponds to the whole features of the image, and small-scale features for the detail information.

2.2   Feature Description

In order to make the descriptor rotation invariant, we need to assign each feature point a direction.

Using gradient direction of feature point's Neighboring pixels and distribution direction, we can get gradient mode value and direction as follows:

$$m(x, y) = \sqrt{(L(x+1, y) - L(x-1, y))^2 + (L(x, y+1) - L(x, y-1))^2}$$
$$\theta(x, y) = \tan^{-1}((L(x, y+1) - L(x, y-1)) / L(x+1, y) - L(x-1, y)))$$

L stands for scales of each key point. We can sample the data in the neighboring windows which take feature points as the center, and use histogram to estimate gradient direction of neighboring pixels. Gradient histogram range is from 0 to 360 degrees, total of 36 directions.

Through the above steps, each feature point has three attributes: location, scale and direction. The next step is to build descriptor for each feature point, which does not change with the various changes, such as illumination changes, perspective changes and so on. And the descriptor should have a high specificity, so that increasing the probability of correct matching between feature points.

3 Improved Algorithm Framework

While SIFT features have many fine features, they still have some drawback as described followed: 1) Feature detection will search in the multi-scale space, which need a lot of convolutions, which result in the computational complexity and the time consuming. 2) SIFT feature set is not very salient, so there are still some instable points in the collection.

According to that, we propose a new algorithm framework to overcome these two shortcomings:

Step1: Feature point extraction

Because SIFT feature points descriptor changed based on the feature point neighborhood of the pixel gradient change, which indicates that the feature vector of the descriptor is more independent points, if the neighborhood gradient of pixels change more sharp, and the probability of correct match is more high. This gives us a inspiration that, if the neighborhood window has significant gradient changes, such as corner points, it will greatly increase the uniqueness of the descriptor.

Step2: Feature Description

Distribute main direction and establish descriptors according to the extracted feature points by the method described in section 2.2.

Step3: Feature Matching

First, we determine the best candidate of each point using nearest neighbor method. Nearest neighbor method is defined as points having the minimum Euclidean distance. However, many features points in the image have not correctly matched, which may be for the reason that they are in the non-overlapping regions of two images or the feature points have not been detected in one of the images. So it's very important to discard these feature points which have no good match points. We can set a threshold to strip out those without good match. Then the rest is stable characteristics descriptor which is relatively easy to be identified. Because of the right match, nearest neighbor distance will be much smaller than the nearest neighbor with matching errors. We found that for the correct matching point, the ratio between the nearest neighbor distance and the second nearest neighbor distance is quite big. But for the outliers, the ratio of nearest neighbor and second nearest neighbor distance is much smaller. Therefore, this ratio can be served as an important threshold to distinguish correct points and outliers. This method can also significantly reduce the number of matching points, thus increasing the rate of correct matching. From the experiments, we give a stable estimated value as 0.5.

Step4: solving the transformation matrix

For the RANSAC algorithm is in a iteration form to solve best geometric transformation model, which can result in the deletion of outliers, the transformation matrix solving is completed at the same time in the previous step.

4 Experiments

To verify the effectiveness of the algorithm, we take a lot of experimental images. Fig.1 is the result from SIFT algorithm and improved algorithm ESIFT. Euclidean distance using SIFT feature vectors and match number from RANSAC algorithm are also not same.

Fig. 1. Top image is the registration result from SIFT algorithm. Bottom image is the one from our ESIFT.

Table 1. Comparison of SIFT and ESIFT algorithm

Image Size	SIFT match number	SIFT time	ESIFT match number	ESIFT time
400×400	325	2.53s	279	1.94s
256×256	253	1.48s	189	1.25s
256×256	227	1.33s	154	0.98s

From the experiment, we can see the SIFT algorithm detected many feature points and the match number is large. This is the character of SIFT. SIFT feature is used in object recognition in which there many small object matching from large number of images. So, the small object's information should also be extracted with sufficient number. This is also very important when the overlapping proportion of image is small, because there is still a need to ensure the images overlap with small region have enough feature points.

5   Conclusion

In this paper we present a effective algorithm for automatic image registration by matching features in images made from different viewpoint. For the SIFT usually bring too many matching points and many of them are not satisfying. We improve the SIFT algorithm by filtering the matching points by a threshold value which is estimated from experiments. From the experiments, we found our algorithm produce much less match points and the correctness ration increased significantly.

Acknowledgments. This work is supported by the National Science Foundation of China (Grant No. 41001305).

References

[1] Mikolajczyk, K., Schmid, C.: Indexing based on scale invariant interest points. In: Proceedings of the 8th International Conference on Computer Vision, Vancouver, Canada, pp. 525–531 (2001)
[2] Mikolajczyk, K., Shmid, C.: An affine invariant interest point detector. In: European Conference on Computer Vision(ECCV), Copenhagen, Denmark, pp. 128–142 (2002)
[3] Schmid, C., Mohr, R.: Local Grayvalue Invariants for Image Retrieval. IEEE Transactions on Pattern Analysis and Machine Intelligence 19(5), 530–535 (1997)
[4] David, L.: Object recognition from local scale-invariant features. In: ICCV, pp. 1150–1157 (1998)
[5] David, L.: Distinctive image features from scale-invariant keypoints. International Journal of Computer Vision 60(2), 91–110 (2004)
[6] Koenderink, J.J.: The structure of images. Biological Cybernetics (50), 363–396 (1984)
[7] Lindeberg, T.: Detecting salient blob-like image structures and their scales with a scale-space primal sketch:a method for focus-of-attention. International Journal of Computer Vision 11(3), 283–318 (1993)
[8] Lindeberg, T.: Scale-space theory:A basic tool for analyzing structures at different scales. Journal of Applied Statistics 21(2), 224–270 (1994)

An Exploration of Research and Innovation in Basic Teaching

TingTing Zhang[*], YongChun Yu, XiaoLi Wu, and YaQin Si

Institute of Science, PLA Univ. of Sci. & Tech., 211101, Nanjing Jiansu China
zhangtings@sohu.com

Abstract. Emphasizing the importance of scientific research to the basic teaching, the authors of this article, based on their experience, first analyze the problems resulting from the disagreement from school's development orientation and its internal management system, and then put forward their own suggestion with the aim to create a formula in which scientific research serves teaching, theory combines with practice and both teachers and students participate in the curriculum innovation.

Keywords: Teaching, Scientific research, Basic teaching.

1 Introduction

Teaching and research are the two core functions in universities[1]. Large amount of researches abroad have indicated that both universities and teachers hold the belief that scientific research can promote teaching. Similarly, college teachers in China also have the conviction that teaching and research are in harmony with each other. However, in practice, separation and even disparity occur. In China, almost all the colleges and universities shoulder the task of basic as well as specialized teaching. Some universities set colleges of basic schooling to fulfill the task of basic teaching to low-grade students. Teachers in these colleges face the problem of one-fold teaching and research tasks. A multi-facet reform is needed to improve the relation between teaching and research and harmonize teaching and research. Authors of this thesis will elaborate on an effective combination of research and teaching in basic teaching and ways to improve teaching quality and research levels.

2 Necessities of Research in Basic Teaching

Although research and teaching are varied activities, they are united and promote each other [2].

---

[*] Corresponding author.

S. Lin and X. Huang (Eds.): CESM 2011, Part II, CCIS 176, pp. 96–100, 2011.

2.1 Research Promotes Teaching by Improving Its Quality and Activates Class-Room Effects

Research-oriented teaching in universities is one important method to improve their teaching qualities. Without the pivot of research, teachers cannot have a timely and thorough grasp of the dynamic development in the subject, and as a result, often teach clichés. It would be difficult to improve teaching quality, let alone innovating education [3]. The promoting effects researches have played are embodies in the following parts:

  ✧ Through research, teachers can include up-to-date research finding into class-room teaching to enable students get informed of the most recent development in certain research field.

  ✧ Through research, teachers can innovate teaching method from traditional spoon-feeding one to an inspiring one, from repeating what books say to case studies. By incorporating thinking of research into classroom, teachers can inspire students' scientific thoughts and cultivate their innovative abilities.

  ✧ Applications of research can boost class-room teaching. Lectures with real cases in life will be more interesting and useful, enabling students to learn relevant knowledge from case studies. Therefore, it greatly boost class-room teaching effect. On the other side, cases of failure in research can also be introduced into classroom to promote students abilities of repetitive practice and thinking.

  ✧ Practice of research encourages students to innovate. With the large increase of research programs among teachers, research levels are constantly upgraded, and researches of varied topics and contents are available among students. Students can further their research based on their interest and train the research innovative abilities.

To sum up, research helps realize a case-centered teaching method dominated by inspiring teaching from teachers and supplemented by self-study from students. Thus an innovative education form students will be achieved.

2.2 Teaching Promotes Research---Students Are the Source of Teacher's Promotion

Generally, people believe research promotes teaching. But in effect, teaching also play an important role in research.

1. Educational background of teachers sometimes makes them over-concentrated in certain areas. As an innovative research needs a comparatively broader scope of knowledge, teachers need study. Therefore, encourage young teachers to give new lectures to enrich their knowledge structure.

2. Teaching provides an opportunity for teachers to explore new research topics. Ideas and questions occur during the process of teaching will stimulate teachers to find new research topics.

3. Teaching pushes teachers to innovate constantly. With the development of society and the ever-increasing knowledge from students, teachers feel it a must to innovate

constantly, to promote themselves through research and to enlarge their knowledge reserves. Students become the impetus of teachers as teaching promotes the development of research.

Therefore, colleges of basic teaching still have to put great attention to scientific research, t promote teaching with research, deepen teaching reforms, optimize curriculum system, update teaching materials and elevate qualities of personnel training. All of the above are the root of innovative higher education among colleges and universities.

3 The Problems for Innovation of Scientific Research on Basic Teaching

In our universities, the teaching and scientific research doesn't combine together, but conflict with each other because of the ambiguous development orientation and internal management system and other unknown reasons.

Firstly, the opportunities participating in research for those teachers assuming the basic teaching is small. In almost all universities in China, the teachers are divided into public class teachers and specialized teachers. Taking the example of our university, we established the College of Science mainly to be responsible for the public classes teaching of low-grade students, which makes those teachers assuming the basic teaching do more basic teaching for the reason of resource, opportunities, qualifications and etc. The specialized college has to focus on the scientific research and academic building under the strong pressure. The unity of teaching and research becomes the empty talk by this way.

Secondly, the current curriculum, teaching resources and the management prevent the combination of teaching and research. Generally the curriculum and teaching resources are managed and planned by the administration department of the nation and universities. The teachers participate in it, but only for the choice of teaching material and methods. Teacher is not the most important part of curriculum and teaching resources creation and setting, so the teachers' research is difficult to go into the curriculum.

Additionally, the management of teaching is not perfect. There is no policy to encourage updating and creating in teaching in some colleges and universities, which make teacher to have no chance to participate in the teaching curriculum innovation. The teachers repeat what the book says and don't guide and promote the teaching. The teaching and research are separate. The teaching is not the one led by research or the one training the explore spirit and ability of the students, but focusing on imparting knowledge of the past, which causes the less improving of teaching.

4 Reforming

It should be clear that the basic classes' teachers have to do scientific research in order to do a good job of teaching. Otherwise the teacher is a porter and they even don't know what to move and how to move without research. Meanwhile, the research should be valuable for the teaching in universities, which means it could be combined with teaching and the students' spirit development. The basic teaching is faced with fewer research projects and heavy teaching task. It is more difficult to get t he projects for the reason of more young teachers and less research experience. Something should be done to solve these problems and create more opportunities for basic teaching teachers.

1. Cooperate with the specialized college, change "passive research" to "active research", and change "individual behavior" to "full participation"

The university should establish some rules to realize the basic class teachers to participate in the research team of the specialized college according to his own major and academic direction to solve the problem of less research task for basic class teacher. In addition, the College advises the young teachers to be the assistant of director of Doctor student, which plays the role of "master train an apprentice", and allow young teachers join in the research team of old faculty to undertake the important research task and make the young teachers grow up quickly on research. Meanwhile, one kind of research team should be established. The team is based on different subject, led by one or several outstanding talents and composed the backbone of outstanding young talent. The different academic backgrounds and different science thought of the team member will lay the foundation for scientific research and form the group advantages. Group promotes the individual and individual drives the group. The research of basic teaching team should desert the pursuit of "first class" and "excellent" and adhere to the principle of "minding small points, having the ability to do and having the potential to tap" based on the characteristics that the research serves for the teaching.

2. Re-define the scientific content and change "Scientific research separate from teaching" to" Scientific research serve for teaching"

The content of scientific research is rich and the scientific research of university is diverse on not only "discovered academic research" but also the academic research of "comprehension", "application" and "teaching". The four types of research is an interdependent whole part. Educational and teaching research should be respected and fit into the areas of scientific research as an important part of scientific research. It should specifically set a project to do some research for those problems to be settled urgently on the teaching front line and the universal and tendentious problem on teaching and the entry point of problem analysis and solving. Improving the system is to let the teachers working in the frontline to participate in summarizing teaching experience timely, solving the teaching problems scientifically and effectively to improve the teaching quality and promote the teacher team changing from "experience" to "research". In addition, the expression form of research is diverse and the scientific research represents an exploration activities. The results could not be published and it is recognized and encouraged to express to the student.

3. Use College Fund to support teachers' scientific research, and emphasize students to join in the teachers' research activities to change act "work behind closed" to "the combination of theory and practice"

College will list some fund to support the teachers to choose the subject by themselves and do some research with the same direction with the college to improve the ability of scientific research. The teachers can choose one small research point for the undergraduate from their research subject to let the students participate in it and increase the chance of practice research. According to research the requirements, the teachers will guide the students to read the literature and allow them to think or take part of the research content. Let the students combine the courses they learned and participate in the research subject applied by the teachers independently and make the students become the learner, cooperator and supervisor of the teachers' research activities. On one hand, this way will achieve the purpose of training innovative talents and students' research innovation. On the other hand, the teachers can guide students more effectively with practice to make up the students' shortage on theoretical knowledge. By this way, the teaching of university is the object and content of scientific research, which make the teachers guide the teaching practice better, optimize the teaching and combine, not opposite, the research and teaching in practice effectively.

5 Conclusion

The basic teaching does not only focus on the teaching quality, but also particularly emphasize the research promoting role for teaching, require and encourage the teachers to combine the research and teaching to bring the research result to the classroom to pass the latest information and knowledge to the students and improve the teaching quality, which is the basic purpose of the fundamental innovation and reform of the teaching and research. In addition, we need to change our idea of research when asked for research. The new research is oriented by quality and combined with theory and practice and full of educational research. Accordingly, when the research becomes the necessary work of the teachers of basic teaching, we need to change the hard management to soft management to the teachers and let the research become the autonomous research for the students and teaching rather than the completion of task or professional title. Otherwise research promoting teaching is empty talk, too.

References

1. Newman, J.H.: The Idea of a University. ZheJiang Education Publishing House (2001)
2. TongChen: Experience of Research Promoting Teaching. Forum on Chinese Culture (SI), 32–33 (2008)
3. BaocunLiu: High-level Teaching Team Building to Promote Improved Quality of Undergraduate Teaching. China Higher Education Informating Network (5) (2007)

An Improvement Method of Fractional-Order Filter Approximation

Yanzhu Zhang[1,2] and Jingjiao Li[1]

[1] College of Information Science and Engineering, Northeastern University
[2] College of Information Science and Engineering, Shenyang ligong University,
Shenyang, China
syzd710471@sina.com

Abstract. In the fractional-order control systems, the fractional-order controller is better than the integer order controller to improve system performance, and design of fractional-order differentiator is the fractional order controller to achieve an important step. Fractional differential for the current problems in design, will improve the genetic algorithm is introduced to approximate the design of fractional filters to Oustaloup filter does approximate system as a starting point, the genetic algorithm optimization of I filter coefficients, To be more accurate integer order system. Simulation results show that the improved genetic algorithm design of fractional order differentiator in a significantly improved performance of the band, designed to avoid the traditional fractional differentiator filter approximate approximation ineffective in the band at both ends of the problem more effectively The approximation of the ideal fractional differentiator frequency response.

Keywords: fractional differentiator, genetic algorithm, fractional-order filter approximation, Oustaloup filter.

1 Introduction

Since the theory of fractional calculus is proposed in 1695, the current study of physical system is divided into fractional-order system and integer-order system, and the fractional-order system is divided into fractional controlled system, whose process controlled object is a fractional model and fractional control system, whose controller is fractional. No matter controlled system or control system, the model parameters or control parameters of fractional-order systems are more than that of integer-order systems, so the research of fractional-order system is apparently difficult. The three hundred years research of fractional order system only results in a theoretical system in pure mathematics direction, furthermore, the physical meaning of fractional calculus is unclear up to today, the research and application of fractional-order system theory is blocked.

In fractional-order systems, owing to the order of calculus is fraction, it can not be used in the theory of the integer-order system. It is one of the main ways in the fraction-order system research that is to do the approximation and discrimination of

S. Lin and X. Huang (Eds.): CESM 2011, Part II, CCIS 176, pp. 101–106, 2011.
© Springer-Verlag Berlin Heidelberg 2011

the fractional-order system. If we follow this way, we could research the fractional-order system as the integer-order system. Many scholars proof that the fractional-order controller can have very well control effect in the fractional controlled system, and the design of the fractional differentiator is an important step in the fractional controller realization. Now the fractional differentiator has been successfully applied in many fields, such as in the fractional-order controller, signal processing, composing and processing of images. The design and improvement method of the fractional-order filter has become a hot topic in the fractional calculus research field.

Genetic Algorithm (GA) is a parallel random search algorithm which has traced the procedure of evolution of living being. Genetic algorithm has the ability of global optimization and can be applied in the Non-convex optimization and multimodal function and many occasions that are difficult to be resolved by tradition method. Therefore, GA has became a useful tool in solve the complex nonlinear problem. Using the Genetic algorithm toolbox which developed by the Field university, the text is doing optimization to the fractional differentiator by genetic algorithm. When we design, we can refer the character of the step response in time domain or frequency domain of the Oustaloup filter as reference, we define fitness function as the error between every best consequence of GA and this reference, also define as performance index. Choosing the 14 best parameters, the system highest did s^7, therefore we can confirm the coefficients of IIR filter, get a more optimized fractional differentiator, given the algorithm simulation experiment result and performance analysis at last.

2   Proposing the Classic Problem of IIR Filter

Nowadays the implementation of direct circuit of fractional order differential has not been resolved. What we do today to solve this problem is to approximate the fractional order system with integral order system, and then to realize it by mature integral order system solutions. So, the approximate computation of the fractional differential became an important step in analyzing fractional order system and designing fractional controller.

An IIR digital filter can be described by system function in the following way:

$$H(z) = \frac{\sum_{k=0}^{M} b_k z^{-k}}{1 - \sum_{k=1}^{N} a_k z^{-k}} \tag{1}$$

In order to design an IIR digital filter, we must work out the system function, which is to work out the coefficient a_k and b_k in formula (1).The design of the optimization of fractional differentiator, also is to optimize these coefficients to get or approach the amplitude-frequency response of the ideal fractional differential. The design method which the text provides can control the procedure during the search by genetic algorithm, and approximate the fractional differentiator from filter form to integral order system. This method gives a recognized and standard performance of fractional differential, it can be the Byrd figure of the frequency domain or the performance indicators of the system time domain phase step, the compare between the search by using genetic algorithm and the consequence before.

The define of the Grünwald-Letnikov fractional calculus is the most widely used definition in the fractional control. Since we can directly deduce the numerical algorithm of the fractional order derivative through the GL definition, and this is very valuable for the research of the fractional control system simulation.

For any real m, refer the integer part of m as [m](which means [m] is the largest integer less than m), so the GL calculus definition of alpha order of function f (t) is:

$$_{\alpha}^{GL}D_t^{\alpha}f(t)=\lim_{h\to 0}h^{-\alpha}\sum_{j=0}^{[(t-\alpha)/h]}(-1)^j\binom{\alpha}{j}f(t-jh)\tag{2}$$

In the equation

$$\binom{\alpha}{j}=\frac{\alpha(\alpha-1)(\alpha-2)\cdots(\alpha-j+1)}{j!}=\frac{\alpha!}{j!(\alpha-j)!}$$

The definition of GL fractional calculus is to find n from the n-order derivative and integral unity out of the starting induction. If $\alpha=n$ (n is a positive integer), then $_{\alpha}^{GL}D_t^{\alpha}f(t)$ is the first derivative. If $\alpha=-n$ (n is a positive integer), then $_{\alpha}^{GL}D_t^{\alpha}f(t)$ is the layer repeated integral of $f(t)$.

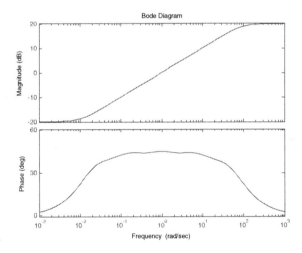

Fig. 1. Oustaloup filter's frequency response

In the study of many existing fractional differentiator filter approximate, Oustaloup filter performance is better, Figure 1 show Oustaloup filter's frequency response. It can be seen Oustaloup can not guarantee to achieve the approximation differentiator in full band filter. By using the definition of Grunwald-Letnikov fractional calculus, figure 2 is 0.8 orders differential of parameter y during the time between 0 and pi It can be seen from the above, Oustaloup filter order approximation performance of 0.8 is very good.

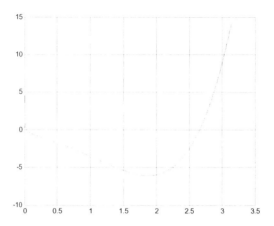

Fig. 2. Oustaloup approximation of the filter y

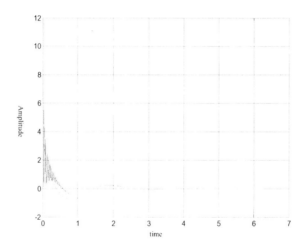

Fig. 3. Classic IIR filtering algorithms and approximate Oustaloup

Figure 3 is the comparison between the approximations of IIR filter which is not applied the classical algorithm and the outcome of Oustaloup filter. It can be seen from the figure that classical IIR filters' value is not constant in the filter fractional signal with low frequency region. The next section proposes the application of genetic algorithm to optimize the classical IIR filter coefficients, can solve this problem.

3   The Coefficients of Genetic Algorithm Optimization IIR Filter

GA (Genetic Algorithm) have the ability in global optimization, and also can be used in the place where the traditional methods can not solve such as convex optimization, multi-function optimization and so on, so GA can be a useful tool to solve complex nonlinear problems. In this article, we use the genetic algorithm toolbox University

Field developed; use the application of genetic algorithm to optimize the fractional order differentiator. In the design put the Oustaloup filter in the time domain or frequency domain characteristics of the step response as a reference, put the error which is the contra of each generation's results of the GA optimization with the reference as fitness function, or performance index, if we optimization of 14 parameters, the system can do the best of s^7, to determine the coefficients of IIR filters, The following will discuss description of the proposed genetic algorithm. The algorithm described as follows:

Step1: Select the population size, weighting factor and the maximum number of iteration $N_I = 100$, and then a set of randomly generated N_p : $x_i \in [0,1]^3, i = 0,1,\cdots,N_p - 1$, to constitute the initial population.

Step2: Decoded the populations of each individual into the corresponding parameter value, and calculate the control vector p and performance indicators $J(p_i)$, to determine the fitness function f=1/J, selected the target function $m = 1$.

Step3: Calculation of reproduction, crossover and mutation, and then recorded as the cost function C_t, if $C_t > J$ established, set $x_m^{new=} = x_m$ and $J^{new}(m) = J(m)$, or set $x_m^{new} = x_t$ and $J^{new}(m) = C_t$.

Step4: Set the target index increased by 1, if $m < N_p$ true, then go to Step2, for $m = 0,1,\cdots N_p - 1$, x_m^{new} will be replaced by X, and $J(m)$ is replaced by $J^{new}(m)$, find the point with minimal value, the number of iterations by 1, if less than N_I, then back to Step3, the best solution is x_m.

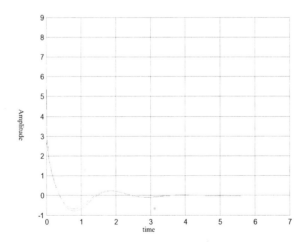

Fig. 4. The approximate comparison between optimized filter and the Oustaloup filter

From the above figure we can see the filter optimized to eliminate the existence of uncertainty interval value in classical IIR filter, the effect is obvious.

4 Conclusion

Fractional fractional-order differentiator is an important tool for computing, it has been successfully applied in the fractional control systems and other fields. In this paper, the design method of IIR filter, using an improved genetic algorithm to optimize the coefficients of fractional order differentiator. The introduction of the fitness population coefficient of variation, using the fitness scaling when no significant difference, overcome the problem of fraud in Genetic algorithms; by retaining part of the population the best individual, ensure the convergence of the algorithm; When the algorithm into a local optimum, through the introduction of new individuals to expand the search space, which makes the algorithm reach the global optimum more quickly. Experimental results show that the algorithm can deal with all cases of fractional differentiator design problem, and made even more outstanding than the traditional design method results.

References

1. Tenreiro Machado, J.A.: Analysis and design of fractional order digital control systems. Systems Analysis Model Simulation 27(2), 107–122 (1997)
2. Vinagre, B.M., Podlubny, I., Hernandez, A.: Some approximations of fractional order operators used in control theory and applications. Fractional Calculus and Applied Analysis 3(3), 231–248 (2000)
3. Shao, M., Nikias, C.L.: Signal processing with fractional lower order moment: stable processes and their applications. Proceeding of IEEE 81(7), 986–1010 (1993)
4. Mathieu, B., Melchior, P., Oustaloup, A., et al.: Fractional differentiation for edge detection. Signal Processing 83(11), 2421–2432 (2003)
5. Oustaloup, A., Mathieu, B., Lanusse, P.: The CRONE control of resonant plants: application to a flexible transmission. European Journal of Control 1(2), 113–121 (1995)
6. Podlubny, I.: Fractional2order systems and controllers. IEEE Transactions Automatic Control 44(1), 208–214 (1999)
7. Chen, Y.Q., Vinagre, B.M.: Continued fraction expansion app roaches to discrediting fractional order derivatives—an expository review. Nonlinear Dynamics 38, 155–170 (2005)
8. Tarczynski, A., Cain, G.D., Hermanowicz, E., et al.: A wise method for designing IIR filters. IEEE Transaction on Signal Processing 49(7), 1421–1432 (2001)
9. Tang, K.S., Man, K.F., Kwong, S., et al.: Design and optimization of IIR filter structure using hierarchical genetic algorithms. IEEE Transaction on Industrial Electronics 45(3), 481–487 (1998)
10. Pu, Y.F., Yuan, X., Liao, K., et al.: Five numerical algorithms of fractional calculus applied in modern signal analyzing and processing. Journal of Sichuan University: Engineering Science Edition 37(5), 118–124 (2005)

Phased Experimental Teaching in the College Course of *Computer and Information Technology*

Nanli Zhu[1], Yu Yao[2], Jianbo Fan[1],
Yongping Zhang[1], Meng Zou[1], and Peng An[1]

[1] College of Electronic&Information Engineer, Ningbo University of Technology,
Cuibai Road 89, 315016 Ningbo, China
nanli.zhu@gmail.com, jbfan@163.com, {zyp,zm,ap}@nbut.cn
[2] Ningbo Institute of Technology, Zhejiang University, Qianhu South Road 1,
315100 Ningbo, China
phoenix.cm@nit.zju.edu.cn

Abstract. The problems of students' starting computer knowledge discrepancy and disconnection of theory and experiment classes pose new challenges to the current teaching practice of college *Computer and Information Technology*. In light of Rogers's non-directive pedagogy and the reality of first-year college students' computer classes, this paper proposes a phased experimental teaching paradigm under the guideline of experiment-initiated teaching mode. This new paradigm divides the course into a number of links, in each the experiments of lower difficulty level placed prior to class lecturing so that students can learn in an epistemologically accumulative process. This paper illustrates how phased teaching paradigm is implemented in the links of *C Programming* module.

Keywords: phased experiment, experiment-initiated, computer education.

1 Introduction

The information society today finds computer technology increasingly creeping into the pedagogy of a wide range of disciplines at college [1]. Computer-centered information technology has become a vital component of curricula in numerous majors. The course *Computer and Information Technology* is offered to elevate students' information literacy as the extension of the related courses at high school level. Different disciplines demand specific IT skills and colleges have more clear-cut curriculum requirements, which show general similarities and diverse individualities [2].

Science and engineering students need intensive knowledge of computer technology, being able not only to use computer but to develop programs competently, [3] namely, algorithm implementation, data analysis, programming, data abstraction and information processing etc [4].On the other hand, students of liberal arts and business management are inclined to take computer as a working tool, [5] so their emphasis is placed on practical application of manipulating and retrieving databases, especially the ability of fulfilling daily work with software, [6] and communicating and learning on computer or internet. Students of arts and athletics intend to learn from computer courses the basic knowledge and dexterous skills of office software operation to the

S. Lin and X. Huang (Eds.): CESM 2011, Part II, CCIS 176, pp. 107–115, 2011.

extent that they will be capable of retrieving information and communicating on internet, processing images and producing animation.

Given the heterogeneous requirements of students' computer and information technology, the curriculum of *Computer and Information Technology* should take into account the respective features of different disciplines and majors. The curricular setup should incorporate customized teaching materials and procedures to make it consistent with teaching reality.

Current problems in the *Computer and Information Technology* are widely identified as follows:

1.1 Discrepancy of Students' Starting Level

The course is normally offered to first-year students whose computer ability differs tremendously due to various reasons, such as the cities and high schools they come from, family background and motivation. The fact is altogether far from the teaching objectives designed in the syllabus of college computer courses and chances are it will remain unchanged for a rather long period of time [7]. It is, hence, essential to strike an optimal point when the course is taught. The reality of the students who just came out of middle school accounts for the widely diversified computer literacy, and it is equally painstaking for teachers to abide by a uniform teaching calendar or syllabus. An indiscriminate teaching paradigm will also breed an even broader gap between top and underachieving students, which both checks favorable outcomes and undermines learning enthusiasm.

1.2 Disconnection of Theoretical and Experiment Classes

Current higher education has enormously improved the phenomenon of "overemphasizing theory and downplaying practice" [9]. However, the highly practical teaching process urges an even greater readjustment in that theory learning and practical experiment are perilously disproportioned, and even mutually disconnected. The common teaching reality usually places theory learning prior to on-computer operation, both of which are allocated equal time block; the former is taught in classroom and the later in computer laboratory. The arrangement seemingly accords to the teaching paradigm of "guiding practice with theory". The fact, however, is that learners need practice to have a solid understanding of theory and in nature practice breeds theory. Students are often misguided and fail to realize the relationship between theory and practice, and even put the cart before the horse.

1.3 Obsoleteness of Course Contents

Information technology is hardly stagnant over the time since new technology, operating system and application flow in and out constantly [10]. It takes a prolonged period of time for a computer textbook to be published, and in most cases when a textbook comes out it becomes out of date. All too often some software evolves into version 2010 while its version 2000 is still being taught at school. The obsolete textbooks greatly wear out students' learning passion.

To solve the above problems we have constructed an experiment-initiated teaching mode and put it into daily teaching practice.

2   Experiment-Initiated Teaching Mode

The mode aims at the problems and dilemma confronted by college computer teaching, which constructs a teacher-student role-switching teaching mode under the guidance of Rogers's non-directive teaching ideology. Its central concept is reflected by two distinctive facets, role-switching and experiment-initiating.

2.1   Role-Switching

In light of Rogers's non-directive teaching, [11][12][13] we have partly switched the learning center from the teacher to the students and solved the problems prevalent in the traditional "teacher-centered" teaching mode, [14] as shown in Fig. 1.

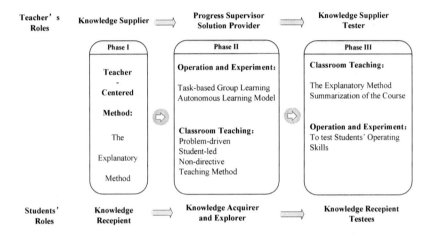

Fig. 1. Framework of Teacher-Student Role-Switching Mode

Phase I is to build up teacher-student affection, after which students are led by the teacher to learn computer science courses. At the time the teacher has a major task of building up a strong bond with students for the purpose that students are willing to communicate with him/her as to problems occurring in their later learning activities.

Phase II emphasizes knowledge acquisition and reinforcement. Students go as the focus of learning activity, and keenly engage in learning and exploring, while the teacher takes the role of both a supervisor to keep a minimum control of the learning process and a trouble-shooter to help solve problems students have encountered.

Phase III is of summary and test as the teacher plays a leading role to recapitulate the entire course's basic and key knowledge, to ensure the completion of teaching activities as planned and to give achievement examinations to track students' learning process.

2.2   Experiment-Initiated Teaching Mode

The experiment-initiated teaching mode in the main (also the second) phase of teaching reverses the traditional methodology of placing class lecturing prior to experiment;

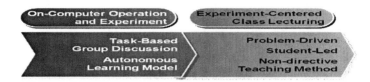

Fig. 2. Flow Chart of Phase II of Experimental Non-Directive Teaching Mode

instead, it gives priority to on-computer operation and experiment, followed by class lecturing and reinforced by group discussion, as shown in Fig. 2.

This mode is highly task-driven and student-centered, with the teacher placed backstage. Meanwhile the group discussion introduces the concept of modern business management and auxiliary evaluation mechanism, effectively organizing and monitoring the learning process of each individual student. The lectures after experiment classes solely focus on the specific problems present in students' experiments [15]. Therefore, students are placed at the center of class lecturing and activities while the teacher monitors the depth and progression of the class by presenting questions and awards.

3   Exploration and Practice of Phased Experimental Teaching

The experiment-initiated teaching paradigm offers an innovative solution to the various problems occurring in *Computer and Information Technology*, clearly animating class activity and stimulating student enthusiasm. However, the fact that the course consists of a series of modules demands differentiated teaching materials to various majors. An indiscriminate methodology of placing the experiment at the very beginning does not work, so we propose the phased experimental teaching paradigm to modulate the experiment-initiated teaching, enabling every teaching module to fit into a proper plan in the paradigm.

3.1   Group Learning

In order to effectively monitor the learning hours and progress of each student we adopt group learning. Each class is divided into six groups of seven students (one monitor and six group members). In-group cooperation facilitates mutual assistance so much so that top students and underachievers will work together and improve an overall learning outcome.

The paradigm compensates for the high teacher-student ratio. We also nominate a group leader and set up a group structure, to organize and monitor the learning performance and progress.

Group leaders organize and arrange the learning and experiment within each group, whose responsibilities include:

1) Coordinating group learning and make experiment schedule;
2) Supervising each group member's assignment in an experiment cycle (particularly in Phase II Experiment);
3) Summarizing and reporting team's achievement.

3.2 Process in Each Link

Some modules in the course of *Computer and Information Technology* has a high level of difficulty and makes it inappropriate to place all experiments before class lecturing, so we chop the relevant experiment into several links and distribute them at different phases.

The entire curriculum is divided into several relatively independent links according to their knowledge relevance. In each link the experiments will be undertaken in blocks according to their difficulty level, as the less difficult ones placed in Phase I while the more difficult and more comprehensive ones in Phase II.

Each link starts from Phase I experiment, which demands each student to complete their own assignment independently, because in most cases the experiment in this section pinpoints a knowledge point. To help students better do the pre-class experiments, the teacher needs to provide them with voluminous references and resources [16]. Students will learn and discuss the assigned chapters in the textbook, coupled with references, to complete the Phase I experiments on their own. Afterwards, they actually are able to do advanced work of preview.

The following class lecturing can be regarded as a transitional phase between Phrase I and II Experiments.

Students should have an overall understanding of the knowledge block after class discussion and learning, and they can complete the one or two more difficult combined experiment in Phase II. Groups of higher level are welcome to research further into the field and present the outcome of optional experiments. The teaching paradigm is each section is shown in Fig. 3.

3.3 Integration

The entire teaching process consists of multiple links, which develops and interlock with each other as a living organism as shown in Fig 4.

Each experiment includes two parts with the exceptions of Experiment One and N at both ends:(1)Phase II experiment in the previous section,(2)Phase I experiment in the present section. Therefore, the knowledge in the previous section is closely associated with that in the present section. This integrated teaching process makes the course go smoothly and continually.

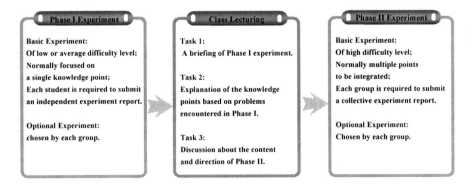

Fig. 3. Flow Chart of Each Link

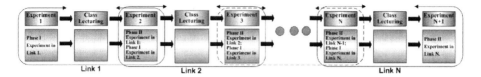

Fig. 4. Flow Chart of Integration

4 Application Examples

Take the course *C Programming* for example. It is a module of *Computer and Information Technology* for most engineering major students in college, such as Electric Information and Automation, Electronic Information, Transportation and Logistics etc.

Pointer is an important but tricky concept for students, so they need constant reinforcement in theory and repeated on-hands experiment to gain a clear awareness. We thereby illustrate by one of its links: *Pointers to Variables and Pointer Variables to Variables*.

4.1 Phase I Experiment

In this phase students are assigned to write basic programs, such as the experiment which demands students to write the outcome of the following code.

```
main()
{    ...
     printf("a:\t%d\n",a);
     printf("*pa:\t%d\n",*pa);
     printf("&a:\t%x(hex)\n",&a);
     printf("pa:\t%x(hex)\n",pa);
     printf("&pa:\t%x(hex)\n",&pa);
}
```

They are also required to complete the following code to realize "input two numbers, and display them in the numerical order".

```
main()
{    int *p1,*p2,*p,a,b;
     scanf("%d,%d",&a,&b);
     p1=&a;   p2=&b;
     ...
}
```

Only if students have a basic understanding of *Pointers and Addresses* can they complete the experiment. Meanwhile their group discussion and material collecting will help them to solve the problems encountered. Some of the problems are supposed to be solved independently while some remain open to answers, which the monitor makes a wrap-up and share with all the class in the following class lecturing.

4.2 Class Lecturing

It starts with the teacher's lecturing of relevant knowledge.

The teacher proceeds to discuss the problems in Phase I experiment. The groups volunteer to share with the rest of class what problems they have in Phase I, and those who know the solutions will offer to help. Since most problems are commonly found, some students can always come up with ingenious ideas. The students who can successfully solve problems will be awarded. The whole class goes in this ask-answer circle. Finally, the teacher draws a conclusion by offering some hints on the unsolved problems.

4.3 Phase II Experiment

Based on what students have learned in Phase I experiment and in the class lecturing, Phase II experiment starts a high level experiment section, in which each group completes the following experiment tasks.

   1)   Complete the unfinished parts of the first phase.
   2)   Do the experiments assigned by the teacher, including outputting the two numbers which are input through keyboard by means of *value passing* and *address passing*.
   3)   Each group has to program multiple codes according to what they have discussed and learned, or what they are interested in.

This section also involves the first phase of the next link's experiment.

4.4 Next Link's Class Lecturing

First the teacher gives answers to Phase II experiment in the link of *Pointers to Variables and Pointer Variables to Variables* for reference. A version of *value passing* is given below. An example of *address passing* is also given.

```
swap(int x,int y)
{    ... }
main()
{    ...
    pointer_1=&a;
    pointer_2=&b;
    if(a<b)  swap(*pointer_1,*pointer_2);
    printf("\n%d,%d\n",a,b);
}
```

Then each group is invited to display the distinctive part of their program to share the achievements and challenges they face in the process, or present their problems for collective exploration in the next section. The teacher starts to introduce the class lecturing about the next phase's knowledge. The circle is concluded by each group sharing their problems, which will be answered by those who know.

This teaching paradigm runs in the cycle of "experimental preview", "discussion and reinforcement in class", "higher level experiment", "outcome display in class", and "further exploration".

5 Conclusion and Future Work

Aiming at the prevalent problems in the current teaching of *Computer and Information Technology*, we propose an experiment-initiated teaching paradigm and explore linked teaching methodology. This paradigm breeds favorable outcomes in the module of *C Programming*, integrating theoretical teaching and practical experiment, solving the discrepancy and stimulating students' learning enthusiasm and performance.

We will further direct our work into various factors which impact the teaching effectiveness, and make detailed readjustment to the experiment-initiated teaching paradigm.

Acknowledgments. Special thanks to Mr. Gang Chen and Mr. Jianguo Tao of Equipment Department, Ningbo University of Technology for their support to the research. This work is supported by Education and Technology Research Project of Zhejiang Province (2011), and partially supported by Project of 21st-century Higher Education and Teaching Reform of Zhejiang Province Grant #yb09077, Educational Science Project of Ningbo City Grant #YGH044.

References

1. Boja, C., Batagan, L.: Analysis of M-learning applications quality. WSEAS Transactions on Computers 8, 767–777 (2009)
2. Wang, F., Deng, H., Liang, B., Zheng, S., Ren, X.: A computer-assisted marking system for enhancing education equity. International Journal of Innovative Computing, Information and Control 5, 4703–4714 (2009)
3. Regli, W., Kopena, J.B., Grauer, M., Simpson, T., Stone, R., Lewis, K., Bohm, M., Wilkie, D., Piecyk, M., Osecki, J.: Semantics for digital engineering archives supporting engineering design education. AI Magazine 31, 37–50 (2010)
4. Yates, J.K.: Engineering knowledge versus skills. Leadership and Management in Engineering 10, 135–136 (2010)
5. Aleksic-Maslac, K., Vasic, D., Korican, M.: Student learning contribution through E-learning dimension at course "management information systems". WSEAS Transactions on Information Science and Applications 7, 331–340 (2010)
6. Lasen, M.: Education and career pathways in Information Communication Technology: What are schoolgirls saying? Computers and Education 54, 1117–1126 (2010)
7. Zhu, N., Yang, S., Ye, W.: Research on the Student-Oriented Role-Shift Teaching Model in the Computer Information Technology Course. In: 1st International Workshop on Education Technology and Computer Science, pp. 256–260. IEEE Computer Society, Wuhan (2009)
8. Alsurori, M., Salim, J.: The status of information and communication technology in the higher education in yemen. International Review on Computers and Software 5, 712–723 (2010)
9. Peng, W.: Experience and ideas on basic computer teaching in independent colleges. In: 2nd International Conference on Education Technology and Computer, pp. V4542–V4544. IEEE Computer Society, Shanghai (2010)
10. Appavoo, P.: The constructivist' approach to teaching computing. International Journal of Continuing Engineering Education and Life-Long Learning 20, 407–417 (2010)

11. Carl Ransom, R.: Freedom to learn for the 80s. Charles Merrill Publishing Company, London (1983)
12. Barrett-Lennard, G.T.: Carl Rogers' helping system. Journey and Substance. Sage, London (1998)
13. Rogers, C.: A theory of therapy, personality, and interpersonal relationships, as developed in the client-centered framework. In: Koch, S. (ed.) Psychology: A Study of a Science, vol. 3, pp. 184–256. McGraw Hill, New York (1959)
14. Zhu, N., Cheng, M., Fan, J., Shu, R.: Applying Role-Switch Model in College Information Technology Course. In: 10th IEEE International Conference on Computer and Information Technology, pp. 2029–2032. IEEE Computer Society, Bradford (2010)
15. Zhu, N., Tang, Y.-T., Xuan, J., Guan, B., Zhao, M.: Construction of Role-Switch Model in College Information Technology Experiment Course. In: 10th IEEE International Conference on Computer and Information Technology, pp. 2025–2028. IEEE Computer Society, Bradford (2010)
16. Zhu, N., Fan, J., Lou, J., Li, W., Zhang, H.: Web-based Negative Selection Algorithm in the Experiment-assisting Information Extraction. In: International Conference on Fuzzy System and Neural Computing, pp. 270–273. IEEE Press, Hongkong (2011)

Modeling and Simulation of the Underground Mining Transportation System

Lei Xu[*], Sheng Ye, Guilin Lu, and Zhen Zhang

School of Mechanics and Civil Engineering,
China University of Mining and Technology,
Xuzhou (221008), Jiangsu, China
cumtxulei@126.com

Abstract. The system simulation is a study hotspot in large underground mines system engineering field. In view to the fact that the underground transportation is a large and complex system, we set Datun horizontal transportation coal mining system as the research object in Xuzhou district, discreting event simulation theory, a transportation system model for certain transportation parameters. Through adjusting some transportation parameters, confirming the best distribution, thus analyzing the transportation system efficiency, carrying on a scientific evaluation on the transportation capacity system.

Keywords: underground mine system, the system simulation, transportation system.

1   Introduction

The system simulation is a new subject which is based on auxiliary system design and management decision-making. The new technology has been widely used in mechanical manufacturing, material processing, transportation, military deployment, flight training, business services, computer, communication, mining engineering system analysis and design works. We use it to carry on reality system test, which can help us accurately evaluate the operation system performance.

One underground mine in South Africa, using simulation technology to do a feasibility simulation research on the gangue-rock shipment system of a new mine to determine the number of crusher and the capacity of adhesive tape machine, it leads to saving at least 4.4 million dollars investment [1].

Because domestic underground mining level of automation transportation system isn't enough, the application of this technology has not come into widely used. This article takes Datun horizontal transportation coal mining system as the research object which is based on PLC control system, adopting discrete event systems simulation principle to build the system simulation model, so as to demonstrate its transportation capability.

---

[*] Corresponding author.

S. Lin and X. Huang (Eds.): CESM 2011, Part II, CCIS 176, pp. 116–121, 2011.

2 Profiles of Mining Transportation System

Datun coal gangue is mainly transferred by each sneak well and transportation flat, finally danger out by different levels. With the decline in the middle of production and limited surface, the transportation level is the lowest of the whole east, most of the mine gangue is transported through this level, and because of its unique geographical position, we hope it can afford a certain amount of transportation capacity of the other mines, and there gangue we urgently needs to make a scientific evaluation for the entire production system, so as to provide reliable basis for the optimization of transportation line. This level is shown in figure 1 below.

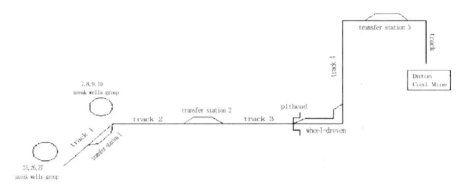

Fig. 1. Transportation route schemes

As can be seen from the graph, whether gangue of 7-10 sneak wells group or 25 to 27 sneak wells groups are required to pass through tracks 2, 3, 4 and rail track rails 5 (tracks 2-5). So, tracks 2-5 is the main bottleneck of the whole transportation system.

3 Model Building

The system is a discrete event systems. According to the discrete event simulation principle [2]: We can look the train as sports entity; Each pack, unloading track respectively means competition resources; Wheel-dreven and transfer station stand for queue waiting sites, queuing rules are first come first serve. Producing entities equal to the train number, after the entity is uninstalled, going back to the install mine dot through the original path, and then execute transportation tasks, so as to keep on circulating in the system. Using events at fostering both propulsion simulation clock step [3], simulating transportation system operation.

To simplify the actual conditions, making modeling gangue convenient, we assums that:

1) 7 to 10 sneak Wells with 25-27 of slip Wells, there is always full of mine.

2) The wheel-dreven can accommodate a sufficient number of trains. There gangue, we can build a transportation model, the logic structure model is shown in figure 2.

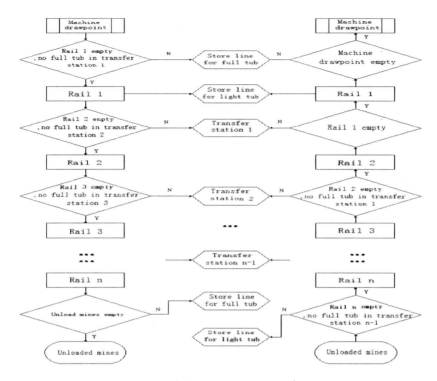

Fig. 2. Logic structure

4 Data Collection and Analysis

What this model requires most is various transportation links, the time needed for that time is usually random variables, such as loading, unloading time and rail train running time in paragraphs. The probability density function that we obtain is shown in table 1.

Table 1. Distribution density function

Parameters	Function
Loading time	$f(x) = \frac{1}{10.1}e^{-\frac{x-10}{10.1}}(x > 10)$
Unloading time	$f(x) = \frac{1}{12.8\sqrt{2\pi}}e^{-\frac{(x-42)^2}{327.68}}(x > 0)$
Tracks (1,2,3) running time/min	$f(x) = \begin{cases} x-5 & 5 \le x \le 6 \\ 7-x & 6 \le x \le 7 \\ 0 & others \end{cases}$
Tracks (4,5) running time/min	$f(x) = \begin{cases} 0.59x - 3.91 & 6.6 \le x \le 7.9 \\ 5.43 - 0.59x & 7.9 \le x \le 9.2 \\ 0 & others \end{cases}$

5   System Simulation and Results Analysis

5.1   The Best Vehicle Number of Various Transportation Line

The system is divided into two transportation line:

Line 1: From 7 to 10 sneak wells to the mill;
Line 2: From 25 to 27 sneak wells to the mill.

Supposing the working time of the system is:

3 classes in 1 day, 7 hours every class, every day works for 21 hours. Simulating a single transportation route, changing vehicle number, making the model run 30 days respectively (21 × 30 = 630 hours, simulating the real time), we can get results as figure 3 shows.

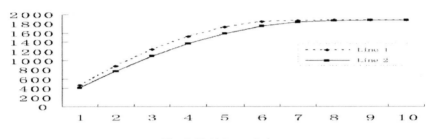

Fig. 3. Vehicles variation

As can be seen from the graph, with the increase of vehicles number, driving ability increases, but the increasing number gradually reduce to a certain number, and driving ability has no gangue improvement, even declined. This is because the fact that with the increase of tracks utilization rate, driving ability can not get unlimited increase, meanwhile, heavy traffic may have leaded to waiting time increased, causing driving ability declined.

From the graph, we can see that line 1 and 2, as long as there is respectively 6 or 7 trains, they will reach saturation.

5.2   Distribution of Total Line Vehicles

Before this, what we get is just the best vehicle number of a single line, line 1 and line 2, they compete to use tracks 2, 3, 4, there must be certain proportion relationship between them. Distributing the vehicle according to the proportion of stable condition, 6:7, changing the total vehicle number, we obtain the relationship between each vehicle combination and drive number, as shown in table 2.

From table 2, we can see the maximum number of vehicle distribution is that line 1 distributes 7 column, line 2 distributes 8 column, but considering convenient for management, under the premise of satisfying the production, (6, 7) combination has reached saturation.

Table 2. The relationship between each vehicle and driving number

Line 1/column	Line 2/column	Vehicle number
5	5	2757
5	6	2823
6	6	2880
6	7	2916
7	7	2949
7	8	2967

5.3 Transportation Efficiency

We use facilities utilization rate (the ratio of facilities busy time with total time)to measure the efficiency of transportation system. The function of B(t) stands for the facilities state of in moment t:

$$B(t)= \begin{cases} 1 & \text{facility is busy.} \\ 0 & \text{facility is not busy.} \end{cases}$$

T: the total systems work time

Through the operation model, drawing facilities utilization under different saturated state as we referred to, such as shown in table 3.

Table 3. Facilities utilization rate

	Datum warehouse %	7-10 sneak wells group %	25-27 sneak wells group %	track 1 %	track 2 %	track 3 %	track 4 %	track 5 %	Waste rate %
Line 1	47	98	--	--	58	58	58	58	16
Line 2	47	--	98	58	58	58	57	57	16
Total line	74	75	80	48	92	92	91	91	25

From the table we can see, railway track 2-5 which is seen as transportation bottlenecks, when we simulate line 1, 2 respectively, due to restriction from7-10 sneak wells group or 25 to 27 sneak wells group, they can only achieve about 58% function. But in the total transportation, they have already reached gangue than 90%. The former state did not reach good condition while the latter transportation capability has been well done.

6 Coal Production Capacity Assessment in Four Years

According to the above results, the system drives 2916 columns in 30 days, 97 columns in a day. Assuming that every day, the car engine several materials is 17 columns, harvesters is 80 columns; Each column can bear 63 t; Every year, they work 330 days. So, we the production capacity is 63 x 80 x 330 = 166. 3 million t.

7 Conclusion

Through the above simulation analysis, we can draw a conclusion that:

1) Using system modeling simulation method, through building model, we can adjust the transportation parameters without interfering with the actual system. To make transportation state achieve the best state, easier to monitor the transportation process, finding out the weak link, thus transforming;

2) Each road transportation route can accommodate limited vehicle number, we'd better put quantity control in its saturation point to make the vehicle distribution achieve the best state;

3) The method can accurately calculate the mining system potential carrying capacity, providing the basis for decision-maker.

References

1. Li, Z.: Foreign Simulation System Technology and Its New Application in Mining Development. Journal of China Mining 7(2), 75–79 (1998)
2. Banks, J., Carson, J.S., Nelson, B.L., Nicol, D.M.: Systems Simulation of Discrete Event (English Version), 4th edn. China Machine Press, Beijing (2005)
3. Lu, Z., Lin, M.: Computer Simulation of Port Service System of [J]. Journal of Hehai University 27(3), 17–21 (1999)
4. Zhang, X.: Logistics System Simulation Principle and Application, pp. 30–43. China Supplies Press, Beijing (2005)
5. Zhao, W., Li, Z.: Simulation System Technology and Its New Progress in Mining. Foreign Metal Mines 3, 51–56 (2000)
6. Li, M., Lu, W.: Production Material Transport System Modeling and Simulation Based on Pet ri Nets. Journal of Anhui University of Technology 21(1), 45–48 (2004)

Database System Development for Cement Factory

Wu Xie[*], Huimin Zhang, Zili Qin, and Huacheng Zhang

Guilin University of Electronic Technology,
541004 Guilin, China
xiewu588@126.com

Abstract. Aiming at reforming the old data management technology of manual work and files document in cement plants, a database system was customized for cement enterprises with Visual Studio and SQL Server. After the steps of demand analysis, conceptual structure design, logical structure design, physical structure design and implementation, the system is developed. Software test results show that all the functional modules are finished. The cement database system is easy to use with intuitional statistical diagrams. The software can improve the level of cement industry and information technology, lowering the management costs, helping to establish strict and standard operation flow and enhancing enterprise efficiency or benefit.

Keywords: Database system, cement plants, software design, information management.

1 Introduction

In recent years, a large number of infrastructure investments have promoted the rapid development of construction industry with a huge boost demand for cement products, highlighted for some attention and research [1, 2, 3, 4, 5]. At present, the cement production, cement capacity, material flow, transports, purchasing and orders are mass for cement plants, and cement logistic is connected with the departments of purchasing, pounds room, sales, warehousing, laboratory, etc. It takes a lot of time to do manual work and process files document data, especially business processes are not standardized, which becomes a big bottleneck during cement enterprises informationizing process. Meanwhile, as high energy consumption and high pollution industries, it is imperative to readjust the cement industrial structure in future. In order to outstand in an invincible position during the company merger or consolidation, it is extremely urgent for cement factories to transform the traditional production management mode with digital and informationalizing technology.

Therefore, a database system is developed for cement enterprises based on SQL Server and Visual Studio. In the following sections, the development process is introduced in detail, which includes the steps of demand analysis, conceptual structure design, logical structure design, physical structure design and implementation. The software will improve the level of industry and information technology for cement enterprises.

---

[*] Corresponding author.

S. Lin and X. Huang (Eds.): CESM 2011, Part II, CCIS 176, pp. 122–127, 2011.

2 Requirement Analysis

Though the business process of cement plants is very complex, some main functional requirements for cement plant database system can be analyzed and divided into several modules as follow.

Information management needs of users registering module. In the cement plant database system, the important data cover user information, the cement product information, material information, customer information and supplier information, etc. The main operations are creating, modifying and deleting the cement database system, and inserting, updating, deleting and selecting the records or tuples in the rows of the database.

Information management needs of raw material purchasing module. The main function of this module is to add, modify, query purchase orders. During the input of the purchasing orders, it can effectively verify whether the input data integrity of the database.

Information management needs of the cement production process module. The main function of this module is to call and transfer the raw materials, manufacturing the cement finished goods. The system is required to add a single bill of raw materials, modifying the corresponding inventory of raw materials. Similarly, when the cement production documents are added, the corresponding stocks bills of cement products also increased. The module also requires a corresponding input validation functions before login.

Information management needs of the sales business module. Just like procurement operations, this module needs the adding and querying functions of the sales order. When they input the sale order, verification is required to check the integrity of input data for the cement database.

Information management needs of the inventory module. This module mainly deals with materials received report and cement products outgoing bills, which includes purchasing order, sales receipts, notes during loading and discharging, weight difference records after cement weighs. The module needs a corresponding input validation functions, too.

Information management needs of the selecting and statistical module. According to purchasing order and sales receipts, the total monthly amount and percent are calculated, and shown in intuitive pie chart.

3 Database System Design for Cement Plants

According to database theory and software engineering, database design is often divided into three phases, namely conceptual structural design, logical structural design and physical structural design.

3.1 Conceptual Structure Design

For the cement database system, there are over six entities, such as supplier, raw materials, workers, warehouse, customers and products, and so on. The global Entity-Relationship diagram is shown as follow in Fig. 1.

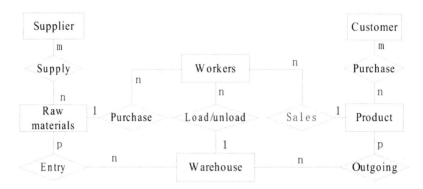

Fig. 1. The Entity-Relationship Diagram of the Database System for Cement Factory

3.2 Logical Structure Design

According to the Entity-Relationship diagram, there are some relation schemas in the cement database system from the view of logical structure.

The relation schema of employees is used to store the information of the registered users, and it is described as: Employees (Emp_Id, Emp_LoginName, Emp_Password, Emp_Name, Emp_Dept), where Emp_Id is the primary key.

The relation schema of customers is used for the client business formation with the cement plants products, and the relational table is customers (Ctm_Id, Ctm_Name, Ctm_Phone, Ctm_Address), where Ctm_Id is the primary key.

The relation schema of providers is applied for the related suppliers formation about raw materials of cement products, and the relational table is providers (Provider_Id, Provider_Name, Provider_Phone, Provider_Address), where Provider_Id is the primary key.

The relation schema of Storage deals with the related formation about raw materials and cement products, and the relational table is Storage (Store_ID, Store_Name, Store_Size, Store_Phone), where Store_ID is the primary key.

The relation schema of RawMaterials collects the formation about diverse rough materials of cement products, and the relational table is RawMaterials (RawMater_Id, RawMater_Name, RawMater_Unit, RawMater_Unit_Price, RawMater_KC_Weight, RawMater_Address), where RawMater_Id is the primary key.

The relation schema of Orders represents the formation of bills about selling cement products between plants and customers, and the relational table is Orders (Order_Id, Product_Name, Ctm_Name, Order_Weight, Letf_Weight, Emp_Name, Order_Unit, Emp_Name, Order_Time, Order_State), where Order_Id is the key.

The relation schema of SellDetails describes the formation about the signed orders in detail and delivery of the factory, and the relational table is SellDetails (Selldetail_Id, Order_Id, First_Weight, Second_Weight, First_Time, Second_ Time, Real_Weight, Left_Weight, Emp_Name), where Selldetail_Id is the primary key.

The relation schema of BuyingOrder affords the formation about cement plants and suppliers, and the relational table is BuyingOrder (BuyOrder_Id, RawMater_ Name, Provider_Name, Buying_Weight, Left_Weight, Buying_Unit, BuyOrder_Price, Emp_ Name, BuyOrder_Time, BuyOrder_State), where Buy Order_Id is the primary key.

The relation schema of BuyDetail stores the formation about the detailed order form between plants and suppliers after purchasing and discharging, and the relational table is BuyingOrder (BuyOrder_Id, RawMater_Name, Provider_Name, Buying_ Weight, Left_Weight, Buying_Unit, BuyOrder_Price, Emp_Name, BuyOrder_Time, BuyOrder_State), where BuyOrder_Id is the primary key.

The relation schema of RawMaterialsConsume just shows the formation transferring raw materials from warehouse during manufacturing in cement plants, and the relational table is RawMaterialsConsume (RawMaterConsume_Id, RawMater Consume_Weight, Raw Mater_Name, Emp_Name, RawMater_Consume_Time), where RawMaterConsume_Id is the primary key.

The relation schema of Productions includes the formation of final cement products that are transferred to warehouse, and the relational table is Productions (Production_Id, Product_Name, Production_Weight, Production_Emp, Production_ Time), where RawMaterConsume_Id is the primary key.

The relationship diagram among the tables of Customers, Employees, Selldetails, Orders and Products is shown as follow in Fig. 2.

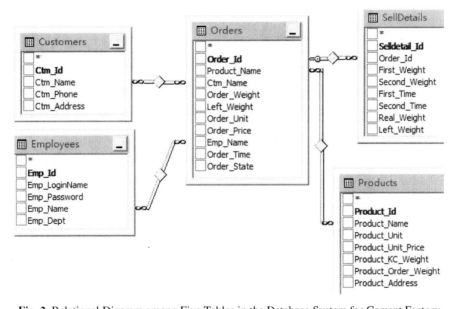

Fig. 2. Relational Diagram among Five Tables in the Database System for Cement Factory

3.3 Physical Structure Design

During the physical structure design of the cement database, the work of selecting storage structure and access methods is usually finished by DBMS, such as SQL Server. Employees often operate the cement systems frequently, and it takes long time to search the whole tables to select some daily information for massive data records, resulting in waste of resources the server. So, to improve query speed for this cement database, it is necessary to create indexes as follows in Table 1.

Table 1. Non clustered and clustered index table in the database for cement factory

Relational tables	Clustered index	Non clustered index
Employees	Emp_Id	Emp_LoginName
customers	Ctm_Id	Ctm_Name
providers	Provider_Id	Provider_Name
Storage	Store_ID	Store_Name
RawMaterials	RawMater_Id	RawMater_Name
Products	Product_Id	Product_Name
Orders）	Order_Id	
SellDetails）	Selldetail_Id	
BuyingOrder	BuyOrder_Id	
BuyDetail	BuyDetail_Id	
RawMaterialsConsume	RawMaterConsume_Id	
Productions	Production_Id	

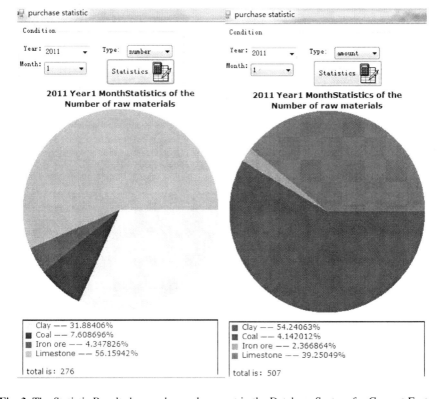

Fig. 3. The Statistic Results by number and amount in the Database System for Cement Factory

4 Programming and Implementation of the Database System for Cement Plants

The database system for cement plants is developed in C# programming language within Visual Studio, and the data are stored in SQL Server. The ADO.net component technology is adopted to connect and bind database. All the functional modules are finished according to demand requirement. The users registering module, raw material purchasing module, cement production process module, sales business module, inventory module, selecting and statistical module are carried out. For example, the user can simply select the appropriate time of the month and year, and the proportion of the amount of sales are derived from the database system of cement plant, shown in statistical interface like Fig. 3.

5 Conclusion

Through several steps of needs analysis, concept design, logic design, physical structure and coding, a complete database for cement plants is gained, and this software runs steadily. Its interface is friendly with easy operation, and each software modules is easy to upgrade with strong portability. Some modules have advantage of corresponding input validation functions with good data integrity and security. The database system software increases the level of enterprise information and business management norm, improving data management and increasing enterprise efficiency significantly.

References

1. Kotini, I.H., Hassapis: A Hybrid Automaton Model of the Cement Mill Control. IEEE Transactions on Control Systems Technology 4, 676–690 (2008)
2. Smith, T.P.: Performing detailed power system studies for designing and analyzing electrical distribution systems - Power system studies for cement plants. IEEE Industry Applications Magazine 4, 56–65 (2007)
3. Melick, T., Robinson, A.D.: Going with the Flow. IEEE Industry Applications Magazine 2, 42–49 (2007)
4. Sahasrabudhe, R., Sistu, P., Sardar, G., Gopinath, R.: Control and optimization in cement plants. IEEE Control Systems Magazine 6, 56–63 (2006)
5. Mirolli, M.D.: Cementing Kalina cycle effectiveness. IEEE Industry Applications Magazine 4, 60–64 (2006)

A Feedback Comprehensive Evaluation Method with Data Mining

Wu Xie[*], Huimin Zhang, and Zengshan Meng

Guilin University of Electronic Technology,
541004 Guilin, China
xiewu588@126.com

Abstract. There was a problem that it was difficult to carry out a synthetic evaluation of mass records in database or data warehouse with traditional ways, and a feedback comprehensive evaluation method based on data mining was presented. It was completed in five steps through a feedback control system. Case study shows that the decision trees or association rules from the mining results can perform the comprehensive assessment. The puzzle that large-scale data objects is too complicate to assess at the same time is solved with this method, which improves assessment efficiency and quality greatly, reducing the workload for decision support. It is an effective complement to the traditional evaluation theory.

Keywords: Evaluation, Data mining, large scale systems, feedback, database system, data warehouses.

1 Introduction

In recent years, comprehensive evaluation methods occur in diverse way [1, 2], such as fuzzy evaluation method, correlation analysis, principal component analysis, factor analysis, etc. With the development of information technology, the data storage of some evaluation objects expands day by day. When faced with complicate objects of large scale systems as huge databases or data warehouse, the evaluation results of with some factors that play a key role are often submerged in a sea of data. Those traditional evaluation methods can not meet the requirements of many extra objects. It is difficult to complete the evaluation tasks of large-scale objects. Moreover, some evaluation information is fuzzy, gray, rough and uncertain with semi-structured or unstructured data, which causes hard scientific computing. So, evaluation theory needs developing itself. A new comprehensive assessment method for some large scale objects is proposed through data mining with a feedback control system, and the massive evaluated information is stored in the database system or data warehouse system.

2 Feasibility of Comprehensive Evaluation with Data Mining

Data mining is a non-trivial process where gets valid, novel, unknown, hidden, potential useful, understood knowledge, law or mode from mass incomplete, noisy,

---

[*] Corresponding author.

S. Lin and X. Huang (Eds.): CESM 2011, Part II, CCIS 176, pp. 128–132, 2011.

fuzzy, random information in database, data warehouse or other data entities [4]. It's named as knowledge discovery from databases, Comprehensive evaluation is a qualitative or quantitative process to determine the level or order of the evaluated objects with multi-index system from many indicators of specific aspects or multiple phenomena, and it is a multidisciplinary interdisciplinary subject. Major theoretical research, significance, role, and methods are covered in it, as decision science [4].

There is much interdisciplinary content and common knowledge in comparison with comprehensive evaluation and data mining. Many data mining algorithms can obtain an objective quantitative analysis of understanding the nature of the excavated objects from a large amount of data or data sets, while comprehensive evaluation method is of advantage of subjective and qualitative analysis. The combination of both will be the highlight of the new interdisciplinary. Therefore, it is feasible to perform synthetic assessment with data mining from accumulated mass data for large scale systems.

3   Feedback Comprehensive Evaluation with Data Mining

For large sample space with massive data objects, a new feedback comprehensive evaluation model with data mining technology is shown in Fig. 1.

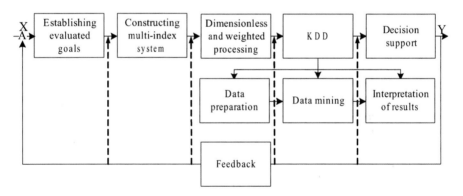

Fig. 1. The Control System Model of the Feedback Comprehensive Evaluation Process with Data Mining, and the five sections implement the forward assessment, improved by feedback.

It is a closed-loop feedback control system. The input of system is from the records in database or data warehouse, and the output is obtained through the results of comprehensive evaluation after data mining results. Forward transfer function during the comprehensive evaluation process is divided into five sections, which includes establishing goals, constructing multi-index evaluation system, dimensionless and weighted processing, KDD (knowledge discovery from databases), decision support. Each stage has a feedback to the input section to improve the quality of evaluation through the negative feedback sections. Solid line stands for the data flow that must pass through the control system for comprehensive assessment, while the dashed lines indicate the feedback data flow available.

In the feedback comprehensive evaluation system, when the results of evaluation does not meet the needs of users, it is necessary to return to the five sections of the forward transfer function by the principle of negative feedback control, adjusting the sample size, or checking the established model to improve the quality of data mining to achieve the user expectations.

3.1 Determining the Synthetic Evaluation Target

The synthetic evaluation goal is to determine the properties and the status of the development or operation for the evaluated objects, which are often classified or sorted by their merits or orders through data mining. Therefore, for the large-scale database or data warehouse objects, the original data are extracted from the feedback control system are considered as an evaluation sample of the environment, and a new database or data warehouse are created to perform assessment. After the feedback comprehensive evaluation process, diverse results can be obtained from data mining of database system, data warehouse system or large data sets.

3.2 Establishing Multi-index System of Comprehensive Evaluation

Diverse indexes are often used to evaluate the system as quantificational parameters or variables, which describe and reflect one aspect of objects, and they are usually divided into qualitative indicators described their values with language or quantitative indicators by data representation.

The evaluation criteria are selected to build to a complete evaluation of the object reflected in the overall properties of the multi-index system. It is composed of multiple indicators system, which measures some features of the system according to the principles of purpose, comprehensiveness, feasibility and independence. Those attributes or attributes group of relational tables in database, or the columns and attributes sets of some specific fact tables and dimension tables in data warehouse can be selected as the multi-index system for some large-scale sample of the evaluated objects.

3.3 Dimensionless and Weighted Processing

In multi-index comprehensive evaluation system, the indicators tend to have different units of measurement. Their dimensions with multiply physical meaning are various. Therefore, it is necessary to transform the actual data of the original indexes to the relative values before assessment to eliminate the influence on overall evaluation of large data objects. To solve the problem of synthesizing the indicators of different units of measurement, the feasible and objective principles should be followed to realize the multi-index sampled data by standardization and normalization process.

Massive data objects often have non-equilibrium, and they are usually described by relation schemas with a lot of attributes. From the view of formal formulas, there are some dependency relationships between primary attributes and nonprime attributes. To adjust the indicators to play the role of evaluation results, it is necessary to process each index with structural relative weighted value, and the importance degree is determined by various factors of evaluated objects.

3.4 Knowledge Discovery in Database

Thousands of records in database or data warehouse objects lead to complicated comprehensive evaluation process, the KDD section is often divided three steps, which are data preparation, data mining and results interpretation, as shown in Fig. 1.

The first is data preparation. There are three sub-steps of the data selection, data preprocessing and data transformation in the data preparation stage.

The second is data mining. Mining algorithms include Bayesian networks, nearest neighbor method, case-based reasoning, decision trees, neural networks, rule induction method, etc. In the data mining results, there are prototype examples, decision tree, neural network weights, and production rules, and so on [3-5]. In order to meet user's assessment needs, it is necessary to use descriptive, appropriate and easy to understand the knowledge of mining results.

The third is interpretation of data mining results. In order to facilitate the users to understand and accept the modes, rules or knowledge in the data mining results for large-scale evaluation objects, it is very necessary to analyze the data mining process referring to the evaluation criteria. The grade, number and boundary in multi-index evaluation results need some consistency tests, eliminating redundant or independent assessment conclusions. Visualization method can be adopted to carry out reasonable interpretation for the data mining results.

3.5 Decision Support

According to the visual results of data mining, a decision model can be created to perform quantitative comprehensive evaluation beyond selected samples for large-scale objects. The association rules, decision trees, charts and other forms of mining results can be intuitively and directly applied to the decision-making and management. Different types of mining results can be interchangeable with the actual needs of decision-making after comprehensive evaluation.

4   Example

To evaluate the quality of graduate design, 30 titles were sampled. The data records were stored in the database systems, which front was developed with Visual Studio 2010, and background was SQL Server 2005. The data mining algorithm is ID3 decision tree. After optimizing the classes of the graduate design titles, a decision tree was gained though feedback assessment. The results are shown in Fig. 2. From the results, all graduated titles can be comprehensively assessed at the same time with ID3 decision tree after data mining, and the grades of these titles are objective, and the results can reflect the quality of 30 graduation project.

ID	Type	Similar	Difficulty	Group
7	Network	new	Easy	yes
8	Network	similar	Easy	no
9	Embedded	new	Easy	yes
10	DataBase	new	Easy	no
11	DataBase	new	Difficult	yes
12	DataBase	similar	Difficult	no
13	Embedded	similar	Difficult	yes
14	Network	new	Easy	no

```
Type
⊟ Network
   ⊟ Difficulty
      ⊟ Easy
         ⋯ high 7  8  14  18  22
      ⊟ Difficult
         ⋯ low 15  17  27  34
⊟ Embedded
   ⋯ low 9  13  20  21  25  26  30
⊟ DataBase
   ⊟ Similar
      ⊟ new
         ⋯ low 10  11  16  19
      ⊟ similar
         ⋯ high 12  23  24  29
```

Fig. 2. Results of Graduate Design Title with the Feedback Comprehensive Evaluation Method

5 Conclusion

A feedback comprehensive evaluation method is obtained through data mining database or data warehouse. It improves the comprehensive evaluation theory. Compared with traditional methods, its characters are as follows: 1) It is fit for large-scale evaluation objects; 2) it can evaluate a subset of the sample space once; 3) It can handle uncertain information for diverse objects; 4) it can use traditional methods in the data preparation process; 5) it can improve continuously assessment quality by negative feedback control; 6) It can find the hidden mass data information, patterns or rules.

References

1. Wei, B., Wang, S.L.: Fuzzy comprehensive evaluation of district heating system. Energy Policy (2010)
2. Jiawei, H., Micheline, K.: Data Mining: Concepts and Techniques. Morgan Kaufmann, San Francisco (2006)
3. Da, G., Martino, S.: Mining Structured Data. IEEE Computational Intelligence Magazine 147, 42–49 (2010)
4. Wu, X., Huacheng, Z., Huimin, Z.: Study of comprehensive evaluation method of undergraduates based on data mining. In: The 2010 IEEE International Conference on Intelligent Computing and Integrated Systems, pp. 541–543. IEEE Press, Guilin (2010)
5. Wu, X., Huimin, Z.: Design and Implementation of Data Warehouse of Minor Chain Supermarkets. In: The 3rd International Conference on Intelligent Computing and Intelligent Systems, pp. 828–830. IEEE Press, Xiamen (2010)

eTOM Business Processes Conception in NGN Monitoring

B. Raouyane[1,2], M. Bellafkih[1], M. Errais[1,2], D. Leghroudi[2],
D. Ranc[3], and M. Ramdani[2]

[1] Institut National des Postes et Télécommunications, RABAT, Morroco
[2] Faculté des Sciences et Techniques, MOHAMMEDIA, Morroco
[3] LOR Laboratory, INT SudParis, Evry, France
{Raouyane_brahim,mbellafkih}@yahoo.fr,
daniel.ranc@itsudparis.eu

Abstract. Networks are growing in complexity because of several factors, including number of user, applications, and different technologies. Indeed the management in this case is relativistic. The QoS management mechanisms proposed by 3GPP allow providing the IMS network entities controls and efficient service delivery; however the 3GPP approach focuses entirely on the step of providing the service without consideration the type of customer, which requires a monitoring architecture. Furthermore the TMForum groups within specification scenario type of monitoring based end to end business process oriented Assurance to a permanent monitoring of the services provided. However these scenarios are generic and haven't specification for IMS networks. We propose in this paper a new approach to monitor IMS networks, which based specifications TMForum and use WS-Composite and XML Communication, and it provides a platform for continuous monitoring of services.

Keywords: IMS (IP Multimedia System); QoS (Quality of services); NGOSS (New Generation Operations Systems and Software); eTOM (enhanced Telecom Operations Map); SLA (Service Level Agreement); SID (Shared Information Data); SOA (Service Oriented Architecture); WS (Web Service); BPEL (Business Process Execution Language).

1 Introduction

QoS management mechanisms as defined by 3GPP [1] can be viewed as a network-centric approach to QoS, providing a signaling chain able to automatically configure the network to provision determined QoS to services on demand and in real time, for instance on top of a DiffServ-enabled network. However, to envision a deployment of such technology in a carrier-grade context would mean significant further effort. In particular, premium paid-for services with SLA (Service Level Agreement) contracts such as targeted by IMS networks would require additional mechanisms able to provide some degree of monitoring in order to asset the SLAs, while IMS by itself does not provide such mechanisms.

S. Lin and X. Huang (Eds.): CESM 2011, Part II, CCIS 176, pp. 133–143, 2011.
© Springer-Verlag Berlin Heidelberg 2011

The work presented in this contribution is an attempt to achieve Assurance functionality for QoS-enhanced IMS services following strictly the eTOM specification [2], thus filling the functional gap as analyzed earlier, and we proposed tow architecture to be compared: centralized and distributed.

2 IMS and Service Monitoring

IMS signaling management adopts policy based approach to satisfy the dynamic, flexible and versatile signaling management requirements. The signalizations between the network entities (Access, Transport, and Control) interested only in the provision of service at the beginning, afterward without mechanism to monitor the conduct of the service. Indeed, the 3GPP defines two entities for the control of QoS services. The both entities PCRF (Policy and Charging Rule Function) and PCEF (Policy and Charging Enforcement Function) also facilitate flow based online and offline charging.

The service delivery model focuses just on the service provisioning and specific type (Video, Audio, etc...), without take into account class of customer (QoS) or the contract between client and operator related (SLA). Where the need for a new monitoring approach that provide ongoing monitoring mechanisms and integrating the importance and the satisfaction of client in decision making.

3 eTOM Functionality and SLA Verification

3.1 eTOM

The eTOM is the functional analysis viewpoint of the NGOSS framework. As such, it provides a common language to describe business processes carried out in telecom activities. The eTOM has three major business process areas: the Strategy, Infrastructure & Product area, the Enterprise area and the Operations area, of which only the latter is relevant to our discussion. The Operations area is furthermore organized in vertical process groupings (Fulfillment, Assurance and Billing) and in horizontal layers (Customer Relationship, Service Management, Resource Management and Supplier/ Partner Relationship). The eTOM model is structured into four abstraction levels allowing viewing processes and tasks in various detail.

3.2 Shared Information Data (SID)

The counterpart in terms of data of the eTOM is the Shared Information and Data (SID) model [3]. This object-oriented information model is composed of UML (Unified Modeling Language) class specifications identifying the entities and the basic elements necessary for each layer in the eTOM. Information modeling provides a common language to represent features and functions of various network devices. SID uses the concepts of capacity to represent functions of an entity and the constraints that the restrictions on features. The model information enables the various features of each device to be represented in a common manner. This allows them be programmed together and cooperate to provide a common service.

3.3 SLA Verification in the eTOM

The eTOM proposes the SLA (Service Level Agreement) Verification [4] as the suitable procedure for monitoring services. It identifies whether the provided QoS meets the requirements specified in the SLA contract from the information collected through the network entities. The verification process is structured into four stages:

- **Performance Indicators Collection:** Key Performance Indicators (KPI) are a relevant means of monitoring the status of delivered services. There are three classes of performance indicators each of which focuses on a particular aspect of media streaming services:
  - *Network Indicators:* such as Jitter (ms) Delay (ms) Bandwidth (kb/s).
  - *Configuration Indicators:* Access Technology, Decoder type, Access line bandwidth, CBR / VBR, Transport protocol.
  - *Service indicators:* Coding protocol, Motion, Video bit rate, Frame size, Number of programs, Media types, Service type, Bit-rate.

- **Mapping of quality indicators:** Unlike indicators of performance, quality indicators are correlated to the service, so they can identify the quality of service more concretely than the performance indicators. The KQI (Key Quality indicator) are calculated after combination or using an algorithm for calculating various performance indicators, which have an impact on this service (Mapping) to identify the quality perceived by the customer. The quality indicators most used for multimedia streaming [5] are: MOS-V (Mean Opinion Scores-Video) and MOS-A (Mean Opinion Scores-Audio).
- **Comparison between quality indicators and SLA:** SLA contracts negotiated between a supplier and a user define the conditions of supply, the targets of the QoS, and actions to take if the delivered service does not comply. The SLA must be designed so that it allows easily comparing with quality indicators.
- **Report overall service and resources:** It is necessary to provide a report on the resource during the provision of service and its status. Likewise for service availability, response times and indicators that measure specific levels of transport infrastructure performance (packet loss, network transit time and transit time variations).

The technical part of SLS (Service Level Specification) defines SLA violation thresholds; depend on the class of service (CoS) for the client. During service delivery KQIs are continuously calculated and compared to the thresholds.

4 Issues

3GPP standards propose a QoS provisioning system lacking any provision for a monitoring mechanism after delivery of services. Indeed, the 3GPP specifications focus on providing services such as reservation of resources, but without worrying about the behavior that follows. If the QoS deteriorates over time the system would be unable to detect and resolve the problem. Moreover, as the entities responsible for QoS management in IMS, in particular PCEF and PCRF, don't support neither class of services nor customer categories, no provision can be made with respect to class-related SLAs. The eTOM functional model together with the NGOSS QoS management framework proposes a working procedure for the Assurance functionality missing in the IMS. A new design is suggested, combining IMS QoS management with eTOM Assurance functionality.

5 Functional Architecture

A first step in this undertaking is to match IMS functionality with eTOM processes. The resulting set has furthermore to be enriched by eTOM processes relevant to Assurance. This broader set forms the basis to select the different SID entities necessary to carry out these processes. The SLA verification procedure as defined in the eTOM model requires the cooperation of several processes belonging to the Assurance column of the 'FAB' area, and spanning the three business layers: Customer, Resource, and Service.

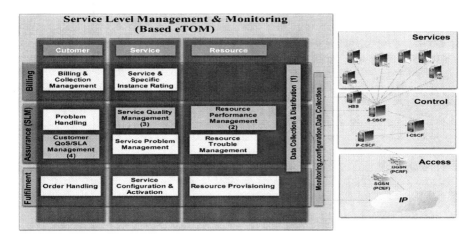

Fig. 1. Operating Processes in the SLA verification: (1) aggregation of information, (2) Extraction of KPIs related to service, (3) Mapping and calculating KQIs, (4) Comparison, estimation of QoS and SLA verification

These eTOM processes will be activated sequentially (Figure 1). The four processes belonging to the Assurance layer correspond to the monitoring aspect of this operation. In order to link the eTOM processes to the IMS network, a new component entitled *Monitoring, Configuration, Data Collection* is required, which clusters the core modules to communicate with these entities. The diversity of entities and their various communication protocols require multi-protocol components which can implement all the necessary monitoring operations. An additional constraint is that the performance data collection and detection of services should be executed in real time or near real.

6   SLA Verification Components

- **Resource Data Collection component:** This component is responsible for collecting performance indicators in communicating with the Monitoring, Configuration, and Data Collection module. The Process contains several secondary processes according to level 4 eTOM decomposition.
- **Resource Performance Management component:** The Resource Performance Management (RPM) component processes collected performance indicators; it provides XML (Extensible Markup Language) reports featuring a structured view of the KQIs as well as threshold detection.
- **Service Quality Management component:** This component performs a mapping of performance indicators; it identifies for each service its quality indicators before determining appropriate operations to be performed to calculate them.
- **Customer QoS/SLA Management component:** This component is responsible for the SLA verification. After the retrieval of quality indicators from the Service Quality Management component and receiving its preliminary report, it imports the client profile as well as SLA parameters to identify threshold levels for comparison purposes.

7   System Architecture

7.1   Centralized Architecture

The WSOA (Web Service Oriented Architecture) [6] appears as a valid choice for such a distributed system. The SOA concepts will allow implementing EJB-based [7] SOA modules supporting the processes of each component, exposing web services communications via SOAP [8] (Simple Object Access Protocol)/HTTP. Three SOA modules have been designed, each of which supporting a part of the targeted eTOM business processes and their associated SID entities. In addition, a BPEL (Business Process Execution Language) [9] component has been designed to orchestrate the various processes and to organize the desired operations.

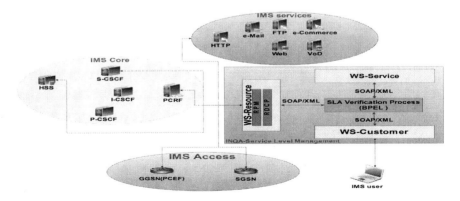

Fig. 2. Centralized Implementation Architecture

The three modules of the monitoring system are: *Resource Management, Service Quality, and Customer Management;* each one exposes a set of web services specified using WSDL (Web Services Description Language) [10]. These web services are invoked and synchronized by the central BPEL component that provides moreover tools such as a web interface that tracks the performance of the SLA verification processes and the monitoring of physical and logical network resources (Figure 2) [11].

7.2 Distributed Architecture

The proposed functional architecture supports three channels of communication between the different modules:

- TCP/IP between agents and Synchronization module,
- SOPA/XML between eTOM layer(Resource, Service, Customer),
- The possibility to use XML-Configuration between Synchronization module and managed entities in SLA violation case.

Figure 3 shows the functional architecture platform which consists of two main modules:

- *Assurance layer* represent the SLA verification process as defined in eTOM. In Assurance layer for each horizontal layer of the eTOM a module that allows the implementation of operations eTOM level higher (level 4) and also to explain the process of level 3 in the form of Web Service Module (Customer, Service). Also we define the synchronization modules and controls necessary for the detection of events in the network such as the provision of service and the timing of a side between the distributed modules (module synchronization) and between the web services exposed (orchestration module).

- *Monitoring Layer* is distributed contains a set of agents and probes are capable to retrieve all data in real-time (signalization, log, reservation, routers status, etc...) and implement all Resource processes layer the both process: *Resource Data Collection & processing* and *Resource Performance Management.*

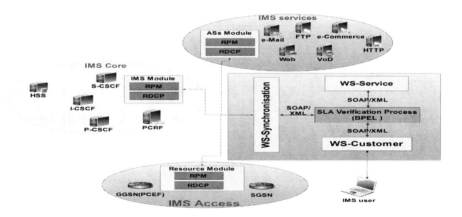

Fig. 3. Distributed Implementation Architecture

Distributed architecture allows the treatment and comparison of the parameters collection retrieved in real time from network entities, which differs from the centralized architecture, this gives intelligence to different entities and allows a real time management of data, and allows reduction of communication between the two layers assurance and monitoring.

8   Implementation and Results

The platform has been validated by performing practical cases of multimedia services (IPTV) in an IMS network.

The monitoring activity is triggered by the IMS agent detecting the launch of a service: the Assurance phase begins. Communication with the Application Server agent allows identification of customer parameters. The Router and the Customer agents are started in order to retrieve performance indicators.

Meanwhile, the BPEL engine starts the web services, in particular the *Resource Data Collection Processing* that will retrieve the KQIs via sockets from the *Customer* and *Router* agents. These values are forwarded to the *Resource Performance Management* web service via SOAP. This service generates a XML report that is transmitted to the *Service Quality Management* web service.

The latter performs the first step of stage 2 of eTOM's SLA verification procedure: KQI mapping. The results are forwarded to the *Customer QoS/SLA management* web service that retrieves the customer profile and compares the actual KQIs to threshold values to determine if the QoS matches the SLA.

8.1   Trial Infrastructure

The test bed is composed of a core router and two edge routers (Linux boxes) defining a DiffServ-enabled network on which are connected an IMS terminal ad an Application Server[12]; This network is controlled by the OpenIMS[13] system which is deployed in the core router Linux box. A management server supports the QoS monitoring/Assurance functionality (Fig 4).

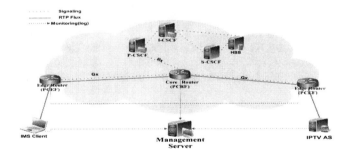

Fig. 4. Test bed infrastructure

8.2 Scenarios

Bob has registered in the IMS system with QoS classes Platinum and Gold respectively. The goal is to perform SLA Assurance tests in three representative cases and to compare the results:

- No or only few competing services (FTP)
- Significant load of competing services
- Maximum load of competing services up to bandwidth saturation

For the tree cases, we compare the results and response time of architecture: centralized and distributed.

8.3 Results

- *Case 1*: The QoS offered to Alice and Bob matches the SLA contract, perceived video quality is satisfying (Figure 5)

Fig. 5. Video bandwidth =128kbps, MOS-A = 4.75, MOS-V = 4.58

- *Case 2:* the network conditions, hence the video quality, deteriorate proportionally to the mass of competing services for lost packets and reduced flow rate (Figure 6).

Fig. 6. Video bandwidth =76kbps, MOS-A = 4,07 MOS-V = 3.0

- *Case 3:* competing services overload the routers: the queues fill in the gateways, impacting delay and jitter. Routers discard packets in excess, this causes static pixels in the video (Figure 7) and in some cases service cancellation.

Fig. 7. Video bandwidth =40kbps, MOS-A = 3,14, MOS-V = 1.17

The formulas for MOS audio and Video demonstrate their effectiveness to evaluate the perceptual quality of the service. The values for these indicators clearly are sensitive to the network load induced by competing services. Indeed the quality of the video in fig 5 is deemed well where the value exceeds the threshold 4.0 MOS-V when the quality of the video becomes critical (figure 6 and 7) MOS-V takes that reflects values.

9 Discussion

The platform succeeds in identifying accurately the deterioration of delivered services. The cost in terms of response time has been evaluated as well. It is observed that the response time for the Resource web service is much longer than for other web services, due to the complexity of its tasks [12].

The number of web services and their internal functionality has a considerable impact on the running time of the SLA verification. This led to limit the exposed eTOM processes to level 3 and to implement sub processes via internal java methods.

The execution time of the verification is composite; it depends on time checking for each web service. This time varies depending on the number of provided operations and the time of the audit. Thus, during the first operations of SLA verification we note that the time synchronization module (exceeds 500 ms) is large that reflecting the message exchange with the entities of controls to get the parameters of services. The number of Web services invoked by the BPEL has a significant impact on the execution time of the SLA verification process .This explains our choice to expose the processes of the eTOM level 3 all by implementing the sub-process via regular duties. Similarly, the nature of the communication technology between entities plays a vital role in reducing the complexity and verification time, which highlights the advantage of using TCP/IP for exchange of parameters service and transmission performance indicators to upper layers.

The response time of WS-Synchronization and other agents in resource is short compared to the WS-Resource (Fig 8), due of processing performed in each devise that offer an opportunity to reduce traffic between the Assurance and Monitoring layer, plus decreases the time response, further processing of flux parameter in entities level permit a real-time control of multiple QoS service but at the same time overloads the entity, e.g. a router must have sufficient memory to condition the traffic and use the control function as a treatment and comparison with the thresholds may reduce its capacity in terms of CPU and memory.

Fig. 8. Response time (ms) for centralized and disturbed architecture

Plus this disturbed architecture may alert Assurance layer in a very short time or almost quasi-real, and allowed speedy processing of SLA violations, compared with another architecture that has made several processing to detect the responsible entity.

10 Conclusion

The proposed approach leverages the 3GPP QoS provisioning architecture with eTOM Assurance features monitoring the delivered QoS in real time. The platform will act as proactive supervisor of the IMS network to monitor the network behavior, to correct and to anticipate degradations before failures occur at customer premises. The requirements are not only to produce, to manage and to send alarms based on events and thresholds in real time, but also to correlate network performance and the proposed root solution.

Using SOA concepts and BPEL in Assurance and monitoring functions bridges the conceptual gap between the eTOM model and the actual implementation. Its modularity and openness will moreover facilitate the design and deployment of future problem-solving, decision making modules. The system monitoring should provide proactive service assurance that include plus performance monitoring based root-cause correlation and service impact analysis, a capacity to automates problem resolution by using BPEL based a predefined steps and knowledge base. Therefore the system monitoring moves from a reactive to proactive system and ensure an enormous potential to offer new benefits and revenue for IMS network operators.

References

1. 3rd Generation Partnership Project; Evolution of policy control and charging (Release 7), 3GPP TR 23.803 V7.0.0 (September 2005)
2. Enhanced Telecom Operations Map (eTOM) The Business Process Framework for the Information and Communications Services Industry, Addendum D: Process Decompositions and Descriptions Release 6.0 GB921 D; TMF
3. Shared Information/Data (SID) Model, Addendum 2, Customer Business Entity Definitions, NGOSS Release 4.0, GB922 Addendum-2, TMF Approved Version 3.2 (August 2004)

4. SLA Management Handbook, Volume 4: Enterprise Perspective, TMF document reference GB917, Version 2.0, vol. 4. Open Group (October 2004)
5. Bellafkih, M., Raouyane, B., Errais, M., Ramdani, M.: MOS evaluation for VoD service in an IMS network. In: 2010 5th International Symposium on I/V Communications and Mobile Network (ISVC), September 30-October 2, pp. 1–4 (2010)
6. Hansen, M.D.: SOA Using Java Web Services. Prentice Hall PTR, Englewood Cliffs (2007)
7. EJB 3.0 Specification,
   `http://openejb.apache.org/3.0/ejb-30-specification.html`
8. Latest version of SOAP Version 1.2 specification, W3C Recommendation, 2nd edn. (April 27, 2007), `http://www.w3.org/TR/soap12`
9. Business Process Execution Language Version 2.0.Public Review Draft (August 23, 2006), `http://docs.oasis-open.org/wsbpel/2.0/`
10. Web Services Description Language (WSDL) Version 2.0, W3C Recommendation (June 26, 2007), `http://www.w3.org/TR/wsdl`
11. Raouyane, B., Errais, M., Bellafkih, M., Ranc, D.: SLA Management & Monitoring Based-eTOM and WS-Composite for IMS Networks. In: 2011 4th IFIP International Conference on New Technologies, Mobility and Security (NTMS), February 7-10, pp. 1–6 (2011)
12. Rouyane, B., Bellafkih, M., Ranc, D.: QoS Management in IMS: DiffServ Model. In: 2009 Third International Conference on Next Generation Mobile Applications, Services and Technologies, Cardiff, Wales, UK. IEEE Computer Society/ACM (2009)
13. Open IMS Core, `http://www.openimscore.org/`

Identifying Oligomeric Proteins Based on a Self-constructed Dataset

Tong Wang[1,*], Wenan Tan[1], and Lihua Hu[2]

[1] Institute of Computer and Information, Shanghai Second Polytechnic University,
Shanghai, 201209, China
tongwang0818@yahoo.cn
[2] School of Computer Science and Technology, Taiyuan University of Science and Technology,
Taiyuan, 030024, China

Abstract. Oligomeric proteins are very common in nature. They can be divided into two classes: homo-oligomers and hetero-oligomers. In this paper, a new method for the prediction of oligomeric protein types is proposed based on a self-constructed dataset. This stringent benchmark data set were screened strictly in which none of proteins has ≥60% pairwise sequence identity to any other in the same subset. DC (Dipeptide Composition) is used as sequence encoding scheme for the construction of decision system. A supervised linear DR (Dimensionality Reduction) algorithm, the so-called LDA (Linear Discriminant Analysis) is introduced to reduce the decision system, which can be used to classify new objects. The results thus obtained in predicting the types of oligomeric proteins are quite encouraging.

Keywords: oligomeric proteins, dipeptide composition, Linear Discriminant Analysis.

1 Introduction

Proteins are at the center of the action in biological processes, several proteins are a combination of two or more individual polypeptide chains. The arrangement according to which such subunits assemble is called the protein quaternary structure. Quaternary structure is the fourth levels of structural hierarchy of proteins. The other three structural hierarchies of proteins are: primary, secondary and tertiary. Primary structure is defined by the amino acid sequence. Secondary structure is the local spatial arrangement of a polypeptide's backbone, without regard for the conformations of its side-chains. Tertiary structure refers to the three-dimensional structure of an entire polypeptide. Quaternary structure refers to the non-covalent interaction of protein subunits to form oligomers. Oligomeric proteins are very common in nature. They can be divided further into two classes: homo-oligomers and hetero-oligomers. The former are composed of identical subunits while the latter are composed of non-identical subunits. Oligomeric structure can also vary through arrangement of subunits. Thus, in the protein universe, there are many different

---

* Corresponding author.

S. Lin and X. Huang (Eds.): CESM 2011, Part II, CCIS 176, pp. 144–148, 2011.

classes of subunit construction, such as monomer, homo-dimer, hetero-dimer, homo-trimer, hetero-trimer, homo-tetramer, hetero-tetramer, and so forth. Single subunit or polypeptide chain is called a monomer, two subunits a dimmer, three a trimer, four a tetramer etc. The homo-dimer, homo-trimer, homo-tetramer, hetero-tetramer and so on are all called homo-oligomers. Otherwise, they are called hetero-oligomers. The Oligomeric proteins have more advantages than the monomers in terms of functional evolution of biomacromolecules [1]. It is easier for multi-subunit proteins to repair their defects by simply replacing the flawed subunit. Moreover, in many biological processes the oligomeric proteins is an interesting field in bioinformatics.

Given an oligomeric protein, will it a homo-oligomer or a hetero-oligomer? Some efforts have been made in developing computational tools to predict types of oligomeric proteins from its sequence. To explore this problem, Garian [2] developed a method which used decision-tree models and a feature extraction approach (simple binning function) to successfully predict homodimers and nonhomodimers. Recently, Xiao et al. [3] introduced a 2-layer predictor to this problem.

In this study, we constructed a new data set in which all the protein samples annotated with ambiguous or uncertain terms were removed. Based on such a stringent data set, DC [4] is used as sequence encoding scheme for the construction of decision system. A supervised linear DR algorithm, the so-called LDA [5] is introduced to identify whether the given protein is a homo-oligomer or a hetero-oligomer.

2 Methods

2.1 Data Set

Protein sequences were taken from the latest UniProtKB(UniProt Knowledgebase) database. It can be accessed from the web at http://www.uniprot.org and downloaded from http://www.uniprot.org/database/download.shtml (UniProtKB Release 2011_03 (08-Mar-2011)). The detailed protein collected procedures are as follows. (1) Those annotated with "subunit" were extracted typing in "homo-dimer", "homo-trimer", "homo-tetramer", "homo-pentamer", 'homo-hexamer", "homo-heptamer", "homo-octamer", "homo-dodecamer", "hetero-dimer", "hetero-trimer", "hetero-tetramer", "heteropen-tamers", "hetero-hexamer", "hetero-heptamer", "hetero-octamer" or " hetero-dodecamer".

In order to collect as much desired information as possible and meanwhile ensure a high-quality for the benchmark dataset, the data were screened strictly according to the following criteria and order. (1) Sequences annotated with "fragment" were excluded; also, sequences with less than 50 amino acid residues were excluded because they might just be fragments. (2) Sequences annotated with ambiguous or uncertain terms, such as "potential", "probable", "probably", "maybe", or "by similarity", were removed for further consideration. (3) Those entries which annotated with more than one quaternary attribute were removed because of lacking uniqueness. (4) To reduce the homology bias, a redundancy cutoff was operated by the PISCES program to winnow those sequences which have >60% sequence identity to any other in a same oligomeric protein type. Finally, we obtained a dataset containing 4869 sequences of which 3468 to homo-oligomers, and 1401 to hetero-oligomers.

2.2 Dipeptide Composition

DC can be considered as a representative form of proteins incorporating sequence neighborhood information. This method extracts and computes the occurrences of two consecutive residues from a sequence string. Therefore, a fixed pattern length obtained is 400-D (dimensional) vector. It can be calculated by Eq.1.

$$\text{Fraction of dipeptide(i)} = \frac{\text{total number of dipeptide(i)}}{\text{total number of all possible dipeptides}} \tag{1}$$

2.3 LDA

LDA attempts to maximize the linear separability between datapoints belonging to different classes. In contrast to most other dimensionality reduction techniques, LDA is a supervised technique[5]. LDA finds a linear mapping M that maximizes the linear class separability in the low-dimensional representation of the data. The criteria that are used to formulate linear class separability in LDA are the within-class scatter S_W and the between-class scatter S_B, which are defined as:

$$S_W = \sum_c p_c \operatorname*{cov}_{X^c - \bar{X}^c} \tag{2}$$

$$S_B = \operatorname*{cov}_{X - \bar{X}} - S_W \tag{3}$$

where p_c is the class prior of class label c, $\operatorname{cov}_{X^c - \bar{X}^c}$ is the covariance matrix of the zero mean datapoints x_i assigned to class $c \in C$, and $\operatorname{cov}_{X - \bar{X}}$ is the covariance matrix of the zero mean data X. LDA optimizes the ratio between the within-class scatter S_W and the between-class scatter S_B in the low-dimensional representation of the data, by finding a linear mapping M that maximizes the so-called Fisher criterion

$$\phi(M) = \frac{\left| M^T S_B M \right|}{\left| M^T S_W M \right|} \tag{4}$$

This maximization can be performed by computing the d principal eigenvectors of $S_W^{-1} S_B$. The low-dimensional data representation Y of the datapoints in X can be computed by mapping them onto the linear basis M, i.e., $Y = (X - \bar{X})M$.

3 Experimental Results

The accuracy of the low dimensional representations of the high dimensional data obtained by the LDA method was evaluated via KNN algorithm. Accordingly, the jackknife test has been increasingly and widely adopted by investigators to test the power of various predictors. Therefore, in this study, jackknife test was performed with the current approach in predicting the types of oligomeric proteins.

Comparison results of original high dimensional vector and dimension-reduced vector generated by LDA are listed in Table 1. As shown in Table 1, the overall jackknife success rates obtained by the LDA method in identifying the types of oligomeric proteins are higher than the ones obtained without using the LDA.

Table 1. Success rates in identifying the types of oligomeric proteins by the jackknife test

Method	Input form	Test method (%)
		Jackknife
K-NN(K=1)	Original vector	$\dfrac{3416}{4869} = 70.16$
LDA& K-NN (K=1)	Dimension-reduced vector by LDA	$\dfrac{3918}{4869} = 80.47$

Table 2. The jackknife success rates for each of the 2 oligomeric proteins

Types of oligomeric proteins	Original vector (%)	Dimension-reduced vector by LDA (%)
Homo-oligomer	$\dfrac{2575}{3468} = 74.25$	$\dfrac{2919}{3468} = 84.17$
Hetero-oligomer	$\dfrac{841}{1401} = 60.03$	$\dfrac{999}{1401} = 71.31$
Overall	$\dfrac{3416}{4869} = 70.16$	$\dfrac{3918}{4869} = 80.47$

The detailed jackknife success rates of original high dimensional vector and dimension-reduced vector extracted by LDA method for each of the two oligomeric proteins are shown in Table 2. All these indicate that the LDA method is indeed very useful in dealing with the complicated biological problem of predicting the types of oligomeric proteins.

4   Conclusions

In this paper, we constructed a new data set. Based on such a stringent data set, DC is used as sequence encoding scheme for representing the protein sequence. We apply the LDA algorithm to discriminate the types of oligomeric proteins. The results obtained are encouraging, which are higher than the ones obtained without LDA method.

Acknowledgments. This work was supported by shanghai university scientific selection and cultivation for outstanding young teachers in special fund (EGD10003) and This work was supported by Chenguang Program of Shanghai Municipal Education Commission (10CG61).

References

1. Price, N.C.: Assembly of multi-subunit structures. In: Pain, R.H. (ed.) Mechanisms of Protein Folding, pp. 160–193. Oxford University Press, New York (1994)
2. Garian, R.: Prediction of quaternary structure from primary structure. Bioinformatics 17, 551–556 (2001)
3. Xiao, X., Wang, P., Chou, K.C.: Quat-2L: a web-server for predicting protein quaternary structural attributes. Molecular Diversity (2010) (in press)
4. Lin, H., Li, Q.Z.: Using pseudo amino acid composition to predict protein structural class: approached by incorporating 400 dipeptide components. J. Comput. Chem. 28, 1463–1466 (2007)
5. v. d. Maaten, L.J.P., Postma, E.O., v.d. Herik, H.J.: Dimensionality Reduction: A Comparative Review (2007)

The Effect of IT Capability on Firm Performance

Ping Fan

School of Information Engineer, East China Jiaotong University,
Nanchang, China
fp_ecjtu@163.com

Abstract. In the recent years, the dynamic capability view has become topical in
IS field to model the relationship between IT investments and company results.
The paper try to propose the indirect impact mechanism of IT capability on firm
performance from dynamic capability view, and test empirically the relationship
of IT capability, dynamic capability and firm performance. Based on data from
China, the research finds that IT capability impact firm performance via dynamic
capability and IT capability impacts dynamic capability significantly, is the key
antecedent of dynamic capability building. Some suggestions for the future study
related to the IT business value research from dynamic capability view are also
included in the last section.

Keywords: IT capability, Dynamic capability, firm performance.

1 Introduction

One of the principal topics in the IS field has been the relationship between the use of
IT and firm competitiveness. The resource based theory become topical in the IS
research. But the increase in uncertain and competitive markets has made the concepts
of dynamic capability receive much attention recently (Eisenhardt and Martin 2000,
Teece et al. 1997). The conventional wisdom is that IT is necessary for business
survival and that prudent deployment and management of IT capabilities leads to
enhanced value for the firm. However, for many firms, existing IT assets and
capabilities pose a serious impediment to strategic agility in turbulent environments,
while other recent work illustrates that IT capability can enable a firm's strategic
abilities to respond to changes in the competitive marketplace (Sambamurthy 2000,
Weill et al.2002). If indeed dynamic capability have become critical imperatives for
businesses, then a critical question for IS researchers and practitioners is what can be
done to better position IT capability to enable dynamic capability and require better
firm performance?

In this paper, we draw from the dynamic capability view to examine the indirect
impact of IT capabilities on firm performance. The purpose of this study is to advance
understanding of the relationships among IT capability, dynamic capability, and firm
performance. The paper is structured as follow: Literature is reviewed to build the
rationale for our research model. Research framework and hypotheses is brought out in
the third section. The research method including data collection and data analysis is
discussed in the following section. This is followed by the study conclusions and
directions for future research in the last section.

S. Lin and X. Huang (Eds.): CESM 2011, Part II, CCIS 176, pp. 149–154, 2011.
© Springer-Verlag Berlin Heidelberg 2011

2 Literature Review

2.1 Dynamic Capability

The dynamic capabilities perspective, a theoretical extension of the RBV, combines ideas from resource-based theory and evolutionary economics theory to explore the source of competitive advantage in rapidly changing environments (Teece et al.1997, Barney 2001). Dynamic capability can be defined as the firm's ability to integrate, build, and reconfigure internal and external competences to address rapidly changing environment. Dynamic capabilities develop from the firm's assets, evolutionary path, and managerial routines (Teece et al. 1997, Zello and Winter 2002). Whereas the firm's asset positions and its evolutionary path impact competitive advantage, its organizational processes transform the capabilities of the firm over time (Teece et al. 1997). Dynamic capabilities thus are viewed as the organizational and strategic routines by which firms achieve new resource configuration as markets emerge, collide, split, evolve, and die. Dynamic capability consists of organizational and managerial processes with three roles: coordination /integration; learning; and reconfiguration (Teece et al.1997). Coordination/ integration refers to the process by which firms efficiently and effectively integrate internal and external resources and competences. Learning refers to the process by which repetition and experimentation enable tasks to be performed better and better. Reconfiguration refers to the ability to sense the need to reorganize the firm's asset structure, and accomplish the necessary internal and external transformation.

2.2 IT Capability

Following the resource-based perspective, several scholars provide the definitions of IT capability. Bharadwaj (2000) defined IT capability as "a firm's ability to mobilize and deploy IT-based resources in combination or copresent with other resources and capabilities." Sambamurthy et al. (2003) defined IT capability as "the organizational base of IT resources and capabilities and describes a firm's capacity for IT-based innovation by virtue of the available IT resources and the ability to convert services into strategic applications." From this point of view, a firm was successful not because it implemented a leading-edge IT application, but because it has developed a capability for applying IT to changing business opportunities.

Previously thought to be a single dimension concept, researchers now increasingly argue that IT capability is a multidimensional concept (Santhanam and Hartono 2003). Bharadwaj (2000) divides IT-based resources into three categories: IT infrastructure, human IT, and IT-enabled intangibles. Sambamurthy et al. (2003) suggest that IT capability includes four dimension: the level of IT investments, the quality of the IT infrastructure, IT human capital, and the nature of IS/business partnerships. Ganesh and Varun (2005) divides IT capability into three dimensions: IT infrastructure, IT management competence, relation infrastructure. According to the research above, It seems that IT capability not only encompasses the tangible and intangible elements of IT capability, but also introduces the business operations and IT leverage.

3   Research Framework and Hypotheses

Based on the literature reviewed in the previous section, a research framework is presented and depicted in Fig.1. In this framework, we attempt to provide an integrated model that explicitly links IT capability and dynamic capability to firm performance. Some evidence from literature is further presented to elucidate these hypotheses among various constructs, such as IT capability and dynamic capability, IT capability and firm performance, dynamic capability and firm performance.

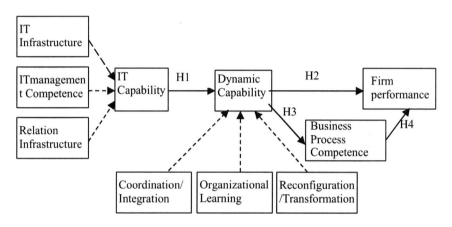

Fig. 1. Research Framework

3.1   IT Capability and Dynamic Capability

Recently, there is a focus on building dynamic capabilities by leveraging IT. For instance, Sambamurthy et al. (2003) view IT as a platform for building new innovative resource combinations. Straub and Watson (2001) argue that IT-enabled organizations are more agile and capable of competing in turbulent environments. There is also empirical evidence that firms can use IT to enable change. Hence, we propose the following hypothesis 1:

Hypothesis 1: IT capability positively influences dynamic capabilities.

3.2   Dynamic Capability and Firm Performance

Because of the complexity, causal ambiguity, and path dependence of dynamic capability, dynamic capabilities have the potential to be a source of competitive advantage. Many studies demonstrated a positive relationship between dynamic capabilities and organizational performance. For example, Danneels (2002) found that dynamic capabilities improve firm performance. Zott (2003) found that dynamic capabilities can generate significant firm performance. Hence, we propose the following hypothesis2:

Hypothesis 2: Dynamic capability is positively associated with organizational performance.

3.3 Dynamic Capability and Business Process Competence

The true value of dynamic capabilities lies in quickly and efficiently replacing ineffective configurations of business process competencies and architecting more promising ones that better match the environment (Eisenhardt and Martin 2000). Dynamic capabilities can be used in various ways to enable the adaptation process to the environment. Hence, we propose the following hypothesis 3:

Hypothesis 3: Dynamic capability is positively associated with business process competence.

3.4 Business Process Competence and Firm Performance

Superior business process competencies can serve as the basis for competitive advantage (Clark and Fujimoto 1991, Danneels 2002, Krishnan and Ulrich 2001). On the other hand, outdated or inept business process competencies (termed 'rigidities') (Leonard-Barton 1992) would result in poorer process efficiency and product effectiveness, and therefore inferior firm performance. Hence, we propose the following hypothesis4:

Hypothesis 4: Business process competence is positively associated with firm performance.

4 Method

4.1 Data Collection

A survey design was used for this study and questionnaires were sent to 300 top or senior IT executives (CIO, vice president of IT, director of IT) in a variety of industries randomly when a IT application meeting is held in shanghai in 2009. A total of 178 usable responses were received, resulting a response rate of about 60 percent. We conducted a Chi-square test to determine whether responses varied by the industry and their revenues. No significant differences in Chi-square at the .05 level were noted, which suggests that perceptual measures are unbiased by variations in the industry and their revenues.

4.2 Operationalization of Measures

According to the literature review in the section 2, IT capability is a second-order construct which include three first-order construct: IT infrastructure, IT management competence, relation infrastructure. Dynamic capability is also defined as a second-order construct generated from a set of specific variables measuring coordination/integration, organizational learning; and reconfiguration/ transformation. Firm performance is a first-order construct which measure financial indicators of the firm. Business process competence is a first-order construct too, which measure the efficient and effective of business process.

4.3 Reliability Analysis and Convergent Validity

Cronbach's alpha, composite reliability, and the average variance extracted were computed to assess the internal consistency of each dimension. The results show that all

Cronbach's alpha and composite reliabilities exceeded Nunnally's (1978) criterion of 0.7 while the average variances extracted for these constructs were above the recommended 0.5 (Hair et al. 1998).

Convergent validity ensures that all items measure a single underlying construct (Bogozzi and Fornell 1982). To test the convergent validity, we performed confirmatory factor analyses of the eight multiple- items constructs using LISREL 8.7. A high value of composite reliability, ranging from .724 to .902, suggests the convergent validity of the constructs. The model fit indices also provide adequate evidence of the unidimensionality of the items.

4.4 Testing the Structural Models

Having demonstrated that our measures possessed adequate validity and reliability, we then proceeded to test hypotheses in a structural equation model. Fig.2 shows the standardized loadings of the items on each construct, as well as the path loadings between constructs. The overall model fit (RMSEA =0.049, CFI=0.962, AGF=0.912 and χ2/d.f.=2.872) shows that our structural model has good model validity according to the heuristics for statistical conclusion validity (Gefen et al 2000).Therefore, the model is acceptable. The hypotheses that we proposed have been proved for the results show that all the hypotheses are supported at the P<0.001level.

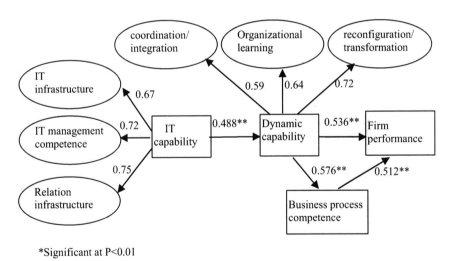

*Significant at P<0.01

Fig. 2. SEM Analysis Result

5 Discussions and Conclusions

During the past years, the competitive environment prompted most corporations to reexamine their strategic logic and the role of information technologies in shaping their business strategies. Many firms begin to share a common understanding that IT play a fundamental role in their ability to enhance their business performance through dynamic capabilities (Sambamurthy et al.2003, Palvou 2004). Therefore, the goal of the paper is to develop a theoretical perspective for understanding the connections among IT capability, dynamic capability and firm performance. The paper construct a theory framework that describes IT capability can enhance dynamic capability which can improve firm performance. Based on empirical investigation, our results show that dynamic capability plays a mediating role in the relationship between IT capability and firm performance, IT capability impacts indirectly firm performance from upgrading organization dynamic capability, IT capability impacts dynamic capability significantly, is the key antecedent of dynamic capability building.

Although this study provided a profound theoretical foundation for investigating the value of IT and a thoroughly empirical data analysis, there is still more work to do in the future. First, we could adopt qualitative methods such as case study to strengthen the potential for greater generalizability of the research findings. Second, since we examined IT capability and dynamic capability with cross-sectional data, we do not examine the long-term role of IT-enabled dynamic capability. Longitudinal research is needed to trace the dynamics of business activities over time. In conclusion, this study provides not only a profound theoretical foundation for investigating the value of IT but also examines these empirical findings in a way which might help companies make wise decisions about IT adoption and use.

Acknowledgments. The research was supported by the National Natural Science Foundation of China under Grant 70761003.

References

1. Bharadwaj, A.: A Resource-Based Perspective on Information Technology Capability and Firm Performance: An Empirical Investigation. MIS Quarterly 24(1), 169–196 (2000)
2. Bhatt, G.D., Grover, V.: Types of Information Technology Capability and Their Role in Competitive Advantage: An Empirical Study. Journal of Management Information Systems 22(2), 253–277 (2005)
3. Danneels, E.: The Dynamic of Product Innovation and Firm Competences. Strategic Management Journal 23(9), 1095–1121 (2002)
4. Eisenhardt, K., Martin, J.: Dynamic Capability: What are they? Strategic Management Journal 21, 1105–1121 (2000)
5. Grant, R.M.: The resource-based theory of competitive advantage: Implications for strategy formulation. California Management Review 33(3), 114–135 (1991)
6. Helfat, C.E., Peteraf, M.A.: The Dynamic Resource-Based View: Capability Lifecycles. Strategic Management Journal 24, 997–1010 (2003)
7. Keen, P.G.W.: Shaping the Future: Business Design through Information Technology. Harvard Business School Press, Boston (1991)

The Development and Deployment of a Computer Network Laboratory Education Service Platform

Chenyang Yan

Ningbo City College of Vocational Technology, Faculty of Computer, Xuefu Road. 9,
315200 Ningbo, China
yanchenyang@nbcc.cn

Abstract. In Computer Network courses, it is necessary to provide a proper laboratory where instructors or learners could carry out hands-on pedagogical activities associated with the lectures. However, pedagogical experience in a traditional physical lab often suffered from shortage of network devices, poor lab maintenance and restrictions imposed on practical procedure to prevent potential dangerous operations. With this constraint comes the need for more flexible lab architecture. This paper explores using open source Cloud Computing technologies to build a Computer networks Laboratory Education Service Platform (CLESP) that provides an entire virtual computer networks practical environment with uniformed deployment and management as an online service to learners and instructors. The effectiveness of the system has been investigated by introducing a student survey. The survey results indicated that students had a favorable view of the CLESP and regarded it as a useful learning tool.

Keywords: computer network education, cloud computing, Xen Cloud Platform, virtual laboratory.

1 Introduction

Practical experience through lab work has long been recognized as an important part of the computer network education. Equipment is one of the most important and crucial factors in the computer network laboratory practice. A successful computer network practical course requires not only a well-designed class but also a full range of facilities with necessary maintenance. Unfortunately, it is not easy to achieve this objective due to shortage of network devices, poor lab maintenance and restrictions imposed on practical procedure to prevent potential dangerous operations.

We are aimed at creating a versatile "virtual computer network lab" where every student is provided root access to an entire network of virtual machines, created for their use in the computer network course.

The rest of the paper is organized as follows: Section 2 provides brief background information and presents description of related work in the field of virtual labs for ICT/IT courses and section 3 presents the core technologies used in CLESP and the architecture of a prototype system. Next, we analyze and discuss the technical advantages/disadvantages which CLESP provided, and their pedagogical influence in Section 4. Finally, we conclude and give an outlook on future work in Section 5.

S. Lin and X. Huang (Eds.): CESM 2011, Part II, CCIS 176, pp. 155–160, 2011.
© Springer-Verlag Berlin Heidelberg 2011

2 Background and Related Work

There are several ways to utilize virtualization in teaching ICT/IT disciplines; in fact, this subject has been studied since the 80s [1]. However, the recent advances in virtualization technology [2] explain the growing interest on using it as an important teaching aid in the ICT/IT courses. There is large amount of literature about the implementations of virtual lab for various ICT/IT disciplines [3, 4, 6, 7]. In this regard, two conventional approaches to organize a virtual lab have been investigated.

The Type I virtual lab [3,4] just requires ordinary PCs connected by a LAN. Each PC would have locally installed several desktop virtual machine monitor, like UML[5] or VMware Workstation. Such a system could be configured to allow the students treat the virtual hosts as real machines or even setup simple LANs. This approach is more inexpensive and easier to implement at the expense of its flexibility and scalability. For example, when deploying longer or incremental experiments, the student still need the exclusive access to the same computer in which she started it. Also, this system is harder to maintain and almost impossible to operate remotely. The Type II virtual lab [6,7] demands much more computing and storage resources and industry standard machine monitors are deployed in central servers, accessible to the students through the network. Although the specific functions can be very different according to its architecture and implementation, this approach generally provides a remote access interface and a centralized management unit. Students will be able to perform their practical work remotely and the teachers/administrators also can prepare the experiment or maintain the lab facility remotely.

3 Architecture

3.1 Overview of CLESP

Our approach, CLESP, can be basically classified as the Type II virtual lab but more advance. It is accomplished through the use of the Xen Cloud Platform (XCP) [8] to provide the core functionality. CLESP leverages the power of virtualization to implement a cloud computer networks lab infrastructure, which can offer the entire experiment environment as an online laboratory service to both on-campus and off-campus students.

For example, students can use the web-based interface to connect to the CLESP to apply to the teachers/administrators for virtual devices and networks they consider necessary for their practical work. After the application is approved, students will be able to login the CLESP and work freely with full control over the virtual resources they applied. CLESP also enables teachers to predefine and generate an entire configured computer networks and ask the students to observe the network behavior or verify/troubleshoot the settings of the devices included in these networks.

CLESP consist of several components that work together to deliver the whole computer network laboratory platform to the users: Xen Cloud Platform (XCP), OpenXenManager (OXM), experiment workflow Engine (EWE), hosts/virtual network devices based on VMs and hardware. Figure 1 below shows the basic architecture of CLESP.

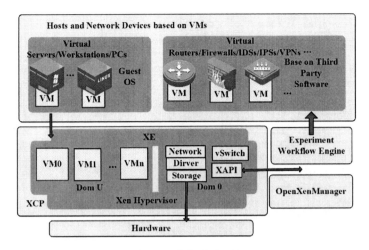

Fig. 1. Current CNLSP Architecture

3.2 XCP

XCP is the foundation of CLESP. The CLESP use the XCP to provide the virtualization functionality. XCP consists of Xen Hypervisor, Dom0 privileged domain including support for network, storage and drivers, XE command line, XAPI and XAPI Lib [8]. Xen Hypervisor virtualizes and aggregates the underlying physical hardware resources across multiple systems and provides pools of virtual infrastructure to users. Dom0 Linux kernel includes drivers, rich virtual networking capabilities via Open vSwitch and support for cloud storage infrastructures. XE command line tool offers an interface to control Xen virtual machines and resource pools. XAPI and XAPI Lib provide a program interface for configuring and controlling Xen-enabled hosts, resource pools and co-ordinates resources within the pool.

3.3 OXM

OXM, which is part of the open source XenseMaking project (http://www. xensemaking.com/), is a client application to connect to the XCP Host through the network. The OXM provides a primary GUI interface for basic virtual machine management and configuration as well as a console access to virtual machines. To improve the usability of CLESP, the XE command line interface in XCP was replaced with OXM. This simplifies the Xen administrative tasks by eliminating the need to learn the underlying command syntax.

3.4 EWE

To simplify the design, creation and administration of the virtual networks in teaching/practicing, a custom middleware called EWE was developed to simplify necessary tasks and manage the lifecycle of practical assignments. EWE is a simple Python workflow engine server based on XenAPI. It was developed by Faculty of Department of Computer Science at Ningbo City College and has been released under the GNU GPL. EWE is required to be deployed on Linux and work with the support of Mysql. Combined with OXM, teachers can access to EWE to prepare experiments, assign tasks, examine experiment results and give feedback to students through web browser. Students also can access to EWE to apply for practical resource, accept tasks, submit results and get feedbacks.

3.5 Hardware

According to the tests, given the hardware shown in Table 1, CLESP will support 120 VMs in normal circumstances. Under extreme conditions, CLESP can even provide 220-240 VMs simultaneously by decreasing the performance of VMs. This number of hosts would be impractical in a dedicated physical lab. Therefore, without virtualization, the experiment described in Section 4 of this paper could not be assigned in anything but the smallest of classes.

Table 1. CLESP hardware and their usage

Hardware	Usage
Dell PowerEdge R710 2U Rack Server (Quad-core Intel Xeon/16GB Memory/Intel PRO/1000 VT Quad Port Server Adapter/2TB hard drive space with integrated RAID controller) × 2	Deploy XCP 1.0
PC(AMD AthlonII/4GB Memory/Gigabits Ethernet NIC)×1	Deploy EWE Server and its Database (Mysql) / Apache HTTP Server 2.0
Cisco Catalyst 2960S × 1	Connect XCP Servers / EWE Server to the Campus LAN

4 Survey Results

The potential of the CLESP was demonstrated with the implementation of a prototype system that hosted VMs and experiment network infrastructure for 2 classes, total 76 students, for an entire semester. Students provided their feedback and comments on the survey at the end of semester.

The survey was conducted with students at the Department of Computer Science at Ningbo City College in the spring semester of 2010. The questionnaires were intended gauge the students' attitudes toward CLESP. Students received a paper-based questionnaire at the end of the semester. 76 sophomore students participated in the study. Very high response rates (> 97%) were achieved for student feedback. The possible responses to the survey could be agree, neutral or disagree. The questionnaire is listed below:

(1) CLESP can increase your CN practical exercise time. (2) CLESP can help you deepen your understanding of the new concepts. (3) CLESP can make the CN experiments more open and flexible. (4) You NEVER fail to connect to the CLESP. (5) You NEVER feel the reaction speed of CLESP is unacceptable and imposes negative effect on your experiment procedure. (6) You NEVER failed to deploy your experiment due to unfriendly user interface. (7) You NEVER feel that the virtual infrastructures offered by CLESP are different with the physical ones in their

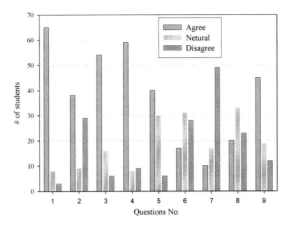

Fig. 2. Students' opinion on CNLSP, total number of attendances is 76 and total number of valid responds is 75

functionality or operability. (8) You NEVER feel that the CLESP is too complex and makes you confused about your experiment procedure. (9) You enjoy using CLESP in your CN class. (10) Please write down your suggestion on how to improve the CLESP.

As can be seen from the survey results, the overall experience is favorable with students and many students consider it convenient and valuable learning environment (question 9). A majority of students believed that the CLESP can improve their experiment experience (question 1, 2 and 3) and provide reliable and stable service as well (question 4 and 5). However, there are still a significant number of students hold an unfavorable attitude toward the functionality, operability and usability of CLESP (question 6, 7 and 8). 25 of the 76 students gave their suggestions. Of these suggestions, 20 requested to improve the operability of CLESP, especially the unfriendly interface of EWE. 22 complained about the different functionality and behavior between virtual devices provided by CLESP and physical devices. 4 considered the practical assignment workflow was confusing, 2 off-campus students indicated that the VPN service was unstable.

5 Conclusion and Future Works

In this paper, we presented our approach toward building a Computer Networks Laboratory Service Platform (CLESP) where students can freely practice on designing, configuring, and troubleshooting a network scenario. First, it outlined the architecture as well as main components of CLESP, which was created to provide a virtual lab environment for education in the areas of computer networks. It is a flexible learning environment that is simple to use and is equally accessible by on- and off-campus students. Second, we also presented a practical assignment workflow on CLESP for reference, and discussed a typical assignment that can be given using the CLESP but would be difficult to conduct in a physical lab. In addition, we presented the results of a student survey that indicates a favorable view of the platform as a convenient tool for learning. Given the feedback on how to improve the CLESP, future work will develop a friendly user interface for EWE, and consider providing pre-defined practical scenario "template library".

Acknowledgments. This material is based in part upon work supported by the Scientific Research Fund of Ningbo City College of Vocational Technology (SRFNCC), Grant No. ZWX10094.

References

1. Donaldson, J.: Teaching operating systems in a virtual machine environment. In: 18th SIGCSE Technical Symposium on Computer Science Education (1987)
2. Li, Y., Li, W., Jiang, C.: A Survey of Virtual Machine System: Current Technology and Future Trends, Electronic Commerce and Security, International Symposium. In: 2010 Third International Symposium on Electronic Commerce and Security, pp. 332–336. IEEE Press, New York (2010)
3. Armitage, G.: Maximizing student exposure to networking using FreeBSD virtual hosts. ACM SIGCOMM Computer Communications Review 33(3), 48–57 (2003)
4. Balamuralithara, B., Woods, P.C.: Virtual laboratories in engineering education: The simulation lab and remote lab. Computer Applications in Engineering Education 17, 108–118 (2009)
5. Dike, J.: A user-mode port of the Linux kernel. In: Proceedings of the 4th Annual Linux Showcase and Conference (2000)
6. Border, C.: The development and deployment of a multi-user, remote access virtualization system for networking, security, and system administration classes. In: 38th SIGCSE Technical Symposium on Computer Science Education, pp. 576–580. ACM, New York (2007)
7. Wannous, M., Nakanom, H.: NVLab, a Networking Virtual Web-Based Laboratory that Implements Virtualization and Virtual Network Computing Technologies. IEEE Transactions on Learning Technologies 3, 129–138 (2010)
8. Xen Cloud Platform, http://www.xen.org/products/cloudxen.html

Obscene Picture Identification Based on Wavelet Transform and Support Vector Machine

Chun Liu[*], Changsheng Xie, Guangxi Zhu, and Qingdong Wang

Dep. of computer science, HUST, Dep. of optoelectronic storage, WNLO
Wuhan Hubei, P.R. China
chun_liu@tom.com

Abstract. An obscene picture detection algorithm is presented based on wavelet transform and SVM. The algorithm combines the pre-process including quickly color space transform, skin color detection, and texture detection, then a Haar wavelet transform of pictures is performed to decrease the dimension. The LL dataset is input to SVM and classify according to the eigenvector trained and built by given samples. The test results show that the system not only achieves high detection rate, but also reduces the computational complexity, has practice ability to be applied in embedded platform.

Keywords: image detection, wavelet transform, support vector machine.

1 Introduction

The high profits of sex industry and the interconnectivity, opening of internet, large numbers of sex information and erotica videos had already seriously interfered the normal network living, harmed the teenager's mind and the body's health. Accompany with overall transition of digital TV in more and more countries, and the internet function integrated in the STB devices, the sex videos or pictures used almost only appeared in PC domain have penetrated to and appeared at home public domain like lobby. So constructing identification and filter technology based on embedded platform had became a kind of strong requirement.

The difficulty in such application is compromise between accuracy and response time. Hung Chih Lai, and Junguk Cho etc [1][2][3] had presented a SOC chipset architecture based on FPGA used to face detection. They analyzed and trained the face feature with Haar wavelet and ANN (Artificial Neural Network) algorithm, and accelerate the computation with pipeline and parallel process. The realtime performance reached to 625frame/s. While Zhang [4] also utilized the wavelet and SVM (Support Vector Machines) to analyze face feature. But compared to face recognition, if there includes sex content in a picture is a high-level semantic characteristic, moreover because of the indeterminacy of object size and complexity of picture's background, it's very hard to filter the picture or video in short time. So the key to identifying sex picture is to decrease the gap between high-level semantic characteristic and low-level vision characteristic, in an other word, it's much easy to convert the identification to judge if there includes specific sexual organs in a picture.

---

[*] Corresponding author.

S. Lin and X. Huang (Eds.): CESM 2011, Part II, CCIS 176, pp. 161–166, 2011.

In this paper we transition the key frame of a video with Haar wavelet, and then classify with the eigenvector of SVM based on the trained specific sex organ's samples, combined with fast algorithms of skin detection and texture detection, and time-sharing identifying strategy of different sex organs, we can catch the optimum effect between detection effective and time.

2   Sex Video Detection Based on Wavelet Transform and SVM

2.1   Key Frame Pick Up and Pre-process

To meet the run-time claim before the video output to screen a key frame need to be picked up and pre-process, including color space transforming, skin detection and texture detection, then a gray scalar graphic of skin area is building to perform the Haar wavelet transforming and SVM analysis.

The aim of picking up key frame is to convert the analysis of motion video to static picture. The fastest strategy to decrease system load and accelerate detection in embedded SOC decoder is to pick up I frame of input video every 1 second or 0.5s on

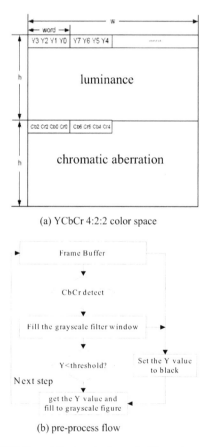

(a) YCbCr 4:2:2 color space

(b) pre-process flow

Fig. 1. The YCbCr architecture in frame buffer and pre-process flow

time. At the same time skin detection model based on color range is also the fastest method currently. Because of the scuro feature of sex organs, in this paper we present a restricted color space as: $C_r \in$ [140; 183] and $C_b \in$ [86: 117]. All pixels fall into this rectangle area are seen as skin pixels. Furthermore we apply a gray scalar filter window with 20 pixels width to detect texture, whose essence is first order gray level statistic method which compares the gray level value of current pixel and statistic gray level value of area or window, then judges if current pixel and around area have smooth-skined feature. It can decrease the probability of false detection if deleting those pixels whose gray level value is low than the threshold of texture model.

So combined with YUV color space used in output frame buffer of current video decoder, a flow is shown as Figure 1 to finish the all pre-process actions and build gray level graphic in one-time scanning.

After transforming an 2D image with wavelet, it results in 4 different frequency bands: LL, LH, HL, HH, each has only 1/4 size of original image size[5]. LL brings the original content information; the energy of entire image is concentred on these frequency bands. HL band bring the high frequency edge information at horizontal direction, LH keep the high frequency edge information at vertical direction, and HH keep the high frequency edge information at diagonal direction. In this paper we collect mammiferous pictures with different directions and different poses and transform them to 82×82 pixels size, and then they were delete edge and corner pixel to decrease noise, form an 80 dimensions vector as an input train vector of support vector machine introduced later. Figure 2(a) shows the mammiferous pictures and 2(b) shows the effect after Haar wavelet transform.

(a) sample gray level mammiferous pictures

(b)The LL sub picture after Haar wavelet transform

Fig. 2. The sample picture and LL sub picture

After trained, the test picture are also transformed by Haar wavelet transform with Mallat fast algorithm, and then the LL sub-picture are input to SVM and perform detection. The Mallat algorithm filter the input signals with a series decompose low-pass filter H and high-pass filter G, then down sample every other sample from output set to realize the wavelet transform.

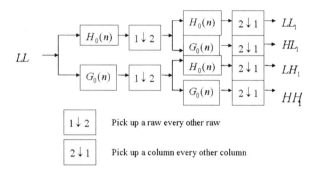

Fig. 3. The two dimension wavelet decompose process. $H_0(n)$ and $G_0(n)$ are low-pass filter and high-pass filter respectively.

2.2 Support Vector Machine

SVM is a statistic learning method presented by Vapnik and based on SRM (Structural Risk Minimization principle), has special advantages when solve the recognition problems at small samples, non-linear and high dimension conditions[6].

Assumed that a train sample set with given size l is $\{(x_i, y_i), i=1,2,...,l\}$, and composed by 2 classes. If $x_i \in R^N$ belongs to the first class, and marked as $+(y_i=1)$; If $x_i \in R^N$ belongs to the second class, then marked as $-(y_i=-1)$. If the train sample set is linear separable, then a classify hyperplane $w \cdot x_i + b = 0$ exists and makes:

$$y_i (w \cdot x_i + b) \geq 1, \quad i = 1, 2, \cdots, l \tag{1}$$

in which $w \in R^N$. From the statistics for machine learning theory, if all samples can be correctly separated by hyperplane, and the distance from the nearest sample to hyperplane is the longest, then the hyperplane is the optimum hyperplane, and the classic distance is $2/\|w\|$. So to maximize the classic distance is equivalent to minimize $\|w\|^2/2$, thus the solution to optimum hyperplane is converted to quadratic programming problem like equation (2):

$$\min_{w,b} \frac{1}{2} \|w\|^2, \tag{2}$$

$$s.t.: y_i (w \cdot x_i + b) \geq 1, \quad i = 1, 2, \cdots, l$$

In our research the identification of obscene picture belongs to non-linear classification problem. When the train sample set is non-linear separable, the train data x can be mapped to a high dimension space, and a an optimum hyperplane $w \cdot \phi(x_i) + b = 0$ can be constructed even the dimension maybe infinite.

If considered the slack variable l and punishment parameter C, the optimum hyperplane problem (2) is equivalent to equitation (3). In which $\xi_i, i=1,2,...,l$ is the nonnegative slack variable. With Lagrange multiplier method the solution to this quadratic programming problem restricted by linear constraint condition is given in (4):

$$\min_{w,b} \left(\frac{1}{2} \|w\|^2 + C \sum_{i=1}^{l} \xi_i \right),$$

(3)

$$s.t.: y_i \, (w \cdot \phi(x_i) + b) \geq 1 - \xi_i, i = 1, 2, ..., l, \xi_i \geq 0$$

$$w^* = \sum_{i=1}^{l} \alpha_i^* \, y_i \, \phi(x_i), \ s.t.: \sum_{i=1}^{l} \alpha_i \, y_i = 0, 0 \leq \alpha_i \leq C$$

(4)

So the discriminant function is:

$$y(x) = \text{sgn} \left\{ \sum_{i=1}^{l} \alpha_i^* \, y_i \, K(x_i, x) + b^* \right\}$$

(5)

While $K(x_i, x) = \phi(x_i)\phi(x)$ is kernel function. We need only compute the kernel function thus to avoid the disaster resulted by too high dimension eigenspace. In this paper we choose Gaussian RBF (radial basis function) with kernel width σ as our kernel function:

$$K(x_i, x) = \exp(-\| x - x_i \|^2 / 2\sigma^2)$$

(6)

3 Simulation Experiments and Analysis

Because there is no standard test picture set currently, we collect pictures from internet and capture screenshot, the pictures are good quality and all uniform lighting. Totally 80 pictures include 65 obscene scenes and 146 exposed breast characteristics, others include scenic and seaside resort scenes. The system judgment method is listed in Table 1. The system performance indexes can be described as (7):

$$\begin{cases} \text{Abandon True Rate: } R_a = C/(A+C) \\ \text{Take fasle Rate: } R_t = B/(B+D) \\ \text{Correct Recognition Rate: } R_c = A/(A+C) \\ \text{Error Rate: } R_e = (C+B)/(A+B+C+D) \end{cases}$$

(7)

Table 1. The System Judgment Table

	obscene picture	*normal picture*
correct recognition No.	A(obscene&identified)	B(normal but confused)
error recognition No.	C(bscene but omit)	D(normal&identified)

The test pictures' classified results are shown in Table 2. The simulation test results indicate that the most time consumption action is Haar transform, but because we can not operate the output frame buffer in PC and consider that the picture format is bmp or jpg which need decoding time and transferring time, so the actual time is approximately about 1~2 second and still need to improve. Although the train time is quite long but actually it's no impact to our system because the train process can be finished firstly. The reason about high take false rate is almost resulted from the seaside resort scene pictures, means that the model need to enhance skin detection. But this system present a practice ability which can be applied in embedded platform. In our paper we only give the method to detect women breast characteristic, but the method can be easily used to detect other obscene feature just add a time spare sub module, which can control the system to detect different feature every several seconds.

Table 2. Test Result

Time	Value(s)	Rate	Value
pre-process time	<1s	R_e	0.077
haar transfrom time	<3s	R_t	0.2
train time	230s	R_c	0.923
SVM classify time	<1s	R_e	0.135

4 Conclusion

In this paper an obscene picture detection algorithm is presented based on wavelet transform and SVM. The algorithm combines the color space transform, skin color detection and texture detection, after that a Haar wavelet transform of pictures is performed, and then the LL data is input to SVM and classify according to the eigenvector trained and built by given samples. The test results show that the system has practice ability which can be applied in embedded platform.

Acknowledgments. This work is financially supported by National 973 Program (contract No. 2011CB302303) and National 863 Project (contract No. 2009 AA01A402).

References

1. Lai, H.-C., Savvides, M., Chen, T.: Proposed FPGA hardware architecture for high frame rate (>100 fps) face detection using feature cascade classifiers. Biometrics: Theory, Applications,and Systems, 1–6 (2007)
2. He, C., Papakonstantinou, A., et al.: A Novel SoC Architecture on FPGA for Ultra Fast Face Detection. In: IEEE International Conference on Issue Computer Design, ICCD 2009, pp. 412–418 (2009)
3. Cho, J., Kastner, R., Oberg, J., Kastne, R.: FPGAbased face fetection system using Haar classifiers. In: International Symposium on Field Programmable Gate Arrays (2009)
4. Zhang, X.Y., Zhao, X.Y., Li, X.: Face Detection Based on Wavelet Trans form and Support Vector Machine. Microcomputer Information 34 (2007)
5. Ji, H., Sun, J.-X., Yao, W.: Wavelet moment for images. Journal of Circuits and Systems 6 (2005)
6. Burges, C.J.C.: A Tutorial on Support Vector Machines for Pattern Recognition. In: Data Mining and Knowledge Discovery (February 1998)

The Design and Implementation of a Course Scheduling System

Ping Guo, Lin Zhu, and Shuai-Shuai Chen

School of Computer Science, Chongqing University, Chongqing, 400044, China
guoping@cqu.edu.cn

Abstract. The course timetabling problem is a very difficult problem. There have used many different heuristic approaches to solve it. One of the efficient solution methods for this problem is Tabu Search. In this paper, greedy algorithm and Tabu Search algorithm are combined to obtain a feasible solution. Firstly, use greedy algorithm to achieve automatic course arrangement and obtain a feasible initial solution. Secondly, use Tabu Search algorithm to optimize the course timetable which have obtained in the first step.

Keywords: Tabu Search algorithm, Timetable, greedy algorithm, course scheduling.

1 Introduction

The course timetabling problem is an activity of assigning subjects to time and space such that all constraints are satisfied simultaneously. It is begin in the late 20th century 50. In 1963, Gotlieb made a formal description of the course timetabling problem, and proposed a mathematical model. While at the beginning, because of the difficult of the problem people begin to distrust whether the solution is exist. In 1976, S.Even and Cooper proved it is a NP complete problem.

Solving the course timetabling problem is a very difficult task because of the large size of the problem and different kinds of constraints; in many cases conflict is inevitable. The solution techniques range from graph coloring to metaheuristic algorithm, including linear programming formulations and heuristic approaches[1]. MirHassani has developed an integer programming approach. Gueret et al. have developed a different approach, constraint logic programming[5]. The more efficient procedures which have appeared in recent years are based on metaheuristics. Dowsland and Elmohamed et al. have used simulated annealing[4], Corne et al. have developed procedures based on variants of genetic algorithms[8] and Alvarez et al. have used tabu search techniques[6,7].

One of the most efficient algorithms for solution of the problem is Tabu Search algorithm. It is a meta-heuristic search method which has proved its efficiency in solution of combinatorial optimization problems[2]. It contains several important components, such as tabu list, tabu length, aspiration criterion, and neighborhood

S. Lin and X. Huang (Eds.): CESM 2011, Part II, CCIS 176, pp. 167–173, 2011.

structures, and so on. One of the most important factors which affect the efficiency of the algorithm is a defined neighborhood structures pertained to the nature of the problem [3].

In this paper, greedy algorithm and Tabu Search algorithm are combined to solve the timetabling problem and obtain a feasible solution. It is organized as follows. In section 2, we present the elements, objectives and constraints of the problem. The solution method to obtain the feasible initial solution is presented in section 3. In section 4, the Tabu Search algorithm is used to optimize the solution which has obtained in the last step. Finally, the conclusions are summarized in the last section 5.

2 Elements, Objectives and Constraints

2.1 The Elements of the Problem

A course timetabling problem has the following elements:

(1) A set of courses $A= \{A_1, A_2,..., A_j,..., A_s\}$. Each course has a fixed number of hours per week. Besides this, each course also contains the following elements: the class ID, the instructor ID of the courses, the needed room type and capacity, the number of weeks, the course type and so on.

(2) A set of classes $C= \{C_1, C_2,..., Cj,..., C_{an}\}$. Each class will have quite a stable set of students and it is therefore very important that lessons will not be taught simultaneously. Each class has several components, such as class ID, class name, student number.

(3) A set of teachers $T= \{T_1, T_2,...,T_j,..., T_r\}$. Each course will have a teacher previously assigned and each teacher have several components, such as teacher ID, teacher name and so on.

(4) A set of rooms $R= \{R_1, R_2,,..., R_j,...,R_m\}$, which have different types, including computer rooms and laboratories and general rooms. Each room contains several elements, such as room ID, room name, room type, and the capacity of room.

(5) A week, made up of a set of periods $P= \{P_1, P_2,..., P_j,..., P_p\}$, and divided into days. Each day has the same number of the periods of equal length.

(6) A set of lessons $L= \{L_1, L_2,..., L_j,..., L_k\}$, which stand for all courses belong to set A are assigned at k periods.

The course timetabling problem consists of k lessons L to be scheduled in a set of p periods P and a set of m rooms R. To schedule each lesson, variables X_{lpr} should be defined:

$$X_{lpr} = \begin{cases} 1 & \text{if lesson } l \text{ start at period } p \text{ in room } r \\ 0 & \text{otherwise} \end{cases}$$

Besides the sets defined before, the parameter definition in table 1 also needed.

Table 1. Parameter definition

Elements	Description
L	Set of lessons per week
Y_{jk}	Set of k lessons of course j
$P(l)$	The period of lesson l
LT_k	Set of lessons teacher k teach
LC_k	Set of lessons of class k
L_{cd}	The number of lessons of class c in day d
Z	Set of weeks
D	Set of days per week
P_l	Set of periods of day l
$Max(R_i)$	Max capacity of room R_i
$Num(Y_{jk})$	Student number of the lesson Y_{jk}
$Type(R_i)$	The type of room R_i
$NeedType(l)$	The type of room lesson l needed

2.2 Problem Formulation

When we think of a good timetable we consider several types of conditions, these conditions are not the same import. If we want to obtain a timetable, same conditions we must meet, we call these conditions hard constraints. These constraints are:

(1) Each lesson must assign to a period or several period, depending on the lesson's length.

$$\forall l \in L, \sum_{r \in R} \sum_{p \in P} X_{lpr} = 1 \tag{1}$$

(2) No teacher can give two simultaneous lessons.

$$\forall t \in T, \sum_{l \in LT_t} \sum_{r \in R} \sum_{p \in P} X_{lpr} \leq 1 \tag{2}$$

(3) Each room has no more than one lesson in a period.

$$\forall r \in R, \sum_{l \in L} \sum_{p \in P} X_{lpr} \leq 1 \tag{3}$$

(4) Each class has no more than one lesson in one period.

$$\forall c \in C, \sum_{l \in LC_c} \sum_{r \in R} \sum_{p \in P} X_{lpr} \leq 1 \tag{4}$$

(5) The room assigned to a given lesson must be of the required type and its capacity should not less than the number of students.

$$\forall r \in R, \forall l \in L, Max(r) \geq Num(l), Type(r) = NeedType(l \tag{5}$$

On the other hand, some conditions are helpful but not essential in a good timetable. The more these conditions are met, the better the timetable will be. We called this type of conditions soft constraints. We group the objectives according to the elements they involve. The soft constraints are:

(1) Different lessons of the same course should be assigned as average as possible in one week. For instance, a course has three lessons per week (called LPW for short), be assigned at Monday, Wednesday, Friday will be the best. If a course have two LPW, be assigned at Monday and Wednesday or Tuesday and Thursday or Wednesday and Friday are better. Assign different lessons of the same course at different days as far as possible.
(2) Class timetables should be as compact as possible, eliminating idle times for students.

When a feasible timetable is obtained, an objective function which is grouped according to the elements soft constraints involve will be used to judge whether it is a good timetable. According to the soft constraints described before, we define the objective function $f(x)$ like this:

$$f(x) = \sum_{j=1}^{s} \sum_{m=1}^{k} (P(Y_{jm}) - \frac{1}{k} \sum_{r=1}^{k} P(Y_{jr}))^2 \tag{6}$$

So the problem is: Min $f(x)$.

3 Obtain a Feasible Solution

In the last section, some constraints have been proposed and described it in mathematic formulation .In this section, an algorithm will be proposed which based on greedy algorithm to obtain a feasible initial solution.

3.1 Data Structures

In order to reduce the complexity of the algorithm, preprocessing is necessary. It contains two parts: course sort and time preprocessing.

(1) Course sort. According to the definition before, each course have a fixed number of hours per week (HPW). So the course can be sorted by HPW, the larger week hours is, the higher priority will be. Some courses, such as Common Course or PE (Physical Education) or other special courses should be preassigned, so the priority of those courses will be the highest.
(2) Time preprocessing. Suppose that every day have 5 periods and there are five days every week. So there are 25 periods every week. Suppose that variable j stand for the number of periods in one week, so $j \in [1, 25]$, variable z stand for the number of weeks in one semester.

3.2 Algorithm Achieve

The algorithm of Obtain a feasible solution is achieved by a sequential greedy heuristic starting from an empty timetable, from which course assignments are constructed by inserting one appropriate lesson into the timetable at each time. At each step, two distinct operations are carried out: one is to select an unassigned lesson which has sorted by the priority; the other is to find a period and a room for this lesson.

A course which has odd number of hours per week is also very common in course timetabling problem. In this case, if two courses of this kind can be finding, for example, two courses have three hours per week. It is clearly that the timetable will be like this: Each course have two lessons in the first week and one lesson in the second week .To deal with this situation, we can combine two courses as single one. So two courses have three lessons in one week , this will improve the utilization of the room, only the timetable will be different in neighboring two weeks .

Conflict is very common in course timetabling problem. In order to deal with conflict, one semester can be divided into two sections .Some courses can be assigned in the first section while others which can not be assigned in the first section can be assigned in the second one. Using this strategy, to some extend, it can deal with the conflict.

4　Optimize Timetable by Tabu Search Algorithm

Tabu Search algorithm which was introduced by Glover is a well know heuristic method[1]. In this study, the Tabu Search algorithm is used to optimize the initial timetable. The elements of the Tabu Search procedure are as follows.

4.1　The Key Parameters

(1) The solution x

Each solution x is a vector whose elements are variables of X_{lpr} that is previously defined. The number of elements taking the value of course ID is equal the number of lessons. The rest of the elements are equal to 0.

(2) The initial solution

The proposed Tabu Search algorithm begins with an initial solution. The initial solution is which obtained in the last section.

(3) The solution space X

It is set of solutions satisfying constraints (1)-(6).

(4) The objective function f(x)

This is the combination of objectives given by the user as appears in Section 2.

(5) The neighborhood N(x)

Two alternative neighborhoods are created by the following moves: The simple move in which a solution $x' \in X$ is a neighbor of solution $x \in X$ if it can be obtained from x by changing the assignment of one lesson i from one period t to another t'. The swap or interchange of lessons, in which a solution $x' \in X$ is a neighbor of solution $x \in X$ if it can be obtained by interchanging the periods assigned to two lessons i and i' .The simple move and the swap move are illustrated in Table 2 and 3, respectively.

Table 2. The simple move

Monday	Tuesday	Wednesday	Thursday	Friday
1	6	11	16	21
2	7 lesson *i*	12	17	22
3	8	13	18	23
4	9	14	19	24
5	10	15	20	25

Table 3. The swap move

Monday	Tuesday	Wednesday	Thursday	Friday
1	6	11	16	21
2	7	12 lesson *i'*	17	22
3	8	13	18	23
4 lesson *i*	9	14	19	24
5	10	15	20	25

(6) Candidate list strategy

For a given solution *x*, it is computationally too expensive to explore its whole neighborhood *N(x)*. Therefore, each course is moved randomly and the best one is chosen. For example, in a simple move, a period to which a course is assigned is chosen randomly among all empty periods. However, randomness herein is restricted, because the chosen next solution *x'* has to be a feasible solution satisfying hard constraints. Thus, for solution *x*, instead of examining of all neighborhood *N(x)*, a candidate list, consist of neighbors which are equal to the number of courses is examined.

(7) The tabu list

The tabu list keeps, for every iteration, the course starting the change and its initial period. Beside this, a tabu length is needed to define .For the tabu list, "first in first out"*(FIFO)* rule is used as a data structure.

(8) The aspiration criterion

If an explored move produces a solution *x'* with objective function lower than the best current solution, the move is made in spite of its tabu status.

4.2 The Steps of Tabu Search Algorithm

According to the key parameters defined 4.1, the steps of Tabu Search algorithm for solving course timetabling optimizes are as follows:

a) Obtain an initial solution *x*, set the tabu list, candidate list empty, define a variable *iter←0* to record the iterations, suppose that the maximum iterations is *Iter_Max*, set the best solution *best_x←x*, the best objective function is *best_fun←fun(x)*.

b) Determine whether *iter≥Iter_Max* established, if it is, the algorithm is over, otherwise, *iter←iter+1*.

c) For the given solution x, explore its neighborhood $N(x)$, choose some neighbors and obtain a candidate list.
d) For every candidate solution x' compute its objective function, choose the best one, if it is lower than the best current solution x, then the aspiration criterion is satisfied, set the $best\_x \leftarrow x'$, $best\_fun \leftarrow fun(x')$, and put the solution to tabu list. Then go to step b). Otherwise, go to next step.
e) Choose a best candidate solution which is not in tabu list. And set the $best\_x \leftarrow x'$, $best\_fun \leftarrow fun(x')$, Then go to step b).

At this point, a feasible timetable will be obtained. If some courses are not assigned in section one, it should be assigned in section two and an optimize of the timetable will be needed again.

5 Conclusion

In this paper, a greedy algorithm is used to obtain a feasible initial solution first, then in order to obtain a more reasonable solution, Tabu Search algorithm is used. To a certain extent, it can meet the actual requirements. However, the constraints are different in different universities, even in the same university, different departments may have different constraints. So it is difficult to design an algorithm which meets all constraints. In order to design a good algorithm to meet the actual it should be carefully analyze the situation and study, master them. The actual situation is changing, the algorithm must be constantly adjusted to meet the new situation demands.

Acknowledgment. This work was supported by the National Natural Science Foundation of China-Youth Fund (Grant No. 1010200220090070).

References

1. Alvarez-Valdes, R., Crespo, E., Tamarit, J.M.: Design and implementation of a course scheduling system using Tabu Search. European Journal of Operational Research 137, 512–523 (2002)
2. Aladag, C.H., Hocaoglu, G., Basaran, M.A.: The effect of neighborhood structures on tabu search algorithm in solving course timetabling problem. Expert Systems with Applications 36, 12349–12356 (2009)
3. Lü, Z., Hao, J.-K.: Adaptive Tabu Search for course timetabling. European Journal of Operational Research 200, 235–244 (2010)
4. Dowsland, K.A.: A timetabling problem in which clashes are inevitable. JORS 41(10), 907–918 (1990)
5. Gu_eret, C., Jussien, N., Boizumault, P., Prins, C.: Building university timetables using constraint logic programming. In: Burke, E., Ross, P. (eds.) PATAT 1995. LNCS, vol. 1153, pp. 130–145. Springer, Heidelberg (1996)
6. Hertz, A.: Tabu Search for large scale timetabling problems. EJOR 54, 39–47 (1991)
7. Hertz, A.: Finding a feasible course schedule using Tabu Search. Discrete Applied Mathematics 35, 255–270 (1992)
8. Paechter, B., Cumming, A., Norman, M.G., Luchian, H.: Extensions to a memetic timetabling system. In: Burke, E., Ross, P. (eds.) PATAT 1995. LNCS, vol. 1153, pp. 251–265. Springer, Heidelberg (1996)

An Simulate Micro Hard Disk Read-Write Channel Servo Signal System Design on FPGA

Qingdong Wang[*], Changsheng Xie, Dexiu Huang, and Chun Liu

Dep. of Computer Science, HUST, Dep. of Optoelectronic Storage, WNLO
Wuhan Hubei, P.R. China
wangqingdong@tom.com

Abstract. It's important to simulate micro hard disk read-write channel servo signal for design and test. This paper researches a programmable signal generator by an high integrated direct digital frequency synthesis (DDFS) technology to simulate servo signal for read-write channel of micro hard disk. This device use very large-scale integrated circuit FPGA (field-programmable logic) to integrate high speed PDSP (programmable digital signal processor) design and DDFS design. Test results indicate that this device has higher precision and sequence of signal, and the circuit need not connect filter and can output 2-100 order harmonious. The circuit design is simply, reliable, and programmable, compared with general design by separate parts design.

Keywords: servo signal, PDSP, FPGA, direct digital frequency synthesis (DDFS).

1 Preface

It plays an important role in the studying of read-write channel of micro hard disk by simulating all kinds of servo signal through high-quality signal generator. The direct digital frequency synthesis (DDFS) is the key technology of designing the signal generator for the time being, which influence the indexes of signal precision, resolution, stability and wave distortion.

Currently, we generally use the traditional design solution of discrete device and integrated circuit, but with complicated circuit design, big circuit consumption and noise interference, less points of each wave circle, and also need to connect to filter circuit, so it has the disadvantage of low signal precision and unable to repair on site.

This paper introduces a kind of 0.0001Hz-15MHz servo signal generated by high-integrated direct digital frequency synthesis, which adopts the total design of high precision.

24bit D/A converter and signal generator, please refer to Fig. 1(a) for the general design principle. The extra-large scale FPGA integrates the high-speed PDSP, 2K*24bit RAM and digital frequency synthesis calculation. It utilizes the signal discrete points calculated by PDSP, which contains the amplitude value and phase information, and then store the points in RAM. There are 1024 points in each cycle

---

[*] Corresponding author.

S. Lin and X. Huang (Eds.): CESM 2011, Part II, CCIS 176, pp. 174–179, 2011.

for this solution. Signal wave table is stored in RAM, which size is 2K, the pulse signal generates the cycling address through the counter, and then fetch the 24bit binary code from RAM, and then send into D/A converter and output the smooth and continuous signal. Amplitude precision of signal is 0.02%, stability is 0.002%/min, phase precision is 0.02°, and frequency precision is 0.0001Hz, can overlay 2 to 100 harmonic.

2 Direct Digital Frequency Synthesis

Direct Digital Frequency Synthesis, short for DDFS, is a kind of new frequency synthesis technology developed in recent years, which imports the advanced digit treatment theory into the field of signal synthesis, and signifies the synthesis technology enters the third generation. Its feature is to synthesize frequency by PC, and change the digit signal into analogue signal by D/A converter, and then carry out the frequency synthesis in the time domain. DDFS has the main advantage of: short time of frequency convert (to ns grade), phase and amplitude can be program controlled, same stability of output frequency and clock. Fig. 1(b) is the basic schematic diagram of DDFS system.

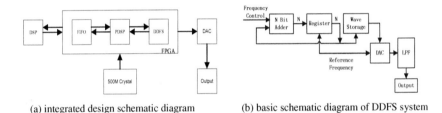

(a) integrated design schematic diagram   (b) basic schematic diagram of DDFS system

Fig. 1. Integrated design schematic diagram and basic schematic diagram of DDFS system

2.1 Traditional Design of Direct Digital Frequency Synthesis

Frequency divider works in the way of 74LS191 4-digit addition-subtraction counter and cascade connection with four chips. Addressing addition counter circuit is realized by using 74LS283 all adder cascade mode. If Module 1024 adder circuit needs to use three chips 74LS283, signal wave pre-calculate it and put into the storage. The disadvantage of this solution is: complicated circuit design, unable to change the design on site, high circuit consumption, bad precision and signal quality.

2.2 Design of DDFS Based on FPGA High Integration

Frequency divider, adder and lookup table is realized by FPGA, and the information of signal wave form, such as frequency, phase and amplitude, should be real time converted by DSP, and send into FPGA. Because of the programmability, flexibility and fast-speed of FPGA, it has been developed rapidly and widely applied in the design of digit circuit and digit signal process [2] [3]. The PDSP based on FPGA integration design and the Direct Digital Frequency Synthesis is becoming increasingly salient in the field of digit signal process, because of it high-speed process, flexible modification, especially the capability at digit signal process [4][5]. This paper bases on the technology of Direct Digital Frequency Synthesis [1], and it designs the special PDSP and Direct Digital Frequency Synthesizer according to the advantages of FPGA. Compared with realization mode in the past, it can reduce the quantity of components and disturbance on circuit, and increase the signal stability and also can be modified on line.

3 Realization of PDSP and Direct Digital Frequency Synthesizer in FPGA

Compared with external connection to DSP, it has the advantage of higher flexibility, more convenient modification, and lower cost to realize PDSP in FPGA. Here we only use the basic function of DSP. Direct Digital Frequency Synthesis is based on concept of phase, and it is a new frequency synthesis technology to directly synthesize the wave form in need. It far surpasses the traditional frequency synthesis technology in series of indexes, such as relative bandwidth, frequency conversion time, continuity of phase, quadrature output, high resolution and integration, etc.

3.1 Realization Course of DDFS

The phase adder is cascade connected by N-digit full adder and N-digit accumulation register, which is capable for accumulation calculation of binary code of frequency control word. It is a kind of typical feedback circuit, and the high M-digit of accumulation result generated can be the sampling address value of RAM of look-up table, in this way, a periodical signal wave value is stored in the look-up table. Obviously, here the storage RAM can be considered to be a converter from phase to amplitude value. So, it can drive the D/A converter by RAM output value, and then convert into the simulation signal wave form in need through the filter. At the same time, the N-digit accumulation output can also be considered to be the next round date of full adder to add with the frequency data, until the 16 bit phase adder is full with overflow, and finally a circle is finished, this is the frequency circle of DDFS signal.

3.2 Realization of DDFS in FPGA

The design of FPGA contains three parts:

(1) Design of look-up table calculation

To calculate 1024-point dispersed wave form according to the frequency, phase, and amplitude of signal, and then store in RAM, so it is needed to design a 1K*24bit RAM and 24bit*24bit multiplier unit.

(2) Design of DDFS calculation

Use 16 bit frequency divider as the clock of 32 bit adder to input, 300MHz clock is adopted for frequency divider to input, so the high bit of adding result of adder can be the addressing of RAM.

(3) Design of read-write controller of RAM and D/A converter

Design of data bus, address bus, control bus of read-write operation for RAM and D/A converter.

3.3 Realization of PDSP in FPGA

The PDSP function is realized by designing a 24bit*24bit multiplier and a 32bit summator.

In this design, we adopt FPGA chip Stratix IIIE EP3SE50 provided by ALTERA Company to realize DDFS and PDSP. EP3SE50 is the latest product of ALTERA for DSP and multi storage application, which supports high speed core and I/O, with optimized internal storage and flexible I/O. The number of Adaptive Logic Module (ALM) of EP3SE50 is 19000, the number of logical equivalence unit (LE) is 47500 and 1836(Bits) embedded array block, which can provide max. 144KB ROM/RAM bit, so it can meet the design requirement of DDFS and PDSP.

The circuit design of FPGA is realized by using VHDL hardware description language, because VHDL hardware description language can be planted into different FPGA chips conveniently. In this system, the external connected crystal of FPGA has the highest frequency of 500MHz, can be said as a high speed system. So when laying the PCB, should pay attention to isolation in case of the noisy disturbance, and also should avoid the burs when inducting the clock. In addition, also need to take some measures to increase the running speed, such as the flow line technology and design the high speed circuit by using the carry chain of FPGA device. Fig. 2(a) shows the simulation of DDFS realization course, among of them, signal ADDER is the coursing of address adding, 80M_CLK is the clock after frequency dividing, OUT is the pulse output. Fig. 2(b) is the design simulation of look-up table calculation, RAMADDRESS is the address generator of RAM, and INTEGER_COUNTER is the multiplier.

3.3.1 Design of Main Module Design of DDFS
DDFS can refer to above principles, to describe by VHDL, and below is part of the original program of calculation.

```
BEGIN
PROCESS(CLK)
BEGIN
COUNTER[31..0]=COUNTER[31..0]-1;
CLK=COUNTER[31];
IF(CLK'event AND CLK='1') THEN
\\ clock rising edge trigger
FREQ< =FREQINPUT;
AC0< =AC0+FREQ; \\adding
END IF;
END PROCESS;
RAMADDR< =AC(ADDER WIDTH-1 DOWN TO ADDER WIDTH-16);     \\
high 16-digit of adding result is the address bit of look-up table
RAM: LPM_RAM\\ calling of RAM look-up table
```

3.3.2 Design of DDFS Control Module
The system control of DDFS is designed based on the necessary functions, such as phase modulation and amplitude modulation, this is a kind of utilization of flexibility of FPGA. The schematic diagram is referred to Fig. 3(a).

3.3.3 Design of PDSP Control Module

PDSP is designed for look-up table, also a kind of utilization of flexibility of FPGA. The schematic diagram is referred to Fig. 3(b).

(a) DDFS simulation   (b) PDSP simulation

Fig. 2. DDFS simulation and PDSP simulation

(a) DDFS design schematic diagram   (b) PDSP design schematic diagram

Fig. 3. DDFS design schematic diagram and PDSP design schematic diagram

3.3.4 Comparison of Test Result

The comparison test result of this design and tradition design is referred to Table 1, 2 and 3, for the comparison of precision of amplitude, phase and frequency. It can be indicated that the precision is increased a lot, and the design has meet the expected result.

Table 1. Improved scheme test result compare with traditional scheme on amplitude

Amplitude(V)	Improved scheme (V)	Error(%)	traditional scheme(V)	Error(%)
0.1	0.10002	0.02	0.10050	0.50
0.5	0.50008	0.01	0.50200	0.40
1	1.00010	0.01	1.00350	0.35
2	2.00025	0.01	2.00640	0.32
3	3.00036	0.01	3.00910	0.33
5	5.00700	0.01	5.01503	0.30

Table 2. Improved scheme test result compare with traditional scheme on phase

Phase(°)	Improved scheme (°)	Error(°)	traditional scheme(°)	Error(°)
30	30.015	0.015	30.031	0.031
90	89.983	-0.017	90.027	0.027
120	120.020	0.020	119.034	0.034
240	240.011	0.011	240.022	0.022
270	270.013	0.013	270.036	0.036

Table 3. Improved scheme test result compare with traditional scheme on frequency

Frequency(Hz)	Improved scheme (Hz)	Error(Hz)	traditional scheme(Hz)	Error(Hz)
1	1.00008	0.00008	0.89154	0.1085
10	10.00001	0.00001	9.76552	0.2354
50	50.00008	0.00008	50.39732	0.6027
100	100.00009	0.00009	100.25752	0.7435
400	400.00005	0.00005	400.46903	0.4310
700	700.00005	0.00005	700.67723	0.3228

4 Conclusion

This paper is an simulate micro hard disk read-write channel servo signal system design on FPGA, and the test result proves the quality of output signal is highly increased compared with the traditional designs, and the effectiveness of this solution is gradually recognized.

Acknowledgments. This work is financially supported by National 973 Program (contract No. 2011CB302303) and National 863 Project (contract No. 2009 AA01A402).

References

1. Liu, L., Hu, Y.-S.: Digital Signal Processing with Field Programmable Gate Arrays. Tsinghua University Press, Beijing (2003)
2. Wang, C.-M., Shun, H.-B., Ren, Z.-H., et al.: TMS320C5000 Serial DSP System Design and Research Example. Electronics Industry Press, Beijing (2004)
3. Qi, C.-J.: Arithmetic Analyse and Application Digital Signal Processing Technology. Machine Industry Press, Beijing (2005)
4. Ren, X.-D., Wen, B.: CPLD/FPGA Advanced Application Design Guide. Electronics Industry Press, Beijing (2003)
5. Zhu, Z.-Y., Weng, M.-Y.: FPGA Design and Application. Xian Electronics Science and Technology University, Xian (2002)

A New Method for Constructing Concept Maps in Adaptive E-Learning Systems

Mohammed AL-Sarem[1], Mostafa Bellafkih[2], and Mohammed Ramdani[1]

[1] Faculty of Sciences and Techniques, Mohammadia, Morocco
[2] National Institute of posts and Telecommunications, Rabat, Morocco
mohsarem@gmail.com

Abstract. With the enormously progress of information technology, more and more adaptive learning and testing systems based on concept map have been proposed. Because the existing method to construct concept maps is time consuming and needs extra space to store the result of calculations or dependents on the threshold value given by learner that sometimes constructs incorrectly relationships or miss some relationships. In this paper, we present a new method based on Chen and Bai's method to automatically construct concepts maps. Firstly, we apply the Apriori Algorithm to mine some information then we construct two kinds of questions-relationship maps and combine them into the one combined questions-relationship map. Finally, we calculate the relevance degree between any two concepts to construct concepts map. The proposed method overcomes the drawbacks of Chen and Bai's method and gets more reasonable results than the one constructed by Chen and Bai's method.

Keywords: Adaptive learning systems, Concept map, Apriori algorithm, Data mining.

1 Introduction

With the enormously progress of information technology, more and more adaptive learning and testing systems based on concept map have been proposed to offer learners customized courses in accordance with their learning results. In [6], Novak presented a method for using concept maps as facilitative tools in schools and corporations. In [7], Tseng et al. proposed a heuristic algorithm to automatically construct the concept map. In [2], Bai and Chen proposed a method for automatically constructing concept maps based on fuzzy rules. In [5], Lee et al. proposed a method to automatically construct concepts maps for conceptual diagnosis based on Apriori algorithm [1]. In [4], Chen and Sue proposed a method to automatically construct concepts maps based on four kinds of association rules. In [3], Chen and Bai proposed a method to automatically construct concept maps based on data mining techniques to overcome the drawbacks of Lee al.'s method, however, Chen and Bai's method [3] used two questions-relationship maps to calculate the relevance degree between concepts. Furthermore, the count of operations needs to complete this process is dependant on the count of conceptual weight of concept in questions-concepts matrix,

S. Lin and X. Huang (Eds.): CESM 2011, Part II, CCIS 176, pp. 180–185, 2011.

therefore we can say certain method is time consuming and needs extra space. Firstly, Chen and Bai's method used the "failure-to-failure questions-relationship map" and "questions-concepts mapping matrix" to calculate the relevance degree between concepts and store the results in "failure-to-failure concepts-relationships table". Then, it used the "correct-to-correct questions-relationship map" and "questions-concepts mapping matrix" to calculate the relevance degree between concepts and store the results in "correct-to-correct concepts-relationships table". Finally, they combined the two tables in one to get "combined concepts-relationship table". Therefore, Chen and Bai's method presented in [3] is time consuming and needs extra space, furthermore, number of relationships in completed concept mapping depends on the threshold value given by user, some correctly relationships between concepts maybe lose in the constructed concepts map or will be cause to build unnecessary relationships in the constructed concept maps. Therefore, we can summarize the drawbacks of Chen and Bai's method presented in [3], as follows:

1. It is time consuming and needs extra space to store the result of calculations;
2. Based on the threshold value given by user, it will build unnecessary relationships or lose some relationships between concepts in the constructed concept maps.

In this paper, we present a new method based on Chen and Bai's method [3] to automatically construct concepts maps for adaptive learning systems. First, we apply the Apriori Algorithm [1] to mine some information then we construct two kinds of questions-relationship maps based on the associated rules derived in previous step and combine them into the one combined questions-relationship map. Finally, we calculate the relevance degree between any two concepts to construct concepts maps for adaptive learning systems. The proposed method provides us with a useful way to construct concept maps in adaptive learning systems, overcomes the drawbacks of Chen and Bai's method [3] and gets more reasonable results than the one constructed by Chen and Bai's method.

2   A New Method for Automatically Constructing Concept Maps

Assume that there are n learners $S_1, S_2,..., S_n$, there are m questions $Q_1, Q_2,..., Q_m$, and there are p concepts $C_1, C_2,..., C_p$, then we can transform the test portfolio of the learners and the conceptual weight relationships to the matrix G and the matrix QC, respectively[3].

Let Q_x denote the xth question, where $1 \leq x \leq m$, and let S_z denote the zth student, where $1 \leq z \leq n$. Then, we can get the grade matrix G, shown as follows:

$$
G = \begin{matrix} & \begin{matrix} S_1 & S_2 & \cdots & S_n \end{matrix} \\ \begin{matrix} Q_1 \\ Q_2 \\ \vdots \\ Q_m \end{matrix} & \begin{bmatrix} g_{11} & g_{12} & \cdots & g_{1n} \\ g_{21} & g_{22} & \cdots & g_{2n} \\ \vdots & \vdots & \ddots & \vdots \\ g_{m1} & g_{m1} & \cdots & g_{mn} \end{bmatrix} \end{matrix}
$$

where $g_{xz} \in [0,1]$, $g_{xz} = 1$ denotes the student S_z gets the right answer in question Q_x, and $g_{xz} = 0$ denotes the student S_z has a wrong answer in question Q_x, where $1 \le x \le m$ and $1 \le z \le n$. In the same way, we can construct the questions-concept matrix QC, shown as follows:

$$QC = \begin{matrix} & Q_1 \\ & Q_2 \\ & \vdots \\ & Q_m \end{matrix} \begin{bmatrix} C_1 & C_2 & \cdots & C_p \\ qc_{11} & qc_{12} & \cdots & qc_{1p} \\ qc_{21} & qc_{22} & \cdots & qc_{2p} \\ \vdots & \vdots & \ddots & \vdots \\ qc_{m1} & qc_{m1} & \cdots & qc_{mp} \end{bmatrix}$$

where qc_{st} denotes the degree of relevance of question Q_s with respect to concept C_t and $0 \le qc_{st} \le 1$. The proposed method to construct concept maps in adaptive learning systems is now presented as follows:

Step 1: Based on the testing records of the learners and the Apriori algorithm [1], we extract all association rules type "$Q_x \rightarrow Q_y$". Firstly, we extract rules, where the question Q_x is incorrectly learned by the learner and then the question Q_y is also incorrectly learned by the same learner, we will call these rules "wrong-to-wrong association rules". Similarly, we extract also the rules, where the question Q_x is correctly learned by the learner and then the question Q_y is also correctly learned by the same learner and call these rules "correct-to-correct association rules". We can find the association rules by applying the Apriori algorithm as follows:

Firstly, we construct the association rules from each question in the large 1-itemset to all other questions (an itemset is called a large-itemset if its support value is greater or equal to the user-specified support threshold called minSupport), then calculate the confidence of each rule obtained by the Apriori algorithm, where the confidence $conf(Q_x \rightarrow Q_y)$ of an association rule $Q_x \rightarrow Q_y$ is calculated as follows:

$$conf(Q_x \rightarrow Q_y) = \frac{Sup(Q_x, Q_y)}{Sup(Q_x)}. \tag{1}$$

where Q_x is a question in the large 1-itemset, Q_y is a question in the test paper, conf $(Q_x \rightarrow Q_y)$ denotes the confidence of the association rule "$Q_x \rightarrow Q_y$", $Sup(Q_x, Q_y)$" denotes the support of the 2-itemset (Q_x, Q_y)," $Sup(Q_x)$" denotes the support of the large 1-itemset Q_x ; $x \ne y$; $1 \le x \le m$ and $1 \le y \le m$.

Step 2: Based on the associated rules derived in Step 1, we construct two kinds of questions-relationship maps [3]. For the wrong-to-wrong association rules that the learner failed the question "Q_i" and failed the question "Q_j", we build a relationship from question "Q_i" to question "Q_j". For the rules that the question "Q_i" is correctly learned and the question "Q_j" is also correctly learned by the same learner (the correct-to-correct association rules), we build a relationship from question "Q_j" to question "Q_i", and let the confidence of an association rule be the confidence of the relationship between questions build from it.

Step 3: Based on the questions-relationship maps derived in Step 2, combine the tow questions-relationship maps into the combined questions-relationship map, described as follows:

1. If the relationship "$Q_i \rightarrow Q_j$" only exists in one of questions-relationship maps, we simply keep it without any change.
2. If the relationship "$Q_i \rightarrow Q_j$" exists in both questions-relationship maps, we keep the relationship whose the confidence is smallest.

$$Conf(Q_i \rightarrow Q_j) = Min(Conf(C_i \rightarrow C_j)^*, Conf(C_i \rightarrow C_j)^{**}). \qquad (2)$$

where $Conf(C_i \rightarrow C_j)$ denotes the confidence of the association rule"$Q_i \rightarrow Q_j$", $Conf(C_i \rightarrow C_j)^*$ denotes the confidence of the association rule"$Q_i \rightarrow Q_j$", where the learner failed the question Q_i and then failed the question Q_j and $Conf(C_i \rightarrow C_j)^{**}$ denotes the confidence of the association rule "$Q_i \rightarrow Q_j$", where the learner answered correctly in the question Q_i and then also correctly answered in the question Q_j.

For any two question Q_i and Q_j if the confidence of the questions-relationship between them is smaller than the minimum confidence θ, then we delete the relationship between the questions Q_i and Q_j to get the completed question-relationship map.

Step 4: Calculate the relevance degree between concepts.
For all kept association rules type"$Q_x \rightarrow Q_y$" obtained in Step 3, we calculate the relevant degree [5] $rev(C_i \rightarrow C_j)_{Q_x Q_y}$ between concepts C_i and C_j from the relationship"$Q_x \rightarrow Q_y$", shown as follows:

$$rev(C_i \rightarrow C_j)_{Q_x Q_y} = W_{Q_x C_i} \times W_{Q_y C_j} \times conf(Q_x \rightarrow Q_y). \qquad (3)$$

where" $rev(C_i \rightarrow C_j)_{Q_x Q_y}$"denotes the relevance degree of the relationship "$C_i \rightarrow C_j$"converted from the relationship "$Q_x \rightarrow Q_y$", $rev(C_i \rightarrow C_j)_{Q_x Q_y} \in [0,1]$, C_i denotes a concept appearing in the question Q_x, C_j denotes a concept appearing in the question Q_y, $W_{Q_x C_i}$ denotes the weight of the concept C_i in the question Q_x, $W_{Q_y C_j}$ denotes the weight of the concept C_j in the question Q_y," $conf(Q_x \rightarrow Q_y)$" denotes the confidence of the relationship "$Q_x \rightarrow Q_y$", $x \neq y; 1 \leq x \leq m, 1 \leq y \leq m, 1 \leq i \leq p$ and $1 \leq j \leq p$. Furthermore, let "$conf(Q_x \rightarrow Q_y)$" be the confidence of the relationship "$C_i \rightarrow C_j$". If there is more than one relationship between any two constructed concepts, then the relationship between the two concepts chosen as follows:

$$rev(C_i \rightarrow C_j) = Max(rev(C_i \rightarrow C_j)_{Q_x Q_y}). \qquad (4)$$

Step 5: Create a new concept-concept matrix C' based on the conceptual weights found in matrix QC, shown as follows:

$$
\begin{array}{c}
\begin{array}{cccc} C_1 & C_2 & \cdots & C_n \end{array} \\
C' = \begin{array}{c} C_1 \\ C_2 \\ \vdots \\ C_n \end{array}
\begin{bmatrix} b_{11} & b_{12} & \cdots & b_{1n} \\ b_{21} & b_{22} & \cdots & b_{2n} \\ \vdots & \vdots & \ddots & \vdots \\ b_{n1} & b_{n1} & \cdots & b_{nn} \end{bmatrix}
\end{array}, b_{ij} = \begin{cases} 0, & i = j \\ \min\,(qc_i, qc_j), & i \neq j \end{cases}
$$

where "b_{ij}" denotes the minimum nonzero values in a concept C_i's column and C_j's column for all questions from matrix QC, $b_{ij} \in [0, 1]$ and $1 \leq i, j \leq n$.

Step 6: Construct the concepts-relationship map between concepts

Let $\mu = Min(b_{ij})$, where "μ" denotes the minimum nonzero value of the relevance degree in C' matrix and "μ" $\in [0, 1]$. For each relationship "$C_i \rightarrow C_j$", calculate the relative questions-concepts values between concepts C_i and C_j shown as follows:

$$
Ret(C_i \rightarrow C_j) = \frac{N_i}{N_j}. \tag{5}
$$

Where $Ret(C_i \rightarrow C_j)$ denotes the relative questions-concepts values between concepts C_i and concept C_j, N_i denotes the number of the questions which have concept C_i and N_j denotes the number of the questions which have concept C_j. if

$$
Ret(C_i \rightarrow C_j) \times b_{ij} \geq \mu. \tag{6}
$$

Eq. (6) true, add an edge from C_i to C_j into the concept map as with the relevance degree of relationship "$C_i \rightarrow C_j$" to construct a concept map. Otherwise, delete it.

Step 7: If there are more than one concepts- relationship between concepts C_i and concept C_j, then we only keep the concept-relationship with the maximum relevance degree and delete the others.

3   Conclusion

In this paper, we have presented a new method based on Chen and Bai's method to automatically construct concepts maps for adaptive learning systems. Firstly, we apply the Apriori Algorithm to mine some information. Then, based on the associated rules derived in previous step we construct two kinds of questions-relationship maps. After that, we combine them into the one combined questions-relationship map. Finally, we calculate the relevance degree between any two concepts to construct concepts maps for adaptive learning systems. The proposed method overcomes the drawbacks of Chen and Bai's method and gets more reasonable results than the one constructed by Chen and Bai's method.

References

1. Agrawal, R., Srikant, R.: Fast algorithms for mining association rules. In: Proceedings of the 20th International Conference on Very Large Database, Santiago, Chile, pp. 487–499 (1994)
2. Bai, S.M., Chen, S.M.: Automatically constructing concept maps based on fuzzy rules for adapting learning systems. Expert Systems with Application 35(1-2), 41–49 (2008)

3. Chen, S.M., Bai, S.M.: Using data mining techniques to automatically construct concept maps for adaptive learning systems. Expert Systems with Applications 37, 4496–4503 (2010)
4. Chen, S.M., Sue, P.J.: A new method to construct concept maps for adaptive learning systems. In: Proceedings of the Ninth International Conference on Machine Learning and Cybernetics, Qingdao, pp. 2489–2494 (2010)
5. Lee, C.H., Lee, G.G., Leu, Y.H.: Application of automatically constructed concept map of learning to conceptual diagnosis of e-learning. Expert Systems with Application 36(2), 1675–1684 (2009)
6. Novak, J.D.: Learning, creating, and using knowledge: Concept maps as facilitative tools in schools and corporations. Lawrence Erlbaum Associates, NJ (1998)
7. Tseng, S.S., Sue, P.C., Su, J.M., Weng, J.F., Tsai, W.N.: A new approach for constructing the concept map. Computers & Education 49(2), 691–707 (2007)

Abnormal Event Detection Method for ATM Video and Its Application

Min Yi[*]

College of Computer Science and Technology,
Chongqing University of Posts and Telecommunications,
Chongqing 40065, China
shirley1920032003@yahoo.com.cn

Abstract. The paper proposes an abnormal event detection approach based on intelligent video content analysis, and applies it to ATM video forensics analysis. It aims at the surveillance video of payee's abnormal behaviors, based on the advantage combined the weighted geometric characterization with the PCA method, and discusses a new algorithm, namely improved PCA algorithm. This algorithm in the ATM can detect abnormal event under the influence of obstruction, such as hat, and the light. Experimental results show that the above approach is proved to be effective and robust in real videos event analysis.

Keywords: Video forensics, Abnormal event detection, Geometric characterization, PCA.

1 Introduction

The development of video surveillance system experiences three stages: analog video surveillance system (VCR), semi-digital video surveillance system (DVR/NVR) and digital video surveillance system[1-2]. With the development of network and multimedia technologies, intelligent video content analysis has become a key component in video surveillance system. Meanwhile, the video and image forensics has been become an indispensable function in security area[3]. More and more digital video surveillance systems are used, more and more complex criminal scene investigation and evidence collection related to video analysis have become.

We have a case description as following: after a criminal suspect robbed a victim for a bank card and password, he appears in front of a bank ATM wearing a hat, mask or sunglass. Thus external video camera above ATM cannot take a clear picture with recognizable facial features. This kind of intentionally face-hiding behavior is an abnormal event and typically found in all kinds of criminal scenes. In this case we need intelligent surveillance system is able to automatically monitor, give proper warning feedbacks in real time, such as recording the time and criminal process for forensic personnel, and secure ATM.

---

[*] Corresponding author.

S. Lin and X. Huang (Eds.): CESM 2011, Part II, CCIS 176, pp. 186–192, 2011.

This paper uses real data collected from ATM camera and applies abnormal event detection in video forensic to find abnormal behaviors in ATM transactions. The algorithm needs to be very robust and does accurate recognitions at different angels and on different scenes.

2 Design and Implementation of Abnormal Event Detection System for ATM

The major component of ATM abnormal event detection system is video content analysis. The analyzing process is divided into 3 phases: image preprocessing, characteristics extraction and abnormal behavior analysis, illustrated as following Fig.1.

1) Image preprocessing: the system needs to do some pre-processing, such as light compensation, face positioning and face rotation correction, etc.

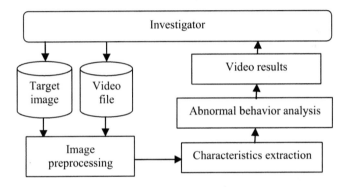

Fig. 1. The framework of abnormal event detection

2) Characteristics extraction: characteristics extraction is mainly based on some facial characteristics which is different among people and thus a stable measurement for each person. Facial characteristics metrics includes geometric characteristics (Euclidean distance, curvature and angel) and algebra characteristics (matrix characteristic vectors) etc[4-5].

3) Abnormal behaviors analysis: abnormal behaviors is a critical task today. We need to monitor large areas, manage camera sensor data, and use this data for detecting behaviors, detecting the abnormal behaviors and classifying the normal behaviors.

2.1 Facial Image Preprocessing

2.1.1 Self-adjustable Light Compensation
Since face color is changed with light strength, self-adjustable light compensation algorithm should be used: First, the light strength average $\overline{x}_1$ of all pixels in the target image is calculated; then we choose a reference image with homogeneous

lighting and also calculate the average $\overline{x}_{\text{ln}}$ for this reference image. If $\overline{x}_{\text{ln}} - \overline{x}_{1} > 7$, we do compensation by using the following formulas:

$$\begin{cases} r' = r + (m_r - m_r')(s_r / s_r') \\ g' = g + (m_g - m_g')(s_g / s_g') \\ b' = b + (m_b - m_b')(s_b / s_b') \end{cases} \quad (1)$$

In the formulas, r, g, b are values of RGB components respectively in the reference image; r', g', b' are for the target image; m_r, m_g, m_b are the averages of RGB components respectively for all pixels in reference image; m_r', m_g', m_b' are for the target image; s_r, s_g, s_b are the variances of RGB components respectively in the reference image; s_r', s_g', s_b' are for the target image.

2.1.2 Radiation Template Method for Face Rotation and Correction

Radiation template method is used to calculate facial rotation angel before characteristics extraction. Then human face is rotated and straightened, if necessary, by coordinate transformation. As illustrated in Fig.2(a), radiation template is a circular template divided into 16 circle sectors with the same size, which are numbered from 0 to 15 counter-clockwise starting from top. In order to adapt to faces with different sizes, concentric circles are used in the radiation template as illustrated in Fig.2(b). To calculate radiation template histogram, we put the face center at the center of radiation template and count the number of edge pixels falling in each circle sector. We can derive the face rotation angle based on the angel of circle sector 0.

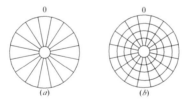

Fig. 2. Radiation template

2.2 Facial Characteristics Extraction

2.2.1 Eye Characteristics Extraction

Eye characteristics includes coordinates of two eyes, height and width of eyes and distance between eyes, etc. Eyes coordinates are composed of the four boundary-points x1, x2, y1, y2 and the center. The height of an eye h=y1-y2 is the difference between y1 and y2; the width of an eye w=x2-x1 is the difference between x1 and x2. The distance between two eyes is the distance between the left boundary-point of right eye and the right boundary-point of left eye.

2.2.2 Nose Characteristics Extraction

Nasal characteristics includes width, height and x-coordinates of leftmost and rightmost boundary points. The first projection below eyes is nasal area. The y-coordinate of nasal tip is the point where the horizontal projection value is the maximum. From the point downward, the lowest point of nasal area is the place when horizontal projection value reaches zero. Based on searching path we can obtain the coordinates of nasal center and height. Start from the nasal center leftward and rightward with a fixed step length and take vertical projections.

2.2.3 Mouth Characteristics Extraction

Mouth characteristics includes width, height and x-coordinates of leftmost and rightmost boundary points. First we obtain the maximum values of horizontal (x) and vertical (y) projections in mouth area. Point (x, y) is a inner point of the area. The leftmost and rightmost boundary points of mouth can be found by the same way as what we did for nasal area. Mouse width is the difference of the x-coordinates of the two points.

3 Abnormal Event Detection Based on Geometric Characteristics and PCA Method

3.1 Definition of Abnormal Events

In situations as traffic crossroads, banks, and shopping malls etc., abnormal events are all of those different from normal events such as rule-broken driving, robbery, shoplifting, wandering, and fire etc. Currently most abnormal events happened at such locations as banks, hospitals, airports, and other crowed public areas etc. For example, in banks intellectual surveillance system should be able to automatic security monitoring without human intervention and prevent robberies. This paper focuses on ATM. Abnormal events are defined as all of those that prevent faces from being detected normally, such as wearing hats, scarves or sunglass to hide face.

3.2 Geometric Characterization

Central moment is a typical geometric characteristics. Histogram normalization is applied on images before we calculate their central moments. If $F(m \times n)$ is a grayscale matrix of a preprocessed image, normalization is done based on the following formula:

$$G(i,j) = F(i,j) / \sum_{i=1}^{m} \sum_{j=1}^{n} F(i,j) \tag{2}$$

$$G(i,j) \in [0, 1] \quad \text{and} \quad \sum_{i=1}^{m} \sum_{j=1}^{n} G(i,j) = 1. \tag{3}$$

p + q matrix of G(i, j) is defined as:
$$m_{pq} = \sum_{i=1}^{m} \sum_{j=1}^{n} i^{p} j^{q} G(i,j) \tag{4}$$

Where (i, j) is the coordinates of the pixel G(i, j), (x_c, y_c) is the center of a target image. $x_c = m_{10}$, $y_c = m_{01}$.

p+q matrix is p+q matrix is
$$\mu_{pq} = \sum_{i=1}^{m} \sum_{j=1}^{n} (i - \chi_c)^p (j - y_c)^q G(i,j) \qquad (5)$$

Because different central moment identity matrices are used against the same sample, there will be a great value difference. Characteristics with greater variance shield those with smaller variance if we apply them for detection directly. Normalization is needed before further processing. μ_{ij} is the i_{th} characteristics of the j_{th} training sample, $U_i = \left[\mu_{i1,} \cdots \mu_{in,} \right]^T$. We use the following formula to normalize characteristics: $V_i = U_i / sqrt\left(\sum_{j=1}^{n} \mu_{ij}^2 \right)$

One thing should be pointed out that training and testing samples should use the same normalization factor, otherwise they are not comparable.

3.3 PCA Method Based on Local Characteristics

Principal component analysis (PCA)[6] is a widely used linear mapping method. It obtains identity vector of sample space along the direction along which the greatest variance changes exist. The vector is used for characteristic extraction. The essence of the method is to treat rows or columns of face image as high dimensional vectors and then obtain K-L bases of sample space by K-L transformation. We call a base "characteristic face" if it has the greatest characteristic value and has the shape of face. The base is corresponded to principle component of original sample space. When using relatively small characteristic face sub-spaces to describe face, face sample is a lower-dimensional weighted vector. Therefore face recognition will be done in sub-space with decreased dimensions. Data redundancy is dramatically decreased and most information is kept from original data although they are transformed into lower-dimensional characteristic space. When doing recognition, original face is projected into a characteristic face sub-space. Similarity and distance measurement are used in the sub-space as metrics. The data are compared with those from known face to derive the identity of target face.

3.4 Improved PCA Method

Geometric characterization has less computation and easier to implement. There are no high requirements on the capability of computer system. Moreover, this method has certain degree of adaptability to facial expressions. Therefore, we use this method to detect abnormal behaviors in face. But this method neglects information of other components in face, which results in multiple detection results when training sample quantity increases. Light strength has negative effects on grayscale information of face characteristics and causes incomplete local characteristic extraction. PCA characterization can extract global features of whole faces although it is also affected easily by light and expression[7-11]. In order to obtain better face detection results, we combine weighted geometric characterization with PCA method.

4   ATM Application of Abnormal Event Detection

In order to test our theory we take ATM as example. Considering the security of ATM, we need to monitor the person appearing before ATM and tell whether an event is normal or not. If detection result is normal, authentication follows; or warning is to be issued right away. This paper uses improved PCA method to detection faces under four different circumstances: hat only hides little face, hat does not hide eyes, hat hides partial eyes and hat hides eyes completely, as illustrated in Fig.3.

In this paper, all the experimental data used video of AVI format, resolution of the video is 320×240, and frame rate is 30fps. Experimental environment is the Intel (R) Pentium (R) 4, CPU 2.66 GHz, Memory 1GB, windows XP. The video data being used in experiment was taken with hand-held video camera or from the real case under the complexity situation of environment that people are moving or the leaves are swing. Practically used video information of examples follows: results are compared and listed in table1. 80 ATM avi video streams are used in the experiment and all are the same abnormal behaviors by 8 persons. We use the precision ratio A and recall ratio R and the frame ratio to compare the three methods' detection effects of covering facial behavior. Calculated as follows: $A = \dfrac{N_C}{N_C + N_w}$, $R = \dfrac{N_C}{N_C + N_m}$, Where, N_c is the number of accurately detecting abnormal behaviors, N_w is the number of mistakenly regarding as abnormal behaviors and N_m is the number of missing detected abnormal behaviors. From table 1, A, R and the frame ratio are all improved significantly for improved PCA. It shows that improved PCA is practical to be used in video surveillance systems. The experimental results of improved PCA are also illustrated in Fig.3.

Table 1. Comparison of Three Methods

Methods	A/%	R/%	Frame/s
Improved PCA method	92.9	94.6	15.2
PCA method	85.1	88.4	13.3
Geometric characterization	76.4	81.2	7.6

Fig. 3. Experimental results

This paper uses improved PCA method to analyze some behaviors in abnormal events. The event of payee wearing hat is taken as example to analyze the degree of how much hat hides face. If hat hides a big portion of face and severely affects the detection of important facial features, then it is an abnormal event; on the contrary, if hat does not affect the detection of important facial features, it is decided as a normal event.

5 Conclusions

This paper proposes an abnormal event detection method based on intelligent video content analysis and applies it in ATM video forensic. Weighted geometric characterization is combined with PCA method, i.e. improved PCA method that is used for abnormal event detection of video surveillance system. Experimental results show that improved PCA method can provides the best detection results. Improved PCA method provides a way to obtain effective detection when target is partially hidden by something and light with angle is a little strong. This method is also very robust.

Acknowledgment

This research is supported both by the National Natural Science Foundation of China under grant number 60573068 and the Key Project of Chongqing Natural Science Foundation of China under grant number CSTC 2008BA2017, 2008BA2041.

References

1. Kim, Y., Lee, H.S., Morales, A.W.: A video camera system with enhanced zoom tracking and auto white balance. IEEE Trans. Consumer Electron 48, 428–434 (2002)
2. Deng, W., Wang, J.A.: Design and implement of the Computer image detect system. Application Research of Computers, 79–80 (2000)
3. Nusimow, A.: Intelligent Video for Homeland Security Applications. In: Proc. of the 7th Technologies for Homeland Security, Boston, pp. 139–144 (2007)
4. Weng, C.-C., Chen, H., Fuh, C.-S.: A Novel Automatic White Balance Method For Digital Still Cameras. IEEE Trans. Consumer Electron
5. Samal, A.: Automatic Recognition and Analysis of Human Faces and Facial Expressions. Pattern Recognition 25(1), 65–77 (1992)
6. Wang, H.M., Ou, Z.Y.: The face recognition of PCA/ICA feature and SVM classification. Aid Design and Graphics of Computers (04), 411–414 (2003), National Center for Biotechnology Information, http://www.ncbi.nlm.nih.gov
7. Long, F., Ye, X.Y., Li, B., et al.: Gabor feature describe approach and the face recognition based on blocking statistic. Pattern Recognition and Artificial Intelligence 19(5), 585–589 (2006)
8. Duan, X., Zhang, X.L.: The face recognition method of a symmetry spread matrices space. Application Research of Computers 19(5), 1557–1559 (2010)
9. Zheng, D.Z., Cui, F.Y.: The face recognition of the wpfun feature extract and variance similarity. Optical Technology 36(2), 2178–2224 (2010)
10. Mahoor, M.H., Abdel-Mottaleb, M.: A Multimodal Approach for Face Modeling and Recognition. IEEE Transactions on Information Forensics and Security 3(3), 431–440 (2008)
11. Su, Y., Shan, S., Chen, X.: Hierarchical Ensemble of Global and Local Classifiers for Face Recognition. IEEE Transactions on Image Processing 5, 18(8), 1885–1896 (2005)

Web Service-Based Enterprise Data Service Center for Exchanging Common Data of Enterprise

WenLin Pan, TieHu Tang, and ChangHua Qiu

College of Mechanical and Electrical Engineering, Harbin Engineering University
150001 Harbin, China
Panwenlin@hrbeu.edu.cn, Tangtiehu@163.com,
Qiuchanghua@hrbeu.edu.cn

Abstract. Web Service is a kind of platform independent application which can support the distributed system. There are two disadvantages of traditional data centers, one is coupling, the other is data synchronization, and proposed a Web Service-based architecture to address these two problems. This architecture adopts Web Service to exchange data among different applications and data centers, and applies version control method to ensure data synchronization between different applications and data centers. Finally, the flexibility and availability of our architecture are tested by the case study of exchanging organization structure data.

Keywords: enterprise data center, data exchange, data synchronization, Web Service, enterprise organization structure.

1 Introduction

EDC (Enterprise Data Center) is based on Internet and LAN (Local Area Network); internally, it is a system for enterprise data management and decision support; externally, it is an enterprise-level e-commerce platform[1]. EDC achieves enterprise data sharing and rational use of resources based on unified data definition, data naming conventions and centralized environment.

Data center provides intelligent processing, information processing, knowledge exchanging and other functions for each enterprise. Moreover, it can effectively solve the issue of "data islands" and improve the integration between systems. The construction of EDC represents the direction of enterprises informatization, and becomes an international trend to promote core competitiveness of enterprises.

From the evolution of EDC's function, the data center has experienced three forms of development: computer center, the stage of data storage and simple calculation, appeared in the 1960s; information center, the stage of data processing and business applications, appeared in the 1980s; service center, the stage of data center services, appeared in the early 21st century.

2 Architecture and Shortcomings of Traditional Data Centers

Traditional data center centralizes and manages enterprise data in all applications which interact with the data center to read the needed data. Dedicated administrators

S. Lin and X. Huang (Eds.): CESM 2011, Part II, CCIS 176, pp. 193–199, 2011.
© Springer-Verlag Berlin Heidelberg 2011

are usually distributed to charge for data updating and maintenance in traditional data centers. Traditional data center is not only very difficult to achieve automatic management, but also constantly needs more dedicated administrators to maintain it.

The architecture of traditional data center is shown in Fig. 1.

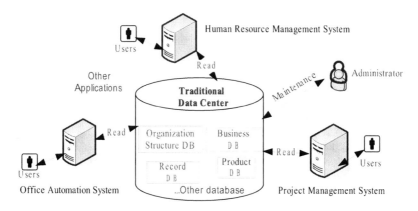

Fig. 1. The Architecture of Traditional Data Center

Recently, with the development of distributed computing, the RMI (Remote Method Invocation), CORBA (Common Object Request Broker Architecture), DCOM (Distributed Component Object Model) gradually appeared. Although they have made some success in enterprise integration application, they still have many fatal flaws, making their applications limited in a narrow range of research areas. The implementation of RMI requires both ends having the JAVA runtime environment, which has fundamentally impeded its promotion. Although CORBA has successfully defined a language-independent communication, it fails to achieve the object request broker (ORB) and leaves the problem to the supplier. Meanwhile, when the enterprises' firewall notices the new protocol of IIOP (Internet Inner-ORB Protocol), sometimes, it will prevent the ORB communication. Soon, IIOP brings CORBA a bad reputation having difficulty to work with firewalls. DCOM relies on the strict management of the environment. If developers want to develop DCOM applications, they have to make sure all distributed applications supported by Windows system. In addition, programmers must deal with the only rules protocol of message format required in data alignment and data types. DCOM and CORBA are suitable protocols for communicating between servers to servers; however, there are serious flaws when they come to deal with communication between clients to servers.

During the construction of EDC, it is urgent to solve the following issues: the integration of traditional data centers, heterogeneous data, data compression performance and system automation.

3 Related Research Works

With the development of information technology in recent years, multi-core, virtualization, and intelligent management software, constantly emerge. Together they generate a new generation data center. The on-demand new generation data center is the real Service-Oriented Architecture (SOA), having sufficient flexibility and scalability to supply, according to the changes in enterprise's business operation, enough support for the enterprise's operation and development[2].

The current preeminent problem is how data centers can be consolidated to host large numbers of servers economically. It is found that the scalability challenge is primarily a governance bottleneck. Research focus has been placed on streamlining the on-boarding processes with visual accountability of the delivery roles and collaboration with clients, Web technologies can be utilized in a new governance model for both productivity and quality improvements [3]. Through strengthening collaborations among clients, management and data transmission as well as establishing a SOA platform to integrate all the business and operating support systems, a visualized portal system can be delivered.

Virtualization breaks the shackles between IT users and IT resources and simplifies complex systems. Virtualization effectively improves data center's efficiency, reduces the investment cost, and integrates and optimizes resources and performance of the existing server. Therefore, it can meet business needs flexibly and dynamically. The business model closely related to virtualization is cloud computing whose core is sharing of virtual resources. The use of cloud computing infrastructure (centralization, virtualization and automation) can achieve traditional data centers' dynamic consolidation [4]. The application of dynamic architecture can integrate the data center network. Storage virtualization effectively solves the integration of multiple operating systems, heterogeneous data, and passive response to management.

At the same time, Web Service is becoming more and more popular for applications. Web Service provides the distributed computing which is implemented by several open Internet standards such as WSDL (Web Services Description Language), UDDI (Universal Description, Discovery and Integration), SOAP (Simple Object Access Protocol) and WSFL (Web Services Flow Language). Web Service eliminates interoperability issues in the existing solutions, such as CORBA and DCOM. Based on Web Service, applications can be quickly developed, released, discovered, and dynamically bound.

4   Our Approach

In the architecture of Web Services-based enterprise data center (WSB-EDC) we proposed, enterprises register the sharing business data in UDDI registration center, and publish them through Web Services, then, other collaboration companies can retrieve the service in UDDI registration center to find out the services they need, and then the service can be bound in the enterprise application systems to achieve enterprises application integration. The enterprise already existing legacy applications developed by other distributed component platform, can be packaged with Web Services specifications, without changing existing applications. After Web Services were registered in the UDDI registration center, UDDI classifies the registered services and restricts the security of registration and access; through the UDDI center, enterprise applications can find appropriate services and the bound operations they need, re-package their own protocols (such as IIOP, ORPC, RMI, etc..) with SOAP through SOAP protocol adapter, which transforms their protocols to the SOAP protocol achieving to interact with the bound services.

To provide services for various departments, WSB-EDC publishes the application as Web Services using the WSDL description specifications, providing uniform call interfaces; when a SOAP request message is received, the built-in XML parser in Web Service will analyze it, and then sends the results to the foreground Web Services after handled by the background business logic, and finally the results are shown to the users after processed by the client[5].

Present researches for Web Service are mostly aimed at Internet and other distributed environments, such as the simple task-oriented service request processing, Web information integration and other issues. However, the implementation of services is not only simple message flow in middleware layer, but also involves the management of bottom data, which require accurate and rich semantic information.

WSB-EDC has a well-packaged, loosely-coupled, standard protocols supported, and highly integrated architecture. Therefore, it is an ideal data center system.

WSB-EDC is a kind of lightweight data center architecture which is designed to manage and share the enterprise data, as shown in Fig. 2. Based on the enterprise actual situation, we adopt Web Service to construct the core architecture of EDC for enterprise, and choose data integration methods different from the traditional WSB-EDC, primarily managing data and innovating data management and maintenance mechanisms through the updating in data versions.

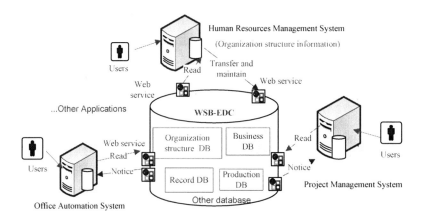

Fig. 2. The Architecture of WSB-EDC

WSB-EDC integrates the databases of the application information systems; each enterprise application manages and stores the data in each respective application database; applications exchange data with WSB-EDC through Web Service interfaces. The updating and maintenance of data in various applications rely on their own management. When the data version updates, the application send the updated data version to the data center, and then data center notifies the application of the updating of the data version; when the related application receives the updating notification, they can choose whether to update the data version depending on their own need.

Compared with the architecture of traditional data center, the obvious improvement in WSB-EDC is the abolition of full-time administrator, i.e., WSB-EDC no longer needs full-time administrators to maintain and update the data, in other words, the data producer should maintain that data. WSB-EDC can effectively improve the management efficiency of data center and save manpower resources, enable data manipulation more intelligent. Therefore, the automation of Web Service composition is improved, the dynamic interaction between the service components becomes more stable and efficient.

5 Case Study: Exchanging Organization Structure Data

The core of WSB-EDC is to storage and exchange data, which consists of series of middleware, Web Service interface, and data management, storage, and backup system. In order to test the framework of WSB-EDC we proposed, we adopt organization structure data to carry on case study.

Within the enterprise, human resources department is in charge of managing enterprise organizational structure data, and therefore in the database of EDC, HRMS (Human Resource Management System) is responsible for the enterprise organization structure data.

The implementation process of organization structure data in the traditional EDC is shown in Fig. 3. Organization structure information is stored in the database of EDC. All data center applications, such as OAS (Office Automation System), PMS (Project Management System), HRMS (Human Resources Management System) and so on, interact with the data center database through the middleware and read the required data from the data center. Maintenance and updating of the database is managed by dedicated administrators. When the organization structure information needs to be updated, Human Resources Department will notice data administrators to update the organization structure data.

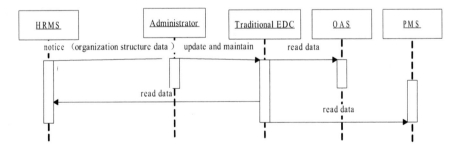

Fig. 3. The Implementation Process of Organization Structure Data in the Traditional EDC

However, in our framework of WSB-EDC, the organization structure data is stored in the database of HRMS. The storing and reading process of organization structure data in WSB-EDC are shown in Fig. 4. HRMS sends organization structure data to the WSB-EDC and enterprise application systems such as OAS, PMS and so on, and then the application reads the organization structure data from WSB-EDC.

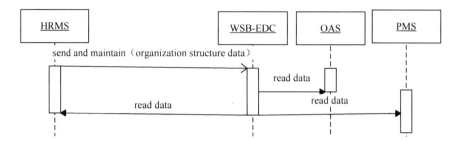

Fig. 4. The Reading Process of Organization Structure Data in WSB-EDC

When organization structure data updates, HRMS will send the new version of data to WSB-EDC, and then the center informs the applications of the new version, as shown in Fig. 5. After receiving the updating notification, the applications can choose to read the desired data version V1 or V2, based on their own needs. WSB-EDC manages the data relying on the updating of the data version, and uses Web Service to achieve the data synchronization without requiring interactivity. Each application can choose the data version in need, even if the data has been updated to the higher version in WSB-EDC; external applications are still using the earlier data version. Even the data version in WSB-EDC has been updated to V2 or more advanced, the applications such as OAS, PMS and so on, still use the original version.

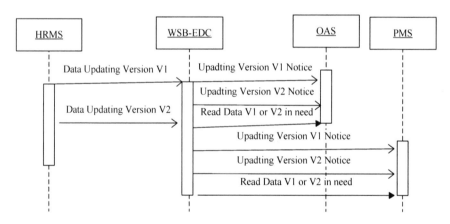

Fig. 5. The Updating Process of Organization Structure Data in WSB-EDC

6   Conclusion

EDC is the IT infrastructure of enterprise informationization. As the running center and disaster recovery center of enterprise information systems, it bears tasks of company's core business operations, information resources services, data storage and backup. Based on Web Service interfaces, WSB-EDC is able to solve heterogeneous environment, business integration and other issues in the traditional EDC. We only proposed application framework of WSB-EDC, the future work is to develop the data center based on our framework.

References

1. Luo, P.: Planning and Implementation of Large Scale Enterprise Data Center: The Case of China National Petroleum Company. In: 5th IEEE International Conference on Management of Innovation and Technology, ICMIT 2010, June 2-June 5, pp. 101–106. IEEE Computer Society, Singapore (2010)
2. Qin, W.: Research and Plan on the Next-Generation Data Center's Construction Based on Maturity Model. Master. Institute of Scientific and Technical Information of China, Beijing (2008)
3. Liu, Y., Wu, F.Y., Yih, J.: Enterprise Data Center Governance Using Web 2.0 Portal and Services Integration. In: IEEE International Conference on Service-Oriented Computing and Applications, SOCA 2009, December 14-December 15, pp. 158–161. IEEE Computer Society, Taipei (2009)
4. Tsai, D., Lin, S.: Building Enterprise Data Centers Using Virtual and Cloud. In: 6th International Conference on Intelligent Information Hiding and Multimedia Signal Processing, IIHMSP 2010, October 15-October 17, pp. 716–718. IEEE Computer Society, Darmstadt (2010)
5. Xianghui, P.: The Research and Implementation of Enterprise Application Integration Based on Web Services. Master. Northwestern University, Xi'an (2005)

Research on Addition of Aluminum Fluoride for Aluminum Reduction Cell Based on the Neural Network

Shuiping Zeng, Rongjuan Wang, and Yuqi Guo

North China University of Technology, Beijing, 100144
zshp@ncut.edu.cn

Abstract. Addition of aluminum fluoride can regulate molecular ratio and temperature of aluminum reduction cell, therefore, the cell could be kept working steady and effectiveness. To calculate the amount of the aluminum fluoride added to the aluminum reduction cell, this paper made a model of BP neural net work which has 7 inputs and 1 output. Genetic algorithm was used to optimize the initial weight and the threshold value. And the software was designed to decide the quantity of aluminum fluoride. The results computed based on 20 groups of data sampled in production indicated the absolute error less than 3kg and relative error less than 0.1, which can be satisfied in aluminum production.

Keywords: Aluminum reduction, aluminum fluoride addition, neural network, genetic algorithm.

1 Introduction

To reduce the crystallized (liquids) temperature, which in turn would reduce the temperature of the electrolysis and the solubility of aluminum in the electrolyte, and to increase the current efficiency, modern aluminum production commonly use electrolyte with low molecular proportion .But excessive low molecular ratio would go ill with the dissolution of alumina and cause sludge, in severe cases it may lead to the occurrence of anode effect [1]. Aluminum is a system with a big time lag, nonlinear and strongly coupling. There is complex nonlinear relationship between the heat balance within the cell and the addition of aluminum fluoride. Aluminum Fluoride addition, which would affect the crust of cell by reducing the temperature of primary crystal and electrolysis, lowering the conductivity of electrolyte and the solubility of alumina, has a great impact on the physical chemistry properties and electrochemical properties of the electrolyte. The amount of fluoride added every day, which is being decided by operators' general experience or by using a simple regression model, has great influence on the parameters of electrolysis process. Accurate mathematical model is difficult to get due to the strong coupling parameter and big time lag. Thus, how to give a reasonable addition of aluminum fluoride seems to be difficult [2]. Once the addition of aluminum fluoride lead the structure irrational, physical field inside the cell would change, and, the stability of the cell damages [3].

S. Lin and X. Huang (Eds.): CESM 2011, Part II, CCIS 176, pp. 200–206, 2011.

2 Establishment of Neural Network Model

2.1 Parameters of Input and Output

Neural network can approximate any complex nonlinear mapping accurately, but efficiency and effectiveness of the network depend on the structure of the network and parameters. Studies have shown that delay exists during the electrolytic process, aluminum fluoride added to the electrolyte deposited in the inner part and sidepiece, and then, released under certain conditions [4, 5]. Having considered the effect of the amount of aluminum fluoride and the impact that aluminum fluoride addition imposed on parameters of electrolysis process, input layer adapts seven neurons: aluminum levels, crystallized (liquids) temperature, electrolyte temperature, the amount of aluminum fluoride added that day, and the amount of aluminum fluoride added, crystallized (liquids) temperature, electrolyte temperature of the day before that day. The output is the amount of aluminum fluoride added the day after that day. Level of the aluminum amount and the temperature of the aluminum reduction cell are measured everyday in the aluminum electrolytic plant, then, a mean value could be gained. To measure or calculate crystallized (liquids) temperature is more complex and expensive. So, the crystallized (liquids) temperature is gained regularly. In this paper the everyday crystallized (liquids) temperature has been estimated by analyzing crystallized (liquids) temperature and the factors of the electrolyte that had been collected twice [6, 7].

2.2 Identification of the Hidden Layer and BP Network Algorithm

The number of the hidden layer neurons can be first selected by formulas as follow: $n = \sqrt{n0 + n1} + a$ and $n \geq n0$ In the equation, n stands for the node number of hidden layer, n0 stands for the number of neurons that input, n1 stands for the number of neurons that output, a is a constant between 1 and 10 [8].

According to the formula, n is a number between 7 and 12.8. After several trials, here n choose 10.

Thus, the topology of the three layers BP neural net work is like this:

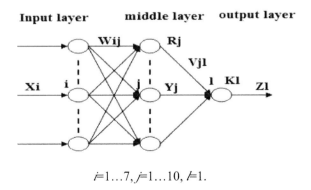

$i{=}1...7, j{=}1...10, l{=}1.$

Fig. 1. Topology with 7 inputs and 1 output

W_{ij} is connect weight of the node of input layer i and the node of hidden layer j. V_{jl} is connect weight of the node of hidden layer j and the node of output layer j. Rj is threshold of the hidden layer node j, K_l is threshold of the output layer node l, X_i is the input of the node i of input layer Y_j is the output of the node j of hidden layer. Z_l is the output of the node l of the output layer.

Output of hidden layer: $y_j=f(\sum x_i*W_{ji}+R_j)$, f is the transfer function and function tansig is used.

Output of output layer: $Z_l=g(\sum V_{lj}*y_j-K_l)= g(\sum V_{lj}* f(\sum x_i*W_{ji}+R_j)-K_l)$, g is the transfer function and function purelin is chosen.

We assume the expectation of the output is T_l, thus, the error of the output is:
$E=0.5*\sum(t_l-Z_l)^2=0.5*\sum(t_l- g(\sum V_{lj}* f(\sum x_i*W_{ji}+R_j)-K_l)^2$

To minimize the error, weights and threshold are revised constantly by network training. Training process takes adaptive learning rate. And the initial learning rate set to 0.5.

3   Optimization of the Neural Network Initial Weights and Threshold with the Genetic Algorithm

The initial weights and threshold of neural network are produced randomly. They can fall into the local extreme value points easily during the training process. What's more, the convergence speed is slow. To tackle this problem, genetic algorithm is put into use.

3.1   Determination of the Initial Population

The BP neural network has three layers. The input layer has 7 neurons, the intermediate layer has 10 neurons and the output layer has 1. The weights and thresholds need to be optimized are 91(7*10+10*1+10+1=91) totally. This paper utilizes real number coding. An individual is composed of 91 real numbers. The former 70 ones represent all the weights between 7 input layer neurons and 10 intermediate layer neurons. Then the number 10 represent the weights between 10 intermediate layer neurons and 1 output layer neurons. After that another number 10 indicates the threshold of intermediate layer neurons. The last one is the threshold of output layer neuron. According to the empirical data of references and the individual coding length, after constantly repeated comparisons we determine that the scale of population is 30.

3.2   Fitness Function

The objective function of genetic algorithm is the output error squares of forward computing network. Because of the evolution of genetic algorithm moves towards the direction of increasing the fitness function, the aim of regulating weights and threshold is to reduce the error squares to the lowest. Therefore the fitness function fi equals to 1/E.

3.3 Selection, Intersection and Mutation Operations

We use the fitness proportion selection method (Roulette) to calculate the probability of individuals selected. The larger the fitness, the higher the probability of selection. We use the arithmetic crossover modes to accomplish the intersection operation. Tow new individuals are produced through two chromosome linear combination. Mutation operation rules how genetic algorithm change the individuals in population through the small random and create the new individuals. We choose the Gaussian mutation operator to accomplish the mutation operation. At the same time, the random which obeys Gaussian distribution $N(\mu, \sigma_2)$ is used to replace the original genes values.

3.4 Process of the Genetic Optimization

The process of optimizing network with genetic algorithm is as above:

Using the optimal value of the decoding above, weight matrices W1 constitutes of the input layer and middle layer, weight W2 constitutes of the middle layer and output

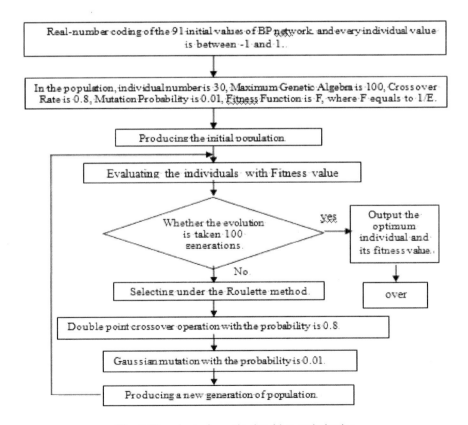

Fig. 2. Flowchart of genetic algorithm optimization

layer, threshold value matrix B1 constitutes of the middle layer, threshold matrix B2 constitutes of the output layer. Training the Network with BP Algorithm, the network's expectation error is 0.005. The initial learning rate is 0.08, the maximum training times are 4000. Running with MATLAB Programming, the specified accuracy could be gained after 2500 times of training.

4   Designation of Software Used to Decide the Quantity of Aluminum Fluoride

4.1   Function and Structure of the Software System

Functions that the software achieved:

(1). Accessing to the database server of aluminum electrolysis on the client, then, read it

(2). Calculating the amount of Aluminum fluoride added next day by data that has been read

(3). Data management

(4). User registration, login system

SQL Server, Visual C++ and MATLAB are all used in this system. The structure of the software program is as follow:

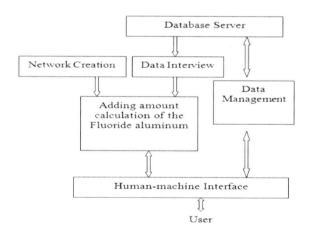

Fig. 3. Structure of software

When system is running the calculation of the amount of aluminum fluoride and data management are as follows.

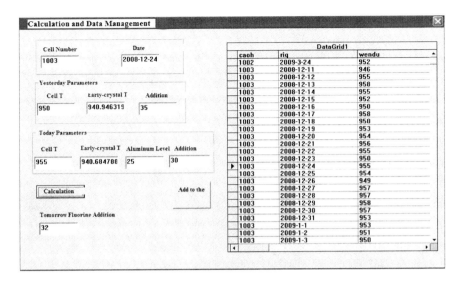

Fig. 4. Data display and management interface

4.2 Results

20 groups of data of aluminum reduction cell choosing from Oct. 2nd to Oct.22nd have been used. During this period, the cell runs well and the result is satisfactory. With the data above, the amount of aluminum fluoride needed everyday came out:

TT=31.93   29.42   35.66   35.73   40.11   48.89   41.19   43.83
  42.94   43.39   36.17   30.78   32.71   32.16   32.87   24.94
  27.52   36.25   34.28   40.06

The real amount of aluminum fluoride is:

t=33 30 33 37 41 50 43 44 42 45 35 30 32 35 32 25 25 35 35 42.

The absolute errors are:

$e1$= 1.07   0.58   -2.66   1.27   0.89   1.11   1.81   0.17
  -0.94   1.61   -1.17   -0.78 -0.71   2.84   -0.87   0.06
  -2.52   -1.25   0.72   1.94

The relative errors are:

$e2$= 0.032   0.019   -0.081   0.034   0.022   0.022   0.042   0.004
  -0.022   0.036   -0.033   -0.026 -0.022   0.081   -0.027   0.001
  -0.101   -0.036   0.021   0.046

Compared TT with t, the absolute error between counterparts is within 3kg. And the relative error is of less than 0.1. With consideration of actual production, the difference would not affect the electrolysis. Therefore, the decision made by the system can meet the actual need.

5 Conclusions

(1). Establishing the model for calculating the amount of Aluminum fluoride by using BP neural network according to the characteristics of aluminum reduction cell.

(2). Optimizing initial values and weights of neural network through Genetic Algorithm.

(3). Developing the application of calculating the amount of Aluminum fluoride should be added.

(4). Validating the reliability of this method through actual data gained from Aluminum Production.

References

1. Liu, Y., Li, J.: Modern Aluminum Production. The Metallurgical Industry Press, Beijing (2008)
2. Zeng, S., Li, J., Ren, B.: Aluminum Fluoride Addition through Electrolytic Process and the Fuzzy Decision of Aluminum Content 32(1), 1 (2008)
3. Nong, G.: System of Aluminum Heat Balance Based on BP Neural Network Control. Light Metal, 8 (2006)
4. Huang, Y.: Aluminum Fluoride Addition Control Strategy Based on the Analysis of Aluminum Heat Balance. PhD thesis, Central South University, 11 (2008)
5. Berezin, A.I., Piskazhova, T.V., Gritsko, V.V.: Bath superheat to control electrolysis process. Light Metals (2007)
6. Zeng, S., Li, J., Wei, Y.: Calculation and Control of Equivalent Superheat for 300kA Prebake Aluminum Electrolysis. In: 8th World Congress on Intelligent Control and Automation, WCICA 2010, pp. 4755–4760 (2010)
7. Meghlaoui, N.A.: Aluminum Fluoride Control Strategy Improvement. Light Metals (2003)
8. Berezin, A.I., Poliakov, P.V., Rodnov, O.O., et al.: Neural Network Qualifier of Noises of Aluminum Reduction Cell. Light Metals (2003)

Hot Topic Detection on Chinese Short Text

Cheng Zhang[*], Xinghua Fan, and Xianlin Chen

Institute of Computer Science and Technology,
Chongqing University of Posts and Telecommunications, 400065, Chongqing, China
zcailmy@163.com

Abstract. Concerning the short length, weak ability to describe the characteristics of short text, an approach of hot topic detection of Chinese short text was put forward by using hyponymy extending the key-feature vectors. First, cluster Chinese short texts and extract keywords, then, use "HowNet" hyponymy to extend the keywords, finally, cluster the extended short texts to obtain hot topics. The experimental results show that this approach can overcome the disadvantage of short text and can improve Chinese short-text detection performance.

Keywords: short-text, key words, hyponymy relation, clustering.

1   Introduction

With the Internet and the rapid development of communication industry, various forms of information rushs toward us. BBS, chat rooms, instant messaging all affect such people's daily lives. Usually the length of the text short text is less than 160 characters, and in the form of the general mobile phone text messages, web reviews and Internet chat text. Short text has the inherent disadvantage of weak signal to describe and short length. Currently a hot topic for the short text found abroad, not mature enough, and domestic just in its infancy, most of the research is only in phase for the users' behavior, such as Click rates, but few studies are designed for content of the short text. If you can find a hot topic and track its development trend, it will be play an important role in governmental control and maintaining social stability.

In this paper, with the characteristics of the short text itself and using hyponymy relation of HowNet to extend the key words of the short text, we put forward a new hot topic detection method, that is, HTDKFEH (Hot Topic Detection based on Key Features Extension by using Hyponymy).

2   Questions to Solve

The basic idea of topic detection comes of the 1996 topic detection and tracking, when the U.S. Defense Advanced Research Projects Agency (DARPA) proposed to

---

[*] Corresponding author.

S. Lin and X. Huang (Eds.): CESM 2011, Part II, CCIS 176, pp. 207–212, 2011.

automatically determine the need for a news topic of the structure of information flow technology, the establishment and development of the idea are carried out under the impetus of Topic detection and tracking (TDT) [1] [2] [3] meeting. Topic detection that can be seen as a clustering according to the event, the researchers often used algorithms: incremental k-means clustering, agglomerative clustering, single-pass clustering, etc. [4].

Question1: How to obtain keywords from the short documents?

Keyword extraction, there are support vector machine (SVM) [5], text-based index map of the CorePhrase method [6], clustering based on keywords tag method [7]. Support vector machine is a supervised learning method, in advance the subject of assumptions is made, and the training data set of tags in a document and use the support vector machine learning to constructed training models to extract key words. Text-based index map of the CorePhrase method requires the establishment of the text index map; cluster labeling methods based on extracting a number of mass components (candidate keywords construct a number of mass components), select the frequency characteristics of the larger center of mass terms for the key words. This method is simple, easy to implement, is considered more typical of the document keyword extraction method.

Question2: How to extend the short texts by using Keywords library and hyponymy relation of HowNet[8]?

Wang Sheng [9] put forward a concept to measure the relationship between words and word relationships between the concepts of upper and lower, through this relationship to extend the short text, so as to achieve the purpose of feature expansion.

We extend a certain threshold frequency keywords, which have a higher intensity in HowNet. This can not only overcome the short length of the text and the birth defects of weak signal, but also can effectively distinguish the type of text and can reduce much noise. See detailed propagation process model in Section 3 Step 4.

3   Model of Hot Topic Detection by Using Feature Expansion

3.1   Model of Traditional Hot Topic Detection

The traditional hot topic[10] process shown in Figure 1. The text is mainly for long text, because the characteristics of long text contains more information, the text can be directly clustered to obtain topics.

Fig. 1. Model of traditional hot topic detection

3.2 Model of HTDKFEH

Referring to hot topic detection on short texts, this paper presents a new model of hot topic detection on Chinese short text, shown in Figure 2. The basic steps of the model are as follows:

1) Import the initial corpus, process the corpus, including segmentation, getting rid of stop words, etc. Finally obtain text S.
2) Cluster the text S and extract the keywords from the result, and obtain keyword library H.
3) Through determining the threshold θ of hyponymy relation of HowNet and term frequency TF of keyword library H, format term expansion library I. Storage model(word 1, word 2).
4) Using the term expansion library I got from Step 3 to extend text S got from Step1. And then obtain extended text set T. More detailed description of the process is as follows:

   ① As to the word A in the short text W to be extended, lookup the word A from the term expansion library I. If there is a pair(A, B), go to Step ②, else go to Step ⑤.

   ② Extract the right word B, if the short text W doesn't contain the word B, then go to Step ③, else go to Step ④.

   ③ Add the word B to the term set of the short text W.

   ④ Do not add the word B to the term set of the short text W.

   ⑤ Do not extend the word A, and go on searching the next word.

5) Then cluster the extend texts set T, and ultimately get a list of hot topics.

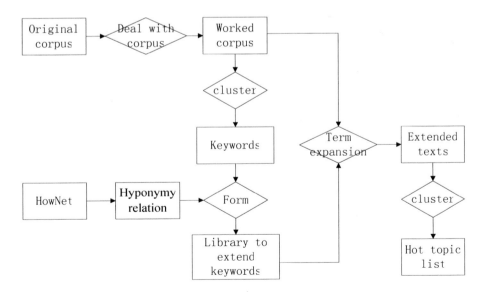

Fig. 2. Model of HTDKFEH

4 Experiment Result and Analysis

4.1 Experimental Setting

4.1.1 Experimental Corpus

Experimental corpus are all collected from Sina, Sohu and Tianya. They are web user reviews about news headlines or topics. We collect 3006 short texts of 4 topics. They are 807 about Yushu earthquake, 689 about conflict between North Korea and South Korea, 790 about Diaoyu Islands, 840 about event of Li Gang.

4.1.2 Measure Standard

This paper adopts a measure standard that is similar to text classification evaluation. There are 3 parameters: Precision (P), Recall (R), F measure and Macro-F. Defined as follows:

$$P = \frac{\text{number of the returned right texts}}{\text{number of all texts about a topic}} \tag{1}$$

$$R = \frac{\text{number of the returned right texts}}{\text{number of all the returned texts}} \tag{2}$$

$$F = \frac{2\ P\ R}{P\ +\ R} \tag{3}$$

$$Macro - F = \left(\sum_{i=1}^{n} F_i\right) / n \tag{4}$$

4.1.3 Experimental Parameter Setting

We have done 12 experiments on extended texts and 1 experiment on un-extended texts. And the 12 experiments' parameters are as follows: TF = {1, 2, 3}, θ={0.5,0.6,0.7,0.8}.

4.2 Experimental Results and Analysis

From the above Table 1, compared with the un-extended experiment, the HTDKFEH Experimental results have significantly improved. Each topic's precision, recall has improved about 5 percents compared with the Un-extended short texts. We can see that, the precisions are all over 90%. The topic corpus are collected from different web site and has obvious boundary. However, when θ=0.5, the extended experiment result is lower than the un-extended. Why? Because θ was set too low, there is too much noise in the extended short texts, the cluster result is lower.

Table 1. Experimental Data

Expansion		Yushu Earthquake			Conflict (N and S)			Diaoyu Islands			Event of Li Gang		
		P	R	F	P	R	F	P	R	F	P	R	F
	$TF=1$, $\theta=0.5$	97.50	48.33	64.62	98.09	52.25	68.18	96.05	61.65	75.09	97.01	69.52	80.99
	$TF=1$, $\theta=0.6$	98.12	58.24	73.09	98.37	52.54	68.49	96.25	61.77	75.25	97.34	69.64	81.19
H	$TF=1$, $\theta=0.7$	98.17	59.73	74.27	98.36	52.11	68.12	96.25	61.77	76.05	97.50	69.64	81.25
T	$TF=1$, $\theta=0.8$	97.97	59.85	74.31	97.76	44.41	61.08	96.66	62.28	75.75	95.01	63.45	76.09
D	$TF=2$, $\theta=0.5$	97.50	48.33	64.62	98.09	52.25	68.18	96.25	61.77	75.25	97.18	69.64	81.14
K	$TF=2$, $\theta=0.6$	98.14	58.74	73.49	98.36	52.39	68.37	96.46	62.02	75.50	97.34	69.64	81.19
F	$TF=2$, $\theta=0.7$	98.79	60.72	75.21	98.90	52.25	68.38	97.49	63.79	77.12	97.50	69.64	81.25
E	$TF=2$, $\theta=0.8$	98.17	60.09	74.59	97.76	44.41	61.08	97.06	62.78	76.25	95.01	63.45	76.09
H	$TF=3$, $\theta=0.5$	97.50	48.33	64.62	98.09	525.25	68.18	96.05	61.65	75.09	97.34	69.64	81.19
	$TF=3$, $\theta=0.6$	97.93	58.49	74.23	98.37	52.39	68.37	96.25	61.77	75.25	97.50	69.64	81.25
	$TF=3$, $\theta=0.7$	97.96	59.48	74.02	98.35	51.96	67.99	96.25	61.77	75.25	96.99	69.17	80.75
	$TF=3$, $\theta=0.8$	97.96	59.73	74.21	97.76	44.41	61.08	97.07	62.79	76.25	95.00	63.33	76.00
Un-extended		96.96	55.39	70.51	96.70	42.53	59.73	94.96	54.81	69.50	94.14	59.29	72.75

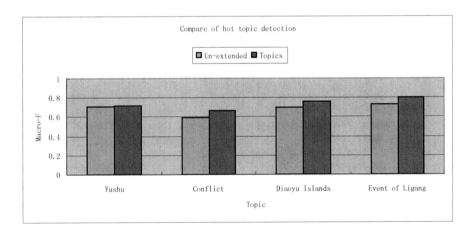

Fig. 3. Macro-F Measure

Generally speaking, most cases of extended precision, recall, F values have a greater degree of improvement. That is to say, HTDKFEH can improve the performance of hot topic detection. And when the threshold value of the TF to take 2, θ=0.7, it takes the most significant effect. Figure 3 shows Macro-F between un-extended and extended (TF=2, θ=0.7) short texts.

5   Conclusions

The technology of hot topic detection on short texts is important. It plays an more and more important role in monitoring public opinion and information retrieval. This paper put forward a method. We extend the keywords of the texts. There are 3 key steps: First, build a keywords library. Then, extend the short texts by using the library and hyponymy relation of HowNet. Finally, cluster the extended texts to obtain hot topic list. Through the experiments, we can get the conclusions as follows: HTDKFEH can improve the performance of hot topic detection, setting the threshold can affect the experiment. In the future, our next work is to find a new method of short texts detection.

References

1. Li, B., Yu, S.: The Study on Topic detection and tracking. Computer Engineering and Applications 39(17), 7–10 (2003) (in Chinese)
2. Hong, Y., Zhang, Y., Liu, T., Li, S.: Topic Detection and Tracking Review. Chinese Information, 71–87 (2007) (in Chinese)
3. James, A., Jaime, C., George, D., Jonathan, Y., Yang: Topic Detection and Tracking Pilot Study: Final Report. In: Proceedings of the DAPPA Broadcast News Transcription and Understanding Workshop, pp. 194–218. Morgan Kaufmann Publishers, Inc., San Francisco (1998)
4. James, A.: Topic Detection and Tracking: Event-based information organization. Kluwer Academic Publishers, Dordrecht (2002)
5. Blaz, F., Dunja, M., Marko, G.: Semi-automatic Construction of Topic Ontology. In: Gómez-Pérez, A., Euzenat, J. (eds.) ESWC 2005. LNCS, vol. 3532. Springer, Heidelberg (2005)
6. Khaled, M.H., Diego, N.M., Mohamed, S.K.: CorePhrase: Keyphrase Extraction for Document Clustering. Machine Learning and Data Mining in Pattern Recognition, 265–274 (2005)
7. Neto, J., Santos, A., Kaestner, C., Freitas, A.: Document Clustering and Text Summarization. In: Proc. 4th International Conference Practical Applications of Knowledge Discovery and Data Mining (PADD 2000), London, UK, pp. 41–55 (2000)
8. Dong, Z., Dong, Q.: HowNet (EB/OL) (September 01, 2008), http://www.Keenage.com (in Chinese)
9. Wang, S., Fan, X., Chen, X.: Chinese Short Text Classification based on Hyponymy relation. Computer Applications (3), 603–606 (2010) (in Chinese)
10. Luo, W., Yu, M., Xu, H., Wang, B., Chen, X.: The Study of Topic Detection Based on Algorithm of Division and Multi-level Clustering with Multi-strategy Optimization. Chinese Information 20(1), 29–36 (2006) (in Chinese)

Research on Digital Campus Based on Cloud Computing

Nian Liu[1] and Geng Li[2]

[1] School of Electrical Engineering And Information, Sichuan University,
Chengdu, Sichuan, China
liunianis@gmail.com
[2] Sichuan Provincial Office of State Administration of Taxation,
Chengdu, Sichuan, China
ligeng27@163.com

Abstract. Along with the networking and diversification of the campus digital applications, the problems that obstruction of data sharing and the increase of maintenance cost are brought out. In this paper, the application model of cloudy computing in campus digitalization is discussed and the operation flow of campus digitalization is analyzed in details. The existing problems and difficulties lie in the work flow and the features of IT needs is discussed. Combining cloudy computing application structures with actual needs of campus digitalization, A solution of campus digitalization platform structure is put forward in details, which adopt the model of SOA plus cloud computing basic structure and realized by virtualization technology to meet universal IT needs of campus digitalization.

Keywords: Cloud Computing, Campus Digitalization, SOA, Virtualization.

1 Introduction

As the education informatization degree increases, all sorts of applications appear in the campus network and therein information management and network resources play a significant role in every college or university. But due to the poor integral planning while building those system and also differences of system structure, data structure, operation platform and access pattern among systems, it's very difficult to exchange data and share resources among systems. Firstly, college departments had developed and adopted relevant operation flow by their own needs and then stored their own data but there is no uniform data base that results in data decentralization and storage repetition. Secondly, departments didn't adopt the same standard while storing data and those results in the difficulty of data exchange between different operation systems and the 'Information Island'. Those problems become obstacles for campus digitalization construction. How to utilize information and network technology to share information, eliminate 'Information Island' and accelerate the campus digitalization has become emergent for present campus digitalization construction.

Cloud computing appearance offers a new solution for this problem. Cloud computing can carry out virtual big-scale scientific or commercial cooperation, remote test, and high-performance distributed computing and data analysis among different organizations, also can results in the combination of experts from different areas and all

S. Lin and X. Huang (Eds.): CESM 2011, Part II, CCIS 176, pp. 213–218, 2011.

sorts of resources to solve problems and save time and cost to a big scale. Meanwhile, the design and application of cloud computing structure in campus will not only take a good advantage of all computing resources in the campus, expand some expensive and non-resource-duplicatable user group but also eliminate resource and information islands, offering a safe, reliable and expandable Web application environment for users.

2 Related Work

As the fast development of cloud computing and with its own advantages, cloud can help campus to gain high-performance IT service with the lease IT investment and also help all sort of users to gain all degrees of IT services. And it will release the IT burden of user which can focus on the core operation. Based on cloud computing flow optimization, the big-scale re-structure of campus digitalization can be achieved and the integral IT level and competition of campus will increase.

Cloud computing is kind of computing pattern which is offered to user in terms of "service" through internet resources and users don't need to learn, know or control the technology basic structure "cloud" which support those services[1]. Cloud computing is kind of commercial computing model. It distributes task into the resource pools composed of massive computing organization and allow all sorts of application systems to gain computing capacity, storage room and all kinds of software services based on their needs [2]. A cloud computing platform is to dispose of a serial of IT resources and distribute them dynamically according to users' needs. Users can use all sorts of terminals to access services offered by cloud platform through simple service interfaces.

Campus informatization needs server at three aspects: general information service, digitalization teaching application and scientific computing. The general information service is the traditional internet service like email, portals and information management system. Digitalization teaching application is the teaching, course and teaching resource management concerning to teaching. Those two aspects suit virtualization more. Scientific computing is about high-performance and grid computing concerning to science research and the cloud computing adopting will be better for adequate usage and application of resource advantages.

Cloud computing can aggregate computing resources from different structures on the internet high-efficiently and realize auto-management and mobilization, and therefore make the supercomputing capacity a possibility through the gathering of network resources. And the "Cloud" terminal users don't need to understand realization details but gain flexible IT services by needs. Virtualization offers cloud computing a good basic technology platform: when enterprise realized its own virtualization, it will naturally realize its internal self-service IT service through campus cloud construction and virtualization offers a seamless connection to cloud computing development.

3 Structure Model

With features of cloud platform and campus digitalization, the high-education industry cloud computing application of cloud computing with SOA structure is mentioned in this paper through analysis and demonstration [3].

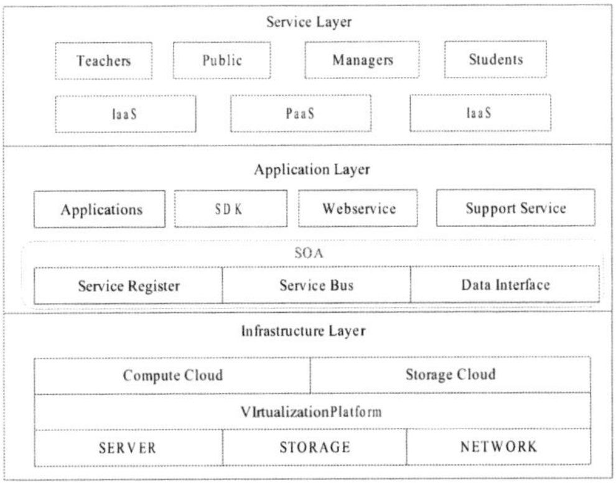

Fig. 1. Model of Digital Compus based on Cloud Computing Application

It's described in this paper that high-education cloud computing platform basic structure should include three layers: infrastructure layer, application layer and service offering layer.

3.1 Infrastructure Layer

It includes platform-supporting hardware and software resources. Hardware includes computers, storage devices, and network equipments and so on. These hardware resources are managed by a distributed computing frame appearing as a uniform service to outside, and behind which scattered hardware resources hide. Software includes storage, alignment, application and other services concerning to users.

Virtualization technology pushes the network exchange tech development. And the server virtualization drives the network virtualization [4]. The virtualization from physical server into many virtual servers would result in the integration of switchboard to virtualization platform by software simulation to form virtual switchboard and other components offering network connection for communications among virtual servers. Another alteration of server virtualization to network topological tech is the change from connection of physical servers through switchboards to the connection of virtual servers through "virtual switchboards" at campus network. Virtualization tech adopting and integration of physical servers descend the physical port quantity and thus the campus cloud can improve efficiency and capacity at a lower cost[5].

3.2 Application Layer

Users want to develop, operate service at cloud platform which needs to offer basic operation environment. And that environment should meet requirements at three aspects: service definition, management and mobilization. Service definition will allow user to define service to meet operation requirement. Service management offers combination, compiling, monitoring functions and so on to define particular operation flow definition. And service mobilization will offer user the uniform access of its services and convenience to utilize the services at this cloud platform.

SOA structure meet cloud computing life circle management requirements mentioned above and also it's a mature structure [6]. Standing at the point of needs of high-education industry to IT service and SOA features, SOA could respond to IT changes of campus digitalization users by needs and other needs like realizing the fast re-organization of flow plan. And the combination of SOA tech and cloud computing platform can sufficiently meet the IT requirements of campus digitalization users. Meanwhile, the combination of their features will bring out a lot of advantages at aspects like service design, service isolation degree, service management quality and other composite user applications.

3.3 Service Layer

Service offering pattern: as a fresh commercial model, cloud computing is offered to users in an IT instant service way [7]. And IT instant service could be divided into: infrastructure as a service (IaaS), platform as a service (PaaS) and software as a service (SaaS), three patterns.

Under the pattern, IT instant service, service supplier offers users hardware, software and consultant service through network. And users can order services in cloud by their particular need. And user can pay supplier based on how much service or how long they want. Then campus digitalization users don't need to maintain software while cloud computing supplier does.

4 Key Network Technology

Besides these advantages of cloud computing to campus informatization mentioned above, the desktop virtualization tech will bring up revolutionary alteration to campus users' maintenance and management. Utilizing desktop offered by campus network cloud computing in a collocation way, the efficiency, reliability and availability could be improved. Desktop virtualization is kind of collective computing pattern which

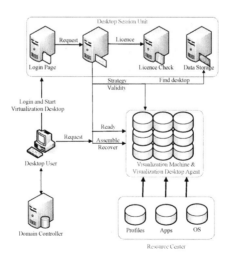

Fig. 2. Desktop Virtualization System Operation Principle under Collocation Pattern

transfers the PC computing to server-cored computing and thus disconnect desktop application with local computing. And the application pattern change will bring up the substantial alteration and improvement to computer management.

Known from the picture, desktop virtualization plan gets a lot of advantages.

In the deployment of desktop virtualization plan, the desktop user will conduct identity definition at first, and then enter personal virtualization desktop at different safety degrees and application authorities. These task executions will be supported by agencies and communication management software that is the desktop virtualization core software system, which is responsible for definition and communication connection between front and back, and also in charge of management, resource distribution, allocation, user definition and so on for the entire system.

Desktop virtualization makes it a possibility that data could be totally reserved at back with only visual appearance in front. Terminal users could access to system in a likely traditional way, but their IT authorities would be managed and controlled efficiently and besides, the terminal desktop information operation tracks could be monitored and recorded. This could solve data safety problem bothering us many years.

The appearance and improvement of desktop virtualization supplies a very effective tech solution for disaster recovery and continuity of campus network applications and operations. The front collective management model brings great benefits for upgrade, maintenance and migration of system. The desktop virtualization plan adopting will not only support present desktop, laptop and other traditional users' terminals, but also make thin client an option for user terminal. Through the tech, user could use thin client to ensure the high-speed network connection, application flexibility and data safety.

5 Advantages

Traditional model takes a back seat to cloud computing for campus digitalization construction. Cloud computing application would improve the integral informatization level with a lower cost, fasten industry IT revolution, and responds to market alteration more quickly. Specific meanings are as follows:

All-orientated IT service: cloud computing can supply uniform and all-orientated IT service for big, middle and small users, colleges, teachers, students and other relevant departments in the high-education industry.

Alteration by needs: quick respondence and following alteration to needs improve the IT flexibility and expandability for users. The openness of cloud computing platform allows users to deploy application developed by them at platform and to aggregate different application. The service of cloud computing platform is based on the SOA structure which could match IT and operation totally through SOA flexibility.

Descend IT cost: the platform is maintained by a professional third-part that allows the adopting of modern information tech achievements and then realize the scale effect to reduce IT investment cost for users.

6 Conclusion

The application pattern of cloud computing in high-education industry is sufficiently explained in this paper. That mainly includes cloud infrastructure construction, application software construction, service patterns, and service maintenance patterns and so on. Based on the application structure of cloud computing, the close relation of virtualization and cloud computing techs is especially described. The operation flow of campus digitalization users is explained in this paper and then the present IT problems confronted are summarized. Also relevant cloud computing plan solutions addressing those problems are pointed out here. This paper starts with the features of cloud computing digital campus, then develops the cloud computing model for high-education industry, following that the new key network communication tech and directions caused by virtualization tech are described in the process, at the end great benefits of cloud computing for digital campus construction are analyzed briefly. That plan will take advantage of cloud computing to a big scale and improve the integral IT level in high-education industry.

References

1. Information (2010), http://en.wikipedia.org/wiki/Cloudcomputing
2. Information (1981), http://baike.baidu.com/view/1316082.htm
3. Web Services Description Language (WSDL) Version 2.0 (2007), http://www.w3.org
4. (2008),   http://www.microsoft.com/windowsserver2008/en/us/hyperv-main.aspx
5. Chen, H., Chen, R., Zhang, F., et al.: In Live updating operating system using yirtualization. In: Proceedings of the 2nd International Conference on Virtual Execution Environments, pp. 35–44 (June 2006)
6. (July 2004), http://www-128.ibm.com/developerworks/cn/Websevices/ws-theme/ws-soa.html
7. Eibach, W., Kuebler, D.: In: Metering and accounting for Web Services. IBM Developer Works 2, 726–730 (2001)

The Computer Modeling of the Ball Gear of Concave Cone Teeth

Huran Liu

Dept. of Mechanical Engineering, Zhejiang University of Science and Technology, Hangzhou, P.R. China

Abstract. The ball gear or globular gear is a ball; on the ball there are a series of holes. The ball gear is the key component of the robot's wrist. As shown in fig.1, by using the ball crowns of two different ball centers as a joint curve surface, and their ball center as a rotational center, the ball gearing can be formed on two ball surfaces with convex teeth and concave teeth engaging each other. The robot's wrist differs from the wrist of human kind in that, it can transmit rotational movement from the upper arm to the lower arm continuously, while the angle between the upper arm and the lower arm is changing. In the formal papers, the protruding teeth have the shape of a cone, while the concave teeth are the conjugate surface of them. The protruding teeth with straight surface are of cause easy to be machined. But the concave teeth are very hard to be machined. The special machining method such as the electric spark machining has to be employed to deal with this kind of work.

Keywords: Cone tooth, ball, gear Motion, Power Transmission, profile.

1 The Machining of the Concave Teeth of the Ball Gear

The concave teeth are shown in Fig.1 As shown in Fig1, the concave tooth is a hole, with the shape of a cone. A tapered miller with helical cutting edges can finish such a machining task easily. The tapered miller with helical cutting edges is a standard cutting tool as shown in Fig.1. Sine that the taper angle of the standard tool may be not the same as our required we must produce the tool by ourselves.

Another standard tapered miller can realize the machining of the tapered miller with helical cutting edges on a NC machine tool, as shown in Fig.2 and Fig.3. But in the former occasion, the manufacturing of concave tooth surface remains complex. To drill a hole with complicated surface, the miller with helical cutting edges and complicated surface is required, as shown in Fig.5. Such tool is much more expansive than the first one.

2 The Machining of the Convex Teeth of the Ball Gear

The convex teeth is made independently, and then installed on the ball one by one. In the former occasion, the manufacture process of convex tooth surface is relatively easy.

In our scheme, the profile of the convex tooth is a rotary surface with complicated profile, as shown in Fig.7.

S. Lin and X. Huang (Eds.): CESM 2011, Part II, CCIS 176, pp. 219–224, 2011.

3 Geometrical Calculations of Concave Cone Teeth and Tooth Profile Equation

For concave teeth the cone tooth profile with a tooth profile angle α are used. Fig.2 shows the axle section. ABCD stands for the profile of cone concave teeth. CD is bottom of tooth groove, O' is cone top. The teeth top circle is coincided with pitch circle. R_{f1} is radius of tooth root circle. Given that hypotenuse length of AB is s. Then

$$O'O = \sqrt{R^2 + (\frac{S}{2})^2} - \frac{S}{2} ctg\,\alpha$$

(1)

In Fig.2, The tooth profile equation of concave tooth section BD side

$$x_1 = u\sin\alpha \qquad y_1 = O'O + u\cos\alpha$$

(2)

On the pitch circle, we have

$$x_1^2 + y_1^2 = R^2$$

$$u_{max} = -(O'O_1)\cos\alpha + \sqrt{R^2 - (O'O_1)^2\sin^2\alpha}$$

(3)

For the same reason

$$u_{min} = -(O'O_1)\cos\alpha + \sqrt{R_{f1}^2 - (O'O_1)^2\sin^2\alpha}$$

(4)

$$u_{min} \le u \le u_{max}$$

(5)

In substance, the ball gearing of ratio 1 is equivalent to two pitch spheres of the same size rolling against each other in space. The engagement of concave teeth with convex teeth along the meridian line of the pitch-curved surface is equivalent to that of a couple of planar gears of ratio 1. Therefore, the convex tooth profile can be found in the same way as the tooth profile of engaged planar gears is calculated.

As is shown in Fig.3, 1 and 2 are two pitch circles with the same radius. P refers to pitch point. The centers of the two pitch circles are expressed by O and O'. The center distance a=2R. The coordinate system $O_1 x_1 y_1 z_1$ is fixed to gear 1, while the coordinate system o2x2y2z2 is fixed to gear 2. XPY is a static coordinate system. The three axles $y_1 y_2 y$, are coincided in initiative position. The coordination equations are:

$$\begin{bmatrix} x \\ y \\ 1 \end{bmatrix} = \begin{bmatrix} \cos\varphi & -\sin\varphi & 0 \\ \sin\varphi & \cos\varphi & -R \\ 0 & 0 & 1 \end{bmatrix} \begin{bmatrix} x_1 \\ y_1 \\ 1 \end{bmatrix}$$

$$\begin{bmatrix} x_2 \\ y_2 \\ 1 \end{bmatrix} = \begin{bmatrix} \cos\varphi & -\sin\varphi & R\sin\varphi \\ \sin\varphi & \cos\varphi & -R\cos\varphi \\ 0 & 0 & 1 \end{bmatrix} \begin{bmatrix} x \\ y \\ 1 \end{bmatrix} = \begin{bmatrix} \cos 2\varphi & -\sin 2\varphi & a\sin\varphi \\ \sin 2\varphi & \cos 2\varphi & -a\cos\varphi \\ 0 & 0 & 1 \end{bmatrix} \begin{bmatrix} x_1 \\ y_1 \\ 1 \end{bmatrix}$$

(6) (7)

In order to see the profile of the convex tooth more clearly, a local coordinate system $O_g x_g y_g z_g$ on the pitch circle of gear2 is established.

$$\begin{bmatrix} x_g \\ y_g \\ 1 \end{bmatrix} = \begin{bmatrix} 1 & 0 & 0 \\ 0 & -1 & -R \\ 0 & 0 & 1 \end{bmatrix} \begin{bmatrix} x_2 \\ y_2 \\ 1 \end{bmatrix}$$

(8)

e 3 Setting of coordinate system.

4 Sectional Profile of the Convex Tooth

Normal vector of concave tooth profile:

$$\vec{n_1} = (\cos\alpha, -\sin\alpha)$$

(9)

The equation of conjugate condition:

$$\vec{n} \cdot \vec{v}^{(12)} = 0$$

(10)

$$\vec{v}^{(1)} = \vec{\omega}^{(1)} \times \vec{r}^{(1)} = x\vec{j} - y\vec{i} \quad \vec{v}^{(2)} = \vec{\omega}^{(2)} \times \vec{r}^{(2)} = -[x\vec{j} - (y-a)\vec{i}]$$

Substitute these equations into equation (10), we can get:

$$(yn_x - xn_y) - Rn_x = 0$$

(11)

$$yn_x - xn_y = (oo')\cos\alpha + u , \quad n_x = \cos(\alpha - \phi)$$

Substitute them into equation (11), we can get:

$$\cos(\alpha - \varphi) = \frac{(O'O_1)\cos\alpha + u}{R}$$

(12)

From the above equation, the α, ϕ are defined for all values of u. If we now transform the profile of concave tooth of gear1 into the system fixed on gear2, we can obtain the profile of convex tooth of gear 2.

$$x_g = x_2 = x_1 \cos 2\varphi - y_1 \sin 2\varphi + a\sin\varphi ,$$

$$y_g = -y_2 = -x_1 \sin 2\varphi - y_1 \cos 2\varphi + a\cos\varphi - R$$

(13)

The rotation surface of the convex tooth profile can be obtained by rotating this curve around the symmetric line of the tooth.

The condition of undercut

I considered the situation: when the Robot joint changes his angel between two arms, one ball gear roll relate to another, if there will undercut or not. If not, there will no undercut in 3D movement as well.

Suppose that, in the his own system, the profile of gear1 (generator) can be expressed as:

$$F(x_1, y_1) = 0$$

The conjugate condition can be written as:

$$f(x_1, y_1, \varphi) = 0 \tag{14}$$

When foot-cut occurred on the second surface (the surface being generated), the velocity of engagement:

$$\overrightarrow{v}_r^{(3)} = 0, \quad \overrightarrow{v}_r^{(1)} + \overrightarrow{v}^{(12)} = 0 \tag{15}$$

Where: $\overrightarrow{v}_r^{(1)}$ — the engagement velocity of generating surface;

$\overrightarrow{v}^{(12)}$ — the relative engagement velocity of generated; In the coordinate system 1, equation (15) can be written as:

$$\overrightarrow{v}_{r1}^{(1)} + \overrightarrow{v}_1^{(12)} = 0 \tag{16}$$

From above equations, we can get:

$$\overrightarrow{v}_{rx_1}^{(1)} = -\overrightarrow{v}_{x_1}^{(12)}, \quad \overrightarrow{v}_{ry_1}^{(1)} = -\overrightarrow{v}_{y_1}^{(12)}, \quad \overrightarrow{v}_{rz_1}^{(1)} = -\overrightarrow{v}_{z_1}^{(12)} \tag{17}$$

Derivate the equation (14) respect to time t, we can get:

$$\frac{\partial f}{\partial x_1}\frac{dx}{dt} + \frac{\partial f}{\partial y_1}\frac{dy_1}{dt} + \frac{\partial f}{\partial \varphi}\frac{d\varphi}{dt} = 0 \qquad \frac{dx_1}{dt} = \overrightarrow{v}_{rx_1}^{(1)}, \quad \frac{dy_1}{dt} = \overrightarrow{v}_{ry_1}^{(1)}, \quad \frac{d\varphi}{dt} = 1$$

We can obtain the discriminate of the undercutting condition.

$$\frac{\partial f}{\partial x_1}v_{x_1}^{(12)} + \frac{\partial f}{\partial y_1}v_{y_1}^{(12)} = -\frac{\partial f}{\partial \varphi} \tag{18}$$

In the Fig.2, the larger the value s, the thinker the convex tooth root, and the greater the strength. However, if the value s had been too big, the top of concave tooth will be pointed. So that we choose: s=7.3978, the top of the gear would not become too pointed. In the meantime the convex tooth will have enough strength.

In order to prevent convex tooth from becoming too pointed and to satisfy the requirements of the contact ratio, the profile angle of concave tooth should not be too big. It is calculated that: $\alpha = 12°$ would be the most appropriate.

According to our calculation, every pairs of convex tooth and concave tooth engage area $\phi = -0.2236 \rightarrow 0.1029\text{rad}$. Since this area is larger than 15, the gearing can act continuously.

The convex tooth surface is a curved rotate surface. The axle sectional profile is shown in Fig.1. According to equation (3), we have:

$$u_{max} = 17.7909$$

According to equation (25), on the undercutting limited point, we have:

$$u_c = 17.7042$$

Since $u_c > u_{max}$, there is no undercutting.

Fig. 1. The concave teeth of the gear

Fig. 4. The cutter of concave teeth of the gear

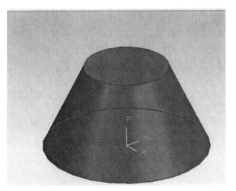

Fig. 2. The concave teeth of the gear

Fig. 5. The convex teeth of the gear

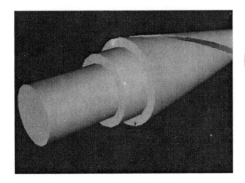

Fig. 3. The cutter of concave teeth of the gear

Fig. 6. The simulation of the gear mesh

5 Conclusions

Ball gear is the key part of a robot wrist. As showed in figure.1, the two balls are the pitch surfaces, the centers of the balls are the revolve centers. On two ball surfaces, there are concave and convex teeth respectively which can engage into meshing with each other. So that realized the ball gear transmission.

The theoretical analysis [1] prove that the concave tooth of the ball gear can be the rotational involutes, which is the surface formed in the process of double parameters involution. But both the concave and convex teeth are hard to generate. Reference [2] presented a new kind of ball gear, in which the convex tooth has the shape of a cone. The convex teeth are easy to manufacture while the concave teeth are still hard to manufacture. This paper presented a new kind of ball gear transmission. The concave tooth has the shape of a cone, which is easy to be machined with a milling cutter machine tool. The convex tooth is the conjugate surface of it. It is obvious that the convex tooth with complicated surface is much easer to be machined than the concave tooth with complicated surface. This kind of gear can increase the accuracy of machining and simplify technology, by means of analysis and calculation of tooth form of cone cave tooth ball gear, undercut and the matching degree and so on, prove that ball gear's construction is reasonable. (2) The advantages are that ball gear have good processing, easily improve machining precision and simplify machining processing.

Acknowledgments

This project is supposed by the natural scientific foundation of China, No.2006-50675235.

References

1. Liu, Z.: Research to cone tooth Ball Gear Transmission of Robot Flexible Joint. The ASME 26, 419–422 (1990)
2. Litvin, L., Fuentes, A.: Gear Geometry and Applied Theory, 2nd edn. by Litvin & Fuentes. Cambridge University Press, Cambridge (2004)
3. Qimi, J., et al.: The Feed Calculation in the Electric Discharge Generating machining of Quasi ellipsoid Gear. Journal of Harbin University (Janaury 2000)
4. Liu, Z.Q., Li, G.X., Li, H.M.: Research on cone tooth ball gear transmission of robot flexible joint. The American Society of Mechanical Engineers 26(5), 56–60 (1990)
5. Li, G.X., Li, H.M., Bi, Z.M.: Machining analysis on the quasi-ellipsoidal gear transmission with inner toroidal teeth in the flexible joint of robot. Chinese Journal of Mechanical Engineering 5(2), 79–86 (1992)
6. Zhang, K., Feng, L.Q.: The research of the design of ball gear transmission used in flexible wrist of robots. Journal of Tsinghua University 34(2), 1–7 (1994)
7. Li, G.X.: Computer simulation on quasi-ellipsoidal gear transmission. Journal of Harbin Institute of Technology 2(4), 42–45 (1995)

The Computer Simulation of the "SFT" and "HFT" Method on the CNC Hypoid Cutting Machine

Huran Liu

Dept. of Mechanical Engineering, Zhejiang University of Science and Technology,
Hangzhou, P.R. China

Abstract. The "SFT" (Spiral, Formate, Tilt; means the spiral gear is generated by the Formate method, while the pinion is generated by the method of envelope with the tool pan tilted) and "HFT" (same as mentioned above but for the Hypoid gears) is a highly effective means of forming spiral-bevel and hypoid gears. The current paper presents a method for realizing, and indeed improving, the conventional gear cutting method associated with a traditional machine tool upon a CNC Hypoid Cutting Machine.

1 Introduction

Nowadays, considerable effort is being expended upon the further development of CNC control of machine tools. Currently, the Hypoid Cutting Machine tool is the most advanced machine tool available for the manufacture of spiral bevel gears. Through an effective CNC realization upon this machine, it is possible to increase the quality and precision of gear manufacture, increase the volume of production, and

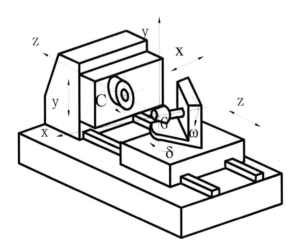

Fig. 1. Schematic of Machine Tool Showing Principal Axes of Motion

S. Lin and X. Huang (Eds.): CESM 2011, Part II, CCIS 176, pp. 225–230, 2011.
© Springer-Verlag Berlin Heidelberg 2011

improve the meshing of the finished gears. An overseas manufacturer by the name of Gleason has developed a CNC Hypoid Cutting machine, which has the ability to coordinate machine tool movements in 6 axes of motion. The development of this machine represents, possible, the greatest advance made in the approximately 100 year history of spiral bevel gear manufacture, and is highly significant by both a theoretical and a practical consideration. It looks like revolutionizing the gear manufacturing process and the performances of so achieved gears. This new development has caused the most part of the traditional machine tools to become obsolete, or at best, old-fashioned.

2 Machine Adjustments for the Method of "SFT"

When using the "SFT" Method and "HFT" to generate gears, the appropriate parameter adjustment of the conventional machine tool can be described as follows:

The plane which passes through the center of the cutter spindle, Oo, and which is perpendicular to the axis of the virtual crown gear, is referred to as the Machine Tool Plane, or simply, M plane. The intersection point of this plane and the swinging table axis, b, is designated as Om, and is identified as the Center of the Machine Tool. The plane which passes through point Om and which is parallel to the axis of the virtual crown gear and the work axis a is called the Horizontal plane or simply H plane. The radial Cutter Position is given by OmOo, OmOo=S. The angle between OmOo and Horizontal Plane represents the angular Position of the cutter Q. The angle between the axis of the virtual crown gear and the axis of the cutter spindle b is referred to as the Total Tilted Angle λ .

The angle between OmOo and the projection of axis a on the Machine Tool Plane is called the Basic rotational Angle of the cutter.

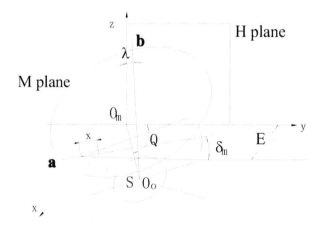

Fig. 2. The machining of the gear in the traditional machine tool

3 Realization of the Method on a CNC Hypoid Machine Tool

On the traditional machine tool, the center point of the swinging table, i.e. Om, is specified as the origin point, and a coordination system is established, as shown in Fig.2. The coordinates of the cone point of the bevel gear may then be expressed as:

$$x1= E \quad y1= - X \cos\delta m \quad z1= -X \sin\delta m \tag{1}$$

The vector of the gear axis is given by:

$$b=(0, \cos\delta m, \sin\delta m)= (p1, q1, r1) \tag{2}$$

The coordinates of the cutter spindle center are:

$$x0= S \sin (Q0+Q) \quad y0= S \sin (Q0+Q) \quad z0=0 \tag{3}$$

The cutter spindle axis is expressed by the following vector:

$$a=(\sin \lambda \cos (Q0+Q+\mu), \sin \lambda \sin (Q0+Q+\mu), \cos \lambda)$$

$$=(p0, q0, r0) \tag{4}$$

The intersection angle of the two axes is expressed by:

$$a \bullet b =\cos\delta m \sin \lambda \cos(q+q0+\mu) + \sin\delta m \cos \lambda \tag{5}$$

The length of the common vertical line is given by:

$$e = \frac{\begin{vmatrix} x_1 - x_0 & y_1 - y_0 & z_1 - z_0 \\ p_0 & p_1 & r_0 \\ p_1 & q_1 & r_1 \end{vmatrix}}{\sqrt{\begin{vmatrix} p_0 & q_0 \\ p_1 & q_1 \end{vmatrix}^2 + \begin{vmatrix} q_0 & r_0 \\ q_1 & r_1 \end{vmatrix}^2 + \begin{vmatrix} r_0 & p_0 \\ r_1 & p_1 \end{vmatrix}^2}} \tag{6}$$

In order to find the distance between O1 and the foot of the perpendicular d1, considering a plane passing through its common vertical line and the axis a, the normal vector of this plane can be given by:

$$(A1, B1, C1)=(a \times b) \times a \tag{7}$$

The equation of the plane is expressed as:

$$A1 (x-x0)+B1 (y-y0)+C1 (z-z 0)=0 \tag{8}$$

The coordinate of the intersect line of this plane with b are:

$$x = x1 + p1\, t \quad y = y1 + q1\, t \quad z = z 1+ r1\, t \tag{9}$$

From the Equ.(8) and Equ.(9), it is possible to derive the following expressions:

$$t1 = \frac{A_1(x_0 - x_1) + B_1(y_0 - y_1) + C_1(z_0 - z_1)}{A_1 p_1 + B_1 q_1 + C_1 r_1}$$

$$d1 = \sqrt{(x-x_1)^2 + (y-y_1)^2 + (z-z_1)^2} = \sqrt{p_1^2 + q_1^2 + r_1^2} \quad t1 = t1 \qquad (10)$$

From seminal reduction, it can be shown that the distance from O0 to the perpendicular foot is given by:

$$d\,0 = t\,0 = \frac{A_0(x_1 - x_0) + B_0(y_1 - y_0) + C_0(z_1 - z_0)}{A_0 p_0 + B_0 q_0 + C_0 r_0} \qquad (11)$$

Where $(A0, B0, C0) = (b \times a) \times b$

In the case of the CNC hypoid machine, the intersection point, G, of the swinging base axis and the work axis is fixed when the machine tool is working. G is specified as the origin point, and the let xGy plane to be parallel to the cutter. A coordinate system is established to describe the various movements of the machine. In this system:

$$a' = k \quad b' = \cos\delta\, i + \sin\delta\, k \quad a' \bullet b' = \sin\delta \qquad (12)$$

The expressions given above are equivalent to Eqn. (5), i.e.

$$a' \bullet b' = a \bullet b, \cos\delta m \sin\lambda\ \cos(Q + Q0 + u) + \sin\delta m \cos\lambda = \sin\delta \qquad (13)$$

Let $x_0^{'}$, $y_0^{'}$, $z_0^{'}$ represent the cutter center coordinates. The equation of the cutter axis then becomes:

$$\frac{x - x_0^{'}}{0} = \frac{y - y_0^{'}}{0} = \frac{z - z_0^{'}}{1} \qquad (14)$$

Furthermore: $(p_0^{'},\ q_0^{'},\ r_0^{'}) = (0,\ 0,\ 1)$

The coordinates of the cone point of the bevel gear are given by:

$$x_1^{'} = G_{O1} \cos\delta \quad y_1^{'} = 0 \quad z_1^{'} = G_{O1} \sin\delta \quad (p_1^{'},\ q_1^{'},\ r_1^{'}) = (\cos\delta, 0, \sin\delta) \qquad (15\text{-}17)$$

Why are the x', y' and z' coordinates given by two Eqns rather than by just one? Answer is: they are Corresponded to two kind of machine.

The axis of the work piece is given by:

$$\frac{x - x_1^{'}}{\cos\delta} = \frac{y - y_1^{'}}{0} = \frac{z - z_1^{'}}{\sin\delta} \qquad (18)$$

With Equation (6), (10) and (11), it is possible to determine the values of e', $t_0^{'}$ and $t_1^{'}$. The values of these invariable parameters should be the same for both machining methods, i.e.

$$e = e' \quad t\,0 = t_0^{'} \quad t1 = t_1^{'} \qquad (19)$$

Using a series of values of Q, which represents the position of the cutter in the traditional machine tool, Equ.(13) can be used to determine the required values of the swinging base movement δ. Meanwhile, applying the expressions given in Eqn.(19)

allows x_0', y_0' and z_0' to be determined, thus specifying the corresponding positions of the CNC cutter center. Finally, from the rolling motion, i.e. $\dfrac{Q}{\varphi} = \dfrac{z}{z_p}$, it is possible to establish the corresponding rotational angle of the work piece φ.

4 The Computer Simulation of the "SFT" and "HFT" Method on the CNC Hypoid Cutting Machine

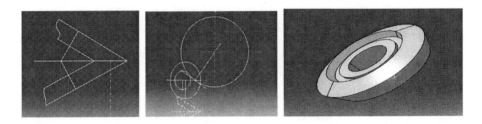

Fig. 3. The pitch cone and the pitch plane

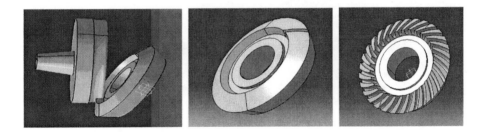

Fig. 4. A right handed generating surface cut a left handed bevel gear, and a left handed generating surface cut a right handed bevel gear

5 Conclusions

In the 1990's there was a significant interest within gear manufacturing circles in Taiwan in the interpretation and understanding of the Gleason manufacturing method for spiral-bevel gears. Nowadays, it is still felt that there remains a considerable need to further understand this method, and indeed it is has been proposed by the National Science Foundation that further research is required in order that Taiwan and the main land of China may be able to produce its own domestic CNC Hypoid Cutting Machine for the manufacture of spiral gears.

References

1. Fan, Q., DaFoe, R.: Gleason Expert Manufacturing System (GEMS) Opens a New Era for Digitized Manufacturing of Spiral Bevel and Hypoid Gears. World Manufacturing & Market (WMEN) 79(4), 87–93 (2005)
2. Fan, Q., DaFoe, R., Swanger, J.: 'New Developments in Computerized Design and Manufacturing of Spiral Bevel and Hypoid Gears'. In: The International Conference on Mechanical Transmissions, Chongqing, China, pp. 128–133 (2006)
3. Litvin, F.L., Fan, Q., Fuentes, A., Handschuh, R.F.: Computerized Design, Generation, Simulation of Meshing and Contact of Face-Milled Formate-Cut Spiral Bevel Gears, NASA Report, /CR-2001-210894, ARL-CR-467 (2001)
4. Fan, Q., DaFoe, R., Swanger, J.: Development of Bevel Gear Face Hobbing Simulation and Software. In: VDI International Conference on Gears, Munich, Germany (2005)
5. Fan, Q., Wilcox, L.: New Developments in Tooth Contact Analysis (TCA) and Loaded TCA for Spiral Bevel and Hypoid Gears. AGMA Fall Technical Meeting, 05FTM08, Detroit, USA (2005)
6. Fan, Q.: Computerized Modeling and Simulation of Spiral Bevel and Hypoid Gears Manufactured by Gleason Face Hobbing Process. ASME J. Mech. Des. 128(6), 1315–1327 (2006)
7. Huran, L.: Contact Deformation and Pre-control of Transmission properties of point conjugate gear. J. of Mechanical Engineering (January 2000)
8. Huran, L.: The improvement of the STF and HTF method in gearing. In: Conference in Mechanical Engineering at HongKong

The Computer-Aided Assembly of Pneumatic Motor with Offset Swinging Planetary Drives of Bevel Gear

Huran Liu

Dept. of Mechanical Engineering, Zhejiang University of Science and Technology,
Hangzhou, P.R. China

Abstract. A new kind of pneumatic motor with offset swingiang planetary drive of bevel gears and the application in Capstan is presented; the researched of the calculation of the efficiency of the mechanism is made. Compared to the former structure, new kind of structure has many advantages over that of the old structure. The pneumatic driving system in the traditional derrick car is: pneumatic motor drives a reducer, and then the reducer in turn drives a capstan. Another pneumatic driving system is: an axial piston motor and an internal cycloid pinwheel drive are applied, so that the reducer and the capstan are combined into one so that simplified the transmission system. In the third version, a pneumatic motor is applied, which can be considered as the combination of pneumatic motor with axial piston and the planetary reducer and then drives the capstan, so that simplified the transmission system as well. The new kind of pneumatic motor with offset swing planetary drive of bevel gears, which combined the pneumatic motor, the internal planetary reducer with bevel gears, and the capstan together, is the most compact structure. It is of more advantage in the occasion when space is extremely limited. In the paper, a new kind of construction of this mechanism is presented. The computer-aided assembly of pneumatic motor with offset swinging planetary drive of bevel gear is presented in this paper.

Keywords: Pneumatic Motor, Planetary Drive of Bevel Gears, Capstan.

1   Introduction

This paper present a new kind of pneumatic motor with offset swing planetary drive of bevel gears and the application in Capstan, and researched the calculation of the efficiency of the mechanism. Compared to the former structure, new kind of structure has many advantages over that of the old structure. The pneumatic driving system in the traditional derrick car is: pneumatic motor drives a reducer, and then the reducer in turn drives a capstan [1, 2, 3]. Another pneumatic driving system is: an axial piston motor and an internal cycloid pinwheel drive are applied, so that the reducer and the capstan are combined into one so that simplified the transmission system [4,5]. In the third version, a pneumatic motor is applied, which can be considered as the combination of pneumatic motor with axial piston and the planetary reducer and then drives the capstan, so that simplified the transmission system as well. The new kind of pneumatic motor with offset swing planetary drive of bevel gears, which combined

S. Lin and X. Huang (Eds.): CESM 2011, Part II, CCIS 176, pp. 231–234, 2011.

the pneumatic motor, the internal planetary reducer with bevel gears, and the capstan together, is the most compact structure. It is of more advantage in the occasion when space is extremely limited. In the paper, two kind of construction of this mechanism is presented, and the analysis of the efficiency of this kind of transmission is made as well. The authors are to emphasize the relevance work to the mechanism rather than just introducing a pneumatic motor.

2 The Structure of the Pneumatic Motor with Offset Swinging Planetary Drive of Bevel Gears

As showed in fig.1 Z1 and W2 formed the internal bevel gearing, Z1 =47, Z2=48, Z3 and Z4 formed the periphery constraint pair, Z3 = Z4 = 84, Z1 and Z3 are fixed with each other, and driven by the spindles through the linkages. The spindles are periphery spaced evenly on the pneumatic cylinder. So that Z3 would make pure rolling along the pith taper of the fixed bevel gear and swinging. In practice it is the revolving about a fixed point of the tip of the pith taper. Since Z1 and Z2 formed the gearing with few teeth difference, Z2 would rotate in opposite direction at low velocity. Z2 was installed on the skew axis 5. The offset swinging of Z2 and Z3

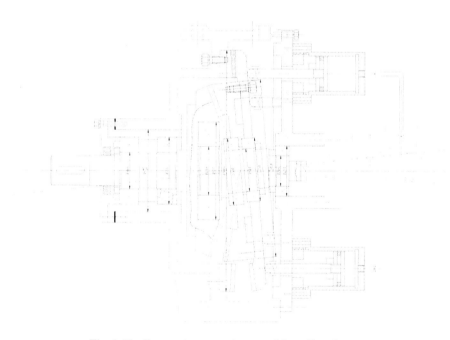

Fig. 1. The Pneumatic motor planetary drive of bevel gears

Z1 and Z2 formed the internal bevel gearing
Z3 and Z4 formed the periphery constraint pair
Z1 and Z3 are fixed with each other, and driven by the spindles through the linkages.

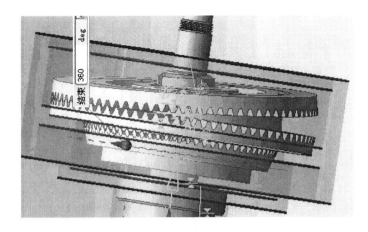

Fig. 2. The mesh of the bevel gear

would make skew axis 5 to rotate, in turn, drive the cylinder distributor 4 to rotate as well, so as to realize the distribution of liquid and, through the spindle and linkages, made the internal bevel gear Z1 to swing circulatory. The driver is Z1 the driven member is Z2 and skew axis 5 is equivalent to carrier H. [1,2,3].

3   The Total Explosion Figure of the Pneumatic Motor is Showed as Following

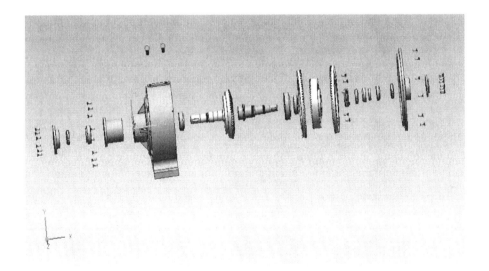

Fig. 3. Explosion figure

4 Conclusion

The new kind of pneumatic motor with offset swing planetary drive of bevel gears, which combined the pneumatic motor, the internal planetary reducer with bevel gears, and the capstan together, is the most compact structure. It is of more advantage in the occasion when space is extremely limited.

Acknowledgments

This project is supposed by the natural scientific foundation of China, No.2006-50675235. Translated by Ms. Quanhong Liu.

References

1. New technique in Pneumatic field. American Pneumatic and Pneumatic Drive (January 1972)
2. Pneumatic motor with swinging bevel gear transmission. American Product Engineering (January 1972)
3. USA Patent No.3675539
4. Huran, L., Dragomir, D.: Calculul randa mentului motor hidtanlic cu angrenaj conjc precesional (January 1996) <<MMTC>> (in Romania)
5. Huran, L.: Pneumatic motor with swinging bevel gear transmission. Drive System Technique (February 1998)
6. Huran, L., Dragomir, D.: Precontrolul angrenarii punctuale cu abateri la angrenaje spirale conice. Tehnologll Calitate Masini Materiale (January 1996) (in Romania)
7. Huran, L.: Contact deformation and pre-control of transmission properties of point conjugate gear. Drive System Technique (March 1999)
8. Huran, L.: Internal cylindrical-bevel gear transmission Drive System Technique (February 1999)
9. Huran, L.: The conjugation of a new kind of transmission. Drive System Technique (January 1999)
10. Huran, L.: The deduction of the forms of the planetary transmission of bevel gear. Drive System Technique (March 1998)
11. Huran, L.: The inversion of the Planetary Drive of Bevel Gear. In: ICMT 2006, ISTP (2006)
12. Lambeck, R.P.: Pneumatic Pumps and Motors: Selection ang Application for Pneumatic Power control System. Marcel Dekker Inc., New York (1983)
13. Vehicle Pneumatic System and Digital/Electropneumatic Controls, SAE SP-882 (1991) ISBN 1-56091-174-3

Programming Calculation of Slope Stability Safety Coefficient

Wei Lei

Chang chun Institute of Technology,
Changchun130012, China
lwlwlw2086@sina.com

Abstract. The soil stabilization is an important problem in the soil mechanics research. Calculation analysis of sticky slope stability becomes complex due to unpredictable crack of slope and complication of ground receiving pressure. The previous calculation models are simplified in order that we can handle it by hands. Now three methods are used: Slices Method are used, Tayerlor's Method and Bishop's Method. The three methods only discuss simple slopes, while too much simplification of computer models can't reflect reality of the slope. Analysis of slope stability by electronic calculation can make the results of calculation more accurate.

Keywords: Clay Soil Slope, Strip Division, Stability Safety Coefficient.

1 The Selection of Mathematical Model of Slope Stability Safety Coefficient

As for the viscous soil slope which is complicated in appearance with $\varphi>0$ especially when the slope is constituted of layers of soil, it is complex to define the weight of the sliding soil mass and its center-of-gravity position. The distribution of shearing strength on the sliding surface is uneven and it is related to the normal pressure. Therefore, in the stability analysis of the soil slope, usually, researchers will divide the sliding soil into several vertical soil bars, get the resisting moment and slip moment each bar has on the slippery arc circle, calculate the total of each and then the slope stability safety coefficient can be got. This is the commonly used strip division method. The analysis diagram which is often used in it is as shown in the Figure 1.

In order to simplify the calculation in engineering practice, we assume that the join force of P_i, H_i and the join force of P_{i+1}, H_{i+1} on the two sides of the soil bar i are equal in magnitude and opposite in direction and their action lines are doubling. Therefore, only the force of W_i, N_i and T_i that act on this soil bar takes advantage of the balance condition of this soil bar and it can be concluded that $N_i =W_i*\cos\alpha_i$　$T_i=W_i*\sin\alpha_i$. On the sliding surface, the slip moment (against the sliding circle) produced by the tangential force caused by the dead weight of all soil bars is $\sum T_i*R=\sum W_i*\sin\alpha_i *R$.

The resisting moment (against the sliding circle) produced by the shearing strength of all the bottoms of the soil bars is $\sum T_{fi}*L_i*R=\sum(N_i *tg\varphi_i+C_i*L_i)*R$.

S. Lin and X. Huang (Eds.): CESM 2011, Part II, CCIS 176, pp. 235–240, 2011.

Thus, the slope stability safety coefficient is

$$F_s = \sum(C_i*L_i + W_i*\cos\alpha_i*tg\varphi_i)/\sum(W_i*\sin\alpha_i) \qquad (1)$$

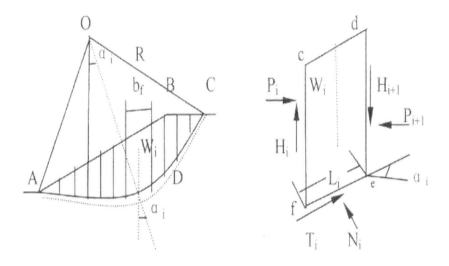

Fig. 1. (a) Numeration of strip division   (b) Numeration of strip division

The formula is proposed by Terzaghi (1936) which is used widely. Calculation experiences show that this formula does not consider the thrust from the two sides of the soil bars so that the stability safety coefficient is on the low side (which is on the safety side) but the measurement error is below 15%. If the soil tested is homogeneous and the width of each soil bar is equal, the (1) can be written in the most concise form:

$$F_s = (\sum C_i*L_i + \sum ri*b_i* H_i *\cos\alpha_i *tg\Phi_i)/ (\sum ri*bi* H_i *\sin\alpha_i)$$

$$= (C*L + r*b*tg\Phi*\sum H_i*\cos\alpha_i)/(r*b*\sum H_i*\sin\alpha_i) \qquad (2)$$

L: Slippery arc length
C, Φ: Soil shearing strength index
r: Soil volume-weight
b: Width of the soil bar

In programming calculation, the formula of stability safety coefficient used is (2) and this is suited to computer calculation.

2   The Program Charts Achieving the Algorithm Above

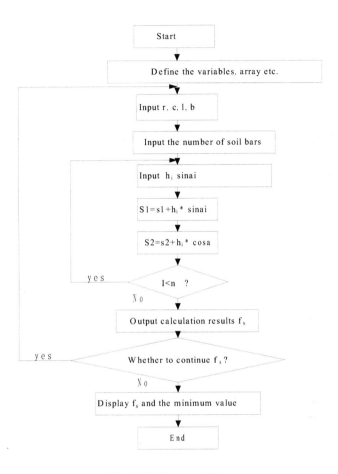

Fig. 2. The Program Charts

3   Application Programming

To define all the variables in the program, it can be known according to analysis that:

The value of r, c, φ is unchangeable during the calculation of the slope stability safety coefficient.

The variables used in the program, if you want to calculate Fs continually when the calculation of slope stability coefficient is finished, the variable value needed to be input is the number of soil bars n, slippery arc length L and soil bar width b, so that a set of values of Fs can be got and the user can choose the minimum one.

Based on the above algorithm, using Visual Basic language programming, the variable needed in the calculation can be input by the user when the screen prompts during the program and the results can be stated on the screen, the program is shown below:

```
Private Sub Command1_Click()
Do
r = Val(Text1.Text)
c = Val(Text2.Text)
fi = Val(Text3.Text)
n = Val(Text4.Text)
l = Val(Text5.Text)
b = Val(Text6.Text)
m = Val(Text10.Text)
For i = 1 To n
H_i = InputBox("input H_i ""input date", 1)
sinai = InputBox("input sinai"" input date ", 1)
s1 = s1 + H_i * sinai
cosai = (1 - sinai * sinai) ^ 0.5
s2 = s2 + H_i * cosai
Next i
m = m + 1
fs(m) = (c * l + r * b * Tan(fi * 3.14159 / 180) * s2) / (r * b * s1)
Adodc1.Recordset.AddNew
Text1.Text = r
Text2.Text = c
Text3.Text = fi
Text4.Text = n
Text5.Text = l
Text6.Text = b
Text7.Text = H_i
Text8.Text = sinai
Text9.Text = s2
Text10.Text = m
Text11.Text = fs(m)
Adodc1.Recordset.Update
ss = MsgBox("Whether to continue calculation ", 1, " Calculating slope stability factor ")
 Loop W H_i le (ss = vbOK)
    End Sub
```

Minimum FS as a subroutine :

```
Private Sub Command6_Click()
Dim fs(21) As Single
Adodc1.Refresh
Adodc1.Recordset.MoveFirst
```

```
r = Val(Text1.Text)
c = Val(Text2.Text)
fi = Val(Text3.Text)
n = Val(Text4.Text)
l = Val(Text5.Text)
b = Val(Text6.Text)
Hᵢ = Val(Text7.Text)
sinai = Val(Text8.Text)
s2 = Val(Text9.Text)
m = Val(Text10.Text)
Adodc1.Refresh
Adodc1.Recordset.MoveFirst
i = 1
Do W Hᵢ le (Not Adodc1.Recordset.EOF)
If Adodc1.Recordset.Fields("fs") <> 0 Then
fs(i) = Adodc1.Recordset.Fields("fs")
i = i + 1
Text12.Text = Adodc1.Recordset.Fields("fs")
End If
Adodc1.Recordset.MoveNext
Loop
Min = fs(1)
For j = 1 To i - 1
If Min > fs(j) Then
Min = fs(j)
End If
Next j
Text12.Text = Min
Adodc1.Refresh
Adodc1.Recordset.MoveFirst
Adodc1.Recordset.Fields("fs value of the minimum ") = Min
End Sub
Data maintenance routines are as follows :
Private Sub Command1_Click()
Adodc1.Refresh
cc = MsgBox("Really delete all data ", 1, " Message")
If cc = vbOK Then
Do W Hᵢ le (Not Adodc1.Recordset.EOF)
Adodc1.Recordset.Delete
Adodc1.Recordset.MoveNext
Loop
Adodc1.Refresh
End If
End Sub
```

4 Conclusion

The program is tested by the input statistics and it is accurately correct. I hope that personnel in using of this program can understand the using situation in order to use it properly. The program is comparatively succinct and easy to use for the users with its visual programming language.

References

1. Yue, Q.: Visual Basic Development Tools Professionals. Economic Industry Press, Beijing (2000)
2. Zhang, S.: Visual Basic 6.0 Introduction and Improvement. Tsinghua University Press, Beijing (1999)
3. Qian, J.: Soil Mechanics, 2nd edn. Hehai University Press, Nanjing (1995)

Qualitative Assessment of the Influence of 2010 Shanghai World Expo on the Tourist Industry in World Expo Circle

Xiujuan Gao

Department of Mathematics, Baicheng Normal College,
Baicheng of Jilin, China
gaoxiujuan578@sohu.com

Abstract. This paper, tourist industry makes a qualitative assessment of the influence of the Shanghai World Expo based on the number of tourists and the tourism revenue in the World Expo circle. The main conclusions are: (1) The total number of visitors to 2010 Shanghai World Expo is about 74.56 million, which is 1 0.34 million more than the historical high number of 64.22 million visitors, with an increase rate by 16.1%; (2) The Year-on-year growth rate of the number inbound visitors in the 2010 Shanghai World Expo Circle from June to December increases by 13.98% averagely than that from January to May; (3) The annual average of the tourism income of 2010 Shanghai World Expo Circle is around 11.1128 million Yuan, which is 15.45 % higher than the annual average 9.6254 million Yuan in 2009, and 65.90% higher than the average revenue 6.6981 million Yuan over the last six years; (4) The tourism revenue of Shanghai in 2010 is about 24.3783 million Yuan, 6.69% higher than the average revenue of 2009, and 38.40% higher than the average revenue over the last six years.

Keywords: Shanghai World Expo, Tourism Industry, Quantitative Assessment.

1 Background

The 41st World Expo, with the theme of *Better City, Better Life*, was held in Shanghai, China in 2010, and it is the first registered World Expo held in developing countries, the first World Expo held in downtown of oversize cities, a World Expo with the biggest area of site, and also the first World Expo opening up the Internet. During the exhibition of 184 days, Shanghai World Expo made full use of the *edges* by building large riverside oasis on the Huangpu River, with two green belts formed and a wedge belt in middle extending into the Expo site. Buildings such as China Pavilion, Theme Pavilion, and Conference Centers etc will become the future landmarks of Shanghai, and take shape of the tourist belt along the River together with the original tourism resources, thus drives the overall development and utilization of tourism resources of Pudong. There is no doubt that, Shanghai World Expo will bring historic opportunities and tremendous promotion to Shanghai, the around tourism circle, and even the entire China's tourism industry. Therefore, taking the opportunity to better develop the tourism industry is an issue worthy of thinking and research for the departments in

S. Lin and X. Huang (Eds.): CESM 2011, Part II, CCIS 176, pp. 241–246, 2011.
© Springer-Verlag Berlin Heidelberg 2011

charge of tourism industry, tourism entrepreneurs and tourism academic circles in China. There is extremely important instructive and practical significance to evaluate the influence of Shanghai World Expo on the tourism industry.

2 Model Building and Solving

2.1 The Number of Visitors during the Exhibition of the Shanghai World Expo

According to the survey on the Internet, there are 8 registered World Expos having been selected for final statistic, and the statistical results are shown in Table 1.

Table 1. Basic Information of Integrated World Expos

No	TimeY ear	Venue (City, Nation)	Session (Days)	Number of visitors (million)		Countries and regions at exhibition
				Totalnumber	Daily number	
1	1933	Paris, France	170	3887	22.86	47
2	1937	Paris, France	185	3104	16.78	46
3	1958	Brussels, Belgium	186	4145	22.28	51
4	1967	Montreal, Canada	185	6040	32.65	62
5	1970	Osaka, Japan	183	6422	35.09	77
6	1992	Sevilla, Spain	175	6082	34.75	110
7	2000	Hannover, Germany	153	5926	38.73	187
8	2010	Shanghai, China	184	----	----	246

According to data in Table 1, a trend line model of the daily number of visitors during exhibition of previous sessions of integrated World Expos has been built up:

$$b_i = 0.1725a_i^2 - 0.5829a_i + 3.3506 \qquad (1)$$

Based on Model (1), the daily number of visitors of the current Shanghai World Expo is predicted out to be 405.2 thousand, with the total number of visitors for 74.56 million, which is 10.34 million more than the record high number of 64.22 million visitors (Osaka, Japan), with a rate of increase by 16.1%, and 41.50067 million more than the average number of 34.04933 million visitors of the previous sessions, with a rate of increase by 118.9%. By 0:00 on September 13, 2010, the cumulative number of visitors to Shanghai World Expo has been up to 50.8653 million, and the daily number of visitors on 12th was 361.5 thousand, which proves that the model prediction is basically in light of the realistic situation.

2.2 Number of Inbound Tourists in Shanghai Expo Circle

During the 2010 World Expo, a World Expo Circle has been formed with Shanghai as the center, including three parts, namely the inner circle, close circle and outer circle, as shown in Table 2.

Table 2. Shanghai World Expo Circle

Shanghai World Expo Circle	Inner Circle	Close Circle	Outer Circle
	Shanghai City and the counties and districts	Nanjing,Hangzhou, Suzhou, Huangshan	Qingdao,Hefei, Zhengzhou ,Nanchang

Take the inner circle and close circle as the object of study, the reception number of 2010 has been estimated out based on the growth rate of the first five months, as shown in Table 3.

Table 3. Reception Number of Inbound Tourism in Major Cities in Shanghai World Expo Circle from January to May of 2010 and the Year-on-year Growth Rate

City		Jan.	Feb.	Mar.	Apr.	May	Monthly average	Yearly average
Shanghai	Reception number	439339	793694	1361190	2004736	2625096	2625096	17337732
	growth rate	25.70	14.79	24.41	25.78	28.90	28.90	23.92
Nanjing	Reception number	39944	99671	230416	377711	452189	452189	2879832
	growth rate	6.25	5.88	9.53	13.03	14.83	14.83	9.90
Suzhou	Reception number	117453	223813	393511	580073	769938	769938	5003484
	growth rate	25.72	20.94	21.92	20.32	22.46	22.46	22.27
Hangzhou	Reception number	114186	247158	479173	754404	971992	971992	6160584
	growth rate	5.18	6.80	7.89	9.08	11.15	11.15	8.02
Huangshan	Reception number	23200	78000	123203	204307	276406	276406	1692276
	growth rate	10.49	36.85	33.05	21.76	19.71	19.71	24.37

A trend line model has been built up for the average growth of inbound tourism in Shanghai World Expo Circle from January to May of 2010:

$$n_j = 2.1857 \ln(m_j) + 16.86 \qquad (2)$$

According to Model (2), the growth of inbound tourism in Shanghai World Expo Circle from June to December has been predicted out and processed in average number, as shown in Table 4.

Table 4. Trend Forecast of the Growth of Inbound Tourism in Shanghai World Expo Circle from June to December

Month	6	7	8	9	10	11	12	Average Rate of Growth
Growth Rate	20.77	21.11	21.40	21.66	21.89	22.10	22.29	21.60

According to the statistical data, it can be predicted that the year-on-year growth rate from June to December has been increased by 13.98% compared with that from January to May of 2010.

By querying the relevant data in Shanghai Statistical Yearbook and the annual average in Table (3), the data table has been accessed including the reception number and Year-on-year growth of Shanghai World Expo Circle in major cities from 2004 to 2010, as shown in Table 5.

Table 5. Reception Number and Year-on-year Growth of Shanghai World Expo Circle in Major Cities from 2006 to 2010

City		2006	2007	2008	2009	2010
Shanghai	Reception number	3812538	19176747	5264727	19082319	17337732
	growth rate	4.90	14.59	1.23	-2.44	23.92
Nanjing	Reception number	816294	5006407	1191813	5166457	2879832
	growth rate	3.60	18.74	2.67	-1.45	9.90
Suzhou	Reception number	1125069	4937866	1682267	5412126	5003484
	growth rate	15.94	14.12	4.34	2.30	22.27
Hangzhou	Reception number	1497230	5568310	2213319	6617700	6160584
	growth rate	18.76	19.10	6.10	9.69	8.02
Huangshan	Reception number	493200	790249	810405	1337633	1692276
	growth rate	24.92	23.71	18.22	15.27	24.37

It can be seen that the number of inbound tourists in major cities shows a fluctuated growth. As a result of the impact of SARS in 2003, the number of inbound tourists in 2004 was relatively low. With the lifting of the epidemic and increase the income of residents, tourist arrivals showed slow growth. Between 2005 and 2006 due to the global spread of bird flu, the number of tourist arrivals declined substantially, but after the bird flu, tourist arrivals increased gradually. In 2008, tourism was influenced by the side effect of the great Wenchuan earthquake and Beijing Olympic Games from different levels and the number of tourists dropt to its lowest point. But in 2009 the number of tourists was quickly pulled up by the World Expo and reached the peak of the period in the first half of 2010.

2.3 Tourism Revenue of Shanghai World Expo Cycle

By querying the relevant information on Internet, a data table has been accessed including the tourism revenue of Shanghai World Expo Cycle in major cities from 2005 to 2009, as shown in Table 6.

Table 6. Tourism Revenue of Shanghai World Expo Cycle in Major Cities from 2004 to 2009 (RMB ten thousand Yuan)

	2005	2006	2007	2008	2009
Shanghai	1598.85	1612.23	1875	1958	2285
Nanjing	379	390.56	654.9	714.69	822.16
Suzhou	400	407.25	552	735.06	830
Hangzhou	465	465	597.22	707.22	803.12
Huangshan	147	187.98	287.49	389.65	416

According to data in the table above, it can be seen a good upward trend in six cities including Shanghai, Nanjing, Wuxi, Hangzhou, Suzhou and Huangshan with the growth in inbound visitors. The tourism revenue of these six cities has been processed in annual average, fitted with quadratic function, to build up a trend line model of the annual average of tourism revenue of Shanghai World Expo Circle:

$$q_k = 5.3872 p_k^2 - 74.059 p_k + 328.9 \qquad (3)$$

In addition, the annual average of the tourism revenue of Shanghai City has been fitted with quadratic function separately, to build up a trend line model of the tourism revenue of Shanghai.

$$t_k = 2.1121 s_k^2 - 8288.4 s_k + 1124.6 \qquad (4)$$

According to Model (3), it has been predicted that the annual average of the tourism revenue of 2010 Shanghai World Expo Circle will be 11.1128 million Yuan, 15.45%

higher than the 9.6254 million Yuan in 2009, and 65.90% higher than the average 6.6981 million Yuan over the last six years.

According to Model (4), it has been predicted that the tourism revenue of Shanghai in 2010 will be 24.3783 million Yuan, 6.69% higher than the 22.85 million Yuan in 2009, and 38.40% higher than the average 17.6148 million Yuan over the last six years.

3   Model Assessment and Improvement

To carry a quantitatively assessment of the influence of Shanghai World Expo, this paper makes a longitudinal assessment from the perspectives of number of tourists of Shanghai World Expo and the tourism revenue of the World Expo Circle. The Model making use of the methods of trend line fitting and chart analysis, makes a survey and evaluation on the visitor number and tourism revenue.

There are still in need of some improvement for this model: Due to the subjective factors such as the lack of statistical data and the exclusion of special data, there is deviation in the data needed for modeling, thus there is still much room for improvement of the reliability of this model.

References

1. Hao, Y., Li, Z.: Excel Statistic and Analysis. Posts and Telecom Press, Beijing (2006)
2. Chen, H., Lu, L.: A Contrastive Analysis of the Effect of Bejing Olympic Games and Shanghai World Expo. Economic Geography 23(6), 843–853 (2003)
3. Xu, M.: World Expo Yearbook (1851-2000). World Architecture (11), 10–12 (2000)
4. Dai, G.: Qualitative Estimation of the Effect of Kunming World Expo: Background Trend Line Model. Geographical Science 27(3), 426–433 (2007)
5. http://www.expo2010.cn/ Shanghai World Expo Official Website (September 10, 2010)

An Optimized Color Image Steganography Using LFSR and DFT Techniques

Asghar Shahrzad Khashandarag[*], Ahmad Habibizad Navin, Mir Kamal Mirnia, and Hamid Haji Agha Mohammadi

Young Researchers Club of Tabriz, Islamic Azad University Tabriz Branch, Tabriz, Iran
a.shahrzad@iaut.ac.ir

Abstract. A color image steganography method to conceal a secret data into the cover image in the frequency domain is suggested. In this method, Lempel–Ziv–Welch (LZW) compression is used to obtain a low bit rate; Also Linear Feedback Shift Register (LFSR) technique is used to enhance the security of the scheme. In the embedding process, an Adaptive Phase Modulation (APM) mechanism and Discrete Fourier Transform (DFT) are used for secret data embedding. Abilities of the proposed method are high speed and security, because of using hardware element LFSR and Data Encryption Standard (DES) cryptography.

Keywords: data hiding, steganography, linear feedback shift register, discrete fourier transform, data encryption standard.

1 Introduction

Image, sound, and etc are known as digital data. The first application of Steganography can be predicted 440 BC by Herodotus. Fig. 1 shows the structure of Steganography. Steganography techniques [1-6] are used to hide digital data in coverage media so that no one can find it. The phrase steganography is derived from Greek and means concealed writing. Other technique of data hiding is called watermarking. Water marking techniques [7, 8] is a process to embedding data into a coverage media that is difficult to remove. Da-Chun Wu [9] proposed a steganography scheme that used pixel-value differencing for secret data embedding. E. Besdok [10] proposed a method in multispectral spatial images to embed a secret data into a cover image. M.A.B Younes [11] published a method of hiding data in images by using the Least Significant Bit insertion. Y.C. Hou [12] explained the Steganography technique as an efficient data hiding method. In this paper, an optimized data-hiding scheme in Frequency domain is presented. This method used Discrete Fourier Transform (DFT) to transfer the cover image from spatial domain into frequency domain. In frequency domain, the phase is a good location for secret data embedding because it has high noise immunity [13]. In this

---

[*] Corresponding author.

S. Lin and X. Huang (Eds.): CESM 2011, Part II, CCIS 176, pp. 247–253, 2011.

method, Lempel–Ziv–Welch (LZW) compression is used to obtain a low bit rate; Also Linear Feedback Shift Register (LFSR) technique is used to enhance the security.

This paper is organized as follows: In section 2, we present the related works. In sections 3 and 4, we propose and analyze our method and present the conclusion.

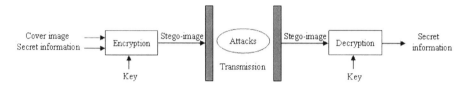

Fig. 1. The structure of steganography is shown

2   Related Works

In this section, two methods color image steganography in frequency domain are demonstrated.

2.1 The First Method

Fig. 2 shows the conceptual model of proposed algorithm by Wen-Yuan Chen [13]. The secret image S is parted into R, G, and B planes. Then they are encoded by SPIHT into the bit stream $\{m_s\}$ respectively. A chaotic mechanism (CM) is used to hash $\{m_s\}$ into $\{m_c\}$ to enhance their security by using PNG as a pseudo random number generator [13]. Also cover image X is parted into R, G, and B planes. Then they are transmitted from spatial domain to frequency domain. A Coefficients selection and frequency hopping algorithm (CSFH) is used to hashing the selected DFT coefficients into a random order. Then the $\{m_c\}$ is embedded into $\hat{X}'$ by Adaptive phase modulation (APM). Then by IDFT $\hat{X}''$ transmitted to spatial domain and finally they are merged and stego-image is created.

2.2 The Second Method

A color image steganography method has been proposed by Asghar Shahrzad Khashandarag [14]. Fig. 3 shows the conceptual model of this method. It used a hybrid method in spatial and frequency domain. The disadvantage of this method is:

- The high complexity because using EMI method (showed in red ellipse)

- The low capacity of Cover image for embedding (showed in green ellipse)

An optimized version of this method is presented in the next section.

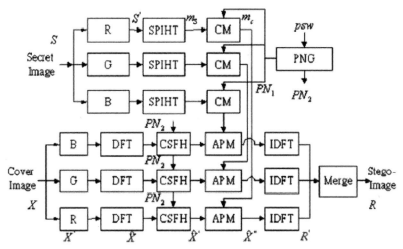

PNG: Pseudo random Number Generator   DFT: Discrete Fourier Transform
SPIHT: Set Partitioning in Hierarchical Trees   APM: Adaptive Phase Modulation
IDFT: Inverse Discrete Fourier Transform   CM: Chaotic Mechanism
SSFH: Coefficient Selection and Frequency Hopping

Fig. 2. The conceptual model of data embedding algorithm is shown [13]

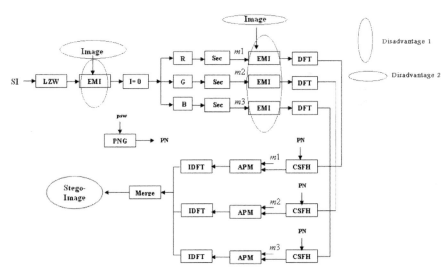

Sec: Security; SI: secret information; EMI: embed with image

Fig. 3. The conceptual model of the data embedding algorithm is shown [14]. In this Figure the disadvantages (Disadvantage 1: The high complexity because using EMI method and Disadvantage 2: The low capacity of Cover image for embedding) of previous method [14] is shown.

3 The Proposed Method

3.1 Data-Embedding Algorithm

A steganography process must be completely secure, and does not reduce the visual quality of the cover image when the secret data is concealed. The overall concealing process of our proposed scheme is shown in Fig. 4. On the other hand cover image also is parted into R, G and B and after by transmitting into frequency domain by DFT, hashing and modulation algorithms are applied. The Secret information (SI) is compression by LZW technique [17]. The Result of compression stages, with pseudo-random number is xor, and then bit streams are split into three parts (SI1, SI2 and SI3) and then Sec block is used for security. Fig. 5 shows the details of Sec block. In Fig. 5 the Data Encryption Standard (DES) is used for enhance security of data hiding. The Data Encryption Standard (DES) is a block cipher that uses shared secret encryption. For more information about DES algorithm see [15]. Then the result of the Sec block stage is embedded into the CSFH results. Then they are transmitted to spatial domain by Inverse Discrete Fourier Transform (IDFT). Finally they are merged and stego-image is created.

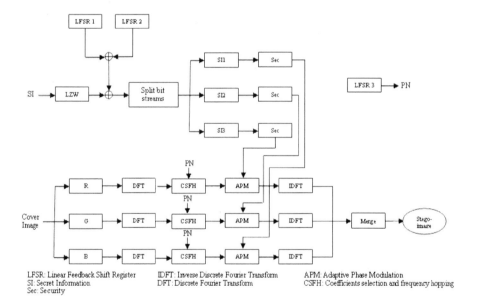

LFSR: Linear Feedback Shift Register   IDFT: Inverse Discrete Fourier Transform   APM: Adaptive Phase Modulation
SI: Secret Information   DFT: Discrete Fourier Transform   CSFH: Coefficients selection and frequency hopping
Sec: Security

Fig. 4. The conceptual model of the optimized algorithm is shown

3.1.1 Linear Feedback Shift Register (LFSR)

A linear feedback shift register (LFSR) is a shift register whose input bit is a linear function of its previous state. The only linear function of single bits is xor, thus it is a shift register whose input bit is driven by the exclusive-or (xor) of some bits of the overall shift register value [16]. The initial value of the LFSR is called the seed, and because the operation of the register is deterministic, the stream of values produced by the register is completely determined by its current (or previous) state. Both hardware and software implementations of LFSRs are common. In Fig. 6 the structure of LFSR is shown, which D_i is a register for save bit and a_i is a Coefficient. LFSR is an n-bit shift register which pseudo-randomly scrolls between $2^n - 1$ values, but does it very quickly because there is minimal combinational logic involved. In formula (1) the polynomial of LFSR is shown.

$$G(x) = x^n + a_{n-1}x^{n-1} + ... + a_i x^i + ... + a_1 x + a_0$$

(1)

$$a_i = 0 \text{ or } 1$$

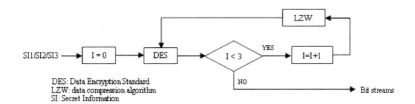

DES: Data Encryption Standard
LZW: data compression algorithm
SI: Secret Information

Fig. 5. The details of sec block are shown

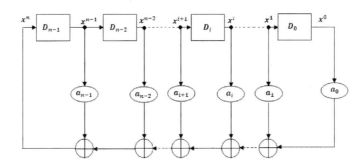

Fig. 6. The structure of LFSR technique is shown

3.1.2 Discrete Fourier Transform (DFT)

We need DFT to transfer an image from spatial domain into frequency domain. In the formula (2) the DFT is shown. Note that $f(x, y)$ is image in spatial domain (host-image) and $F(u, v)$ is image in frequency domain (stego-image).

$$F(u,v) = \sum_{x=0}^{M-1}\sum_{y=0}^{N-1} f(x, y) e^{-j2\pi\left(\frac{ux}{M} + \frac{vy}{N}\right)}$$

(2)

$$u = 0,1,2,...,M-1 \text{ and } v = 0,1,2,...,N-1$$

3.1.3 Inverse Discrete Fourier Transform (IDFT)

The formula (3) the DFT is shown. Note that M and N are the size of image.

$$f(x, y) = \frac{1}{MN} \sum_{u=0}^{M-1} \sum_{v=0}^{N-1} F(u, v) e^{j 2\pi \left(\frac{ux}{M} + \frac{vy}{N} \right)}$$

$$x = 0, 1, 2, ..., M - 1 \text{ and } y = 0, 1, 2, ..., N - 1$$

(3)

3.2 Inverse Data-Embedding Algorithm

The process of inverse data embedding is shown in Fig. 7. We demonstrate the ISEC block of Fig. 7 in Fig. 8. We used three session of DES technique that is called triple DES in data embedding process, therefore three session of Inverse DES is needed for inverse data embedding. Note that APD and ILZW are the inverse of APM and LZW technique which explained in [13].

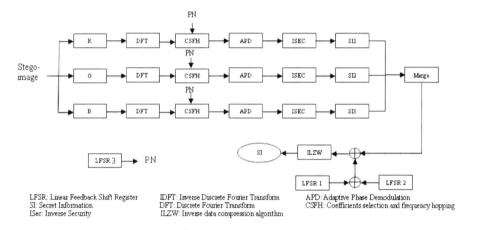

Fig. 7. The conceptual model of inverse data-embedding algorithm is shown

Fig. 8. The reverse of sec block is shown

4 Conclusion

In this paper a color image steganography method to conceal secret data into the cover image in the frequency domain is suggested. The proposed method has high speed and security in comparing with previous method. Because of using secure and fast hardware element LFSR and Data Encryption Standard (DES) cryptography.

References

1. Wang, R.Z., Lin, C.F., Lin, J.C.: Image hiding by optimal LSB substitution and genetic algorithm. Pattern Recognition Society (2001); Published by Elsevier Science Ltd. All rights reserved
2. Marvel, L.M., Boncelet Jr., C.G., Retter, C.T.: Spread spectrum image steganography. IEEE Transactions on Image Processing 8(8), 1075–1083 (1999)
3. Chandramoul, R., Kharrazi, M.N.: Image Steganography and Steganalysis: Concepts and Practice Memon. Springer, Heidelberg (2004)
4. Lin, C.C., Tsai, W.H.: Secret image sharing with steganography and authentication. The Journal of System and Software 73, 405–414 (2004)
5. Mcbride, B.T., Peterson, G.L., Gustafson, S.C.: A new blind method for detecting novel steganography. Digital Investigation 2, 50–70 (2005)
6. Cetin, O., Ozcerit, A.T.: A new steganography algorithm based on color histograms for data embedding into raw video streams (2009), Published by Elsevier Ltd., doi:10.1016/j.cose.2009.04.002
7. Ni, R., Ruan, Q., Cheng, H.D.: Secure semi-blind watermarking based on iteration mapping and image features. Pattern Recognition 38(3), 357–368 (2005)
8. Chen, W.Y., Chen, C.H.: A robust watermarking scheme using phase shift keying with the combination of amplitude boost and low amplitude block selection. Pattern Recognition 38(4), 587–598 (2005)
9. Wu, D.-C., Tsai, W.-H.: A steganographic method for images by pixel-value differencing. Pattern Recognition Letters 24, 1613–1626 (2003); 0167-8655/03/$ - see front matter _ 2002 Elsevier Science B.V. All rights reserved, doi:10.1016/S0167-8655(02)00402-6
10. Besdok, E.: Hiding information in multispectral spatial images (2005), Elsevier GmbH. All rights reserved, doi:10.1016/j.aeue.2004.11.040
11. Younes, M.A.B., Jantan, A.: A New Steganography Approach for Image Encryption Exchange by Using the Least Significant Bit Insertion. IJCSNS International Journal of Computer Science and Network Security 8(6) (June 2008)
12. Hou, Y.C., Chiao, Y.F.: Steganography: an efficient data hiding method. Journal of Technology 15(3), 363–372 (2000)
13. Chen, W.-Y.: Color image steganography scheme using set partitioning in hierarchical trees coding. In: Digital Fourier Transform and Adaptive Phase Modulatio. Elsevier, Amsterdam (2006), doi:10.1016/j.amc.2006.07.041
14. Khashandarag, A.S., Ebrahimian, N.: A new method for color image steganography using SPIHT and DFT, sending with JPEG format, 978-0-7695-3892-1/09 $26.00 © 2009 IEEE DOI 10.1109/ICCTD.2009.14
15. http://en.wikipedia.org/wiki/Data_Encryption_Standard
16. http://en.wikipedia.org/wiki/Linear_feedback_shift_registe
17. http://en.wikipedia.org/wiki/Lempel_Ziv_Welch

Evaluation for the Flawlessness of New Energy Industry Chain Based on Rough Sets and BP Neural Networks

Wei Li, Dan Wang, and Yunqiao Ti

College of Business Administration, North China Electric Power University,
071003 Baoding, China
maggie8992@tom.com, {hd11111,tiyunqiao1986}@126.com

Abstract. As one of the key factors which mankind depends on for existence, energy is the necessary strategic material which plays an important role in national economic and social development. In order to cope with changes the energy situation, the Chinese government and the domestic provinces have gradually began to vigorously develop new energy industry, and the study on new energy industry has been given more and more important significance. Therefore, this paper takes the energy industry as the researching object and makes an evaluation index system of flawlessness to evaluate the flawlessness of new energy industry chain, combining Rough Sets with BP Neural Network Theories.

Keywords: New energy industry, Industry Chain, flawlessness, Rough Sets, BP Neural Networks.

1 Introduction

In the current world, the development of energy is an important issue that the mankind pays close attention to, and along with the development of economy, the energy shortage and energy security issues are protruding, therefore, all countries are developing new energy to realize the sustainable development. Some achievements in new energy industry has been made in China. As one of the important standards to evaluate the development of an industry, the flawlessness of industry chain can implies the ability of a province to develop new energy industry.

According to this, this paper focus on the flawlessness of new energy industry chain, establishes evaluation index system to evaluate the flawlessness of new energy industry chain and puts forwards to the problems and countermeasures about new energy industry chain.

S. Lin and X. Huang (Eds.): CESM 2011, Part II, CCIS 176, pp. 254–260, 2011.
© Springer-Verlag Berlin Heidelberg 2011

2   Basic Theories

2.1 Rough Set Method

Rough set theory is a new mathematical approach to data analysis and data mining.
   Some theory and definition about rough set are introduced as followed:

(1) Information system

An information system is expressed by a quaternary function, $S=(U,A,V,f)$. And
$U=\{x_1, x_2, x_3,...,x_m\}$ is non-empty finite set of objects called the universe, where x_i is
the element object for the system; A is the non-empty boundary set of attribute a; V is
the value set of information function f; and f: $U \times A \rightarrow V$ is a information function of S,
which assigns information value to attributes, that is, $\forall a \in A$, $x \in U$, $f(x,a) \in V$.

(2) Importance of Attributes

A method to get the importance of attributes is to remove some attributes and then to
which the changes of the investigation The bigger change represents higher
importance, while smaller change represents lower importance. C and D denote the
attribute sets and decision attribute sets.

(3) Decision table

Decision table is a special and important information system. For information system
$S=(U,A,V,f)$, $A=C \cup D$, $C \cap D=\emptyset$. C is called condition attribute set and D is called the
decision attribute set.

2.2 BP Neural Network

(1) Basic concepts

Artificial neural network is a kind of dynamic study system, designed with the way the
brain works, and it is mainly divided into feed forward neural networks, feedback
network, and self-organizing network etc. At present, the BP network, with the function
of error back-propagation learning, is the most widely used and most in-depth study.
BP neural network consists of two processes: feedback transmission of Information and
back propagation of error

(2) BP neural network structure

The BP neural network concludes input layer, hidden layer and output layer, composed
of simple nerve cells. BP neural network structure is as shown in Fig1:

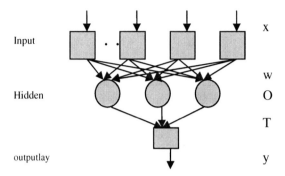

Fig. 1. BP Neural Network Structure

(3) Process of BP neural network

The basic process is as follows shown in Fig 2:

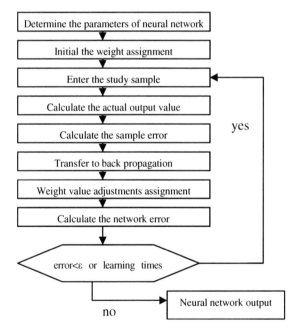

Fig. 2. BP neural network Process

3 Construction of Index System and Reduction of Attributes

3.1 Construction of Index System

The new energy industry chain of Hebei province can be revealed via four categories, including economic factors, resource factors, technical factors, and Cultural factors. Thus this paper makes the four one-class to the evaluation system. Based on the analysis of the internal and external conditions related to new energy industry chain, establishes the evaluation system which as follows.

Table 1. Index system

Evaluation index system of flawlessness of new energy industry chain	economic factors E	Regional economic evaluation E1	regional economic strength E11
		new energy enterpriseE2	proportion of leading enterprises E21
			company strength E22
		new energy productsE3	variousness E31
			unique nature E32
	resource factors F	resource endowment F1	technical exploitation amount F11
		infrastructure F2	development of supporting industries F21
	technical factors G	application technology G1	popularization of new energy products G11
		development Technology G2	utilization rate of resources G21
		innovation Ability G3	patent number G31
	Cultural factors H	government H1	local government Performance H11
			local government support H12
		public H2	the local people's culture quality H21
			the local people's sense of energy conservation H22
		foreign exchange H3	cooperation with the foreign counterparts H31
		education H4	universities H41
			relevant professional H42

3.2 Reduction of Attributes Based on Rough Set

Selected 15 evaluators do evaluation of each index and the decision attribute. and then discretize the data to obtain the discretized decision table, as shown in Table 2.

Table 2. Discretized Decision Table

Evalu-ators	Condition Attributes C																	Decis-ion Attri-bute D
	E					F		G			H							
	E1	E2		E3		F1	F2	G1	G2	G3	H1		H2		H3	H4₄		
	E11	E21	E22	E31	E32	F11	F21	G11	G21	G31	H11	H12	H21	H22	H31	H41	H42	
x1	4	3	4	4	7	6	6	4	6	6	8	7	7	6	7	3	5	D1
x2	5	3	4	4	7	6	6	4	6	6	8	7	7	6	7	3	5	D2
x3	5	6	4	4	7	6	6	4	6	6	8	7	7	6	7	3	5	D1
x4	5	6	4	4	7	6	6	4	6	6	8	7	7	6	6	3	5	D3
x5	5	6	4	5	7	6	6	4	6	6	8	7	7	6	6	3	5	D1
x6	5	6	4	5	6	6	6	4	6	6	8	7	7	6	6	3	5	D3
x7	5	6	4	5	6	7	6	4	6	6	8	7	7	6	6	3	5	D1
x8	5	6	4	5	6	7	7	4	6	6	8	7	7	6	6	3	5	D1
x9	5	6	4	5	6	7	7	5	6	6	8	7	7	6	6	3	5	D2
x10	5	6	4	5	6	7	7	5	5	6	8	7	7	6	6	3	5	D3
x11	5	6	4	5	6	7	7	5	5	7	8	7	7	6	6	3	5	D3
x12	5	6	4	5	6	7	7	5	5	7	8	7	7	6	6	3	6	D1
x13	5	6	4	5	6	7	7	5	5	7	8	6	7	6	6	3	6	D3
x14	5	6	4	5	6	7	7	5	5	7	8	6	6	6	6	3	6	D2
x15	5	6	4	5	6	7	7	5	5	7	8	6	6	5	6	3	6	D1

The decision attribute D is divided into three levels: good, middle and bad.

According the principle of attribute reduction, in the table above, we reduce E22, H11 and H41, so the index system is adjusted as shown in the following table.

Table 3. Adjusted Index System

one-class index	E				F		G			H				
two-class index	E1	E2	E3		F1	F2	G1	G2	G3	H1	H2		H3	H4
Three-class index	E11	E21	E31	E32	F11	F21	G11	G21	G31	H12	H21	H22	H31	H42

4 Evaluation Process Based on BP

As well as the index system is reduced, next, we take Hebei province, Jiangsu province, Neimeng province, Xinjiang province and Zhejiang province as evaluation objects to evaluate the flawlessness of new energy industry chain via BP Neural Networks.

First, we can take 12 group data in Table 1 as the testing data of BP neural networks, and get the weight of each index. And then we get the first 12 group data as shown in Table 4.

Table 4. Testing Data

1	2	3	4	5	6
0.4803	0.4870	0.5070	0.5070	0.5137	0.5070
7	8	9	10	11	12
0.5103	0.5170	0.5237	0.5170	0.5237	0.5237

Next, we make BP simulation, using the testing data above, and in the simulation the times of training is 10000 and the accuracy is1e-3. The calibration results is shown in Table 4.

Table 5. Training Result of BP

Expectation data	0.5170	0.5103	0.5070
Forecast data	0.5170	0.5102	0.5068

We can get that the error meets the accuracy requirement, and it meets the requirement when the training get to the 84th, as shown in Figure 2.

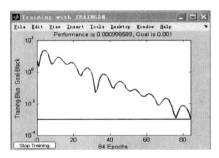

Fig. 3. The results of network training

Finaly, we make a evaluation of the flawlessness of new energy industry chain in the five provinces, the results are shown in the following table.

Table 6. Evaluation Results

Province	Hebei	Neimeng	Jiangsu	Xinjiang	Zhejiang
Evaluating values	0.5436	0.4836	0.5503	0.4569	0.5403
Sort	2	4	1	5	3

The above evaluation results gives a general evaluation to the flawlessness of new energy industry chain. It shows that The province which develops best in new energy industry chain is Jiangsu, and the next is Hebei. The new energy industry in Jiangsu and Hebei province is well developed and has the leading position.

5 Conclusion

This paper uses establishes the index system of flawlessness of new energy industry chain, and makes a attribute reduction with Rough Sets, and then make a evaluation with BP neural network. Finally, it obtain the development state of new energy industry chain in the five provinces, which have far-reaching practical significance for the development of new energy industry.

Acknowledgments

This paper is supported by the fund project (09457272D) of Department of Science and Technology in Hebei province.

References

1. Sun, W., Niu, D.-X., Shen, H.-Y.: Comprehensive evaluation of power plants' competition ability with BP neural networks method. Machine Learning and Cybernetics, 4641–4644 (August 2005)
2. Zhou, X., Zhuang, Y.: Study on Evaluating Method of Entreperise Independent Innovation Ability Based on BP Neural Network. Value Engineering, 7 (2008)
3. Chen, C.T.: Extensions of the TOPSIS for group decision-making under fuzzy environment. Fuzzy Sets and System (114), 1–9 (2000)
4. Li, W., Li, S., Wang, D.: The Wind Power Project Investment Risk Evaluation Based on BP Neural Networks. Advanced Materials Research (05), 108–111 (2010)

Optimizing Industry Structure of HeBei Province Based on Low Carbon Economy

Wei Li, Zuxin Zhang, and Man Wei

College of Business Administration, North China Electric Power University,
071003 Baoding, China
hd11111@126.com, 277239292@qq.com, lishichao7878@tom.com

Abstract. Concerning climate change and security of energy supply, many countries are in the pursuit of low-carbon economy, aim to achieve development of both economic and low carbonization environment by adjusting the industrial structure. This article describes the concepts of low carbon, combining industry economics, gray, regression analysis, using the qualitative and quantitative theory, draw a conclusion that the status quo of the hebei province industrial structure is not conducive to development of a low-carbon economic, in the end study on adjusting direction and propose advice of hebei industrial structure.

Keywords: low carbon economic, industrial structure, energy, optimization.

1 Introduction

The British government first give the concept of low-carbon economic in 2003, it can be easily understood as to decrease the emissions of greenhouse gases, not to affect social welfare and sacrifice economic development. High emission lead to global climate warming, threatening the humanity survival.

In order to Develope low-carbon economic, per energy consumption has shrinked from 1.895tons in2006 to 1.727tons in2008,but the absolute is still significantly higher than the average national level, the main reason is that the industrial structure of hebei province is not reasonable, highly dependent on fossil energy, etc. Industrial structure impacts the amount of energy consumption, in order to reduce energy consumption and carbon emission intensity, optimize and upgrade the industrial structure, realizing low carbon and efficient economic development.

2 Low Carbon Economic

2.1 Definition

Low carbon economy is a combination of "low carbon" and" economic development".
Low carbon economic is a economic mode based on the low emission, low pollution, low energy consumption, emphases the changes of economical development, energy

S. Lin and X. Huang (Eds.): CESM 2011, Part II, CCIS 176, pp. 261–266, 2011.
© Springer-Verlag Berlin Heidelberg 2011

consumption and human life. The substance of low carbon economic is to improve energy utilization, develop clear energy, set up new energy structure and pursue green GDP; the core is to promote social sustainable development and achieve a win-win situation of social development and ecological environment, by doing a fundamental shift on energy and technologies, industrial structure.

2.2 The Possibility of Developing Low Carbon Economic

(1) Energy security

Energy security is a main indicator on both economic and social security, directly affects social stability and sustainable development. Per energy consumption of hebei is below the average level, with the economy developing rapidly, the energy requirements will be further increased, energy is facing the threat. To alleviate the energy crisis, hebei needs to reduce the rely on fossil energy, develop low carbon economic, realize the sustainable development of energy, environment and economic.

(2) The effect of imposing carbon tax

In order to develop low carbon economic, the European and American countries adjust successively policies, imposing carbon tax on the imported which not conforms to the CO_2 emssion level.

In hebei province, steel products, chemical, nonferrous metals and minerals and raw materials are exported in a very significant proportion, these products contain low technology content, cause high emission. Once imposed, the cost of export enterprises increases, trading advantages decrease, the market space narrows, apart from direct impact on industrial development, also leade to a negative impact on employment, welfare of hebei province, etc. In order to reduce carbon tariffs effects, hebei province should give priority to the development of industry, seeking low carbon road, promoting economic development and environmental protection.

3   Analysing the Relationship between the Status Quo of Hebei Industrial Structure and Low-Carbon Economic Development

3.1 The Status Quo of Hebei Industrial Structure

The industry structure of hebei province completed gradually from "one, two, three" to "two, three, one".

(1) Hebei is a big agriculture province, in recent years , husbandry and fishery grew steadily, according to the research that green plants absorb about 150 billion tons CO_2 and produce about 4000million tons O2, if spend investment on forests, it will promote process of realizing low carbon economic.

Agricultural industrialization of hebei provincial level is low, product are apparently short of competition. Pesticides and fertilizers are basic element in agricultural production, but it consume fossil energy in its own process of production, therefore, in a certain sense, modern agriculture can be understood as fossile agriculture in Hebei.

(2) The proportion of manufacturing is high, high-tech industries and mechanization develop slow, heavy industry consume amounts of energy, supporting industries highly depend on resources, carbonization features significantly.

Hebei province is the biggest steel output province, account for 20%t. It produces steel and iron about 31.663 million tons in 2007, Coal is the main energy consumption in its production, proportion of total energy consumption is 69.9%; six highly energy consumption industry account for 50.7%of the total industries, comprehensive energy consumption up to 15.156million tons, account for 89.2%; heavy industry is in the proportion of 78.6%; sulphur dioxide emission of power, steel, building materials, chemicals, paper, account for 86.7% in the whole province.

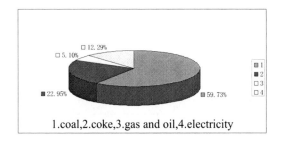

1.coal,2.coke,3.gas and oil,4.electricity

Fig. 1. Hebei province scale industrial enterprises energy consumption in 2007

(3) Travel, communications and information, the third industry has developed rapidly, and formed various categories, and become an important driving force in the national economy. From the service structure, traditional service develope prosperly, modern service develope slowly; from layout, rural services far from behind the overall level; from supply situation, competitiveness of service level is not strong.

Comprehensively, Hebei province now has formed famous-brand industry and developed relative superiority. But the industrial structure is not reasonable, high carbonization and highly depending energy resources features are prominent, the esiting problem restricts low-carbon economic development.

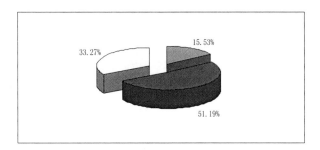

Fig. 2. The proportion of three industrial structure in hebei province

3.2 Analysing the Relationship of the Status Quo of Hebei Industrial Structure and Low-Carbon Economic Development

(1) Associated Analysis

Based on the grey models, study the relation between three major industries and energy consumption. Choosing energy consumption from 1999 ~ 2007 as variables, agricultural, manufacturing and service sectors as arguments, having the following associated coefficient (ρ =0.3).

Table 1. Relationship parameter

Time	△01	△02	△03
1996	0.905162	0.407876	0.404439
1997	0.646255	0.539063	0.538764
1998	0.584524	0.687849	0.643081
1999	0.590625	0.939796	0.769007
2000	0.790922	0.665497	0.602907
2001	0.902171	0.743877	0.581114
2002	0.636886	0.768134	0.543408
2003	0.530869	0.662766	0.663073
2004	0.766188	0.758161	0.623418
2005	0.927717	0.70174	0.632177
2006	0.686489	0.412739	0.390427
2007	1	0.245409	0.235536
Relationship parameter	0.747317	0.627742	0.552279

According to the table shows, associated sequence between three major industries and energy costs are in the follows as agricultural, manufacturing and service industries, illustrating that basic industries and energy costs are in the same follow.

(2) Regression Analysis

Treat agricultural, manufacturing and service industries output and carbon emissions in Hebei provinc as time sequence, using eviews software to calculate the relation of three major industrial structure and carbon emissions. x1 x2 x3 respectively are on behalf of the first and second, the third industries, y represents carbon emissions, four relationships can be given by eviews software as $Y=0.05-1.16X_1+1.71X2-0.07X_3$

Variable	Coefficient	Std. Error	t-Statistic	Prob.
X1	-1.163500	0.329697	-3.528997	0.0168
X2	1.718525	0.500837	3.431309	0.0186
X3	-0.072694	0.339723	-0.213981	0.8390
C	0.057519	0.011415	5.038947	0.0040

R-squared	0.995758	Mean dependent var	0.111111
Adjusted R-squared	0.993213	S.D. dependent var	0.037508
S.E. of regression	0.003090	Akaike info criterion	-8.420207
Sum squared resid	4.77E-05	Schwarz criterion	-8.332551
Log likelihood	41.89093	F-statistic	391.2505
Durbin-Watson stat	2.992352	Prob(F-statistic)	0.000002

Fig. 3. Regression analysis

According to the results of analysis: three major industries increase by 1% make carbon emissions changes -1.16%, 1.71%, -0.07% respectively, reduce manufacturing or increase service industries can effectively promote economic development.

(3) Comprehensive Analysis Between Industrial Structure and Low-carbon Eeconomic

Agricultural industry consume a lot of energy in the production process, due to its proportion and fertilizers excessively; but with the proportion becoming smaller, technological innovation development and production facilities has improved steadily, the dependent on fossil energy will wear down correspondingly, the promoting role will stand out;

Now Hebei province is in the process of industrialization and urbanization, manufacturing is in the proportion of 52% steadily, heavy industries ,which cost highly energy consumption as the support of manufacturing, rely on high fossil energy, figure 3 shows the heavy industrial and resources consumption structure will cause carbon emissions increase in accordance with the speed of1.71%; the optimization and upgrading of manufacturing , carbonization transformation in developing low carbon economic process is especially important;

Service industry depend on energy minimumly, as the main impetus of the hebei economy, its current proportion and the overall level are low, the role to promot low carbon economic is still not obvious.

Manufacturing is key industries to energy reduction and conservation, service industry is in low proportion, carbonization features stand out and limited low-carbon economic development. In order to expedite the process of realizing a low-carbon economic, technology innovation and policy is needed to adjust the three major industries, optimizing and upgrading of the industrial structure, change the status quo of the heavy industrial structure and resources consumption. Adjusting the industrial structure is one of the implementations to realize a low-carbon economy.

4   Adjustment Hebei Industrial Structure Based on Low Carbon Economy

The core is technological advances, adjusting and optimizing industrial structure, forming an advanced industrial structure with modern services and advanced manufacturing industry; developing green agriculture, high and new-tech industries, the third industry and eliminating high energy consumption, low efficiency and poor competitiveness industries.

From the perspective of sustainable development, developing low carbon agriculture should follow aspects as to: full use of agricultural resources, such as the survival of the gas; developing low carbon manufacturing is based on low-carbon energy; whereas it will take a long period, therefore it is difficult to make fundamental shrink to change our energy structure. So in low-carbon industrial development process, not only to develop clean energy, should study how to improve energy accessibility ,as to accelerate process of low-carbon energy; government formulate preferential policies to promote low-carbon manufacturing change; Hebei should vigorously develop modern services, new energy, new material, new medicine, and biological breeding, information network industries, quicken the development of tourism, transportation.

Implementing low-carbon economic development strategy, Hebei province will inevitably turned to low consumption industry as new industries; energy industry, nuclear power industry will become leading industry; using revenue policy to encourage the reduction of energy conservation, technology innovation, realizing the standard of low-carbon economy; adjust the structure and gradually form industrial structure with modern services and manufacturing, realizing low carbon economy. As our province is in the process of the industrialization and urbanization, the manufacturing still will be dominant industry at a longer period, restructuring can not be completed overnight.

Acknowledgments

This paper is supported by the fund project (09457272D) of Department of Science and Technology in Hebei province.

References

1. Zheng, Y.-G.: CGE Model and Policy Analysis. Social and Press (1999)
2. Liu, D.-Z.: Optimizing Industry Structure of HeBei province Based on Energy Cost. Economic Forum (2009)
3. Wei, T.-Y.: Imposing Carbon Taxes On Economy And Greenhouse Gas Emission. World Economic and Political (2002)
4. Chen, W.-J.: Hebei Present Industry Structure. Economist (1) (2007)
5. Sun, J.-H.: Developing Low Carbon Economic, Developing Low Carbon. Nanning. Local Research (9) (2009)

The Competitiveness of Photovoltaic Industry in Hebei Province Fuzzy Comprehensive Evaluation of the AHP

Wei Li, Man Wei, and Zuxin Zhang

College of Business Administration,
North China Electric Power University,
071003 Baoding, China
hd11111@126.com, Happywm888666@163.com, lishichao7878@tom.com

Abstract. This article uses diamond mode to analysis the influence of factors of industrial competitiveness in the qualitative, and thus build the photovoltaic industry competitiveness evaluation index system of Hebei Province, as a result of evaluating indicator multi-level, As well as majority of target's with difficulty quantification and the fuzziness, adopts the fuzzy comprehensive evaluation model to analyze the Hebei photovoltaic industry competitive power, And from the results of analysis.

Keywords: Hebei Province, The diamond mode, AHP fuzzy quality synthetic evaluation, Photovoltaic industry, Industrial competitiveness.

1 Introduction

Porter argued that whether a country's specific industries with international competitiveness depends on six factors: factor conditions, demand conditions, related to the status of industry and supporting industries, firm strategy, structure and competitors, government actions and opportunities. Diamond model is a dynamic, two-way to strengthen the system. It emphasizes the creative power of the elements of industry, the competitiveness of the role of a factor more important than simple.

1.1 Based on Diamond Model of Hebei Province Photovoltaic Industry Power Industrial Competitiveness, Analyzing the Influential Factors

Industrial production factor is the input of the various elements required, it is the basic conditions for industrial development. Porter argued that factors of production can be summarized as: natural resources, human resources, knowledge resources, capital resources and infrastructure top-five.

Annual sunshine hours in Hebei Province from 2500 to 3063 hours, the radiation is about 1384 ~ 1657kwh / m, is very rich with solar energy resources, Hebei Province, photovoltaic power generation industry in terms of resource endowments have more advantages.

Demand refers to the domestic market for the products or services provided by industry, the demand is. Porter believes that the domestic market demand will stimulate

S. Lin and X. Huang (Eds.): CESM 2011, Part II, CCIS 176, pp. 267–272, 2011.
© Springer-Verlag Berlin Heidelberg 2011

business improvement and innovation. China's solar PV market demand conditions, directly on the solar PV industry a significant impact on the competitiveness, the continuing rise in demand is the driving force behind the industrial scale was expanded, but also the determinants of industrial competitiveness.

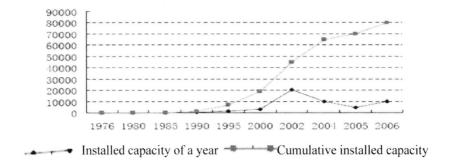

Fig. 1. 1976-2006 of annual installed capacity of photovoltaic solar cells and cumulative installed capacity

Related industry mainly refers to the raw materials, parts and other upstream industries and other industries, related and supporting industries is a necessary condition for industrial development. Advantage of related industries will play each other for a particular industry, there may be advantages to play groups; then, may have driven the demand for complementary products; Photovoltaic power generation industry, mainly for the upstream industry of silicon, wafer manufacturing industry, due to Baoding, Hebei, "China Power Valley" in the building, including China, Yingli PV, including more than a dozen companies are located in Baoding.

Corporate strategy, structure and competitive enterprises in a country is the foundation, organization and management forms, and the performance of the domestic market competition. Porter argued that to create sustainable competitive advantage and the biggest factor is the existence of a strong domestic market, competitors, business improvement and innovation can provide the fundamental driving force.

Government action can have an impact on industrial competitiveness, the factors of production such as government investment, industrial policy on the competitive structure and development strategies, the Government of the process industry, the role competition is sometimes positive and sometimes be negative.

2   AHP and Fuzzy Comprehensive Evaluation Based on Comprehensive Evaluation of Photovoltaic Industry in Hebei Province

2.1   Diamond Model Based on the Evaluation Index System

"Diamond Model Management perish" put forward gives us a good basis to establish the evaluation index. We are under the "Diamond Theory" put forward by the four elements and two variables, the establishment of factors of production, market demand, related industries and support industries, business strategy, structure and peer competitors, government policy and opportunities for a six Level indicators (see Table 1).

Table 1. Photovoltaic Industry in Hebei Province Competitiveness Evaluation System

Level indicators	Secondary indicators	Third indicators
Factor of production A1	Natural Resources A11	Natural endowments A111
	Human ResourcesA12	The number of training institutions A121
		Number of R & D A122
	Knowledge Resources A13	Number of patentsA131
		Number of research projects A132
	Capital resources A14	Industrial output A141
	Infrastructure A15	Number of industrial parks A151
		Business equipment A152
Demand conditions A2	Market size A21	Market potential A211
	The structure of demand A22	Domestic market demandA221
		Product Exports A222
Related and supporting industries A3	Equipment A31	Equipment manufacturing standards A311
		Power generation applications facilities A312
	Technical Services A32	
Corporate strategy, structure and competitive A4	Industrial concentration A41	Clusters of Enterprises A411
	Competitive conditionsA42	Industry Competition A421
	Corporate Structure Strategy A43	Degree of structural optimization company A431
	Regional competitive position A44	The location of economic strength A441
Opportunities with the Government A5	Technological invention and innovation A51	
	Industrial restructuring A52	
	Government policies A53	
	Government Procurement A54	

2.2 PV Industry Structure in Hebei Province Fuzzy Comprehensive Evaluation Model

(1) Establishment of a comprehensive evaluation factors

a factor set: A = {A1, A2, A3, A4, A5}; second factor set: $A_1 = \begin{pmatrix} A_{11} & A_{12} & A_{13} & A_{14} & A_{15} \end{pmatrix}$, three factors: $A_{11} = \begin{pmatrix} A_{111} \end{pmatrix}$

(2) The establishment of rating scale set

The evaluation is defined as 5 grades, ie V = {V1, V2, V3, V4, V5}, where v1; excellent, v2; good; v3; general; v4; poor, V5 poor; the corresponding scores were V = (1, 0.8, 0.6, 0.4, 0.2).

(3) To determine the weight set to build single-factor evaluation matrix and make a comprehensive evaluation of

Using the Delphi method. Determine the levels of factor weights. 10 experts, respectively, then the factors for each level of evaluation. Levels of factor weights and rating scale in Table 2.

Table 2. Photovoltaic Industry in Hebei Province Competitiveness Evaluation System evaluation results

Level indicator	Secondary indicators	Third indicators	Evaluation results				
			Excellent	Good	General	Fair poor	poor
A1 （0.3）	A11 （0.25）	A111(0.15)	2	4	3	1	0
	A12 （0.3）	A121(0.15)	1	4	5	0	0
		A122(0.1)	0	4	4	1	1
	A13 （0.2）	A131(0.2)	3	5	1	0	1
		A132(0.1)	1	3	4	2	0
	A14 （0.15）	A141(0.2)	1	7	1	1	0
		A142(0.05)	2	5	2	1	0
	A15 （0.1）	A151 0.05	3	3	3	1	0
A2 （0.25）	A21 （0.4）	A211(0.3)	2	5	2	1	0
	A22(0.6)	A221(0.35)	3	4	1	2	0
		A222(0.35)	4	4	2	0	0
A3 （0.15）	A31(0.45)	A311(0.45)	0	4	3	2	1
	A32(0.55)	A321(0.55)	0	5	5	0	0
A4 0.2	A41(0.2)	A411(0.2)	3	5	1	0	1
	A42(0.3)	A421(0.3)	2	2	2	4	0
	A43(0.1)	A431(0.1)	4	2	2	0	2
	A44(0.4)	A441(0.4)	3	3	1	2	1
A5 （0.1）	A51(0.15)		7	2	0	1	0
	A52(0.25)		0	5	5	0	0
	A53(0.3)		8	2	0	0	0
	A54(0.4)		5	2	2	1	0

① On the "Factor" for comprehensive evaluation. First on the "Factor A" factor set in as the third stage evaluation: f: A12 (V), A121 = (0.1,0.4,0.5,0,0), A122 = (0,0.4,0.4,0.1, 0.1) was the single factor evaluation matrix for the weight of A12 = (0.15,0.1) with a model for comprehensive evaluation of synthetic operation was:

$$B_{12} = A_{12}, B_{12} = A_{12} \circ R_{12} = (0.15 \quad 0.1) \circ \begin{pmatrix} 0.1 & 0.4 & 0.5 & 0 & 0 \\ 0 & 0.4 & 0.4 & 0.1 & 0.1 \end{pmatrix} = (0.1 \quad 0.15 \quad 0.15 \quad 0.1 \quad 0.1)$$

Similarly:

$B_{11} = (0.15 \quad 0.25 \quad 0.15 \quad 0 \quad 0), B_{13} = (0.1 \quad 0.2 \quad 0.2 \quad 0.1 \quad 0.1), B_{14} = (0.1 \quad 0.2 \quad 0.1 \quad 0.1 \quad 0), B_{15} = (0.4 \quad 0.25 \quad 0.25 \quad 0.1 \quad 0)$

To arrive

$$R_1 = \begin{pmatrix} B_{11} & B_{12} & B_{13} & B_{14} & B_{15} \end{pmatrix} = \begin{bmatrix} 0.15 & 0.25 & 0.15 & 0 & 0 \\ 0.1 & 0.15 & 0.15 & 0.1 & 0.1 \\ 0.1 & 0.2 & 0.2 & 0.1 & 0.1 \\ 0.1 & 0.2 & 0.1 & 0.1 & 0 \\ 0.4 & 0.25 & 0.25 & 0.1 & 0 \end{bmatrix}$$

The same reason, the "production factor" in the second and make a comprehensive evaluation of factors:

$$B_1 = A_1 \circ B_1 = \begin{pmatrix} A_{11} & A_{12} & A_{13} & A_{14} & A_{15} \end{pmatrix} \circ \begin{bmatrix} 0.25 \\ 0.3 \\ 0.2 \\ 0.15 \\ 0.1 \end{bmatrix}^T \begin{bmatrix} 0.15 & 0.25 & 0.15 & 0 & 0 \\ 0.1 & 0.15 & 0.15 & 0.1 & 0.1 \\ 0.1 & 0.2 & 0.2 & 0.1 & 0.1 \\ 0.1 & 0.2 & 0.1 & 0.1 & 0 \\ 0.4 & 0.25 & 0.25 & 0.1 & 0 \end{bmatrix} = (0.15 \quad 0.25 \quad 0.15 \quad 0.1 \quad 0.1)$$

② The A2, A3, A4, A5 for comprehensive evaluation. Similar to the above first to third grade for the comprehensive evaluation factor set, and then on the second level factor set for comprehensive evaluation, the steps above. Available:

$B_2 = (0.35 \quad 0.35 \quad 0.2 \quad 0.2 \quad 0), B_3 = (0 \quad 0.5 \quad 0.5 \quad 0.2 \quad 0.1), B_4 = (0.3 \quad 0.3 \quad 0.2 \quad 0.3 \quad 0.1), B_5 = (0.4 \quad 0.25 \quad 0.25 \quad 0.1 \quad 0)$

so a single factor matrix:

$$R = \begin{pmatrix} B_1 & B_2 & B_3 & B_4 & B_5 \end{pmatrix} = \begin{pmatrix} 0.15 & 0.25 & 0.15 & 0.1 & 0.1 \\ 0.35 & 0.35 & 0.2 & 0.2 & 0 \\ 0 & 0.5 & 0.5 & 0.2 & 0.1 \\ 0.3 & 0.3 & 0.2 & 0.3 & 0.1 \\ 0.4 & 0.25 & 0.25 & 0.1 & 0 \end{pmatrix}$$

factor set for the first stage evaluation. The first level factor set $A = \begin{pmatrix} A_1 & A_2 & A_3 & A_4 & A_5 \end{pmatrix}$ of weight

$A = (0.3 \quad 0.25 \quad 0.15 \quad 0.2 \quad 0.1), B = A \circ R = (0.25 \quad 0.25 \quad 0.2 \quad 0.2 \quad 0.1)$

by the rating scale scores corresponding to $V = (1 \quad 0.8 \quad 0.6 \quad 0.4 \quad 0.2)$ calculated total score

$$(0.25 \quad 0.25 \quad 0.2 \quad 0.2 \quad 0.1) \circ \begin{pmatrix} 1 \\ 0.8 \\ 0.6 \\ 0.4 \\ 0.2 \end{pmatrix} = 0.67$$

3   Conclusions

According to the principle of maximum degree. Hebei Province, could be the evaluation of the competitiveness of the PV industry as a good result. Fuzzy Comprehensive Evaluation Based on the above analysis can be drawn in the PV industry in Hebei Province of factors of production and corporate strategies have an advantage, you can see the demand factors influence the competitiveness of the industry, the greatest degree, in improving competitiveness should play to our strengths, on the important factors breakthrough.

Acknowledgments

This paper is supported by the fund project (09457272D) of Department of Science and Technology in Hebei province.

References

1. Esmaeili, M., Aryanezhad, M.B., Zeephongseku, P.: A game Theory approach in seller-buyer supply chain. Euorpena Journal of Operation Research (195) (2009)
2. Nye, J.S.: Soft Power. In: The Means to Success in World Politics. Public Affairs, New York (2004)
3. Jiang, l.-Q., Wu, R.-M., et al.: Evaluation of sub-industrial cluster competitiveness Index System Design and Analysis of I-J. Economic Geography (1), 37–4O (2006)
4. Yong, Z., Wang, S.-L.: Soft power and hard power: Competitiveness in a new theory Framework. Heilongjiang Social Sciences (4), 60–63 (2009)

Design of Distributed Communications Data Query Algorithm Based on the Cloud Computing of Hadoop

Luo Jun[*]

Center of Computer and Netware, Guangdong Polytechnic Normal University,
293 Zhongshan Avenue, Guangzhou, 510665
Guangdong, China
itczhj@126.com

Abstract. This paper firstly analyzes the algorithm of extension inquires based on traditionally relational database communication social network data, Then analyzes some shortcomings, and puts forward problems need to be solved. This paper presents design thought based on Hadoop Map/Reduce function model .Combining with the original Map/Reduce programming model and the actual demand of visualization systems, designs extension query algorithm based on Hadoop platform and proves that the algorithm has improved more efficiency in data query than the traditional expansion inquire algorithms.

Keywords: Hadoop, cloud computing, distributed expansion inquire algorithms.

1 Research Background

Along with the graph theory, stochastic network knowledge continuously involved, social network analysis technology has greatly developed. In the implementation of visualization technology, communication social network data set is so huge that it demands its visualization system should have strong data processing ability Efficiency of the traditional relational data in dealing with large datasets is not ideal, especially in figure layered expanding, because of involving query processing of massive data, each layer extending of figure all needs to wait for a long time. So it is urgent to solve that a better mode of data processing comes up.

2 Traditional Algorithm of Expansion Inquires

2.1 Overview of Algorithm of Expansion Inquires

In a relational database, it is simple to realize communicate social network analysis and visualization system ,and we could borrow breadth first search thoughts to design layered expansion, Firstly in the client memory the following two Hash Table data structure is defined to save the nodes of being extended out and edges:

```
public HashTable nodeSet ;
public HashTable edgeSet ;
```

---

[*] Corresponding author.

S. Lin and X. Huang (Eds.): CESM 2011, Part II, CCIS 176, pp. 273–280, 2011.

Among them, node Set deposits expansion nodes, and key value is a Mobile Phone number, and value is the relevant information of Mobile Phone accounts.EgdeSet deposits extension edge, and key is the combinations of the Mobile Phone numbers or fetion numbers of the senders and receivers, adding a time-mark behind to ensure that key will not repeat. Value is the communication information. After all date is taken out, Use firstly mechanics algorithm to make the facial point of nodeSet set cover the outer layout of the figure. Then take out edge information from edgeSet to complete the whole map layout. Among them initial data of nodeSet is the set of nodes to expand of visible graphic, and edgeSet is initially empty. Expanding process as seen in figure 1:

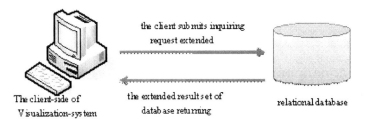

the client submits inquiring
request extended

The client-side of
Visualization-system

the extended result set of
database returning

relational database

Fig. 1. Basic flow chart

1) client uses nodes-set to be expanded initialized nodeSet data sets of memory, and will make query request submit to the database server.

2) database searches the nodes and edges to meet the requirements according to the search queries submitted, and then returns pI results to visualization client.

3) Make the edge collection insert into the edgeSet, and the node collection into nodeSet. During combining by inserting nodes, it will traverse nodeSet. If the node already exists, we will give up insertion operation, if not, we will make it insert in the nodeSet.

4) Do use tension algorithm to make nodes deploy to visual diagram, and use the data of edgeSet to connect related node.

5) If it is multilayer expansion, we will empty edgeList, and then again submit queries to database taking the data of nodeSet of last layer expanded as the condition.

2.2 Problems

Use a relational database to store and manage social networks date, and use last section of the algorithm to realize the visualization systems ,which on the function can meet the required, but there are the following questions:

1) Query efficiency is low, in the system of the realization of the Oracle, when handling inquiries submitted of the client; we could realize it by in-sentence. When data quantity is very large, velocity of inquiry is quite slow.

2) Storage space spending is big, in order to optimize query, so we can create index. But as the data quantity increases, the number of index is exponential increase, which occupied a big part of the storage space of the server.

3) when query to node and then set back memory, we need to traverse the initial nodes to ensure no repetitive nodes. Data quantity of Initial nodes and returning-result set is large, and this traverse process is very time-consuming.

4) when there are a lot of repetitions between returning nodes set and initial nodes set, data from the server back to the client will contain much repetitive information (i.e. nodes that are repetitive with initial nodes). So it is a waste of network broadband to transmit these data to the client.

3   The Realization of Hadoop of Extended Algorithm

3.1 Design Thought

Now commonly use parallel computing method to solve the problem of low efficiency, but both traditional distributed system and parallel algorithm are too complex, and it is so difficult to implement .Hadoop realized Google Map /Reduce programming model, which makes the part of parallel application development package to the inner part of Hadoop platform.We do extend in view of layer, also basing on the ideas of breadth first search algorithm, and in Hadoop platform realize expanse. Design idea as figure2 shows:

1) Submit the client query-request to name nodes of Hadoop platform, and distribute to Map function every name-node.

2) Map function directly output query-edge-collection back to the client, while point-set to combine functions.

3) Combine function does sorting and eliminating repetition on the nodes set and intermediate result that Map () function generates, and then hands result to Reduce function.

4) Reduce function does some comparing between intermediate result set and initial nodes which are passed by Combine function , if the set of initial nodes has already existed, we will eliminate it. If not, return to client.

The resulting edge sets and point sets are not repeated. It is not necessary to use HashTable data types to inner storage structure of the client, and we can Change it for Aryls-type. Structure-type of client in-memory updates to the following:

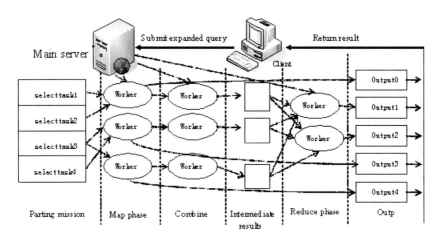

Fig. 2. Overall flowchart

```
public Aryls nodeList ;
public ArryList edgeList ;
```

Efficiency of breadth first search algorithm will be greatly improved. Because the outputing of Map and the Reduce process is the key /value pair, objects of the node and edge class are stored in array of nodeList and edgeList:

```
//node class
public class node
{ string key ;
string value ;
}
//egde class
public class edge
{ string key ;
string value ; }
```

3.2 Map Function Design

Map number is used to execute inquiries, and generates intermediate results. Put query operation of Hbase into the Map () function. Query result can be divided into two parts: edge sets and node sets. Map function directly combining with edge outputs and using node set generates intermediate result set, and then gives it to the middle Combine function to process.

Below it is the pseudo-code of Map function:

```
Map (String node, String cond)
        for each n in node
        nodekey = getcollabel (n, cond);
nodevalue = getValue (nodekey, "Info");
egdekey = n+nodekey+getTimeStamp (n, nodekey);
        egdevalue = getValue (n, nodekey);
        output.collect (nodekey, nodevalue);
        output.collect (edgekey, edgevalue);
```

3.3 Combine Function Design

Combine function is optional in the MapReduce algorithm model. Generally only in dealing with large data, Combine function is used to optimize the whole process. There are two main reasons to lead in Combine in the design:

1) It is permitted to exist some repetitive key values in results that Map function outputs. Especially for communication social network data, there are lots of repeated nodes. Combine function operates in machine of each Map task, so if Combine function in first eliminate repetition to nodes before transfer to Reduce function, which will greatly reduce the network consumption.

2) Here by the thought of breadth first search algorithm to develop the level expanse, new nodes expanded must be compared with initial nodes. If you can first do sorting to nodes in Combine, and again hand it to Reduce function to process, which will greatly improve the efficiency of Reduce function.

We can conclude that there are two main tasks for Combine function from the above two points: eliminating repetition and sorting, the following is pseudo-code to realize Combine function:

```
Combine (String nodekey, String nodevalue):
     for each a in nodekey
     if a exist;
     sort (nodekey);
output, collect (nodekey, nodevalue);
```

From Reduce function it can be seen, the above design does not remove traverse process of the memory while it puts traverse process into Reduce function and improves the ergodic efficiency through the way of parallel computing.

3.4 Run Function Design

In run () function, create JobConf, define input and output of communication social network analysis system, and then submit the Job to JobTracker, waiting for the Job to finish working. Both Map function and Reduce function have output, so we should set up two output directories. For the implementers of Reducer, we need re-write JobConfigurable. JobConf configure(), this method needs to pass a JobConf parameter, whose purpose is to perform initialization of Reducer of. Invoke the method of Reduce (String nodekey, String no devalue). Later, application can execute the corresponding cleaning up by rewriting Closeable. close(). Pseudo-code of run function is below:

```
run ():
     JobConf conf = new JobConf (getConf(), Snv.class);
     conf.setJobName ("snvt");
     conf.setOutputKeyClass (Test.class);
     conf.setOutputValueClass (Test.class);
     conf.setNumMapTasks (Integer.parseInt (m));
     conf.setNumCombineTasks (Integer.parseInt (m));
     conf.setNumReduceTasks (Integer.parseInt(r));
     conf.setOutputPath (new Path (Map.get (0)));
     conf.setOutputPath (new Path (Reduce.get (1)));
     JobClient.runJob (conf);
     Closeable.close ();
```

Hadoop system is responsible for operation of the next things. Its main work is:

1) JobTracker, creates mission of Hbase query, and invokes getSplits0 method, and divides the mission of query to each Mapper task. Put Mapper task Generated Queue into Queue.

2) Mapper task does pass query task to Mapper function, and Mapper function outputs the edge sets inquired to the client while query divides the node sets inquired into middle results, handing to Combine function for processing.

3) Combiner Task does eliminating repetition and sorting with the intermediate results on the machines with the same of Mapper Task, by which the results are output to Reduce Task.

4) Reducer Task acquires intermediate result sets needed from Jetty of TaskTracker to run the Combiner by using HTTP protocol, and then does eliminating repetition.After performing Reducer function, finally outputs the node sets to the client according to Outpufformat.

5) TaskTracker every 10 seconds feeds back operation condition to JobTracker, and once it completes one task, 10 seconds later, it will ask JobTracker for the next Map/Reduce Task.

4 Map/Reduce Related Preparation

4.1 Task Granularity

The determination of task granularity concerns query efficiency, load balancing of the system and many other problems. Conventionally speaking, the number of the Map is usually determined by input-data, which is commonly the total number of input file total.

In fact, when plenty of Map functions work together, there exist different states. Some Map functions are in Hbase database query state, and some are in edge collection output state, and others are in generating the intermediate result set of the node set state. Normal parallel scale is roughly that each node is about 10 to 100 Maps, and for CPU consumption small, Map tasks can be set to 300 or so. Each task initialization need certain time, therefore, more reasonable situation is that the time of Map execution is at least more than 1 minute. For Combine task, generally it should be set up the same number with Map tasks. But for us, because part of the Map function directly is output, and the other part is deal with by Combine function, we should increase the number of Map function.

Reducer makes a group of intermediate numerical set associated with Nodekey Reduce a smaller numerical set, eliminate repetitive nodes of node set. Through JobConEsetNumReduceTasks (int) users can set the number of Reduce task of one homework. When there are 10 million items of communication data, the number of tasks is 50.

4.2 Fault-Tolerant Mechanism of the System

Programming model of Map/Reduce operates in hundreds of thousands of ordinary machines to help deal with large scale data, so the library must be able to deal well with the malfunction. Common failures include Master fault and Worker fault.

If the mission of Master fails, we can start another Master process from the last checkpoint of last time. However, there is only one Master, so its failure is quite troublesome. So now our reality is that if Master failed, we would suspend the computing of Map/Reduce. Visualization-client can check this condition, and also may, according to our needs, resume executing the operation of Map/ Reduce. When we start Master task backuped, it would resume executing Map task.

For Worker, Master periodically pings each worker. If the Master in a certain period has not received information returned by Worker, it will mark this Worker as failure.

Set Data replication factor of communication visualization system Data nodes to 3, the same Data Node should save a copy, and another Data node save a copy. Assume that the work of some node failed, it will not guarantee the reliability of the data.

5 Comparison of Realizing of the Two Systems

Assume that a relational data chooses Oracle database, then the consumption of time Oracle data doing single-layer-extending mainly includes:

1) the time complexity of inquiring in the database is: $Ts1=O$ (ned).
2) the time complexity of sorting for extension nodes is: $Tq1=O$ (e*loge).
3) the time complexity of removing new extension nodes, initial node-set and repetitive nodes in memory is: $Tr1=O$ (n*log (e-s)).
4) network-transmission-time of extending nodes returned to the memory: Tt1

Let's analyze the consuming time on the ground of Hadoop as follows. We suppose that the number of Map mission is m, the number of Combine function is c, the number of Reduce mission is r.

1) The time complexity of finding extension node in Hbase is: $Ts2=O$ (nd/m).
2) The time complexity of removing the repetitive part in the new extension nodes set in the Combine function is: $Tr2=O$ ((e*loge)/c).
3) The time complexity of sorting in Combine function is: $Tq2=O$ (((e-s)*log (e-s))/c).
4) The time complexity of removing the repetitive part between the extension nodes and the initial nodes set by Reduce function is: $Tr3=O$ (n*log (e-s))/r).
5) The network transmission time of extension node set returning to the memory is: Tt2.

Next, take the time complexity of two parts above into compare. The data of the communication network social analysis and visual system is usually huge. This indicates when the system is implemented in the Hadoop platform, m, c and r, the number of mission of Map, Combine and Reduce is respectively a great positive integer. So Ts1+Tq1+Tr1 is more bigger than Ts2+Tq2+Tr3. It has removed the repetitive parts between extension node and initial node set when the data which has been deal with on the Hadoop platform is given back to the client-side. However, the Oracle version makes the new extended data set of all back to the client and eliminates repetition in memory. Therefore, as to the network load, the former is smaller than the latter, that is Tt1> Tt2. So, with regard to this part of the data, the higher the value of m, c, r is, the higher the efficiency is.

Now, we only need to consider the time to eliminate repetition of Combine function on the Hadoop platform. Actually, this time is far less than the previous time difference. Because in these two systems, the two most consuming parts are the data query and data transmission. The eliminating repetition of Combine function is in order to reduce the repetitive part of middle result set that the Map function handles, lower the number of nodes that inputs to Reduce function, and reduce the network consumption of data transmission. At the same time⬡ there is a $Tr2 = O$ ((e * loge) / c) expression, we can see that performance gap of two versions relates to the number of newly extended nodes. In the case that the number of Combine task remains unchanged, the more nodes expanded out, the worse the relative performance of Hadoop platform is. Because eliminating repetition of Combine function increases some time. Without doubt, this is not the Hadoop its own problem, but because we put the operations of eliminating repetition in the Combine function, to affect the treatment efficiency. However, this effect is very small, relative to the efficiency that Hadoop platform has improved can be ignored. Therefore, it can be concluded, Hadoop platform can more improve efficiency in contrast with the traditionally extended algorithm when treating the large data sets.

References

1. Dean, J., Ghemawat, S.: Map/Reduce : Simplified Data Processing 011 Large Clusters. In: OSDI 2004: Sixth Symposium on Operating System Design and Implementation (2004)
2. Chang, F., Dean, J.: Bigtable: A Distributed Storage System for Structured Data. OSDI (2006)
3. Orossman, R., Gu, Y.: Data mining using high performance data clounds: experimental studies using sector and sphere. In: Conference Oil Knowledge Discovery in Data, USA (2008)
4. Liu, J.: Social Network Analysis Introduction. Social Science Literature Press, Peking (2004)
5. Zhu, Z.: Mass Data Processing Research and Practice Based on the Hadoop [Degree Thesis]. Peking. Beijing Post and Human (2008)

Information Technology and "Meaningful Transfer - Led Explore" Teaching Concepts

PingHua Huang[1,2] and SuMin Han[3]

[1] College of Civil Engineering, Hehai University , Nanjing, 210098, China
[2] Wanfang College of Science & Technologe, Henan Polytechnic University
Jiefang Road,142 454000 Jiaozuo, China
hph2001@hpu.edu.cn
[3] Institute of Electrical Engineering, Henan Polytechnic University
Century Avenue.2001 454000 Jiaozuo, China
hansumin@hpu.edu.cn

Abstract. In order to achieve success both in learning and teaching, and take to the advantages of both "pass - accept" type and "self – explore" style, the new teaching concepts "meaningful transfer-led explore" were proposed. More importantly, that information technology being integrated into the new teaching concepts can really increase complementary strengths. Advanced information technology not only enriches the teaching media, especially in terms of optimizating instructional design plays a decisive role. The paper also analyzes the role of information technology on process assessment initiated by the new teaching concept and individualized teaching. New teaching concepts according with applying information technologies can be effective and enhance teaching effectiveness.

Keywords: meaningful transfer-led explore teaching concepts, information technology, teaching design.

1 Introduction

Into the 21st century, the international education technology community about educational technology theory focus on be little the theory of educational technology in China. They think that the concepts are "neither Chinese nor Western", "also East and West", and the traditional "teacher centered" type is now praised as student as the center. Kekang HE Professor of Educational Technology Certificate dialectically think that the two ideologies have both advantages and disadvantages, are not diametrically opposed, and supporting one is not necessarily opposed to a another, and the two just can learn from each other, complement each other. Therefore "teacher-oriented-student-centred", a education thought combination of the two was proposed. Corresponding teaching concepts that is "Meaningful transfer-led explore" also appeared[1,2]. The new teaching concepts in the present of rapid developing information technology, that must be integrated with information technology can take effect. How information technology to promote the implementation of "meaningful transfer - led explore" teaching concepts, a few shallow view will be proposed in this paper.

S. Lin and X. Huang (Eds.): CESM 2011, Part II, CCIS 176, pp. 281–286, 2011.
© Springer-Verlag Berlin Heidelberg 2011

2 "Meaningful Transfer-Led Explore" New Teaching Concepts and Appearing Background

Since the 1960's, the educational technology (Formerly "Electronic Education") in China is developed of absorbing the main content of educational technology of western countries, that Mainly focusing on the theory and application of teaching media. Since the 1980's, it absorbed the connotation of foreign advanced technology , focusing on teaching process and teaching resources in design, development, utilization, management and evaluation. Accordingly, the educational thought of educational technology with Chinese characteristics was formed, that is "teacher-oriented-student-centred". The new teaching thought is neither a "teacher-centered", not "student-centered", but both make teachers play the leading role in the teaching process, and students be highlighted the cognitive subject position in the learning process. Corresponding teaching concepts that is "Meaningful transfer-led explore" also appeared. The new concepts take to the advantages of both "pass – accept" type and "self – explore" style, but not the simple accumulation or combination of them. The new concepts is the improvement and development of the two, And can be effective for using the proper way to implement[1,2].

3 The Analysis of Annotation of "Meaningful Transfer-Led Explore" Teaching Concepts

"Meaningful tranfer-led explore" teaching concepts take to the advantages of the two, and criticize and inheritance from them.

On the one hand, the "pass – accept" teaching concepts emphasis on the traditional teaching and learning activities which regarde "pass – accept" as a symbol. Teachers still through lectures, writing on the blackboard, ppt presentations, and other instructional media to explain subject knowledge, professional skills, and clear up doubts, highlight the key and difficult, and grasp knowledge and context, clarifying system characteristics; Students listen carefully, recorde key, and ask questions, answer, appropriate practice, in order to achieve understanding, digesting, and ultimately to accept, master teaching content.

The only improvement is that the theory of Ausubel Should be strictly followed In the implementation of the "pass – accept", the teaching process of "Meaningful tranfer" be practically accomplished. Ausubel thought that the key to effectively achieve meaningful learning, is establish any substantial non-contact between the new concepts, new knowledge and cognitive structure of learners .That is how to achieve meaningful transfer In the framework of prior knowledge and interests driving[1,2].

On the other hand, the "self - explore" teaching concepts emphasis on emphasis on the traditional teaching and learning activities which regarde "self – explore-cooperate" as a symbol. But the teacher should become organizers, leaders in classroom teaching, helpers and facilitators students constructing meaning independently, the developers and providers of teaching resources. Here only the teacher is became as "leaders". This one word led to very different meaning, "leaders" stressed the autonomous learning, self-building and collaborative exchanges and deepen the process of meaning construction. Teachers still need to play a leading role ("director" do not emphasize the leading role), that is for the subject of independent study, the focus of collaborative exchanges, the learning difficulties deepen the meaning construction process of and other key issues, teachers must make the necessary guidance, inspiration, analysis, coaching, including appropriate classroom instruction[1,2].

The new concepts absorbed the advantages of Western education, and abandoned the shortcomings of the two. Namely the "spoon-fed", "indoctrination" teaching of the traditional classroom teaching and lack the enthusiasm and initiative is improved, and also avoid the blindness of pure self-study, the lack of systematic and forward-looking. But whether the new teaching concepts is implemented smoothly at this stage and achieve need teachers to carefully study and try to make more efforts. Here for that the implementation of information technology in the new teaching concepts can play a role in fueling the author will have a simple discussion.

The online version of the volume will be available in LNCS Online. Members of institutes subscribing to the Lecture Notes in Computer Science series have access to all the pdfs of all the online publications. Non-subscribers can only read as far as the abstracts. If they try to go beyond this point, they are automatically asked, whether they would like to order the pdf, and are given instructions as to how to do so.

Please note that, if your email address is given in your paper, it will also be included in the meta data of the online version.

4   Information Technology Will Greatly Promote the Implementation of "Meaningful Transfer-Led Explore" Teaching Concepts

On July 29, 2010, State Council Information Office issued the "National education reform and development of long-term planning programs''. Chapter19 (Including 59, 60, 61)of which referred to aspects of the planning of educational information mainly relate to the speeding up infrastructure construction, strengthening the development and application of high-quality education resources and building national education management information system in three aspects. It can be seen that my county pay more attention to information education, and the direction for future is clearer[3].

Advanced information technology is the summationv of acquiring, processing, storaging, transmissing and using a variety of text figure audio-visual information ,using computer, network, radio, television and other hardware devices and software tools and scientific methods. Information technology and education are inseparable, the relation is very close. Information Technology in the implementation of "meaningful transfer - led explore" teaching concepts is significant. Effective integration between the two is bound to improve teaching effectiveness, efficiency and effectiveness.

4.1   Information Technology Has Greatly Enriched the Teaching Media

Traditional teaching medias, include language, writing, printed materials, pictures, blackboard, models, and physical and teachers of various facial expressions, posture, etc. Developing with information technology, Modern teaching media mainly include optical projection, tape recorders televisions, computers, a variety of network equipment and the environment etc[4]. Modern teaching media for the rich rendering power, the strong representation power, a wide range of transmission power, ease controllability, the friendly interactivity in teaching has played a not inconsiderable role, especially in instructional design and developing teaching resources. Instructional design is the core and the primary link in the "meaningful transfer - led explore" teaching concepts.

4.2 Information Technology Has Optimized Instructional Design

If information technology teaching environment supported by multimedia and network is still using the traditional teacher-centered teaching methods of passive acceptance, the result is hundreds of billions of dollars will be wasted without success. Therefore, the information teaching is carried on under the direction of "pass meaningful - led explore" teaching concepts.

Integrating effectively information technology in teaching process in various subjects, an information technology teaching will be created, and a teaching and learning mode in that " self – explore-cooperate "is the characteristics, not only teachers can play a leading role but also students can fully reflect the status of student body is achieved to stimulate student initiative, enthusiasm and creativity, and change basically the traditional classroom teaching structure.

Teaching information technology to optimize the teaching design should be adopted the following ways and means:

1) Applicate advanced the construction theory to guide.

2) Use advanced "meaningful transfer - led explore" teaching concepts to build and design the teaching content and process;

3) Design of teaching around the "study and education" ideas;

4) Stress construction of various subjects resources, and collection and open of learning tools.

4.3 Information Technology Make the Learning Process, More Interesting, and Enrich the Learning Resources

Learning process is no longer mechanical acceptance, but is combining of Independent research under the guidance of the teacher. And because the with the rich teaching media of information technology and network resources, the learning process is no longer boring. Web resources include: Online course, e-lesson plans, e-books, CAI courseware, test database and database, the relevant figures, cultural information. Updateing these online resources enable students independently explore directionally, and will not be pointless[5]. By a lively and convenient means of and simulation process of teaching media, the image of audio visual impact, and exploring initiatively (using a variety of resources for information search, information Classification, information consolidation, collaboration, discussing, reporting), the teaching design under the guidance of "Meaningful transfer - led explore" teaching concepts make the learning process is no longer boring, passive, but active, learning effectiveness, efficiency must be improved.

4.4 Information Technology Make Evaluation and Assessment Develope Multidimensionally

The traditional way of written examination results to weaken the learning process and strengthen the examination results. Because the monitoring adversely is inconvenient to determin the process scores. But in the information environment, the process assessmen can be achieved through software and networks. "Meaningful transfer - led explore" teaching concepts also stress the process assessment, such as online tests, exploring the completion of course work, project reports and so can be used as an element of assessment. That is the multidimensional assessment strengthening the process of assessing while weakening the performance appraisal.

4.5 Information Technology Strengthen the Teacher-Student Interaction, Contribute to Individualized Instruction[6]

Education in large classes is the teaching mode of standardized, modular, teaching centered. It ignores the individual differences of learners, curbs the personality of learners. However, the emergence of information technology will reform of this drawback to some extent. Distance education, live classroom, and network class, BBS, electronic lesson plans, test database and database software, and even chat can enhance teacher-student interaction, achieve individualized instruction, personalized counseling, so as to enhance teaching effectiveness.

5 Conclusion

Based on the analysis of "significant transfer - led explore" teaching concepts, the key importance of information technology to teaching was deeply analized. It is conclused that Information technology application in education must be guided by the new teaching concepts for teaching design, teaching resources development, application.

Acknowledgement

This paper is partially supported by 2009 National Teaching Team Project "Henan Polytechnic University," Three Eelectricity" Basic Course Team" (to teach high letter (2009) 18); of Teaching Team for 2009 construction projects in Henan Province "Henan Polytechnic University," Three Eelectricity "Team Basic Course" (to teach high (2009) 483); Henan Polytechnic Univer emphasisly funded projects," for the electrical engineering majors "Three Eelectricity" "Basic Curriculum Reform and Practice "(2009JG037).

References

1. He, K.-K.: Educational technology on the development of the theory with Chinese characteristics, Deep Thoughts (Part One). Electronic Education (5), 5–19 (2010)
2. He, K.-K.: Educational technology on the development of the theory with Chinese characteristics, Deep Thoughts (Part Two). Electronic Education (6), 39–77 (2010)

3. Zhang, Y.-G., She, Y.-Y.: 2010 National Educational Technology Plan And Its Implication. Journal of Distance Education (4), 47–50 (2010)
4. Zhu, Y.-L.: Teaching Analysis of Media Selection and Application. Ault Education in China (7), 153–155 (2010)
5. Li, Z., Wang, H.-X.: Vocational education and curriculum integration of information technology Practice and Thinking. Ault Education in China (3), 99–100 (2010)
6. Tang, G.-H.: Individualized instruction: the teaching methods of information age surely pointing to. Education Research, 101–103 (June 2010)

The Research and Application
of Generating 3D Urban Simulation Quickly
in a Single-View Way

Long-Bao Mei and Chuan Gao

Digital Media Institute of Jiujiang University,
Jiangxi, China
meilb@jju.edu.cn, gaochuan@jju.edu.cn

Abstract. The paper cardings and analyzes the advantages and disadvantages of simulation technology of some major cities at present. Through carrying forward their advantages and avoiding their weaknesses. It puts forward a methods of generating 3D urban simulation quickly in a single-view way. And it discusses the technical principle and process approach, and then proves the advantages and effectiveness of the technique through its application.

Keywords: three-dimensional (3D) modeling, single-view, generating quickly, urban simulation, technical principles, the advantages of technology.

1 Introduction

The core technology of Digital City is the geographic information system (GIS). Digital City not only serves urban planning, construction and management, but also the government, enterprises and the public; It also serves the population, resources and environment, and the sustainable information infrastructure and the use system of the economic society through using global positioning system (GPS), remote sensing system(RS) and other key technologies, developing and applying the spatial information resources. What's more, the urban simulation technology, as one of the key technologies of Digital City, has become the current focus of research.

2 The Comparison of Three-Dimensional Urban Simulation

Through combing and analyzing, the present three-dimensional urban simulation can be divided into: three-dimensional geometry-based modeling method, image-based modeling method and virtual reality-based modeling method.

2.1 Based-on Three-Dimensional Geometric Modeling Method

Three-dimensional geometry-based modeling method is adopted to build the three-dimensional body contours of the environment and object through some basic modeling elements, and then to generate three-dimensional modeling scenarios through

S. Lin and X. Huang (Eds.): CESM 2011, Part II, CCIS 176, pp. 287–292, 2011.

the steps of scenario modeling, viewing transformation, the field cutting, eliminating the hidden surfaces, the brightness calculation of the side we can see and so on. They give the body contours of the environment and object material and texture, and then configure the lighting and so on, to form the three-dimensional model simulation.

The sense of reality of the three-dimensional scene created by this method is based on the light model of the geometric body's surface material. Its shadow and texture are calculated by this light model. Users can get stronger sense of reality in the process of using it. But the construction of the three-dimensional scene is relatively complicated and largely calculated. Every observation point or observation direction needs complex image calculation, so that the interaction between users and virtual space can not be achieved, with simultaneousness greatly affected and unbearable long time delay.

2.2 Image-Based Modeling Method

Image-based modeling refers to getting the spatial samples by means of camera, video and so on in the real space to be built, and constructing a scenario similar to the current three-dimensional scene through some graphic algorithms and computer virtual simulation algorithm. The study discovered that people always stop moving when they're observing something carefully and the position of the fixed object in the scene is unchanged relative to that people observe. And the perspective relationship between the objects in the image resulted in visual is also unchanged. Thus the visual scene generated by the observation points can be used to generate the scene to take place of full three-dimensional concrete model.

Environment mapping makes the center of the scene as the fixed point of view, and records the images around the scene on the sphere of environment mapping or cube surface centering on that point to form panoramic views. The theory basis of image-based modeling is all-optical function, which is used to describe all of the information of the whole scene. And all of the information is the all the radial energy that an observer has received in a particular space. The process of image-based modeling is the process of re-sampling after directly sampling the all-optical function, reconstructing the all-optical function on the sample collection, which is the process of generating images under the viewpoint according to the sample image under the known viewpoint. The original all-optical function is a seven-dimensional function:

$$\mu = \text{Plenoptic}\ (\theta,\ \varphi,\ \lambda,\ Vx,\ Vy,\ Vz,\ t)\ . \tag{1}$$

It is defined as the light intensity across the viewpoint for any viewpoint (Vx, Vy, Vz), in an arbitrary azimuth and elevation angle (θ, φ), and at arbitrary length λ at any time t.

Two-dimensional panoramic fixed viewpoint image is the simplest full-optical function:

$$\mu = \text{Plenoptic}\ (\theta,\ \varphi)\ . \tag{2}$$

Because image-based modeling of three-dimensional scene is generated directly after processing the collection of images already in the scene by means of image perspective transformation, image mosaic, image distortion, image synthesis, image cutting and other methods, comparing to geometric modeling method, its calculation is less, and it doesn't subject to the restriction of the complexity of the scene, and needs lower requirements to computers' hardware. However, the virtual objects in the scene are the two-dimensional objects in the image, so the users may very difficultly, or even can't, interact with these two-dimensional objects, and can't update the changes of the objects in time.

2.3 Based on Virtual Reality Modeling

VRML (Virtual Reality Modeling Language) is a kind of file format which describes interactive 3D environment and objects. VRML allows us to describe the objects and integrate them into the virtual scene, which can realize the simulation systems, simulation animation and the objects with the dynamic characteristics. And the objects in VRML can response to the external events, and walk across any corner in it. In the dynamic exchangeable space and time, multi-dimensional interactive urban simulation environment, the objects can simulate the human's way of understanding and perception of space through multiple sensory modalities. But the virtual simulation technology is still the international relative forefront science and technology, and it has a lot of problems, such as massive 3D data processing, the integration of 2D spatial data and 3D spatial data, and the very slow speed of data browsing and so on.

Thus, the live realistic scene of 3D geometry-based modeling method is relatively strong, but the process of 3D scene modeling is relatively complicated and largely calculated with unbearable relative long time delay between the users and the virtual scene. Although image-based 3D scene modeling with less calculation is not subject to restrictions of the complexity of the scene, the virtual objects in the scene are 2D objects, and the users very difficultly or even can't, interact with these 2D objects. It's very difficult for virtual reality-based modeling method to process the problems, such as massive 3D data, the integration of 2D spatial data and 3D spatial data and data browsing speed.

3 Generating Quickly 3D Urban Simulation Technology in a Single-View Way

3.1 Technical Principles

Through analyzing the advantages and disadvantages of current several kinds of 3D urban simulation technologies and overcoming the disadvantages of multi-view modeling, such as large computation, models' generation and very slow browsing speed, a kind of generating quickly 3D urban simulation method in a single-view way has been put forward. Single-view quick generation technology combines the vector modeling with images texture paste technology and maps and renders the 3D geometric model of urban environment buildings in a fixed-view way, in order to greatly reduce the computation of modeling, quickly generate urban model and improve the web browsing speed. Its principles include three steps: first of all, establish the 3D geometric model of urban buildings by using 3D geometric modeling method; secondly, put the single unit building's model on the 2D vector map by using calling established 3D models with the 2D vector map the large-ratio GIS generates as the base map; thirdly, generate quickly a simulation 3D city by mapping and rendering in the same view.

3.2 The Method of the Process

In the development process of the fund project "the public service platform of WEBGIS-based digital cities' names", take a city area of Ecological Economic Zone of Poyang Lake for example, which has been applied. And the process and methods are as follows:

3D modeling. Collect the data of the building entities of urban simulation area by the way of multi-angle digital camera or video, and so on, and then model quickly to establish 3D vector model base by using the universal design software, such as 3DSMAX and so on, with the 3D modeling of every unit building-entity, non-building body, and the special terrain, etc.

Generating two-dimensional vector base map. Adjust the original satellite map and original surface map proportionately to meet the production ratio, which is usually converted by that 1024 pixels equals to 300 meters. And make the 2D vector map generated by large-ratio GIS as the base map through using Photoshop, cad or 3dsmas

Establishing the basic framework of urban simulation. By calling the models in the 3D vector model base, put the single building entity, scenic spot, road and bridge, mountain, lake, river, green ground, ways of transport and other unit building model on the 2D vector map, and then determine the model's correct position and direction through rotation and movement. At this time it needn't display the results of model's rendering, and only shows the outline's results of models for the purpose of quick display and configuration to generate a 3D simulation urban frame system.

Configuration and properties of hotspot. The operation hotspot and property of the building entity's configuration are to realize the interactive operation between the users and the building entities in the city and obtain the relevant information of entities. Each unit in the 3D vector model base has a unique ID corresponding to the hotspot area record and its operation property record in the database. Select different property types for each building unit to distinguish the function of its operation, and set the effective range of operating hotspot zone. The rang of hotspot area can match automatically the four-side external walls of the building entities, and manually adjust each side, adding the number of nodes to polygon-shaped or curved hotspot area in order to meet the external characteristics of different building entities.

Single-view rendering and mapping. Render and map the configured 3D simulation urban scene in single view (overlooking 45 degrees) to adapt to the operation of the map in the Web interface. In the rendered single-view 3D urban simulation, configure the operating hotspot and property for each building entity, by using the transparent method of overlay in the image on each hotspot region.

Quick browse. In order to achieve quick browse in the WEB, decompose the images produced by 3D big scene rendering, and make the urban simulation scene decompose into continuous small pictures with the same size. To make the browser' quickly loading optimized requirements, these pictures' size makes the script procedures in the browser quickly and dynamically create and remove the nodes, meanwhile occupying as little memory as possible, and its algorithm is that the width or height equals to N multiplying two to the power of n, which is divided by size. In this equation, N is the network bandwidth factor N equaling to the users' bandwidth divided by 128 KB per second, and n is a positive integer, and size is the capacity of the intended small picture, and its unit is Kbyte. Decompose the small pictures, the ones of different focal lengths of the same view, from different perspectives of the whole scene through the width and height of 3D scene, to zoom limited 3D scenes of many perspectives in the interface of Web. Technical principles and methods as the following figure 1.

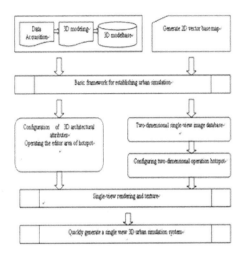

Fig. 1. Technical principles and methods to zoom limited 3D scenes of many perspectives in the interface of Web

4   The Advantages of Generating Quickly 3D Urban Simulation Technology in a Single-View Way

4.1   Fast Browsing and Real-Time Interaction

When the ordinary users of Internet access to the simulation city by using IE, according to the data relationship stored in the database and the set loading parameter, the server will load a certain area of the gallery around the users' access points, and form single-view 3D scene by JS splicing of IE terminal, and read the corresponding hot block, and the hot block is the linking bridge by which the users interact with the entities. Achieve the storage and access of the data in the database.

4.2   The Interaction and Sharing of Multi-content

Single view 3D urban simulation segments the image scene in the background, and integrate the urban information resources to achieve integrated and embedded interaction and sharing of multi-content, and make them get universal application in the Web, through the storage of the database and the hotspot layout processing in the browser, by using the distributed loading model integrating with the database.

4.3 Large-Scale Quick Generation

Generate 3D urban simulation modeling quickly in a single-view way is to have a three perspectives standardized sampling of the urban entities. Through the scene based on the model-pool modeling way, form the model block, and then render it, by single-view drawing and cutting, then into the background editor gallery. Stitch and combine the 3D scene in the gallery by the editing software to achieve large-scale quick generation of single-view 3D urban simulation system.

The Fund Project. The science and technology key project of Educational Office of Jiangxi Province [GJJ09348].

References

1. Zhao, Q.: Review of virtual reality. In: 1st ed Science of China (F Series: Information Science) (2009)
2. Luan, X.: The progress of three-dimensional modeling technology, 2nd edn. Computer Science (2008)
3. Zhang, Y.: The research of the virtual urban simulation technology based on MultiGen Creator and Vega
4. Liu, Y.: The research and design of digital three-dimensional simulation city. In: Full Text Database of China's Outstanding Master'S Degree Thesis (2009)

Numerical Analysis of Twist for
a Horizontal Axis Turbine Blade

Youfeng Zhu and Yongsheng Ren

School of Mechatronics Engineering, Shandong University of Science and Technology,
266510 Qingdao, China
zhuyf1976@163.com

Abstract. The paper extends Hodger-Dowell's partial differential equations of blade motion, by building a new blade model of large horizontal axis turbines. New model describes twisting aerodynamic equations of rotating blades, by means of a finite difference discretization and Greenberg aerodynamic theory. The model can be proved valid, by analyzing time response graphs and stability of variable parameters such as wind velocities, rotor Speeds and shear modului.

Keywords: horizontal axis, blade, twist, stability.

1 Introduction

The paper develops the structural model of kallesøe [1], by containing the unsteady aerodynamic forces on blade section undergoing arbitrary motion. The model includes not only the effects of pitch action, rotor speed variations and blade motion, but also the effects of air density, blade thickness and wind speed. The approach is to couple the structural model with the nonlinear aerodynamic system model (Greenberg's theory). Thus, the stability of twisting blades can be investigated by solving a differential eigenvalue problem where the eigenvalues give the frequency and damping of the blade vibrations. According to maximum of real part of eigenvalues, stable graphs can be made, which shows the effect of variable parameters such as wind velocities, rotor speeds and shear modului. Finally, the time response graphs describe stability, flutter and divergence of rotor blades, and also prove the model and the algorithm valid.

2 Model and Equations

By demanding that any admissible variation of the action integral $\partial H \equiv \int_{t_1}^{t_2} (\partial T - \partial V_{eta} - \partial V_{gra} + \partial Q)dt$ is zero[2], a set of partial differential equations of motion and a set of boundary condition equations are derived (extended Hamilton's principle). First, the partial differential equations of blade bending and torsional motion are presented, followed by the corresponding boundary conditions. Second, the equations of motion for the rotor azimuth angle and the pitch angle are presented.

S. Lin and X. Huang (Eds.): CESM 2011, Part II, CCIS 176, pp. 293–298, 2011.

The blade torsion equation of motion becomes:

$$(I_{cg} + ml_{cg}^2)\ddot{\theta} - ml_{cg}^2\Omega^2 \sin(\overline{\theta} + \beta)\theta$$
$$-(GJ\theta')' + M = 0 \tag{1}$$

The polar moment of inertia is described by:

$$J = \iint_A (\eta^2 + \xi^2) d\eta d\xi \tag{2}$$

2.1 Aerodynamic Model

The aerodynamic lift and pitching moment acting on the blade in wind rotor are based on Greenberg's theory [3] for a two-dimensional airfoil undergoing sinusoidal motion in pulsating incompressible flow. The rotor blade aerodynamic forces are formulated from strip theory in which only the velocity component perpendicular to the blade span-wise axis influences aerodynamic forces. A quasi-steady approximation of the unsteady theory for low reduced frequency is employed, in which the Greenberg's theory is taken to be unity. The steady induced inflow for the rotor is calculated from classical blade element-momentum theory. These simplifying assumptions are judged to be adequate for low frequency stability analyses of wind rotor blades.

If $\lambda = v_{in}/(\Omega R)$, neglecting bending distortion of (x, y)- directions, by method of coordinate transformation, air velocities of (x_2, y_2)-directions lead to the following terms:

$$v_{x2} = \Omega x \cos \beta$$
$$v_{y2} = \lambda \Omega R \cos \beta \tag{3}$$

The tangential velocity is given by:

$$V_t = \left[\Omega x \cos(\beta)\right] j_2 + \left[\lambda \Omega R \cos(\beta)\right] k_2 \tag{4}$$

The modulus of tangential velocity is described by:

$$|V_t| = v_t \approx \Omega x \cos(\beta) + 0.5\lambda^2 \Omega (R^2/x) \cos(\beta) \tag{5}$$

The angle of attack is little, so it can be described by:

$$\dot{\alpha} = \dot{\theta} + \Omega \beta$$
$$\ddot{\alpha} = \ddot{\theta} \tag{6}$$

According to Greenberg's theory, the distributed aerodynamic moment becomes:

$$M_0 = (\rho a_0 c/2)\left\{-(c/4)(c/2)v_t\dot{\alpha} - (c/4)(3c^2/32)\ddot{\alpha}\right\} \tag{7}$$

According to equation (3),(4),(5),(6),(7), the distributed aerodynamic moment becomes:

$$M_0 = 0.125\rho a_0 c^2 (3c^2/32)\ddot{\theta}$$
$$+0.0625\rho a_0 c^3 (\Omega x \cos\beta + 0.5\lambda^2 \Omega(R^2/x)\cos(\beta))\dot{\theta}$$
$$+0.0625\rho a_0 c^3 (\Omega x \cos\beta + 0.5\lambda^2 \Omega(R^2/x)\cos(\beta))\Omega\beta \tag{8}$$

3 Calculation and Results

The boundary conditions for the blade are given by the equation:

$$\theta(0,t) = \theta'(R,t) = 0 \tag{9}$$

Because the coordinate frame used to describe the blade follows the root of blade. The boundary conditions for the tip of the blade are determined by the boundary condition equations derived by demanding any admissible variation of the action integral to be zero. Most modern wind turbine blades are tapered at the tip, making the time variation of the boundary conditions negligible.

The spatial derivatives of a linearized version of the partial differential equations of motion are approximated by a second-order finite difference approximation. According to the equation (1), (8) and the boundary condition equation (9), the resulting approximating ordinary differential equation can be written as:

$$M\ddot{q} + C\dot{q} + kq = 0 \tag{10}$$

Where M, C and K hold the constant coefficients from the discretization and $q = [\theta_1, \theta_2 ..., \theta_n]$ holds the deformations at the n discretization points. Equation (10) is a differential eigenvalue problem [4], where the eigenvalues give the frequency and damping of coupling vibrations of the blade.

3.1 Search Parameters

VTB4_3 in vibration tools of MATLAB is used to calculate the real and imaginary part of eigenvalues, and then draws the locus of roots by varying parameters, such as rotation speed, air speed, the angle of attack and so on. Based on interpolation or curve fitting, all variable parameters[5].of turbine blades can be described .the angle of pre-twist is described by:

$$\theta = 2\pi(s - 60)^2 120 / 360 \tag{11}$$

The cross-section of the turbine blade is simplified as an ellipse. The chord length is given by:

$$c = 4 - 3s \times 2.8 / 180 \tag{12}$$

Blade Thickness is given by:

$$b = 0.25c \tag{13}$$

The core quality of the blade is given by:

$$m = \rho_0 \pi bc / 4 \tag{14}$$

Stability of rotor blades can be described by changing parameters of turbine blades. The typical parameters of turbine blades are given by Table 1.

Table 1. The related parameters

Items	Values
Tip radius R	60
Rotor speed Ω	0.8
Air density ρ	1.27
Chord length c	4
Lift slop a	0.3
Air velocity v	10
Blade thickness b	1

3.2 Analysis of Stability

When the real parts of eigenvalues have all negative numerical values, the system is stable; or it is unstable. For better study of the stability of the blade system, the maximum real part of eigenvalue is used to plot curves as follows.

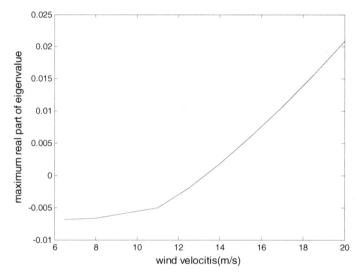

Fig. 1. Stability of varible wind velocities, the flutter wind velocity is 13.6. When v<13.6, the system is convergent; when v>13.6, the system is divergent.

Other parameters, for instance rotor Speeds , shear modului, air density, chord length, pitch angel, lift slop and attack angle have also effect on the stability of the rotor blade. Because of the limitation of words, the other figures aren't plastered on this paper.

When designing the composite core turbine blades, we must search optimum design of ply angles and contours to enhance shear modulus of the rotor blades. For ensuring the stability of turbine blades, the rotor speeds should be changed with different wind velocities.

3.3 Time Response

For verifying the stable curves of variable parameters such as wind velocities, rotor speeds and shear modului, the time response curves are plotted with different wind velocities as follows. Because of the limitation of words, the other figures aren't plastered on this paper.

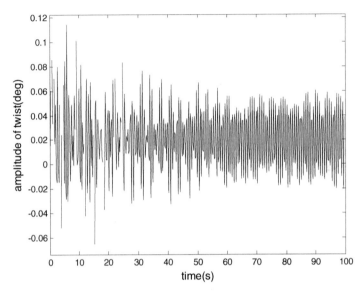

Fig. 2. Time Response (v=12.6), the system is flutter

When v<12.6, the system is convergent. When v>12.6, the system is divergent. The stability of time response is identical with the curves of variable parameters, which also proves the model and the algorithm valid.

4 Conclusion

As wind turbines become larger, the interaction between blade motion, shear modului, rotor speeds and wind speeds becomes more pronounced. These interactions can result in increased fatigue loads on the turbine blades .A fundamental analysis of the stability of rotor blade can help in the design of the wind turbine blades or solve controlling operation situation problems.

The approach gives detailed and relatively precise information about a given blade to a given operation situation. It can, however, be comprehensive to achieve general information about trends and the physical interpretation behind the observed effects, because such information relies on a series of simulations such as the stable curves of variable parameters and time response curves.

The contribution of this work is, not only to analyze of the stability of the rotor blades by varying parameters, but also to present a model which will be used to analyze nearly all properties of interaction between what we choose.

In further work, the equations in the model will consist of a rotating inextensible blade with flap-wise, edgewise and torsion degrees of freedom, then the analysis of the turbine blades will be more reasonable.

Acknowledgement

Sponsor: National Natural Science Foundation of China (under Grant: 10972124) and the Science & Technology Project of Shandong Provincial Education Department of China. (under Grant: J08LB04).

References

[1] Kallesøe, B.S.: Equations of motion for a rotor blade, including gravity, pitch action. Wind Energy 10, 211–216 (2007)
[2] Hodges, D.H., Dowell, E.H.: Nonlinear equation of motion for the elastic bending and torsion of twisted nonuniform rotor blades. NASA Tecnical Note, 19–25 (1974)
[3] Hodges, D.H., Robert, A.: Stability of elastic bending and torsion of uniform cantilever rotor blades in hover with variable structural couping. NASA Technical Note, 15–21 (1976)
[4] Hansen, M.H.: Aeroelastic stability analysis of wind turbines using an eigenvalue approach. Wind Energy 7, 133–143 (2004)
[5] Derek, B., Kevin, J.: Parametric study for large wind turbine blades. Sand 2002–2519 Unlimited Release Printed, 12–18 (2002)

The Computer Simulation of the Half- Forming Principle of Carbide Bur

Huran Liu

Zhejiang University of Science and Technology, China
liuhr53@163.com

Abstract. This paper researched the forming theory and computer simulation of the cutting tools with helical teeth and complex surfaces. Deduced the nonlinear equations of the movement of NC system to generate such tools, presented the way to find the solution of the equations, calculate the cross section graphics of the teeth profile and made computer simulation for NC machining. In the former research, the position of the work, the point to be machined, and the position of the grinder are undetermined. They must be solved out by a group of mathematical equations, so that the method can be called as analytical method. In this paper, the position of the work, the point to be machined on the work, are deliberately determined before hand, while the position of the grinder is determined by solving a group of mathematical equations. Because of these, this method can be called as the half analytical method, or the half-forming method. The cutting edge A is deliberately turned to special position, some kind like the forming method, while contact point on the cutting edge B is determined by the contact condition, so that this method can be also called as half- forming method. The concept of this method is very clear, the mathematical form is very simple, and the calculation is very easy.

Keywords: rotary cutting tools, helical teeth, computer simulation.

1 Introductions

All the rotary bur machine tool producers did not provide their theory or the principle of how to produce this kind of tool. They just seal machine. So that, we need to research the principle of how to produce this kind of tool.

With the present method, the surface formed by the revolution of rotary bur differs from what we desired. While in my theory, the surface formed by the revolution of rotary bur is exactly the same as what we desired. Just consider, in one paper there are so much creations and important significances. I wish your journal could be kind to review this paper of mine.

The establishment of the coordinate system.

In the Fig. 2, a grinder is generating a rotary cutting tool. Two coordinate system need to be established. The fixed coordinate system Oxyz; The x- axis of this system is the rotation axis of the work; the original point O of this system is at the rotation center of the larger end of the work; Grinder coordinate system Oxyz; The original point Os is

S. Lin and X. Huang (Eds.): CESM 2011, Part II, CCIS 176, pp. 299–304, 2011.

at the center of grinder wheel, the ys axis is parallel to y -axis, the angle between xs and x equal to $\pi/2-\Sigma$. The coordinates of point Os in fixed system are x_c, y_c, z_c. The coordinate transformation of two systems can be state as

$$
\begin{bmatrix} x \\ y \\ z \end{bmatrix} = \begin{bmatrix} \sin\Sigma & 0 & \cos\Sigma \\ 0 & 1 & 0 \\ -\cos\Sigma & 0 & \sin\Sigma \end{bmatrix} \begin{bmatrix} x_s \\ y_s \\ z_s \end{bmatrix} + \begin{bmatrix} x_c \\ y_c \\ z_c \end{bmatrix}
\tag{1}
$$

The surface equation and normal vector of grinder.

The surface of grinder is a circular cone, let Mb represent any point on the cone, the coordinates in local system of Mb can be expressed as following: (see Fig.2)

$$
x_{MB}^{(S)} = -(R - r_{mB})tg\alpha_B, \quad y_{MB}^{(S)} = -r_{mB}\cos\theta_B, \quad z_{MB}^{(S)} = r_{MB}\sin\theta_B
\tag{2} \text{(3) (4)}
$$

Where r_{mb}: The radius of point Mb; θ_b: The angle position parameter; α_b: The bottom angle of the grinder

The coordinates in the fixed system are

$$
x_{MB}^{(0)} = -(R - r_{MB})tg\alpha_B \sin\varepsilon + r_{MB}\sin\theta_B \cos\varepsilon + x_c,
$$

$$
y_{MB}^{(0)} = -r_{MB}\cos\theta_B + y_c,
$$

$$
z_{MB}^{(0)} = (R - r_{MB})tg\alpha_B \cos\varepsilon + r_{MB}\sin\theta_B \sin\varepsilon + z_c
\tag{5}
$$

The normal vector in the local system is:

$$
n_{MB}^{(S)}\left(-\cos\alpha_B, -\sin\alpha_B \cos\theta_B, \sin\alpha_B \sin\theta_B\right)
\tag{6}
$$

The normal vector in the fixed system is:

$$
n_{MB}^{(0)} = \left(-\cos\alpha_B \sin\Sigma + \sin\alpha_B \sin\theta_B \cos\Sigma, -\sin\alpha_B \cos\theta_B, \cos\alpha_B \cos\Sigma + \sin\alpha_B \sin\Sigma\right)
\tag{7}
$$

Let Ma represent any point at the largest circle of the grinder, the coordinate of point Ma in local system can be expressed as following:

$$
x_{MA}^{(S)} = 0, \quad y_{MA}^{(S)} = -R\cos\theta_A, \quad z_{MA}^{(S)} = R\sin\theta_A
\tag{8}
$$

Where R: the radius of the largest circle of the grinder, θ_A: The angle position parameter, The coordinates of the same point in the fixed system are

$$
x_{MA}^{(0)} = R\sin\theta_A \cos\varepsilon + x_c, \quad y_{MA}^{(0)} = -R\cos\theta_A + y_c, \quad z_{MA}^{(0)} = R\sin\theta_A \sin\varepsilon + z_c
\tag{9}
$$

The moving equations of nc system

The problem to be solved by this thesis is: when use a grinder with curtain shap to generate the teeth of the cutter, the two neighborhood cutting edges A and B should be made out by the two sides of the grinder in the same time, so that, the relative movement of the work and grinder should satisfy special mathematical and geometrical relationship.

First of all, for the convenience of machining, we deliberate to let the work rotate in the horizontal plane, until the tangential line parallel to the axis x(0), when any point PA on the cutting edge A is under machining.

$$-\frac{dr_A}{dx_A} = tg\,\tau \tag{10}$$

Secondly, for the convenience of machining, we deliberate to let the work rotate about tis axis, until the point to be machined at the plane of z(0)=0, when any point PA on the cutting edge A is under machining. In the other words, the deviation angle ψA is just compensated by the rotation angle φ.

$$\psi A + \varphi = 0 \tag{11}$$

By the coordinate transformation, the coordinates of point PA in the system S(2) are:

$$x_A^{(2)} = x_A, \ y_A^{(2)} = r_A, \ z_A^{(2)} = 0, \ t_{Az}^{(2)} = 1, \ t_{Ay}^{(2)} = \frac{dr_A}{dx_A}, \ t_{Az}^{(2)} = r_A\frac{d\phi_A}{dx_A} \tag{12}$$

By the coordinate transformation, the coordinates of point PA in the system S(0) are:

$$t_{Az}^{(0)} = t_{Az}^{(2)}\cos\tau - t_{Ay}^{(2)}\sin\tau = \cos\tau - \frac{dr_A}{dx_A}\sin\tau = \cos\tau + tg\,\tau\sin\tau = \frac{1}{\cos\tau}$$

$$t_{Ay}^{(0)} = t_{Az}^{(2)}\sin\tau + t_{Ay}^{(2)}\cos\tau = \sin\tau + \frac{dr_A}{dx_A}\cos\tau = \sin\tau - tg\,\tau\cos\tau = 0$$

$$t_{Az}^{(0)} = t_{AZ}^{(2)} = r_A\frac{d\phi_A}{dx_A} = r_A\frac{tg\beta}{r_A}\sqrt{1+(\frac{dr_A}{dx_A})^2} = \frac{tg\beta}{\cos\tau}$$

So that $\bar{t}_A^{(0)} = (\cos\beta, 0, \sin\beta)$

Since that the bottom of the grinder must tangential with the cutting edge

$$A: \bar{n}_A^{(0)} \bullet \bar{t}_A^{(0)} = 0 \tag{13}$$

$$\cos\beta\sin\Sigma - \sin\beta\cos\Sigma = 0$$

This means $\Sigma=\beta$

Since that on the contact point, the bottom of the grinder and the cutting edge A must have the same coordinates:

$$x_s = x_A^{(0)} - R_A \sin\theta_A \cos\Sigma \, ,$$

$$y_s = y_A^{(0)} + R_A \cos\theta_A \, , \quad z_s = z_A^{(0)} - R_A \sin\theta_A \sin\Sigma \qquad (14)$$

$$x_s = x_A^{(0)} + z_s / tg\Sigma \qquad (15)$$

For a rotary bur of the shape of a cone, $\dfrac{dr_A}{dx_A} = -tg\xi = $const,

In the equation ξ is the conical angle, so that $t = \zeta = $ const

In the machining process only xs,ys,φ three coordinates simultaneous control are needed.

For a rotary bur of the shape of a ball,

$$x_A = R_1 \sin\eta \quad r_A = R_1 \cos\eta \quad \frac{dr_A}{dx_A} = -tg\eta \quad \text{so that} : \tau = \eta$$

When the horizontal axis passing through the center of the ball,

$$x_A^{(0)} = x_A^{(2)} \cos\tau - y_A^{(2)} \sin\tau = x_A \cos\tau - r_A \sin\tau = R_1 \sin\eta\cos\tau = 0$$

So that : $x_s = x_A^{(2)} + z_s / tg\Sigma = z_s / tg\Sigma$

2 The Computer Modeling and Simulation of the Generation of the Rotary Tools

In generation, the relative displacement of the grinder and the work is very complicate. Only by numerical control operator can realize such motion requirement. For testifying the theoretical deduction and numerical calculation, we used the imported I-DEAS software to simulate the cutting movement of the work and the grinder at the SUN-CAD workstation. This is the first time to use computer solid modeling in research of the rotary tools with complex surfaces, and we made the best use of the new achievement in computer graphics, and computer Aid Design at home and abroad.

The I-deas soft ware system contains 5 families: 1) solid modeling, 2) system assembly, 3) engineering analysis, 4) system dynamics and 5) drafting. The research of this thesis used two of them: solid modeling (Geomod) and engineering drafting (Geodraw)

First, create the object of the work and grinder, according to their shapes, and stored them with Geomod; secondly, made grinder and work to move relate to each other; than do the Boolean operation, at every position. The generation of the work corresponds to "cut object" operator, one of the Boolean calculation. Finally, after the grinder goes through all move positions the teeth profile of the work was formed.

In the beginning, we choose hand operation, by select menu with mouse, let the grinder and work go several steps according to the required replacement, and recorded our operation into a program file. A passage of the I-deas program corresponds to one cutting step is as follows:

Return to main menu---get the stored work----orient it this time----rotate about its axes---give the value of rotate angle---store it the second time---get the stored grinder---translate it along x and y direction respectively ---give the value of the translate amount ---store the grinder once more ---return to main menu again--- select Boolean operation ---select cutting operation ---define the cutter, the grinder---define the object to be cut, the work---store the new cutter work the third time

In running this short passage of program, we can see from the sceen of the computer a series of pictures in consequence:

The original shape of the work;

The original position of the grinder;

The rotation of the work;

The translation of the grinder relate to the work;

The grinder in cutting with the work;

The shape and the size of the chip formed from cutting, it is growing larger and larger every moment;

The work cut is waiting for further cutting;

Than, let the Fortran program, with which the coordinates of grinder center were calculated, to output automatically a passage of program as mentioned above, whenever a displacement is calculated. Every movement is corresponding to one passage of I-deas format exactly. In this way, the whole generate progress can be simulated. The shape of the work with one groove showed in Fig.3. The sectional curvature of the tooth profile showed in Fig.4.

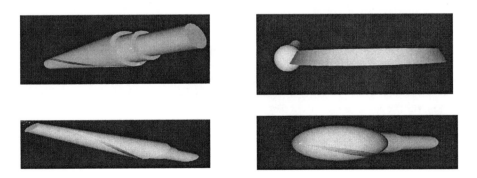

Fig. 1. Computer simulation of the rotary cutting tools

From the analysis and research mentioned above, following conclusions can be arrived at:

1) The forming theory of the rotary tools with helical teeth and complex surfaces is correct. To generate such a kind of tools, three coordinates numerical control manufacturing system is needed.

From computer simulation, we can testify the formulas of theoretic deduction and result of numerical calculation presented in this paper.

We can examine if the interference and other problem. Which are often caused by incorrect parameter selection, would take place and the way to prevent it before hand.

3 Conclusions

The concept of this method is very clear, the mathematical form is very simple, and the calculation is very easy. With my method, the cutting edges are precisely generated on the surface of the cutter blank, so that we can save the cost of production, the material, the grinding wheel and the machine time. In other words, with the method of present, the cutting edges are generated below surface of the cutter blank. The cost of production, the material, grinding wheel and the machine time are much higher than my method.

Acknowledgments

This paper is supported by the natural scientific foundation of China, grant No. 2006-50675235 and the natural scientific foundation of Zhejiang province, China, grants Nos. Y106047 and Y1080093.3. This project is also supported by the State Engineering Center of China.

References

1. Bao, Q.-S.: A study on a virtual manufacturing model of a revolving milling cutter in 2-axis numerical control processing. J. Mater Process Tech. 120, 107 (2000)
2. Chen, C.-G.: A manufacturing model of carbide-tipped spherical milling cutter. Proc. Instu. Mech. Engrs. 213, 45 (1999)
3. Liu, H.: The Forming Theory and the NC Machining for the Rotary Burs on the 5-axis NC machine tool. Journal of Machine Tool and Manufactureing 17, 39 (1998)
4. Liu, H.: The cutting edge of the rotary tool with complex surface. Journal of Cutting Tool 19, 47 (1994)
5. Zhou, J.: The moldering and design of the transitional cutting edges. Journal of Chinese Mechanical Engineering 25, 18 (2003)

The CNC Simulation of the End Milling of the Sculptured Surfaces

Huran Liu

Department of Mechanical Engineering, Zhejiang University of Science and Technology,
Hangzhou 310013, China

Abstract. In order to increase the efficiency in the machining of the sculptured surfaces, the contact principle of differential geometry is applied to the 5-axis NC machining; the best contact condition between tool and the surfaces was researched. Through analysis the contact degree of the intersection line of the cutter and the surfaces is known. In comparison to previous studies, the theory of this paper is more restricted going beyond second order parameters into the third order, suiting both the primary surfaces of analytical geometry and the computer-generated surfaces of the computation geometry. It has definite procedure of calculation, and the equations are easy to solve. My thought process is very clear: first, suppose that there is a surface of third order, the coefficients of which are arbitrary. Then find out the best posture of the circle in order that the circle and the surface will most closely contact with each other at the origin position. Finally, develop the surface into a 3-order surface at every point of machining and employ the results mentioned above to find the best cutter posture at every point of machining. So that, the equations are easy to solve and clear in concept.

Keywords: Surface, Contact, NC machining.

1 Introduction

The concept of "contact" in differential geometry is applied into the machining of the sculptured surface, presented the third order contact principle of the machining of complicated surfaces, using the circumference circle of the flat-end mill (as shown in Fig.1) to sweep the curved surface instead of ball-end-mill. This is a highly effective method. In comparison to previous studies, the theory of this paper is more restricted going beyond second order parameters into the third order, suiting both the primary surfaces of analytical geometry and the computer-generated surfaces of the computation geometry, it has definite procedure of calculation, and the equations are easy to solve.

2 3-Order Approximation of the Surface

Use the Maclaulin series to develop the surface in the adjacent reign of point

S. Lin and X. Huang (Eds.): CESM 2011, Part II, CCIS 176, pp. 305–311, 2011.
© Springer-Verlag Berlin Heidelberg 2011

$$\partial r = \sum_{m=1}^{3} \sum_{i=1}^{m} \frac{\Delta u^i \Delta v^{m-i}}{i!(m-i)!} \frac{\partial^m}{\partial u^i \partial v^{m-i}} r \tag{1}$$

where:

r —— Position vector of surface

u, v —— Two parameters of the surface respectively

Δu, Δv —— Differentia of the two parameters

The distance from any surface point M to the tangential plane of tangential point

$$\delta = n\partial r = \sum_{m=1}^{3} \sum_{i=1}^{m} \frac{\Delta u^i \Delta v^{m-i}}{i!(m-i)!} \frac{\partial^m}{\partial u^i \partial v^{m-i}} \partial mrn \tag{2}$$

where:

n —— Normal vector of surface

With the non-vertical transformation the local approximate surface can be expressed as following:

$$z = ax2 + bxy + cy2 + dx3 + ex2y + fxy2 + gy3 \tag{3}$$

where a,b,c,d,e,f,g ——Coefficients of the 3-order approximate surface.

3 Definition of Contact

Suppose we have a surface $F (x, y, z) = 0$

And a curve: $x = x(\theta)$ $y = y(\theta)$ $z = z(\theta)$

where

x,y,z —— Three coordinates

F —— Implicit function of surface

θ —— Parameter of the curve

establish a function:

$$\Phi(\theta) = F(x(\theta), y(\theta), z(\theta))$$

At contact point $\theta = \theta 0$, the differentials of function $\Phi(\theta)$ is expressed as follows

$\Phi'(\theta) = 0$ $\Phi''(\theta) = 0$…… $\Phi(N)(\theta) = 0$

(N=1,2 ,3……)

N is the non-negative integer, while $\Phi(N+1)(\theta) \neq 0$, then we say that the curve and the surface are in Nth order contact with each other .The point must be on the surface, and the N must be positive. The higher the order, the closer the contact is.

4 Posture of the Cutter

As shown in Fig.1, Oxsyszs is the grinding coordinates. The coordinate transformation in the local system

$$\begin{cases} x = R(\cos\theta - 1)\cos\lambda\cos\omega - r\sin\theta\sin\omega \\ y = R(\cos\theta - 1)\cos\lambda\sin\omega + r\sin\theta\cos\omega \\ z = -R(\cos\theta-1)\sin\lambda \end{cases} \quad (4)$$

where:

R —— Radius of cutter

θ —— Parameter of cutter circle

λ, ω —— Posture parameters of cutter axis

At the local contact point, where $\theta=0$, we have

$x\theta'= -R\sin\theta\cos\lambda\cos\omega- R\cos\theta\sin\omega= -R\sin\omega$

$y\theta'= -R\sin\theta\cos\lambda\sin\omega+ R\cos\theta\cos\omega= -R\cos\omega$ $\quad (5)$

$z\theta'= R\sin\theta\sin\lambda$

$x\theta''= -R\cos\theta\cos\lambda\cos\omega+ R\sin\theta\sin\omega= -R\cos\lambda\cos\omega$

$y\theta'' = -R\cos\theta\cos\lambda\sin\omega+ R\sin\theta\cos\omega= R\cos\lambda\sin\omega$ $\quad (6)$

$z\theta'' = R\sin\theta\sin\lambda$

The coordinates of the tool center in the local system

$(xc, yc, zc)=(R\cos\lambda\cos\omega, -R\cos\lambda\sin\omega, R\sin\omega)$

4 Condition for the Local Contact

Put the equation of the cutter into the equation of the surface

$F(\theta)= ax2+bxy+cy2+dx3+ex2y+fxy2+gy3-z$

At the point of $\theta=0$, the cutter and the surface make contact with each other. Thus, $F(\theta)=0$ will be satisfied. The derivative of F about θ

$F'(\theta)=2axx'b(x'y+xy')+2cyy'+3dx2x'+e(2xx'y+x2y)+f(x'y2+2xyy')+3gy2y'-z'$

At the contact point, the cutter and the surface are tangential with each other, the condition of $F'(\theta)=0$ will be satisfied as well. The second order derivative

$F''(\theta)=2a(x'2+xx')+b(x''y+2x'y'+xy'')+2c(y'2+yy'')+$
$3d(x2x'+2xx'2)+e(2xx''y+x2y''+2x'2y+4xx'y')+$
$f(x'2y2+2xyy''+4xyy'+2xy'2)+3g(y2y''+2yy'2)-z''$

At the contact point, there are

$$F''(\theta) = 2ax'2+b2x'y'+2cy'2 - z'' \quad (7)$$

The third derivative

$F''(\theta)=2a(3x'x''+xx''')+b(x'''y+3x''y'+3x'y''+xy''')+$
$2c(yy'''+3y'y'')+3d(2x'3+6xx'x''+x'''x2)+$
$e(2x'3y+6x'2y'+6x'x''y+2xx'''y+6xx''y'+ 6x'x''y+x''y3) +$
$f(6xy'y''+6x'y'2+2xyy'''+6x'yy''+6x''yy'+x'''y2)+$
$3g(2y'3+6yy'y''+y'''y2)-z'''$

At the contact point

$F''(\theta)=6ax'x''+3b(x''y'+x'y'')+6cy'y'''+$

$$6dx'3+6ex'2y' +6fx'y'2+6gy'3-z''' \qquad (8)$$

Taking Eq.(5) and Eq.(6) into Eq. (7) we obtain

$$R=sin\lambda/2(asin2\omega+ccos2\omega+bsin\omega cos\omega) \qquad (9)$$

When the parametrical net is curvature net, the numerator is the curvature, the above equation is a form of Meusnier theorem. Take Eq.(5) and Eq.(6) into Eq. (8) we obtain
$2(a–c) cos\lambda sin\omega cos\omega+b(sin2\omega– cos2\omega) cos\lambda+$

$$2R[-dsin3\omega+gcos3\omega+esin2\omega cos\omega- f sin\omega cos2\omega] = 0 \qquad (10)$$

Eliminating the λ from the above two equation, we obtain

$$[4R2(asin2\omega+ccos2\omega+bsin\omega cos\omega)2][2(a–c)sin\omega cos\omega+b(sin2\omega–cos2\omega)]$$
$$2+4R2[-dsin3\omega+gcos3\omega+esin2\omega cos\omega-fsin\omega cos2\omega]2=0 \qquad (11)$$

Example: Use the method to machining the surface of Eq.(3), when a = 0.15, b = 0.0, c = 0.03, d = 0.002, e = 0.0015, f = 0.0015, g = 0.001, R =5mm, at the contact point (0,0,0), the angular $\lambda=17.89°$,$\omega=11.3°$, while in the 4-coordination and 2-order contact machining $\lambda=53.13°$, $\omega=0°$. Fig.2 shows the cross section line of the surface to be machined and the cross section line of the surface machined in one travel. From Fig.2 we can find that the surface machined in one travel by the new method is much closer to the surface to be machined than by the other method.

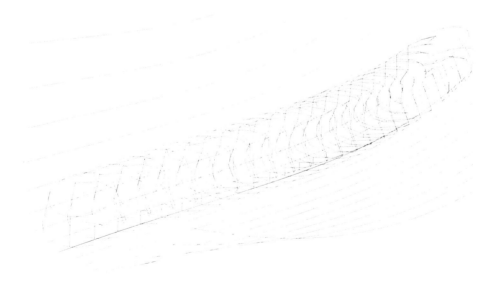

Fig. 1. A series of the strip of the milling cutter of a cone

Fig. 2. The posture of the end milling cutter

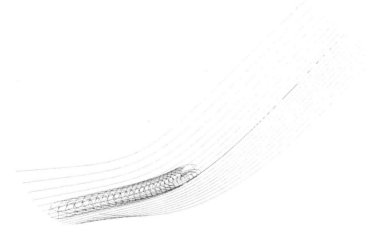

Fig. 3. The strip of the end milling cutter

Fig. 4. The surface formed by NC machining

Fig. 5. The closeness Comparison between the machined surface and that of the surface to be machined

1. Cross section line of the surface to be machined
2. Cross section line of the surface machined in one travel by old method
3. Section line of the surface machined in one travel by new method

5   Conclusions

(1) By applying the concept of "contact" of Differential Geometry into the machining of sculptured surfaces, this new method may be more effective than previous methods.

(2) In comparison to previous studies, the theory of this paper is more restricted going beyond second order parameters into the third order,
(3) Suiting both the primary surfaces of Analytical Geometry and the computer-generated surfaces of the Computation Geometry,
(4) It has definite procedure of calculation, and the equations are easy to solve.

References

1. Miyazawa, S., Takada, K.: Micro milling of three-dimensional surface. Trans. Jap. Soc. Precision Eng. 47(2), 94–99 (1981)
2. Kishinami, T., Suzuki, H.: Theoretical analysis of cutting speed components on the rake face of circular cutting edge of ball end milling. Trans. Jap. Soc. Precision Eng. 46(10), 115–122 (1980)
3. Fujii, Y., Iwabe, H.: Relation between cutting force curve and working accuracy with ball-nose end mills. Trans. Jap. Soc. Precision Eng. 48(5), 105–110 (1982)
4. Vickers, G.W., Bedi, S., Haw, R.: The definition and manufacture of compound curvature surfaces using G-surf. Computer Idust. 6(2), 173–183 (1985)
5. Vickers, G.W., Quan, K.W.: Ball end mill verus end-mills for curved surface machining. Trans. ASME J. Eng. Idust. 25(2), 22–26 (1989)
6. Susan, X., Li, R., Jerard, B.: 5-axis machining of sculptured surfaces with a flat-end cutter. Computer-Aided Design 126(3), 120–125 (1994)
7. Marcinak, K.: Influence of surface shape on admissible tool positions in 5-axis face milling. Computer-Aided Design 19(5), 24–30 (1987)

The Computer Simulation for the Pneumatic Motor with Planetary Drive of Bevel Gear

Huran Liu

Zhejiang University of Science and Technology, China

Abstract. This thesis presented a new kind of pneumatic motor with swing planetary drive of bevel gears, and researched the calculation of the efficiency of the mechanism. The main significant or the main difficulties are: firstly, this is a kind of planetary drive of mechanism with space gearing; secondly, the driving component is the planetary gear with special movement. This paper solved this new kind problem of efficient calculation.

Keywords: Computer Simulation, Pneumatic Motor, Planetary Drive.

1 Introduction

This is a new kind of efficiency calculation; the paper researched the calculation of the efficiency of the mechanism. The main significant or the main difficulties are: firstly, this is a kind of planetary drive of mechanism with space gearing; secondly, the driving component is the planetary gear with special movement rather than central component. This paper solved this new kind problem of computer simulation.

2 The Structure

As showed in fig.1 Z1 and Z2 formed the internal bevel gearing, Z1= 47, Z2 = 48, Z3 and Z4 formed the periphery constraint pair, Z3 = Z4= 84, Z1 and Z3 are fixed with each other, and driven by the spindles through the linkages. The spindles are peripheral spaced evenly on the pneumatic cylinder. So that Z3 would make pure rolling along the pith taper of the fixed bevel gear and swinging. In practice it is the reviving about a fixed point--the tip of the pith taper. Since Z1 and Z2 formed the gearing with few teeth difference, Z2 would rotate reversal at low velocity. Z2 was installed on the skew axis 5. The offset swing of Z2 and Z3 would make skew axis 5 to rotate, in turn, drive the cylinder distributor 4 to rotate as well, so as to realize distribution of liquid; and, through the spindle and linkages, made the internal bevel gear W1 to swing circulatory. The driver is Z1, the droved is Z2 and skew axis 5, which is equivalent to carrier H.

S. Lin and X. Huang (Eds.): CESM 2011, Part II, CCIS 176, pp. 312–317, 2011.

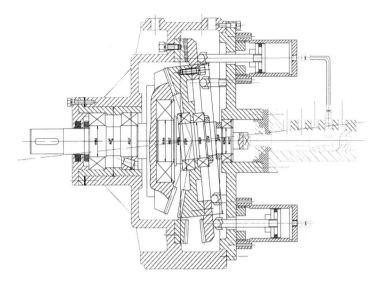

Fig. 1. The structure

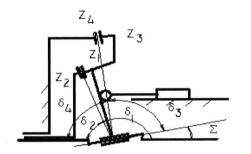

Fig. 2. The kinematical graph

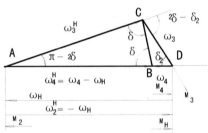

Fig. 3. Kinematical analysis

3 Kinematical Analysis

The vector ω_H and ω_2 parallel to the level direction, ω_3 is coincide with the generative line of pitch taper of W4, ω_3 is along the axis of skew shaft, all these vectors formed the velocity polygon as showed in Fig.3.

from triangle $\triangle ABC$ we may get:

$$2\omega_H \cos\delta = \omega_3 \tag{1}$$

from triangle $\triangle BCD$ we may get:

$$\frac{\omega_2}{\omega_3} = \frac{\sin(\delta - \delta_2)}{\sin \delta_2} \tag{2}$$

From (1) and (2) we may get:

$$\frac{\omega_2}{\omega_H} = \frac{\cos \delta \sin(\delta - \delta_2)}{\sin \delta_2} \tag{3}$$

Since that:

$$\delta_1 + \delta_2 = 2\delta, \ \delta = \frac{(\delta_1 + \delta_2)}{2}, \ \delta - \delta_2 = \frac{(\delta_1 - \delta_2)}{2}$$

So that:

$$\frac{\omega_2}{\omega_H} = \frac{2\cos\dfrac{(\delta_1 + \delta_2)}{2}\sin\dfrac{(\delta_1 - \delta_2)}{2}}{\sin \delta_2} \tag{4}$$

$$= \frac{(\sin \delta_1 - \sin \delta_2)}{\sin \delta_2} = \frac{(Z_1 - Z_2)}{Z_2} \tag{5}$$

If $\delta = 85 \ \ \delta_2 = 65 \ \ \delta_1 = 105 \ \ \dfrac{\omega_2}{\omega_3} = 0.3774$

$\dfrac{\omega_2}{\omega_H} = 0.6578 \ \ \dfrac{\omega_2}{\omega_4} = 1.06578$

4   The Computer Simulation of the Movement

The simulation of the gears:

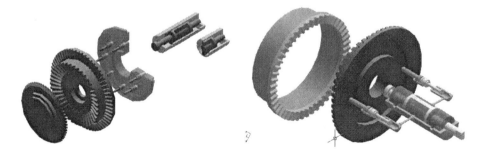

Fig. 4. The dismembers of the mechanism   **Fig. 5.** The driving of the pneumatic power

Fig. 6. The modeling of the gear

The simulation of the pneumatic system:

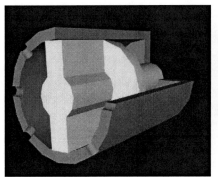

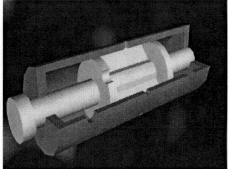

Fig. 7. The air distributor   **Fig. 8.** The air distributor

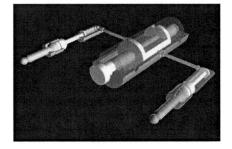

Fig. 9. The piston   **Fig. 10.** The pneumatic system

The simulation of the mechanisim:

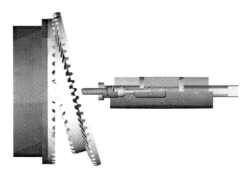

Fig. 11. The structure of the mechanism

Fig. 12. The movement of the mechanism   **Fig. 13.** The movement of the mechanism

5 Conclusions

The new kind of pneumatic motor with offset swing planetary drive of bevel gears, which combined the pneumatic motor, the internal planetary reducer with bevel gears, and the capstan together, is the most compact structure. It is of more advantage in the occasion when space is extremely limited.

References

1. New technique in Pneumatic field. American Pneumatic and Pneumatic Drive (January 1972)
2. Pneumatic motor with swinging bevel gear transmission, American Product Engineering (January 1972)
3. USA Patent No.3675539
4. Liu, H., Dragomir, D.: Calculul randa mentului motor hidtanlic cu angrenaj conjc precesional (January 1996) 《MMTC》 (in Romania)

5. Liu, H.: Pneumatic motor with swinging bevel gear transmission. Drive System Technique (February 1998)
6. Liu, H., Dragomir, D.: Precontrolul angrenarii punctuale cu abateri la angrenaje spirale conice. Tehnologll Calitate Masini Materiale (January 1996) (in Romania)
7. Liu, H.: Contact deformation and pre-control of transmission properties of point conjugate gear. Drive System Technique (March 1999)
8. Liu, H.: Internal cylindrical-bevel gear transmission. Drive System Technique (February 1999)
9. Liu, H.: The conjugation of a new kind of transmission. Drive System Technique (January 1999)
10. Liu, H.: The deduction of the forms of the planetary transmission of bevel gear. Drive System Technique 1998.3
11. Liu, H.: The inversion of the Planetary Drive of Bevel Gear. ICMT2006ISTP1

Prediction of Homo-oligomeric Protein Types by a Dimension Reduction Method

Tong Wang[*], Xiaoxia Cao, and Xiaoming Hu

Institute of Computer and Information, Shanghai Second Polytechnic University,
Shanghai, 201209, China
tongwang0818@yahoo.cn

Abstract. Homo-oligomeric proteins are probably divided into the following seven subtypes: (1) homo-dimer, (2) homo-trimer, (3) homo-tetramer, (4) homo-pentamer, (5) homo-hexamer, (6) homo-octamer, and (7) homo-dodecamer. Given a new uncharacterized homo-oligomer, a biologist may want to know which type it belongs to? Knowing the type of an uncharacterized homo-oligomer often provides useful clues for finding the biological structure of the query protein, developing the computational methods to address these questions can be really helpful. In this paper, a new method for the prediction of homo-oligomeric protein types is proposed based on a self-constructed dataset. The overall success rate was 80.1%.

Keywords: PSSM, homo-oligomeric proteins, LLE.

1 Introduction

A protein may be formed by a single peptide chain or multiple peptide chains. Multiple-chain proteins may be formed as a homo-oligomer by identical peptide chains (subunits). The present study focuses on the homo-oligomers. Homo-oligomeric structure can also vary through arrangement of subunits. Thus, in the protein universe, there are probably divided into the following seven subtypes: homo-dimer, homo-trimer, homo-tetramer, homo-pentamer, homo-hexamer, homo-octamer and homo-dodecamer. Two same subunit or polypeptide chain is called a homo-dimmer, three same subunits a homo-trimer, four a homo-tetramer etc. The Oligomeric proteins are more important in terms of functional evolution of biomacromolecules [1]. For example, the sodium channel is formed by a monomer, whereas the potassium channel is formed by a homotetramer; the acetylcholine-binding protein (AChBP) is formed by homopentamer [2], whereas the gammaaminobutyric acid type A (GABAA) receptor is formed by a heteropentamer [3].

With the number of protein sequences entering into data banks rapidly increasing, the challenge to develop such an automated method to predict the type of a homo-oligomer has become even more critical and urgent. In view of this, our study was initiated in an attempt to explore the problem.

---

[*] Corresponding author.

S. Lin and X. Huang (Eds.): CESM 2011, Part II, CCIS 176, pp. 318–322, 2011.

Firstly, we constructed a valid benchmark data set, in which all the protein samples annotated with ambiguous or uncertain terms were removed. Based on such a stringent data set, an effective sequence encoding scheme for the samples that can truly reflect their intrinsic correlation is used. Finally, a powerful prediction algorithm is introduced to identify the types of the given homo-oligomers.

2 Methods

2.1 Data Set

To use an algorithm for statistical prediction, one has to first construct a training data set. We did this by using the latest UniProtKB(UniProt Knowledgebase) database (UniProtKB Release 2011_03 (08-Mar-2011)). It can be accessed from the web at http://www.uniprot.org and downloaded from http://www.uniprot.org/database/download.shtml. Those annotated with "subunit" were extracted typing in "homo-dimer", "homo-trimer", "homo-tetramer", "homo-pentamer", 'homo-hexamer", "homo-heptamer", "homo-octamer", "homo-dodecamer". The data set construction was governed by strictly criterias. Finally, we obtained a dataset containing 3468 homo-oligomer sequences of which 2259 are homo-dimer, 276 homo-trimer, 631 homo-tetramer, 25 homo-pentamer, 185 homo-hexamer, 62 homo-octamer and 15 homo-dodecamer.

2.2 PSSM

A protein sequence containing N amino acids can be represented by a 420-D (Dimensional) vector, i.e.,

$$\mathbf{P}_{\text{PSSM-420}} = \begin{bmatrix} \overline{\mathbb{A}}_1 & \overline{\mathbb{A}}_2 & \cdots & \overline{\mathbb{A}}_{20} & \mathbb{S}_1 & \mathbb{S}_2 & \cdots & \mathbb{S}_{400} \end{bmatrix}^{\text{T}} \tag{1}$$

where the first 20 components are the average scores of every column in $\mathbf{P}_{PSSM}$ matrix. $\mathbf{P}_{PSSM}$ is shown as below:

$$\mathbf{P}_{PSSM} = \begin{pmatrix} \mathbb{A}_{1\to 1} & \mathbb{A}_{1\to 2} & \cdots & \mathbb{A}_{1\to 20} \\ \mathbb{A}_{2\to 1} & \mathbb{A}_{2\to 2} & \cdots & \mathbb{A}_{2\to 20} \\ \vdots & \vdots & \vdots & \vdots \\ \mathbb{A}_{N\to 1} & \mathbb{A}_{N\to 2} & \cdots & \mathbb{A}_{N\to 20} \end{pmatrix} \tag{2}$$

where $\mathbb{A}_{i\to j}$ represents the score of amino acid residue at the i-th position of the protein sequence being substituted to the amino acid type $j(1 \le j \le 20)$ during evolution process. Here, the numerical codes 1, 2,…, 20 represent the 20 native amino acid types according to the alphabetical order of their single-residue codes. N denotes the length of the protein. In this study, $\mathbf{P}_{PSSM}$ is generated by carrying out

PSI-BLAST. This process will search the Swiss-Prot database through three iterations for multiple sequence alignment against the protein $\mathbf{P}$. Every element in $\mathbf{P}_{PSSM}$ was scaled by a standardization procedure. The components $\mathbb{S}_1, \mathbb{S}_2, ..., \mathbb{S}_{400}$ in Eq.1 are obtained by summing up all rows in the $\mathbf{P}_{PSSM}$, each of which corresponds to the same amino acid in the primary sequence $\mathbf{P}$. It means for each column in $\mathbf{P}_{PSSM}$, there are 20 values instead of N. Hence, we will have a vector of dimension 20×20 for a $\mathbf{P}_{PSSM}$.

2.3   LLE

LLE [4] is a fast nonlinear dimensionality reduction algorithm, which finds local geometry in high dimension space and generates a projection to lower dimension space that preserves original local geometry. LLE algorithm is introduced briefly.

The input is matrix $X = \{x_1, x_2, ..., x_N\}$, where $x_i \in R^D$. The output is matrix $Y = \{y_1, y_2, ..., y_N\}$, where $y_i \in R^d$ and $d << D$. For each vector y_i, repeat following three steps:

(1) Find K nearest neighbors $\{x_{i1}, x_{i2}, ..., x_{iK}\}$;

(2) Find weight matrix $W = \{W_{ij} | i = 1, 2, ..., N; j = 1, 2, ..., K\}$, which minimizes following cost function,

$$\varepsilon(W) = \sum_{i=1}^{N} \left| x_i - \sum_{j=1}^{K} W_{ij} x_{ij} \right|^2 \qquad (3)$$

where W also satisfies conditions: $\sum_{j=1}^{K} W_{ij} = 1$ and $W_{ij} = 0$ if x_j is not a neighbor of x_i;

(3) Find d dimension embedding vector y_i, which minimizes following cost function,

$$\Phi(Y) = \sum_{i=1}^{N} \left| y_i - \sum_{j=1}^{K} W_{ij} y_j \right|^2 \qquad (4)$$

3   Experimental Results

The jackknife test is deemed the most objective that can always yield a unique result for a given benchmark dataset, and hence has been increasingly used and widely recognized by investigators to examine the accuracy of various predictors.

Table 1. The jackknife success rates in identifying the types of homo-oligomeric proteins based on original 420-D feature vector and dimension-reduced 70-D feature vectors generated by K-NN and LLE&K-NN

Method	Input form	Test method (%)
		Jackknife
K-NN(K=1)	Original 420-D vector	$\dfrac{2513}{3468} = 72.5$
LLE& K-NN (K=1)	Dimension-reduced 70-D vector by LLE	$\dfrac{2778}{3468} = 80.1$

Table 2. The jackknife success rates for each of the seven homo-oligomeric protein type based on original 420-D feature vector and dimension-reduced 70-D feature vectors generated by LLE&K-NN

Types of oligomeric proteins	Original 420-D vector (%)	Dimension-reduced 70-D vector by LLE (%)
Homo-dimer	$\dfrac{2012}{2259} = 89.1$	$\dfrac{2211}{2259} = 97.9$
Homo -trimer	$\dfrac{135}{276} = 48.9$	$\dfrac{136}{276} = 49.3$
Homo-tetramer	$\dfrac{290}{631} = 46$	$\dfrac{350}{631} = 55.5$
Homo-pentamer	$\dfrac{5}{25} = 20$	$\dfrac{8}{25} = 32$
Homo-hexamer	$\dfrac{45}{185} = 24.3$	$\dfrac{40}{185} = 21.6$
Homo-octamer	$\dfrac{23}{62} = 37.1$	$\dfrac{28}{62} = 45.2$
Homo-dodecamer	$\dfrac{3}{15} = 20$	$\dfrac{5}{15} = 33.3$
Overall	$\dfrac{2513}{3468} = 72.5$	$\dfrac{2778}{3468} = 80.1$

During the jackknife test, each protein sample in the dataset is singled out in turn as a "test sample" and all the rule-parameters are determined from the remaining N-1 samples. The success rates by jackknife test for the aforementioned 3468 proteins are given in Table 1, where for facilitating comparison the corresponding rates obtained by the LLE and KNN are also listed. As shown in Table 1, the overall jackknife success rates obtained by the LLE method in identifying the types of homo-oligomeric proteins are higher than the ones obtained without using the LLE.

The success rates by jackknife test for the aforementioned 3468 homo-oligomeric proteins classified into seven classes are given in Table 2, where for facilitating comparison the corresponding rates obtained by the LLE and without LLE are also listed. All these indicate that the LLE method is indeed very useful in dealing with the complicated biological problem of predicting the types of homo-oligomeric proteins.

4   Conclusions

It is demonstrated in this study that the overall success rate in predicting the types of homo-oligomeric proteins can be remarkably improved by using the LLE. It has not escaped our notice that the similar approach can be also used to deal with many other complicated problems in biology, such as predicting signal peptides, protein subcellular localization, enzyme functional class and membrane protein type.

Acknowledgments. This work was supported by shanghai university scientific selection and cultivation for outstanding young teachers in special fund (EGD10003) and This work was supported by Chenguang Program of Shanghai Municipal Education Commission(10CG61).

References

1. Garian, R.: Prediction of quaternary structure from primary structure. Bioinformatics 17, 551–556 (2001)
2. Brejc, K., van Dijk, W.J., Klaassen, R.V., Schuurmans, M., van der Oost, J., Smit, A.B., Sixma, T.K.: Crystal structure of an ACh-binding protein reveals the ligand-binding domain of nicotinic receptors. Nature 411, 269–276 (2001)
3. Tretter, V., Ehya, N., Fuchs, K., Sieghart, W.: Stoichiometry and assembly of a recombinant GABAA receptor subtype. J. Neurosci. 17, 2728–2737 (1997)
4. Roweis, S.T.: Nonlinear Dimensionality Reduction by Locally Linear Embedding. Science 290, 2323–2326 (2000)

Research of Optimal Design for Gravity Dam Based on Niche Genetic Algorithm

Liangming Hu[1], Feng Chen[1,2], and Yizhi Li[1]

[1] Zhengzhou University School of Water Conservancy & Environment,
Zhengzhou 450002, China
[2] China Water Resources Pearl River Planning Surveying & Designing Co., Ltd.,
Guangzhou 510610, China

Abstract. Niche genetic algorithm (NGA) is recommended for optimal design of gravity dam section and to overcome the defects of constant crossover probability and mutation probability, appearing precocious phenomena in the optimizing process in simple genetic algorithm (SGA). Thanks to NGA, the calculations are rapid and easy, and the optimization results are more close to the global optimal solution. Thus, it has been successfully applied to the optimal design of gravity dam section. The optimal results indicate that NGA is available in optimal designs of gravity dam section, and the results are safe, economical and rather ideal. Thereby, the optimal results can directly apply to engineering designs, and can provide reference for optimal design of gravity dam.

Keywords: gravity dam, optimal design, niche, GA.

Genetic Algorithm (GA), which was put forward by professor Holland and his student Bagley of Michigan University of American, is a calculation model based on Darwin's biological evolutionary theory of genetic selection and natural elimination. GA provides a universal framework for solving complex system optimization problem. Besides, it is independent of problems of specific areas and has good robustness to the question of species, so it has been widely used in many subjects[1]. Although GA has many advantages, it cannot avoid precocious phenomena, and uncertainty of precision [2]. As a kind of practical, highly efficient and robust optimization technique, NGA has been widely used at home and abroad [3-6]. For above, NGA is adopted in the section optimization design of gravity dam in this article.

1 Principles of NGA

1.1 The Basic Principles

The basic principles of Niche Genetic Algorithm (NGA for short) are: First of all, comparing the distance between each individual of the group. If the distance is within the predefined distance L (hamming distance), then comparing their fitness size and exerting a strong penalty function to the lower fitness individuals for the purpose of greatly reducing their fitness, so their probability of being eliminated in the later evolving process is great. That is, through genetic selection and natural elimination

S. Lin and X. Huang (Eds.): CESM 2011, Part II, CCIS 176, pp. 323–328, 2011.
© Springer-Verlag Berlin Heidelberg 2011

process in evolution, there will be only one fine individual existed within hamming distance L. In this way, it is not only maintaining the diversity of groups, but also making every one keep a certain distance between individuals and making individuals scatter throughout the constraint space, thus completing the NGA. The GA, in which the niche technique is introduced, can not only maintain the group's diversity, but improve genetic algorithm precocious phenomena and accelerating genetic algorithm convergence as well.

1.2 Implementation Procedure

The control variables sequences $(x_1^1, x_2^1, \cdots, x_n^1)$, $(x_1^2, x_2^2, \cdots, x_n^2)$, $(x_1^Z, x_2^Z, \cdots, x_n^Z)$ are randomly generated according to the characterization of gravity dam shape. Z is group size; n is the number of control variables. Making the control variables series of Z groups as matrix, then through certain encoding rules to make them expressed as number series of individuals. In the condition of meeting given constraint conditions, evaluating according to the predetermined fitness evaluation function, calculating the fitness of each individual, and then conducting genetic operation (Selection, crossover and mutation) according to the fitness of each individual and niche eliminated calculation [7]. Eliminating low fitness individual, retaining high fitness individual, thus obtaining the new group, repeatedly, until meeting given termination rules.

1.2.1 Parameters Code and Generating Initial Groups

In order to simplify the calculation, this article adopts the binary-coded method. Predetermining one allows variable interval $[U_{min}, U_{max}]$ of parameter, supposing parameters number as n, using binary string with length of l to represent the parameters. Supposing an individual code is: $X : b_l b_{l-1} b_{l-2} \cdots b_2 b_1$. Then the individual actual value is x: $x = U_{min} + (\sum_{i=1}^{l} b_i \cdot 2^i - 1) \cdot \dfrac{U_{max} - U_{min}}{2^l - 1}$.

Where, U_{min} is the parameter of minimum, U_{max} is the parameter of the maximum, b is binary symbols 0 or 1. Initially, a series of groups (Z group) composed of n variables are randomly generated which represents optimal solution to the possible combinations. Because this group is generated randomly, its fitness is generally low.

1.2.2 Fitness Function

In GA, the probability of each individual inherited to the next generation is determined by the individual fitness. Fitness function is required nonnegative, and for the sake of maximum, optimization problems should be made. To seek the minimum, target function and fitness function are needed to be transformed. The general expression of fitness function is:

$$F(x) = \begin{cases} C_{max} - f(X), & if \quad f(X) < C_{max} \\ 0, & if \quad f(X) \geq C_{max} \end{cases}$$

Where: C_{max} is properly a relatively large number, $f(X)$ is the objective function values.

In addition, GA can only be used to handle unconstrained optimization problems, so the constrained optimization problem is need to transformed into a no-constrained optimization problem according to certain rules. Usually adopting penalty function to deal with the constrained optimization problem, the fitness function expression is:

$$F'(x) = F(x) + k \sum_{j=1}^{p} W_j$$

Where : k is a penalty factor related to evolution algebra; p is the number of constraint conditions; W_j is the default value to be in relations with the constraint of number j, when the constraint of number j meets the constraints, W_j is 0, or W_j takes the larger value.

1.2.3 Niche Eliminating Operation

The basic process of Niche eliminating operation is:

Step (1) Setting evolutionary algebra counter t, randomly generating Z individuals composed initial group $P(t)$, then calculating the individual fitness.

Step (2) Ranking the order based on the fitness of each individual, then recording the first N individuals ($N < Z$).

Step (3) Carrying out roulette choice to groups, getting group $P'(t)$; operating single-point crossover to selected individuals, getting $P''(t)$; making a basic position variation operation to $P''(t)$, getting M new individuals.

Step (4) Getting the N individuals in step (2) and the M new individuals produced in step (3) together; for $N + M$ individuals, carrying out the hamming distance L [8] of the every two individuals $X(i)$ and $X(j)$ according to the formula below:

$$\|X(i) - X(j)\| = \sqrt{\sum_{k=1}^{l} (X_{ik} - X_{jk})^2} \quad \begin{pmatrix} i = 1, 2, \cdots, Z + N - 1 \\ j = i + 1, \cdots, Z + N \end{pmatrix}$$

When $\|X(i) - X(j)\| < L$, comparing the fitness size of individual $X(i)$ and $X(j)$, implementing penalty function ($F_{min}(x_i, x_j) = $ Penalty) to the individuals whose fitness is relatively low. In this article, hamming distance L takes 0.5, penalty takes 10^{-30}.

Step (5) Ranking the order based on the new fitness of $N + M$ individuals produced in step (4), recording the first N individuals.

Step (6) Judging the conditions of termination. If results cannot satisfy the conditions of termination, updating evolutionary algebras, and making the ordered N individuals of step (5) as a new generation P (t), and then turning to step (3).

2 The Optimization Section Design of Gravity Dam

2.1 The Basic Information of Engineering

Gushan Lake Reservoir is a medium comprehensive utilization water conservancy project, whose main task is supplying water to urban, generating power, tourism and flood control for a position of subordination. The dam is a concrete gravity dam, with its overflow segment 76m height, design level 71.83m, downstream tail-water level 26.36m , sediment elevation before dam 31.7m, silt elevation behind the dam 22.5m, silt float density r_s10kN/m^3, anti-sliding friction coefficient f 0.64, anti-cutting friction coefficient f 1.0, cohesion C'0.9Mpa. The constraint conditions are as follow:

(1) Upstream dam slope rate :$0 \le n \le 0.2$;

(2) Downstream dam slope rate :$0.6 \le m \le 0.8$;

(3) The proportion of upstream fold slope height to dam height: $0 \le H1/H \le 1$;

(4) The proportion of downstream fold slope height to dam height:

  $0 \le H2/H \le 1$;

(5) Anti-sliding stability constraint : $K = f(\sum w - U)/\sum P \ge K_s = 1.05$;

(6) Anti-cutting stability constraint: $K' = \dfrac{f'(\sum W - U) + C'A}{\sum P} \ge K_s' = 3.0$;

(7) Dam heel stress constraint: $\sigma_u = \sum W / B + 6 \sum M / B^2 \ge 0$;

(8) Dam toe stress constraint: $\sigma_d = \sum W / B - 6 \sum M / B^2 \le \sigma_{allowable} = 4.0$M pa.

2.2 Establishment of Optimization Model

The Gravity dam basic cross-section is shown as Fig.1. Dam height is H , dam top width B is commonly constant. Design variable X taking upstream dam slope rate x_1, downstream dam slope rate x_2, the proportion of upstream fold slope height to dam height is x_3, The proportion of downstream fold slope height to dam height is x_4; Make target function according to concrete dam volume of per unit length in the direction of dam axis, calculating the minimum volume of the concrete dam, that is $V(x) = A(x) \times l \to min$, where $x_1 = n$, $x_2 = m$, $x_3 = H_1/H$, $x_4 = H_2/H$,

$$A(X) = \frac{1}{2} H^2 x_1 x_3^2 + \frac{1}{2} H^2 x_2 x_4^2 + BH$$

In this article, H of the dam is 76m; the width of the dam top is 5m; the length of the dam is 43m.

Optimization model: calculating the design variables $X = \{x_1, x_2, x_3, x_4\}$, making $V(X) \rightarrow \min$, and satisfying the constraint conditions of (1) ~ (8) above.

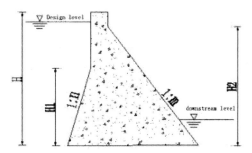

Fig. 1. Gravity dam basic sectional drawing

2.3 The Optimization Results and Analysis

In order to check the feasibility of NGA as well as pros and cons of the optimization results, complex method is adopted to optimize the model in this article, optimization results can be seen from table 1 and table2. According to table 1: NGA's safety coefficient is the smallest satisfying the precondition constraints. According to table 2: NGA $V(X)$ =8.51×10⁴ m³, initial plan $V(X)$ =1.01×10⁵m³, complex method $V(X)$ =9.14×10⁴m³; It is saved 18.45 % dam volume per meter in the direction of dam axis than initial plan, saved 7.43 % compared to complex method, producing significant economic benefits. Therefore, the optimizing results of NGA are more ideal, and have certain practical value for preliminary design of project.

Table 1. The cross-references of NGA compared to the compound algorithm to dam shape parameter optimization results

Scheme	Section parameters of Gravity dam				Stress（MPa）		Safety coefficient	
	Upstream dam slope rate	Downstream dam slope rate	upstream fold slope height	downstream fold slope height	Dam heel	Dam toe	*Ks*	*Ks'*
Initial plan	0.2	0.75	40	52	0.24	1.02	1.14	4.32
NGA	0.196	0.646	63.688	60.952	0.513	1.463	1.05	3.874
Complex method	0.157	0.783	58.14	61.484	0.677	1.224	1.092	4.153

Table 2. The cross-references of NGA compared to the compound algorithm to dam volume optimization results

Scheme	Concrete dam volume (m3)	The increase rate of dam volume
Initial plan	100749	18.45%
NGA	85054	0.00%
Complex method	91375	7.43%

3   Conclusion

(1) The application of NGA to engineering structure optimization design is useful, because initial solution does not suffer limits, and crossover probability and mutation probability can change as evolution process changes. The GA, in which the niche technique is introduced, is favorable to maintain the group's diversity as well as improve genetic algorithm precocious phenomena and accelerate genetic algorithm convergence. Therefore, NGA is a simple, rapid algorithm. And the optimization results are more accessible to global optimal solution.

(2) NGA in this article contributes a lot to target function according to concrete dam volume, makes the gravity dam stability, dam heel and dam toe stress for the main factors to design optimization model. The optimization results show that this algorithm can be used for gravity dam shape optimization, and the optimization results are economy, security and ideal. Therefore, there is a broad application prospect for NGA to be used in large hydraulic structure optimization, which is worth to be promoted in engineering design field.

Acknowledgments. The natural science research grants program of Department of education of Henan province, China (2011A570010).

References

[1] Zhou, M., Sun, S.: Genetic Algorithm Principle and Application, pp. 15–78. National Defense Industry Press, Beijing (1999)
[2] Lei, Y., Zhang, S., Li, X., et al.: MATLAB GA Toolbox and Its Application, pp. 3–22. Xi'an University of Electronic Science and Technology Press, Xi'an (2005)
[3] Sacco, W.F., Lapa, C.M.F., Pereira, C.M.N.A., et al.: A niching Genetic Algorithm Applied to a Nuclear Power Plant Auxiliary Feedwater System Surveillance Tests Policy Optimization. Annals of Nuclear Energy 33, 753–759 (2006)
[4] Alugongo, A.A., Lange, J.M.: Optimization of Multimodal Models in Mechanical Design by a Niche Hybrid Genetic Algorithm. In: IEEE AFRICON 2009, Nairobi, Kenya, September 23-25, pp. 1–6 (2009)
[5] Tu, Q.: Based on Niche Genetic Algorithm of Regional Water Resources Optimization Allocation. Water Technology and Economy 14(3), 209–1609 (2008)
[6] Chen, C., Gong, X.: Based on niche genetic algorithm on soft soil ground embankment stability analysis. Engineering Geological Journals 2(4), 520–2938
[7] Zhao, J., Li, S., Fu, Y., et al.: Based on Adaptive Genetic Algorithm Gravity Dam Shape Optimization Design. Hong Shui He 23(3), 44–46 (2004)
[8] Chen, S.-K., Zhu, Y.-M., Shuai, W.: Back Analysis of Thermal Field of Concrete and Its Application Based on Niche Genetic Algorithms. In: The 2nd IEEE International Conference on Information Management and Engineering (ICIME), Chengdu, China, April 16-18, pp. 403–407 (2010)

A Pilot Study on Comprehensive Evaluating Indicators System for Acceptability of Real Time Communication Software Based on AHP

Jifeng Guo[*]

School of Software, Zhongyuan University of Technology, West Zhongyuan Rd.,
450007 Zhengzhou, China
Jifengguo@yeah.net

Abstract. Real-time communication software has been playing an increasingly important role in our work and life. With the rapid progress of computer and network technique, it is needed to develop the adaptable and reliable real-time communication software for users. This paper is a pilot study on constructing a comprehensive evaluating indicators system for assessing acceptability of real time communication software. Analytic Hierarchy Process is applied for evaluating those indicators. All weight coefficients for evaluating indicators system are from an investigation on specialists on software engineering. The results show that there are two indicators mostly influencing acceptability of real time communication software.

Keywords: Comprehensive Evaluating Indicators System, Analytic Hierarchy Process, Real Time Communication Software.

1 Introduction

Real time communication software (RTCS) has played an important role in our jobs, lives and other social works. Until now, there have been many commercial RTCSs, such as QQ, MSN and NetMeeting. Millions of persons may use the RTCS to exchange the words, voice and picture simultaneously around the world. Therefore, how acceptable to the users are those RTCSs may be an interesting topic for software designers. In the past years, several researchers have analysed the factors influencing RTCS' network security, dependability and so on. Guo et al. puts forward a model of computer forensics based on Multi-Agent for RTCS. It presents the structure of the system, the design and implement of the key modules and technologies. They use distributed technology accurately recovers, collects and analyses the communication records of real time communication soft and makes forensics reports[1]. Li and Gao think that the software dependability evaluation index's weight may affect the accuracy and the validity of the results greatly. They apply a new comprehensive evaluation model with combinational weight based on rough set theory to evaluate software's dependability. This model, taking both of the objective information of

---

[*] Corresponding author.

S. Lin and X. Huang (Eds.): CESM 2011, Part II, CCIS 176, pp. 329–335, 2011.
© Springer-Verlag Berlin Heidelberg 2011

index and the experts' judgment into consideration, can effectively avoid subjectivity about weighing coefficient in fuzzy comprehensive evaluation[2]. However, the studies on comprehensive evaluating indicators system for acceptability of RTCS are fewer. Analytic Hierarchy Process (AHP) may be a good method to analyse the weight of evaluating indicators. Liu and Xu reviewed the development of the theory and applications of the Analytic Hierarchy Process (AHP) in China[3]. Even then, AHP was mostly applied for software designing to evaluating other things except RTCS[4], such as applied economics research[5][6]. The study tries to apply AHP method for comprehensive evaluating indicators system for acceptability of RTCS. Especially, several key indicators with throng influences on acceptability are selected by the AHP method.

2   Method and Materials

2.1   AHP

AHP is a method to decision making that involves structuring multiple choice criteria into a hierarchy. AHP assesses the relative importance of these criteria, compares alternatives for each criterion, and determines an overall ranking of the alternatives. Thomas L. Saaty found the AHP method in late 80's[7]. In next 20 years, AHP has found its way into various decision areas. As a technique not firmly rooted in utility theory, AHP, for the most part, has remained outside the mainstream of decision analysis research. However, the practical nature of the method, suitable for solving complicated and elusive decision problems, has led to applications in highly diverse areas and has created a voluminous body of literature.

Using AHP in solving a decision problem involves four steps. a. setting up the decision hierarchy by breaking down the decision problem into a hierarchy of interrelated decision elements. b. collecting input data by pair-wise comparisons of decision elements. c. using the eigenvalue method to estimate the relative weights of decision elements. d. aggregating the relative weights of decision elements to arrive at a set of ratings for the decision alternatives.

The decision analyst should break down the decision problem into a hierarchy of interrelated decision elements.

2.2   Comprehensive Evaluating Indicators System for Acceptability of Real Time Communication Software

This paper developed the comprehensive evaluating indicators system for assessing acceptability of RTCS. The indicators are divided into two sub-levels. The first sub-level set has the representative letter as "E", which includes indicators as Ease of installation and use (E1), Educational content of the software (E2), Presentation/organization of the content (E3), User interaction (E4), Technical presentation (E5), Management of the software operation (E6) and Free of bias and objectionable content (E7). The second sub-level set is assigned as the letter of "F", which has 44 indicators in this level set. The total comprehensive evaluating indicators system can be shown in Table 1.

Table 1. Comprehensive evaluating indicators system

The first sub-level set	The second sub-level set
Ease of installation and use (E_1)	f_1– Installation process f_2– Instructions/documentation to begin use f_3– Ease to understand basic controls, major features organization f_4– Technical assistance available
Educational content of the software (E_2)	f_5– Presents accurate, current information f_6– Depth of information f_7– Breath/range of information f_8– Sensitive/respectful of diversity (income, gender, age, race, physical/mental ability) f_9– includes additional curriculum support/lesson plans
Presentation/organization of the content (E_3)	f_{10}– Presents materials in an organized manner f_{11}– Provides consistent, easy to use on screen instructions f_{12}– Provides consistent, easy to use help screens f_{13}– Search methods and results easy to understand f_{14}– Multiple levels of use/difficulty f_{15}– Use of multimedia to provide multiple channels for information f_{16}– Multiple ways to move through information (sequentially, random, search, hyperlinks) f_{17}– Exhibits diversity with characters, graphics, etc.
User interaction (E_4)	f_{18}– Helps user link new info to existing knowledge f_{19}– Helps user remember information f_{20}– Encourages user to practice to whole skill and/or see the big picture f_{21}– Ease of user interaction f_{22}– Provides appropriate feedback to user responses f_{23}– Allows/encourages user to apply knowledge/skills to real life situations f_{24}– Lends itself to repeated use
Technical presentation (E_5)	f_{25}– Runs smoothly without long delays f_{26}– Spelling/grammar accurate f_{27}– Visual quality of graphics/text f_{28}– Quality of audio f_{29}– Quality of video f_{30}– Avoids unnecessary screens, sounds, graphics f_{31}– Use of multimedia f_{32}– Use of hyperlinks
Management of the software operation (E_6)	f_{2}– Information can be printed f_{2}– Information can be saved to a file f_{2}– On screen notebooks, bookmarks f_{2}– Allows user to exit/resume use at another time f_{2}– Keeps performance records for each user f_{2}– Keeps information on more than one individual (not necessarily simultaneous users) f_{2}– Allows control of various aspects (e.g. sound) f_{2}– Operations can be undone, steps retraced f_{2}– Clear instructions on how to return to main menu, exit program
Free of bias and objectionable content (E_7)	f_{33}– Race/gender/age views f_{34}– Extremist views f_{35}– Objectionable content (nudity, excessive violence, offensive language)

2.3 Investigation

A score methodology was applied for an investigation on specialists in software research. The importance of the indicators in all sub-level sets was evaluated corresponding values in the investigation. Twenty eight specialists were consulted for getting the importance criterion for pairwise comparisons of the indicators in the first sub-level set and the second sub-level set.

3 Results

3.1 Weight Coefficient of the Indicators Set in the First Sub-level Set and the Second Sub-level Set

The importance of the indicators in the first sub-level set to another has been given as listed in Table 2.

Table 2. Pairwise comparison matrix for the first sub-level set

Comparison value	E_1	E_2	E_3	E_4	E_5	E_6	E_7
E_1	1	1/2	1	2	3	1/2	1/3
E_2	2	1	2	4	5	1	1/2
E_3	1	1/2	1	2	3	1/2	1/3
E_4	1/2	1/4	1/2	1	2	1/3	1/5
E_5	1/3	1/5	1/3	1/2	1	1/5	1/7
E_6	2	1	2	3	5	1	1/2
E_7	3	2	3	5	7	2	1

The results of pairwise comparisons for the second sub-level sets can be gotten by the same investigation on the advices from the specialists in software research. Table 3 is the pairwise comparison matrices for the second sub-level sets.

Table 3. Pairwise comparison matrix for the second sub-level set of E_1 to E_7

Comparison value	f_1		f_2		f_3		f_4
f_1	1		2		5		3
f_2	1/2		1		3		2
f_3	1/5		1/3		1		1/2
f_4	1/3		1/2		2		1

Comparison value	f_5	f_6	f_7	f_8	f_9
f_5	1	1/2	1/2	1/3	1
f_6	2	1	1	1/2	2
f_7	2	1	1	1/2	2
f_8	3	2	2	1	3
f_9	1	1/2	1/2	1/3	1

Comparison value	f_{10}	f_{11}	f_{12}	f_{13}	f_{14}	f_{15}	f_{16}	f_{17}
f_{10}	1	2	2	5	3	1	1	1
f_{11}	1/2	1	1	3	2	1/2	1/2	1/2
f_{12}	1/2	1	1	3	2	1/2	1/2	1/2
f_{13}	1/5	1/3	1/3	1	1/3	1/5	1/5	1/5
f_{14}	1/3	1/2	1/2	3	1	1/3	1/3	1/3
f_{15}	1	2	2	5	3	1	1	1
f_{16}	1	2	2	5	3	1	1	1
f_{17}	1	2	2	5	3	1	1	1

Table 3. (*continued*)

Comparison value	f_{18}	f_{19}	f_{20}	f_{21}	f_{22}	f_{23}	f_{24}
f_{18}	1	2	1/2	3	3	1	2
f_{19}	1/2	1	1/3	2	2	1/2	1
f_{20}	2	3	1	5	5	2	3
f_{21}	1/3	1/2	1/5	1	1	1/3	1/2
f_{22}	1/3	1/2	1/5	1	1	1/3	1/2
f_{23}	1	2	1/2	3	3	1	2
f_{24}	1/2	1	1/3	2	2	1/2	1

Comparison value	f_{25}	f_{26}	f_{27}	f_{28}	f_{29}	f_{30}	f_{31}	f_{32}
f_{25}	1	1	1/2	1/3	1/3	1/3	1/3	1/3
f_{26}	1	1	1/2	1/3	1/3	1/3	1/3	1/3
f_{27}	2	2	1	1/2	1/2	1/2	1/2	1/2
f_{28}	3	3	2	1	1	1	1	1
f_{29}	3	3	2	1	1	1	1	1
f_{30}	3	3	2	1	1	1	1	1
f_{31}	3	3	2	1	1	1	1	1
f_{32}	3	3	2	1	1	1	1	1

Comparison value	f_{33}	f_{34}	f_{35}	f_{36}	f_{37}	f_{38}	f_{39}	f_{40}	f_{41}
f_{33}	1	1	1/2	2	2	1	2	3	5
f_{34}	1	1	1/2	2	2	1	2	3	5
f_{35}	2	2	1	3	3	2	3	5	7
f_{36}	1/2	1/2	1/3	1	1	1/2	1	2	3
f_{37}	1/2	1/2	1/3	1	1	1/2	1	2	3
f_{38}	1	1	1/2	2	2	1	2	3	5
f_{39}	1/2	1/2	1/3	1	1	1/2	1	2	3
f_{40}	1/3	1/3	1/5	1/2	1/2	1/3	1/2	1	2
f_{41}	1/5	1/5	1/7	1/3	1/3	1/5	1/3	1/2	1

Comparison value	f_{42}	f_{43}	f_{44}
f_{42}	1	1	1
f_{43}	1	1	1
f_{44}	1	1	1

3.2 Comprehensive Evaluating Results of Acceptability for Real Time Communication Software Based on AHP

With the comprehensive evaluating, weight coefficients for all hierarchies for comprehensive evaluating indicators system can be reached. Table 4 gives those weight coefficients and the overall ranks of indicators on the second sub-level.

Table 4. Weight coefficients and ranks of all indicators

The first sub-level set	Weight coefficient	The second sub-level set	Weight coefficient	Overall weight coefficient	overall rank
E_1	0.1200	f_1	0.0909	0.0109	28
		f_2	0.1818	0.0218	17
		f_3	0.4545	0.0545	5
		f_4	0.2727	0.0327	10
		f_5	0.3000	0.0180	20
E_2	0.0600	f_6	0.1500	0.0090	31
		f_7	0.1500	0.0090	31
		f_8	0.1000	0.0060	40
		f_9	0.3000	0.0180	20

Table 4. (*continued*)

		f_{10}	0.0625	0.0075	33
		f_{11}	0.1250	0.0150	23
		f_{12}	0.1250	0.0150	23
E_3	0.1200	f_{13}	0.3125	0.0375	9
		f_{14}	0.1875	0.0225	16
		f_{15}	0.0625	0.0075	33
		f_{16}	0.0625	0.0075	33
		f_{17}	0.0625	0.0075	33
		f_{18}	0.0800	0.0192	18
		f_{19}	0.1600	0.0384	7
		f_{20}	0.0400	0.0096	30
E_4	0.2400	f_{21}	0.2400	0.0576	3
		f_{22}	0.2400	0.0576	3
		f_{23}	0.0800	0.0192	18
		f_{24}	0.1600	0.0384	7
		f_{25}	0.2400	0.0864	1
		f_{26}	0.2400	0.0864	1
		f_{27}	0.1200	0.0432	6
E_5	0.3600	f_{28}	0.0800	0.0288	11
		f_{29}	0.0800	0.0288	11
		f_{30}	0.0800	0.0288	11
		f_{31}	0.0800	0.0288	11
		f_{32}	0.0800	0.0288	11
		f_{33}	0.0571	0.0034	41
		f_{34}	0.0571	0.0034	41
		f_{35}	0.0286	0.0017	44
		f_{36}	0.1143	0.0069	37
E_6	0.0600	f_{37}	0.1143	0.0069	37
		f_{38}	0.0571	0.0034	41
		f_{39}	0.1143	0.0069	37
		f_{40}	0.1714	0.0103	29
		f_{41}	0.2857	0.0171	22
		f_{42}	0.3333	0.0133	25
E_7	0.0400	f_{43}	0.3333	0.0133	25
		f_{44}	0.3333	0.0133	25

4 Discussion

The research calculated weight coefficient of each level indicator set based on the results of the investigation on specialists in software research. Then, AHP was applied for evaluating the comprehensive evaluating indicators system for acceptability of real time communication software.

Table 4 shows us the overall weight coefficients. It can be gotten that the top influential two indicators are in turn as runs smoothly without long delays (f_{25}) and spelling/grammar accurate (f_{26}).

Table 4 also displays that one indicator with the weakest influence on the system. It is objectionable content (f_{35}). It can explain that some objectionable content may be not the key factors for operating software.

As to the first sub-level set of the comprehensive evaluating indicators system, the indicators in technical presentation have the highest weight coefficient among the seven sets. It partially contributes to that users prefer remarkably to the operating feeling of real time communication software.

5 Conclusions

This study evaluated the comprehensive evaluating indicators system for acceptability of real time communication software based on AHP. The results show that AHP can enable the decision-makers to structure a complex problem in the form of a simple hierarchy. The AHP helps analysts to organize the critical aspects of a problem into a hierarchy rather like a family tree.

It can be concluded that running smoothly without long delays and spelling/ grammar accurate are the important indicators for contributing to the acceptability of software to users. A software designer may use the above results according to his particular needs and interests which are the measurements to promote the acceptability of software.

Acknowledgments. The work is partly supported by Education Department of Henan Provincial Government, No.2008B480006.

References

1. Guo, J.F., Pan, L., Miao, F.J.: The Study of Computer Forensics System for Real Time Communication Soft. J. Zhongyuan Inst. Technol. 16(5), 10–12, 37 (2005)
2. Li, B., Yang, C.: An Improved Comprehensive Evaluation Model of Software Dependability based on Rough Set Theory. J. Software 4(10), 1152–1159 (2009)
3. Liu, B., Xu, S.: Development of the theory and methodology of the analytic hierarchy process and its applications in China. Math. Modell. 9(3), 179–183 (1987)
4. Wu, Y., Du, D.: AHP Evaluation Software Design and Empirical Research. Comput. Syst. Appl. 17(11), 35–39 (2008) (in Chinese)
5. Wu, M.: Topsis-AHP simulation model and its application to supply chain Management. World J. Modell. Simul. 3(3), 196–201 (2007)
6. Yang, L., Zhang, Y.: Application of Fuzzy-AHP Method in the Evaluation of Logistics Capability in E-Commerce Environment. In: Proceedings of 2010 Communications and Intelligence Information Security, pp. 228–231. IEEE Press, New York (2010)
7. Saaty, T.: The Analytic Hierarchy Process. Wiley, New York (1980)

The Research on a New Image Enhancement Algorithm Based on Retinex Theory

Qin Guang

Network Management Center, Xichang College, Xichang, China

Abstract. On the basis of Retinex theory, We know that SSR (SSR, Single Scale Retinex) algorithms mainly consists of two steps: estimation and normalization of illumination. The illumination is estimated as a smooth version of input image using gaussian low-pass filters. In this paper, We propose a method to improve SSR algorithm. We used Butterworth low-pass filter instead of gaussian low-pass filter to smooth the image, Compared with traditional Retinex algorithm, The experimental results shows that, The result images using modified SSR algorithm have greater entropy and average gradient.

Keywords: Retinex theory, SSR algorithm, Gaussian low-pass filter, Butterworth low-pass filter.

1 Introduction

Image enhancement has long been a topic of interest in the image processing field. The goal of image enhancement is to improve the visual quality of an image. Any image can be expressed as a product of two components⫿ the illumination image and the reflectance image.

On the basis of it, Retinex theory was bring forward in the 70s 20th century by Edwin Land [1], this theory is a regulation on how the human visual system to perceive color and brightness of the object model.

The Retinex Theory shows that the human visual system can identify the color of objects in a scene irrespective of the color of the illumination [2-4]. This phenomenon is called color constancy. Trying to recover the illumination is an under-constrained problem and various methods have been proposed to address it.

Retinex theory is different from the traditional image enhancement algorithms, such as the spatial enhancement of pixel-based image processing; the frequency domain enhancement based on Fourier transform; the wavelet enhancement based on wavelet transform. They can only enhance the one type of features in the image, such as the dynamic range of images or the details such as edges of images. While the Retinex algorithm can keep a balance in several aspects such as the image dynamic range, image detail and image color keep. So the Retinex algorithm had been applied in many areas, such as medical image processing, remote sensing image processing and video image processing.

S. Lin and X. Huang (Eds.): CESM 2011, Part II, CCIS 176, pp. 336–342, 2011.

2 Retinex Basic Theory

The Retinex theory consider that the human visual system to the object color and reflection inherent has a very close relationship, while had small relationship with the reflected light which come into human eyes[5-8].

Because of this perception, Retinex theory mainly compensate for the impact of images affected by illumination. Based on Retinex image formation model:

$$I(x, y) = L(x, y) \cdot R(x, y) \tag{1}$$

An image is pixel-by-pixel product of the ambient illumination and the scene reflectance. As the ambient illumination is independent of object itself, Only the scene reflectance reflect the inhesion characteristic of object itself. Illumination is a kind of low-frequency image information which is slow changing, and reflectance contains the most high-frequency detailed image information. The Retinex theory deal with the problem of separating the two quantities: first estimating the illumination and then obtaining the reflectance by division. From the mathematical point of view based on logarithmic domain, complex multiplication can be converted to a simple addition operation. So the first step taken by most Retinex Algorithms is the conversion of the given image into Logarithmic domain. As shown in formula 2:

$$\log I = \log L + \log R \tag{2}$$

Therefore, as shown in formula 3, the logarithm of the reflectance can be obtained by the logarithm of the image subtract the logarithm of the illumination.

$$\log R = \log L - \log I \tag{3}$$

Then the reflectance can be obtained by taken its index form, as shown in formula 4 The reflectance is inherent properties of object itself.

$$R = \exp(\log L - \log I) \tag{4}$$

The overall diagram of the Retinex theory is given in Fig.1.

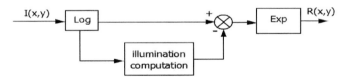

Fig. 1. The Retinex theory

As the illumination compared with the reflectance is low frequency component, so the Retinex Algorithm uses the low-pass filter to estimate the illumination .However, as Gaussian filter used in the filtering process will inevitably lose some high-frequency components, image will lose some of the details and edges, resulting in image distortion. In this paper, We introduce a new method to estimate the illumination. The method is that We use Butterworth low-pass filter algorithms instead of gaussian low-pass filter algorithms to smooth the images [9].

3 Modified SSR Algorithm

Using SSR algorithms with Gaussian low-pass filter to make image enhanced, details of the image reflected are not very obvious. When images are fuzzy and have thin cloud, enhancing effect with this method is not ideal. The reason is that Gaussian low-pass filter used in the filtering process will inevitably lose some high-frequency components, Image will lose some of the details and edges, resulting in image distortion.

We use Butterworth low-pass filter instead of gaussian low-pass filter to smooth the image, Compared with traditional Retinex Algorithm with Gaussian low-pass filter, The experimental results shows that, the result images have greater entropy and average gradient, as well as smaller standard deviation, which indicating that the images contain more details and information, and have more uniform illumination.

Butterworth low pass filter transfer function:

$$H(u,v) = \frac{1}{1+[D(u,v)/D_0]^{2n}} \tag{5}$$

In the formula (5), D_0 is Cut-off frequency, where $D(u,v) = \sqrt{u^2 + v^2}$, and when $D(u,v) = D_0$, $H = \frac{1}{2}H_{max}$, n is the order and take a positive integer to control the frequency ecay rate. Filter characteristics determined entirely by the order of n, the filter characteristics curve becomes steeper when n increases. The greater n becomes the range of the pass band is closer to 1, stop-band close to 0 more quickly, while the amplitude characteristics closer to the ideal rectangular frequency characteristics.

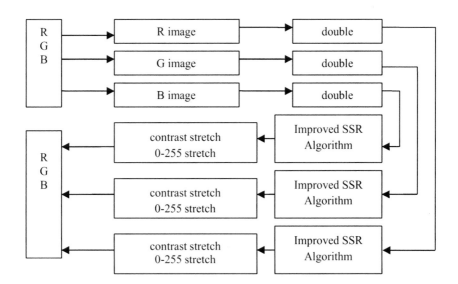

Fig. 2. Proposed SSR Algorithm flow-process diagram

4 Experiments and Results

Image enhancement is a crucial step in image processing. To illustrate the effectiveness and superiority of the modified SSR Algorithm on image enhancement, the modified SSR Algorithm is compared with traditional SSR Algorithm by enhancing three groups of images with poor visibility and little visual contrast. The performances have demonstrated that modified SSR algorithm method achieves higher score than traditional method based on entropy and average gradient, as well as smaller standard deviation.

Low contrast images taken through thick smoke. Processing brings out dramatic detail that was not even visible to the observer.

Fig. 3. Original image

Fig. 4. SSR algorithms image

Fig. 5. Modified SSR algorithms image

Fig.3 is a original image with poor visibility and thick smoke, figure 4 is the result image which has been processed by SSR Algorithm, figure 5 is output image which has been processed by modified SSR Algorithm. It can be found, compared with the image processed by traditional SSR Algorithm and original image, the image processed by modified SSR Algorithm brings out dramatic detail and more uniform illumination.To further illustrate the effectiveness of our modified SSR algorithm, We have compared the parameters of these images which include information entropy, Standard deviations and average gradient.

Table 1. Parameters of images comparison

	Entropy	Standard deviations	average gradient
Original image	5.2101	9.8166	0.0019
SSR	5.5534	12.9657	0.0058
Modified SSR	6.6981	26.6934	0.0199

It can be found from table 1, compared with the image processed by SSR Algorithm, the value of entropy, Standard deviations and average gradient of the image processed by modified SSR Algorithm is the biggest, So, The effect of the image enhancement by modified SSR algorithm is the best. The greater entropy, Standard deviations and average gradient indicating that the image contains more details and information, and the smaller variance indicating that the image has more uniform illumination.

Dark original caused by Lack of light, Processing brings out detail and color in the shadows.

Fig. 6. Original image

Fig. 7. SSR algorithms image

Fig. 8. Modified SSR algorithms image

Fig.6 is a original image with poor visibility and lack of details, figure 7 is the result image which has been processed by SSR Algorithm, figure 8 is output image which has been processed by modified SSR Algorithm. It can be found, the image processed by modified SSR Algorithm brings out brightness and some new details which hidden in black background.

Table 2. Parameters of images comparison

	Entropy	Standard deviations	average gradient
Original image	5.7612	0.000115	3.8661
SSR	7.2127	52.2723	0.0233
Modified SSR	7.6351	51.9137	0.0417

According to table 3, we also get conclusion that improved SSR algorithm is the best.

5   Conclusions

As the illumination compared with the reflectance is low-frequency component, Therefore, the modified SSR Algorithm can overcome the shortcoming of traditional SSR Algorithm, and get a better enhanced image. The results show that the modified SSR Algorithm is satisfying and superior over the other traditional SSR algorithm.

References

1. Land, E.H.: The Retinex theory of color vision. Scientific American 237(6), 108–129 (1977)
2. Land, E.H., McCann, J.J.: Lightness and retinex theory. J. Opt. Soc. A 61(1), 11 (1971)
3. Land, E.H.: The retinex theory of color vision. Sci. Am. 237(6), 108–128 (1977)
4. Land, E.H.: Recent advances in retinex theory and some implications for cortical computations: color vision and the natural image. In: Proc. Natl. Acad. Sci. USA, vol. 80, pp. 5163–5169 (1983)
5. Anustup, C., Gerard, M.: Perceptually Motivated Automatic Color Contrast Enhancement. In: IEEE ICCV International Conference on Computer Vision Workshops, pp. 1893–1900 (2009)

6. Jean, M.M., Ana, B.P., Catalina, S.: A PDE Formalization of Retinex Theory. IEEE Transactions on Image Processing 19(11), 2825–2837 (2009)
7. Cui, L.Y., Xue, B.D., Cao, X.G.: An Improved Retinex Image Enhancement Technique for Dim Target Extraction in Infrared Images. In: IEEE a Grant from the Aeronautical Science Foundation of China (2009)
8. Wu, J., Wang, Z., Fang, Z.: Application of Retinex in Color Restoration of Image Enhancement to Night Image. In: IEEE Colleges Natural Science Research Project of Anhui (2010)
9. Anustup, C., Gerard, M.: Color Constancy Using Denoising Methods And Cepstral Analysis. In: IEEE ICIP 2010 (2010)

Application of Combined Grey Neural Network for the BTP Forecasting in Sintering Process

Rui Wang[1] and Qiang Song[2]

[1] Mechanical and Electrical Engineering Xinxiang University, Xinxiang, China
[2] Mechanical Engineering Department of Anyang Institute of Technology, Anyang, China

Abstract. The Burning-Through-Point is affected by many reasons and difficult to be controlled to the required precision by conventional control methods. This paper presents a better prediction model by the integration of neural network technique and grey theory for the BTP in sintering process. This paper constructs a model of Burning-Through-Point and the simulation results prove that the model has a good performance and can improve the prediction accuracy. It is concluded that great improvement comparing with any method of BTP in combined model of grey system and neural network comparing with the any model of grey system.

Keywords: Grey theory, Improved GM (1,1) model, Artificial neural network.

1 Introduction

The Burning-Through-Point (BTP) is an important parameter in sintering process. In the iron and steel enterprises, sintered ore is the main raw material for blast furnace. In the sintering process, stability and quality of sinter is a decision factor to production efficiency of blast furnace. The sintering process is a preprocess for blast-furnace materials. The quality of sinter is very important for smooth operation and high productivity of the blast furnace since it improves the permeability and reducibility of the burden material. Burning-Through-Point for judging the quality of sinter important indicator is a measure of good and bad sintered minerals important parameters. The BTP is a very important parameter in the sintering process. The sinter quality can be improved, and the energy consumption can be reduced, if one can accurately predict the BTP value. That means the accurate prediction of BTP can bring significant economic benefits and is of important practical significance. Traditional methods using features such as exhaust gas temperature, negative pressure and exhaust gas composition to predict the BTP [1].

2 The Principles of Grey Forecasting Model

2.1 Original GM (1,1) Forecasting Model

A grey system is a system that is not completely known, i.e., the knowledge of the system is partially known and partially unknown. In recent years, grey models have

S. Lin and X. Huang (Eds.): CESM 2011, Part II, CCIS 176, pp. 343–348, 2011.

been successfully employed in many prediction applications. The GM (1,1) model means a single differential equation model with a single variation. The modeling process is as follows: First of all, observed data are converted into new data series by a preliminary transformation called AGO (accumulated generating operation). Then a GM model based on the generated sequence is built, and then the prediction values are obtained by returning an AGO' s level to the original level using IAGO (inverse accumulated generating operation).

A grey modeling algorithm is described as follows.

Suppose there is a set of discrete data that is unequal intervals as follows:

$$x^{(0)} = \left(x^{(0)}(1), x^{(0)}(2), \ldots\ldots, x^{(0)}(n) \right) \tag{1}$$

Accumulate the discrete data above once to get a new serial, that is

$$x^{(1)} = \left(x^{(1)}(1), x^{(1)}(2), \ldots\ldots x^{(1)}(n) \right), x^{(1)}(\kappa) = \sum_{i=0}^{k} \left(x^{(0)}(k) \right) \tag{2}$$

The GM (1,1) model can be constructed by establishing a first order differential equation for $x^{(1)}(t)$ as:

$$\frac{d\, x^{(1)}}{dt} + a\, x^{(1)} = u \tag{3}$$

The equation's general solution is:

$$x^{(1)}(t) = Ce^{-at} + \frac{\mu}{a}$$

The grey parameter a and u can be obtained by using the least square method: where:

$$\hat{\alpha} = \begin{bmatrix} a \\ u \end{bmatrix} = \left(B^T B \right)^{-1} B^T Y_N \tag{4}$$

where

$$B = \begin{bmatrix} -0.5\left(x^{(1)}(2)+x^{(1)}(1)\right) & 1 \\ -0.5\left(x^{(1)}(3)+x^{(1)}(2)\right) & 1 \\ \vdots & \vdots \\ -0.5\left(x^{(1)}(n)+x^{(1)}(n-1)\right) & 1 \end{bmatrix} \qquad Y_N = \begin{bmatrix} x^{(0)}(2) \\ x^{(0)}(3) \\ \vdots \\ x^{(0)}(n) \end{bmatrix}$$

Grey parameters $\hat{\alpha}$ will be substituted into the time function, then:

$$\hat{x}^{(1)}(k+1) = \left(x^{(0)}(1) - \frac{u}{a} \right) e^{-ak} + \frac{u}{a} \tag{5}$$

Dealing $\hat{x}^{(1)}(k)$ for derivative and return to original equation then obtain

$$\hat{x}^{(0)}(k+1) = (1 - e^a)\left(x^{(0)}(1) - \frac{u}{a}\right)e^{-ak} \tag{6}$$

Calculating the difference of $x^{(0)}(k)$ and $\hat{x}^{(0)}(k)$ and the relative error

$$\varepsilon^{(0)}(k) = x^{(0)}(k) - \hat{x}^{(0)}(k)$$

However, the potency of the residual series depends on the number of data points with the same data, which is usually small when there are few observations. In these cases, the potency of the residual series with the same data may not be more than four, and a residual GM(1,1) model cannot be established. Here, we present an improved grey model to solve this problem.

2.2 Residual Forecasting Model

To evaluate modeling performance, we should do synthetic test of goodness

$$C = \frac{S_2}{S_1} \tag{7}$$

Where $S^2{}_1 = \frac{1}{n}\sum_{k=1}^{n}(x^{(0)} - \overline{x}^{(0)})^2$; $S^2{}_2 = \frac{1}{n}\sum_{k=1}^{n}(\varepsilon(k) - \overline{\varepsilon})^2$ deviation between original data and estimating data:

$$\varepsilon^{(0)} = \{\varepsilon(1), \varepsilon(2), ..., \varepsilon(n)\} =$$

$$\left\{x^{(0)}(1) - \hat{x}^{(0)}(1), x^{(0)}(2) - \hat{x}^{(0)}(2), \cdots, x^{(0)}(n) - \hat{x}^{(0)}(n)\right\}$$

$$P = P\{|\varepsilon(k) - \overline{\varepsilon}| < 0.6745S_1\} \tag{8}$$

The precision grade of forecasting model can be seen in Table 1. Finally, applying the inverse accumulated generation operation (AGO), we then have prediction values

$$\hat{x}^{(0)}(k) = \hat{x}^{(1)}(k) - \hat{x}^{(1)}(k-1) \tag{9}$$

Table 1. Precision grade of forecasting model

Precision grade	P	C
Good	$0.95 \leq p$	$C \leq 0.35$
Qualified	$0.80 \leq p < 0.95$	$0.35 < C \leq 0.5$
Just	$0.70 \leq p < 0.80$	$0.5 < C \leq 0.65$
Unqualified	$p < 0.70$	$0.65 < C$

2.3 Artificial Neural Network (ANN)

In recent years, Artificial Neural Networks can be applied to a wide variety of problems, such as storing and recalling data or patterns, classifying patterns, performing general mapping from input patterns to output patterns, grouping similar patterns, or finding solutions to constrained optimizations problems. Artificial Neural Network is typically organized in layer where the layers made up of a number of interconnected 'nodes' which contain an "activation function". Patterns are presented to the network via the "input layer", which communicates to one or more "hidden layers" where the actual processing is done via a system of weighted "connections". The hidden layers then link to an "output layer" where the answer is output. Commonly Neural Networks are adjusted, or trained, so most ANN contains some form of "learning rule" which modifies the weights of the connections according to the input patterns that it is presented with. BP neural network is a gradient descent algorithm. It tries to improve the performance of the neural network by reducing the total error by changing the weights along its gradient.

2.4 The Combined Model of Grey Neural Network

We could see from the example that the difference value between forecasting value and practical value is large if the single model GM (1, 1) is employed to forecast. In order to make the forecasting result as close as the real value, literature[2] provide a combined grey neural network model. This kind of model could make the forecasting value as the input sample (learning sample) of the neural network, and make the real value as the target sample of the neural network. Adopting suitable structure and training on the neural network. Then we could get a series of authority value threshold value which correspond some corresponding crunodes. This kind of combined method mainly use the characteristics such as three BP neural network layers carries the network which contains at least one concealed layer of S style and one linear output layer could approach any rational function. Through training we endow the neural network the ability of simulating the relation between sequence data and sequence respectively. Meanwhile, literature provides the way that compensating the modeling error by neural network and blur logic, and doing some study training of network using heredity arithmetic. Thus we bring forward a new combined model of grey neural network synthesizing the literature.

3 The Simulation Result and Analysis

Firstly, we selected forty-eight groups of data of well controlled results. Secondly, in order to get a full appreciation of the grey network, we will normalize the real data and transform the physical quantities into [0 1] zone values. Then using normalized training data to train the network, input layer, hidden layer transfer function is Sigmoid type, and the output layer is Purelin transfer function. The range of Sigmoid function is [0,1],Setting the maximum study number for 5000 times, the learning goal takes 0.001 as the square error and setting the initial value of network connection weights is the random number between[-1,1]. It converges to the error range after 28 training times based on Levenberg-Marquardt optimization algorithm, the predicted results shown in Table 2. In order to compare the difference accuracy of three model forecasting, three evaluation criteria were used: Mean relative error, Mean absolute error, and Mean square error, The corresponding calculated results shown in Table 2.

Table 2. The comparison of forecasting model accuracy of the BTP

Model name	Mean relative error	Mean absolute error	Mean square error
GM(1,1)	1.77	0.59	2.224
BP neural network	0.68	-0.034	8.4218e-004
Grey neural network(GMNN)	0.041	0.0286	4.6077e-004

From Table 2 it can be seen that three models present quite satisfactory forecasting results. By comparing the Mean relative error, Mean absolute error and Mean square error of GNNM is smaller than that of GM (1,1) and BP neural network, we can find that grey neural network (GMNN) has higher precise prediction than GM(1,1) and BP neural network.

4 Conclusion

In this paper, we have applied an improved grey GM(1,1) model by using a technique that combines residual modification with ANN. Our study results show that this method can yield more accurate results than the original GM(1,1) model and Artificial Neural Network. In short, the GMNN model proves to be a more effective way than any simple model. However, some problems such as adapting conditions and parameters of model is worthy of studying.

References

[1] Fan, X.-h., Wang, H.-d.: Mathematical model and Artificial Intelligence of sintering process. Central South University Press (2002)
[2] Wang, Y.-w., Gui, W.-h., Wang, Y.-l.: Integrated model for predicting burning through point of sintering process based on optimal combination algorithm. The Chinese Journal of Nonferrous Metal 12(1), 191–195 (2002)

[3] Zhang, X.-l.: forecasting method and application of BTP based on neural network. Central South University (2006)

[4] Hsu, C.-C., Chen, C.-Y.: Applications of improved grey prediction model for power demand forecasting. Energy Conversion and Management 44, 2241–2249 (2003)

FMH and Its Application in Chinese Stock Market

Yuling Wang[1], Juan Wang[2], Yanjun Guo[1], Xinjue Wu[1], and Jing Wang[3]

[1] School of Science, Tianjin University of Commerce, Tianjin 300134
[2] Beijing Institute of Tracking and Telecommunications Technology, 100094
[3] Department of Math, Bengbu University, Bengbu 233030

Abstract. A demonstrative research in Chinese stock markets is given by stable software. The results show that the Chinese stock markets have obviously fractal characteristics. It is difficult to describe with efficient market hypothesis. On the contrary, the fractal market hypothesis can deal with this problem very well.

Keywords: FMH, fractal distribution, stock returns, fat tail.

1   The Proposition of FMH

Among financial and economic theories, the most authoritative and most influential theory further to the efficiency of capital market is undoubtedly the Efficiency Market Hypothesis (EMH)[1]. However, with the development of financial market, more and more phenomenon such as rush thick tail, scale effect and seasonal effect cannot be explained properly in the theoretical framework of the EMH. The Fractal Market Hypothesis (FMH) based on nonlinear dynamics thus comes into being[2-6].

Fractal Market Hypothesis thinks: 1. when the market is composed of invertors of various investment terms, it is stable. In a stable market, adequate liquidity can guarantee the normality of security trading; 2. Information brings about different effects on the investors of different investment time scales. The short term influence of information collection on data and technique analysis is greater than the long term one. Along with the increase of investment period, the longer-term fundamental analysis becomes more important. Therefore, there is no internal consistency between short-term market tendency and long-term economic development trend; 3. When the appearance of a certain event makes the effectiveness of basic analysis questionable, the long-term investors may stop the operation of entering the market, or buying and selling based on short-term information. When all the investment periods shrink to the same investment level, the market will volatile, because there are no long-term investors to provide this kind of liquidity for short-term investors to stabilize the market; 4. The price is the combined reaction by both the short-term technical analysis and long-term base analysis. Thus, the short-term price fluctuates more greatly, or "creates more noises". But the potential market trend reflects the expected returns which change along with the economic environment. 5. If a certain security is irrelevant to economic cycle, then it itself doesn't have long-term trend. At this time, transactions, market liquidity and short-term information will be in domination. And different from EMH, FMH emphasizes that there exists different investment time scales in the market, that the impacts of information on the investors of different investing time scales are different and that the diffusion of information is not balanced thus prices cannot reflect all information with linear ways.

S. Lin and X. Huang (Eds.): CESM 2011, Part II, CCIS 176, pp. 349–355, 2011.
© Springer-Verlag Berlin Heidelberg 2011

Fractal Market Hypothesis uses a plenty of empirical analysis to prove that security market is in a coexisting state of stability and instability and puts forward the condition of transformation between stability and instability.

2   R/S Analysis and Related Theory

In the fractal study, an important method, the heavy standard poor law (R/S), is a kind of statistic put forward by the Britain hydrologist of 1950s, H.E. Hurst, usually used to analyze the fractal features and the long-term memory process of time series. In 1972 Mandelbrot initially applied R/S analysis for the American Stock Exchange to analyze the changes of stock earnings[2]. Peters[6] discussed in detail and further developed this method as the most important research tool of the Fractal Market Hypothesis, and did a lot of empirical researches.

2.1   The Calculation Process of R/S

Supposed there is a time series $x = (x_1, x_2, \ldots, x_n)$, cut it into subsequences with the number of d, each at the length of n, represented separately by $m = 1,2,3 \cdots d$;

(1) Calculate the mean and variance of each subsequence, noted as E_m, S_m ;

(2) Normalize the sample data of each subsequence

$$(Z_{im}), x_{im} = z_{im} - E_{im}, i = 1,2,3,\ldots\ldots n;$$

(3) Establish a cumulative time series, $y_{im} = \sum_{j=1}^{i} x_{j,m}, i = 1,2,3,\cdots n$

(4) Calculate the range: $R_m = \max\{y_{1,m}, y_{2,m}, L, y_{n,m}\} - \min\{y_{1,m}, y_{2,m}, L, y_{n,m}\}$;

(5) Calculate the rescaled range R_m / S_m ;

(6) Calculate the average value of rescaled ranges of the subsequences at the length of n , $(R/S)_n = \dfrac{1}{d}\sum_{m=1}^{d}(R_m / S_m)$;

(7) For $(R/S)_n = C * n^H$, take logarithms from both sides and use the least squares method to build a regression equation

$$\log(R/S)_n = \log C + H \log n$$

From the regression equation, estimate the value of H, called Hurst index.

2.2   Hurst Index

As an inference for traditional statistics, if the process is a independent stochastic process sequence with limited variance, Hurst and Feller prove: $(R/S)_n = (n * \pi / 2) = 1/2$ that is $H = 1/2$, and get the relevant function of time series incremental: $C_n = 2^{(2H-1)} - 1$, to inspect the independence of time series and conclude the relation between fractal statistics D (used to identify whether the system is at random) and Hurst Index: $D = 1/H$. Three different values of Hurst Index can tell three different types of time series:

When $H = 0.5$, $C_n = 0, D = 1.5$, it is standard Brownian motion. This suggests that the previous incremental is not related to the future incremental, it is actually an independent random process.

When $0 < H < 0.5$, $C_n < 0, D > 1.5$, it is the anti-persistent fractal Brownian motion. This marks a persistent or trend enhanced sequence, that the future incremental and past increment is in positive correlation. Conversely, a decreasing trend in the past means a decreasing trend in the future. Fractal time series is different from random walk. It is a biased random process. The deviation degree depends on level that H is greater than 1/2.

When $0.5 < H < 1$, $C_n > 0, D < 1.5$, it is anti-persistent fractal Brownian motion. This marks that the past incremental and future incremental is negatively correlated, that is to say, the increasing trend of the past means the decreasing trend in the future.

Mandelbrot points out: The smaller H is, the more complicated the system means to be. Fractal time series has a long-term but limited memory [2].

2.3 Statistic V_n

Statistic V_n was originally used to test the stability of R/S analysis method. Peters expanded it to accurately measure the critical point N and average cycle length.

$$V_n = (R/S)_n / \sqrt{n} \tag{1}$$

For the time series of independent stochastic process, the curve of V_n concerning $\log(n)$ is a straight line. If the sequence possesses a state persistence, i.e. when $0.5 < H < 1$, V_n concerning $\log(n)$ is upward raked; if the sequence has an inverse state persistence, i.e. when $0 < H < 0.5$, V_n concerning $\log(n)$ is sloped downward. When the graphic shape of V_n changes, it produces the sudden mutation, and the long-term memory also disappears. Therefore, we can see directly the influence time boundary of the value of time series at a certain moment on the future values with the relation curve of V_n concerning $\log(n)$.

2.4 Significance Test

The greatest fault of the early-period R/S analysis is the lack of significance test. As to random walk hypothesis, $H = 0.5$ is a gradual process. When the study sample is limited, the value of H of random sequence always deviates from 0.5. At this time the expectation value of H can be derived from the following formula

$$E(R/S)_n = \frac{n - 0.5}{n}(0.5\pi n)^{-0.5} \sum_{r=1}^{n-1} \sqrt{(n-r)/r} \tag{2}$$

From the regression analysis of $\log E[(R/S)_n] \sim \log(n)$ we can get the value of $E(H)$.

$(R/S)_n$ is the random variable of normal distribution, thus $E(H)$ also follows the normal distribution, expectation variance $Var(H)_n = 1/T$, T is the total sample capacity. The null hypothesis of this significance test is $H_0 : H = E(H)$ that is the Gaussian process of random walk; the alternative hypothesis: $H_1 : H \neq E(H)$ that sequence is biased random walk and has persistence and memory effect. The statistic t of hypothesis test:

$$t = \frac{H - E(H)}{\sqrt{1/T}} \tag{3}$$

2.5 Long-Term Correlation Inspection

For a time series, when $H \neq 0.5$, corresponding to the case of $V_n(q) \neq 1$ in variance analysis, the yield is no longer following normal distribution, and each observation of time series is not independent. The latter observations are catching with the "memory" of previous observations; this is what we call the long-term memory feature. Mandelbrot introduced an index of correlation measurement C_n, and it means corresponding to H:

$$C_n = 2^{(2H-1)} - 1 \tag{4}$$

C_n represents the correlation at interval M. Therefore when $H = 0.5$, the series is not correlated; when $C_n > 0$, it is positively correlated; When $C_n < 0$ it is negatively correlated.

2.6 Data Processing

The original data must be processed in order to eliminate their autocorrelation influence. For capital markets, analyzing the residual AR (1) of logarithm yield can better reveal the intrinsic characteristics of data. AR (1) residual can be used to eliminate or reduce linear reliance degree, i.e. autocorrelation. Because linear reliance will deviate from Hurst index H or easily lead to the first kind of error. By taking the AR (1)'s residual, we can reduce deviation degree and this may hopefully reduce insignificant degree of the results. This process is usually called the pre white noise treatment or trend expunction method.

2.7 Processing Methods

If the time series composed of original data is represented by {Pt}, we can get the series of logarithm yield

$$S_t = \log(P_t / P_{t-1}) \tag{5}$$

S_t represents the logarithm yield at t, Pt represents stock index at t. Take S_t as dependent variable, S_{t-1} as independent variable, do a regression analysis with S_t to S_{t-1}, and get AR(1) residual series of S_t : $X_t = S_t - (a + b \cdot S_{t-1})$ At this time, the length of time series X_t is T- 2, thus the problem transforms into doing R/S analysis on series X_t.

Firstly make factorization on T - 2 and obtain $A \bullet n = T - 2$, thus dividing the time series X_t into A groups of subsamples within which there are n observations. From the first factor of $n \neq 1, 2$, calculate each subsample's rescaled range R and standard deviation S, then obtain R/S in the number of A, thus calculate the averages, and record them as $(R / S)_n$. For the next factor n, please repeat the above process until $n = (T - 2) / 2$. Finally estimate the Hurst index H, and further analyze the periodic problem.

2.8 Results of Analysis

We use MATLAB programming language to complete the process above. Take respectively $n=5,10,15,20\ldots300$ to calculate and find the Hurst indexes we get are not greatly differed. So we can uniformly take $n=20$ for calculation. The analysis results are as following charts:

Table 1. R/S analysis parameter estimation results of equation

Parameter estimation values of equation(6)		Constant term	Coefficient	R	H	Fractal dimension	Correlation dimension
Shang hai compo site index	**Day returns**	-0.33	0.68	0.96	0.68	1.47	0.28
	Weekly returns	-0.30	0.71	0.99	0.71	1.40	0.35
	Monthly returns	-0.29	0.75	0.88	0.75	1.33	0.42

The day returns statistic of Shanghai composite index is V_n. The graphs of $\log(R / S)$, $\log E(R / S)$ related to $\log(n)$ are showed in Figure 1 and 2.

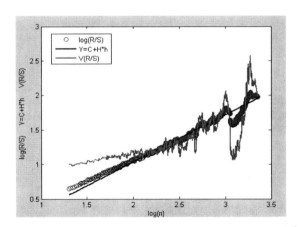

Fig. 1. R/S analysis: daily yields of SSE Index Graph of $\log(R / S)$ and statistic V related to $\log(n)$

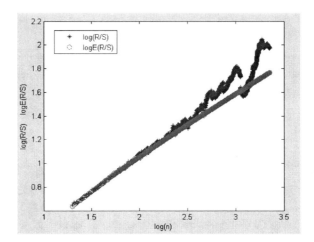

Fig. 2. R/S analysis: daily yields of SSE Index Graph of $\log(R/S)$ and $\log E(R/S)$ related to $\log(n)$

3 Conclusion

The normality test which takes daily, weekly, monthly logarithmic yields of Shanghai stock market as the research object illustrate that it does not submit to normal distribution, but typical fractal distribution.

(1) From Jan1 2000 to May 8 2009, the Hurst index H of SSE daily yield is 0.6801, the correlation degree is 28.36%, the fractal dimension D is 1.4704; the Hurst index of weekly yield is 0.7143, the correlation degree is 34.59%, the fractal dimension D is 1.3999; the Hurst index of monthly yield is 0.7518, the correlation degree is 41.78%, the fractal dimension D is 1.3301.

(2) Shanghai Stock Market exits persistence in state and the time series composed of stock indexes present nonlinearity. This indicates that the historical information in China Stock Market will have certain impact on stock market and to investors it is provided with the expectations to some extent.

(3) The state persistence feature of stock market allows it to have certain risks, in the form of prices increasing or falling continually, showing fluctuating clustering, i.e. the wide fluctuations of endogenous variables are focused on certain periods while small-scope fluctuation on the process and the process itself involves certain policy implications. Whether the investors can gain from stock market and how they can get maximum gain, in a certain extent, depend on the investors' profound understanding on features of stock market.

To sum up, R/S analysis indicates that the yields of Shanghai stock market is a persistent series submitting to fractal distribution; they follow biased random walk, instead of mean reversion behavior. Fractal market means that there exists memory, enhancement and continuity in the variation of stock market. The changes in asset prices increase and continue on the basis of previous state. They may continue rising or falling, or go on the horizontal price movement. Therefore, studying the risk control theory and method based on fractal market has significant realistic guidance functions and application values.

Acknowledgments

The paper is supported by 1. Research Fund for the Doctoral Program of Higher Education of China No.20090032110031; 2. Natural Science Foundation of Hubei under Grant No. D20105001; 3. Research Fund for Young Talents of Higher Education of Anhui No. 2011SQRL164.

References

[1] Fama, E.: The Behavior of Stock Market Prices. Journal of Business 38, 34–165 (1965)
[2] Mandelbrot, B.: The fractal geometry of nature. Freeman, San Francisco (1982)
[3] Lintner, J.: The Aggregation of Investor's Diverse Judgments and Preferences in Purely Competitive Security Markets. Journal of Financial and Quantitative Analysis 4, 347–400 (1969)
[4] Richard, G.R.: The Fractal structure of exchange rates: measurement and orecasting. Journal of International Financial Markets, Institutions and Money 10, 163–180 (2000)
[5] Mandelbrot, B.: The Variation of Certain Speculative Prices. J. Bus. 36, 394–491 (1963)
[6] Peters, E.: Fractal Market Analysis: Applying Chaos Theory to Investment and Economics. John Wiley & Son Lnc., New York (1994)

Sentiment Classification of Documents Based on Latent Semantic Analysis

Lan Wang[1] and Yuan Wan[2]

[1] School of Foreign Language, Wuhan University of Technology,
Wuhan, Hubei, 430070, P.R. China
echolinda777@yahoo.com.cn
[2] Mathematical Department School of science, Wuhan University of Technology,
Wuhan, Hubei, 430070, P.R. China

Abstract. Sentiment classification has attracted increasing interest from natural language processing. The goal of sentiment classification is to automatically identify whether a given piece of text expresses positive or negative opinion on a topic of interest. Latent semantic analysis (LSA) has been shown to be extremely useful in information retrieval. In this paper, we propose a new method, based on LSA and support vector machine (SVM) to improve the sentiment classification performance. This method takes the advantage of both LSA and SVM. During the training process, SVM makes use of its excellent classification ability to conduct the sentiment classification first. To show that our method is feasible and effective, we designed two experiments and the experimental result shows that the introduction of SVM outperforms the other experiment in precision of the polarity analysis.

Keywords: sentiment classification, polarity analysis, support vector machine, latent semantic analysis.

1 Introduction

Sentiment classification has been a focus of recent research. It has been applied on different domains such as movie reviews, product reviews, and customer feedback reviews [1]. The most basic task in sentiment classification is to classify a document into positive or negative sentiment. The difficulty of sentiment classification is the context-dependency of the sentiments of linguistic expressions.

As efficient business intelligence methods, data mining and machine learning provide alternative tools to dynamically process large amounts of data available online. Another most recent technique called sentiment analysis, also referred to as emotional polarity computation, has always been simultaneously employed when conducting online text mining [2]. The purpose of text sentiment analysis is to determine the attitude of a speaker or a writer with respect to some specific topic. The attitude can be any forms of judgment or evaluation, the emotional state of the author when writing, or the intended emotional communication. It is recognized that the performance of sentiment classifiers are dependent on domains or topics [3,4].

S. Lin and X. Huang (Eds.): CESM 2011, Part II, CCIS 176, pp. 356–361, 2011.

Latent semantic analysis (LSA) has been applied to text categorization in many previous works. LSA uses singular value decomposition (SVD) to decompose a large term-document matrix into a set of k orthogonal factors. It is an automatic method that can transform the original textual data to a smaller semantic space by taking advantage of some of the implicit higher-order structure in associations of words with text objects. These derived indexing dimensions can greatly reduce the dimensionality and have the semantic relationship between terms [5].

In this paper, for each document, after preprocessing, we use LSA to convert the original feature space to a new lower-dimension space, so that it is more effective for the semantic understanding of sentiment orientation. We then introduce support vector machine (SVM) to classify the polarity of document. The polarities of words are afforded by Tansongbo's resource that can be downloaded at [6].

The remainder of this paper is organized as follows: Section 2 explains how to generate latent semantic space. In section 3, we discuss the techniques about support vector machine for sentiment classification. Experiment results are given in section 4. Conclusions are given in Section 5.

2   Latent Semantic Analysis

Latent semantic analysis considers documents that have many words in common to be semantically close and those with few words in common to be semantically distant. Once a term-document matrix is constructed, LSA requires the singular value decomposition of this matrix to construct a semantic vector space which can be used to represent conceptual term-document associations.

2.1   Singular Value Decomposition (SVD)

From the training documents, we can get the term by document matrix $A(m{\times}n)$, it means there are m distinct terms in a n documents collection $m{\geq}n$. The singular value decomposition of A is defined as

$$A = U\Sigma V^{\mathrm{T}} \tag{1}$$

where U and V are the matrices of the term vectors and document vectors. $\Sigma{=}\mathrm{diag}(\sigma_1,\ldots,\sigma_n)$ is the diagonal matrix of singular values[9].

2.2   Reduced Vector Space

For reducing the dimensions, we can simply choose the k largest singular values and the corresponding left and right singular vectors, and the best approximation of A with k-rank matrix is given by

$$A_k = U_k \Sigma V_k^{\mathrm{T}} \tag{2}$$

where U_k is comprised of the first k columns of the matrix U and V_k^{T} is comprised of the first k rows of matrix V^T, $R_k = \mathrm{diag}(\sigma_1,\ldots\sigma_k)$ is the first k factors. The matrix A_k is the best k-rank approximation matrix of A in the sense of 2-norm.

The context-sensitive terms have higher similarity thus they will be close to each other in the new term space. This indicates that these terms are synonymous or multivocal. Then by recombining the information in the initial feature space, LSA reduces vector space dimensions with most information retained. Similarities between two documents and between term and document can be calculated in the new reduced vector space.

3   Analysis of Sentiment Orientation of Document

According to the recent research of natural language processing, it is difficult to both totally comprehend the theme of a passage and give a explicit analytic expression. Even though we conduct the grammar or semantic analysis to the whole document, the procedure always fails due to the constraint of resource or response time.

Since many arguments from forums or blogs are random or not specific, it is not necessary to adopt complete syntactic analysis for them. In this paper, we choose the strategy of polarity analysis that is similar to the TSOU BKY[9], i.e. method about width, density and intensity. This method uses the distribution of the oriented words to decide the argument's orientation. For each word of each sentence, i.e. noun, verb, adjective, the orientation will be calculated one by one, and the modification prefixes are also considered as well. After that, taking a global consideration of density and intensity of these polar words of this comment, we come to a conclusion of the orientation of this passage [10]. The process of analysis of orientation with support vector machine algorithm is shown as Figure 1.

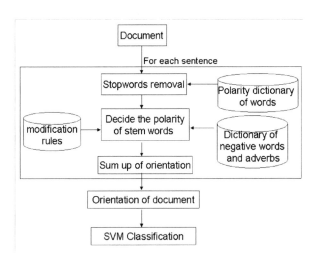

Fig. 1. The flow chart of the method of sentiment classification based on SVM

More detailed steps are depicted as follow:

Step 1: Construct the dictionary of oriented words and dictionary of negative words and adverbs.

Step 2: Transform each comment toe the format of vector space model after the stop words are removed.

Step 3: Conduct SVD for each comment to generate the latent semantic space.

Step 4: For each sentence, for each noun, verb and adjective, check its polarity according the dictionary in step 1. Then check its modification prefix, and calculate the polarity of the context.

Step 5: Calculate the density and the intensity of the oriented words in the whole comment, then use these two values to determine the orientation grade of this passage.

Step 6: For each passage of one class, use support vector machine to classify the polarity.

4 Experiments and Results

4.1 Data Collection

We select randomly 2% news comments, 300 passages, from Tencent net (http://news.qq.com) about five categories, education, entertainment, vehicle, society, movies. The initial analysis finds that there are 20 passages have no apparent argument existing in the longer passages, so among the effective web comments, the smaller passages have more proportion. Then In these comments, there are 170 passages (about 61%) have less than 3 sentences, 52 passages(about 19%) have 3 to10 sentences and 58 passages (about 20%) have more than 10 sentences. We denote these three type A, B, C, respectively.

For each passage, the following preprocessing stages are performed. Text segmentation is used to divide the whole passage into meaningful units. Stop words that are of high frequency and provide no discriminative information are removed, then the left words are almost nouns, adverbs, and adjectives which are all need to be discriminated by polarity analysis.

4.2 Experiment Design and Performance Measure

We designed two experiments to compare our method in this paper. The first experiment directly uses the algorithm shown in the figure 1. The second introduces support vector machine to classifies the polarity first and then use the same algorithm to analyze sentiment of documents.

To evaluate the text classification result, we use the F1 measure. This measure combines recall and precision in the following way:

$$\text{Recall} = \frac{\text{number of correct positive predictions}}{\text{number of positive examples}}$$

$$\text{Precision} = \frac{\text{number of correct positive predictions}}{\text{number of positive predictions}}$$

4.3 Experiment I

In this experiment, each passage has labeled first by positive or negative. Then using the algorithm shown in the figure 1, we get the experimental result as shown in Table 1.

From Table 1, we find that the recalls of each type are relatively high. This mainly because that this algorithm can easily recognize the passage provided that any sentence has the oriented words. But the polarity analyses of these passages are not so good. We find that the comments always include the sentimental expression which has no direct relationship to the topic, or can not behalf the argument of the author. So we improve our method by increasing the affectivity of how to determine the sentimental expression about the whole topic. Then we introduce the support vector machine.

Table 1. Result of Experiment I

	Polarity	Labeled	Recognition	Recall	Precision
Type A	Positive	92	86	93%	63%
170	Negative	78	71	91%	54%
Type B	Positive	29	26	88%	61%
52	Negative	23	19	82%	59%
Type C	Positive	31	26	84%	54%
58	Negative	27	22	81%	51%

4.4 Experiment II

Basic idea of the SVM is to map data into a high dimensional space and find a separating hyperplane with the maximal margin. The general form of support vector machine is used to separate two classes by a function, which is induced from available examples [7]. The main goal of this classifier is to find an optimal separating hyperplane that maximizes the separation margin between it and the nearest data point of each class.In experiment II, the total 300 passages have been classified into two categories, i.e. positive and negative. We first choose 200 of them as the training set and the rest 100 as the test set. The 5-fold cross is used in our experiment and then we retain the best precision to classify them into two categories. Then in these two categories of three types, we use the algorithm as shown in the figure 1. the experimental result is shown in the Table 2.

Table 2. Result of Experiment II

	Polarity	Labeled	Recognition	Recall	Precision
Type A	Positive	87	92	95%	75%
170	Negative	73	78	93%	63%
Type B	Positive	27	29	92%	77%
52	Negative	20	23	86%	69%
Type C	Positive	27	31	87%	65%
58	Negative	23	27	85%	62%

In Table 2, the recalls of each type are increased a little. This is reasonable since they are already at a relatively high level. Compared with the experiment 1, the precisions of each type are increased greatly. Especially in type B, the precision of the positive sentiment are increased to 26%. In type C, the precision of positive and negative sentiment are both increased more than 20%. The experimental results indicate that the introduction of support vector machine to conduct classification first is effective. The results can be explained. Because support vector machine has mined the context relationship between sentences, it has a better performance.

5 Conclusion

Sentiment classification is a hot topic in the natural language understanding. In this paper, we propose a new method, based on LSA and SVM to improve the classification performance. This method uses the LSA to mine the latent semantic meaning of each passage, also reducing the dimensions of them. Then we utilize the high quality of classification of SVM to conduct classification first. To show that our method is feasible and effective, we designed two experiments of which one chooses SVM to do classification first and the other one does not choose. The experimental result shows that the introduction of SVM is more effective in precision of the polarity analysis.

Acknowledgments. This paper is supported by the Fundamental Research Funds for the Central Universities (2010-1a-037).

References

1. Wiebe, J., Wilson, T., Bell, M.: Identifying collocations for recognizing opinions. In: Proceeding ACL 2001 Workshop on Collocation: Computational Extraction, Analysis and Exploitation, pp. 79–87 (2001)
2. Riloff, E., Wiebe, J.: Learning extraction patterns for subjective expressions. In: Proceedings of EMNLP-2003, pp. 105–112. ACL, Morristown (2003)
3. Pang, B., Lee, L., Vaithyanathan, S.: Thumbs up? Sentiment classification using machine learning techniques. In: Proceedings of EMNLP-2002, pp. 79–86. Now Publishers Inc., Hanover (2002)
4. Choi, Y., Cardie, C.: Learning with compositional semantics as structural inference for subsentential sentiment analysis. In: Proceedings of the Empirical Methods in Natural Language Processing, pp. 793–801. ACL, Morristown (2008)
5. Deerwester, S.C., Dumais, S.T., Landauer, T.K., Furnas, G.W.: Indexing by latent semantic analysis. Journal of the American Society of Information Science 41, 391–407 (1990)
6. http://www.searchforum.org.cn/tansongbo/corpus-senti.htm
7. Vapnik, V., Golowich, S., Smola, A.: Support vector method for function approximation, regression estimation, and signal Processing. Neural Information Processing Systems, 281–287 (September 1997)
8. Xiong, Z.Y., Li, Z.H.X.: Text Classification Model Based on Orthogonal Decomposition. Computer Engineering (July 2009)
9. Tsou, B.K.Y., Yuen, R.W.M.: Polarity classification of celebrity coverage in the Chinese Press. In: Hitemational Conference on Intelligence Analysis, Virgina (2005)
10. Yao, T.F., Nie, Q.Y., Li, J.C.: An Opinion Mining System for Chinese Automobile Reviews. In: Cao, Y.Q., Sun, M.S. (eds.) Frontiers of Chinese Information Processing, pp. 260–281. Tsinghua University Press, Beijing (in Chinese with English abstract)

Product Innovative Development for the Laser Orientation Projection Device

Ruilin Lin

Department of Commercial Design, Chienkuo Technology University,
No. 1, Chieh Shou N. Rd., Changhua City 500, Taiwan
linrl2002@gmail.com

Abstract. This study developed a creative produce, a projection device with orientation using the laser theory. The product is composed of a hollow case and a luminous floating body. Inside the hollow case there are liquid, a light-pervious part, and a magnetic part. The luminous floating body can be placed inside the case and float. The body comes with a top part which is always on the top and the bottom part which is always at the bottom. The light which goes through the light-pervious part of the luminous floating body can be controlled by matching the position of the bottom part of the luminous floating body with the magnetic part of the hollow case. This innovatively developed product is designed for divers. It shows the location of the user in a sea. In case of emergency, rescue can be conducted with the information of his location. Therefore this product makes water activities safer.

Keywords: laser orientation, projection device, product innovative development.

1 Design Concept

Taiwan is surrounded by the sea with the length of the coast line being 1,566km. The seashores and the oceans are beautiful. The resources for sea recreation are rich. In the recent years, the number of sea recreation activities has been increasing. Seashores have become major scenic spots. In the early days, diving was considered as a dangerous activity. Recently, it has become a hot sport. There are more and more people diving. And now it's much easier to go to diving zones with convenient communications. All these natural conditions make Taiwan a perfect place to develop diving activities [1] [3].

However, the sea is abysmal. It is still very dangerous to work under water or to engage in diving activities. Once something goes wrong, if a diver cannot help himself immediately, he would definitely need help from his companions or a rescue team. Therefore, it is extremely important to find out a way to let companions who are also in a dark sea or a rescue team which is on the water to know where this diver is, in order to help him as soon as possible. Yet, among all the diving equipment and items brought by divers, none can offer information on real time location of a diver. Thus, this study develops a laser orientation projection device for divers to show their locations underwater and thus make it safer for them to dive.

S. Lin and X. Huang (Eds.): CESM 2011, Part II, CCIS 176, pp. 362–367, 2011.
© Springer-Verlag Berlin Heidelberg 2011

2 Theoretical Foundations

Safety is the first consideration when it comes to diving. Safety regarding natural factors, equipment, technology, and regulations for diving can be controlled by men. Management strategies of diving safety are imputed to human factors. Divers must be careful and confident, but they cannot be arrogant, flaunt, or try to be heroes. Key human factors related to diving safety including: ignorance, wrong attitude, over-confidence, bad physical condition, tiredness, insufficient sleep, and inability to respond to crises. These factors are important for not only general divers, but also divers with coaching licenses. The key to management strategies of diving safety is the development of safety concepts, which should be delivered through basic diving education and training. Simulation courses should be included in daily training, so that divers can learn more safety concepts, education can be improved, and divers will raise their self-standards. Diving safety management relies on complete education and coordination of psychological and physical development [1] [6].

Divers engage in leisure activities frequently. Their focus is on professional techniques and knowledge. And their purpose is to experience and watch beautiful underwater scenery and lives. According to the result of this study, it is suggested that when promoting leisure diving activities, diving safety should be improved by increasing diving safety cognition, individual internal cognition, and activity feature cognition through education [4]. Some scholars had surveyed shore environmental engineering safety constructions for the diving issue. They hoped that the burden of guaranteeing divers' safety can be shared by a safe environment which ensures divers' safety in the sea. This way, people's perception of diving can be changed [2]. As for the functions and efficiency of diving regulators, there is no theory as the basis for design improvement. The only possible way is the trial-and-error method with repeated experiments. In the experiments, the dynamic mechanism (MSC Adams) and simulation analysis software (FLOW-3D) were used to simulate the internal air pressure and air velocity while using a regulator. Through tuning key parameters, the influences on the regulator can be analyzed. As a result, time spent on product development can be reduced and the performance of the regulator can be improved [5].

3 Content

The innovative product developed by this study is a laser-orientation projection device. It consists of a hollow case filled with fluid and a luminous floating body inside the case. The hollow case contains a light-pervious part and a magnetic part. There is an empty space inside the luminous floating body with the balance weight, luminous object, a battery, and magnetic switch connecting the luminous object and battery. When the magnetic switch of the luminous floating body matches the magnetic part of the hollow case, the luminous floating body is triggered to send out light through the light-pervious part of the hollow case. When the magnetic switch of the luminous floating body moves away from the magnetic part of the hollow case and the distance is larger than the threshold, the switch is turned off and the light from the luminous floating body goes out.

The laser-orientation projection device developed by this study does not have an extra switch, for changing the relative positions of the magnetic switch of the luminous floating body and the magnetic part of the hollow case by rotating the hollow case can turn on or off the luminous floating body. This design makes it impossible for water to get inside the projection device and damage it. This product is suitable for divers to use underwater. The light from the luminous floating body shows the location of the user so that his companions the rescue team can find out where he is in a short time to help him once there is an emergency.

The magnetic switch of the laser-orientation projection device developed by this study includes a spring piece. The first conductance section of the spring piece is connected to the positive or negative terminal of the battery. The second conductance section can be controlled by magnetic force and touch the positive or negative terminal of the battery. Once the magnetic force is gone, it moves away from the terminal. Thus, when the spring piece inside the luminous floating body matches the magnetic part of the hollow case, the second conductance section is pulled to the terminal of the battery by the magnetic force. And the light from the luminous floating body goes through the light-pervious part of the hollow case. When the spring piece inside the luminous floating body moves away from the magnetic part of the hollow case, the magnetic force would disappears. The circuit is broken. And the light goes out. In addition, the light from the luminous floating body should be red/green light laser for the purpose of identification.

4 Mechanical Application

Figure 1 shows the parts of the product and figure 2 is a simple illustration of the product. No1 is the case when the spring piece inside the luminous floating body matches the magnetic part of the hollow case, the light from the luminous floating body goes through the light-pervious part of the hollow case. No2 is the case when the spring piece inside the luminous floating body moves away from the magnetic part of the hollow case, without any light coming from the luminous floating body. No3 shows a laser-orientation projection device installed on a gas cylinder which a diver carries. And the light goes out of the surface of the sea. The laser-orientation projection device shown in No1 includes a hollow case and a luminous floating body. Inside it is a plastic injection ball. In fact, the hollow case doesn't have to be a ball. It can be a cube or other forms. Secondly, the hollow case contains a light-pervious part, and a magnetic part on the opposite side. The light-pervious part is made by installing a light-pervious cover on the hollow case, while the magnetic part is made by embedding a magnet into the hollow case. Inside the hollow case there is a space which is filled 80% full with liquid. The type and amount of liquid chosen must be able to make the luminous floating body float inside the hollow case. Possible choices include oil, water, etc.

The luminous floating body is a plastic injection ball with an empty space, forming the balance weight. Also there are the luminous object, battery, and magnetic switch. The luminous object is on the opposite side of the balance weight. The battery and magnetic switch are inside the empty space. The battery provides power required by the luminous object. The magnetic switch connects the battery and the luminous object. When the luminous floating body floats inside the hollow case, the side with balance weight is always the down side, while the side with the luminous object is always the top side. This study provides an example of product innovative development. The magnetic switch is made with a spring piece with the first conductance section connected to the positive/negative terminal of the battery and located between the battery and the balance weight. The second conductance section is connected to the first conductance section. Whether it is conductive depends on whether the magnetic power causes the connection to the positive/negative terminal of the battery. The battery can be a nickel hydrogen battery, an alkaline battery, a mercury battery, a nickel cadmium battery, a lithium ion battery, a lithium polymer battery, or a dry battery. The luminous object can be anything which can emit light to a certain distance (light other than laser beam is also fine). The luminous object must emit light which goes out of the surface of the sea while the object is underwater. After considering the cost, this study suggests red/green light laser which can be identified more easily.

In No1 and No2, the luminous floating body is placed and floats inside the hollow case. No3 shows a real application with the laser-orientation projection device installed on the gas cylinder which a diver carries. The device can also be attached to the diver's arm or wrist. The magnetic part of the hollow case helps to fix the device to the diver. When the diver is underwater, he may adjust the relative positions of the hollow case and the luminous floating body (No1). The diver can adjust the position of the luminous floating body to match the magnetic part of the hollow case, so that the second conductance section of the spring piece inside the luminous floating body will be connected to the battery due to magnetic force. Then light from the luminous floating body goes through the light-pervious part of the hollow case and out of the surface of the sea. Other underwater diving companions may find the location of this diver. And the rescue team may get to the diver more quickly for he can be located more easily. The diver may also cut off the light by having the magnetic switch of the luminous floating object away from the magnetic part of the hollow case so that the spring piece inside the luminous floating body will be disconnected from the battery. This way power can be saved (No2). Whether the floating body of the laser orientation projection device developed by this study emits light through the

(10) Laser orientation projection device	(20) Hollow case	(21) Light-pervious part
(23) Magnetic part	(25)(31) Empty space	(27) Fluid
(30) Luminous floating body	(32) Battery bearing seat	(33) Balance weight
(35) Luminous object	(37) Battery	(39) Magnetic switch (spring piece)
(391) Conductive pad (first conductance section)	(393) Conductive pad (second conductance section)	(50) Gas cylinder

Fig. 1. Mechanical Component Diagram

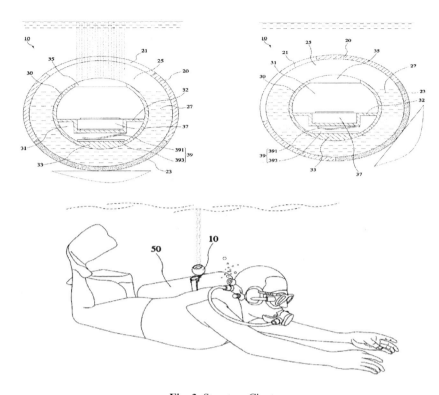

Fig. 2. Structure Chart

light-pervious part can be controlled by the positions of the magnetic switch of the luminous floating body and the magnetic part of the hollow case. And the luminous object emits light to a distance far enough for other diving companions or a rescue team above water to find out where the diver is. This product improves the safety of divers while engaging in underwater activities.

5 Contribution

Through the innovative product development of this study, the laser device developed can be equipped on divers to show their locations in the sea. In case of emergency, other people can find out where they are to help them immediately. Generally speaking, the features of this innovative product include.

(1) Caring Design

The safety of divers working underwater or tourists who love diving is the major consideration for the innovative product development of this study. The dangers divers may face while diving are taken into account while designing the product using a laser orientation projection method. This shows caring for human safety. It is hoped that people can be saved when being in trouble underwater. This product which is invented to help people shows humane caring. It is worth praise.

(2) Conceptual Innovation

The dangers which might be encountered by divers while engaging in underwater activities, such as losing direction, are considered for the innovative product development of this study. New technology and materials are used for better protection of their lives. The developed product should be promoted.

(3) Energy Saving and Carbon Reduction

The concept and idea of energy saving and carbon reduction are adopted in this study. An orientation projection device for divers engaging in underwater activities is developed with a low-cost mechanism. The device helps people to find out where the diver with the device is in a short time when he is in trouble in order to assist him, reducing unnecessary regrets.

(4) Market Expansion

Unexpected situations and dangers during underwater activities are issues to be concerned for those who work underwater or those who enjoy diving. Through the innovative product design of this study, the developed laser orientation projection device can be carried by divers. In case of emergency, other people can find out where the diver in trouble is and proceed to rescue him. Nowadays, the number of divers has been increasing, which makes the priority of the market development for this product very high.

References

1. Mei, C.C.: The Research of Scuba Diving Safety Management, Department of Sport Business Managemen. Dayeh University, Master dissertation (2009)
2. Meyers, D.T.: Safe Diving Operations on Near-shore Coastal Construction Projects, Underwater Technology. In: International Symposium on Digital Object Identifier: 10.1109/UT.2000.852594, pp. 499–502 (2000)
3. Li, J.Y.: Study on the Scuba Diver Recreation Activities in Reefs of Taiwan, Department of Environmental Biology and Fisheries Science. National Taiwan Ocean University, Master dissertation (2007)
4. Chang, P.L.: Study of Cognition, Motivation and Leisure Constraints on the Recreational Diving, Department of Leisure Recreation Studies, Aletheia University, Master dissertation (2009)
5. Hu, W.C.: Analysis and Improvement of SCUBA Diving Regulators, Mechanical Engineering, National Chiao Tung University, Master dissertation (2008)
6. Wang, Y.: A study of instructor's risk management for recreational scuba diving, Department of Physical Education, National Taitung University, Master dissertation (2006)

An Improved Quantum Genetic Algorithm for Knapsack Problem

Ning Guo, Fenghong Xiang, Jianlin Mao, and Rui Wang

Ning Guo, Kunming University of Science and Technology, 65000 Yunnan, China
124328466@qq.com

Abstract. Quantum genetic algorithm (QGA) is a new optimization algorithm developed recent years, but the standard QGA is easy to get into a local optimal solution. To solve the problem, an improved quantum genetic algorithm (IQGA) is proposed in this paper. IQGA codes the chromosome with probability amplitudes represented by sine and cosine functions, and uses an adaptive strategy of the rotation angle to update the population. Simulation results based on 0-1 knapsack problem demonstrate the effectiveness of IQGA, especially the superiority in terms of optimization quality and population diversity. Moreover, results show the improved algorithm has better comprehensive performance than traditional genetic algorithm (GA) and standard quantum genetic algorithm (QGA).

Keywords: IQGA, 0-1 knapsack problem, adaptive quantum rotation angle.

1 Introduction

QGA is a kind of efficient optimization algorithm based on certain concept and principles of quantum computing. A.Narayanan who introduced the concept of quantum Multi-universe to genetic algorithm firstly in 1996 proposed quantum inspired genetic algorithm[1],and applied the algorithm to TSP problem successfully. In the year 2000, K.H.Han who introduced the concept of quantum bit and quantum gate to genetic algorithm proposed Quantum genetic algorithm[2], and verified the superiority of the algorithm by a class of Combinatorial optimization problem. Two years later, K.H.Han proposed the population migration mechanism[3] based on literature [2] ,and the algorithm is named quantum—inspired evolutionary algorithm.

0-1 knapsack problem is a typical NPC problem[4]. It has a broad background of practical application. Nowadays, kinds of methods are applied to solve the problem. For example, Ref. [5] proposes a differential evolution algorithm which uses greedy transform algorithm to fix the infeasible solutions, then the accuracy of solutions is improved obviously. Ref. [6] adopts QGA for 0-1 knapsack problem, though the optimal solution is obtained, the population diversity should be enhanced.

2 0-1 Knapsack Problem Description

Suppose that there are n goods can be selected into a backpack which have the total limited weight c, and the item number is $1, 2, \ldots, n$. If the weight and value of item i

S. Lin and X. Huang (Eds.): CESM 2011, Part II, CCIS 176, pp. 368–373, 2011.

are known as w_i and P_i, how to select the goods in order to make the total value maximum while can't be overweight. The mathematical model can be expressed as:

$$
\begin{cases}
Maxinize \sum_{i=1}^{n} p_i x_i \\
S.t \sum_{i=1}^{n} w_i x_i \le c
\end{cases}
\tag{1}
$$

Where $x_i = 1$ (represents that the item is selected) or $x_i = 0$ (represents that the item isn't selected).

3   Improved Quantum Genetic Algorithm (IQGA)

In QGA, all qubits are initialized with the same value which brings less randomness for initial population. And the method of changing rotation angle is based on a lookup table which doesn't consider the difference of each chromosome. These shortcomings can result in lower population diversity, so we propose a quantum genetic algorithm which has improvements in the population coding and evolution strategy.

3.1   Trigonometric-Functions-Based Encoding

Suppose a quantum population is:

$$
Q(t) = \left\{ q_1^t, q_2^t, \ldots, q_n^t \right\}
\tag{2}
$$

Where n represents the size of the population, t represents the evolutionary generation.

The algorithm in this paper codes the chromosomes with probability amplitudes represented by sine and cosine functions. It can be shown in equation (3).

$$
q_i = \begin{bmatrix} \cos(t_{i1}) & \cos(t_{i2}) & \cdots & \cos(t_{in}) \\ \sin(t_{i1}) & \sin(t_{i2}) & \cdots & \sin(t_{in}) \end{bmatrix}
\tag{3}
$$

Where $i = 1, 2, \ldots, m$, and m is the population size; $j = 1, 2, \ldots, n$, and n represents the quantum bits; $t_{ij} = 2\pi \cdot rand$, $rand$ is a random number between $(0,1)$. This method of encoding makes the code of initializing population more random and enhances the diversity of population.

3.2   Adaptive Rotation Gate Updating

IQGA uses the same rotation gate U, but for the angle $\Delta\theta$, the specific adjustment strategy is defined as [4]:

$$\Delta\theta_{ij} = -sign(A) \cdot \Delta\theta_0 \cdot \exp(-\frac{\left|\nabla f(X_i^j)\right| - \nabla f_j \min}{\nabla f_j \max - \nabla f_j \min}) \tag{4}$$

Where $\Delta\theta_0$ is the initial value, $sign(A)$ is a sign function which determines the direction of $\Delta\theta_{ij}$.

Here, we define A as follows:

$$A = \begin{vmatrix} \alpha_0 & \alpha_1 \\ \beta_0 & \beta_1 \end{vmatrix} \tag{5}$$

Where α_0 and β_0 are the probability amplitudes of the global optimal solution α_1 and β_1 are the probability amplitudes of a quantum bit in the current solution.

The direction of the rotation angle is selected by the following rules: while $A \neq 0$, the direction is $-sign(A)$; while $A = 0$, the direction can be both positive and negative.

In equation (4), $\nabla f(X_i^j)$, $\nabla f_j \max$ and $\nabla f_j \min$ separately represent the first difference, the maximum and the minimum of the first difference which is adjacent to two generations. They are described by the following equations:

$$\nabla f(X_i^j) = f(X_{pi}^j) - f(X_{ci}^j) \tag{6}$$

$$\nabla f_j \max = \max\left\{\left|f(X_{p1}^j) - f(X_{c1}^j)\right|, \dots, \left|f(X_{pm}^j) - f(X_{cm}^j)\right|\right\} \tag{7}$$

$$\nabla f_j \min = \min\left\{\left|f(X_{p1}^j) - f(X_{c1}^j)\right|, \dots, \left|f(X_{pm}^j) - f(X_{cm}^j)\right|\right\} \tag{8}$$

Where $i = 1, 2, \dots, m$; m is the population size; j represents the quantum bit; X_p and X_c represent the parent and offspring chromosomes.

The aforementioned adjustment strategy considers the differences of each chromosome in the population, but also takes advantage of the trend of the objective function. It is an adaptive rotation angles computing method.

4   Experiments and Tests

To test and evaluate the performance of IQGA and make a comparison with QGA and GA, two classical tests of knapsack problem examples commonly found in many papers are employed.

4.1   Experiment 1

We have known the optimal solution [5][6]: the total value and weight are 3103 and 1000. Categories of item n are equaled 50, the corresponding value and weight are:

p={220,208,198,192,180,180,165,162,160,158,155,130,125,122,120,118,115,110,105,
101,100,100,98,96,95,90,88,82,80,77,75,73,72,70,69,66,65,63,60,58,56,50,30,20,15,10,
8,5,3,1};w={80,82,85,70,72,70,66,50,55,25,50,55,40,48,50,32,22,60,30,32,40,38,35,32,
25,28,30,22,50,30,45,30,60,50,20,65,20,25,30,10,20,25,15,10,10,10,4,4,2,1}

The maximum capacity c is equaled 1000.

A. Parameter Settings

We fixed some shared parameters: the maximum generation of three algorithms was
set to 500, the population size of QGA and IQGA was set to 10. Some other specific
parameters: the population size of GA was 50, the crossover and mutation
probabilities of GA were 0.8 and 0.05. The initial value $\Delta\theta_0$ of IQGA was 0.001π.

B. Results and Analysis

We run each algorithm independently 50 times for the experiment. The statistical
results were listed in Table 1. We also painted Fig.1, Fig.2 and Fig.3. They all
contained two optimization results: the global optimal fitness and the average fitness.

Table 1. Simulation Results and Comparisons for Experiment 1

Kinds of algorithm	Optimal value (total value / total weight)	Worst value	Average value	percents of hitting 3103
GA	3099/999	3096	3098.7	0%
QGA	3103/1000	3097	3101.5	80%
IQGA	3103/1000	3103	3103	100%

Table 1 shows the comparison of some solutions gained by three algorithms. It is
found that the result accuracy of IQGA is much better than the other two algorithms.
After running 50 times, GA can't achieve the optimal value known as 3103.QGA and
IQGA can all get optimums, but as to the number of hitting 3103, QGA is less than
IQGA, IQGA can hit the optimal value 3103 every time.

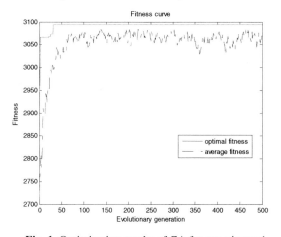

Fig. 1. Optimization results of GA for experiment 1

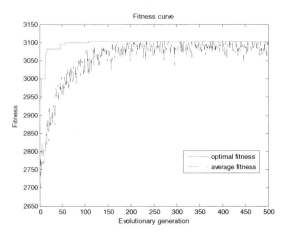

Fig. 2. Optimization results of QGA for experiment 1

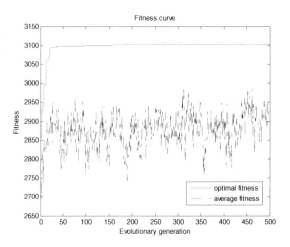

Fig. 3. Optimization results of IQGA for experiment 1

4.2   Experiment 2

Parameters of the item in this experiment are known as below [6] [7]: Categories of item n are equaled 100. The item's weights w are random numbers generated between (0, 10), the corresponding values are obtained from formula (9). The maximum capacity C is defined by equation (10).

$$p_i = w_i + 5 \tag{9}$$

$$c = \frac{1}{2} \sum_{i=1}^{n} w_i \tag{10}$$

Table 2. Simulation Results and Comparisons for Experiment 2

Kinds of algorithm	Optimal value	Worst value	Average value
GA	612.11	584.60	599.58
QGA	613.61	592.52	599.80
IQGA	633.03	622.46	627.41

All the parameters' values are established the same as experiment 1. We also run each algorithm independently for 50 times. The results are recorded in Table 2.

Table 2 shows three kinds of solutions in IQGA are all better than other two algorithms.

In summary, IQGA is superior to QGA and GA. Comparing with them, IQGA can get higher quality of solutions, perform more stably and have better population diversity.

5 Conclusions

In this paper, we propose an improved quantum genetic algorithm, IQGA. It codes the chromosome with sine and cosine functions, and adopts an adaptive strategy to adjust the rotation angle. This algorithm takes the difference of each chromosome into account, so the diversity of the population is enhanced and the accuracy of the solutions is improved. By two experiments of 0-1 knapsack problem, we can see that IQGA has better performance than other two algorithms in searching for the optimal solution. Therefore, IQGA is an effective algorithm to solve the knapsack problem, and also can be used to solve other discrete optimization problems. In the future, we will consider the crossover and mutation operations and discuss their influence on IQGA.

References

1. Narayanan, A., Moore, M.: Quantum-inspired genetic algorithms. In: Proceedings of IEEE International Conference on Evolutionary Computation, Nagoya, Japan (1996)
2. Han, K.H., Kim, J.H.: Genetic quantum algorithm and its application to combinatorial optimization problems. In: Proceedings of International Congress on Evolutionary Computation, pp. 1354–1360. IEEE Press, Los Alamitos (2000)
3. Han, K.H., Kim, J.H.: Quantum: Inspired evolutionary algorithm for a class of combinatorial optimization. IEEE Trans. on Evolutionary Computing 6, 580–593 (2002)
4. Karp, R.: Reducibility among combinatorial problems. J. Complexity of Computer Computations, 85–104 (1972)
5. Deng, C., Liang, C.: Mixed coding greedy differential evolution algorithm for 0-1 knapsack problem. J. Computer Engineering 35, 24–26 (2009)
6. Zhu, X., Zhang, X.: A quantum genetic algorithm with repair function and its application in knapsack question. J. Computer Application 27, 1187–1190 (2007)
7. Li, S., Li, P.: Quantum Computation and quantum optimization algorithms. Harbin industry university press, Harbin (2009)

Innovations in the Teaching of Building Physics with Ecotect

Jian Yao and Chengwen Yan

Faculty of Architectural, Civil Engineering and Environment,
Ningbo University, Ningbo, China
yaojian@nbu.edu.cn

Abstract. Building physics focuses on the analysis of the physical phenomena affecting buildings such as sound control and daylight as well as solar shading. The purpose of this paper is to enhance the teaching quality of building physics with computer simulation technologies. Compared with experiments, using the program Ecotect in teaching, an innovative method, shows its great advantages including its cost-effectiveness, visual display and capability of dealing with complex physical phenomena, which help students improve the adoption of knowledge.

Keywords: Building physics, Teaching, Computer simulation, Ecotect.

1 Introduction

Building physics that applies the principles of physics to buildings brings a fundamental understanding of physics to improving the design of acoustic, daylighting and thermal behaviour of a building. Good knowledge in building physics is a key factor for designing energy-efficient buildings with the highest comfort and lowest impact on the environment. The learning objectives for students of civil engineering and architecture are to command the basic concepts of building physics and building technologies that allow buildings designed more sustainable. In China, classroom teaching of the theory of building physics with few and simple experiments is the main teaching method that becomes more and more dull due to lack of visual teaching. Therefore there is a great need for innovations in the teaching of building physics to enhance the teaching quality. With the development of computer technologies, computer simulation plays a significant role in reducing experimental costs and time as well as improve students' adoption of knowledge about complex phenomenons of building physics. A wide range of programs are available for building simulations such as Ecotect, Designbuilder and Energyplus etc [1-3]. Among them, however, only Ecotect is more suitable for simulation application due to its capacity for simulating the three major parts of building physics (the acoustics, daylighting and thermal performance of a building). The following of this paper will present these simulation based teaching methods with Ecotect.

S. Lin and X. Huang (Eds.): CESM 2011, Part II, CCIS 176, pp. 374–378, 2011.

2   An Innovative Method with Ecotect

2.1   Daylighting Analysis

A commonly used teaching method for daylighting analysis is an experiment carried out on a room with ten test points as shown in Fig.1. Its drawback is that the measurement duration may unacceptable long if we want to determine the daylighting performance of the room at different climate conditions. Simulation based teaching for daylighting analysis can easily overcome this problem as it can change the climate conditions by selecting different time in the program. In addition, determining the daylighting performance of different room dimensions are also convenient through inputting different room designs, and an illustration of this method is graphically shown in Fig.2 that helps students understand daylighting design.

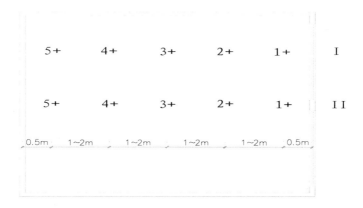

Fig. 1. An experiment of daylighting measurement

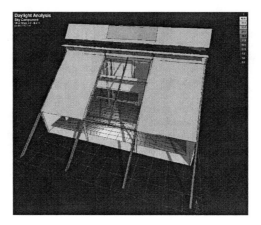

Fig. 2. A computer simulation of daylighting performance with Ecotect

2.2 Solar Shading Analysis

Solar heat gain is a key factor in determining the energy efficiency and thermal performance of building envelope [4-5]. Therefore solar shading is extremely important for building energy conservation and is also a major part of building physics teaching. Traditionally, an experiment with a light source, a mirror and a flat plate with building models, as shown in Fig.3, provide a simple test for solar shading. Apparently, this method can not perform accurate analysis as the light reflected by mirror is not parallel enough. Fig.4 shows different solar shading effects of different buildings at summer and winter in Ecotect. We can see that solar altitude is high at summer, however it is low at winter. So the optimum dimension of an overhang on the south facade can be determined according to the detailed analysis of solar shading at different time. Therefore this method can help students compare quantitatively shading between buildings at any time, allowing a better understanding of the effect of solar altitude and azimuth on solar shading.

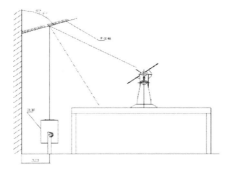

Fig. 3. An experiment of solar shading measurement

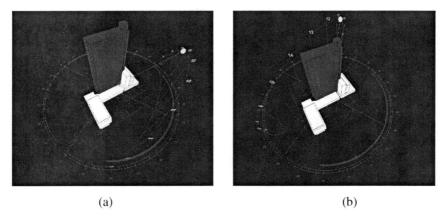

(a)   (b)

Fig. 4. A computer simulation of solar shading performance with Ecotect at winter (a) and summer (b) conditions

2.3 Acoustic Analysis

Acoustic analysis in buildings can help to improve the uniformity of a sound field and reduce noise. Fig. 5 presents the equipment and connections of basic acoustic measurements (reverberation time, sound insulation), which is a complex and expensive system. The disadvantage of this system is that it is inconvenient to move it from a room to another for measuring different types of rooms as it is very heavy. Thanks to Ecotect, because it can perform various acoustic simulation accurately for any kind of buildings such as classrooms, concert halls and theaters etc. Moreover it can record the track of sound at any direction and demonstrate it graphically as shown in Fig.6, which helps students identify the defects of building designs. This is a great advantage of Ecotect compare with experiments.

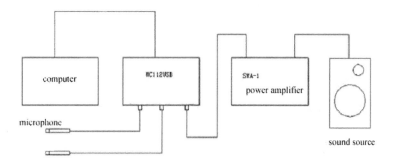

Fig. 5. The equipment connection of acoustic measurement

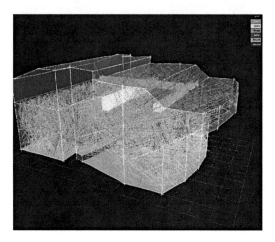

Fig. 6. A computer simulation of acoustic performance with Ecotect

3 Conclusions

Building physics is the collection of knowledge about the description and control of physical phenomena affecting buildings. It includes the detailed analysis of sound control, and daylight as well as solar shading for building envelope. The purpose of building physics teaching is to provide skills to students, leading to optimization of building performance. Traditionally, experiments are commonly used to enhance the adoption of knowledge, which has its limitations due to several factors. However, computer simulation shows its great advantages in analysing complex physical phenomena in buildings. This paper presents an innovative method in teaching building physics by using Ecotect as simulation tool to help students understand knowledge. There are several big advantages to performing simulations rather than experiments. The biggest of these advantages is money. Because most of the time the simulation analysis is cheaper and faster than tests. The second biggest advantage of simulations is that they can give you results that are not experimentally measurable at a laboratory.

Acknowledgement

This work was sponsored by Teaching and Research Fund in Ningbo University.

References

1. Marsh, A.: Ecotect. Square One Research. Software 5 (2006)
2. Xin, L., Zhang, H.: Graphic Interface Designing Software Design Builder of Energy Plus and its Application. Journal of Xi'an Aerotechnical College 5 (2007)
3. Tindale, A.: DesignBuilder and EnergyPlus. The Building Energy Simulation User News 25, 2–5 (2004)
4. Zhou, Y., Ding, Y., Yao, J.: Preferable Rebuilding Energy Efficiency Measures of Existing Residential Building in Ningbo. Journal of Ningbo University (Natural Science & Engineering Edition) 22, 285–287 (2009)
5. Yao, Yuan, Z.: Study on Residential Buildings with Energy Saving by 65% in Ningbo. Journal of Ningbo University (Natural Science & Engineering Edition) 23, 84–87 (2010)

Study of Microwave Attenuation from Dust Particle

Qianzhao Lei

Department of Physics and Electronic Engineering, Weinan Normal University,
Weinan, Shaanxi, China
leiqzh@126.com

Abstract. Microwave propagation in the atmosphere can be influenced by dust particles; in order to be acquainted with this effect, we need to calculate the microwave attenuation caused by dust particle. According to the relation between microwave wavelengths and atmospheric dust particles sizes, Rayleigh scattering theory can be used. The scattering field of particle is equivalent dipole radiation. First microwave scattering angle distribution around a dust particle is calculated, it correctly reflects the relation of the differential scattering section with scattering angle, wavelength and radius. Then the average scattering and absorption cross sections are calculated at a dust particle; as the wavelength decreasing or the radius increasing, both of the two sections increase. The simulation results can provide practical basis for overcoming the dust's impact on microwave propagation.

Keywords: dust particle, dipole radiation, scattering cross section, absorption cross section.

1 Introduction

The atmosphere is as electromagnetic wave propagation channel, in which microwave and millimeter waves are more affected. When the wavelength is less than 1 mm, the resonance absorption of molecules of nitrogen and oxygen will be significantly increased. When the wavelength is that of microwave which greater than 1 mm, the effect of oxygen and nitrogen to electric wave can be ignored, but that of dust and sand can not be ignored [1, 2, 3]. Suspended particle radius in dust is general in 0.001 ~ 0.1 mm range; when the wavelength greater than the upper limit of microwave region, dust effects can be ignored. Dust effect leads to the attenuation of electric wave mainly through dust grains' electromagnetic wave absorption and scattering [4], among them especially the scattering and absorption of microwave is evidently. The relevant research is currently less, still needs to strengthen.

2 Microwave Scattering Angle Distribution around a Dust Particle

2.1 Differential Scattering Cross Section of Microwave around a Particle

Dust particle sizes and microwave wavelengths satisfy the Rayleigh approximation $ka \leq 0.1$, which to ensure the particle in a uniform field

S. Lin and X. Huang (Eds.): CESM 2011, Part II, CCIS 176, pp. 379–383, 2011.

approximatively, and the phase difference between the internal and external field very small.

A particle in free space, its relative dielectric constant $\varepsilon_r(r')$ is as $\varepsilon_r(r') = \varepsilon'_r(r') + i\varepsilon''_r(r')$. According to Rayleigh approximation, when a particle is under the irradiation of line polarization plane incident wave with unit amplitude, particle's internal field $\bar{E}(\bar{r}') = 3/(\varepsilon_r + 2)\bar{E}_i$ will be uniform. Polarization direction parallels to the incident electric field polarization direction, equivalent to dipole radiation, the scattering amplitude is as [5]:

$$\bar{f}(\bar{o},\bar{i}) = \frac{k^2}{4\pi}\left|\frac{3(\varepsilon_r - 1)}{(\varepsilon_r + 2)}\right| V \left|-\bar{o} \times \bar{o} \times \bar{e}_i\right| \bar{E}_i \tag{1}$$

Where, $\left|-\bar{o} \times \bar{o} \times \bar{x}_i\right| = \sin\chi$, χ is the angle between the polarization unit vector of incident electric field and the scattering direction. The differential scattering cross section is [6]:

$$\sigma_d(\bar{o},\bar{i}) = \frac{k^4}{(4\pi)^2}\left|\frac{3(\varepsilon_r - 1)}{\varepsilon_r + 2}\right|^2 V^2 \sin^2\chi = \frac{16\pi^4 r^6}{\lambda^4}\left|\frac{(\varepsilon_r - 1)}{\varepsilon_r + 2}\right|^2 \sin^2\chi \tag{2}$$

Here, $\sin^2\chi = 1 - \cos^2\phi\sin^2\theta$, V is the volume of spherical grain of sand.

2.2 Simulation Results and Analysis

Incident electromagnetic wave $\bar{E}_i = \bar{e}_x E_0 e^{ikz}$, propagation along the z axis, x-axis polarization, let the relative permittivity of the dust particle ε_r be 2.635+ 0.735i.

Radiuses of sand grains are taken 0.0004 cm, 0.0006 cm, 0.0008 cm and 0.001 cm, incident wavelength takes 0.78cm. The scattering cross section changing with scattering angle follows as shown in Fig. 1 (a).

Radius of sand grain take 0.0005 cm, incident wavelengths are taken 0.4 cm, 0.6 cm, 0.8 cm and 1.0 cm. The scattering cross section changes with scattering angle as shown in Fig. 1 (b) below.

It can be seen from Fig. 1, when the scattering angle is from 0 degrees to 90 degrees, the scattering cross section decreases gradually; scattering angle from 90 to 180 degrees, the scattering cross section increasing; in Rayleigh scattering, absorption is main, pure scattering few. From Fig. 1, we can roughly get the

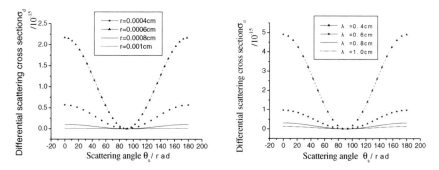

a) Differential scattering cross section-angular b) Differential scattering cross section-angular
distribution for particles of different radius   distribution for different wavelengths

Fig. 1. Differential scattering section-angular distribution around a dust particle

conclusion, that the Rayleigh scattering cross section is proportional to the particle radius of the power of 6, and is inversely proportional to the incident wavelength of the power of 4.

3   Microwave Scattering and Absorption Cross Section at a Dust Particle

3.1   Particle Electromagnetic Scattering and Absorption Cross Section

From formula 2, single particle scattering cross section is:

$$\sigma_s = \int_{4\pi} \sigma_d d\Omega = \frac{128\pi^5 a^6}{3\lambda^4} \left| \frac{(\varepsilon_r - 1)}{\varepsilon_r + 2} \right|^2 \tag{3}$$

Under unit intensity of incident waves, single scatterer's absorption cross section is [7]:

$$\sigma_a = \int_V \text{Im}[\varepsilon_r (r')] |E(r')|^2 \, dV' = \frac{24\pi^2 a^3 \varepsilon_r''}{\lambda} \left| \frac{1}{\varepsilon_r + 2} \right|^2 \tag{4}$$

3.2   Simulation and Analysis

Radiuses are taken 0.001 cm; 0.0015 cm; 0.002 cm; 0.0025 cm, variation of average scattering and absorption cross section with wavelength [8], as shown in Fig.2.

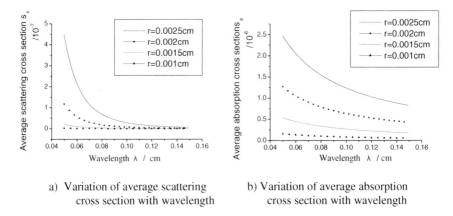

a) Variation of average scattering
cross section with wavelength

b) Variation of average absorption
cross section with wavelength

Fig. 2. Variation of average cross section with wavelength

Wavelengths are taken 0.2cm, 0.3cm, 0.4cm and 0.5cm, average scattering and absorption cross section changes with radius [9], as shown in Fig. 3.

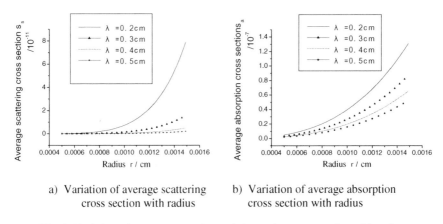

a) Variation of average scattering
cross section with radius

b) Variation of average absorption
cross section with radius

Fig. 3. Variation of average scattering and absorption cross section with radius

Sum of absorption and scattering cross sections is the extinction cross section σ_t [10], $\sigma_t = \sigma_s + \sigma_a$ for the total incident loss by uneven body. Using Rayleigh scattering principle gets the simulation results, which show: for a dust particle, its microwave scattering and absorption cross sections weaken with the wavelength increasing, increase with the particle radius increasing. It also shows incident wave scattering and absorption by dust particle leading to extinction cross section, which follows the same pattern. In the microwave range, the dust particles well satisfy the Rayleigh scattering approximation.

4 Conclusion

Rayleigh scattering suits for study of the microwave scattering and absorption at dust particles, from this get microwave scattering angle distribution and microwave average scattering and absorption cross section around or at a dust particle. This can be used for understanding the attenuation of dust particles, and then providing practical basis for overcoming the impact of dust storms.

Acknowledgements

This work is partially supported by Weinan Normal University Research Funding (11YKS016).

References

1. Zhou, W., Zhou, D.F., Hou, D.T., Hu, T., Weng, L.W.: Dust attenuation calculation and simulation in the course of microwave transmission. High Power Laser and Particle Beams 17(8), 1259–1262 (2005)
2. Yang, R.K.: Influence of multiple scattering on attenuation of millimeter wave propagation in sand and dust storm. Chinese Journal of Radio Science 23(3), 530–533+579 (2008)
3. Dong, Q.S.: Physical Characteristics of the Sand and Dust in Different Deserts of China. Chinese Journal of Radio Science 12(1), 15–25 (1997)
4. Ye, Y.X., Fan, D.Y.: Theoretical Analysis and Numerical Calculation of Transmitted Light Intensity of Light Scattering from Nano Particle Random Scatterers. Acta Optica Sinica 27(5), 951–956 (2007)
5. Li, Y.L., Wang, M.J., Dong, Q.F., Tang, G.F.: Anisotropic Rayleigh Scattering for a Dielectric Sphere. Acta Photonica Sinica 39(3), 504–507 (2010)
6. Lei, Q.Z.: Study of Electromagnetic Scattering of Plane Wave by Atmospheric Particles. Journal of Changchun University of Science and Technology 33(3), 65–67 (2010)
7. Xiong, H.: Electromagnetic wave propagation and space environment, p. 93. Electronic Industry Press, Beijing (2004)
8. Zhang, P.C.: Characteristics Of Microwave Attenuation For Groups Of Small Spheroid Particles. Acta Meteorologica Sinica 59(2), 226–233 (2001)
9. He, X.S., Zhou, Y.H., Zheng, X.J.: The scattering field of charged sand and its effect on electromagnetic wave propagation. Science in China Ser. G Physics, Mechanics & Astronomy 35(3), 308–317 (2005)
10. Jiang, C.G., Lin, K.Z., Tian, G.C.: The research of Mie scattering peculiarity of metal particles. Journal Of Atomic And Molecular Physics 23(5), 978–980 (2006)

A Linear Localization Algorithm for Wireless Sensor Network Based on RSSI

Feng Liu[*], Hao Zhu, Zonghai Gu, and Yan Liu

Zheng Zhou University, Zheng Zhou, He Nan, China
feng5373@sina.com

Abstract. Node localization and tracking is a highlight research in wireless sensor networks(WSN), and localization algorithm plays the most important role in improving the localization accuracy. To overcome the drawback of the low localization accuracy of conventional Least Squares(LS) with small number reference nodes, this paper proposes a linear algorithm based on received signal strength indicator (RSSI), which implements Taylor Series Expansion to linearize binary quadratic equations. With the same number reference nodes, simulation result shows, compared to conventional LS, the linear algorithm can highly enhance the localization accuracy.

Keywords: Wireless Sensor Networks, Linear Localization Algorithm, RSSI.

1 Introduction

Wireless sensor networks(WSN)[1] [2] contain a large number of tiny sensor nodes deployed in the monitored area, the wireless sensor nodes communicate with each other through a multi-hops ad-hoc network, which aims to collaborate, perceive and process the environmental information of covered network area. However, the positions of WSN nodes are the basic elements for other applications. Only the sensor nodes are positioned correctly, can they be monitored and tracked to external targets. WSN positioning technology is widely used in instrument, industrial control, medical, military, aviation and aerospace and other fields.

Usually, there are two kinds of nodes self-localization algorithms[3]: rang-based and rang-free. Rang-free localization algorithms, such as centroid, DV-HOP, convex programming, and MDS-MAP etc, roughly calculate the nodes' positions through the wireless communication connection among nodes. Though the algorithms require a lower hardware of the sensor nodes, they have a relative low precision position [4]. Range-based localization algorithms, which measure the actual distance or angle between the wireless sensor nodes, usually have a good positioning precision. Distance-based methods are commonly implemented in RSSI[5][6], TOA, AOA, TDOA, etc. Distance-based localization algorithm on RSSI is often applied in WSN.

This paper proposes a linear algorithm based on RSSI, applying Taylor Series to overcome the low accuracy of the conventional LS algorithm. Simulation results

---

[*] Corresponding author.

S. Lin and X. Huang (Eds.): CESM 2011, Part II, CCIS 176, pp. 384–389, 2011.

show that our linear localization algorithm has a high accuracy, and it can also solve the problem of lower accuracy when environment changes greatly. So it has good robustness.

2   Signal Propagation Models

There are two wireless signal propagation models, which are the free space propagation model and the log-distance distribution model. The free space propagation model's path-loss formula is shown below:

$$Loss = 32.4 + 10\lg(d) + 10k\lg(f) \tag{1}$$

d means the distance from the source node, the unit is km; f is the frequency of the signal with the unit of MHz; k is the fading factor of the wireless signal. Because of the complexity of the actual environment with node properties of dispersion, wireless propagation path-loss is not very consistent with the theoretical value. So, the log-distance distribution model is more reasonable as follow:

$$PL(d) = \overline{PL(d_0)} + 10k\lg(d / d_0) + X_0 \tag{2}$$

$PL(d)$ is the wireless signal loss after the distance of d ; X_0 is a random number of Gaussian distribution with its mean 0; k is the fading factor of the wireless signal, the range of k is 2 to 4; if d = 1, according to equation (1), $Loss$ is $\overline{PL(d_0)}$, then , the wireless sensor node received signal strength indicator (RSSI) as follow:

$$RSSI = -(10k\lg d + A) \tag{3}$$

k is the fading factor of the wireless signal, the range of k is 2 to 4; d means the distance from the source node, the unit is km; A, whose range is usually 45 to 49, is the received signal strength indicator when the distance from the source is 1m.

As we must put the average value of $\overline{RSSI}$ into the embedded hardware, so, we must use the absolute value, according to the absolute value from the source:

$$d = 10^{\frac{\overline{RSSI} - A}{10k}} \tag{4}$$

3   Linear Algorithm Based on RSSI

The basic principle of linear algorithm: assuming that the true positioning coordinates of the unknown node was (x, y) , the unknown node could receive n pairs of reference nodes' location coordinates and $RSSI$ values, then we could get the d value from (4), so due to Phthagorean proposition ,we educed equations (5) below:

$$\begin{cases} (x-x_1)^2 + (y-y_1)^2 = d_1^2 \\ (x-x_2)^2 + (y-y_2)^2 = d_2^2 \\ \quad\quad ...... \\ (x-x_n)^2 + (y-y_n)^2 = d_n^2 \end{cases} \tag{5}$$

Changed (5) in the following ways:

$$d_i = \sqrt{(x_i - x)^2 + (y_i - y)^2} , \quad i = 1, 2, ..., n \tag{6}$$

We assumed that:

1. The approximate coordinate of the unknown node was $(\hat{x}, \hat{y})$

2. $(\Delta x, \Delta y)$ was the position offset between (x, y) and $(\hat{x}, \hat{y})$

3. Equation (6) was expanded by Taylor Series in the approximate location.

$$d_i = \sqrt{(x_i - x)^2 + (y_i - y)^2} = f(x, y) \tag{7}$$

$$\hat{d}_i = \sqrt{(x_i - \hat{x})^2 + (y_i - \hat{y})^2} = f(\hat{x}, \hat{y}) \tag{8}$$

The true position was the sum of the approximate location and the offset. Thus,

$$x = \hat{x} + \Delta x , \quad y = \hat{y} + \Delta y \tag{9}$$

then,

$$f(x, y) = f(\hat{x} + \Delta x, \hat{y} + \Delta y) \tag{10}$$

Expanded (6) with Taylor's Series in the approximate location.

$$f(\hat{x} + \Delta x, \hat{y} + \Delta y) = f(\hat{x}, \hat{y}) + \frac{\partial f(\hat{x}, \hat{y})}{\partial \hat{x}} \Delta x + \frac{\partial f(\hat{x}, \hat{y})}{\partial \hat{y}} \Delta y + ... \tag{11}$$

We just saved the first-order partial derivative and eliminated Taylor Series expansions of the nonlinear term, partial derivatives of higher orders were ignored, then $f(\hat{x}, \hat{y})$ on the x and y partial derivatives are below:

$$\frac{\partial f(\hat{x}, \hat{y})}{\partial \hat{x}} = -\frac{x_i - \hat{x}}{\hat{r}_i} , \quad \frac{\partial f(\hat{x}, \hat{y})}{\partial \hat{y}} = -\frac{y_i - \hat{y}}{\hat{r}_i} , \quad \hat{r}_i = \sqrt{(x_i - \hat{x})^2 + (y_i - \hat{y})^2} \tag{12}$$

Introduced (8) (9) (10) (11) (12) into (7) then arranged the result:

$$d_i = \hat{d}_i - \frac{x_i - \hat{x}}{\hat{r}_i} \Delta x - \frac{y_i - \hat{y}}{\hat{r}_i} \Delta y \tag{13}$$

Assuming that:

$$\Delta d_i = \hat{d}_i - d_i, \quad a_{xi} = \frac{x_i - \hat{x}}{\hat{r}_i}, \quad a_{yi} = \frac{y_i - \hat{y}}{\hat{r}_i} \tag{13}$$

then, we could calculate the two unknowns with the linear equations as the following:

$$\begin{cases} \Delta d_1 = a_{x1}\Delta x + a_{y1}\Delta y \\ \Delta d_2 = a_{x2}\Delta x + a_{y2}\Delta y \\ \quad \cdots\cdots \\ \Delta d_n = a_{xn}\Delta x + a_{yn}\Delta y \end{cases} \tag{14}$$

We assumed that:

$$\Delta d = \begin{bmatrix} \Delta d_1 \\ \Delta d_2 \\ \cdots \\ \Delta d_n \end{bmatrix}, \quad H = \begin{bmatrix} a_{x1} & a_{y1} \\ a_{x2} & a_{y2} \\ \cdots & \cdots \\ a_{xn} & a_{yn} \end{bmatrix}, \quad \Delta\rho = \begin{bmatrix} \Delta x \\ \Delta y \end{bmatrix} \tag{15}$$

then, (14) could be expressed like following:

$$H\Delta\rho = \Delta d \tag{16}$$

We Applied LS to solve the matrix:

$$\Delta\hat{\rho}_{LS} = (H^T H)^{-1} H^T \Delta d \tag{17}$$

Once we got Δx and Δy, with (9) we could get the true coordinate $(\hat{x}, \hat{y})$ of the unknown node. If the displacement of $(\Delta x, \Delta y)$ was a point of near-line, our linear method is feasible. Acceptable displacement depended on the accuracy in need. If the displacement exceeded the acceptable value, we could return $(\hat{x}_{LS}, \hat{y}_{LS})$ as initial coordinate of the unknown node, and implemented our linear algorithm to repeat iterations until the value was acceptable.

4 Algorithm Simulation

We compared the network performance of our linear algorithm to the conventional LS method based on RSSI on MATLAB, and the basic initial conditions for the wireless sensor networks are in a 100 m × 100 m area, 30 randomly distributed reference nodes within the region, and each simulation was experimented 50 times. The simulation results are shown below:

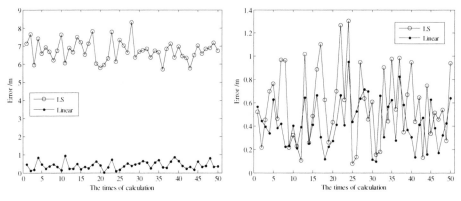

Fig. 1. The same number reference nodes   **Fig. 2.** Different number reference nodes

As Fig.1 showed, both algorithms selected the same three reference nodes, LS almost could not locate the unknown node, while the linear algorithm could meet the desired accuracy. As Fig.2 showed, six reference nodes selected in the LS algorithm and three reference nodes in our linear algorithm, the simulation results showed that LS had some limitations and our linear algorithm was better than LS algorithm. As we intended to improve the accuracy, our linear algorithm was more complex than the LS. But our linear algorithm could be applied in different environments, and it had higher accuracy than LS.

The problem of linear algorithm was the iterative times. Fig.3 showed the relationship between the times of iterations and error.

It could be seen in Fig.3, when the iteration was the fifth, the error became stable.

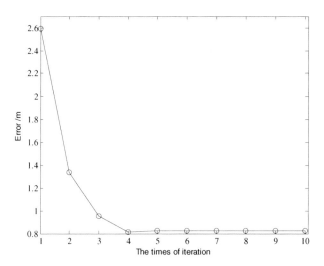

Fig. 3. Localization error converges

5 Summary

This paper discusses the two algorithms in two-dimension, and simulation results show that our linear algorithm is superior to the conventional LS algorithms. Further more, our linear algorithm has good robustness.

References

1. Akyildiz, I.F., Su, W., Sankarasubramaniam, Y., et al.: Wireless sensor networks: a survey. Computer Network 38, 932422 (2002)
2. Callaway, E.H.: Wireless Sensor Networks Architectures and Protocols, p. 1210. CRC Press, Boca Raton (2004)
3. Wang, F., et al.: Self-Localization Systems and Algorithms for Wireless Sensor Networks. Journal of Software 16(5), 857–866 (2005)
4. Mao, G.Q., Fidan, B., Anderson, B.: Wireless sensor network localization techniques. J. Computer Networks 51(10), 2529–2553 (2007)
5. Fang, Z., Zhao, Z., Guo, P., Zhang, Y.: Analysis of Distance Measurement Based on RSSI. Chinese Journal of Sensors and Actuators 20(11), P2526–P2530 (2007)
6. Zheng, J.: The Location of the WSN-Nodes Based on RSSI 2010. In: International Conference on Computational Intelligence and Industrial Application (PACIIA), pp. 322–325 (2010)
7. Rappaport, T.S.: Wireless communications: principles and practice, 2nd edn. Prentice Hall PTR, New Jersey (2002)

Database System of University Sports Meet

Wu Xie[*], Huimin Zhang, and Tong Li

Guilin University of Electronic Technology,
541004 Guilin, China
Xiewu588@126.com

Abstract. There was a problem of inefficient management for university games, and the tools of Microsoft Visual Studio and SQL Server were adopted to develop a management information system for sports meet on campus. The main work of the software development process included requirements analysis, preliminary design, detailed design and implementation. Software test results show that the database system meets the requirements of each module with user-friendly interface and simple operation. The instant data can be updated efficiently, accurately and safely during university games in a variety of data forms, reducing the labor intensity of organization staff greatly and lowering data management costs dramatically. It is very useful for the committee to deal with the organization and schedule of college sports.

Keywords: Database system, software design, sports meet, information management.

1 Introduction

In recent years, the number of students for many universities increased from several thousand to over ten thousand in China. In order to improve the physical quality of teachers and students, a regular sport meet is held every year. Sports and games are considered and researched [1, 2, 3, 4]. Yet the data from university games is usually processed in hand, leading to poor data management way with some disadvantages of high cost, wrong data, low efficiency, heavy workload and massive information. Especially, the data of game time, location and competing performance for some athletes and teams can not be updated in real time. It tends to spend a lot of financial, material and human resources for sports commissions, and the game items and sections are too many to organize and arrange in good order and perfect schedule. The sport staff is usually very hard and tiring, so the development of a university information system for the Games is essential. The following sections will focus on the development work of needs analysis, summary design, detailed design and implement for the game systems.

2 Requirement Analysis

According to the actual needs for university, the requirements of sports database system are described as follows.

---

[*] Corresponding author.

S. Lin and X. Huang (Eds.): CESM 2011, Part II, CCIS 176, pp. 390–395, 2011.

Games information is integrated into a unified platform to meet the integrity constraints. The faculty for the college athletes, student athletes, referees, organizers, leaders, administrators and other member can select their information from the system instantaneous, which can insert, delete and modify their records of sport games. The diverse information is stored centrally with a high degree of sharing.

The multi-level security management system is established for a variety of users with effective security information to ensure system. From the previous games of university, the useful experience is summed up to simplify every flow or process for entry, competing, remark and rank, etc. Human resource of game management is rationally allocated by the actual situation, improving the work efficiency and reducing the information collection cost for sports.

The establishment of sports service chain management system is indispensable for the application of signing, querying and announcing game results. All information is input into the management database system to ensure the smooth flow of sports information to select from the various hyperlinks of users. Information sharing and optimizing management are important, and the system module diagram is shown below.

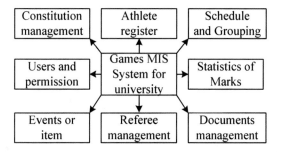

Fig. 1. System Modules of Database System of University Sports Meet

The regulation management module is mainly for the committee information of sports meet, just like other games [5, 6], and relevant game rules are described with unified regulation. The work of organizing sport games are carried out by the staff of the school or department in turn.

The athlete and delegation registering module is mainly for these users to log in the sports game management system, and getting the printed entry card. They can select their personal or team member information randomly.

The referee module is mainly for the judges to register and log in the system, and affording to select the reasonable schedule information of time, location and group, etc. It is necessary to assure the responsibility of the different game referee. It can be also selected or printed everywhere with many terminals.

The game item modules is for administrator and committee to insert, update, delete and select all the competing information, which is usually divided into field and track events. Every item is listed with relation table, or exported with Excel.

The scheduling and grouping module is for the athletes, referees and committee to arrange diverse information of item, time, events, batch and fields, etc. It is important for the distinction between team and individual competitions, men's and women's competitions.

The results and statistics module is for the competitions of a team or individual performance, and it can print, export report, and sort or scoring.

Altogether the system dataflow for sports meet on campus is show as Fig. 2.

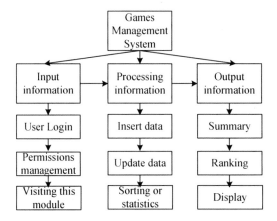

Fig. 2. IPO (Input-Processing-Output) Diagram of Database System Dataflow

3 Preliminary Design

In order to clarify the relation among the modules of user logging, the organizing committee information management, players and referee registration, team information management, events classification, games arrangement, results entry and summary, document management, the entity-relationship (E-R) diagram for these functional modules of the whole system of university sports meet is designed and shown as Fig. 3.

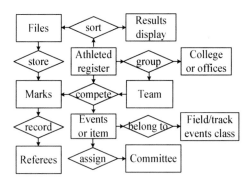

Fig. 3. Entity-Relationship Diagram of Database System of University Sports Meet

4   Detailed Design

Every entity and relationship for preliminary design is corresponding to a relational table. So, in the step of detailed design, the relevant relational schemes are described, such as attribute, type, field, length, constraints or description. A few software constraint conditions are in the design process of the following relational scheme of database system.

The user table is used to store detailed information of all users for the sports meet system, and the relational scheme is User (UserID, UserName, UserPassword, UserRoleName, UserSex, UserTel). It can manage users to insert, delete, update or select records from games. The users can only maintain their own information, such as account, password and personal secrets.

The Athlete member table describes the information of athlete, team and member, and the relational scheme is Athlete member (AthleteID, TeamID, AthleteName, AthleteSexl). It is easy to select the instant data change from sport game after competing. The rank, score and order can be known to all members in time.

The table of competition team is mainly about information from some teams and delegations, including mane, number, score, rank and order, etc. The relational scheme is Competition Team (TeamID, ItemID, ItemChangCiNum, TeamCheck, TeamName, TPScore, ItemRank, TeamCompany).

The item table is for the information of ID, name, record or record keeper from game data available, and the relational scheme is Item (ItemID, ItemName, Item_ Property, ItemRecord, RecordKeeperName).

The detailed item arrangement table covers the attributes of item, referee, location, time, and the relational scheme is Detailed Item (ItemID, RefereeID, ItemAddress, ItemCheckTime, ItemTime).

The referee information table records the attribute of ID, name, sex, etc, and the relational scheme is Referee Information (RefereeID, RefereeName, RefereeSex).

The table of athlete information has ID, number, sex, rank, score, etc, and the relational scheme is Athlete Information (AthleteID, ItemID, ItemChangCiNum, AthleteCheck, AthleteName, AthleteSex, APScore, ItemRank, AthleteCompany).

5   Implementation

The software of college sports games is carried out with the tool of Visual Studio in C# programming language, and the data records are stored in the back-end of Microsoft SQL Server 2005. Some of the software of the database system are shown in Fig.4, 5, and 6.

The ADO.net technology is used to connect the database with the front-end. All the modules from requirement are completed, and the input data can be shown in time after processing by the database with SQL binding technology. The score, rank, team results can be updated shortly.

The database system can deal with the information from committee, team, players and referees during sports meet. The competing items, arrangement, and scores can be processed and announced in time.

Fig. 4. The Software Interface of Database System of University Sports Meet as a Whole

conditions   All   ▼   [Query]

TeamID	ProjectID	ProjectNum	TeamCheck	TPScore
000001	000006	1	unchecked	12
000002	000006	1	unchecked	18
000003	000009	1	unchecked	4
000004	000008	2	unchecked	1
000005	000008	2	unchecked	2
000006	000008	2	unchecked	3

TeamID 000001   ItemID 000006   ItemNum 1

                                              [Add]
TeamCheck unchecked   TeamName AGT   [Del]
                                              [Modify]

TPScore 12   ProjectRank 5   TeamCompany China

Fig. 5. One of the Results Interface of Database System of University Sports Meet

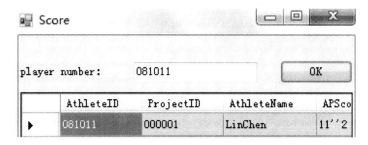

Fig. 6. One of the Score Results Interface of Database System of University Sports Meet

6 Conclusion

The management information system for college sports meet is powerful during processing the data from games. Its interface is beautiful with easy selection and simple operation, greatly reducing the manual workload of the sports staff, and improving efficiency during the organization of scheduling and competitions of various items. The data management capability is promoted, effectively ensuring the just, fair and open games for universities.

References

1. Mileham, R.: Let the Games Begin. Engineering & Technology 14, 20 (2008)
2. Sheahan, M., Andrews, P.: Inventors' inbox (Innovation Football). Engineering & Technology 8, 28–29 (2010)
3. Douglas, L.: Olympics watch. Engineering & Technology 6, 28–31 (2009)
4. Rusdorf, S., Brunnett, G., Lorenz, M., Winkler, T.: Real-Time Interaction with a Humanoid Avatar in an Immersive Table Tennis Simulation. IEEE Transactions on Visualization and Computer Graphics 1, 15–25 (2007)
5. Guangzhou Asian Games Organizing Committee information,
   http://www.gz2010.cn
6. The London, Olympic and Paralympic Games (2012),
   http://www.london2012.com

Shoe Last Free-Form Surface Reconstruction Technique Based on Reverse Engineering

Xiang Chen[1] and Xin Zhang[2]

[1] School of Civil Engineering, Xi'an Technological University,
710032 Xi'an, China
[2] School of Fashion & Art Design, Xi'an Polytechnic University,
710048 Xi'an, China
xichen0801@163.com, xianzhangxin@sina.com

Abstract. Shoe last is the benchmark of shoe style in the shoemaking technology and the foundation of shoemaking. At present, how to constitute the last 3D free-form surface model rapidly is one of the important subjects about the last design and the sole mould manufacture. On this basis, the reverse engineering technology was introduced to expatiate its application in the shoemaking industry. The key techniques of the last 3D free-form surface reconstruction were focused. And the reverse processing procedure of the last was set up; the fast reconstruction of the last 3D free-form surface model was also realized. The research has certain directive significance to the concrete application and further popularization of reverse engineering technology in the shoemaking industry.

Keywords: last, free-form surface, reverse engineering, surface reconstruction.

1 Introduction

Last of shoe is style benchmark of shoemaking technology and basis of shoemaking. Changes in styles of shoes directly dependent on the design of shoe last, and the quality of shoe last directly affects quality of the shoe and wearing comfort. In traditional last production, old master produced the first last with standard size in manual according to design drawing, and then last cutting machine was used to produce lasts with different sizes. Although the production process can quickly produce large amount of lasts with full sizes, there is no available 3D design for assistant design for CAD of uppers and soles. Using reverse engineering [1], we can quickly obtain complete 3D point data and rebuild curves and surfaces. After these data was inputted into CAD/CAM system, 3D shoe last model can be achieved, which can not only aids design of uppers and soles, but also provides adjustment basis for afterwards design, so as to improve speed and efficiency of last design and production. So the reverse engineering was introduced into design of last, the design result of which can be applied in production or researches in other fields. The U. S., Britian, Italy and other countries has developed many shoe last for spefical uses and related system, which provided a complete set of last aid design solution. We also actively engaged in researches on last in recent years.

S. Lin and X. Huang (Eds.): CESM 2011, Part II, CCIS 176, pp. 396–402, 2011.

In the past researches, A. M. Jimeno el at researched NC machining of shoe last with virtual discrete methods [2]; Yang researched on 3D modeling of shoe last with reverse engineering [3]; Gao focused on shoe last modeling and local modification techniques [4]; Liu presented shoe last surface digital features information recognition method with reverse engineering [5]; Chen proposed a complete set of shoe last reverse design and NC machine method with general-purpose CAD/CAM software [6]; Chen researched on last CAD system modeling technique based on surface data of shoe last [7]; Wang developed shoemaking CAD system with reverse engineering [8] and Xu developed customized shoe last CAD system [9].

But how to quickly establish 3D surface model of shoe last is still an important topic in shoe last design and soles mold design that. On this basis, reverse engineering technology was introduced to research on key techniques in shoe last 3D free-form surface reconstruction. Reverse engineering software as *Imageware* was used in the paper, so as to illustrate specific application of reverse engineering in shoe last 3D free-form surface reconstruction.

2   3D Free-Form Surface Reconstruction of Shoe Last

Now, there are three programs to construct surface in reverse engineering, one is rectangular parametric surface fitting, which construct surface with B-Spline or NURBS; the second is discrete data points, which construct surface on the basis of triangular Bezier surface; the third describe surface entity with polyhedral [10]. As the most professional reverse engineering software, *Imageware* follow the data processing procedures of point-curve-surface, which adapt the first surface construction scheme.

2.1   Data Collection and Input

Data collection is the first step in reverse engineering modeling. Good measurement data can greatly improve speed and quality of surface reconstruction. The paper selected 25 men shoe last model to collect shoe last data with Vitus 3D laser scanner, which can rapidly collect complete data. Obtained large amount of point cloud data, the simple scattered points were removed. Then Construct‖Polygon Mesh‖Polygonize Cloud method was used to compute point cloud data into triangular mesh format. Distribution of light and shadow on object can be used to observe shoe last shape, is shown in Fig. 1.

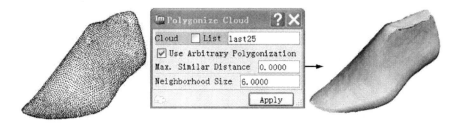

Fig. 1. Shoe last point aloud data

2.2   Shoe Last Cusp Identification and Bottom Surface Reconstruction

In model reconstruction, we need to segment all point cloud according to feature lines. Each point cloud was fitted with specific surface and operations as surface extension and splicing were performed to form complex surface. But the feature lines are usually submerged in the obtained point cloud data. How to effectively extract feature lines and improve accuracy and speed of reverse processing is a problem of keen interest by engineers [5, 11, 12].

Shoe last is a free-form surface body, which has the following features. One is that it is a complete free-form surface and different surface patches everywhere. The second is that it has large change curvature. The third is that it has sharp corners and edges. After shoe last data collection, the key is to identify cusps. We used the similar curvature identification method to point out range of large curvature according to point cloud curvature distribution by Construct‖Feature Line‖Sharp edges. Then the required angular point group is shown in Fig. 2 can be obtained based on the curvature distribution. After smoothing, we can construct a closed even curve to generate turning sharp edge feature line of shoe last. With this line, we can segment

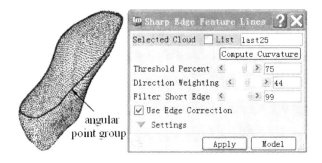

Fig. 2. Sharp edge point cloud of last bottom

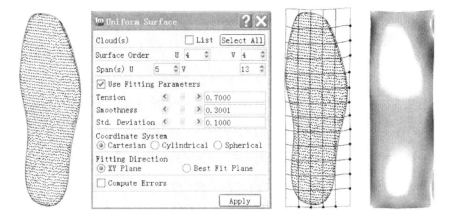

Fig. 3. Free-form surface reconstruction of last bottom

bottom point data of last with method of Construct||Surface From Cloud||Uniform Surface to construct free-form curve is shown in Fig. 3. Finally, these feature lines were projected onto surface to form 2D curve. Then we can prune external surface with 2D curve to reconstruct free-form surface model of last.

2.3   Last Surface Reconstruction

(1) Boundary line construction of last surface. There is no special feature be used as reference for surface segmentation. We used 4 boundary line and point cloud within boundary to reconstruct last surface. The key is how to build a boundary line. Firstly point cloud data was transferred to side-glance. Based on inside and outside shape, a section was roughly cut and divided into 2 parts, and then 2 uniform curves can be construct with these point group data. Repeat the above process to finish point cloud of each section and then construct 3 even curve according to shoe forefoot, heel and top of the shape of a cross section.

(2) Top surface construction of last. With closed curve in top of last, we ca segment point data in the top and delete unnecessary points to construct a plane. The closed curve was then projected to the plane. With the projected 2D curve, the plane can be cut into the required last top shape.

(3) Last surface reconstruction. Firstly transfer the obtained 2D curves of last bottom and top surface into 3D curve, and then cut it into 4 curves according to side, upper palm and follow boundary. Then Modify||Continuity||Match 2 Curve method was used to fix broken curves. Move boundary line on last surface to link with each other to form closed loop. The key of boundary line connection is to ensure continuity of G0 among curves. After match connection completed, segment 4 parts of point data according to a closed boundary line is shown in Fig. 4. Then each surface can be constructed with the method of 4 closed boundary curve and inside point cloud.

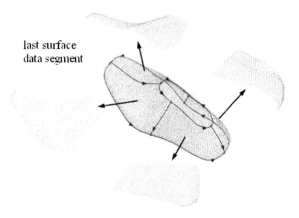

Fig. 4. Point data segmentation within 4 boundary scope of last surface

2.4 3D Free-form Surface Model of Last

The continuous among 4 reconstructed last surfaces should be processed with the method of Modify||Continuity||Match 2 Surface. If the connection processing was not very good, it needs to adjust control points near surface boundary till the subsequent processing result meet requirements. In general, it needs at least G1 be continuous and there is no traces on the surface boundary after coloring. After these processing, the 3D free-form surface model of shoe last is shown in Fig. 5. The product was output in *Iges* surface format. It can be inputted into CAD/CAM system to perform upper design, sole design or to generate process routes.

Fig. 5. 3D free-form surface model of shoe last

3 Accuracy Analysis on Last Reconstruction Model

In the reverse engineering, it inevitably exist error from data measurement to model reconstruction. Error model of reverse engineering is mainly made up of prototype error, measurement error, data processing error, modeling error and so on. It is an simple way to evaluate accuracy of reconstruction model by checking distance from measurement point to surface model. The evaluation index does not include measurement error, which is an approximation and expedient method. In the current technical conditions, evaluation on reverse model still uses the method. We also compared difference by computing distance from point to model so as to conduct accuracy analysis. With error analysis of distance from surface to point group in the bottom of last, the corresponding distance error from last surface to point group was statistic in Table 1.

From Table 1, we can know that maximum standard error of absolute distance between last reconstruction model and measurement point group is 0.1830mm and maximum absolute distance between single point and model is 1.3320mm. We can also know from further analysis that point with large error appears turning sharp edges of shoe last. There are two reasons leading to such error. One is that the sharp point information included in collected point aloud data of shoe last is not accurate enough and comprehensive. The identification of sharp point caused the error. Another is that there is fitting error of feature curve construction according to cusp point group, so the matching between reconstructed feature line and sharp edges of last caused the error. Therefore, we should further improve cusp point data collection and solve error control problem of curve and surface fitting.

Table 1. Shoe last reconstruction model accuracy statistics (Unit. mm)

Reconstruction surface measure		Model accuracy analysis indexes			
Surface part	Measure points number	Type	Forward distance	Negative distance	Absolute distance
Last bottom	2028	Maximum	0.6370	-1.2250	1.2250
		Mean	0.0838	-0.0797	0.0817
		Standard error	0.0978	0.1148	0.1066
Last surface	1 895	Maximum	0.6822	-1.3212	1.3212
		Mean	0.0865	-0.1219	0.1039
		Standard error	0.1157	0.2321	0.1830
	2 958	Maximum	0.8840	-1.1832	1.1832
		Mean	0.0731	-0.1339	0.1051
		Standard error	0.1103	0.2050	0.1683
	3 1047	Maximum	0.4333	-1.0831	1.0831
		Mean	0.0880	-0.1273	0.1099
		Standard error	0.0883	0.1726	0.1423
	4 795	Maximum	0.6451	-1.3320	1.3320
		Mean	0.1100	-0.1338	0.1196
		Standard error	0.1143	0.2494	0.1815

4 Conclusion

The paper introduced reverse engineering technique to construct reverse processing flow of last according to design idea of original designers to implement quick construction of 3D free-form surface model of last, so as to improve speed and efficiency of last design. The reconstructed last model can be inputted into shoemaking CAD/CAM system. It not only helps follow-up uppers and soles design, but also can achieve higher size accuracy in production to produce higher quality shoes. It will help to specific application and deepen promotion of reverse engineering technique in the whole shoemaking.

References

1. Wu, J.-j., Wang, Q.-f., Huang, Y.-b., Zhou, J.: Review of Surface Reconstruction Methods in Reverse Engineering. Journal of Engineering Graphics 2, 133–142 (2004)
2. Jimeno, A.M., Chamizo, J.M.G., Salas, F.: hoe Last Machining Using Virtual Digitising. Int. J. Adv. Manuf. Technol. 17, 744–750 (2001)
3. Yang, G.-q., Li, S.-y., Cao, X.-j.: Nurbs Surface in CAGD-Theory and Application CAGD. Journal of Northwest University of Light Industry 19, 62–65 (2001)
4. Gao, C., Li, J., Guo, Y.-c.: Local Deformation Technique in Shoe Last Modeling. Journal of Computer Aided Design & Computer Graphics 14, 890–893 (2002)
5. Liu, D., Lin, S.-w.: Characteristic Recognition and Data Compression for the Last of Shoe. Modular Machine Tool & Automatic Manufacturing Technique 3, 9–11 (2003)

6. Chen, J.-h., Tong, S.-l., Chen, J.-l.: Inverse Design and NC Machining of Shoe Last Based on General Motor's CAD/CAM Software. Modular Machine Tool & Automatic Manufacturing Technique 8, 31–32 (2003)
7. Chen, J.-l., Tong, S.-g., Jin, T.: Research on Modeling Technologies of Shoe Last CAD System. Journal of Engineering Design 11, 197–200 (2004)
8. Wang, L.-p., Qiu, F.-y.: Shoemaking CAD System Based on Reverse Engineering and Layout Algorithm. Journal of Zhejiang University of Technology 32, 363–366 (2004)
9. Xu, C.-f., Liu, Y., Jiang, Y.-l., Pan, Y.-h.: Design and Realization of Customized Shoe Last CAD System. Journal of Computer Aided Design & Computer Graphics 16, 1437–1441 (2004)
10. Luan, Y.-g., Li, H.-f., Tang, B.-t.: Reverse Engineering and its Technologies. Journal of Shandong University (Engineering Science) 33, 114–118 (2003)
11. Hu, X., Xi, J.-t., Jin, Y.: Segmentation and Surface Reconstruction of Scattered Data in Reverse Engineering. Journal of Shanghai Jiaotong University 38, 62–65 (2004)
12. Lu, Y.-p., Chen, L.-q.: Techniques for Acquiring the Key Lines in Reverse Design. Die & Mould Industry 277, 14–18 (2004)

Product Innovative Development for the Datum Orientation Triangle

Ruilin Lin

Department of Commercial Design, Chienkuo Technology University,
No. 1, Chieh Shou N. Rd., Changhua City 500, Taiwan
linrl2002@gmail.com

Abstract. This study is the product innovative development for the datum orientation triangle using a triangle, an indicator, and a scale ring. The indicator is fixed to a proper location near the center of the triangle inside the scale ring. The scale ring and the indicator hand share the same center. A triangle is also used. This product can be used for orientation and used as a traditional triangle or ruler. The hand of the indicator always points to the same direction. Therefore this product can be used as a compass as well. This product with multiple functions developed by this study can solve the problems of traditional drawing tools being too heavy, costly, and difficult to carry.

Keywords: triangle, indicator, scale ring.

1 Design Concept

When drawing a graph or a chart, it is usually necessary to draw some lines. Traditionally, lines can be drawn with appliances on a drawing table. However, when there is no drawing table, the only way to do so is to use a ruler, a triangle, and a protractor together. This way, one can draw lines which are parallel to a datum line or lines with any included angle with a datum line. A traditional drawing table comes with two fixed rulers and a protractor. The two rulers can slide along the tracks on the table to change their positions. With the protractor, the included angle of the rulers can be changed. Then all kinds of lines can be drawn.

Although drawings can be made on drawing tables, drawing tables are still too heavy and impractical. Also datum lines are required. However, without drawing tables, carrying many appliances is an inconvenient choice with rather low precision. This study considered the problems with traditional methods and designed a new product in hopes of creating an innovative structure which is ideal and practical for related developers to make breakthroughs in research and development of mechanical design. As a result, consumers may this innovative product which is lighter and more precise. The goal of benefiting people is then reached. The researcher has years of experiences in product manufacturing, development, and design. After careful consideration and evaluation according to the goal mentioned above, a practical invention was finally born. The innovative product developed by this study helps drawing personnel to draw by providing them the datum orientation triangles for

S. Lin and X. Huang (Eds.): CESM 2011, Part II, CCIS 176, pp. 403–408, 2011.
© Springer-Verlag Berlin Heidelberg 2011

design. Technically, triangles with an orientation function can be used to draw all kinds of lines, including those parallel to a datum line or those with any included angle with a datum line.

2 Theoretical Foundations

When it comes to constructions, no matter their sizes, engineering drawing has been playing an important role. From planning, to measuring, experiments, designing, subcontracting, production, checking, maintaining, and re-production, every phase requires cooperation of staffs from different fields with different specialties. Achievements are shown on drawing papers. Thus, using good tools to creating drawings is particularly important [1]. In the recent years, 3D CAD systems have matured. Gradually, 3D methods have been applied in design and development of industrial objects. However, sometimes 2D engineering drawings are still needed. It is possible to create engineering drawings using 3D object projection. Still, scales have to be marked on these drawings. Thus, some scholar proposed a way to create 2D engineering drawings through projection using axis transformation based on characteristics model. Also, information of object's characteristics and projection is used for automatic labeling, so that users can obtain 2D engineering drawings with labels from 3D objects in a short time. Once an object is modified, users only have to regenerate engineering drawings without modifying labels on those drawings. And by referencing drawings of different elevation angles, unnecessary labels can be removed to make labeling more reasonable and efficient [8].

CAD/CAM software is widely used and has helped to develop and apply many technologies, such as digital manufacturing, rapid prototyping, computer integrated manufacturing, virtual reality, enterprise resources planning, concurrent engineering, and mass customization. However, drawing staffs create 2D production drawings as bases of productions. These advanced technologies can hardly be applied. They wish there can be a way to smoothly transform 2D drawings into 3D ones [4]. Practically, engineers use 2D sheet metal part designs. But later they have to use 3D CAD software to build object models manually for progressive die design software. Due to this fact, some scholar tried to develop a system to automatically create 3D object models from 2D sheet metal engineering drawings, in order to save time, manpower, and money required for 3D model building [3] [6].

Also, some people developed systems by combing hand drawings with fuzzy logic concepts, in hope that users can quickly construct objects and understand structures of drawings, to save time spent on trial and error and cost on production [2]. The frameworks of drawing software used in the industry are usually AutoCAD or Access. However, to learn engineering drawing, school students should begin with hand drawing. They should learn about meanings of lines on drawings and how to draft and draw before learning computer drawing software [5]. After all, knowing how to correctly use tools to create drawings helps to apply deeper professional knowledge in the future [7]. According to the documentation, using computer software is the trend in the job market. However, the ability of hand drawing for engineering drawing is the ticket to 3D drawing. Under the premise that the ability of hand drawing is a must, developing a light, convenient, and precise drawing tool is very important.

3 Content

Traditionally, to make a drawing, one must slide the two fixed rulers on a drawing table along the tracks and change their included angle using the protractor to draw all kinds of lines. Drawing tables or drawing boards are expensive, heavy, and hard to carry. It is also inconvenient to put them away. There is space for improvement. The innovative product developed by this study is a monocoque triangle for drawing which can also be used for orientation without any limitation on angles. Drawing personnel can do orientation and use the functions of a triangle without bringing any extra drawing tools. This invention combines a drawing table and a triangle (or just a ruler, a triangle, and a protractor) for drawing. The problem of traditional tools, being hard to carry, can be solved, and so can the technical problems such as datum line setting and drawing from different angles.

Due to many difficulties and disadvantages to make drawings using the traditional method, the researcher finally found a solution after detailed design and several tries and improvements, developing a datum orientation triangle which is precise in orientation and convenient to use. The problem with the traditional method to make drawings can be solved. This study developed a datum orientation triangle. The indicator is fixed to a proper location near the center of the triangle inside the scale ring. The scale ring and the indicator hand share the same center. A triangle is also used. This product can be used for orientation and used as a traditional triangle or ruler. This product is an invention with multiple functions.

4 Mechanical Application

This study developed a datum orientation triangle including a triangle, which is a board with certain thickness. Scales are marked on the edges of the board. In a proper place by the center, an indicator and a scale ring is installed. The indicator is fixed inside the triangle, and its hand always points to the same direction like a compass. The indicator with a hand is inside the scale ring, sharing the same center. Both the indicator and the scale ring are inside the triangle. Both sides of the triangle are flat. Therefore it can be used with either side on top.

The scale ring can be rotated. When using this product, one side of the triangle should be adjusted to overlap the datum line, as the datum side. When the indicator hand stops, the scale ring should be rotated until the hand points at the "0". Then move the triangle to where you'd like to draw a line, and place it there for a while until the indicator hand stays still. After that, rotate the triangle to match the indicator hand with the "0". To draw a line parallel to the datum line, all you have to do is to draw a line along the datum side of the triangle.

To draw a line which is not parallel to the datum line, follow the above-mentioned steps and then rotate the triangle so that the indicator hand points at the angle of your choice, say 30 degrees. Then move the triangle so that its datum side is on where the line should be drawn. If, due to the movement, the indicator hand is not pointing at 30 degrees at the moment, the position of the triangle should be slightly adjusted so that the hand can be exactly on 30 degrees. Now, if you draw a line along the datum side of the triangle, the included angle between the line and the datum line would be exactly 30 degrees. Figure 1 shows the parts of the product and figure 2 is a simple illustration of the product.

(1) Triangle	(2) Indicator	(21) Indicator hand
(3) Scale ring	(111) Datum line	(112) Datum side

Fig. 1. Mechanical Component Diagram

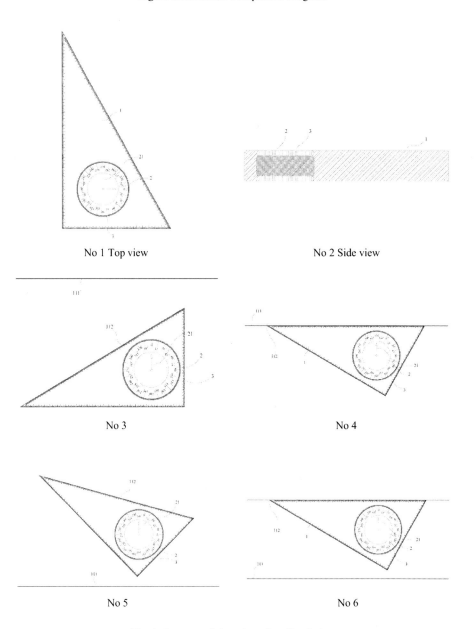

No 1 Top view   No 2 Side view

No 3   No 4

No 5   No 6

Fig. 2. Pressure-tight palette for oil painting

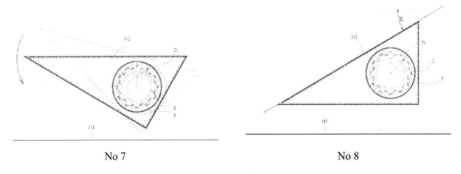

No 7   No 8

Fig. 2. (*continued*)

5 Contribution

The datum orientation triangle developed by this study helps drawing staffs to make drawings more conveniently and precisely, solving many problems with the traditional tools or hand drawing. Generally speaking, the features of this innovative product include:

(1) Conceptual Innovation

This study looked into the difficulties of traditional drawing methods and summarized the problems. By thinking beyond the frame of the traditional tools, some solution was developed. The result of the research and development is worth promoting.

(2) Energy Saving and Carbon Reduction

The innovative product developed by this study helps to make drawings more conveniently and precisely. Unnecessary manpower, resources, and money can be saved to achieve the environmental protection goal of energy saving and carbon reduction.

(3) Caring Design

The innovative product developed by this study helps drawing staffs to make drawings more conveniently and precisely, showing caring by observing details of small things in our daily lives. The contribution of this product to engineering drawing is very substantial and meaningful.

(4) Market Expansion

This study developed an innovative product by solving the inconvenience problem of the traditional drawing tools, offering drawing staffs a product with more convenient and precise drawing function. It is necessary to develop the market for this innovative product.

References

1. Wu, C.H.: Application of Object-Oriented Technology to Building Relationships among Engineering Drawings, Civil Engineering, National Taiwan University, Master dissertation (1997)
2. Chen, C.L.P., Xie, S.: Freehand Drawing System Using a Fuzzy Logic Concept. Computer-Aided Design 28(2), 77–89 (1996)

3. Pu, J., Ramani, K.: On Visual Similarity Based 2D Drawing Retrieval. Computer-Aided Design 38(3), 249–259 (2006)
4. Chen, K.Z., Feng, X.A.: Solid Model Reconstruction from Engineering Paper Drawings Using Genetic Algorithms. Computer-Aided Design 35(13), 1235–1248 (2003)
5. Weng, M.C.: Study of Engineering Drawing Management System, Department of Electrical Engineering, National Changhua University of Education, Master dissertation (2008)
6. Chen, M.Y.: Automatic Construction of 3D Solid Model from 2D Sheet Metal Drawing, Graduate Institute of Automation and Control, National Taiwan University of Science and Technology, Master dissertation (2004)
7. Varley, P.A.C., Martin, R.R., Suzuki, H.: Frontal Geometry from Sketches of Engineering Objects: Is Line Labelling Necessary? Computer-Aided Design 37(12), 1285–1307 (2005)
8. Tsai, S.Y.: Dimensioning of Engineering Drawing from Solid Model, Department of Mechanical Engineering, National Taiwan University, Master dissertation (2007)

A Distributed Certification Method for Peer-to-Peer System Based on Biological Information

Zhenhua Tan[1], Guangming Yang[1], Zhiliang Zhu[1], Wei Cheng[1],
and Guiran Chang[1,2]

[1] Software College, Northeastern University, Shenyang City, Liaoning, China
[2] Computing Center, Northeastern University, Shenyang City, Liaoning, China
tanzhenhua192@126.com, {tanzh,yanggm,zzl,
chengw}@mail.neu.edu.cn, chang@neu.edu.cn

Abstract. Peer-to-Peer network takes more and more important role in the internet life and is studied by more and more researchers. The security mechanism is the core technology for P2P service network. In order to improve P2P System's security, this paper proposed a method named P2PBioC to use P2P biological information for certification. Two kinds of nodes are defined in this paper, communication node and authenticate node, using human face information as the biological features. Algorithms and communication processes based on the two types are described in this paper.

Keywords: peer-to-peer, network security, certification, biological information.

1 Introduction

Peer-to-peer (commonly abbreviated to P2P) service network, which is self-organized and distributed, is composed of participants that make a portion of their service resources directly available to other network participants, without the need for central coordination instances [1-7], and developed very fast recently.

In the current p2p system [7-9], there exists many unsafe nodes because of the anonymity and concealment of the p2p itself. For example, some nodes just got services from the p2p system but contributed never; some nodes share evil services and some nodes destroy the p2p resources using virus and etc; even, some nodes associated as a team to commit an offence in the p2p system. Some authentication mechanisms were used to control evil nodes. The central authentication was used most universally. However, the central authentication violated the p2p reciprocity and p2p equity. Moreover, the central authentication has the inherent problem, such as exceeding load, crowding band-width, and bottle-neck for the whole p2p system.

This paper proposes a distributed method to improve P2P System's security using P2P biological information, and this method is named P2PBioC (Peer-to-Peer Biological Certification). Users who take part in P2P system should provide their biological features for certification.

S. Lin and X. Huang (Eds.): CESM 2011, Part II, CCIS 176, pp. 409–414, 2011.

2   P2PBioC Topology

P2PBioC topology is formed with bicyclic circle adapt to structured p2p overlay network. There are two kinds of node, one is communication node and one is authentication node, separately short as Comm-Node and Auth-node. The communication node (Comm-Node) is responsible for providing or getting p2p services while the auth-node responsible for the certification.

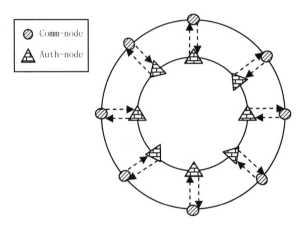

Fig. 1. This is the topology for P2PBioC. This topology is designed by bicyclic which is constructed by Comm-Node and Auth-Node. The Comm-Node and Auth-Node are one-on-one with same node-id and different port in same terminal.

3   Node Architecture

3.1   Architecture of Comm-Node

Comm-Node takes part in the communication and get or share data, such as video, mp3, files or just a text message. Figure 1 shows its structure. Generally speaking, Comm-Node includes two general components.

The first one is responsible for receiving and forwarding, just like the left part in figure 2, including five sub components.

(1) Receiver: to receive data from the upper net (or another peer).

(2) Data Sharing: to is responsible for sharing data by disc.

(3) Routing Policy: who is responsible for the routing activities, including maintaining the route table, storing policies in cache and selecting next hop.

(4) Sender: to send data to the next node.

(5) Forwarder: to forward data to the next node.

The second part is to take biological information. This paper uses human face as the biological features during to user could get a camera easily instead of a fingerprint. This part also includes five sub components.

(1) Photo taker: to take a human face as biological information from video camera for Auth-Node.

(2) Timer: to set up a frequency for photo taker.

(3) Extractor: to extract the face feature and cache the feature.

(4) Register: Use bio feature to register in the Auth-node.

(5) Detector: To detect the current bio information is whether remain the same one.

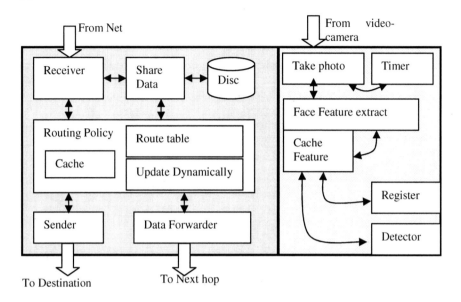

Fig. 2. This is the general structure of Comm-Node

3.2 Architecture for Auth-Node

Auth-Node is responsible for register the node that wants to join in the p2p system, and is also responsible for storing the users' biologic features. Figure 3 shows the structure of the Auth-node, including message receiver, feature getting, decision maker, credit computing, routing policy and sender.

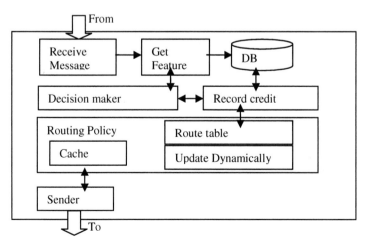

Fig. 3. This is the general structure of detecting node, including message receiver, feature getting, decision maker, credit computing, routing policy and sender

3.3 Process for Comm-Node Joining In

When the Comm-Node wants to join in such p2p system, it must provide a photo which has his face. The system in the node can extract his face feature from the photo, and then send this feature in the message to the detecting node. Each node can only submit the photo one time for register. When the Auth-node receives the register message, it gets the face feature and node identifier information from the message, and stores them to a database.

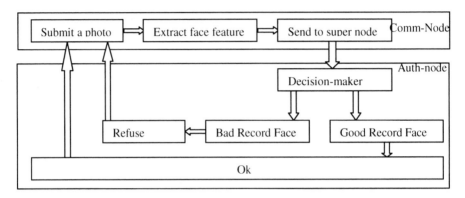

Fig. 4. This is a demonstration of the processes for a Comm-node to join in a P2PBioC system

The register will be failed when such face feature has bad record. Of course, the Auth-node then sends a message to allow this Comm-Node to join in the system for communication when the face has good record.

By the way, a node who has bad record in the Auth-node can recover its credit by some other mechanism which can be defined for special purpose. Figure 4 shows the processes.

4 Processes of P2PBioC Communication

After the register successfully, the node can use any resource in the p2p system via searching or sharing. During the communication, every user should have a video-camera, and take the user's face photo by timer. Then, the system will extract the face features, and then send the feature to the Auth-node by Auth-Node (see in figure 2). When the Auth-node receives the feature of the uses' face, it compares the feature with the existed face feature in database.

Once the current face is unmatched with the feature in database, the Auth-node will send refuse message to the user, and forbids such node's communication continued (See in figure 3, 4). At the very same time, the Auth-node will record it in the credit database with bad record of this node. Later, all of the node in the p2p system will get this message, and refuse the related message. Of course, the Auth-node can give a good credit for the user node whose feature is matched, and support its communication.

The algorithm for P2PBioC could be described as figure 5.

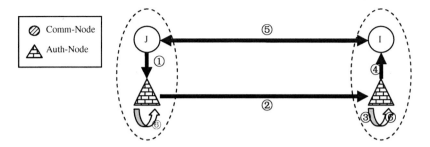

Fig. 5. This is the communication processes for P2PBioC, including six steps

Step 1: The comm-node J want to start the session to communicate with comm-node I, it sends the request message (req-msg) to the auth-node J.

Step 2: The auth-node J sends the req-msg and the comm-node J's bio feature forward to the destination auth-node I.

Step 3: After received the req-msg and Trust-Degree-Net of node I and J, the auth-node I calculates the rightness of the bio information by detector.

Step 4: The auth-node I compares its receive bio feature, the session will start between node I and J when the feature is right, go to step 5. Or else, refuse and end the communication.

Step 5: The comm-node I receives the request and begin the service for comm-node J.

Step 6: After the service, feature cache can be update according to the feedback from J.

Step 7: End.

5   Conclusions and Future Work

P2PBioC defined a bicyclic P2P Topology, the Comm-node and Auth-node one-on-one, running in separated p2p system. During the communication, P2PBioC uses human face as biological feature for certification to prevent impostor, so as to improve P2P system's security. Of course, lots of further works need to study, for example, how to ensure the bio information's accuracy.

Acknowledgement

This work is supported by the National Natural Science Foundation of China under Grant No. 61070162, No. 71071028, No. 60802023 and No. 70931001; the Specialized Research Fund for the Doctoral Program of Higher Education under Grant No. 20070145017; the Fundamental Research Funds for the Central Universities under Grant No. N090504003 and No. N090504006. This paper also supported by Intellectual Ventures Asia Pte. Ltd.

References

1. Joung, Y.J., Yang, L.W., Fang, C.T.: Keyword Search in DHT based Peer-to-Peer Networks. IEEE Journal on Selected Areas in Communications 25(1) (2007)
2. Farag, A., Ahmad, R.: Recommendation Retrieval in Reputation Assessment for Peer-to-Peer Systems. J. Electronic Notes in Theoretical Computer Science 244(1), 13–25 (2009)
3. Do, T.T., Hua, K.A., Jiang, N., Liu, F.Y.: PatchPeer: A scalable video-on-demand streaming system in hybrid wireless mobile peer-to-peer networks. J. Peer-to-Peer Networking and Applications 2(3), 182–201 (2009)
4. Ranka, S., Aluru, S., Buyya, R.: Security Issues in Cross-Organizational Peer-to-Peer Applications and Some Solutions. Communications in Computer and Information Science 40, 422–433 (2009)
5. Nakashima, T., Ono, A., Sueyoshi, T.: Performance framework for P2P overlay network. In: 2008 Fourth International Conference on Intelligent Information Hiding and Multimedia Signal Processing (IIH-MSP), Piscataway, NJ, USA, pp. 101–104 (2008)
6. Do, T.T., Hua, K.A., Lin, C.S.: ExtRange: Continuous Moving Range Queries in Mobile Peer-to-Peer Networks. In: Proceedings of the Tenth International Conference on Mobile Data Management: Systems, Services and Middleware, Taipei, Taiwan (2009)
7. Steinmetz, R., Wehrle, K.: Peer-to-Peer Systems and Applications. Springer, Heidelberg (2005)
8. Stoica, I., Morris, R., Karger, D.: Chord: A Scalable Peer-To-Peer Lookup Service for Internet Applications. In: Proceedings of the 2001 ACM Sigcomm Conference, pp. 149–160. ACM Press, USA (2001)
9. Ratnasamy, S., Francis, P., Handley, M.: A Scalable Content-Addressable Network. In: SIGCOMM, pp. 161–172. ACM Press, New York (2001)

Characters of a Sort of Finitely Supported Wavelet Bases for Sobolev Space[*]

Yongcai Hu[1,**] and Qingjiang Chen[2]

[1] Department of Fundamentals, Henan Polytechnic Institute, Nanyang 473009, China
[2] School of Science, Xi'an University or Architecture Technology, Xi'an 710055, China

Abstract. The rise of wavelet analysis in applied mathematics is due to its applications and the flexibility. Finitely Supported wavelet bases for Sobolev spaces is researched. Steming from a pair of finitely supported refinale functions with multi-scale dilation factor in space $L^2(R^3)^s$ satisfying a very mild condition, we provide a general approach for designing wavelet bases, which is the generalization of univariate wavelets in Hilbert space. An approach for designing a sort of biorthogonal vector-valued ternary wavelet wraps is presented and their biorthogonality traits are characterized by virtue of iteration method and time-frequency analysis method. The biorthogonality formulas concerning these wavelet wraps are established. Moreover, it is shown how to draw new Riesz bases of space $L^2(R^3)^s$ from these wavelet wraps. The pyramid decomposition scheme based on pseudoframes is established.

Keywords: B-spline function; Sobolev space; multi-scale dilation factor; Riesz bases; iteration method; oblique dual frames.

1 Introduction

The latest two decades or so have witnessed the development of wavelet theory. Wavelet analysis has been applied to signal processing, image compression, and so on. The main advantage of wavelets is their time-frequency localization property. Construction of wavelet bases is an important aspect of wavelet analysis, and multiresolution analysis method is one of important ways of constructing various wavelet bases. There exist many kinds of scalar scaling functions and scalar wavelet functions. Every frame(or Bessel sequence) determines an analysis operator, the range of which is important for a lumber of applications. Multiwavelets can simultaneously possess many desired properties such as short support, orthogonality, symmetry, and vanishing moments, which a single wavelet cannot possess simultaneously. This suggests that multiwavelet systems can provide perfect reconstruction, good performance at the boundaries (symmetry), and high approximation order (vanishing moments). Already they have led to exciting applications in signal analysis [1], fractals [2] and image processing [3], and so on. Vector-valued wavelets are a sort of special multiwavelets Chen [4] introduced the notion of orthogonal vector-valued wavelets.

---

[*] Foundation item: The research is supported by the Science Research Foundation of Education Department of Shaanxi Provincial Government (Grant No:11JK0468).
[**] Corresponding author.

S. Lin and X. Huang (Eds.): CESM 2011, Part II, CCIS 176, pp. 415–420, 2011.
© Springer-Verlag Berlin Heidelberg 2011

However, vector-valued wavelets and multiwavelets are different in the following sense. Pre-filtering is usually required for discrete multiwavelet transforms [5] but not necessary for discrete vector-valued transforms. Wavelet wraps, owing to their nice characteristics, have been widely applied to signal processing [6], code theory, image compression, solving integral equation and so on. Coifman and Meyer firstly introduced the notion of univariate orthogonal wavelet wraps. Yang [7] constructed a-scale orthogonal multi wavelet wraps that were more flexible in applications. It is known that the majority of information is multi-dimensional information. Shen [8] introduced multivariate orthogonal wavelets which may be used in a wider field. Thus, it is necessary to generalize the concept of multivariate wavelet wraps to the case of multivariate vector-valued wavelets. The goal of this paper is to give the definition and the construction of bioorthogonal vector-valued wavelet wraps and desing new Riesz bases of $L^2(R^3)^s$.

2   Notations and Vector-Valued Multiresolution Analysis

Frame multiresolution analysis is not the most general way to obtain frames via multi-scale techniques, but it provides us with a natural link from the classical constructions.We begin with some notations. Set $Z_+ = \{0\} \cup N$, s, $n, v \in N$ and $s, n, v \geq 2$, $Z^3 = \{(z_1, z_2, z_3): z_\sigma \in Z, \sigma = 1, 2, 3\}$, $Z_+^3 = \{\{(n_1, n_2, n_3):$ $: n_\sigma \in Z_+, \sigma = 1, 2, 3\}$. For any U, $U_1, U_2 \subset R^3$, denoting by $3U = \{3u : u \in U\}$, $U_1 + U_2 = \{x_1 + x_2 : x_1 \in U_1, x_2 \in U_2\}$, $U_1 - U_2 = \{u_1 - u_2 : u_1 \in U_1, u_2 \in U_2\}$. There exist 27 basic elements μ_0, $\mu_1, \cdots, \mu_{26}$ in Z_+^3 by finite group theory such that $Z^3 = \bigcup_{\lambda \in \Gamma_0} (\lambda + MZ^3)$; $m = \det(M)$, $(\lambda_1 + MZ^3) \bigcap (\lambda_2 + MZ^3) = \varnothing$, where $\Gamma_0 = \{\lambda_0,$ $\lambda_1, \cdots, \lambda_{26}\}$ denotes the set of all different representative elements in the quotient group $Z^3/(MZ^3)$ and λ_1, λ_2 denote two arbitrary distinct elements in Γ_0, M is a 3×3 matrix Set $\mu_0 = \underline{0}$, where $\underline{0}$ is the null of Z_+^3. Let $\Gamma = \Gamma_0 - \{\underline{0}\}$ and Γ, Γ_0 be two index sets. By $L^2(R^3)^s$, we denote the aggregate of all vector-valued functions $H(x)$, i.e., $L^2(R^3)^s := \{\Phi(t) = (\phi_1(t), \phi_2(t), \cdots, \phi_s(t))^T : \phi_l(t) \in L^2(R^3), l = 1, 2, \cdots, s\}$, where T means the transpose of a vector. Video images and digital films are examples of vector-valued functions where $\phi_l(t)$ in the above $\Phi(t)$ denotes the pixel on the l th column at the point t. For $\Phi(t) \in L^2(R^3)^s$, $\|\Phi\|$ denotes the norm of vector-valued function $\Phi(t)$, i.e., $\|\Phi\| := (\sum_{l=1}^s \int_{R^3} |\phi_l(t)|^2 dt)^{1/2}$. In the below * means the trans-pose and the complex conjugate, and its integration is defined to be

$$\int_{R^3} \Phi(t)dt = (\int_{R^3} \phi_1(t)dt, \int_{R^3} \phi_2(t)dt, \cdots\cdots, \int_{R^3} \phi_s(t)dt)^T.$$

The Fourier transform of $\Phi(t)$ is defined as $\hat{\Phi}(\omega) := \int_{R^3} \Phi(t) \cdot e^{-it \cdot \omega} dt$, where $t \cdot \omega$ denotes the inner product of real vectors t and ω. For $\Phi, \Upsilon \in L^2(R^3)^s$, their *symbol inner product* is defined by

$$[\Phi(\cdot), \Upsilon(\cdot)] := \int_{R^3} \Phi(t) \Upsilon(t)^* dt, \tag{1}$$

Definition 1. A sequence of vector-valued functions $\{\Phi_n(t)\}_{n \in Z^3} \subset U \subset L^2(R^3)^s$ is called a Riesz basis of U if it satisfies (i) for any $\Upsilon(t) \in U$, there exists a unique $s \times s$ matrix sequence $\{Q_n\}_{n \in Z^3} \in \ell^2(Z^3)^{s \times s}$ such that

$$\Upsilon(t) = \sum_{n \in Z^3} Q_n \Phi_n(t), \quad t \in R^3, \tag{2}$$

where $\ell^2(Z^3)^{3 \times 3} = \{Q : Z^3 \to C^{u \times u}, \|Q\|_2 = \sum_{l,j=1}^{v} \sum_{n \in Z^3} |q_{l,j}(n)|^2)^{\frac{1}{2}} < +\infty\}$, (ii)   there exist

two constants $0 < C_1 \le C_2 < +\infty$ such that, for any matrix sequence $\{M_n\}_{n \in Z^3}$, the

following equality follows. i.e.,

$$C_1 \|\{M_n\}\|_* \le \| \sum_{n \in Z^3} M_n \Phi_n(t) \| \le C_2 \|\{M_n\}\|_*, \tag{3}$$

Definition 2. We say that a pair of vector-valued functions $\Upsilon(t), \tilde{\Upsilon}(t) \in L^2(R^3)^s$ are bi orthogonal ones, if their translations satisfy

$$[\Upsilon(\cdot), \tilde{\Upsilon}(\cdot - k)] = \delta_{0,k} I_s, \quad k \in Z^3, \tag{4}$$

where I_s denotes the $s \times s$ identity matrix and $\delta_{0,k}$ is the Kronecker symbol.

In what follows, we introduce the notion of vector- valued multiresolution analysis and give the definition of biorthogonal vector-valued wavelets of space $L^2(R^3)^s$.

Definition 3. A vector-valued multiresolution analysis of the space $L^2(R^3)^s$ is a nested sequence of closed subspaces $\{Y_\ell\}_{\ell \in Z}$ such that (i) $Y_\ell \subset Y_{\ell+1}, \forall \ell \in Z$;   (ii) $\bigcap_{\ell \in Z} Y_\ell = \{0\}$ and $\bigcup_{\ell \in Z} Y_\ell$ is dense in $L^2(R^3)^s$, where 0 denotes an zero vector of space R^s; (iii) $\Phi(t) \in Y_\ell \Leftrightarrow \Phi(Mt) \in Y_{\ell+1}, \forall \ell \in Z$; (iv) there exists $H(t) \in Y_0$, called a vector-valued scaling function, such that its translates $H_n(t) := H(t - n)$, $n \in Z^3$ forms a Riesz basis of subspace Y_0.

Since $H(t) \in Y_0 \subset Y_1$, by Definition 3 and (4) there exists a finitely supported sequence of constant $s \times s$ matrice $\{P_n\}_{n \in Z^3} \in \ell^2(Z^3)^{s \times s}$ such that

$$H(t) = \sum_{n \in Z^3} P_n H(Mt - n). \tag{5}$$

Equation (6) is called a refinement equation. Define

$$m \cdot \mathcal{P}(\omega) = \sum_{n \in Z^3} P_n \cdot \exp\{-in \cdot \omega\}, \quad \omega \in R^3. \tag{6}$$

where $\mathcal{P}(\omega)$, which is $2\pi Z^3$ function, is called a symbol of $H(t)$. Thus, (6) becomes

$$\hat{H}(M\omega) = \mathcal{P}(\omega)\hat{H}(\omega), \quad \omega \in R^3. \tag{7}$$

Let $X_j, j \in Z$ be the direct complementary subspace of Y_j in Y_{j+1}. Assume that there exist 27 vector-valued functions $\psi_\rho(t) \in L^2(R^3)^s, \rho \in \Gamma$ such that their translations and dilations form a Riesz basis of X_j, i.e.,

$$X_j = \overline{(span\{\Psi_\rho(M^j \cdot -n) : n \in Z^3, \rho \in \Gamma\})}, \quad j \in Z. \tag{8}$$

Since $\Psi_\rho(t) \in X_0 \subset Y_1$, $\rho \in \Gamma$, there exist 26 finitely supported sequences of constant $s \times s$ matrice $\{B_n^{(\mu)}\}_{n \in Z^3}$ such that

$$\Psi_\rho(t) = \sum_{k \in Z^3} B_n^{(\rho)} H(Mt - k), \quad \rho \in \Gamma. \tag{9}$$

By implementing the Fourier transform for the both sides of equation (9), we have

$$\hat{\Psi}_\mu(M\omega) = \mathcal{B}^{(\mu)}(\omega)\hat{H}(\omega), \quad \omega \in R^3, \quad \mu \in \Gamma. \tag{10}$$

$$m \cdot \mathcal{B}^{(\mu)}(\omega) = \sum_{n \in Z^3} B_n^{(\mu)} \exp\{-in\omega\}, \quad \mu \in \Gamma. \tag{11}$$

If $H(t), H(t) \in L^2(R^3)^s$ are biorthogonal vector-valued scaling functions, then

$$[H(\cdot), \widetilde{H}(\cdot - n)] = \delta_{0,n} I_v, \quad n \in Z^3. \tag{12}$$

We say that $\Psi_\mu(t), \tilde{\Psi}_\mu(t) \in L^2(R^3)^s, \mu \in \Gamma$ are pairs of biorthogonal vector-valued wavelets associated with a pair of biorthogonal vector-valued scaling functions $H(t)$ and $\widetilde{H}(t)$, if the family $\{\Psi_\mu(t - n), n \in Z^3, \mu \in \Gamma\}$ is a Riesz basis of subspace X_0, and

$$[H(\cdot), \tilde{\Psi}_\mu(\cdot - n)] = O, \quad \mu \in \Gamma, \quad n \in Z^3. \tag{13}$$

$$[\widetilde{H}(\cdot), \Psi_\mu(\cdot - k)] = O, \quad \mu \in \Gamma, \quad k \in Z^3. \tag{14}$$

$$[\Psi_\lambda(\cdot), \tilde{\Psi}_\mu(\cdot - k)] = \delta_{\lambda,\mu} \delta_{0,k} I_s, \quad \lambda, \mu \in \Gamma, \quad k \in Z^3. \tag{15}$$

$$X_j^{(\rho)} = \overline{Span\{\Psi_\rho(M^j \cdot - n) : n \in Z^3\}}, \quad \rho \in \Gamma, \quad j \in Z.$$

Similar to (5) and (9), there exist 27 finitely supported sequences of $s \times s$ complex constant matrice $\{\widetilde{P}_k\}_{k \in Z^3}$ and $\{\tilde{B}_k^{(\mu)}\}_{k \in Z^3}$, $\{\tilde{B}_k^{(\rho)}\}_{k \in Z^3}, \rho \in \Gamma$ such that $\widetilde{H}(t)$ and $\tilde{\Psi}_\rho(t)$ satisfy the refinement equations:

$$\widetilde{H}(t) = \sum_{k \in Z^3} \widetilde{P}_k \widetilde{H}(Mt - k), \tag{16}$$

$$\tilde{\Psi}_\rho(t) = \sum_{k \in Z^3} \tilde{B}_k^{(\rho)} \widetilde{H}(Mt - k), \quad \rho \in \Gamma. \tag{17}$$

3   The Features of a Class of Biorthogonal Wavelet Packs

Frames have fascinated many researchers since they appeared. A frame for a vector space equipped with an inner product also allows each element in the space to be written as a linear combination of the elements in the frame, but linear in-dependence. Denoting by $G_0(x) = H(x), G_\mu(x) = \tilde{\Psi}_\mu(x), \tilde{G}_0(x) = \widetilde{H}(x), \tilde{G}_\mu(x) = \tilde{\Psi}_\mu(x), Q_k^{(0)} = P_k,$ $Q_k^{(\mu)} = B_k^{(\mu)}, \tilde{Q}_k^{(0)} = \widetilde{P}_k, \tilde{Q}_k^{(\mu)} = \tilde{B}_k^{(\mu)}, \mu \in \Gamma, k \in Z^3, M = 3I_s.$ For any $\alpha \in Z_+^3$ and the given vector-valued biorthogonal scaling functions $G_0(x)$ and $\tilde{G}_0(x)$, iteratively define, respectively,

$$G_\alpha(x) = G_{3\sigma+\mu}(x) = \sum_{k \in Z^3} Q_k^{(\mu)} G_\sigma(3x - k), \quad \mu \in \Gamma_0, \tag{18}$$

$$\tilde{G}_\alpha(x) = \tilde{G}_{3\sigma+\mu}(x) = \sum_{k\in Z^3} \tilde{Q}_k^{(\mu)} \tilde{G}_\sigma(3x-k), \quad \mu\in\Gamma_0. \tag{19}$$

where $\sigma\in Z_+^3$ is the unique element such that $\alpha = 3\sigma + \mu$, $\mu\in\Gamma_0$ follows.

Lemma 1 [4]. Let $F(x), \tilde{F}(x) \in L^2(R^3)^s$ Then they are biorthogonal if and only if

$$\sum_{k\in Z^3} \hat{F}(\omega+2k\pi)\hat{\tilde{F}}(\omega+2k\pi)^* = I_s. \tag{20}$$

Definition 4. We say that two families of vector-valued functions $\{G_{3\sigma+\mu}(x), \sigma\in Z_+^3, \mu\in\Gamma_0\}$ and $\{\tilde{G}_{3\sigma+\mu}(x), \sigma\in Z_+^3, \mu\in\Gamma_0\}$ are vector-valued wavelet packets with respect to a pair of biorthogonal vector-valued scaling functions $G_0(x)$ and $\tilde{G}_0(x)$, resp., where $G_{3\sigma+\mu}(x)$ and $\tilde{G}_{3\sigma+\mu}(x)$ are given by (18) and (19), respectively.

Applying the Fourier transform for the both sides of (18) and (19) yields, resp.,

$$\hat{G}_{3\sigma+\mu}(\omega) = Q^{(\mu)}(\omega/3)\hat{G}_\sigma(\omega/3), \quad \mu\in\Gamma_0, \tag{21}$$

$$\hat{\tilde{G}}_{3\sigma+\mu}(3\omega) = Q^{(\mu)}(\omega)\hat{\tilde{G}}_\sigma(\omega), \quad \mu\in\Gamma_0, \tag{22}$$

Lemma 2 [6]. Assume that $G_\mu(x)$, $\tilde{G}_\mu(x) \in L^2(R^3)^s$, $\mu\in\Gamma$ are pairs of biorthogonal vector-valued wavelets associated with a pair of biorthogonal scaling functions $G_0(x)$ and $\tilde{G}_0(x)$. Then, for $\mu,\nu\in\Gamma_0$, we have

$$\sum_{\rho\in\Gamma_0} Q^{(\mu)}((\omega+2\rho\pi)/3)\tilde{Q}^{(\nu)}((\omega+2\rho\pi)/3)^* = \delta_{\mu,\nu}I_s. \tag{23}$$

Lemma 3 [8]. Suppose $\{G_\alpha(x), \alpha\in Z_+^3\}$ and $\{\tilde{G}_\alpha(x), \alpha\in Z_+^3\}$ are wavelet packets with respect to a pair of biorthogonal vector-valued functions $G_0(x)$ and $\tilde{G}_0(x)$. Then, for $\alpha\in Z_+^3$, we have

$$[G_\alpha(\cdot), \tilde{G}_\alpha(\cdot-k)] = \delta_{0,k}I_\nu, \ k\in Z^3. \tag{24}$$

Theorem 1 [8]. Assume that $\{G_\beta(x), \beta\in Z_+^3\}$ and $\{\tilde{G}_\beta(x), \beta\in Z_+^3\}$ are vector-valued wavelet packets with respect to a pair ofbiorthogonal vector-valued functions $G_0(x)$ and $\tilde{G}_0(x)$, respectively. Then, for $\beta\in Z_+^3, \mu,\nu\in\Gamma_0$, we have

$$[G_{3\beta+\mu}(\cdot), \tilde{G}_{3\beta+\nu}(\cdot-k)] = \delta_{0,k}\delta_{\mu,\nu}I_\nu, \ k\in Z^3. \tag{25}$$

Theorem 2. If $\{G_\beta(x), \beta\in Z_+^3\}$ and $\{\tilde{G}_\beta(x), \beta\in Z_+^3\}$ are vector-valued wavelet wraps with respect to a pair of biorthogonal vector scaling functions $G_0(x)$ and $\tilde{G}_0(x)$, then for any $\alpha,\sigma\in Z_+^3$, we have

$$[G_\alpha(\cdot), \tilde{G}_\sigma(\cdot-k)] = \delta_{\alpha,\sigma}\delta_{0,k}I_\nu, \ k\in Z^3. \tag{26}$$

Proof. When $\alpha = \sigma$, (26) follows by Lemma 3. as $\alpha \neq \sigma$ and $\alpha,\sigma\in\Gamma_0$, it follows from Lemma 4 that (26) holds, too. Assuming that α is not equal to β, as well as at least one of $\{\alpha,\sigma\}$ doesn't belong to Γ_0, we rewrite α,σ as $\alpha = 3\alpha_1 + \rho_1$,

$\sigma = 3\sigma_1 + \mu_1$, where $\rho_1, \mu_1 \in \Gamma_0$. **Case 1.** If $\alpha_1 = \sigma_1$, then $\rho_1 \neq \mu_1$. (26) follows by virtue of (24), (25) as well as Lemma 1 and Lemma 2, i.e.,

$$[G_\alpha(\cdot), \tilde{G}_\sigma(\cdot - k)] = \frac{1}{(2\pi)^3} \int_{R^3} \hat{G}_{3\alpha_1 + \rho_1}(\omega) \hat{\tilde{G}}_{3\sigma_1 + \mu_1}(\omega)^* \cdot \exp\{ik \cdot \omega\} d\omega$$

$$= \frac{1}{(2\pi)^3} \int_{[0,2\pi]^3} \delta_{\rho_1, \mu_1} I_v \cdot \exp\{ik \cdot \omega\} d\omega = O.$$

Case 2. If $\alpha_1 \neq \sigma_1$, order $\alpha_1 = 3\alpha_2 + \rho_2$, $\sigma_1 = 3\sigma_2 + \mu_2$, where $\alpha_2, \sigma_2 \in Z_+^3$, and $\rho_2, \mu_2 \in \Gamma_0$. If $\alpha_2 = \sigma_2$, then $\rho_2 \neq \mu_2$. Similar to Case 1, (28) follows. As $\alpha_2 \neq \sigma_2$, order $\alpha_2 = 3\alpha_3 + \rho_3$, $\sigma_2 = 3\sigma_3 + \mu_3$, where $\alpha_3, \sigma_3 \in Z_+^3$, $\rho_3, \mu_3 \in \Gamma_0$. Thus, taki-ng finite steps (denoted by κ), we obtain $\alpha_\kappa \in \Gamma_0$, and $\rho_\kappa, \mu_\kappa \in \Gamma_0$.

$$8\pi^3 [G_\alpha(\cdot), \tilde{G}_\sigma(\cdot - k)] = \int_{R^3} \hat{G}_\alpha(\omega) \hat{\tilde{G}}_{\sigma_1}(\omega)^* \cdot e^{ik \cdot \omega} d\omega$$

$$= \int_{R^3} \hat{G}_{3\alpha_1 + \lambda_1}(\omega) \hat{\tilde{G}}_{3\beta_1 + \mu_1}(\omega)^* \cdot \exp\{ik \cdot \omega\} d\omega =$$

$$= \int_{[0,2 \cdot 3^\kappa \pi]^3} \{ \prod_{l=1}^\kappa \mathcal{Q}^{(\rho_l)}(\omega/3^l) \} \cdot O \cdot \{ \prod_{l=1}^\kappa \tilde{\mathcal{Q}}^{(\mu_l)}(\omega/3^l) \}^* \cdot \exp\{-ik \cdot \omega\} d\omega = O.$$

Therefore, for any $\alpha, \sigma \in Z_+^3$, result (26) is established.

Theorem 3 [7]. Let $\phi(x), \tilde{\phi}(x), \psi_l(x)$ and $\tilde{\psi}_l(x), l \in J$ be functions in $L^2(R^3)$ Assume that conditions in Theorem 1 are satisfied. Then, for any function $f(x) \in L^2(R^3)$, and any integer n,

$$\sum_{u \in Z^3} \langle f, \tilde{\phi}_{n,u} \rangle \phi_{n,u}(x) = \sum_{t=1}^7 \sum_{s=-\infty}^{n-1} \sum_{u \in Z^3} \langle f, \tilde{\psi}_{t,s,u} \rangle \psi_{t,s,u}(x). \tag{27}$$

References

1. Telesca, L., et al.: Multiresolution wavelet analysis of earthquakes. Chaos, Solitons & Fractals 22(3), 741–748 (2004)
2. Iovane, G., Giordano, P.: Wavelet and multiresolution analysis:Nature of ε^∞ Cantorian space-time. Chaos, Solitons & Fractals 32(4), 896–910 (2007)
3. Zhang, N., Wu, X.: Lossless Compression of Color Mosaic Images. IEEE Trans. Image Processing 15(16), 1379–1388 (2006)
4. Chen, Q., et al.: A study on compactly supported orthogo-nal vector-valued wavelets and wavelet packets. Chaos, Solitons & Fractals 31(4), 1024–1034 (2007)
5. Shen, Z.: Nontensor product wavelet packets in $L_2(R^5)$. SIAM Math. Anal. 26(4), 1061–1074 (1995)
6. Chen, Q., Cheng, Z., Feng, X.: Multivariate Biorthogonal Multiwavelet packets. Mathematica Applicata 18(3), 358–364 (2005) (in Chinese)
7. Li, S., et al.: A Theory of Geeneralized Multiresolution Structure and Pseudoframes of Translates. J. Fourier Anal. Appl. 6(1), 23–40 (2001)
8. Chen, Q., Zhao, Y., Gao, H.: Existence and characterization of orthogonal multiple vector-valued wavelets with three-scale. Chaos, Solitons & Fractals 42(4), 2484–2493 (2009)

The Novel Characteristics of Two-Directional Multi-scale Binary Small-Wave Wraps with Short Support

Dong Liao[*] and Guodong Xu

School of Math. and Statistics, Nanyng Normal University, Nanyang 473061
{hjk123zas,zxs123hjk @126.com

Abstract. The rise of wavelet analysis in applied mathematics is due to its applications and the flexibility. In this article, the notion of biorthogonal two-directional compactly supported bivariate wavelet wraps with poly-scale is developed. Their properties is investigated by algebra theory, means of time-frequency analysis method and, operator theory. The direct decomposition relationship is provided. In the final, new Riesz bases of space $L^2(R^2)$ are constructed from these wavelet wraps. Moreover, it is shown how to draw new Riesz bases of space $L^2(R^2, C^v)$ from these wavelet wraps.

Keywords: two-directional; bivariate; small-wave wraps; Riesz bases; iteration method; time-frequency analysis representation.

1 Introduction

At present, image interpolation algorithms based on wavelet transform are mainly based on multiresolution analysis of the wavelet. raditionally, short-time Fourier Transform and Gabor Transform were used for harmonic studies of nonstationary power system waveforms which are basically Fourier Transform-based methods. To overcome the limitations in these existing methods, wavelet transform based algorithm has been developed to estimate the limitations the frequency and time information of a harmonic signal. Multiwavelets can simultaneously possess many desired properties such as short support, orthogonality, symmetry, and vanishing moments, which a sin-gle wavelet cannot possess simultaneously. Already they have led to exciting applications in signal analysis [1], fractals [2] and image processing [3], and so on. Vector-valued wavelets are a sort of special multiwavelets Chen [4] introduced the notion of orthogonal vector-valued wavelets. However, vector-valued wavelets and multiwavelets are different in the following sense. Pre-filtering is usually required for discrete multiwavelet transforms [5] but not necessary for discrete vector-valued transforms. Wavelet wraps, owing to their nice characteristics, have been widely applied to signal processing [6], code theory, image compression, solving integralequation and so on. Coifman and Meyer firstly introduced the notion of univariate orthogonal wavelet wraps. Yang [7] constructed a-scale orthogonal multiwavelet wraps that were more flexible in applications. It is known that the majority of information is multidimensional information. Shen [8] introduced multivariate orthogonal wavelets

---

[*] Corresponding author.

S. Lin and X. Huang (Eds.): CESM 2011, Part II, CCIS 176, pp. 421–427, 2011.

which may be used in a wider field. Thus, it is necessary to generalize the concept of multivariate wavelet wraps to the case of multivariate vector-valued wavelets. The go al of this paper is to give the definition and the construction of bioorthogonal vector-va valued wavelet wraps and designt new Riesz bases of $L^2(R^2,C^v)$.

2 The Preliminaries on Vector-Valued Function Space

Let Z and Z_+ stand for all integers and nonnegative integers, respectively. The multiresolution analysis is one of the main approaches in the construction of wavelets. Let us introduce two-direction multiresolution analysis and two-direction wavelets.

Definition 1. We say that $f(x) \in L^2(R^2)$ is a two-direction refinable function if $f(x)$ satisfies the following two-direction refinable equation:

$$f(x) = \sum_{v \in Z^2} b_v^+ f(5x - v) + \sum_{v \in Z^2} b_v^- f(u - 5x), \qquad (1)$$

where the sequences $\{b_v^+\}_{v \in Z^2} \in l^2(Z^2)$ and $\{b_v^-\}_{v \in Z^2} \in l^2(Z^2)$ are also called positive-direction mask and negative-direction mask, respectively. If all negative-direction mask are equal to 0, then two-direction refinable equation (2) become two-scale refinable equation (1). By taking the Fourier transform for the both sides of (2), we have

$$\hat{f}(\omega) = b^+ \left(e^{-i\omega/5}\right) \hat{f}(\omega/5) + b^- \left(e^{-i\omega/5}\right) \overline{\hat{f}(\omega/5)}, \qquad (2)$$

where $b^+(z) = (1/25) \sum_{v \in Z^2} b_v^+ z^u$, $z = e^{-i\omega/5}$ is called positive-direction mask symbol, and $4b^-(z) = \sum_{v \in Z^2} b_v^- z^u$ is called negative-direction mask symbol. In order to investigate the existence of solutions of the two-direction refinable equation (2), we rewrite the two-direction refinable equation (2) as

$$f(-x) = \sum_{v \in Z^2} b_v^+ f(-5x - v) + \sum_{v \in Z^2} b_v^- f(v + 5x), \qquad (3)$$

By taking the Fourier transform for the both sides of (4), we have

$$\overline{\hat{f}(\omega)} = b^+(e^{-i\omega/5}) \overline{\hat{f}(\omega/5)} + b^-(e^{-i\omega/5}) \hat{f}(\omega/5), \qquad (4)$$

Form the refinement equation (3) and the refinement equation (5), we get that

$$\hat{F}(\omega) = \begin{bmatrix} \overline{\hat{\phi}(\omega)} \\ \hat{\phi}(\omega) \end{bmatrix} = \begin{bmatrix} b^+ \left(e^{-i\omega/5}\right) & b^- \left(e^{-i\omega/5}\right) \\ b^+ \left(e^{-i\omega/5}\right) & b^- \left(e^{-i\omega/5}\right) \end{bmatrix} \begin{bmatrix} \overline{\hat{f}\left(e^{-i\omega/5}\right)} \\ \hat{f}\left(e^{-i\omega/5}\right) \end{bmatrix} \qquad (5)$$

By virtue of the positive-direction mask $\{b_v^+\}_{v \in Z}$ and the negative-direction mask $\{b_v^-\}_{v \in Z}$, we construct the following matrix equation:

$$F(x) = \begin{bmatrix} f(-x) \\ f(x) \end{bmatrix} = \sum_{u \in Z^2} \begin{bmatrix} b_{-u}^- & b_{-u}^+ \\ b_u^+ & b_u^- \end{bmatrix} F(5x - u) \qquad (6)$$

Definition 2. A pair of two-direction function $f(x),, \widetilde{f}(x) \in L^2(R^2)$ are biorthogonal ones, if their translate satisfy

$$< f(x), \widetilde{f}(x-k) > = \delta_{0,k}, \quad k \in Z^2, \tag{7}$$

$$< f(x), \widetilde{f}(n-x) > = 0, \quad n \in Z^2, \tag{8}$$

where $\delta_{0,k}$ is the Kronecker symbol. Define a sequence $V_j \in L^2(R^2)$ by

$$S_j = clos_{L^2(R^2)} \langle 5^{j/2} f(5^j \cdot -k), 5^{j/2} f(l-5^j \cdot) : k,l \in Z \rangle, \quad j \in Z.$$

where "clos" denote the closure of a space by a function $f(x)$.

A two-direction multiresolution analysis is a nested sequence $\{S_j\}_{j \in Z}$ generated by $f(t)$, if it satisfies: (i) $\cdots \subset S_{-1} \subset S_0 \subset S_1 \subset \cdots$; (ii) $\bigcap_{j \in Z} S_j = \{0\}$ $\bigcup_{j \in Z} S_j$ is dense in $L^2(R^2)$, where 0 is the zero vector of $L^2(R^2)$; (iii) $h(x) \in S_0$ if and only if $h(5^j x) \in V_j$, $j \in Z$; (iv)There exists $f(x) \in V_0$ Such that the sequence $\{f(x-k), f(n-x) : k,n \in Z\}$ is a Riesz basis of S_0.

Four two-direction functions $\psi_t(x) (t \in \Lambda \triangleq \{1,2,3,4\})$ are called two-direction-al wavelets with scale 5 associated with $f(t)$, if the family $\{\psi_t(x-k), \psi_t(n-x) : k,n \in Z^2, t=1,2,3,4\}$ forms a Riesz basis of W_j, where $V_{j+1} = V_j \oplus W_j$, $j \in Z$, where $\oplus$ denotes the direct sum. Then $\psi_t(x)$ satisfies the following equation:

$$\psi_t(x) = \sum_{v \in Z^2} q_{v,t}^+ f(5x-v) + \sum_{v \in Z^2} q_{v,t}^- f(v-5x), \quad t \in \Lambda \tag{9}$$

Implementing the Fourier transform for the both sides of (10) gives

$$\widehat{f}_t(\omega) = q_t^+ (e^{-i\omega/5}) \widehat{f}(\omega/5) + q_t^- (e^{-i\omega/5}) \overline{\widehat{f}(\omega/5)}, \quad t \in \Lambda. \tag{10}$$

Similarly, there exist two seq.s $\{\tilde{b}_u^+\}_{u \in Z^2}, \{\tilde{b}_u^-\}_{u \in Z^2} \in l^2(Z^2)$, such that

$$\widetilde{f}(x) = \sum_{u \in Z^2} \tilde{b}_u^+ \widetilde{f}(5x-u) + \sum_{u \in Z^2} \tilde{b}_u^- \widetilde{f}(u-5x). \tag{11}$$

The Fourier transforms of refinable equation (12) becomes

$$\widehat{\widetilde{f}}(\omega) = \widetilde{b_k^+} (e^{-i\omega/5}) \widetilde{f}(\omega/5) + \widetilde{b_k^-} (e^{-i\omega/5}) \overline{\widetilde{f}(\omega/5)}. \tag{12}$$

Similarly, there also exist two sequences $\{\tilde{q}_{u,t}^+\}, \{\tilde{q}_{u,t}^-\} \in l^2(Z)$ so that

$$\widetilde{\psi}_t(x) = \sum_{u \in Z^2} \tilde{q}_{u,t}^+ \tilde{\phi}(5x-u) + \sum_{u \in Z^2} \tilde{q}_{u,t}^- \tilde{\phi}(u-5x). \tag{13}$$

By taking the Fourier transforms for (14), for $\iota \in \Lambda$, we have

$$\widehat{\widetilde{\psi}}_\iota(5\omega) = \widetilde{q}_\iota^+\left(e^{-i\omega}\right)\widehat{\widetilde{f}}(\omega) + q_\iota^-\left(e^{-i\omega}\right)\widehat{\widetilde{f}}(\omega). \tag{14}$$

We say that $\psi_\iota(t), \widetilde{\psi}_\iota(t) \in L^2(R)$ are pairs of biorthogonal two-direction wave-lets associated with a pair of biorthogonal two-direction scaling functions $f(x)$, $\widetilde{f}(x) \in L^2(R^2)$, if the family $\{\psi_\iota(x-n), \psi_\iota(n-x): n \in Z^2\}$ is a Riesz basis of subspace W_0, and they satisfy the following equations:

$$\left\langle f(x), \widetilde{\psi}_\iota(x-u)\right\rangle = \left\langle f(x), \widetilde{\psi}_\iota(u-x)\right\rangle = 0, \ \iota \in \Lambda, u \in Z^2, \tag{15}$$

$$\left\langle \widetilde{f}(x), \psi_\iota(x-u)\right\rangle = \left\langle \widetilde{f}(x), \psi_\iota(u-x)\right\rangle = 0, \quad \iota \in \Lambda, \ u \in Z^2, \tag{16}$$

$$\left\langle \widetilde{\psi}_\iota(x), \psi_v(x-u)\right\rangle = \delta_{u,0}\delta_{v,\iota}, \ u \in Z^2, \ \iota, v \in \Lambda, \tag{17}$$

$$\left\langle \psi_\iota(x), \widetilde{\psi}_v(u-x)\right\rangle = \delta_{u,0}\delta_{\iota,v}, \ u \in Z^2, \ \iota, v \in \Lambda. \tag{18}$$

By replace t by $-t$ in the refinement equation (10), we get

$$\psi_\iota(-x) = \sum_{v \in Z^2} q_{v,\iota}^+ f(-5x-u) + \sum_{v \in Z} q_{v,\iota}^- f(v+5x). \tag{19}$$

The refinement equ. (10) and (20) lead to the following relation formula

$$\Psi_\iota(x) = \begin{bmatrix} \psi_\iota(-x) \\ \psi_\iota(x) \end{bmatrix} = \sum_{k \in Z^2} \begin{bmatrix} q_{-k,\iota}^- & q_{-k,\iota}^+ \\ q_{k,\iota}^+ & q_{k,\iota}^- \end{bmatrix} F(5x-k), \quad \iota \in \Lambda. \tag{20}$$

The frequency fiele form of the relation formula (18) is

$$\widehat{\Psi}_\iota(\omega) = \begin{bmatrix} \widehat{\psi}_\iota(\omega) \\ \widehat{\psi}_\iota(\omega) \end{bmatrix} = \begin{bmatrix} q_\iota^-\left(e^{-i\omega/5}\right) & q_\iota^+\left(e^{-i\omega/5}\right) \\ q_\iota^+\left(e^{-i\omega/5}\right) & q_\iota^-\left(e^{-i\omega/5}\right) \end{bmatrix} \begin{bmatrix} \widehat{f}(\omega/5) \\ \widehat{f}(\omega/5) \end{bmatrix}, \quad \iota \in \Lambda. \tag{21}$$

Similarly for $\widetilde{\psi}_\iota(t)$ $(\iota \in \Lambda)$ and two mask symbols $\{\widetilde{q}_{v,\iota}^+\}, \{\widetilde{q}_{v,\iota}^-\}, \in l^2(Z^2)$ we have

$$\widetilde{\Psi}_\iota(x) = \begin{bmatrix} \widetilde{\psi}_\iota(-x) \\ \widetilde{\psi}_\iota(x) \end{bmatrix} = \sum_{v \in Z^2} \begin{bmatrix} \widetilde{q}_{-v,\iota}^- & \widetilde{q}_{-v,\iota}^+ \\ \widetilde{q}_{v,\iota}^+ & \widetilde{q}_{v,\iota}^- \end{bmatrix} F(5x-v), \quad \iota \in \Lambda. \tag{22}$$

By taking the fourier transforms for the both sides (23), it follows that

$$\widehat{\widetilde{\Psi}}_\iota(\omega) = \begin{bmatrix} \widehat{\widetilde{\psi}}_\iota(\omega) \\ \widehat{\widetilde{\psi}}_\iota(\omega) \end{bmatrix} = \begin{bmatrix} \widetilde{q}_\iota^-\left(e^{-i\omega/5}\right) & \widetilde{q}_\iota^+\left(e^{-i\omega/5}\right) \\ \widetilde{q}_\iota^+\left(e^{-i\omega/5}\right) & \widetilde{q}_\iota^-\left(e^{-i\omega/5}\right) \end{bmatrix} \begin{bmatrix} \widehat{\widetilde{f}}(\omega/5) \\ \widehat{\widetilde{f}}(\omega/5) \end{bmatrix}, \quad \iota \in \Lambda. \tag{23}$$

By $L^2(R^2, C^v)$, we denote the aggregate of all vector- valued functions $H(x)$, i.e., $L^2(R^2, C^v) := \{H(x) = (h_1(x), h_2(x), \cdots, h_v(x))^T : h_l(x) \in L^2(R^2), l = 1, 2, \cdots, v\}$, where T means the transpose of a vector. Video images and digital films are examples of vector-valued functions where $h_l(x)$ in the above $H(x)$ denotes the pixel on the l th column at the point x. For $H(x) \in L^2(R^2, C^v)$, $\|H\|$ denotes the norm of vector-valued function $H(x)$, i.e., $\|H\| := (\sum_{l=1}^{v} \int_{R^2} |h_l(x)|^2 dx)^{1/2}$. In the below * means the transpose and the complex conjugate, and its integration is defined to be

$$\int_{R^2} H(x)dx = (\int_{R^2} h_1(x)dx, \int_{R^2} h_2(x)dx, \cdots\cdots, \int_{R^2} h_v(x)dx)^T.$$

The Fourier transform of $H(x)$ is defined as $\hat{H}(\gamma) := \int_{R^2} H(x) \cdot e^{-ix\cdot\gamma} dx$, where $x \cdot \gamma$ denotes the inner product of real vectors x and γ. For $F, H \in L^2(R^2, C^v)$, their *symbol in ner product* is defined by

$$[F(\cdot), H(\cdot)] := \int_{R^2} F(x)H(x)^* dx, \tag{24}$$

Since $F(x) \in Y_0 \subset Y_1$, by Definition 3 and (4) there exists a finitely supported sequence of constant $v \times v$ matrice $\{\Omega_n\}_{n \in Z^2} \in \ell^2(Z^2)^{v \times v}$ such that

$$F(x) = \sum_{n \in Z^2} \Omega_n F(Mx - n). \tag{25}$$

Equation (6) is called a refinement equation. Define

$$m \cdot \Omega(\gamma) = \sum_{n \in Z^2} \Omega_n \cdot \exp\{-in \cdot \gamma\}, \quad \gamma \in R^2. \tag{26}$$

where $\Omega(\gamma)$, which is $2\pi Z^2$ fun., is called a symbol of $F(x)$. Thus, (26) becomes

$$\hat{F}(M\gamma) = \Omega(\gamma)\hat{F}(\gamma), \quad \gamma \in R^2. \tag{27}$$

Let $X_{j,} j \in Z$ be the direct complementary subspace of Y_j in Y_{j+1}. Assume that there exist 63 vector-valued functions $\psi_\mu(x) \in L^2(R^2, C^v), \mu \in \Gamma$ such that their translations and dilations form a Riesz basis of X_j, i.e.,

$$X_j = \overline{(span\{\Psi_\mu(M^j \cdot -n) : n \in Z^3, \mu \in \Gamma\})}, \quad j \in Z. \tag{28}$$

Since $\Psi_\mu(x) \in X_0 \subset Y_1$, $\mu \in \Gamma$, there exist 63 finitely supported sequences of constant $v \times v$ matrice $\{B_n^{(\mu)}\}_{n \in Z^4}$ such that

$$\Psi_\mu(x) = \sum_{n \in Z^2} B_n^{(\mu)} F(Mx - n), \quad \mu \in \Gamma. \tag{29}$$

We say that $\Psi_\mu(x), \tilde{\Psi}_\mu(x) \in L^2(R^3, C^v), \mu \in \Gamma$ are pairs of biorthogonal vector wavelets associated with a pairof biorthogonal vector scaling functions $F(x)$ and $\tilde{F}(x)$, if the family $\{\Psi_\mu(x - n), n \in Z^3, \mu \in \Gamma\}$ is a Riesz basis of subspace X_0, and

$$[F(\cdot), \tilde{\Psi}_\mu(\cdot - n)] = [\tilde{F}(\cdot), \Psi_\mu(\cdot - n)] = O, \quad \mu \in \Gamma, \quad n \in Z^2, \tag{30}$$

$$[\widetilde{\Psi}_\lambda(\cdot), \Psi_\mu(\cdot - n)] = \delta_{\lambda,\mu}\delta_{0,n}, \quad \lambda, \mu \in \Gamma, \quad n \in Z^2. \tag{31}$$

$$X_j^{(\mu)} = \overline{Span\{\Psi_\mu(M^j \cdot -n) : n \in Z^2\}}, \mu \in \Gamma, j \in Z. \tag{32}$$

Similar to (5) and (9), there exist 64 finitely supported sequences of $v \times v$ complex constant matrice $\{\widetilde{\Omega}_k\}_{k \in Z^2}$ and $\{\tilde{B}_k^{(\mu)}\}_{k \in Z^2}$, $\mu \in \Gamma$ such that $\tilde{F}(x)$ and $\widetilde{\Psi}_\mu(x)$ satisfy the refinement equations:

$$\tilde{F}(x) = \sum_{k \in Z^2} \widetilde{\Omega}_k \tilde{F}(Mx - k) \tag{33}$$

$$\widetilde{\Psi}_\mu(x) = \sum_{n \in Z^2} \tilde{B}_n^{(\mu)} \widetilde{F}(Mx - n), \quad \mu \in \Gamma. \tag{34}$$

3   The Biorthogonality Features of a Sort of Wavelet Wraps

Denoting by $G_0(x) = F(x), G_\mu(x) = \Psi_\mu(x), \tilde{G}_0(x) = F(x), \tilde{G}_\mu(x) = \Psi_\mu(x), Q_k^{(0)} = \Omega_k,$ $Q_k^{(\mu)} = B_k^{(\mu)}, \tilde{Q}_k^{(0)} = \widetilde{\Omega}_k, \tilde{Q}_k^{(\mu)} = \tilde{B}_k^{(\mu)}, \mu \in \Gamma, k \in Z^3, M = 4I_v$. For any $\alpha \in Z_+^3$ and the given vector biorthogonal scaling functions $G_0(x)$ and $\tilde{G}_0(x)$, iteratively define,

$$G_\alpha(x) = G_{4\sigma+\mu}(x) = \sum_{k \in Z^3} Q_k^{(\mu)} G_\sigma(4x - k), \quad \mu \in \Gamma_0, \tag{35}$$

$$\tilde{G}_\alpha(x) = \tilde{G}_{4\sigma+\mu}(x) = \sum_{k \in Z^3} \tilde{Q}_k^{(\mu)} \tilde{G}_\sigma(4x - k), \quad \mu \in \Gamma_0. \tag{36}$$

where $\sigma \in Z_+^2$ is the unique element such that $\alpha = 4\sigma + \mu, \mu \in \Gamma_0$ follows.

Definition 3. We say that two families of vector-valued functions $\{G_{4\sigma+\mu}(x), \sigma \in Z_+^3, \mu \in \Gamma_0\}$ and $\{\tilde{G}_{4\sigma+\mu}(x), \sigma \in Z_+^3, \mu \in \Gamma_0\}$ are vector-valued wavelet packets with respect to a pair of biorthogonal vector-valued scaling functions $G_0(x)$ and $\tilde{G}_0(x)$, resp., where $G_{4\sigma+\mu}(x)$ and $\tilde{G}_{4\sigma+\mu}(x)$ are given by (35) and (36), respectively.

Theorem 1 [8]. Assume that $\{G_\beta(x), \beta \in Z_+^2\}$ and $\{\tilde{G}_\beta(x), \beta \in Z_+^2\}$ are vector-valued wavelet packets with respect to a pair ofbiorthogonal vector-valued functions $G_0(x)$ and $\tilde{G}_0(x)$, respectively. Then, for $\beta \in Z_+^2, \mu, v \in \Gamma_0$, we have

$$[G_{4\beta+\mu}(\cdot), \tilde{G}_{4\beta+v}(\cdot - k)] = \delta_{0,k}\delta_{\mu,v}I_v, \ k \in Z^3. \tag{37}$$

Theorem 2 [8]. If $\{G_\beta(x), \beta \in Z_+^2\}$ and $\{\tilde{G}_\beta(x), \beta \in Z_+^2\}$ are vector-valued wavelet wraps with respect to a pair of biorthogonal vector scaling functions $G_0(x)$ and $\tilde{G}_0(x)$, then for any $\alpha, \sigma \in Z_+^2$, we have

$$[G_\alpha(\cdot), \tilde{G}_\sigma(\cdot - k)] = \delta_{\alpha,\sigma}\delta_{0,k}I_v, \ k \in Z^2. \tag{38}$$

References

1. Telesca, L., et al.: Multiresolution wavelet analysis of earthquakes. Chaos, Solitons & Fractals 22(3), 741–748 (2004)
2. Iovane, G., Giordano, P.: Wavelet and multiresolution analysis: Nature of ε^∞. Cantorian space-time. Chaos, Solitons & Fractals 32(4), 896–910 (2007)
3. Zhang, N., Wu, X.: Lossless Compression of Color Mosaic Images. IEEE Trans. Image Processing 15(16), 1379–1388 (2006)
4. Chen, Q., et al.: A study on compactly supported orthogonal vector-valued wavelets and wavelet packets. Chaos, Solitons & Fractals 31(4), 1024–1034 (2007)
5. Chen, Q., Huo, A.: The research of a class of biorthogonal compactly supported vector valued wavelets. Chaos, Solitons & Fractals 41(2), 951–961 (2009)
6. Chen, Q., Cheng, Z., Feng, X.: Multivariate Biorthogonal Multiwavelet packets. Mathematica Applicata 18(3), 358–364 (2005) (in Chinese)
7. Li, S., et al.: A Theory of Geeneralized Multiresolution Structure and Pseudoframes of Translates. J. Fourier Anal. Appl. 6(1), 23–40 (2001)
8. Shen, Z.: Nontensor product wavelet packets in $L_2(\mathrm{R}^5)$. SIAM Math. Anal. 26(4), 1061–1074 (1995)

Algorithms and Methods for Emotional Mandarin Speech Synthesis

HuaPeng Zhang

Luoyang Institute of Technology,
Luoyang, China
lygzzhp@163.com

Abstract. Attempts to add emotion effects to synthesized speech have existed for several decades now. Several prototypes and fully operational systems have been built based on different synthesis techniques for different languages. This survey first gives an overview of techniques used in synthesizing emotional English or Japanese. Second, the difference lies in Mandarin emotional speech synthesis is stated. The difficulties and how to address them are analyzed.

Keywords: speech synthesis, Mandarin, emotion.

1 Introduction

With the intelligibility of synthetic speech approaching that of human speech, the need for increased naturalness becomes more palpable.

In the past several decades, there has been growing interest in emotional speech synthesis. The goal of speech synthesis systems is to convert ordinary text messages into intelligible and natural sounding synthetic speech. Such systems are often referred to as text-to-speech (or TTS) systems, and their general structure is illustrated in Fig. 1.

Vocal communication of emotion is biologically adaptive for socially living species. When listening to speech, we rely upon a range of cues upon which to base our inference as to the communicative intent of others. To interpret the meaning of speech, how something is said may be as important as what is actually said [1].

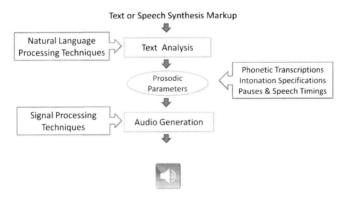

Fig. 1. Block diagram of TTS system

S. Lin and X. Huang (Eds.): CESM 2011, Part II, CCIS 176, pp. 428–433, 2011.

This observation has been motivating attempts to incorporate the expression of emotions into synthetic speech for several decades. Synthetic speech nowadays is mostly intelligible; in some cases, it also sounds so natural that it is difficult to distinguish it from human speech. However, the flexibility and appropriate rendering of expressivity in a synthetic voice is still out of reach: making a voice sound happy or subdued, friendly or empathic, authoritative or un-certain are beyond what can be done today. Still, there is an interesting variety of approaches that adopted in the studies concerned with the expression of emotion.

The first part of this paper introduced the methods and techniques frequently used. Compared to languages like English and Japanese, fewer studies were done on Mandarin. So the second part of this survey focuses on the possibilities of adapting existing techniques applying to mandarin speech synthesis. In the third part, the difficulties in the task are listed. In the fourth part, our method is described, the results are presented. In the last part, conclusion is reached.

2 Existing Approaches and Techniques

Work on emotional expressivity in synthetic speech goes back to the end of the 1980s. As technology evolved, different technologies have been used, each with their strengths and weaknesses. The frequently used approaches and techniques are listed below:

2.1 Rule-Based Formant Synthesis

Rule-based formant synthesis is the oldest speech synthesis technique, predicts the acoustic realization of speech directly using a set of rules, usually designed carefully by experts. As these rules tend not to capture the complexity of natural human speech, the synthetic speech sounds unnatural and "robot like".

Table 1. Examples of Successful Explicit Prosody Rules for Emotion Expression in Synthetic speech [3]

Emotion Study Rec. Rate	Parameter Settings
Joy Burkhardt & Sendlmeier 2000 81%	F0 mean: +50% F0 range: +100% Tempo:+30% Other: wave pitch contour model: main stressed syllables are raised (+100%)
Sadness Cahn 1990 91%	F0 mean: -1 F0 range: -5 Tempo: -10 Loudness: -5 Other: stress frequency :+1 Precision articulation: -5

This type of method creates the acoustic speech data entirely through rules on the acoustic correlates of the various speech sounds. The types of parameter modeled vary greatly between different studies, but all studies agree on the importance of global prosodic settings, such as F_0 level and range, speech tempo and eventually loudness. Some other studies modeled the steepness of the F_0 contour during rises and falls and the number and duration of pauses.

This method seems quite explicit. By its very nature, formant synthesis allows for control over a broad range of parameters, including glottal as well as supraglottal aspects of speech production. But it's really hard to design a set of rules that is suitable for various emotion and sentence types.

2.2 Unit Selection

In the mid-1990s, with the development in power and storage capacity of computers and the efficient searching techniques, the concept of concatenative synthesis was developed further: instead of using just one example of each diphone recorded with a flat pitch, several versions of a speech unit are recorded in natural speech. Through a selection method, the most suitable chain of such units is determined for any given target sentence, hence the name unit selection synthesis. This process is outlined in Fig. 2 [17], which shows how the method dynamically finds the best path through the unit-selection network corresponding to the sounds for the word "two". If suitable units are available in the recordings, no or very little signal processing is needed, resulting synthesized speech can sound highly natural, sometimes difficult to distinguish from natural human speech.

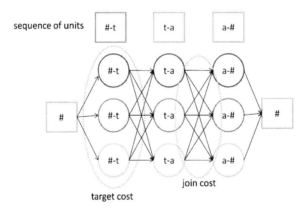

Fig. 2. An example of unit selection speech synthesis

The current trends of this method are: 1) Add symbolic targets (speaking style, cost matrix) for the unit selection process. 2) Apply PSOLA or other signal modification techniques on unit selection output to modify pitch and duration according to emotional prosody rules.

The weakness lies in unit selection method is that only the speaking style recorded in the database can be generated, and little or no control is available over prosody and voice quality. Some research is dealing with voice quality parameters modification for emotional speech synthesis, these algorithms may be useful in that synthesis of expressive speech has demonstrated that convincing natural sounding results are impossible to obtain without dealing with voice quality parameters [5].

3 Special Aspects of Mandarin Speech Synthesis

There are several characters of Mandarin that have strong impactions on emotional speech synthesis process.

3.1 Tonal Aspects

A very special important feature of Mandarin Chinese is the tonal aspects, since Chinese is a tonal language, i.e., the tones in Mandarin Chinese have lexical meaning. There are basically four lexical tones and one neutral tone in Mandarin Chinese, as illustrated in Fig. 4. Although each of four lexical tone types possessed a typical F_0 contour, syllable F_0 contours in continuous speech vary highly and can deviate dramatically from their canonical forms. Many factors have been shown to have major influences on syllable F_0 contours: neighboring tone types (tone sandhi), stress, intonation, semantics, emotion, and so on. These variations make high-quality tone component generation not an easy task.

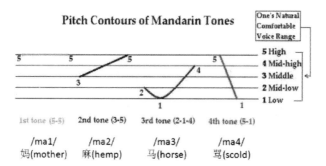

Fig. 4. Four tones in Mandarin

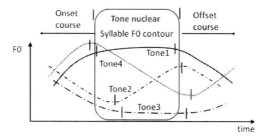

Fig. 5. Tone nuclei for the four lexical tones

There have been several successful methods that modeled the tones in Mandarin. Fig. 5 illustrates tone nucleus model, which only models the stable middle part of a tonal syllable. When it comes to emotional mandarin speech synthesis, Ross, Edmondson and Seibert found that the presence of tone in Chinese significantly inhibits the unrestricted manipulation of acoustic measures of F_0 contour (F_0 slope, F_0 variation and delta F_0) that are involved in vocal emotion expression.

3.2 Structure of Mandarin Speech

As pointed out in 1978 by Mr. Chao Yuan-ren, the F_0 contour is composed of three elements [7], 1. A syllable's tone, 2. The variety of tone in continuous utterance, and 3. The movement caused by mood, so-called intonation of the sentence. Tones are riding on the intonation in a way so-called "algebraic sum of big wave plus small wave". Fujisaki model is consistent with this classic view in that it is a superposition of tone (accent) components on phrase (intonation) components [2]. The tone components should enable listeners to distinguish which syllable is said. The phrase components, which could be deemed as the low frequency part of the F_0, may enable the listeners to determine the basic emotion expressed.

In HMM-based method, both segmental and prosodic features of speech are processed together in a frame-by-frame manner, and, therefore, it has an advantage that synchronization of both features is kept automatically. Although various styles such as attitudes and emotions were realized with rather high quality by the method, frame-by-frame processing of prosodic features, however, includes some problems. It sometimes causes sudden F_0 undulations (not observable in human speech) especially when the training data are limited. Prosodic features cover a wider time span than segmental features, and should be treated differently.

From this consideration, a corpus-based method of synthesizing F_0 contours in the framework of the generation process model (F_0 model) and realized speech synthesis in reading and dialogue styles with various emotions for Japanese language [2]. There have also some published work that model F_0 contour of emotional Mandarin sentences with Fujisaki model. [14] used the framework in [15] to extract tone and phrase commands from F_0 contour. With modification of tone command part of the original model, F_0 contours could be achieved. [16] also modified the tone command part to eight tone patterns in order to make it suitable for Mandarin tones representation. The phrase components were first extracted from recorded speech (read in normal way), and then modified to each emotion type based on rules.

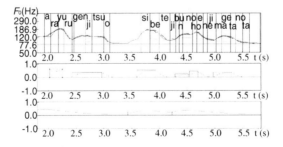

Fig. 6. Example of F_0 contour of Japanese utterance

4 Conclusion

This paper presents a brief overview of emotional speech synthesis. The basic conceptions are demonstrated; current existing methods are illustrated and compared. The current challenge of emotion speech synthesis methods is how to combine naturalness and control flexibility. The special aspects of Mandarin and the possible model are also introduced. The difficulties and challenges are discussed with possible solution.

References

1. Mitchell, R.L., Elliott, R., Barry, M., Cruttenden, A., Woodruff, P.W.: The neural response to emotional prosody, as revealed by functional magnetic resonance imaging. Neuropsychologia 41, 1410–1421 (2003)
2. Hirose, K., Sun, Q., Minematsu, N.: Synthesis of F_0 contours for Mandarin speech by superposing corpus-generated tone contours on rule-generated phrase components. In: Proc. Int. Conf. on Speech Analysis, Synthesis, and Recognition (SASR), Plenary Talk (2008-2009)
3. Schröder, M.: Emotional Speech Synthesis: A Review. In: Proc. Eurospeech 2001, ISCA, Bonn, Germany, pp. 561–564 (2001)
4. Sproat, R., Olive, J.: Text to Speech Synthesis. AT&T Technical Journal 74(2), 35–44 (1995)
5. d' Alessandro, C., Doval, B.: Voice Quality Modification for Emotional Speech Synthesis. In: EUROSPEECH 2003, Geneva, Switzerland, pp. 1653–1656 (2003)
6. Hirose, K., Sato, K., Asano, Y., Minematsu, N.: Synthesis of F_0 contours using generation process model parameters predicted from unlabeled corpora: Application to emotional speech synthesis. Speech Communication 46(3-4), 385–404 (2005)
7. Chao, Y.-R.: Problems of Language. Commercial Press of China (1980)
8. Cowie, R.: Describing the Emotional States Expressed in Speech. In: ISCA Workshop on Speech & Emotion, Northern Ireland 2000, pp. 11–18 (2000)
9. Anscombe, E., Geach, P. (eds.): Descartes_ Philosophical Writings. The Open University, Nelson (1970)
10. Scherer, K.R.: Appraisal theory. In: Dalgleish, T., Power, M. (eds.) Handbook of Cognition and Emotion, pp. 637–663. John Wiley, New York (1999)
11. Cornelius, R.R.: The Science of Emotion. Research and Tradition in the Psychology of Emotion. Prentice-Hall, Upper Saddle River (1996)
12. Cowie, R., Douglas-Cowie, E., Romano, A.: Changing emotional tone in dialogue and its prosodic correlates. In: Proc. ESCA Workshop on Dialogue and Prosody, Eindhoven, The Netherlands, pp. 41–46 (1999)
13. Liscombe, J., Venditti, J., Hirschberg, J.: Classifying subject ratings of emotional speech using acoustic features. In: Proceedings of Eurospeech (2003)
14. Su, Z.L., Wang, Z.F.: An approach to affective-tone modeling for Mandarin. Affective Computing and Intelligent Interaction, 390–396 (2005)

Energy Savings Potential for Buildings in Hot Summer and Cold Winter Zone

Tianhong Wang and Jian Yao

Faculty of Architectural, Civil Engineering and Environment,
Ningbo University, Ningbo, China
nagtive@163.com

Abstract. energy savings potential for buildings in different climate zones differs greatly. This paper carried out computer simulations to determine the energy loss breakdown of a typical building to give solutions to reduction of energy consumption. Results show that energy savings potential of buildings in hot summer and cold winter zone is big and it can be achieved through the improvement of solar shading performance and ventilation.

Keywords: Energy saving; Potential; buildings.

1 Introduction

Hot summer and cold winter zone is an area in which temperature is extremely high in summer with great solar radiation and low in winter. A typical city in this area is Ningbo, and its monthly average temperature is illustrated in Fig.1. Buildings in this area consume a large amount of building energy [1]. The main reason for this high consumption is the poor performance of building envelopeee, so energy loss through building envelopeee can be reduced by good insulation. Although many studies have been done on building energy efficiency [2-5], they did not focus on the energy savings potential in this area. This paper focuses on the energy savings potential of buildings obtained from the breakdown of energy loss from building envelopeee through computer simulation and gives suggestions on the energy saving measures on the basis of the comparison of the energy performance of building envelopeee at different climate zones. A case study of Ningbo was demonstrated in the following context.

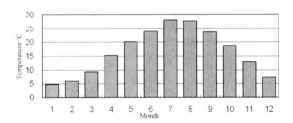

Fig. 1. Monthly average temperature in Ningbo

S. Lin and X. Huang (Eds.): CESM 2011, Part II, CCIS 176, pp. 434–437, 2011.

2 Methodology

A typical six-floor building in Ningbo with the total area of 3544.56m^2 was adopted as a base model in the analysis. The height of each floor is 2.8m, and the area of each household is about 100m^2. The thermal design for envelope of this model is set to the typical building at 1980s in hot summer and cold winter region, in cold zone and in severe cold zone in order to compare the energy savings potential of buildings at different zones. Simulations were carried out with the program DeST-h. Fig. 2 shows the base residential building. Fig.3 illustrates the five climate zones in China.

Fig. 2. The base residential building

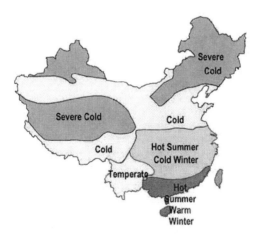

Fig. 3. The five climate zones in China

3 Results and Discussion

Figures 3-5 show the energy loss breakdown of the base model in hot summer and cold winter zone, cold zone and severe cold zone, respectively. It can be seen that each part of building envelopeeee changed a lot from a zone to another, especially for wall, window and ventilation and infiltration. The colder the place is the greater energy loss from wall. The contrast behavior occurs for window and ventilation and infiltration. This means that wall insulation should be designed appropriately, which is not similar to cold zone and severe cold zone. Energy loss from window and ventilation and infiltration indicates that solar radiation increase cooling energy consumption and mechanical ventilation caused energy consumption is the major part. Therefore, energy savings potential in hot summer and cold winter is really different from other climate zones and is concentrated on windows and its ventilation. Thus energy saving measures should be considered on enhancing solar shading and strength the ventilation.

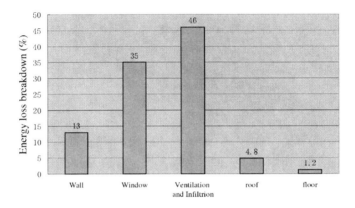

Fig. 3. Energy loss breakdown of the base model in hot summer and cold winter zone

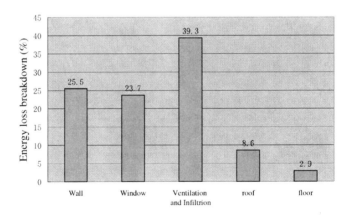

Fig. 4. Energy loss breakdown of the base model in cold zone

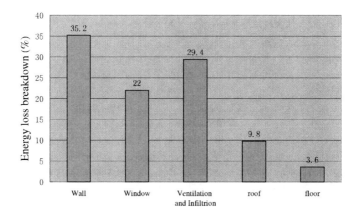

Fig. 5. Energy loss breakdown of the base model in severe cold zone

4 Conclusions

In this paper computer simulations based analysis of energy loss breakdown of a typical building was performed to give solutions. The results show that the energy savings potential of buildings in hot summer and cold winter zone is big and it can be achieved through the improvement of solar shading performance and ventilation.

References

1. Li, Z.Y., Zhang, C.: Prediction and Analysis of the Energy Saving Tendency in China's Building. Economist 3, 20–22 (2010)
2. Yao, J., Xu, J.: Effects of different shading devices on building energy saving in hot summer and cold winter zone. In: 2010 International Conference on Mechanic Automation and Control Engineering, MACE 2010, Wuhan, China, pp. 5017–5020 (2010)
3. Tzempelikos, A., Athienitis, A.K.: The impact of shading design and control on building cooling and lighting demand. Sol. Energy 81, 369–382 (2007)
4. Zhou, Y., Ding, Y., Yao, J.: Preferable Rebuilding Energy Efficiency Measures of Existing Residential Building in Ningbo. Journal of Ningbo University (Natural Science & Engineering Edition) 22, 285–287 (2009)
5. Yao, Yuan, Z.: Study on Residential Buildings with Energy Saving by 65% in Ningbo. Journal of Ningbo University (Natural Science & Engineering Edition) 23, 84–87 (2010)

Research on Initial Trust in a B2C E-Vendor

Hanyang Luo[1,2]

[1] Shenzhen Graduate School, Harbin Institute of Technology, Shenzhen 518055, China
[2] College of Management, Shenzhen University, Shenzhen 518060, China
hanyang@szu.edu.cn

Abstract. One of the most important reasons why many web users do not shop online is the lack of trust in e-vendors. This research proposes a model to examine how new consumers develop their initial trust in a B2C e-vendor after their first experience with the e-vendor's website. The model is empirically tested using an online questionnaire survey. The research results indicate that new consumers' perceived e-vendor reputation and perceived privacy protection and safety assurance significantly positively affect their initial trusting belief in the e-vendor. Disposition to trust, perceived usefulness and ease of use of the e-vendor's website are also significant antecedents of initial trust, which further extraordinarily significantly positively affect consumers' online shopping intention.

Keywords: Initial trust, online consumer, e-business, B2C, e-vendor, perceived reputation, privacy protection.

1 Introduction

According to China Internet Network Information Center's survey, till December 31, 2010, the number of web users in China has reached 457 million. However, only about 35% of those users make purchases online [1]. There are many reasons, such as traditional consumption concept, counterfeit and shoddy products, inefficient logistics system, increasingly frequent network security incidents, and especially, consumers' lack of trust in online companies. Trust in the online vendor is one of the critical factors of success in electronic commerce [2]. In B2C e-business, consumers routinely engage with online vendors with whom they have little or no prior interaction. This exposes consumers to a risk of opportunistic vendor behavior, which has great negative influence on consumers' confidence [3]. Usually, the development of consumers' trust depends on direct physical experiences with the vendor's brick-and-mortar store and its salespeople [4]. How do online consumers develop their trust in e-vendors? It's necessary to study the promotion and cultivation of online consumers' trust.

2 Literature Review

Adapting the definition of trust from Mayer et al. [5] to the context of B2C e-business, we define trust as the belief that an online consumer has in an Internet vendor and is willing to engage in an Internet shopping transaction, even with the possibility of loss, based on the expectation that the vendor will engage in generally

S. Lin and X. Huang (Eds.): CESM 2011, Part II, CCIS 176, pp. 438–444, 2011.
© Springer-Verlag Berlin Heidelberg 2011

acceptable practices, and will be able to deliver the promised products or services. Trust is generally based on the beliefs regarding the ability, integrity, and benevolence of the vendor [5, 6]. In B2C e-business, ability concerns the skills and competencies of the vendor, related to the consumers. Integrity implies that the vendor follows moral and ethical principles that are acceptable to the consumers. Benevolence concerns the degree to which the vendor has goodwill towards the consumers [5, 7].

McKnight et al. defined initial trust as trust in an unfamiliar party [6]. In the context of B2C e-business, when the customer has no prior interaction with an e-vendor, he/she cannot develop trust based on direct experience with or first-hand knowledge of the e-vendor. Instead, the customer will depend on other sources, such as second-hand information, contextual factors, or personal intuition to make trust inferences.

McKnight et al. tested empirically the factors that may influence initial trust in an online company. They found that perceived company reputation and perceived website quality both had a significant positive relationship with initial trust with the company [8]. Marios Koufaris and William Hampton-Sosa proposed a model to explain how new customers develop initial trust in a web-based company after their first visit. Their research results indicated that perceived company reputation, willingness to customize products and services, perceived web site usefulness, ease of use, and security control could significantly affect initial trust [7]. Xin Li et al.'s research results indicated that subjective norm and the cognitive–reputation, calculative, and organizational situational normality base factors significantly influence initial trusting beliefs and other downstream trust constructs [9].

3 Conceptual Model and Theoretical Hypotheses

3.1 Conceptual Model

Based on the review of extant literature and semi-structure interviews, we proposed an integrated conceptual model of consumers' initial trust in a B2C e-vendor (see Fig. 1).

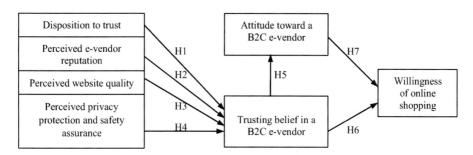

Fig. 1. An integrated model of initial trust in a B2C e-vendor

3.2 Theoretical Hypotheses

Disposition to trust. Defined as a general willingness based on extended socialization to depend on others, disposition to trust had a direct effect on the formation of trust [5, 10]. The effect of trust propensity on trust formation can be especially significant when the trusting party, e.g. an online customer, has no prior information about the trusted party, e.g. the web-based company [5]. This is indeed the case in our study where the online customers are new to the e-vendor and its B2C website and have no prior experience with them. Therefore, we hypothesize that:

H1: Consumers' disposition to trust will positively affect their trusting belief in a B2C e-vendor.

Perceived e-vendor reputation. In markets where experience is not readily available, trust can be built through institution-based mechanisms such as a reputation system. Imitating word-of-mouth communication using online means, a reputation system accumulates and disseminates information about vendors' past trading behavior [11]. In this paper, we define perceived e-vendor reputation as the degree in which people believe in the e-vendor's honesty and concern towards its customers [4]. The positive relationship between reputation and initial trust has been shown in the online environment in McKnight et al.'s study [8]. Based on positive feedback and reputation information, customers should be able to form trusting beliefs in the B2C e-vendor. Therefore, we hypothesize that:

H2: Consumers' perceived e-vendor reputation will positively affect their trusting belief in a B2C e-vendor.

Perceived website quality. McKnight, Choudhury and Kacmar suggested that perceived website quality positively influences both trusting beliefs and trusting intentions because using the website provides the first experiential taste of the e-vendor's presence, solidifying initial impressions [6]. If an online consumer perceives that the B2C website is of high quality, he/she will assume that the e-vendor has positive attributes and will form trusting belief and trusting intentions. Therefore, we hypothesize that:

H3: Consumers' perceived website quality will positively affect their trusting belief in a B2C e-vendor.

Perceived privacy protection and safety assurance. It has been mentioned previously that first-time online consumers have greater concerns about the security and privacy of online transactions than their experienced counterparts [7]. When consumers evaluate the trustworthiness of an online organization, privacy and security are taken as crucial criteria in the assessment [12]. Privacy and security concerns have been pointed out as a significant factor for consumers to trust or distrust e-commerce [13]. An experiment by Pan and Zinkhan even found that the mere presence of a privacy policy would be sufficient to persuade online consumers that an e-vendor can be trusted and would be expected to respect and protect their personal data [14]. Therefore, we hypothesize that:

H4: Consumers' perceived privacy protection and safety assurance will positively affect their trusting belief in a B2C e-vendor.

Trusting belief. Based on TRA(Theory of Reasoned Action) [15], beliefs directly affect attitude. In the context of our study, we suggest that online customers' trusting beliefs in a B2C e-vendor affect their attitudes toward it. Jarvenpaa et al. also demonstrated, through their empirical study, that trust could influence one's attitudes toward shopping at an online store [16]. Therefore, we suppose:

H5: Consumers' trusting belief in a B2C e-vendor will positively affect their attitude toward it.

Consistent with McKnight et al., we define trusting intention as the willingness of a potential online consumer to expose him or herself to the possibility of loss and transact with the e-vendor. In our study context, the trusting intention is willingness to purchase in a B2C website. McKnight et al.'s model suggests that trusting beliefs directly affect trusting intentions [6]. Jarvenpaa et al. also found that trust in online stores could directly affect customers' willingness to buy [16]. Therefore, we suppose:

H6: Consumers' trusting belief in a B2C e-vendor will positively affect their willingness to go shopping in the e-vendor's website.

Attitude. According to TRA [15], favorable attitudes toward an act or event would lead to a positive intention to perform the act or adopt the event. In the online context, Jarvenpaa et al. found that a favorable attitude toward shopping at an Internet store led to a greater willingness to buy from that store [16]. Therefore, we suppose:

H7: Consumers' favorable attitude toward B2C e-vendor will positively affect their willingness to go shopping in the e-vendor's website.

4 Research Methodology

In order to test our model, we conducted a field study and collected data via an online questionnaire. We developed multi-item scales for each variable, most used five-point Likert-type interval scales ranging from strongly disagree (1) to strongly agree (5). Then, we asked subjects to browse a B2C website they had never visited before and searched for a particular product. Subsequently, they answered a series of questions regarding their experience on that site. The primary subjects were undergraduate and graduate students from Shenzhen University. There are other respondents such as school teachers, company employees and governmental personnel and so on. At last, due to some reasons such as incomplete data, 3130 observations could be used in data analysis.

5 Result

5.1 Measurement Model

The reliability and validity of measurement for each construct was tested by using exploratory and confirmatory factor analysis based on the 3130 samples.

Exploratory factor analysis. A principal component analysis with varimax rotation was used to examine measures. The results of the initial PCA showed that the items for the attitude scale loaded on the same factor as those for the willingness scale. We combined the two scales into a new one measuring the integrated construct named online shopping intention. On the other hand, the items for the perceived website quality scale loaded on two different factors, thus we separated the construct perceived website quality into two constructs named perceived usefulness and perceived ease of use. The resulting scales were then evaluated for reliability using Cronbach's a . All had acceptable reliability (a > 0.70).

Confirmatory factor analysis. Confirmatory factor analysis was performed with LISREL 8.70. The fit of the overall measurement model was estimated by various indices. RMSEA showed the discrepancy between the proposed model and the population covariance matrix, to be 0.054, which was lower than the recommended cut-off of 0.08. All other indices (CFI, NFI, IFI, GFI) exceeded the commonly acceptance levels (0.90), demonstrating that the measurement model exhibited a fairly good fit with the data.

5.2 Measurement Model

We examine the path coefficients of the structural model. This involved estimating the path coefficients and R^2 value. Path coefficients indicated the strengths of the relationships between the independent and dependent variables, whereas the R^2 value was a measure of the predictive power of a model for the dependent variables. Fig. 2 shows the structural model.

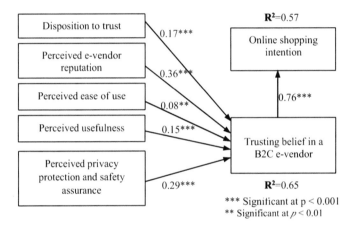

Fig. 2. Structural model

As shown in Fig.2, the path coefficients respectively from trust disposition, perceived e-vendor reputation, perceived usefulness, perceived privacy protection and safety assurance, to trusting belief in a B2C e-vendor, are very significant at the $P < 0.001$ level, the path coefficient from perceived ease of use to trusting belief is significant at the $P < 0.01$ level. Therefore, the data indicate support for H1–H4. But we were unable to directly test H5-H7, because we had combined the two constructs-- attitude toward a B2C e-vendor and willingness of online shopping into a new integrated one named online shopping intention. The path coefficient from trusting belief in a B2C e-vendor to online shopping intention is the most significant at the $P < 0.001$ level, which indirectly support our hypotheses H5-H7.

6 Discussion

The most important antecedent of initial trust was new customers' perceived e-vendor reputation. This is consistent with prior researches in online trust [6, 7]. If new online consumers believe that an e-vendor has a good reputation, they are inclined to trust it despite the lack of more tangible and physical signs.

Another very important antecedent of initial trust in our model is perceived privacy protection and safety assurance. New customers with no prior experience with an e-vendor are likely to be very concerned with the transactions safety and privacy protection. In fact, many web users still don't go shopping online because of fears of the leakage of private information and the occurrence of plenty of security incidents. Thus, believing a B2C website is secure can increase new customers' trust in the e-vendor.

Perceived usefulness and ease of use of a B2C website were also significant antecedents of initial trust in the e-vendor though with smaller path coefficients than other antecedents. New online customers indeed regard the website as a representation of the e-vendor itself. Thus, we suppose that new consumers' perceptions about a B2C website directly affect their perceptions about the e-vendor itself.

Accordant with TRA, our research results indicate that new online consumers' trusting belief in a B2C vendor has an extraordinary strong positive effect on their attitude toward and willingness of online shopping.

There are some limitations in our research. The first limitation is the representative nature of this study. Because trust is intensive and may evolve in e-marketplace, our study faced a limitation of not being able to capture its temporal aspect. The second limitation concerns the measures and generalization. The findings of this study may only reasonably be claimed to generalize to B2C e-business domain. We should be very prudent to apply it more broadly. As for the third limitation, we combined the attitude and willingness constructs into a new one named online shopping intention, whose rationality await further research.

Our research just examined new consumers' initial trust in a B2C e-vendor. We did not explore how their initial trust develops over time through repeated experiences with the web-based company. Therefore, there is an obvious need for future longitudinal research to examine the temporal nature of customer trust.

References

1. China Internet Network Information Center, http://www.cnnic.net.cn
2. Torkzadeh, G., Dhillon, G.: Measuring factors that influence the success of Internet commerce. Information Systems Research 13(2), 187–204 (2002)
3. Luo, H., Lin, X., Wang, S.: Research on Trust in C2C E-marketplace. In: Proceedings of the 2010 International Conference on Management and Service Science, pp. 1–4. IEEE Press, Piscataway (2010)
4. Doney, P.M., Cannon, J.P.: An examination of the nature of trust in buyer–seller relationships. Journal of Marketing 61, 5–51 (1997)
5. Mayer, R.C., Davis, J.H., Schoorman, F.D.: An integrative model of organizational trust. Academy of Management Review 20(3), 709–734 (1995)
6. McKnight, D.H., Choudhury, V., Kacmar, C.: Developing and validating trust measures for e-commerce: an integrative typology. Information Systems Research 13(3), 334–359 (2002)
7. Koufaris, M., Hampton-Sosa, W.: The development of initial trust in an online company by new customers. Information & Management 41(3), 377–397 (2004)

8. McKnight, D.H., Choudhury, V., Kacmar, C.: The impact of initial consumer trust on Intentions to transact with a web site: a trust building model. Journal of Strategic Information Systems 11(3/4), 297–323 (2002)
9. Li, X., Hess, T.J., Valacich, S.J.: Why do we trust new technology? A study of initial trust formation with organizational information systems. The Journal of Strategic Information Systems 17(1), 39–71 (2008)
10. McKnight, D.H., Chervany, N.L.: What trust means in Ecommerce customer relationships: an interdisciplinary conceptual typology. International Journal of Electronic Commerce 6(2), 35–59 (2001/2002)
11. Dellarocas, C.: The digitization of word of mouth: Promise and challenges of online feedback mechanisms. Management Science 49(10), 1407–1424 (2003)
12. Aiken, K., Boush, D.: Trustmarks, objective-source ratings, and implied investments in advertising: Investigating online trust and the context-specific nature of internet signals. Journal of the Academy of Marketing Science 34(3), 308–323 (2006)
13. Hoffman, D.L., Novak, T.P., Peralta, M.: Building consumer trust online. Commun. ACM 42(4), 80–85 (1999)
14. Pan, Y., Zinkhan, G.M.: Exploring the impact of online privacy disclosures on consumer trust. Journal of Retailing 82(4), 331–338 (2006)
15. Fishbein, M., Ajzen, I.: Belief, Attitude, Intention and Behavior: An Introduction to Theory and Research. Addison-Wesley, Reading (1975)
16. Jarvenpaa, S.L., Tractinsky, N., Vitale, M.: Consumer trust in an Internet store. Information Technology and Management 1, 45–72 (2000)

Prediction of Protein O-Glycosylation Sites by Kernel Principal Component Analysis and Artificial Neural Network

Xue-mei Yang

College of Mathematics and Information Science
Xianyang Normal University
712000, Xianyang, China
xmyang412@gmail.com

Abstract. O-glycosylation is one of the main types of the mammalian protein glycosylation, it occurs on the particular site of serine and threonine. It's important to predict the O-glycosylation site. In this paper, we proposed a new method of combining kernel principal component analysis(KPCA) and artificial neural network(ANN) to predict the O-glycosylation site. The samples for experiment are encoded by the sparse coding with window size $w=21$. We first extracted the features of the original data by kernel principal component analysis, and then used artificial neural network to classify the test samples into two classes(positive and negative). The results of experiments show that the proposed method is more effective and accurate than PCA+ANN. The prediction accuracy is about 88.5%.

Keywords: prediction, glycosylation, protein, KPCA, ANN.

1 Introduction

Glycosylation is the most common post-translation modification of protein in eukaryotic cells, and has important functions in secretion, antigenicity, and metabolism of glycoproteins. There are four types of glycosylation: N-linked glycosylation to the amide nitrogen of asparagines side chains, O-linked glycosylation to the hydroxyl of serine and threonine side chains, C-linked glycosylation to the tryptophan side chains and GPI. Here we only focus on O-linked glycosylation protein sequence. In fact, not all serine or threonine residue are glycosylated and about 10%-30% protein can't be glycosylated. There are many factors which affect this process. So it's important to predict the O-glycosylation sites.

Many computational methods based on artificial neural networks and support vector machines [1-3] have been developed for prediction of O-glycosylation sites. The prediction accuracy can be achieved more than 70%. Yukiko N. et al. focused on the distribution of the glycosylation sites, and treated the crowded and the isolated glycosylation separately[4], they found the different glycosylation mechanisms and different statistics for two groups .Yong-zi Chen[5] used a new protein bioinformatics tool, CKSAAP_OGlySite, for prediction under the composition of k-spaced amino acid pairs (CKSAAP) based encoding scheme, with the assistance of Support Vector

S. Lin and X. Huang (Eds.): CESM 2011, Part II, CCIS 176, pp. 445–450, 2011.

Machine (SVM). His method yielded a higher accuracy of 83.1% and 81.4% in predicting O-glycosylated S and T sites, respectively.

In our previous work, we used the nonlinear methods of KPCA[6] and kernel fisher discriminant analysis (Kfisher) [7] to predict the O-glycosylation sites, and obtained good performance.

In this paper, we propoesd a new method of KPCA +ANN to predict the O-glycosylation site in protein sequence. We first extracted the features of the original data by kernel principal component analysis, and then used artificial neural network(ANN)[8] to classify the test samples into two classes(positive and negative).

2   Protein Sequence Data and Encoding

The protein sequence data used in this research is searched from glycosylation database Uniprot (v8.0) [9]. We selected only 99 mammalian protein entries, each entry contains some serine and threonine residue sites which are annotated experimentally as being glycosylated, together with other serine and threonine residue sites which have no such annotations. We call the former a positive site(positive S or positive T), while the latter a negative site(negative S or negative T). Each selected protein entry (sequence) is truncated by a window (window size: w) into several subsequences with S or T residues at the center.

The protein sequence(exclude S or T at the center)with a length of $w-1$ are used for analysis. There are many methods for protein sequence coding, such as sparse coding, 5-letter coding, hydropathy coding and physical properties based coding. In this paper, we use the sparse coding scheme for representation of the protein sequence. In sparse coding, 21-binary sequence is used to code one site of amino acid or vacancy, for example, the site of amino acid I is coded as 100000000000000000000, the site of amino acid V is coded as 010000000000000000000. Thus the total length of coded sequence or dimension of sample vector is $(w-1) *21$.

We randomly choose 100 samples from each class for training, and 50 samples from each class for testing.

3   Kernel Principal Component Analysis and Artificial Neural Network for Prediction

The prediction can be viewed as a 2-class (positive and negative) classification problem. We first construct a feature space of protein sequence by using KPCA, and then project the test protein sequence into the feature space, at last, we classify the test samples into two class by using ANN.

3.1   Kernel Principal Component Analysis (KPCA)

Kernel principal component analysis (KPCA) is the application of PCA in a kernel-defined feature space making use of dual representation. The input data are first projected into a high-dimension feature space by using a nonlinear projection, then the principal component analysis is done in this feature space.

We use $\phi(\mathbf{x}_k)$ to denote the projection of input data $\mathbf{x}_k$, and they are supposed to satisfy the following

$$\sum_{k=1}^{M} \phi(\mathbf{x}_k) = 0 \tag{1}$$

Then the covariance matrix $\mathbf{C}$ of the projected training samples is

$$\mathbf{C} = \frac{1}{M} \sum_{j=1}^{M} \phi(\mathbf{x}_j)\phi(\mathbf{x}_j)^T \tag{2}$$

The eigenvector $\mathbf{V}$ of $\mathbf{C}$ satisfy

$$\lambda\mathbf{V} = \mathbf{C}\mathbf{V} \tag{3}$$

From the reproducing kernel theory, we know that $\mathbf{V}$ must be in the space spanned by $\phi(\mathbf{x}_1),\cdots,\phi(\mathbf{x}_M)$, that is to say

$$\mathbf{V} = \sum_{i=1}^{M} \alpha_i \phi(\mathbf{x}_i) \tag{4}$$

Here α_i is constant. Let $\mathbf{K}$ be a $M*M$ matrix

$$\mathbf{K}_{ij} = \phi(\mathbf{x}_i)^T \phi(\mathbf{x}_j) \tag{5}$$

$\mathbf{K}$ is called kernel matrix, take (2)(4)(5) into (3), we have

$$\mathbf{K}\alpha = M\lambda\alpha \tag{6}$$

Thus, the problem of finding the eigenvector $\mathbf{V}$ of (3) is equal to the problem of finding the eigenvector α of (6). From (6) we know that kernel matrix $\mathbf{K}$ is symmetric and semi-definite matrix with nonnegative eigenvectors. By solving (6), we can obtain nonzero eigenvalues λ_i and the corresponding eigenvectors α^j satisfying

$$(\alpha^j, \alpha^j) = 1 \tag{7}$$

Here $j = 1,\cdots,M',(M' \leq M)$. From (4) we can obtain $\mathbf{V}_j$, let $\mathbf{x}$ be the training sample, then the projection of $\mathbf{x}$ under $\mathbf{V}_j$ is

$$(\mathbf{V}_j)^T \phi(\mathbf{x}) = \sum_{j=1}^{M} \alpha_i^j \phi(\mathbf{x}_i)^T \phi(\mathbf{x}) = \sum_{j=1}^{M} \alpha_i^j \mathrm{K}(\mathbf{x}_i, \mathbf{x}) \tag{8}$$

We need only to know the representation of $\mathrm{K}(\mathbf{x}_i, \mathbf{x})$, $\mathrm{K}(\mathbf{x}_i, \mathbf{x})$ is called kernel function.

If (1) is not satisfied, we need to adjust the projection

$$\tilde{\phi}(\mathbf{x}_i) = \phi(\mathbf{x}_i) - \frac{1}{M}\sum_{j=1}^{M}\phi(\mathbf{x}_j)$$

$$\tilde{\mathbf{K}}_{ij} = (\tilde{\phi}(\mathbf{x}_i)\cdot\tilde{\phi}(\mathbf{x}_j))$$

$$= \mathbf{K}_{ij} - \frac{1}{M}\sum_{p=1}^{M}\mathbf{K}_{ip} - \frac{1}{M}\sum_{q=1}^{M}\mathbf{K}_{qj} + \frac{1}{M^2}\sum_{p,q=1}^{M}\mathbf{K}_{pq}$$

So we have

$$\tilde{\mathbf{K}} = \mathbf{K} - \mathbf{I}_M\mathbf{K} - \mathbf{K}\mathbf{I}_M + \mathbf{I}_M\mathbf{K}\mathbf{I}_M \qquad (9)$$

Here $\mathbf{I}_M$ is a $(M*M)$ matrix

$$(\mathbf{I}_M)_{ij} = \frac{1}{M} \qquad (10)$$

The choice of kernel function must be subject to the Mercer's theorem. Usually we use the following kernel function: (1) linear kernel function, $K(\mathbf{x}_i,\mathbf{x}) = \langle\mathbf{x},\mathbf{x}_i\rangle$; (2)quadratic kernel function, $K(\mathbf{x}_i,\mathbf{x}) = \langle\mathbf{x}\cdot\mathbf{x}_i\rangle(\langle\mathbf{x}\cdot\mathbf{x}_i\rangle+1)$; (3) polynomial kernel function, $K(\mathbf{x}_i,\mathbf{x}) = [\langle\mathbf{x},\mathbf{x}_i\rangle + c]^d$; (4)sigmoid kernel function,

$$K(\mathbf{x}_i,\mathbf{x}) = \tanh[v*\langle\mathbf{x},\mathbf{x}_i\rangle + c]\ ; (5)\ \text{RBF}, K(\mathbf{x}_i,\mathbf{x}) = \exp(-\frac{\|\mathbf{x}_i - \mathbf{x}\|^2}{2\sigma^2})$$

3.2 Artificial Neural Network(ANN)

In our method, we used a one-hidden-layer artificial neural network as a classifier for prediction. The input data is the projection of the protein sequence(the kernel principal components of original data), and the output is 1(means the input sample is positive or glycosylated) or 0(means the input sample is negative or not glycosylated). The number of hidden units can be determined by the following formula

$$n = \sqrt{M'+1} + a \qquad (11)$$

Here, n is the number of hidden units, M' is the number of input units, a is a constant in 1~10. The transfer function of the hidden unit and output units is the following function

$$f(x) = \frac{1}{1+e^{-\beta x}} \qquad (12)$$

The neural network is trained by momentum back propagation (MOBP) algorithm:

$$\Delta\mathbf{w}(k+1) = \eta\Delta\mathbf{w}(k) + \alpha(1-\eta)\frac{\partial\mathbf{E}(k)}{\partial\mathbf{w}(k)} \qquad (13)$$

$$\mathbf{w}(k+1) = \mathbf{w}(k) + \Delta\mathbf{w}(k+1)$$

Here, $\mathbf{w}(k)$ is the connect-weight or bias vector of the kth iteration, $\dfrac{\partial E(k)}{\partial \mathbf{w}(k)}$ is the gradient vector of output error to the connect-weight or bias vector in the kth iteration, α is the learning rate, and η is the momentum factor.

4 Predictions and Validations

We experimented with window size w=21 by using PCA+ANN and KPCA+ANN. The dimension of original data is 21*(w-1)=420, the total number of training samples M=400, so the dimension of kernel space is 400, since the accumulated variance(eigenvalue) of the top 150 kernel principal components is more than 85%, so we took $M' = 150$, namely we extracted the first 150 kernel principal components in feature space for prediction, and 5 kinds of kernel functions are used for projection. When using ANN for prediction, α =0.01~0.05, η =0.1~0.9, β =0.1~0.9, we tested 200 test samples, the results of experiment are shown in Fig.1 and Table1.

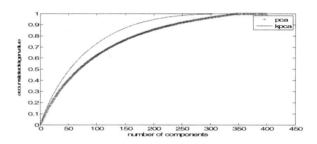

Fig. 1. The accumulated eigenvalue curve

Table 1. Prediction results by PCA+ANN and kpca+ANN

method	PCA+ANN	KPCA+ANN							
kernel function		linear	quadratic	polynomial					
				c=1d=1	c=1d=2	c=10d=2	c=1d=3	c=1d=4	c=1d=5
prediction accuracy	84%	**86.5%**	74.5%	**87%**	**87.5%**	**87.5%**	83.5%	80.5%	78.5%
method	KPCA+ANN								
kernel function	sigmoid			RBF					
	v=0.1c=-1	v=3c=-1	v=8c=-1	σ =7	σ =8	σ =9	σ =10	σ =20	
prediction accuracy	79.5%	80%	79%	**86%**	**87%**	**88.5%**	**87.5%**	**85.5%**	

From Fig.1, we see that the accumulated variance (eigenvalue) of the top 150 principal components of KPCA is more than that of PCA, this indicates that the ability of feature extraction of KPCA is stronger than that of PCA. From Table1, we see that, when using quadratic kernel function or sigmoid kernel function, the prediction accuracy of KPCA+ANN is worse than that of PCA+ANN, this shows that not all kernel functions can improve the prediction accuracy, we should find the fittest kernel function for a given experiment; We also see that, when using polynomial kernel function, the best order d of polynomial is 2, when using gauss radial basis kernel function, the best parameters σ is 9, this shows that it is important to choose parameters.

5 Conclusions

We used a new method of combining kernel principal component analysis (KPCA) with artificial neural network(ANN) to realize the prediction of O-glycosylated sites in protein sequence under window size $w=21$. The protein sequence(training samples and test samples) are projected into the kernel feature space by kernel principal component analysis, then the classification is done by artificial neural network. Since KPCA captures the nonlinear feature of the original data, the performance of prediction is improved. The result of experiments shows that the proposed method is more effective and accurate when using linear kernel function, polynomial kernel function and gauss radial basis kernel function if we choose fit parameters. The prediction accuracy is 88.5%.

Acknowledgments

This work is partially supported by the Scientific Research Project of Education Department of Shaanxi Province (No. 09JK809, No. 2010JK896) and the Nature Science Fund Project of Shaanxi Province (No. 2010JQ1013).

References

1. Nishikawa, I., Sakamoto, H., Nouno, I., Iritani, T., Sakakibara, K., Ito, M.: Prediction of the O-glycosylation sites in protein by layered neural networks and support vector machines. In: Gabrys, B., Howlett, R.J., Jain, L.C. (eds.) KES 2006. LNCS (LNAI), vol. 4252, pp. 953–960. Springer, Heidelberg (2006)
2. Sasaki, K., Nagamine, N., Sakakibara, Y.: Support vector machines prediction of N- and O-glycosylation sites using whole sequence information and subcellular localizition. IPSJ Transactions on Bioinformatics 2, 25–35 (2009)
3. Li, S., et al.: Predicting O-glycosylation sites in mammalian proteins by using SVMs. Computational Biology and Chemistry 30, 203–208 (2006)
4. Yukiko, N., Kazutoshi, S., Masahiro, I., Ikuko, N.: Prediction of the O-glycosylation by Supprt Vector Machines and Characteristics of the Crowded and Isolated O-glycosylation Sites. In: IEEE, Fifth International Conference on Intelligent Information Hiding and Multimedia Signal Processing, pp. 1209–1212 (2009)
5. Chen, Y.-z.: Prediction of mucin-type O-Glycosylation sites in mammaliam protein using the composition of k-spaced amino acid pairs. BMC Bioinformatics, 101–107 (2008)
6. Yang, X.-m., Cui, X.-w., Yang, X.-z.: Prediction of O-Glycosylation Sites in Protein Sequence by Kernel Principal Component Analysis. In: International Conference on CASoN, pp. 267–270 (2010)
7. Yang, X.-m., Li, S.-p.: Prediction of o-glycosylation sites in protein sequence by kernel fisher discriminant analysis. Journal of Computer Applications 30(11), 2959–2961 (2010) (in Chinese)
8. Zhou, K.-l., Kang, Y.-h.: Model of Neural Network and Program Design with Matlab. Tsinghua University Press, Beijing (2005)
9. http://www.ebi.uniprot

Analyzing the Effect and Selecting the Parameter of Bioradar Antenna for Measurement

Hui Xu, Bangyu Li, Xinsheng Che, and Jian Ren

Advanced Online Measurement Technology Key Lab of Liaoning Province,
Shenyang University of Technology, Shenyang, P.R. China

Abstract. Selection of UWB antenna parameters in bioradar measurement, such as antenna VSWR, antenna gain and antenna power leakage, are discussed, and the influences for radar measurement are analyzed. A step frequency ultra-wideband mode is used for access the budge and certain micro doppler information of the target. The double ridge rectangular horn antenna is selected as ultra-wideband antenna. The inconsistencies among various frequencies of antenna and instrument accessory can be eliminated by cancellation method. The effect of power leakage from the rear end is cut off by metal shielding. Test results show that the method is effective, and the distance from human body to the antenna and the respiratory rate can be clearly distinguished by the bioradar.

Keywords: UWB; stepped frequency bioradar; antenna; cancellation method; power leakage.

1 Introduction

Non-contact life detection technology is a new technology with the development of medical engineering, military, social development in recent years, which is used as imaging for target, detecting respiration and heartbeat, and other parameters of living body in the case of non-contact with the body[1,2]. Compared with the infrared, optical and ultrasonic detection technology, radar has its unique advantage in detection of living body, which is not affected by weather, temperature and other environmental factors, and has a strong penetrating ability. Radar can penetrate a certain thickness of the barrier (such as walls, smoke, trees, etc.) for detecting target. This radar is also known as bioradar[3-5]. Ultra-wideband stepped frequency radar has advantages of high resolution, strong penetrating ability, available of subtle features of target and simple hardware implementation, and it is a hot spot of life detection in recent years[6,7].

Antenna is a more important component for bioradar. The performance of antenna demonstrated in the work impact the signal to noise of echo and imaging quality directly. In this paper, problems in use of antenna, such as UWB antenna selection, antenna VSWR, antenna gain and antenna power leakage, are discussed, and the influences for radar measurement are analyzed, and appropriate solutions are proposed.

S. Lin and X. Huang (Eds.): CESM 2011, Part II, CCIS 176, pp. 451–456, 2011.

2 Problems and Solutions in Use of Antenna

2.1 Choice of Ultra-Wideband Stepped Frequency Radar Antenna

Antenna is a sensor for transmitting and receiving electromagnetic signal, and is an important component in radar system. In the application of bioradar, single base mode is used generally, that the same antenna is used for transmitting and receiving electromagnetic signal. A coupler is connected at the back of antenna, which is to separate the transmitted signal and the received signal, make them non-interfering. Firstly, the antenna as ultra-wideband stepped frequency bioradar should be wide bandwidth. Frequency range is used in our research group is 800~2500MHz, and bandwidth is 1700 MHz, so the antenna should cover 800~2500MHz; secondly, the antenna of ultra-wideband stepped frequency bioradar should have better VSWR. Echo in bioradar imaging is often small-signal and low signal to noise ratio. These require antenna to achieve a better match, which makes electromagnetic power be radiated from the antenna port as much as possible, and reduce the reflection. These ensure a certain intensity of radiation power, which can improve signal to noise ratio for the detection of small-signal. General requirement of VSWR for the antenna is less than 2. Finally, the antenna of Ultra-wideband stepped frequency bioradar should have a better gain. Directional radiation is used in the application of bioradar, so better antenna directivity is required. Antenna directivity is corresponding to antenna gain, so good antenna directivity means high antenna gain. However, due to the synthetic aperture technology is used in bioradar imaging, antenna directivity does not require too much concentration. Generally, gain in bandwidth should be more than 4dBi, and the average gain should be 10dBi.

Horn antenna is a commonly used for ultra-wideband antenna, and is a microwave antenna of round or rectangular cross-section that waveguide terminal gradually open. It has a unique time-frequency domain broadband performance, good impedance characteristics and waveform fidelity. The horn antenna is usually used for a medium directional antenna because its structure is simple and pattern is easy to control. Our research group uses a double ridge rectangular horn antenna, and the real is shown in Fig. 1a, the structure is shown in Fig. 1b.

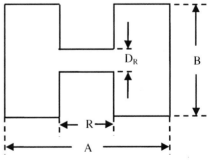

(a) Real of antenna   (b) Structure of antenna

Fig. 1. Real figure and structure chart of antenna

Where, A and B are width and height of rectangular horn respectively, R is the width of the ridge, D_R is the distance between the two ridges. The ridges of horn play a role of resistance gradually changing, which make the impedance gradually change from 50Ω at the feeding point to 377Ω at the aperture out. The shape of ridge affects the performance of horn antenna directly, such as VSWR, etc. The performance of double ridge rectangular horn antenna used in our research group is listed in Table 1, and the antenna meets the requirement of bioradar imaging.

Table 1. Antenna parameters

Antenna parameter	Antenna performance
Working frequency	800~6000MHz
VSWR	<2
Gain	>5dBi
Average gain	10dBi

2.2   Antenna Calibration in Use of Cancellation Method

Microwave device is difficult to achieve parameter consistency for every frequency points in a larger bandwidth, for instance the VSWR in bandwidth will be a great volatility, which is the drawback of UWB signal. For the double ridge horn antenna used in our research group, VSWR of antenna is fluctuating between 1.1 and 2 in the bandwidth of 800 ~ 2500MHz, and the corresponding reflection coefficient (S11) is -26.1 ~-9.6dB. This shows that when the same output power produced by signal source is transmitted to the antenna, the radiated power of antenna for different frequencies is not same, and the reflected signal will be superimposed on the echo signal and detected by receiver. Generally imaging algorithm assume that there is no difference between transmitted signal for every frequency points, so parameter inconsistency of antenna in bandwidth will affect imaging for target, the detection of micromotion and micro-Doppler information of target.

In addition, the residual error of instrument accessory will also affects imaging for target, the detection of micromotion and micro-Doppler information of target. The instrument accessory is cable equipment or other connector which connects the antenna and equipment. The effect of calibration is to eliminate cable inconsistency at each frequency point, and make various parameter performances (output power and phase) of the cable output port maintain consistency when the cable connect instrument. The calibration process is that the output port of cable connects open circuit device and short circuit device respectively, and does open calibration and short calibration. The parameter of each frequency point is recorded in calibration process, and after the measurement the inconsistencies among the various frequencies are eliminated by mathematical method. As calibration process and measurement process exist a certain degree of error, there is a error of parameter performance of each frequency point when 50Ω match load is connected after calibration, that is the residual error. Residual error will be loaded into the echo data, make the echo signal to noise ratio decrease.

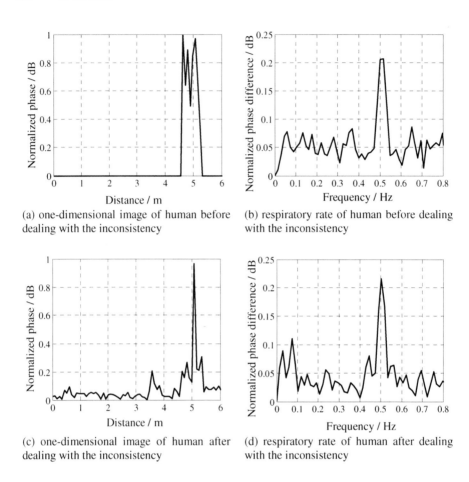

(a) one-dimensional image of human before dealing with the inconsistency

(b) respiratory rate of human before dealing with the inconsistency

(c) one-dimensional image of human after dealing with the inconsistency

(d) respiratory rate of human after dealing with the inconsistency

Fig. 2. One-dimensional image and respiratory rate of human

Fig. 2a and 2b are one-dimensional image of human (Straight-line distance between antenna and human) and respiratory rate of human measured before dealing with the inconsistency. In the experiment, the human body sits on the chair 5m far from the antenna, and respiratory frequency is 0.5Hz. One-dimensional image of human and respiratory rate of human are vague, the resolution is not high. The cancellation method is used to eliminate the two kinds of errors above-mentioned in this paper, which is vector differencing. Before measuring in the target area, echo signal of antenna in free space is measured firstly. The measurement is best carried out in microwave anechoic chamber, which make no reflection of electromagnetic wave radiated by antenna. If there is no microwave anechoic chamber, you can choose a open location to measure. Transmitted power of signal in microwave anechoic chamber is the same as the transmitted power of signal in the target scene. Amplitude and phase difference (phase difference between transmitted signal and echo signal) of every frequency point of echo signal can be measured by vector network analyzer. Assuming that the vector value of echo signal of a frequency point measured is $A_{1,i}e^{-j\varphi_{1,i}}$, which is the reflected power brought by antenna and instrument accessory. Assuming that the vector value of echo signal of a frequency point measured in target area is $A_{2,i}e^{-j\varphi_{2,i}}$. Inconsistencies among the various frequency of antenna and instrument accessory are eliminated by subtracting between them, shown in formula 1.

$$\sum_{i=1}^{N} B_{i}e^{-j\varphi_{3,i}} = \sum_{i=1}^{N} A_{2,i}e^{-j\varphi_{2,i}} - \sum_{i=1}^{N} A_{1,i}e^{-j\varphi_{1,i}} \tag{1}$$

Fig. 2c and 2d are one-dimensional image of human and respiratory rate of human under the same condition, and the one-dimensional image of human and respiratory rate of human can be easy to distinguish.

2.3 Elimination of Antenna Power Leakage Influence

The antenna of bioradar can generate power leakage in use. There are two main aspects of the power leakage. One is that antenna is not completely sealing at connection because of production process, so part of the power radiate at connection, especially leakage power is large at connector back of antenna. For double ridge horn antenna used in our research group, when the power of transmitter is 10dBm, and human body move 20cm back of antenna, as the leakage power of antenna is reflected by human body and received, then the power reflected which is measured by power meter is greater than -13dBm. That impact the measurement of target signal, and make signal to noise ratio of echo be decreased. Second is that there is a certain distance between wall and antenna when penetrating wall imaging for target area. Electromagnetic wave reflected by wall is reflected by bioradar user again, and then received by antenna. That also impact the measurement of target signal, and make signal to noise ratio of echo be decreased.

The solution for the first case of leakage power is to do a good shielding between antenna and user, and use metal to wrap up the antenna. The power which is received by antenna when electromagnetic wave radiated by the back of antenna is reflected by metal can be measured, and is a constant. This part of error will be eliminated in imaging. The solution for the latter case of power leakage is to use the antenna to contact with the wall as much as possible, without leaving any gap. At this time all of power reflected by wall are received by antenna.

3 Conclusion

In this paper application problems of antenna are discussed, such as the selection of UWB antenna, antenna VSWR, antenna gain and antenna power leakage, and the influences of them for radar measurement are analyzed, and also some appropriate solutions are proposed. The conclusions are as follows: (1) The structure of double ridge rectangular horn antenna is simple, meanwhile the pattern is easy to control. The pattern can be made a high bandwidth one, which is more suitable for use in bioradar. (2) Inconsistencies among various frequencies of antenna and instrument accessory can be eliminated by cancellation method. (3) Power leakage of antenna impact the measurement of the target signal, and decrease the signal to noise ratio of echo. This phenomenon can be eliminated by adding metal shielding and contacting with the wall tightly for antenna.

Acknowledgments

The project is supported by the Department of Liaoning Education. No. 2009T074.

References

1. Gaugue, A.C.: Overview of Current Technologies for Through-the-wall-surveillance. In: Proceedings of SPIE, vol. 5989, pp. 1–11 (2005)
2. He, F., Zhu, G.F., Huang, X.T., et al.: Preliminary Results of Ultra-wideband Through-the-wall Life-detecting Radar. In: IEEE National Radar Conference - Proceedings, pp. 1327–1330 (2010)
3. Zhuge, X., Savelyev, T.G., Yarovoy, A.G.: Assessment of Electromagnetic Requirements for UWB Through-wall Radav. In: 2007 International Conference on Electromagnetics in Advanced Applications, pp. 923–926 (2007)
4. Borek, S.E., Clarke, B.J., Costianes, P.J.: Through-the-wall Surveillance for Homeland Security and Law Enforcement. In: Proceedings of the SPIE - The International Society for Optical Engineering, vol. 5778(1), pp. 175–185 (2005)
5. Wang, Y.Z., Kuhn, M.J., Fathy, A.E.: Advanced System Level Simulation of UWB Three-dimensional Through-wall Imaging Radar for Performance Limitation Prediction. In: 2010 IEEE/MTT-S International Microwave Symposium, pp. 16–165 (2010)
6. Wang, D.W., Wang, S.G., Guan, X.P., et al.: Progress in Ultra Wide-band Radar and Target Identification Techniques. Journal of Air Force Radar Academy 21(3), 157–164 (2007)
7. Wu, S.Y., Huang, Q., Chen, J., et al.: Target Localization and Identification Algorithm for Ultra Wideband Through-wall Radar. Journal of Electronics & Information Technology 32(11), 2624–2629 (2010)

Design of a CAI System for Translation Teaching

Zheng Wang

College of Journalism and Communication, Shanghai International Studies University,
550 Dalian West Road, Shanghai 200083
wangzheng021@126.com

Abstract. There has been a lack of consensus on how to build a computer-aided instruction (CAI) system for translation. Reviewing existing researches on computer-assisted translation teaching, the author divides these tools or technologies into "top-quality course" sites, computer-aided translation, general-purpose courseware, data-driven translation learning and intelligent translation learning tools. Combining tools with translation studies, this paper proposes a CAI system for translation teaching. It describes various functional modules that are expected to enable self-access learning of translation learners.

Keywords: computer-aided instruction (CAI); computer-aided translation (CAT); translation teaching; self-access learning.

1 Introduction

Translation has been traditionally regarded as an art or manual craft that cannot be handled with computers. The recent progress of instructional technology has enabled people to learn translation with the aid of computers. With the development of professionalism-oriented translator training programs in China, an increasing number of translation teachers are using computers or online applications to help learners develop their translation competence. However, there has been a lack of consensus regarding what tools and technologies can be utilized in translation pedagogy. On the one hand, computer or online applications that are currently used for translation teaching either cannot fulfill their expected purposes or were not designed specifically for translation teaching. On the other hand, some linguistic or translator tools that can contribute to translation teaching such as corpora, translation memory and machine translation (MT) have been ignored by translation teachers. It is thus necessary to have an overview of all existing tools and study their applicability from the perspective of translation studies and translation pedagogy.

2 Current Researches on CAI Systems for Translation Teaching

2.1 "Top-Quality Course" Sites for Translation Teaching

As Wang (2010:506) noted, university professors are required to establish online course sites if they want to apply for "top-quality courses" from universities and governments. Here "top-quality courses" used in a Chinese context refer to courses that

S. Lin and X. Huang (Eds.): CESM 2011, Part II, CCIS 176, pp. 457–462, 2011.
© Springer-Verlag Berlin Heidelberg 2011

are chosen to be exemplary ones of its field and are funded by the government. IT applications are required for "modernizing" pedagogical efforts. A panel of educational experts judges the eligibility of such courses largely by the quality of these course sites. This is typical to the course of "Theory and Practice of Translation," a core course of English major in Chinese universities. While elaborate efforts have been made on data collection and presentation such as course presentations, test papers, reference materials, teacher-student interaction is largely ignored during this process. Although some course sites are equipped with forums for students, they are hardly used. The modules for Q&A and homework are usually missing from these sites, too. Therefore we regret to note that many of these sites have not fulfilled their designed functions and purposes.

2.2 Computer-Aided Translation as Pedagogical Tools for Translators

In a broad sense, computer-aided translation (CAT) includes any type of computerized tool that translators use to help them do their job (Bowker 2002:6). In a narrow sense, it refers to translation memory tools and related applications. Wu (2006), Xu (2006), Lü and Mu (2007) have proposed that computer-aided translation (CAT) should be incorporated into translation teaching to develop an authentic environment for translation learners and, when accompanied by the boom of Master of Translation and Interpreting (MTI) in recent years, has led to the widespread installation of CAT tools in translation classrooms (Wang 2011). While highly laudable as a move to bridge the ivory tower with the academia, CAT tools should be taught by the right, competent people who, though small in number today in China, are growing by leaps and bounds. It has also to be noted that CAT tools are designed for translators and not specifically for translation learners. Therefore it should be used in combination with various other tools.

2.3 General-Purpose Courseware for Translation Teaching

Unlike the "top-quality courses" described above, general-purpose courseware is actually designed by professional educational engineers or research companies to promote online learning. Some of the best known representatives include Moodle® and Blackboard®. The former is widely used in China because it's open-source and free for use. Some of the most reputed translation training institutions such as the University of Geneva and Monterey Institute of International Studies have also built course sites with Moodle. Some typical features of Moodle are:

- Assignment submission
- Discussion forum
- Files download
- Grading
- Moodle instant messages
- Online calendar
- Online news and announcement (College and course level)
- Online quiz
- Wiki

Developers can extend Moodle's modular construction by creating plugins for specific new functionality. Moodle's infrastructure supports many types of plug-ins:

- activities (including word and math games)
- resource types
- question types (multiple choice, true and false, fill in the blank, etc)
- data field types (for the database activity)
- graphical themes
- authentication methods (can require username and password accessibility)
- enrollment methods

Moodle certainly provides an excellent tool for teachers to build their course sites with relatively small efforts. However, it (as well as most other courseware tools) is not built specifically for translation teaching. To make it more feasible as a tool for translation teachers, some customization efforts such as plug-ins and extensions have to be made. This is where translation theories and pedagogy step in.

2.4 Data-Driven Translation Learning

As a highly reliable source for empirical translation studies, corpora refer to large electronic bodies of texts that can be processed efficiently with computer tools. They can be divided into monolingual corpora and multilingual corpora in terms of languages involved, and into parallel corpora and comparable corpora in terms of alignment. They provide a brand-new data-driven approach to translation learning.. Monolingual corpora of the target language can help translators determine terms or regular expressions used in corresponding contexts; bilingual/multilingual corpora can help them learn translation decisions or skills from existing translations. Therefore translators and learners can either use commercially/freely available corpora to support their translation process or DIY a disposable corpus for their specific purpose (Varantola 2008). Bilingual corpora can also be imported into translation memory (TM) tools such as TRADOS or DejaVu to support new translation decisions or extract terms for future use.

Li (2010) proposed that "corresponding units," or highly modularized parallel chunks, can be extracted manually from bilingual corpora to support translation learning and research. Wang (2011) also points out that the research of TM is undergoing a transition to sub-sentential or chunk-based approach. The utilization of sub-sentential units in translation will provide a useful source of reference for learners.

Translation learners also benefit from a variety of online tools and resources such as search engines, encyclopedia, electronic dictionaries and termbases. They should constitute an indispensible part of CAI system for translation teaching.

2.5 Intelligent Tools for Translation Teaching

Shei & Pein (2002) designed a "Translation Method Tutor" system to help learners understand different translation methods. In the database there are four different ready-made translations of *Pride and Prejudice* that correspond to four different translation methods, and the system does an automatic formal comparison between students' translation against these four translations. In this way students can learn different translation methods by judging from the correspondence between their translation and reference translations (Wang 2010).

Another intelligent tool for translation teaching is computerized translation testing. Wang & Wen (2009) designed a system for computer-assisted scoring of large-scale translation tests and Tian (2011) proposed an online system for automatic scoring of translation exercises. Both tests show satisfactory correlation between human scoring and computerized scoring, though there is still room for improvement.

3   An Integrated CAI System for Translation Teaching

An integrated CAI system for translation teaching should thus be divided into four categories, namely, course management, CAT, data-driven learning and automatic tutoring. The modules that are involved in each category are shown as follows:

Table 1. Functional modules of CAI system for translation teaching

Course Management	CAT	Data-driven Learning	Automatic Tutoring
Assignment submission	Translation Memory	Corpora and tools	Intelligent Translation Method Tutor
Discussion forum	Terminology Management	Termbases	Automatic scoring of translation testing
Files download	Machine Translation	Electronic dictionaries	Interactive teaching aids
Grading	Localization tools	Corresponding units of translation	…
Instant messages	…	Online encyclopedia	
Online calendar		Search engines	
…		Translators' online resources	

I argued for a Client/Server (C/S) structure for the CAI system for translation teaching instead of a Browser/Server (B/S) one, thinking that C/S provides better speed and easier process monitoring (Wang 2010). However, progress in Browser/Server (B/S) structure and hardware upgrading makes it possible to eliminate these problems. The B/S structure provides easy access for learners and supports mobile learning, so it is gaining increasingly popularity in system design in recent years. The C/S structure has been traditionally used for such tools as TM and terminology management tools, but the advancement of technology makes it possible to manage TM online. The Google Translator Toolkit (GTT) and Wordfast ™ Everywhere are good examples of online TM systems. Process monitoring is also possible as long as proper interactive measures are taken in the system. For example, teachers can evaluate students' participation in online discussion by studying the threads they send in forums—the quality, quantity and relevance of threads are rated as contributions to forums (Wang 2010).

One feasible solution to building this CAI system is to adapt a course management system such as Moodle for this purpose. Developers and teachers can easily add new functions and modules to open-source systems such as Moodle. Instead of programming a TM system from scratch, teachers are encouraged to capitalize on existing online tools for free use (GTT, for example) and embed it in this CAI system. Wang (2011) mentioned that ten special bilingual corpora in different fields of business were integrated in a CAI system for business translation teaching. These resources are an excellent basis for mining terminology pairs and corresponding units for reuse by translators.

It is hoped that this system will contribute to self-access learning (SAL) of translation learners. In a SAL environment, learners assume a bigger role in language learning—they actively gain knowledge instead of being crammed by teachers. They can adjust their learning materials and targets by their progress, interest and orientation. In a word, they can customize their learning plan and learn to acquire knowledge in an ocean of (web) information. Teachers, rather, are changed from being the "saint on the stage" to the "guide by the side." (*ibid*) This CAI system has a full-fledged array of functions that are suited not only for learners but also professional translators, so learners can get whatever information that is relevant to their learning project.

4 Conclusion

This paper surveys all existing computer tools and technologies for translation teaching and evaluates their applicability from the perspective of translation. Existing CAI systems are either general purpose course management tools (such as Moodle) or discrete tools to assist translation learning in one aspect or another. Some CAI systems adopt a C/S structure and are usually used in a LAN environment. As a result, students have to go to a special computer lab for translation learning. However, the irrevocable trend for mobile learning and ubiquitous learning will soon make this approach obsolete. Therefore this paper proposes that all applications should be integrated in one system that can be accessed with a regular web browser.

Another trend worthy of notice is the integration of professional CAT tools in translation pedagogy. MT systems today are going increasingly web-based. Greater attention is needed for the interface between translation memory, parallel corpora and machine translation, all of which being driven by the same language data. It would be a big step forward if we can combine them in one single environment to promote the translation competence of learners.

Moreover, greater attention should be paid to the development of intelligent tools for translation learning. Despite progress in automatic scoring of translation tests, a great deal of efforts are needed to make them viable and commercially available. Existing studies have borrowed from the evaluation metrics for machine translation, but more human factors are actually involved in the making of authentic translation. Therefore the place of human and machines in computerized translation teaching deserves further probe.

Acknowledgments. This work is supported by Grant "211YYWZ001" of the 211 Project and by Innovative Research Team of Shanghai International Studies University.

References

1. Bowker, L.: Computer-aided Translation Technology: a Practical Introduction. University of Ottawa Press, Ottawa (2002)
2. Li, W.: The Parallel Corpus Design and the Corresponding Unit Identification. Contemporary Foreign Languages Studies 9, 22–26 (2010)
3. Lü, L., Mu, L.: Computer-aided Translation Technology and Translation Pedagogy. World of Foreign Languages 3, 35–43 (2007)
4. Shei, C.C., Pein, H.: Computer-assisted Teaching of Translation Methods. Literary and Linguistic Computing 3, 323–344 (2002)
5. Tian, Y.: Probes into Automatic Scoring of Online English-Chinese Translation. China Translators' Journal 2, 38–41 (2011)
6. Varantola, K.: Disposable Corpora as Intelligent Tools in Translation. Cadernos de Tradução 2 (2008)
7. Wang, J., Wen, Q.: A model for the computer-assisted scoring of Chinese EFL learners' Chinese-English translation. Modern Foreign Languages 4, 415–420 (2009)
8. Wang, L.: Building the Undergraduate Course of Computer-aided Business Translation and the Research and Development of Its Teaching System. China Translators' Journal 2, 34–37 (2011)
9. Wang, Z.: Design of Project-based Online Translation Teaching. In: Zhang, H., Zhu, Y., Sun, G. (eds.) Web-based Foreign Language Teaching: Theories and Designing, pp. 503–555. Shanghai Foreign Language Education Press, Shanghai (2010)
10. Wu, Y.: The Application of CAT in Translation Teaching. Educational Technology for Foreign Language Teaching 6, 55–59 (2006)
11. Xu, B.: CAT and Translation Research and Teaching. Shanghai Translators' Journal 4, 59–63 (2006)

Author Index